1	Dome of the Rock	**30**	Golden...
2	The Aqsa Mosque	**31**	"Gram..."
3	Western Wall and prayer plaza	**32**	Iron Gate
4	Ablution Gate	**33**	Is`irdiyya College
5	Almalikiyya College	**34**	Islamic Museum (Mosque of the North Africans)
6	Aminiyya College		
7	Archaeological Park	**35**	Jawiliyya College
8	Ashrafiyya College	**36**	Jewish Generations Center
9	Barclay's Gate	**37**	Magharibah Gate
10	Chain Gate and Gate of the Divine Presence	**38**	Manjakiyya College
		39	Mansuri Hospice
11	Davidson Center	**40**	Market of the Cotton Merchants
12	Dawadariyya Convent	**41**	al-Musalla al-Marwani = Solomon's Stables
13	Dome and Prayer Niche of the Prophet		
14	Dome of the Ascension	**42**	Prayer place commemorating the Sabra and Shatila massacre
15	Dome of Joseph		
16	Dome of Moses	**43**	Ramp leading to 37
17	Dome of Solomon	**44**	Remission Gate
18	Dome of the Balance	**45**	Robinson's Arch
19	Dome of the Chain	**46**	Small Western Wall
20	Eastern Cardo	**47**	Solomon's Stables = al-Musalla al-Marwani
21	Fountain of Mustafa Agha		
22	Fountain of Qai'tbay	**48**	Stairs leading down to 41/47
23	Fountain of the Chain Gate	**49**	Superintendent's Gate
24	Fountain of the Superintendent's Gate	**50**	Tankiziyya College (Mahkama) and Wilson's Arch
25	Gate of Darkness (Faysal Gate)		
26	Gate of the Cotton Merchants	**51**	The Cup
27	Gate of the Tribes	**52**	`Uthmaniyya College
28	Ghadiriyya College	**53**	Western Wall tunnel ⸻
29	Ghawanima Gate	**54**	Women's Mosque

Map: Survey of Israel | Course of Western Wall tunnel: Jon Seligman | Place names: Ed.

WHERE HEAVEN AND EARTH MEET:
JERUSALEM'S SACRED ESPLANADE

The Hebrew University
of Jerusalem

École biblique
de Jérusalem

Al-Quds
University

CENTRE FOR JERUSALEM STUDIES

WHERE HEAVEN AND EARTH MEET:
JERUSALEM'S SACRED ESPLANADE

EDITORS:
OLEG GRABAR AND BENJAMIN Z. KEDAR

Yad Ben-Zvi Press
Jerusalem

University of Texas Press
Austin

This book was initiated and supported by the Beracha Foundation and is in the Jamal and Rania Daniel Series in Contemporary History, Politics, Culture, and Religion of the Levant of the University of Texas Press.

SPONSORS

The Hebrew University of Jerusalem and Yad Izhak Ben-Zvi

Al-Quds University and the Centre for Jerusalem Studies

Ecole Biblique et Archéologique Française de Jérusalem

B E꜀R꜀A꜀C꜀H A

Printed in Israel | First edition, 2009

Library of Congress Cataloging-in-Publication Data

Where heaven and earth meet : Jerusalem's sacred esplanade / Oleg Grabar. — 1st ed.
   p. cm. — (Jamal and Rania Daniel series in contemporary history, politics, culture, and religion of the Levant)

ISBN 978-0-292-72272-9 (cloth : alk. paper)
1. Temple Mount (Jerusalem) 2. Jerusalem—History. I. Grabar, Oleg. II. Kedar, B. Z.
DS109.28.W54 2010
956.94'42—dc22
2009027309

EDITORS
Benjamin Z. Kedar | Oleg Grabar

EDITORIAL BOARD
Mustafa Abu Sway | Amnon Cohen | Father Marcel Sigrist OP | Guy Stroumsa | Yoram Tsafrir

Editorial coordinator and copy editor: Yohai Goell
Choice of illustrations (excepting most images in the articles
   by Professors Hurowitz, Patrich, Tsafrir, Kaplony, and Burgoyne): BZ Kedar
Production coordinator: Jonathan Rubin

Book design: Nomi Morag
Pre-press, printing, and binding: Art Plus, Jerusalem

Cover: The Old City of Jerusalem, 1984. Photo: Werner Braun Jerusalem

Title pages: Qubbat al-Sakhra and the Golden Gate (Bab al-Dhahabi) from the Mount of Olives, at dawn. Photo: Saïd Nuseibeh
Small pictures (from left):
1. Abraham about to sacrifice his son Isaac. Mosaic of the sixth-century synagogue of Beth Alpha. Photo: Yad Ben-Zvi Archives
2. The Presentation of Jesus in the Temple. Amiens Cathedral, thirteenth century. Photo: BZ Kedar
3. Muhammad's Ascension from Jerusalem's Rock to Heaven. Khusraw Dilhawi, *Khamseh*. Istanbul, Topkapı Museum, Hazine 798 (sixteenth century), fol. 4v.

ACKNOWLEDGMENTS

We would like to express our gratitude to Khaled Zighari, Baruch Gian, Prof. Laura Minervini and Sarit Uziely for having taken photos on our behalf; to Dr. Nazmi Al-Jubeh, Prof. Dan Bahat, Yuval Baruch, Prof. Michael Burgoyne, Dr. Ejal Jakob Eisler, Prof. Yael Katzir, Gabi Laron, Yoram Lehman, Nadav Mann, Dr. Eilat Mazar, Moshe Milner, Prof. Avner Offer, Ehud Prawer, Prof. Denys Pringle, Ely Shiller, Hayim Shtayer, Jean-Michel de Tarragon, O.P., and Prof. Yoram Tsafrir, as well as to Bayerisches Hauptstaatsarchiv, Abt. IV: Kriegsarchiv (Munich), Deutsches Archäologisches Institut (Berlin), École Biblique et Archéologique Française de Jérusalem, Israel Defence Forces – Film Archives, The Temple Institute, and Yad Izhak Ben-Zvi Photo Archives, for having placed their photos or plans at our disposal; to Meir Ben-Dov, Saïd Nuseibeh, Varda Polak Sahm, Leen Ritmeyer, and Zev Radovan, as well as to Albatross (Tel Aviv), Associated Press, Bibliothèque royale de Belgique, British Museum, Government Press Office (Jerusalem), Historic Views of the Holy Land, Israel Antiquities Authority, Israel Museum, Istanbul Archaeological Museums, Municipal Archives (Jerusalem), National Library of Israel, RMN – Les frères Chuzeville, Vorderasiatisches Museum – Staatliche Museen zu Berlin, and the Tower of David Museum for having granted permission to reproduce their photos or plans; to Dr. Axel Dornemann of the Dr. Ernst Hauswedell & Co. Publishing House, Stuttgart, for permission to reprint a painting of Gustav Bauernfeind; to Haim Gitler, Curator of Numismatics at the Israel Museum, for permission to publish a seal of King Amaury.

Prof. Marcel Sigrist of the École Biblique et Archéologique Française de Jérusalem, Huda Imam of the Centre for Jerusalem Studies of Al-Quds University, and Yael Dinowitz of Yad Izhak Ben-Zvi were instrumental in organizing the Jerusalem sessions of February-March 2006 at which contributors discussed the drafts of most chapters. A year later, Prof. Guy Stroumsa joined us at Princeton while we were discussing the subsequent drafts. Professors Michael Burgoyne, Amnon Cohen, Andreas Kaplony, Jonathan J. Price and especially Benny Morris repeatedly offered counsel and aid during the later stages of the editorial process. Jonathan Miller assisted us during the initial stages of the book's production. Prof. Rachel Milstein helped us obtain reproductions from the Istanbul collections. Jon Seligman, Yael Barschak, Robert Kool, and Silvia Krapiwko located photos in the archives of the Israel Antiquities Authority. Jonathan Rubin exhibited an uncommon ingenuity and perseverance in obtaining the illustrations that appear in the volume, and assiduously coordinated much of the editorial work, while Pnina Arad prepared or updated a number of plans. Deborah Greniman copyedited the first batch of chapters and Yohai Goell—the bulk of the book; he also volunteered to uniformize all texts and proofread them. Nomi Morag took upon herself the complex task of advising our photographers, specifying the plans' layout, and preparing the pre-press for the volume. Michael Glatzer did much of the correspondence with holders of copyrighted material. Dr. Zvi Zameret, director of Yad Izhak Ben-Zvi, the moving spirit behind the project, was always ready with advice and support. We thank them all.

TABLE OF CONTENTS

9   **Introduction**
Oleg Grabar and Benjamin Z. Kedar

HISTORY

14   **Tenth Century BCE to 586 BCE: House of the Lord (*Beyt YHWH*)**
Victor Avigdor Hurowitz

36   **538 BCE–70 CE: The Temple (*Beyt Ha-Miqdash*) and Its Mount**
Joseph Patrich

72   **70–638: The Temple-less Mountain**
Yoram Tsafrir

100   **635/638–1099: The Mosque of Jerusalem (*Masjid Bayt al-Maqdis*)**
Andreas Kaplony

132   **1099–1187: The Lord's Temple (*Templum Domini*) and Solomon's Palace (*Palatium Salomonis*)**
Benjamin Z. Kedar and Denys Pringle

150   **1187–1260: The Furthest Mosque (*al-Masjid al-Aqsa*) under Ayyubid Rule**
Michael Hamilton Burgoyne

176   **1260–1516: The Noble Sanctuary (*al-Haram al-Sharif*) under Mamluk Rule History** — Donald P. Little

188   **1260–1516: The Noble Sanctuary (*al-Haram al-Sharif*) under Mamluk Rule Architecture** — Michael Hamilton Burgoyne

210   **1516–1917: *Haram-i Şerif* - The Temple Mount under Ottoman Rule**
Amnon Cohen

230   **1917 to the Present: *Al-Haram al-Sharif* / Temple Mount (*Har ha-Bayit*) and the Western Wall**
Yitzhak Reiter and Jon Seligman

274   **1917 to the Present: Basic Changes, but Not Dramatic: *Al-Haram al-Sharif* in the Aftermath of 1967**
Nazmi Al-Jubeh

A PHOTOGRAPHIC DOSSIER

290   Saïd Nuseibeh

THEMATIC CHAPTERS

300   **The *Haram al-Sharif* as a Work of Art**
Oleg Grabar

308   **From Priestly (and Early Christian) Mount Zion to Rabbinic Temple Mount**
Rachel Elior

320   **Christian Memories and Visions of Jerusalem in Jewish and Islamic Context**
Guy G. Stroumsa

334   **The Holy Land, Jerusalem, and the Aqsa Mosque in the Islamic Sources**
Mustafa Abu Sway

344   **The Temple Mount in Jewish Thought (70 CE to the Present)**
Miriam Frenkel

THREE PERSONAL VIEWS

362   **The Temple Mount—A Personal Account**
Menachem Magidor, President, The Hebrew University of Jerusalem

366   **The Haram al-Sharif**
Sari Nusseibeh, President, Al-Quds University

374   **What Do I Think about When I Imagine Myself Walking on the Temple Esplanade—al-Haram al-Sharif?**
Carlo Maria Cardinal Martini, S.I.

378   **Epilogue**
Benjamin Z. Kedar and Oleg Grabar

392   **Notes**
408   **Glossary**
411   **Sources of illustrations**

Inside front cover: Detailed area map | **Inside back cover:** Main dates

1   Next spread: An aerial view, from the south, of Jerusalem's sacred Esplanade (July 1997).
In the foreground, the archaeological excavations south and southwest of the Esplanade's walls.
The red arrow at left points at the post-1967 prayer plaza in front of the Esplanade's Western Wall

Introduction

Oleg Grabar
Institute for Advanced Study, Princeton

Benjamin Z. Kedar
The Hebrew University of Jerusalem

The object of this book is to present and explain one of the most extraordinary spaces on earth, the large man-made, more or less rectangular, area which occupies the southeastern corner of the walled Old City of Jerusalem and which takes up almost one-sixth of its surface.

This Esplanade, measuring some 15 hectares or 150,000 meters square, has been regarded as sacred for about three millennia. It has aroused, and continues to arouse, conflicting emotions and passions among many millions of people. For Judaism, it is the holiest space, where the Solomonic and Herodian Temples once stood and where, in the messianic age, the Temple is to be rebuilt at God's behest. For Christendom, it is the site of the Herodian Temple which Jesus repeatedly visited, foretelling its destruction and announcing the advent of a new, spiritual worship of God. For Islam, it is the holy space to which the Prophet Muhammad traveled on his mystical Night-Journey and Ascension, and which holds the Dome of the Rock and the Aqsa Mosque. For Judaism and Christendom the Last Judgment is to take place in the valley just east of the Esplanade; this is not far from Islam's position.

Since the 1920s, the Wailing Wall—which bounds the Esplanade on the west—has been a focus of the Arab–Jewish conflict and, between 1948 and 1967, was inaccessible to Jews; since 1967, the Esplanade itself has repeatedly witnessed eruptions of violence. During the past decade, the site's possession has become one of the thorniest issues impeding an Israeli–Palestinian, and Israeli–Arab, rapprochement. An Israeli lunatic fringe hopes for the imminent destruction of the Muslim shrines and actually makes preparations for rebuilding the Jewish Temple in their stead; an underground cell even plotted, in the 1970s, to destroy the shrines, but was apprehended in time by the Israeli authorities. And while Jewish extremists hope for the destruction of the Muslim shrines standing since the late seventh and early eighth century, a growing number of Palestinians and Arabs deny that the Solomonic and Herodian temples had ever stood there; Yasser Arafat said as much during the Camp David peace talks of 2000. This widespread denial of the Jewish shrines of the past is a mirror image of the extremists' wish to erase the Muslim shrines of the present. But even with moderate Israelis and Palestinians, who shun such

extreme positions, the Esplanade evokes turbulent emotions the nature of which they are sometimes at a loss to rationally explain.

The present endeavor is unprecedented. For the first time an Israeli, a Palestinian and a Dominican institute of higher learning, all located in Jerusalem—namely, the Hebrew University of Jerusalem and the Research Center it runs in common with Yad Izhak Ben-Zvi; Al-Quds University and its Centre for Jerusalem Studies; and the École Biblique et Archéologique Française de Jérusalem—have decided to jointly produce a volume dealing with Jerusalem's sacred Esplanade. And, of course, not only with its monuments, but also with the conflicting emotions they have aroused over the ages and with the passions they ignite today.

To do so, we had to evolve some empathy for all of these emotions—both for sentiments we share to some extent, as well as for those we do not share at all. To empathize can be difficult; but without empathy there can be no true understanding. By launching the enterprise we attested to our confidence that people of varying backgrounds who share a common commitment to truth are capable of producing a book that should be of value for open-minded readers of every persuasion. The book should be of interest to scholars who have studied the site's past and present, for it contains many new findings and hypotheses—from pinpointing a new location for the Herodian Temple to explaining the emergence of the term "Temple Mount" to a new interpretation of the meaning of the early Islamic shrine to information on the site's recent history.

When dealing with passions one must beware of treating them passionately. A historian who chooses to become the enthusiastic spokesman of one side to a conflict inevitably risks a blurring of vision and a subversion of his credibility. We attempted therefore to try to stick to the facts, to avoid partisan assertions and recriminations, to steer clear of oblique references to the present in chapters dealing with the past, and to refrain from supercilious indignation at the doings of present-day protagonists, dismissed as hopelessly unworthy custodians of matchless monuments. Yet with regard to the post-1967 period we did not succeed in inducing our authors to agree on a single narrative and therefore we have been constrained to present two parallel accounts, overlapping with regard to most facts but often diverging in interpretation and fervor.

We believe that the project we have embarked upon is bold, thrilling, and important. Its success could amount to a signal of great significance: if an Israeli university and a Palestinian one, aided by experts from abroad, are capable of co-producing a volume about the past and the present of this extremely emotion-laden Esplanade, less thorny enterprises may become feasible.

Close to the beginning of our enterprise we realized that even the site's name poses a problem. The site has now and has had over the centuries many names. Almost all are loaded with ideological, political, or pious implications and are therefore sources of conflict.

Among Jews and Christians it has long been known as Mount Zion and as Mount Moriah, associated with the Land of Moriah where God commanded Abraham to sacrifice his son (for Muslims, the scene took place in Mecca). The Solomonic Temple was mainly known as the "House of the Lord" (*Beyt elohim*) or the "House of YHWH" (*Beyt YHWH*); the temple rebuilt after the Babylonian exile was usually referred to as "House of the Sanctuary" (*Beyt ha-Miqdash*). In Rabbinic tradition the area is known as "the Temple Mount" (*Har ha-Bayit*; literally: "Mountain of the House"); the same term recurs today in modern European languages. The site may have been called the Capitolium during the few centuries of direct Roman rule because a pagan temple and statues of the emperor stood at the site.

It was called "the Mosque of Jerusalem" (*Masjid Bayt al-Maqdis*) in early Islamic times, reflecting a plethora of names given to the city in the 7th to 9th centuries and in an acknowledgment both of its Jewish past and of its renewal under the aegis of Islam. It was "The Farthest Mosque" (*al-Masjid al-Aqsa*), referring to the passage in the Qur'an (17.1) which mentions the place to which the Prophet Muhammad traveled on his Night-Journey. For the Crusaders, who conquered Jerusalem in 1099, the site contained "The Lord's Temple" (*Templum Domini*) and "Solomon's Palace" (*Palatium Salomonis*).

For the past six hundred years, it has been called al-Haram al-Sharif, the Noble Sanctuary, proclaiming that space to be the third of the uniquely holy places of Islam, after Mecca and Medina. Nowadays, while oral usage of the term Haram persists, Palestinians tend to use in formal texts the name Masjid al-Aqsa, habitually rendered into English as "the Aqsa Mosque."

Each of these names is explicable and has an historical justification. The two most commonly used names—Temple Mount and al-Haram al-Sharif—have also acquired an ideological connotation which makes them unacceptable to many of our contemporaries.

Since our objective is neither to stir up unnecessary controversies nor to buttress ideological positions but to explain the forms, meanings, and uses of a given space through the centuries, we have left each contributor free to use, in his or her chapter, whatever name she or he preferred.

But is there one term that could define the space through time? Probably not. There are only successions of attitudes, shapes, myths, symbols, and practices. These form the web of the history we are trying to tell. Yet something may well have characterized that space, at least since its invention as a sanctuary at the time of the Hebrew monarchy, if not earlier. From then until now, it was a space in which earthbound man found or sought to find the divine. The ways varied enormously, but the hope was and is always there.

And this is why we have been so taken by the fisheye lens photo used for the book's cover jacket, and entitled this volume: "Where heaven and earth meet."

Tenth Century BCE to 586 BCE: The House of the Lord (*Beyt YHWH*)

Victor Avigdor Hurowitz

Ben-Gurion University of the Negev, Beer Sheva

Throughout the Ancient Near East the major religious institution and locus of encounter or contact between man and deity was the temple. Temples were not primarily places of public prayer as are today's synagogues, churches, and mosques, but divine residences or manors; and it is preferable to refer to a temple as "the House of (the divine) John/Jane Doe," referring to temples of foreign deities or as "the House of God" and "the House of the Lord [YHWH],"[1] in the case of Israelite temples. Within the temple, a god would dwell with family members and subordinates in the divine hierarchy, and one could find therein tangible representation of divine presence such as a cult statue, some standard, or symbol. The god in residence could be worshipped and paid homage by offering sacrifices, presenting gifts, uttering prayers, or simple prostration.

Ancient Israelites visited their temples on fixed festivals; sporadic public or private occasions are well attested in biblical literature. So we read about Elqanah and his family frequenting Shiloh (1 Sam. 1), Absalom paying a vow in Hebron (2 Sam. 15.7, 8), and the People of Israel and Judah making annual pilgrimages individually or en masse to Jerusalem or Bethel (1 Kings 12.28–29, etc.). But even in these temples the popular visit was not the important event. Although not excluded from the temples, public presence was not obligatory, had no active role essential to the temples' functioning, and even with no people present at all, the cult could go on. The regular cult was observed by a permanent, professional clergy, be they the Sons of Eli, Abiathar, Zadok, Levi, Moses, or even Aaron.

In Israelite temples, as in those of surrounding cultures, the essential necessity was a permanent divine presence. Cultic activities performed in Israelite temples were performed "before the Lord"; and, of course, there was some sort of sign of divine presence, be it a cult

2   Fragments of ceramic table wares and animal bones, dating from the eighth to the sixth centuries BCE, discovered in August 2007 by Yuval Baruch of the Israel Antiquities Authority while inspecting maintenance work of the Waqf below the southeastern corner of the raised platform surrounding the Dome of the Rock
The finds include fragments of bowl rims, bases and body sherds; the base of a juglet used for the ladling of oil; the handle of a small juglet and the rim of a storage jar. The bowl sherds were decorated with wheel burnishing lines characteristic of the First Temple Period. In addition, a piece of a white washed handmade object was found. It may have been used to decorate a larger object or may have been part of a figurine

statue as in the private temple belonging to an otherwise unknown Micah in Dan (Judg. 17–18), the Golden Calves in Bethel, Dan (1 Kings 28) and Samaria (Hos. 8.6), the pillars at Arad or Bethel (Gen. 28.17, 22; 35.14), or the Ark and *kavod* (Divine Majesty or Glory) in Shiloh (1 Sam. 4.21–22) and subsequently in Jerusalem (1 Kings 8.11).

Temples in the Ancient Near East in general, and in ancient Israel in particular, were built and, to a large extent, maintained by the local rulers, added prestige to the crown, and were considered mediators of blessing to the people and the land. But even this political role was secondary, at least conceptually and theologically, to the temple's primary role as place of divine presence. Divine presence in the temples led, during the first millennium BCE, to temples becoming places of asylum for inadvertent spillers of blood. In Israel and Judah, this function of the temples, and the altar in particular, was eventually eliminated, for as cult became centralized and the number of temples reduced to one, asylum was granted in cities of refuge spread through the land. The temples may also have been centers of justice. Eli the priest is said to have "judged Israel" for forty years (1 Sam. 4.18), assumedly at the Shiloh temple. A law in the Book of Deuteronomy prescribes that judges and scribes be appointed in all cities, but especially difficult cases were to be judged in the central sanctuary (Deut. 16.18–19; 17.8–13). This practice is certainly the basis of the famous vision shared by the prophets Isaiah and Micah of the Mountain of the House of the Lord in the future being an international court of justice where disputes between nations will be adjudicated by the God of Israel, thereby bringing an end to war (Isa. 2.1–4; Mic. 4.1–5).

> In the days to come, the Mount of the Lord's House shall stand firm above the mountains and tower above the hills; and all the nations shall gaze on it with joy, and the many peoples shall go and say: "Come let us go up to the Mount of the Lord, to the House of the God of Jacob, that he may instruct us in His ways, and that we may walk in His paths." For instruction shall come forth from Zion, the word of the Lord from Jerusalem. Thus He will judge among the nations and arbitrate for the many peoples, and they shall beat their swords into plowshares and their spears into pruning hooks: Nation shall not take up sword against nation; they shall never again know war.

The Bible indicates that ancient Israel knew several temples at various sites including Shiloh, Nob, Gilgal, Bethel, Schechem, Hebron, Mitzpah, and, of course, Jerusalem. Even the Tabernacle described in the Book of Exodus that stood at the center of the Israelite camp during their desert wanderings was a temple. To be sure, it was assembled and disassembled from time to time as they traveled from one desert encampment to the next; but despite its portability it was not conceptually or functionally different from any other House of God. The God of Israel was present in it, and served publicly by a family of priests. Archaeologists have uncovered in Arad a building that was apparently a temple; and even outside the Land of Israel, in Elephantine (present day Aswan) in Egypt, there was a temple to YHW the God of Israel, as shown by the documents found at the site. If so, temples were common sights in ancient Israel.

The most prominent and well known of these ancient Israelite Houses of God was the Temple that, according to the Bible, stood in Jerusalem on Mount Zion. This Temple was built in the tenth century BCE by Solomon (1 Kings 5.15–9.9), king of Israel, until plundered and destroyed in 586 BCE by Nebuzaradan, officer of King Nebuchadnezzar of Babylon, a national disaster also marking the beginning of the so-called Babylonian Exile (2 Kings 25.8–21). In light of ancient Near Eastern and even later custom to build new places of worship on the sites of older edifices, even belonging to other religions, some scholars have suggested that the Israelite Temple in Jerusalem was preceded by a Canaanite (Jebusite) temple and that the Israelite kings did no more than expand or refurbish an existing structure. To be sure, there are Canaanite elements in the symbolism and traditions pertaining to the Temple as reported by the Bible. Even so, the Bible itself knows of no predecessors apart from the threshing floor which David reportedly purchased from the Jebusite Araunah for the site of an altar (2 Sam. 24.18–25).

Nothing survives from this glorious Temple, and the site cannot be properly studied because of the political and religious sensitivity of Jerusalem. Moreover, constant occupation and rebuilding at the site has probably obliterated any possible remains; in October 2007 some pottery sherds from the period of the First Temple were discovered on the Temple Mount itself, but their relationship, if any, to the Temple has yet to be established.[2] As a result, the only window into this Temple is the Hebrew Bible, and especially the description in 1 Kings 6–7 and scattered allusions in the Book of Kings, the books of prophets of the First Temple period, and perhaps some Psalms. The description of the Temple in the Book of Chronicles is late and of secondary importance, and imposes on the First Temple certain features of the Tabernacle and perhaps the post-exilic Temple. Even so, some relevant information can be gleaned from it as well as from the descriptions of the Tabernacle in Exodus 25–40, and the Temple of the future in the vision concluding the Book of Ezekiel.

Our generation has witnessed biblical scholars, historians, and archaeologists claiming that the Jerusalem Temple, if it existed at all, was not built by Solomon and certainly did not resemble the magnificent edifice described in the Hebrew Bible.[3] Also, the biblical accounts as they appear before us today are products of literary growth, and may telescope reflections of the Temple as it appeared at various stages of its existence. Be this as it may, the biblical text enables the modern reader to conjure up a coherent portrait of the Temple as envisaged by the biblical authors; with the help of ancient Near Eastern artifacts and textual parallels it is possible to reconstruct its form [fig. 3], visualize it, and understand its

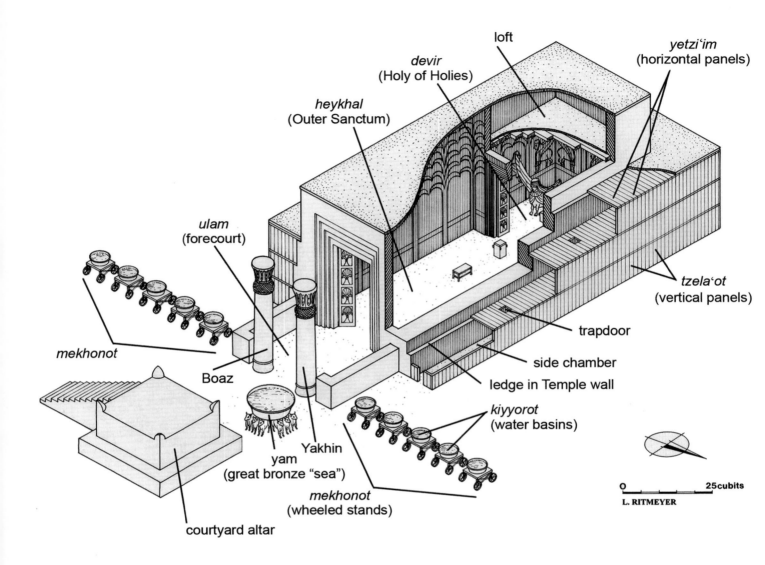

loft

devir
(Holy of Holies)

yetzi'im
(horizontal panels)

heykhal
(Outer Sanctum)

ulam
(forecourt)

tzela'ot
(vertical panels)

trapdoor

mekhonot

side chamber

Boaz

ledge in Temple wall

kiyyorot
(water basins)

Yakhin

yam
(great bronze "sea")

mekhonot
(wheeled stands)

courtyard altar

0   25 cubits
L. RITMEYER

3   Reconstruction of Solomon's Temple

design, significance, and ancient symbolism. In fact, it is the parallels with other temples
of the Iron Age in the Ancient Near East which offer the strongest affirmation that the
Temple described in the Book of Kings did indeed exist even if the picture we can have of
it is not fully exact.[4]

The Bible speaks from time to time of "going up" to Mount Zion or the Mountain of
the Lord. The toponym Zion, whose derivation and meaning remain elusive, originally
designated the fortress captured by King David, indicating that it was the hill overlooking
the royal compound in Jerusalem. The term was applied in the course of time to all of
Jerusalem, and eventually to the entire Land of Israel. The Mountain of the Lord is

therefore not particularly high, and one passage even states that Jerusalem is surrounded by mountains; but the disappointing topographic reality needs not detract from the emotional experience of the ascent. Isaiah, Micah, Ezekiel, and the so-called Deutero-Zechariah (Zech. 9–14) from among the prophets predict, each in his own style, that in the End of Days, as a result of apocalyptic catastrophes and upheavals, "the mountain of the Lord's House shall be established in the top of the mountains, and shall be exalted above the hills."[5] This vision of the future certainly reflects the aspirations and desires of the present, and pilgrims going up to the House of the Lord assumedly saw in their mind's eye and felt themselves symbolically uplifted or spiritually ascending a much loftier promontory.

Sacred mountains are known from ancient Near Eastern sources and the Bible itself. In mountainless Mesopotamia temples were built as artificial mountains in the form of stepped towers known as *ziqqurrat*s, and considered cosmic bonds or staircases linking heaven with earth. The *ziqqurrat* is the architectural form behind the biblical account of the Tower of Babel, as well as the staircase or ladder Jacob saw in his dream at Bethel.[6] The Temple of the Goddess Ishtar in the city of Assur, outside of Mesopotamia proper, stood on Mount Ebih, which a Sumerian myth considers a rebellious mountain believed to have been subdued by the goddess Inanna (= Ishtar).

Of particular significance for Mount Zion is Mount Tzaphon, the mountain upon which the Canaanite deity Baal-Hadad resided according to mythological texts from Ugarit (ancient Ras-Shamra in Syria). In fact, Ps. 48, which is a psalm praising Zion and its Temple, juxtaposes the terms *har Tziyyon*, Mount Zion, and *yarketei Tzafon*, "the recesses of Tzaphon," thus identifying the two (v. 3). The Canaanite deity El also lived at a place designated in Ugaritic *hurshanu* (cf. Akkadian *hurshanu*), or mountain range. El's mountain was at the "source of the rivers; amidst the channels of the two oceans," a concept reminiscent of the biblical Garden of Eden, a divine garden from which four rivers flowed, and having parallels in the bronze vessels in Solomon's Temple (see below). If so, the biblical concept of Jerusalem's Temple Mount as a holy mountain has roots in beliefs of neighboring cultures and in particular those of the Canaanites.

The Bible refers to various holy mountains, or mountains of God. According to some sources, the entire Land of Israel is the "Mountain of God's Inheritance" (Exod. 15.17) or the "Mountain which His right hand created" (Ps. 78.54). Various traditions relating to the period prior to building the Temple in Jerusalem recognize a Holy Mountain located elsewhere. The supplements to the laws of the Book of Deuteronomy (Deut. 27.1–7) and historiography in the Book of Joshua (Josh. 8.30–32) single out Mount Ebal as a place where an altar and several stones inscribed with the laws are erected. Nonetheless, even if Mount Ebal (rather than Jerusalem) is the site which the legislator considers the place where YHWH will eventually choose "to cause his name to dwell," there is no indication that it possesses any natural sanctity or cosmic significance, and Mount Ebal is never called a holy mountain or mountain of God.

Most important is the mountain where God appeared first to Moses and then to the entire People of Israel, called either Sinai or Horeb. Horeb is referred to explicitly by one Pentateuchal author as The "Mountain of God" and in one place "The Mountain of YHWH" (Num. 10.33). Another source provides no appellation for Mount Sinai, but its account of revelation portrays the mountain as a sacred compound at the time of revelation and until the Tabernacle is built; and afterwards several elements from the revelation, especially the Divine Glory (*kavod*), the cloud and the fire upon the Mountain, are transferred to the Tabernacle and eventually end up in Solomon's Temple (1 Kings 8). All this indicates that in the view of that school, Solomon's Temple in Zion is Mount Sinai's heir as a mountain where God dwells, although it had no sanctity prior to the time of David.

There is no hint in the Pentateuch, the books of Joshua, Judges, Samuel, and Kings, or even the Book of Chronicles, that Jerusalem was considered a Mountain of God before the time of David and Solomon, and even the story of the binding of Isaac, which provides a cult legend for this site (Gen. 22.14), offers no indication that the Land of Moriah had any inherent sanctity or cosmic qualities before it was chosen for the test of Abraham. If so, the traditions reflected in Psalms and several of the prophetic books (especially Isaiah) regarding Mount Zion as inherently holy and not only because of the Temple built upon it, developed after the fact because of the Temple. In other words, according to the majority of biblical traditions the Temple was built on Mount Zion because of a human or divine choice and not because of some inherent, natural quality. Yet alongside these traditions, certain biblical authors begin to consider the mountain as having sanctity which antedated the Temple. We should note in particular the story of the binding of Isaac from which the sanctity of the Temple site originates in the Patriarchal period, the identification of Mount Moriah in 2 Chronicles 3.1 with the place where David built an altar after a plague ceased (cf. 1 Chron. 21.15–22.1), the identification of Zion with Mount Tzaphon, and Jeremiah 17.12, "O Throne of Glory (*kavod*), exalted from the very beginning, the place of our Temple!"

The Temple could be entered through a number of gates. One cannot be sure what these gates looked like or their number at the time of Solomon. However, assuming that the gates the prophet Ezekiel envisions for the future Temple reflect those he saw in the Jerusalem Temple on the eve of its destruction in 586 BCE, then we may assume that at some time during its long history the Temple was outfitted with gates resembling those found in excavations at Megiddo and Gezer, the dates of which are still not firmly fixed by archaeologists.

It can be assumed that ritual purity was required of Temple visitors. Men and women alike visited the Temple to worship and participate in sacrificial meals, although women may have come less frequently because of purity restrictions as well as family responsibilities. All were welcome, including Gentiles from distant lands, although certain idealistic Psalms express ethical requirements, and such strictures have parallels in temples of other ancient Near Eastern religions. At the time of Solomon, entering the Temple was free. However, at the time of Jehoash, King of Judah (late 9th century BCE), voluntary contributions were instituted that would be collected by priests watching at the threshold (2 Kings 12). These contributions were collected in a wooden box with a hole in its lid standing beside the altar. This box would be opened when full by a royal scribe and the high priest, and the silver accumulated would be refined, counted, and disbursed to artisans engaged in repairing damages to the Temple. This practice indicates that responsibility for maintaining the Temple had passed, at least partially, from the royal purse to the public pocket. At the same time, oversight of the Temple maintenance fund was shared by King and clergy, as it was in contemporary Assyrian temples as well. This shows certain democratization or popularization of the cult, a phenomenon reflected as well in the account of building the Tabernacle (Exod. 35) and the story in 1 Chronicles about building the Temple in which the people contribute generously from their own property to the construction project.

Scholars sometimes refer to Solomon's Temple as a "royal chapel" – an analogy of the "Royal Sanctuary" at Bethel visited by Amos (Amos 7.12). As illustrative of this designation, archaeologists have pointed out that building complexes encompassing palace and temple such as may have existed in Jerusalem are well known from other sites in the ancient Near East. In fact, the Temple was within earshot of the Palace, as illustrated by a story in which Queen Athalyah goes to the Temple because she hears a tumult coming from its courtyard (2 Kings 11.13). Ezekiel too sees immediate proximity of Temple and Palace as a source of defilement which is to be eliminated from the Temple of the future (Ezek. 43.7–9). Nonetheless, free access and dependence on public funding challenge the accuracy of such an appellation. Although Temple and Palace were next-door neighbors, and this certainly enhanced the prestige of the King and might even have been manipulated by him for his own purposes, they were in fact separate entities. The Royal Palace with its Hall of Pillars, House of the Forest of Lebanon, and Throne Room where the king sat in judgment, was considerably larger than the Temple, certainly no less grand, and took longer to build; but the biblical authors, interested more in religious than in mundane matters, describe it in far less detail. One may wonder, nonetheless, which of the buildings would have made the greater impression.

Upon entering the Temple compound one stands in the large Outer Court. This court is paved with large hewn stones and surrounded by service chambers (*leshakhot*) used by priests, prophets, and courtiers. They serve for eating sacrificial meat, storage, and other assorted functions. The courtyard itself is full of people reciting prayers and psalms, and preparing or consuming sacrifices. Similar structures with like purposes were present at Shiloh (1 Sam. 1.9 Septuagint), Ramah (1 Sam. 9.22) and perhaps Dan. One cannot know how many were in the Temple when first built, but narratives in the Book of Jeremiah and Ezekiel's vision show that by the end of the First Temple's existence they were numerous and were loci of royal and clerical activity of not strictly cultic nature (Jer. 35.2, 4; 36.10, 12, 20, 21; Ezek. 40.17; 42.9, 10; 45.5, etc).

Continuing on, one enters the inner court, something permitted only to priests. In this court stands a large altar of bronze which serves for several types of sacrifices and libations. The priests tend the fire burning on the altar, arrange cuts of sacrificial animals, gather the blood of the victims, and pour it at the base of the altar, all using special bronze implements [fig. 4]. At the time of King Ahaz (mid to late 8th century BCE) this altar was replaced by one in Aramaean style while the older, Solomonic altar was pushed aside, serving now for special rituals, perhaps divination by means of examining the entrails performed for the king (2 Kings 16.10–15). The old altar was simple, having only a single storey and a set of horns, resembling the bronze altar described for the Tabernacle or the stone altar, remains of which were found in Tel Sheva [fig. 5]. The new altar, which Ezekiel saw as the basis for the altar in the future temple, is stepped having three stages, and resembles in form and the names of its parts the Mesopotamian stepped temple towers called *ziqqurrat*s (Ezek. 43.13–17).

The Temple itself stands in the middle of the court. In front of the building, to the right and left of the entrance, stand enormous bronze implements filled with water. Left of the entrance as one faces the building is a huge basin, or Sea (*yam*). This Sea rests on twelve bronze cattle, four facing each direction of the compass. Along with them are ten immense wheeled stands (*mekhonot*) made of bronze [fig. 6]. Each stand is decorated with lions, cattle, and cherubs, and atop each one rests a bronze basin (*kiyyor*). According to a note in the Book of Chronicles, the Sea served for priestly ablutions, while the smaller basins held water for washing the flesh and entrails of the sacrificial animals.

But apart from the practical cultic function of these vessels, their number, size, and decoration indicate that they had a symbolic role. Some scholars have suggested that they symbolized God's war with primeval sea monsters around the time of creation. They would then be trophies from this battle, and one can compare, for example, the Sumerian deity Ninurta's vanquished enemies displayed in the temple at Nippur according to the text "Ninurta's Return to Nippur."

Even if right, this explanation does not exhaust the symbolism. In fact, the key to unlocking the symbolic meaning of the bronze water works is provided by Ezekiel's concluding vision in which he tours and describes the Temple of the future. This Temple contains no such vessels. Instead, at the place where the bronze Sea stood in Solomon's Temple, Ezekiel sees welling up from under the Temple threshold a steady stream flowing

4 Shovels from Tel Dan

5 Altar from Tel Sheva

6 Miniature water wagon from Cyprus
(1225–1100 BCE)
© The Trustees of the British Museum

7 Water basin from Assur

out and down, eastward into a sea in the Jordan Rift Valley ('Arabah) – this is the Salt Sea, known today as the Dead Sea. Only this Sea, after receiving the waters of the stream flowing from the Temple, is no longer dead, for this stream is a source of life for animals and plants grazing and growing on its banks, and the stream "heals" the Salt/Dead Sea itself into which it flows.

This river of the future, also described by Joel (4.18), reminds one of the river flowing from the Garden of Eden where it watered the Garden, and then branched into four streams. Now the Garden of Eden was God's private pleasure garden, tended by newly created Man, where God could walk, enjoying the afternoon breeze. If so, the river flowing from Ezekiel's temple and the bronze water implements in Solomon's Temple symbolized the river flowing forth from the Garden of Eden. Other ancient Near Eastern temples and palaces had in them streams or waterworks of various sorts. An inscription of the Assyrian King Ilu-shuma (early 2nd millennium BCE) tells that from the Ishtar temple in the city of Assur, situated on Mount Ebih, two streams flowed forth to different gates, just as we find in Deutero-Zechariah[7] (Zech. 14.8); and Assyrian kings such as Ashurnasirpal II (883–859 BCE) and Sennacherib (704–681 BCE) dug canals alongside the palaces in their newly built capital cities, Kalhu and Nineveh. The waterworks of the Jerusalem Temple thus mark it as the natural habitat of the Divine resident.

Another important line of meaning is suggested by Ugaritic mythology. El's abode on Mount Tzaphon was located at "the underground wellspring of the rivers, amidst the course of the two seas." Solomon's waterworks consisting of a Sea and two rows of water wagons are comparable, in which case the Temple resembles the abode of the Canaanite deity El, and suits the well known El-YHWH syncretism. Finally, a large water basin found at Assur was decorated with figures of primordial sages, deities holding jugs from which flow streams of water [fig. 7]. The primordial sages mark the basin as belonging to Ea, the Mesopotamian god of wisdom and crafts who is identified eventually with Canaanite El.

An additional aspect of the water vessels connects them to both the ideal world of the future and the divine garden. The water stands are decorated with lions, bulls, and cherubs. Cherubs are winged, mythological denizens of the divine realm and divine gardens. Furthermore, the combination of lions and bulls is reminiscent of Isaiah's prophecy (Isa. 11.6–9):

> And the wolf will dwell with the sheep, and the leopard will crouch with the kid;
> And the calf and the lion cub will graze together and a small boy will lead them.
> And the cow and the bear will graze, together their offspring will crouch down;
> And the lion like the cattle will eat straw.

The prophecy then says "They will no longer be wicked or violent throughout my sacred mountain." If so, harmony and serene coexistence between carnivorous and herbivorous animals is connected with the Holy Mountain where the future Temple will stand. Again, the decorations of the Temple implements in the present reflect the ideal divine dwelling of the future, while the Temple of the future provides the key for understanding the symbolism of the Temple of the present.

Walking between the rows of wheeled stands (*mekhonot*), one reaches the entrance to the House of God. This building, a long-room structure consisting of a forecourt, a large anteroom and a smaller inner room, resembles in overall internal layout various ancient near eastern temples, but in particular two temples from Syria – an early first-millennium temple at Tell-Ta'yinat [fig. 8] and a late second-millennium (or early first-millennium) temple at 'Ayn Dara [fig. 9].

The materials of which this building is constructed contrast sharply with those of the courtyard pavement. It is not made of hewn stone with which the courtyards are paved, but of rough, unhewn, whole stones. The builders seem to have applied to the Temple building itself the ancient altar law prohibiting an altar of hewn stone. If the reason for this prohibition is indeed that given by traditional exegetes, namely that the altar that brings peace should not be desecrated by iron used in war, then it is yet another expression of the Paradise-like tranquility of the Divine dwelling.

Furthermore, the stone structure is encased on its right, rear, and left sides by a three-storey cedar-wood structure reaching half the height of the building. A unique parallel to this wooden surrounding structure is found in the 'Ayn Dara temple which is surrounded on two sides and from behind by a chambered, stone corridor. The upright boards of this structure are called "ribs" (*tzela'ot*), while the ones laying horizontally, connecting the "ribs" with the stone walls, are called "mattresses" (*yetzi'im*). The vertical and horizontal boards made up together a type of cedar-wood box encasing the building, recalling the forest of Lebanon considered by peoples of the Ancient Near East a pure or holy divine residence. So again the Temple resembles the natural habitat of the God dwelling within.

The horizontally laying "mattresses" divide the structure into three stories, the middle story having an opening to the left of the entrance to the Temple itself. One who enters can ascend and descend through trap doors or spiral staircases. This structure houses Temple treasures, including all valuable objects dedicated to God as royal presents or items taken booty from holy wars.

Exiting the side structure and the stores, and returning to the main entrance of the Temple, one finds in front, extending the width of the building, a small forecourt (*ulam*). This court, 20 cubits wide and 10 deep, is enclosed by a low wall whose height equals that of the wall around the Temple courtyard itself.[8] In the forecourt stand two immense hollow pillars cast from bronze and topped with floral motifs [fig. 10]. These pillars support nothing, standing free with no architectural function, being obviously of decorative and symbolic significance. Unfortunately, one can only guess what their meaning might be. On

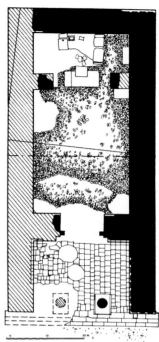

8   Temple at Tell Ta'yinat

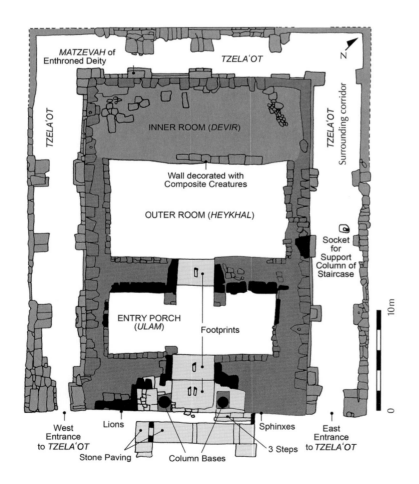

9   Temple at 'Ayn Dara
(after Gunnar Lehmann)

10 Terra cotta temple model showing columns, Tell al-Far`a (biblical Tirzah?), 10th century BCE

11 *Kudurru* (boundary stone) of Eanna-shum-iddina
© The Trustees of the British Museum
The square boxes support divine symbols and represent temple entrances with multiple interlocking door frames

the one hand, they flank the entryway as silent witnesses to the great event of God's entry into the new Temple when it was dedicated. If so, they bear constant witness to God's presence in the Temple, much like the flag flying over Buckingham Palace or Windsor Palace when the Queen is present. If this is their function, then they resemble the giant footprints found in the 'Ayn Dara temple leading from the entry to the inner sancta.

On the other hand, something may be learned from the physical shape of the pillars. Atop each pillar is a lotus-shaped capital, decorated with pomegranates, and intertwined, tangled branches, making them essentially stylized trees. This raises the possibility that they represent the two trees which grew in the middle of the Garden of Eden, namely the Tree of Knowledge and the Tree of Life. This symbolic interpretation accords well, of course, with the other motifs already observed connecting the Temple with the divine garden.

The pillars were given the names Yakhin and Boaz, names no less enigmatic than the pillars that bear them. They may be related to inscriptions often engraved on cult objects; and one might mention an inscription from the Assyrian city Kar-Tukulti-Ninurta describing two wooden pillars dedicated to the god Assur, each one bearing an inscription. They may also be words of some blessing or a prayer for the king who built the Temple and made the pillars. It has been suggested that they are the first words of the prayers, "may YHWH establish (*yikon*) the throne of his David and his kingdom to his descendants forever"[9] and, "by might (*be'oz*) of YHWH may the king rejoice."[10] The first of these names resembles the name of a gate of Nineveh given it by Sennacherib, "Enlil makes my regnal period stable."[11] If this is indeed the name's interpretation, it provides the only explicit link between the Temple design and aspirations of the royal dynasty.

Passing between the two pillars, one reaches the entrance of the Temple building itself. The entrance is framed by four stepped, interlocking doorframes. The frames are of "oil wood," which is either a type of olive wood or pine. Similar stepped doorframes are found in tomb entrances in Cyprus, or windows depicted on ancient ivories such as the famous Woman in the Window from Nimrud. Most importantly, they resemble a feature representing temples *pars pro toto* in divine symbols used in Mesopotamian iconography. Such representations appear in the divine symbols on the so-called "entitlement monuments" (*kudurru*) [fig. 11], on which gods are represented by standard symbols mounted upon square mounts showing several interlocking squares. The same occurs on the relief atop the stele of Hammurabi, King of Babylon, where the Sun-God Shamash sits upon a temple entrance consisting of four interlocking frames. In the doorframe hang two doors, each made of two planks of cypress or juniper wood.

The doors are engraved with cherubs, palmettes, and open calyxes, and the decorations are overlain with gold applied in a way designated enigmatically as "straightened" (*meyyushar*). These doors are opened and closed every morning and evening with golden implements, certainly a type of key. Door opening rituals are known from other ancient Near Eastern temples, and in particular Shiloh where young Samuel, who slept in the temple, opened its doors on the morning after his vision.

Having entered the Temple building, one is found in a long room measuring 20x40 cubits known as the "outer sanctum" (*heykhal*). Similar to the doors from the outside, the floor of this room is of cypress (or perhaps juniper) wood. But the walls and ceiling are of cedarwood, and the room was assumedly somewhat fragrant. The two sidewalls as well as the wall through which one enters from the outside are engraved with gourds and calyxes. But the far wall, at the rear of the *heykhal*, through which one enters the innermost room, or Holy of Holies, is decorated more ornately. It is covered not with gourds and calyxes but with calyxes, palmettes, and cherubs. The cherubs engraved on the doors to the *heykhal* represent, certainly, guards and may be compared in this capacity with the cherubs holding the ever-turning sword guarding the entry to the Garden of Eden and the way to the Tree of Life. The cherubs on the back wall of the *heykhal* represent, in contrast, the honor guard standing outside the throne room in which the Divine King sits enthroned in all His radiant Glory.

The *heykhal*, where the main daily ritual is performed, is equipped with cultic furnishings outfitted with appropriate implements; and the ritual performed aims at arousing the senses and providing the daily needs of the Divine resident.

Along the sidewalls stand ten golden lamp stands (*menorot*), five to the right and five to the left. On each lamp stand rests a golden oil lamp which burns from dusk to dawn, as God's lamp did at Shiloh. The priest tends these lamps with golden implements.

In the middle of the *heykhal* stands a table upon which loaves of bread are arranged as are pouring and drinking vessels, all for the Divine repast. The meals served periodically on this table were accompanied by music played upon gilded-instruments called "music makers" (*mezammerot*).[12]

In front of the doors leading into the inner chamber stands an altar for incense [fig. 12]. This altar is made of cedarwood overlain with gold. The attending priests place incense upon it using golden spoons, called, literally "palms" [fig. 13] and in order to burn the incense coals are brought from the courtyard altar upon golden pans.

To enter the inner chamber called the *devir* or "Holy of Holies," one passes through a short corridor surrounded by interlocking five frames. The doors to the Holy of Holies are made of "oil wood" and decorated with cherubs, palmettes [fig. 14], and calyxes and covered with gold.

The Holy of Holies itself is cubic, twenty cubits to each dimension, and entirely of cedarwood. The walls of this chamber are covered with gold and decorated with calyxes, palmettes, and cherubs representing God's heavenly retinue, reminding one of the Divine throne-room scenes described in the prophecy of Michayahu son of Yimla (1 Kings 22.19–25), Isaiah's Throne Vision (Isa. 6), and the heavenly scene opening the Book of Job (Job 1). Above the Holy of Holies is an attic or loft. This secret room may have been "the bed room," used by Ahaziah's sister Jehosheba to hide her nephew Jehoash from wicked Queen Athalyah (2 Kings 11.2), and one scholar has suggested that it was used for performing a sacred marriage rite. Many scholars suggest, on the basis of comparison with other temples such as those at Arad, 'Ayn Dara and Tell Ta'yinat, that the Holy of Holies was elevated, its floor higher than the floor of the *heykhal*. There is, however, no indication of such an elevation, nor is there one in the Tabernacle or in Ezekiel's temple of the future, which was probably based on Solomon's Temple.

In the middle of the Holy of Holies stand two enormous cherubs, each ten cubits

12 Incense altar from Megiddo

high with a ten-cubit wingspan. The outstretched wings fill the chamber from side to side. These cherubs represent God's throne, and are the basis of the divine epithet "He who sits upon the cherubs" (1 Sam. 4.4). But this throne is not stationary but mobile, and when moving from place to place it serves as God's sedan chair, giving the title "Rider of the Cherubs" (Ps. 18.11). According to the Book of Chronicles, this cherub throne is a model of the *Merkavah*, a term used in post-biblical Hebrew to designate the Divine chariot described in the first and twelfth chapters of Ezekiel.

Under the outstretched wings of the cherubs stands the Ark (*aron*), literally a box. This Ark, brought to Jerusalem from Shiloh where it stood earlier, is God's footstool when He sits upon the cherub throne. As in some other ancient near eastern temples where copies of treaties were placed at the feet of the gods, the Ark stores the tablets of the Covenant recording the covenant between God and His People Israel.

The importance of this inner room is emphasized by the grand door in its entrance, and also by the form of the Temple in its entirety. Looking back on what has been seen thus far one recalls that the way from the courtyard into the Holy of Holies displays cultic

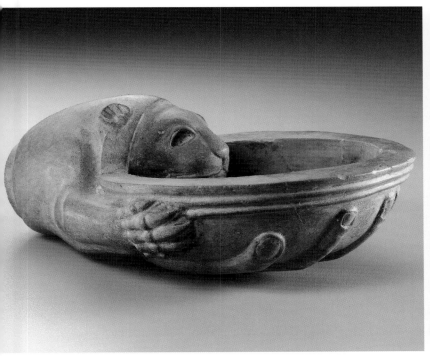

13 Incense spoon from Tel Kinnarot (9th-8th centuries BCE)

14 Cherub on ivory from Samaria

implements and decorations increasing in material worth and technological sophistication as one progressed inward. In the courtyard, everything was made of bronze, but when entering the building one encounters only gold, and the amount of gold increased going from the *heykhal* into the *devir*. The wood in the *heykhal* was both cedar and cypress, while in the Holy of Holies it was cedar with the cherubs of oil wood. The outer doors were surrounded by a four-tiered doorframe, while the frame of the inner door was five-tiered. The walls of the *heykhal* were decorated with gourds and calyxes, while those of the Holy of Holies bore calyxes, palmettes, and cherubs (see table on page 35).

The gradual increase in the value of the materials and the sophistication of design parallels an increase in sanctity and limitations on who may enter. The outer court would have been visited by the public at large, while the inner court was restricted to priests, and the inside of the Temple was open only to the high priest. All in all, Solomon's Temple is a luxurious divine residence in a mountaintop pleasure garden; and its general design focuses on the inner room, and is meant to glorify and magnify the Divine resident sitting on the cherub throne.

One might ask whether the Temple was aesthetically pleasing or visually impressive. The description of the Temple in 1 Kings 6–7 makes no specific allusions to such aspects of the design. This is in keeping with the Bible's general silence on aesthetic matters apart from places where the beauty of a person or an object is of importance in the narrative. It contrasts sharply with Mesopotamian building inscriptions which often praise the beauty or grandeur of the edifices they describe, all this being in line with those inscriptions' tendency to glorify the king and his works. Nonetheless, it is hard to imagine that a visitor to the Jerusalem Temple would not have been overwhelmed by the enormous bronze implements in the courtyard or impressed by the copious gold overlaying the walls and cultic furnishings inside. The bright, eye-catching materials used and the elaborate floral and zoological motifs etched on the implements and the walls are all signs of luxury, and to the extent that luxury items please the aesthetic tastes of their owners, so the Temple would have appealed to its onlooker. The Queen of Sheba is said to have been left breathless at what she saw in Jerusalem, and this included Solomon's processions to (or sacrifices in) the House of YHWH (1 Kings 10.5). The elders of the community of returnees from the Babylonian Exile who had beheld the First Temple in its glory, considered the newly built Second Temple as nothing in comparison, and only Divine intervention, so they believed, could make the Second more sumptuous than the First (Hag. 2.3, 9). Jerusalem is referred to as "crown of beauty, joy of all the Land," and this title would certainly include the city's most prominent building, the Temple (Lam. 2.15; cf. Ps. 50.2 referring to Zion). It seems, therefore, that the building designed to house the Divine king would have been as pleasing to its human visitors as the grand buildings neighboring peoples erected for their kings and gods. These aesthetic qualities would also enhance the religious experience of the visit to the Temple.

But, in what form did God dwell in this Temple? This question has inspired theological speculation and contention for generations, the answer changing from time to time, and even thinkers living in a single generation could answer it in varying manners. As stated above, various Ancient Near Eastern peoples regarded temples as earthly residences for their gods. The gods were manifest in the temples in physical embodiments as cult statues or other sorts of symbols. Such a way of representing the God of Israel in an Israelite temple would be possible as long as it was believed that divinity could be imbued in a physical object; and, indeed, the Book of Judges mentions a cult statue in the private Temple of Micah in the Tribe of Dan, while other temples such as at Bethel and Arad housed stone pillars (*matzevot*) [fig. 15]. Certain contemporary scholars suggest that representing YHWH by an anthropomorphic statue was as common in ancient Israel as it was elsewhere in the ancient near east, and that even the Jerusalem Temple hosted such an icon.

Be this as it may—and it is hardly convincing nor is it the scholarly consensus that the Jerusalem Temple ever housed a statue of the God of Israel—as soon as a cult developed which was free of such physical embodiments of divinity, such a statue would have no place in an Israelite temple. At the same time, however, Solomon pronounces "I have surely built You an exalted house; a place for Your eternal dwelling" (1 Kings 8.13).

So how did God dwell in the exalted house built by Solomon? Since the Ark served as God's sedan-chair and footstool, introducing it into the Temple and placing it in the Holy of Holies, as reported in 1 Kings 8, brought with it the invisible God seated upon it. Where the Ark goes, there goes God! This has been designated "empty seat aniconism." Authors from the so-called "Priestly School" did not suffice with an invisible, transcendent God, and in their opinion God dwelled first in the Tabernacle and subsequently in Shiloh and then Jerusalem in the form of something called *kavod*, often translated glory, or majesty, but preferably "glorious radiance." This term, in its theological usage is not an abstract term meaning "honor" or "glory" as it is in many parts of the Bible, but signifies something quite perceptible. The divine *kavod* is the shining radiance which enveloped God and radiated from Him. It has been compared to the divine radiance called *melammu* in Akkadian and a mark of all gods. This radiance overwhelmed and could knock off his feet anyone who gazed upon it, and it in turn was shrouded by a cloud. Ezekiel, who lived at the time of the destruction of the Temple, describes the step-by-step exiting of the *kavod* from the Temple before its destruction (Ezek. 10), and in his vision of reconstruction he sees it return. Zechariah shares Ezekiel's view, and in rebuilt Jerusalem God promises to be: "A wall of fire round about [...]. And *kavod* in its midst" (Zech. 2.9).

But in striking contrast to the Priestly School and these two prophets, the school responsible for the main part of the Book of Deuteronomy and the redaction of the Former Prophets places God in His heavenly dwelling-place, limiting His presence in the Temple to His name that is called upon the Temple. According to this school, God looks down from His heavenly residence (Deut. 26.15); and Solomon says "The Heavens and the Heavens of Heavens do not contain You, how much less this Temple which I have built" (1 Kings 8.27). When these authors kicked God upstairs, so to speak, they turned the earthly Temple in Jerusalem into a type of switchboard that would redirect heavenwards any prayer directed towards it. God sees the supplicant in the Temple and hears his prayer, but is not present there Himself.

Disagreement often yields compromise, and, to be sure, already the prophet Isaiah sees God sitting on a high and exalted throne, in the Temple, but according to the seraphim whom the prophet hears, God's *kavod* fills the entire earth (Isa. 6).

A similar compromise was accepted by the anonymous prophet of the restoration period, whom scholars call Third-Isaiah. In his opinion, God says "The heavens are My throne and the earth is My footstool; which is the house you will build Me, and which is the place of My resting?" (Isa. 66.1) The same prophet says elsewhere: "My House will be called a House of Prayer for all the peoples" (Isa. 56.7), and in this he accepts the concept of Solomon's prayer and of the school responsible for the main part of the Book of Deuteronomy. As for the concept of *kavod*, Third-Isaiah construes it as the light of God which will shine upon His people as well as the glorious building materials which the peoples will bring to the Temple as we find: "The glorious wealth (*kavod*) of Lebanon will come to you, cypress and pine and box together// to adorn the place of my Sanctuary and the place of my feet I will glorify (*akabbed*)" (Isa. 60.13).

It seems that the prophet Haggai too was a compromiser. He predicts that God's *kavod* will enter the Temple as the heavens and earth quake (Hag. 2.6–9), and as far as these things go he is very close to Ezekiel. But he empties the crucial concept of *kavod* of theological meaning, for the *kavod* that is to fill the Temple is not God's radiant *kavod* that stuns any onlooker, but vast wealth. Similarly, God says that he will be desirous of the Temple and will be "glorified" by it, using the word *ekkabed(ah)* "I will be honored," namely, the new Temple will be for God's glory and honor (Hag. 1.8). It turns out that Third-Isaiah and Haggai as well exploit a play on words, and the multivalence of the word *kavod*, in order to span the theological abyss separating two radically different concepts of Divine presence in the Temple.

In fact, the two concepts exist to this day. The *kavod* has changed, developed, and metamorphosed into the rabbinic *Shekhinah* which is a restricted Divine presence focused in a particular locus, and according to the Rabbis the *Shekhinah* during the Second Temple period was found in one of the lamps burning on the Temple lamp stand, so that the radiance of the *kavod* persists even though it is, so to speak "on a low flame."

But, when the Second Temple was initiated after the Babylonian Exile no hint is recorded that God's *kavod* entered the newly rebuilt Temple as expected; and the initiation festivities of this Temple, which should have climaxed with the entry of the Divine resident into the rebuilt Temple, were limited to offering sacrifices (Ezra 6.16–18). This is because, as it turned out, the Temple is devoid of its Divine resident. And, to be sure, the concept that God is not restricted to the Temple is complementary to the concept that God is found everywhere and can be worshipped anywhere and everywhere, and this is the concept which permits the existence of synagogues, the Jewish institution which eventually inherited and replaced the Temple.

But were one to ask the builder of the First Temple and the architect who designed it the rhetorical question "Will God really dwell with Man upon the earth?" he would be likely to answer "But of course, for the Temple is Heaven on Earth."[13]

The Internal Décor of Solomon's Temple – A Synopsis

Chamber	*Heykhal*	*Devir*/ Holy of Holies
Doors		
Type of wood	Cypress	Oil Wood
Number of boards	2 each rounded?	1
Plating material	Gold	Gold
Plating method	straightened on the engraving	beaten on the cherubs and palmettes
Engraving	Cherubs	Cherubs
	Palmettes	Palmettes
	Open Calyxes	Open Calyxes
Doorposts	Four framed	Five framed
	Oil wood	???
Floor	Cypress	Cedar
Ceiling	Cedar	Cedar
Walls		
Wood type	Cedar	Cedar
Engraving	Gourds	Palmettes
	Open Calyxes	Open Calyxes
	-----------	Cherubs
Plating material	Gold	Gold
Furnishings		
		Huge Cherubs
		Ark
	Incense altar	
	Table of showbread	
	Ten Lampstands	
Wood Type	Cedar	Oil Wood
Plating material	Gold and sāgûr gold	Gold

538 BCE–70 CE:
The Temple (*Beyt Ha-Miqdash*) and Its Mount

Joseph Patrich

The Hebrew University of Jerusalem

Introduction

The prevalent name of the period in the history of the Jewish people dealt with in the present article—The Second Temple Period—reflects the centrality of the Temple in the life of the Jewish nation in this era. This period began with the restoration of the Temple under the Persian Achaemenids and ended with its second destruction by the Romans. Its apogee was during its final century, better known as the Herodian Period. During this lengthy period the Jews enjoyed political independence only for a short time, under the Hasmoneans; the Herodians were client kings of Rome. But Jewish religious autonomy, including conduct of the Temple service according to their Law, was maintained almost throughout without any hindrance on the part of the Persians, Greeks, or Romans.

According to the Roman author Pliny, at the time of its destruction Jerusalem was "by far the most famous city of the East and not of Judaea only."[1] The Temple was the largest and most impressive structure therein, the center of religious and national life and a goal of pilgrimage. In its splendor and importance it eclipsed all other institutions of the Jews, both in the Land of Israel and in the Diaspora. It was the one and only Temple of the entire nation. The Greek historian Polybius, writing in the second century BCE, noted that Jews were a nation residing around a Temple called Jerusalem.[2] The Roman historian Tacitus wrote: "Jerusalem is the capital of the Jews. In it was a temple possessing enormous riches."[3]

This chapter will focus mainly on the architectural history of the Temple and its precinct. There is a variety of literary sources at our disposal: biblical and post-biblical, the writings of the Jewish historian Flavius Josephus, the New Testament, the Dead Sea Scrolls (mainly the Temple Scroll), and rabbinic sources. There are also several allusions by Greek and Latin authors. These sources do not uniformly cover the entire period.

15 Herodian decorated fragment, found ca. 1970 in the excavations of Benjamin Mazar and Meir Ben-Dov south of the Temple Mount. Most probably originating from the Herodian Triple Gate that led up to the Mount from the south. On permanent exhibition in the Hecht Museum, Haifa

We have less information on the Persian period (538–332 BCE) than we have on the Hellenistic era (332–37 BCE), while we are much more informed about the Herodian period (37 BCE–70 CE). The archaeological finds pertains mainly to the Herodian precinct walls and gates, first explored in the nineteenth century.[4] Outside the precinct, large-scale archaeological excavations were conducted on the south and southwest.[5] There are several remains within the area of the Haram al-Sharif that can also be attributed to the Second Temple, including most of the water cisterns, 37 altogether. The Herodian names of three of them are known: *HaGullah*, *hqr*, and the Great Cistern. Water was drawn by a wheel.[6] Of the Temple proper there are no remains. It seems that the floor level of the upper court was higher than the top elevation of the rock within the present Dome, so it never constituted a part of the Temple.[7]

Religious restrictions determined that the Second Temple and the altar should follow the location and the main outlines of the First Temple. The pre-Herodian Temple Mount was delineated on the east by the Kidron valley and on the west by the Tyropoeon valley. The Herodian precinct extended beyond this valley on the southwest. On the north the pre-Herodian Temple Mount was delineated by two tributaries of the Kidron and of the Tyropoeon, with a saddle in between, located in its northwest. The Herodian precinct extended beyond these two tributaries.

The Persian Period (538–332 BCE)

Their Temple destroyed and most of their people exiled, the Jews had only the prophetic words of Jeremiah on which to peg their hopes for redemption. Jeremiah foretold both the impending destruction of Jerusalem at the hand of the Babylonians and the seventy-year length of the Jewish exile in Babylonia.[8]

After thirty years of exile, a series of seemingly insignificant events would bring Jeremiah's vision closer to fruition. While the Babylonians saw the deity Marduk as their supreme God, Nabonidus, who assumed kingship over Babylon in 556 and ruled until 539 BCE, wished to elevate the moon god, Sin, much to the consternation of the Babylonian people. With Nabonidus' standing among the people and priesthood weakened because of this conflict, the ambitious Cyrus, who united the Persian and Median Empires, saw that it was opportune to expand his realm westward. His opportunity came in 539 when Nabonidus set up the statues of many Akkadian deities in the city of Babylon. In the wake of this controversial act, Cyrus conquered Babylonia without resistance and was accepted unanimously as king. The so-called "Cyrus Cylinder," discovered in 1879, asserts that he returned all of the "misplaced" deities to their respective temples. The biblical Book of Ezra quotes, in Hebrew, the decree Cyrus issued to the exiled Jews in Babylon in 538 by which he permitted the Jews to return to Jerusalem, rebuild the Temple, and restore its cult:

Thus said King Cyrus of Persia: The Lord God of Heaven has given me all the kingdoms of the earth and has charged me with building Him a house in Jerusalem, which is in Judah. Anyone of you of all his people—may his God be with him, and let him go up to Jerusalem that is in Judah and build the House of the Lord God of Israel, the God that is in Jerusalem; and all who stay behind, wherever he may be living, let the people of his place assist him with silver, gold, goods, and livestock, besides the freewill offering to the House of God that is in Jerusalem.[9]

In a parallel, more official memorandum, written in Aramaic and addressed to Cyrus' administration, the goal of restoring the Temple and renewing its cult is more specific. Details are given about the Temple's structure, dimensions, building materials, financing, and vessels:

Memorandum: In the first year of King Cyrus, King Cyrus issued an order concerning the House of God in Jerusalem: "Let the house be rebuilt, a place for offering sacrifices, with a base built up high. Let it be sixty cubits high and sixty cubits wide, with a course of unused timber for each three courses of hewn stone. The expenses shall be paid by the palace. And the gold and silver vessels of the House of God which Nebuchadnezzar had taken away from the Temple in Jerusalem, and transported to Babylon shall be returned, and let each go back to the Temple in Jerusalem where it belongs; you shall deposit it in the House of God."[10]

Some of the vessels pillaged by Nebuchadnezzar (the Babylonian king [605–562 BCE] responsible for the destruction of the First Temple), were entrusted by Cyrus to Sheshbazzar, the newly installed governor of the province of Judaea. Sheshbazzar rebuilt the altar on its earlier base and the sacrifices were renewed, though the foundations of the Temple were not yet laid. Then the Feast of Tabernacles was celebrated and sacrifices associated with other feasts and new moons were resumed, as well as freewill offerings.[11] Fifty years after the destruction of the First Temple, the initial foundations of the Second Temple were laid by Sheshbazzar in 536 BCE. At the foundation ceremony priests officiated in their ritual apparel, with trumpets, cymbals, and songs of praise.

However, full realization of Cyrus' declaration was much more difficult to achieve due to the hardships of life in the deserted city, administrative obstacles, the animosity of neighboring nations, and friction between the returnees and those who were not exiled. These impediments led to a delay of over fifteen years in the construction of the Temple. Only after a copy of the official memorandum cited above was found in 520 BCE in the Persian royal archives did Darius I (522–486) allow the resumption of construction. Darius issued another decree, instructing his officials that supervision over the work be entrusted to the hands of the governor of the Jews, together with their elders, and that state funds be provided for the construction and daily provisions of sacrificial animals, wheat, salt, wine, and oil, so that they may pray for the life of the king and his sons.[12] A service for the welfare of the supreme foreign ruler of the time, be he Persian, Greek, or Roman, became common practice throughout the Second Temple period. The regular provision of offerings by the central authorities was a privilege of the Temple city Jerusalem had become. This was a means of guaranteeing the loyalty of the priests, headed by the high priest, and of the people.

Darius' decree, together with the exhortations of the prophets Haggai and Zechariah, expedited the completion of the Temple. On 12 March 515 BCE, more than twenty years after the restoration of the altar and the renewal of sacrifice and about seventy years after the destruction of the First Temple, Jeremiah's year prediction was substantiated and the Second Temple was completed. Built of stones, with timber laid in the walls, it reached a height of 60 cubits (ca. 30m in present-day units).[13] With its completion, the rite was better organized, according to the Law of Moses; priests were set in their divisions, and the Levites in their courses.

The new Temple evidently lacked the splendor of the previous one. Describing the rededication ceremony of the Temple, the Book of Ezra contrasts the ecstatic joy of those who were too young to remember the First Temple with the mournful weeping of the old priests and Levites who had served in it.[14] Moreover, several focal objects were not recovered from the pillaging of the First Temple: the Ark of Covenant, the two tablets of the Law, and the oracle of the high priest.[15]

The sources are largely silent about the fifty years following the completion of the Second Temple. In the wake of a decree of King Artaxerxes I (465–424 BCE) which invited the Jews of his empire to return to Jerusalem, Ezra, a royal scribe and priest, led a group of some 1,500 returnees in 458 BCE. A letter carried by Ezra containing a record of the decree also bears witness to the king's gifts to the Temple and to the authority bestowed upon Ezra. The king recognized the lofty status of Temple personnel by exempting them from tolls, tributes, and customs.

Upon his arrival in Jerusalem, Ezra was distressed to discover that the Jews had been intermarrying with the indigenous nations, in direct violation of biblical law. Ezra's public display of mourning stirred the people to repent and to enter into a new covenantal relationship with God, beginning with the banishment of their "foreign" wives. The covenantal ceremony presided over by Ezra, reading the Pentateuch in a street remote from the Temple courts, marks the emergence of a new expression of Jewish religiosity, alternative to the Temple. In later generations of the period that is at our concern it evolved into the institution of the synagogue.

Nehemiah, a cupbearer in the court of Artaxerxes I, took leave of his position with the king's blessing and made the trek to Jerusalem. Serving as governor of Judah for twelve years (445–433 BCE) he presided over the restoration of the city walls and gates and the rebuilding of the gates of the *bira*—a citadel of the period of Persian rule in Jerusalem—

that was first built by an earlier governor. (The First Temple, being a part of the royal palace, did not have a separate citadel; this was an innovation of the Second Temple.) By the end of his tenure, the Temple was surrounded by a precinct wall with lockable doors.

Nehemiah, like Ezra, emphasized separation from the Gentiles, refraining from mixed marriage, and keeping the Sabbath. Equally emphasized were laws which facilitated the Temple service and provided for the wellbeing of those entrusted with its administration and operation. The most basic of these contributions was the obligation to contribute yearly one-third of a sheqel for the Temple service.[16] The constant need for wood, used in copious amounts for sacrifices, was met by choosing lay families by lot. Finally, the people also affirmed their commitment to provide for the priests and Levites through tithes of both produce and animals.

Under Nehemiah and the prophet Zechariah we already hear about the courts of the House of the Lord, in the plural, indicating that by this time the built complex had already been expanded, including now more than an altar and a Temple. Around the courts were chambers which functioned as storage rooms for various offerings or served high priests and other Temple officials. Since the people gathered in the "Street of the House of God," there was not as yet an outer court for this purpose.

Our next piece of information dates from about a century later. Under the Persian King Artaxerxes III (358–338 BCE), an internal dispute erupted over the high priesthood, as a result of which the high priest John II murdered his elder brother Jeshua. Bagoses, the chief military officer of the Persian king, who had supported Jeshua, defiled the sanctuary by entering the sacred precinct and imposed on the Jews a penalty of 50 drachms (a Greek silver coin) for each lamb of the two daily sacrifices. This penalty continued in force for seven years.[17]

The Hellenistic Period (332–37 BCE)

The imperial and religious stability which typified the waning years of the Persian Empire in the first half of the fourth century BCE ended in a series of bloody bids for royal succession. Simultaneously, Alexander "the Great" of Macedon embarked on an ambitious mission of territorial conquest that would bring an end to the Persian Empire in 330. That same sweeping campaign brought Judaea under Alexander's control in 332 BCE without encountering any resistance. Thus ended more than two centuries of Persian rule over Jerusalem and the Temple.

The tumultuous aftermath of Alexander's death witnessed wars between his successors. Judaea's strategic location between Egypt and Syria turned the area into a flash-point for the succession battles between the Ptolemaic dynasty which controlled Egypt and the Seleucid dynasty which controlled Syria. Judaea was first under Ptolemaic rule (301–198 BCE) and then under the Seleucids (198–142 BCE).

Though information about the condition of Jerusalem and the Temple during the Ptolemaic period is scanty, we do know that the high priest was appointed to serve as governor of Judaea, his principal responsibility being the collection of municipal taxes. The Ptolemies initiated the translation of the Hebrew Bible into Greek. Legend has it that it was commissioned by Ptolemy II Philadelphus (283–246 BCE), with great ceremony and at great expense, and carried out by seventy sages from the Temple circles; hence it is called the Septuagint. It is also said that he contributed to the Temple many golden and silver vessels, and an elaborately worked golden table.[18] Even if a legend, this reflects the Ptolemaic custom of presenting gifts to the Temple, as is attested by other sources.

The reign of Ptolemy IV Philopator (221–205 BCE) is best known for Ptolemy's sound defeat of the Seleucid king Antiochus III the Great (223–187 BCE) at the Battle of Raphiah (217 BCE), on the border with Egypt. After routing Antiochus and his army, Ptolemy continued on an extensive campaign northward, reconquering his territories. He is said to have reciprocated for the gifts bestowed upon him by Jews in celebration of his victory at Raphiah by visiting Jerusalem and offering sacrifices in the Temple. Impressed by the Temple's beauty, he wished to enter the Holy of Holies, a request which was summarily denied by the priests because of the biblical injunction against anyone entering this sacred precinct except for the high priest, and even that only on the Day of Atonement. Ptolemy's insistence on entering aroused a great turmoil among the people who wept and prayed for salvation. Ultimately, legend has it that Ptolemy fell ill, had to be pulled out of the Temple by his bodyguards, and returned to Egypt.[19]

In 198 BCE Jerusalem and the Temple fell to Antiochus III, and after over a century of Ptolemaic control Judaea was now part of the Seleucid Empire. As the Jews came to the aid of Antiochus in his conquest of Jerusalem, the king rewarded his supporters accordingly, granting tax exemptions to Temple personnel, earmarking provisions for the Temple service, and—most importantly—guaranteeing freedom of religion for the Jewish people.[20]

Antiochus III also issued two edicts to guarantee the state of purity of the Temple and city. First, Gentiles were prohibited from entering the Temple, a ban that was in effect also in the Herodian period [fig. 16] (see below). Second, Antiochus forbade the breeding of impure animals within Jerusalem, alongside a ban on bringing their skins or meat into Jerusalem. Antiochus issued a permit for the completion of the restoration of the Temple, including the porticos, and exempted all necessary materials from customs.[21]

That the Temple required renovation is but another testimony to the damage inflicted on Jerusalem during the tumultuous years preceding Antiochus III's decisive victory, in which Jerusalem passed back and forth between the Ptolemies and the Seleucids.[22] The high priest, relegated to cultic duties by the later Ptolemies, returned to prominence under Antiochus III with new diplomatic and economic duties. Simeon II (d. ca. 196 BCE), the high priest who served during Antiochus' reign, is credited with repairing the damage sustained as a result

16 Greek inscription (now in Istanbul) forbidding foreigners, under penalty of death, from entering into the Temple
The inscription reads: "No foreigner is to enter within the balustrade and enclosure around the Sanctuary. Whoever is caught will himself be responsible for [his] consequent death"

of the wars. The extent of Simeon's renovations features prominently in the Book of Ben Sira—a work written in the first quarter of the second century BCE—which provides an elaborate and detailed description of the glorious Simeon arrayed in his vestments, officiating at the altar surrounded by his colleagues, radiant "like the sun shining resplendently on the king's Temple, and like the rainbow which appears in the cloud."[23]

Simeon's renovations included fortification of the Temple, building high retaining walls, and digging a cistern (*miqveh*), which Ben Sira described as vast like a sea.[24] The retaining walls are the deep and high quadrangular foundations for the Temple courts, usually identified with the basic square of the inner court whose dimensions were 500x500 cubits,[25] which was later encompassed within the outer court of the Herodian precinct (see below). The hewn-out reservoir may be one of the huge cisterns under the Haram.

The contemporary *Letter of Aristeas*, written in Greek, provides much information regarding the Temple structure and furnishings. According to the *Letter*, the Temple, built on a grand scale, occupied a prominent position and was enclosed within three precincts. A curtain drawn downward from above, of exquisite workmanship and impressive in its strength, was laid over the doorway of the Sanctuary. The House faced eastward. It was surrounded by a floor paved with sloped stones to permit easy drainage of the water used for cleansing the blood of the sacrifices. Hidden openings installed in the base of the altar also assisted the drainage. Seven hundred priests ministered there. The Temple had an abundant supply of flowing water, as if emerging from a spring located within the precinct. There were also magnificent underground, well-leaded, and plastered reservoirs placed around the foundations.[26]

Antiochus III mounted a final military campaign in 192 BCE which brought Asia Minor and Greece under his control. But a series of defeats at the hands of the Romans nullified Antiochus' newest territorial gains and compelled the latter to accept the terms of the peace treaty of Apamea (188 BCE), by which the Seleucids were forced to pay heavy tribute to the Romans. His treasuries depleted by the costly wars, Antiochus was compelled to loot temple treasuries throughout the kingdom. In 187 BCE Antiochus III was murdered while seeking to loot a temple in Susa.

Despite the circumstances surrounding his father's death in Susa, Seleucus IV Philopator (187–175 BCE) set his eyes on the treasures of the Jerusalem Temple where, in addition to the funds allocated for the daily sacrifices and Temple maintenance, donations, incomes, and deposits were accumulated there along with the trusts of widows and orphans.[27] In 176 BCE Seleucus sent Heliodorus, his highest ranking minister, to confiscate the treasury under the pretext that donations from the royal treasury went well beyond the needs of the Temple. By this action the asylum right of the Temple was violated. The lone account of this episode relates that Heliodorus was stopped by supernatural intervention and punishment so severe that he urged the king to send one of his enemies should he decide to plunder the Temple again.[28] Heliodorus murdered Seleucus IV in 175 BCE, though not before he repatriated his brother Antiochus IV Epiphanes (175–164 BCE), the younger son of Antiochus III, who had been held hostage by the Romans pursuant to the treaty of Apamea.

Under Antiochus IV the high priesthood became a commodity, sold to the highest bidder with the most rigorous program for the Hellenization of Jerusalem, that is, imposing Greek culture. The first was Jason, who offered the exorbitant sum of 440 gold talents for the privilege of serving as high priest. Jason's tenure (175–172 BCE) ended when the priest Menelaus pledged to the king 300 talents over above and above Jason's payments. Antiochus acceded, and Menelaus, following the example of prior Seleucid kings, stole gold vessels from the Temple to guarantee his ability to pay. As if this wasn't enough to spark the rage of Jerusalem's Jews, Onias, who publicly exposed Menelaus' misdoings, was murdered at the latter's urging. Riots ensued in Jerusalem resulting in some fatalities, but Menelaus was acquitted of any misdoing after bribing the appropriate authorities.[29]

Antiochus IV mounted a successful preemptive invasion of Egypt in 169, and turned the Ptolemaic stronghold into a puppet regime. In the autumn of 169, on his way back from Egypt, he stopped in Jerusalem, where Jason, the former high priest, had stirred up a revolt against Menelaus. Driven to avenge Jason's uprising or, perhaps, by the heavy expenditures entailed by the war, and guided by Menelaus, Antiochus plundered the Jerusalem Temple, taking the golden incense altar and the lampstand (*menorah*), with all its vessels, the table and other vessels of gold, as well as the curtain over the sanctuary entrance.[30] A subsequent invasion of Egypt ended prematurely, with Antiochus retreating to Judaea after an embarrassing confrontation with a Roman general who demanded that Antiochus retreat or suffer Roman retaliation. Antiochus, reeling from the devastating ultimatum of the Romans, returned to Jerusalem in 168, and again pillaged the city.[31] Jerusalem's houses and walls were destroyed, and a Seleucid citadel (Akra) was built in the City of David, to the south of the Temple.[32] The Temple was desecrated and dedicated to the Olympian Zeus. The altar was desolated and an "abominating idol" placed there in 167. The perpetual daily offerings ceased for the first time in over three centuries.

Some Jews passively resisted the religious persecution of the Seleucids, preferring to die as martyrs rather than violate the laws of the Torah, while others displayed compliance with the program for Hellenization. A family of priests of the house of Jehoiarib, led by their patriarch Mattathias, embarked on a revolt for the preservation of the Jewish religion. Led by Judas Maccabaeus, one of Mattathias' five sons, this Jewish army emerged victorious in a series of engagements with Antiochus' generals. In 164 Jerusalem was recaptured.

Under the Hasmonaeans (164–37 BCE) a new chapter began. Judas found the Temple deserted, the altar defiled, the gates burnt, the courts covered by wild vegetation, and the chambers ruined. Judas purified the Temple, rebuilt its inner parts, restored the gates of the chambers, and installed their doors. He refortified it, blocking up the thirteen breaches caused by the Greeks.[33] The Temple Mount (that is, Mount Zion) was surrounded by a tall wall with massive towers that encompassed the outer court. It was garrisoned as a means of protection against the Seleucids, still in the Akra.[34] This wall was later removed by Herod [fig. 17].[35] New vessels and a curtain were provided by Judas and the Temple façade was decorated by golden crowns and tablets. The defiled stones of the altar were set in a separate chamber on the northwest of the inner court,[36] a new altar was built, and the liturgy resumed. Exactly three years after Antiochus IV had defiled the Temple the altar was re-inaugurated in an eight-days-long feast, maintained to the present as the feast of Hanukkah, beginning on 25 Kislev 164 BCE.[37]

Meanwhile, political rivalry in the Seleucid court caused a change of attitude towards the Jews. Rivals competing for the throne issued letters granting the Jews the right to conduct their rite according to their laws and privileges to the city and to the Temple, and acknowledging the status of the Hasmonaean ruler as high priest.[38] Thus did the high priesthood of the house of Zadoq come to an end.

In 142 BCE, as a result of the continuing disintegration of the Seleucid state, Simeon, the last brother of Judas Maccabeus, declared the independence of Judaea from Seleucid rule. The new status of Judaea was recognized by the reigning Seleucid monarch. This marked a new stage in the fate of the Temple, the city, the state, and the nation. In 140 BCE Simeon's position as high priest was confirmed by the Great Assembly.[39] From then on the high priesthood became hereditary in the house of the Hasmonaeans until Herod's

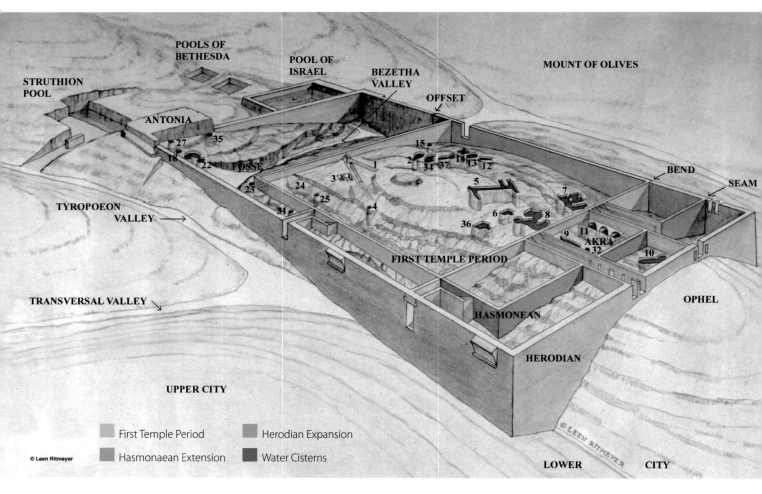

POOLS OF BETHESDA

POOL OF ISRAEL

BEZETHA VALLEY

MOUNT OF OLIVES

STRUTHION POOL

OFFSET

ANTONIA

27   35

18

22   **FOSSE**

1

15

2   14   13   12

34   37

3

5

BEND

SEAM

24

23

25

4

7

TYROPOEON VALLEY →

31

36

6   8

9   11
AKRA
32

10

FIRST TEMPLE PERIOD

TRANSVERSAL VALLEY ↘

HASMONEAN

OPHEL

HERODIAN

UPPER CITY

First Temple Period   Herodian Expansion

© Leen Ritmeyer   Hasmonaean Extension   Water Cisterns

LOWER   CITY

17   Proposed reconstructed development of the Second Temple precinct, set on the topographical relief, including the water cisterns (numbered)

18   A menorah depicted on a Hasmonaean coin of Mattathias Antigonus

time, when it ceased to be so and became an issue of Temple politics. In 139 BCE the independent status of Jerusalem and the Temple was confirmed by a letter of the Seleucid king Antiochus VII Sidetes (139–129 BCE) to Simeon.[40]

Gradually, mainly under the rule of Simeon's son John Hyrcanus I (134–104 BCE) and his grandson Alexander Jannaeus (103–76 BCE), the Jewish state had expanded in all directions. Religious zeal led to the persecution of pagan cults, the destruction of alien cities, and annihilation of their population. Contacts with the Jewish communities in the Galilee and across the river Jordan were improved. Some of them, harassed by Gentiles, were transferred or immigrated to Judaea and into Jerusalem, which subsequently expanded topographically and demographically. The Temple had to serve an ever-growing population, and the rite became more and more intricately organized. This gradual process reached its apogee in the coming generations, under Herod the Great and his successors.

Imitating customs of the neighboring Hellenistic monarchies, Judas Aristobolus—Simeon's second son—was the first to assume a royal title in 104 BCE. The Hasmonaean state became a centralized quasi-Hellenistic kingdom, with the Temple city of Jerusalem as its capital. Its king served simultaneously also as the high priest, arousing protest in some circles. Thus, the demand of the Pharisee sages[41] that Alexander Jannaeus be content with kingship alone resulted in bloodshed.[42] It is also related that once, while officiating at the altar, he was insulted and pelted by the people with their citron fruits on the Feast of Tabernacles. He is said to have built a barrier around the altar so as to protect him from such further altercations with the people.[43] Dispute over the Temple rite as conducted by the Hasmonaeans and the lunar calendar they had adopted in the Temple cult were the major reasons for the splitting off of the Dead Sea Sect and their formation as a separate sect some time in the second century BCE, when the Wicked Priest (apparently Alexander Jannaeus), had persecuted their Teacher of Righteousness. Under Salome Alexandra (76–67 BCE), the widow of Alexander Jannaeus, the non-priestly Pharisees, popular among the masses, assumed supremacy in regulating the Temple rite, which nevertheless continued to be conducted by celebrants of priestly ancestry, comprising mainly the Sadducees—the rival Jewish sect. Besides the high priest, the Temple also had a chief administrator,[44] both in the Hellenistic and the Herodian periods, treasurers, and officers, fifteen in number, in charge of specific tasks.[45] Unlike the regular priests, who served for a week, in rotation, these were tenure posts, some of them hereditary.[46]

The Hasmonaean sacred precinct covered and area of 500x500 cubits, dimensions that might go back much earlier, as was indicated above. There were five gates: two to the south (the Hulda gates), one to the west (Kiponos),[47] perhaps the one at the end of the bridge, one to the north (Tadi), and one to the east (Shoshan).[48] Being fortified, the Temple precinct could withstand a siege. After the death of Salome Alexandra, when the struggle over the throne and the high priesthood erupted between her two sons, the younger Aristobulus II found refuge there in 67 BCE in his struggle against the elderly brother Hyracanus II. Later, in 63 BCE, he managed to escape there from Pompey, the Roman consul who converted Seleucid Syria into a Roman province. Pompey conquered Jerusalem and the Temple after a prolonged siege, bringing Judaea for the first time under the Roman yoke.[49] According to one tradition the sacred precinct was captured on the Day of Atonement. Pompey's forces breached the northern wall, entered the Temple, and are said to have killed 12,000 Jews, including priests in the midst of performing their cultic duties. With some of his men, he entered beyond the curtains of the Holy of Holies, the precinct so sacred that only the high priest was allowed to enter, and only once a year, on the Day of Atonement. But not only did Pompey not touch the Temple vessels and treasures, he even ordered that the Temple be purified, cultic rites be resumed, and that Hyrcanus II be reinstalled as high priest.[50] This example was not followed by another proconsul of Syria—Marcus Licinius Crassus—who plundered the Temple in 54 BCE, in preparation for an advance against the Parthians.

Sometime during the years 48–44 BCE Julius Caesar issued a decree confirming the high priesthood of Hyrcanus II and his sons, and the title of ethnarch, but no longer a king. Hyrcanus was also granted permission to rebuild the walls of Jerusalem which had been breached by Pompey in 63 BCE, and to fortify and control Jerusalem.[51]

In 37 BCE Mattathias Antigonus, the grandson of Alexander Jannaeus and Salome Alexandra, was besieged in the Temple Mount by Herod, the former Hasmonaean governor of Galilee and now the newly nominated king of Judaea on behalf of the Roman senate, assisted by the Roman governor of Syria, Sosius. After the conquest Sosius offered a golden crown to the Temple.[52] In this siege damage was caused to some of the porticos (stoai).

Under the Hasmonaeans the city also largely extended over the western hill. A wooden bridge across the Tyropoeon valley connected the Temple with the upper city,[53] which was encircled by the First Wall—the wall which encompassed Hasmonaean Jerusalem according to Josephus.

The Herodian Period (37 BCE–70 CE)

Herod ruled as a Roman client king appointed by the Roman senate. After his death, and the short rule of his son Archelaus (4 BCE–6 CE), Judaea was administered by Roman governors. With a short interlude between 41–44 CE, when it was reigned by Agrippa I, a grandson of Herod the Great, Roman procurators continued to rule Judaea until the eruption of the Great Jewish Revolt against the Romans in 66 CE. However, religious autonomy relating to the Temple rite was maintained throughout, with one exception: Emperor Caligula (37–41 CE), in a radical departure from the imperial cult of the Roman empire, declared himself a living God, demanding of all—including the Jews—to worship him accordingly. As for Judaea and Jerusalem, in 40 CE he insisted that his statue be set up and worshipped in the

19 The ossuary of "Simon the builder of the Sanctuary"

sanctuary, even fetching Petronius, the governor of Syria, with an army to see it done. This menace of abomination roused a wide protest, and Agrippa I, who was a friend and confidant of Caligula in Rome, was moved to interfere to prevent it. This intention came to an end only when Caligula was assassinated in January 41 CE.[54] Claudius, his successor, issued a letter of toleration, thus restoring the former situation of religious freedom.[55]

Under Roman rule a daily sacrifice for the welfare of the emperor was offered on the altar, comprising two lambs and an ox. This was first instituted by Augustus and financed by the imperial treasury.[56] Its cessation in 66 CE (see below), was an expression of revolt.

The religious freedom, first conferred on the diaspora Jews by Julius Caesar and Augustus, had guaranteed, inter alia, that their sacred funds were to be inviolable and their right to send to Jerusalem legally, and without any hindrance on the part of Roman imperial or municipal authorities, the two drachms contribution to the Temple.[57] However, from time to time, even before the imperial era, there were attempts to confiscate these sums.[58]

In the Herodian period the Temple had reached its highest splendor: "He who has not seen the Temple of Herod has never in his life seen a beautiful structure," claims the Babylonian Talmud.[59] In an address to the people Herod made known his enterprise to rebuild and elaborate the Temple at his own expense—enlarging its precinct and raising it to a more imposing height—as an expression of gratitude to God for making his kingdom prosper. He prepared a thousand wagons that were to bring stones for the building, and chose ten thousand of the most skillful workmen while a thousand priests, dressed in their sacerdotal garments, were taught the arts of stonecutting and carpentry.[60] Interestingly, an Aramaic inscription on an ossuary found to the north of the city identifies it as that of "Simon the builder of the Sanctuary" [fig. 19]. Augustus—the first Roman emperor—and his household also made donations to the Temple.[61]

Construction began in 19 BCE, that of the Temple proper being completed in one year and five (or six) months. According to an oral tradition that reached Josephus, it did not rain in daytime as long as the Temple was under construction, showers falling only at night so that the work was not hindered.[62] Completion of the works coincided with the annual anniversary of the king's inauguration—a customary day of feast, so the two events were celebrated in a most illustrious festival.[63] It took eight more years to construct the porticos, but the work was not completed. The entire refurbishment, including modifications and restorations, continued for approximately 75 years after the completion of the major work by Herod. It is said that they were finished only in the days of the Roman procurator Albinus (62–64 CE), as a result of which 18,000 workers found themselves without a job.[64] And even later on, King Agrippa II had huge timber beams brought from Lebanon to retain the sanctuary and raise it by another 20 cubits.[65]

A detailed description of the Herodian Temple and its precinct is provided by Flavius Josephus.[66] More details are found in the rabbinic sources, mainly Mishnah tractates Middot ("measurements") and Tamid ("the permanent sacrifice"), first compiled immediately after the destruction of the Temple, when hopes for its rebuilding still seemed to be applicable at a not too distant future. Discrepancies between the sources seem to result from pertaining to different historical periods. Josephus' earlier work, *Antiquities of the Jews*, refers to the Temple built by Herod, while his subsequent *War of the Jews* describes the Temple that he actually saw in its final state, before destruction.[67] The rabbinic sources also seem to reflect various periods, although these may not always be easily distinguished. Certain portions of the rabbinic sources may even refer to the Hasmonaean-era Temple.[68]

Herod extended the Hasmonaean precinct to the north [fig. 20], west, and south [fig. 21]. The steep slope down to the Kidron Brook prevented any expansion to the east. His extension is best seen today on the east, near the southeastern corner, adding 32m (i.e., 100 Hellenistic feet) to the previous precinct [fig. 22]. The largest stone uncovered so far *in situ* on the western side, to the north of Wilson's Arch, is 12m long, 3m high, and ca. 4m thick. Its estimated weight is ca. 400 tons. Most stones were much smaller, though still quite heavy: 2–5 tons in weight. Many weigh 10 tons and more. A quarry of stones matching these dimensions was exposed recently ca. two km to the north of the Old City [fig. 23]. The stones were well cut and laid dry one above the other, without any bonding material between them. Stability was attained by founding the platform walls on bedrock and by laying each course 3cm inward relative to the course underneath. The courses, with

20 The northeastern corner of the Herodian precinct, looking northwest; the huge lower courses are Herodian

flat face and draft margins, are regularly ca. 1m in height, with the exception of the first course above ground level on the south, between the Double and the Triple Gates, which is 1.80m high. The retaining walls on the west and south were ca. 4.8m thick, though that on the east was more than 5m thick, built of three successive horizontal rows of stones.

According to Josephus, earth was brought and poured against the walls on the outside, to make it level with the streets within the city. And indeed, the graded streets resting on vaults, shops, wide stairs, ritual baths and other installations which were uncovered in Benjamin Mazar's excavations in 1968–78 to the south and west of the Herodian precinct indicate that this outer area was also an integral part of the building project. On the inside the platform was leveled by a fill poured into a matrix of walls, and by subterranean vaults.[69]

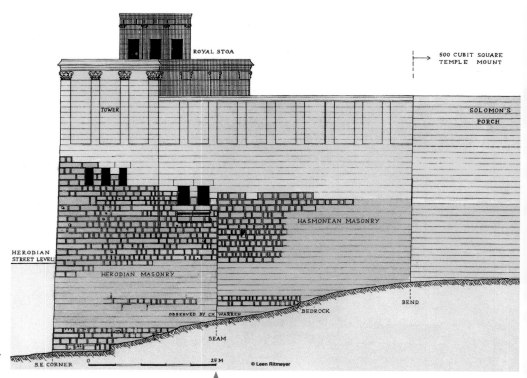

21 Proposed reconstruction of the southern part of the eastern wall during the Herodian period, indicating early visible masonry

22 The eastern wall of the Herodian precinct near its southern end: the seam between the Hellenistic/Hasmonaean masonry and the Herodian extension

23 Quarry of the Second Temple period discovered in 2007 at Ramot Shelomo, about 4 km northnorthwest of the Temple Mount

The quarry stands out for the enormous size of its stones, up to 8 meters long, similar to those composing the lower courses of the Temple Mount's external walls. This is the first quarry that can be linked to the tremendous building projects of the Second Temple period. The elevation of the ridge—about 80 meters above that of the Mount—and its proximity to the main road to Jerusalem, enabled moving the stones down the slope with the help of oxen. The stones, set on bedrock, maintained the walls' stability though no plaster or cement were employed

24 Quarry of the Second Temple period discovered in 2008 in Sanhedria, about 2.5 km northwest of the Temple Mount

25 Northwestern corner of the Esplanade, rock cut by Herod's workmen. Roofing beams of the northern stoa were set in the square sockets (at which the arrows point)

The eastern portico, 400 cubits long and attributed by Josephus to King Solomon, remained lower relative to the level of the Esplanade.[70] This is seemingly the "Solomon's Porch" mentioned in John 10.23. On the other sides the external court was surrounded by double porticos, with pillars 25 cubits (12.5m) in height. Deep, rock-cut, square mortises, 0.5x0.5m in size and set at intervals apart, in which their roofing cedar beams were set, can still be seen on the rock face on the north, ca. 9m above ground level [fig. 25]. Round about the entire Temple were fixed the spoils taken by Herod from barbarous nations, including the Arabs.[71] The Herodian temenos (sacred precinct), 144,000 (or 135,000) sq. m, is one of the largest ancient precincts in the entire Roman world. It was much larger than the later ones of Bel in Palmyra, or that of Jupiter and Bacchus in Baalbek. The lengths of the walls are: western — 488m, southern — 280m [fig. 26], eastern — 460m, northern — 315m. The entire circumference on the outside is 1533m. The space for pilgrims flocking therein from the extended kingdom of Judaea, as well as from the Jewish diaspora, was significantly increased, and it was more conveniently organized than before to serve their needs, providing shelter from rain and sun in the porticos.

The second court of the Temple was square in shape (1x1 stades, which equals 600x600 ft.),[72] and elevated relative to the previous one. Entrance of Gentiles was prevented by a partition (the *soreg* of Mishnah Middot) made of pillars and stone plates, three cubits high all around. Near the gates and upon this partition stood, at equal distances from one another, inscriptions in Greek or Latin declaring the law of purity and stating, under penalty of death, that no Gentile should enter that sanctuary [fig. 16].[73] Two of these warning inscriptions were actually found. The more complete one reads: "No foreigner is to enter within the forecourt and the balustrade around the sanctuary. Whoever is caught will have himself to blame for his subsequent death."[74] Staircases of fourteen steps were located at the *soreg* gates.

The buildings of the inner precinct were surrounded by a high wall with ten gates, seven of them leading to the Court of Israel and of the Priests (135x187 cubits in dimension [fig. 27]):[75] four each on the north and on the south.[76] On the east there were two, the first leading from the east to the Court of the Women, measured 135x135 cubits[77] while the second, on the west side of this court, led to the Court of Israel, into which women were not permitted[78] except during the offering of the sacrifices.

The nine outer gates were plated on both sides, including their jambs and lintels, in gold and silver donated by Alexander, brother of the philosopher Philo of Alexandria.[79] The one leading to the Women's Court was of Corinthian brass and was known as the Gate of Nicanor, named after a wealthy Alexandrian[80] whose family tomb was discovered on Mount Scopus in 1902.

Atop the Gate that led eastwards from the Women's Court, much larger than the rest and overlaid with massive plates of silver and gold, there was a tower Herod built for himself, which he could access safely through a secret subterranean passage that led there from Antonia.[81] Fifteen steps led up to Nikanor Gate, on which the Levites stood with their musical instruments during the libation of the water in the Feast of Tabernacles.[82] Three trumpet blasts, before sunrise, announced the daily opening of the Court's gates.[83]

In the inner court stood the altar, ten cubits high, and of length and breadth equal to 32 cubits,[84] built of unhewn stones.[85] Nearby stood the laver for washing the hands and feet of the ministering priests. Water for the laver was drawn by a wooden wheel from an adjacent subterranean cistern.[86] This particular cistern is of utmost importance for resolving the question of the location and orientation of the altar, the Temple, and the surrounding court.[87] The unique shape of the cistern, designated as Cistern Five by Charles Wilson in the late nineteenth century, with its sets of parallel and perpendicular walls and lengthy corridor on the east-west transversal, indicates that the altar sat snugly between the two northward facing parallel arms of the cistern. Given that the altar and Temple had parallel axiality, the proposed orientation of the altar vis-à-vis the cistern determines the location and orientation of the Temple as well [fig. 28]. The Temple would still face eastward, in accordance with the sources, but with a small deviation to the south which would not render the precinct walls exactly parallel with the Temple itself [fig. 29]. An additional ramification of this conclusion relates to the location of the Temple vis-à-vis the Haram, which would now fall outside, and to the west, of the Temple court.

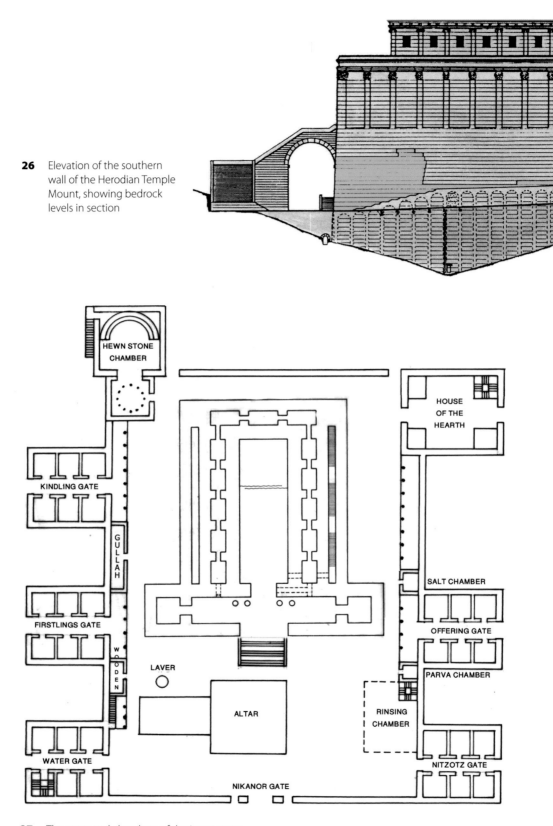

26 Elevation of the southern wall of the Herodian Temple Mount, showing bedrock levels in section

HEWN STONE CHAMBER

KINDLING GATE

GULLAH

FIRSTLINGS GATE

WOODEN

WATER GATE

NIKANOR GATE

LAVER

ALTAR

HOUSE OF THE HEARTH

SALT CHAMBER

OFFERING GATE

PARVA CHAMBER

RINSING CHAMBER

NITZOTZ GATE

27 The gates and chambers of the inner court

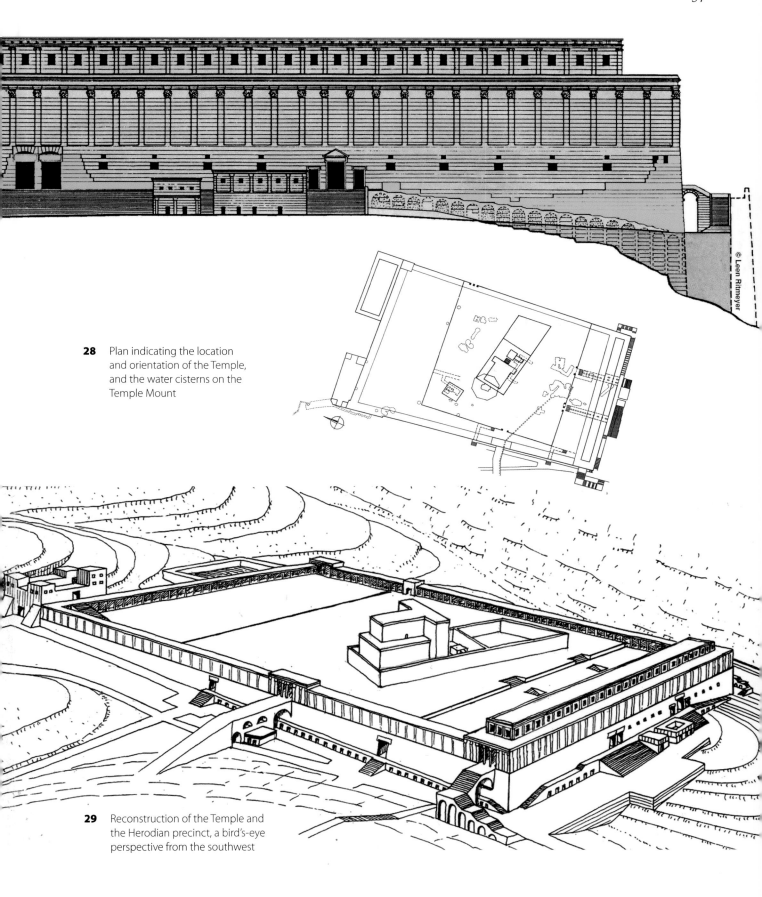

© Leen Ritmeyer

28 Plan indicating the location
and orientation of the Temple,
and the water cisterns on the
Temple Mount

29 Reconstruction of the Temple and
the Herodian precinct, a bird's-eye
perspective from the southwest

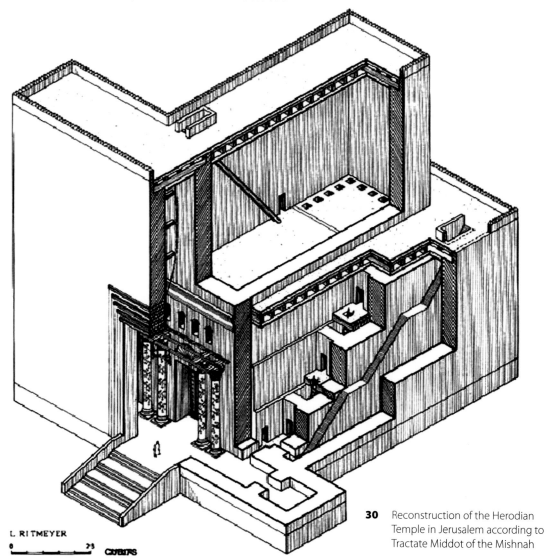

L. RITMEYER

0   25   CUBITS

30   Reconstruction of the Herodian
Temple in Jerusalem according to
Tractate Middot of the Mishnah

The Temple proper [fig. 30] was comprised of three parts: Porch (*ulam*), Sanctuary (*heykhal*) and Holy of Holies, and was ascended by twelve stairs. To the front its height and breadth were 100 cubits, while in the rear it was 30 cubits narrower.[88] On the outside, and over the entire façade, the Temple was plated with tablets of gold of great weight.[89] The façade reflected the rays of the rising sun. On the other sides its upper parts were not gilded, but white, resembling a mountain covered with snow.[90] They were topped by spikes with sharp points, to prevent pollution by resting birds.

The Gate of the Porch had a lintel made of five massive beams.[91] The Sanctuary portal was also surrounded by gleaming gold.[92] A golden vine, from which clusters of grapes hung as tall as a man's height, was hanging on columns over this portal,[93] and a veil covered its golden doors. Helene, the proselyte queen of Adiabene (in present-day northern Iraq), donated a golden chandelier that was placed above this gate.[94] The opening of the doors marked the beginning of the daily rite, and their closure, its end. Inside the sanctuary, 40

31 A portable sundial depicting a menorah on its reverse side

cubits long and 20 cubits broad, stood the lampstand (depicted on bronze coins of the years 40–37 BCE of Mattathias Antigonus [fig. 18] and in other works of art [fig. 31], including on the Arch of Titus in Rome [fig. 42]),[95] which was daily lit, the table of the shewbread (the bread being replaced once a week), and the altar of incense, kindled each day anew by two priests. Then came the Holy of Holies, 20x20 cubits in dimension, separated by two curtains from the Sanctuary. It was empty, except for the stone called the Foundation Rock (*even shetiyyah*), projecting just three fingerbreadths above floor level.[96] Only the officiating high priest was allowed to enter this innermost center of sanctity once a year, on the Day of Atonement.[97] Above the Sanctuary and the Holy of Holies was an Upper Chamber (*aliyah*); on the north, west, and south they were surrounded by three stories of cells, with passages between them, that served for storage. On the north there was a staircase leading to the Upper Chamber.[98] The total height of the Temple was thus 100 cubits, its upper part being narrower than the lower one, resembling in this respect the roofing of the basilical stoa,[99] on which see below.

According to Josephus, there were four gates on the western side of the Temple compound.[100] This is borne out by the actual archaeological finds. The one leading to the king's palace across the Tyropoeon valley was set at the end of a bridge that ran parallel to the present-day Wilson's Arch; two more, that led to the suburbs of the city, are today called Barclay's Gate [figs. 32–35] and Warren's Gate, located in the lower parts of the precinct wall. They opened on to the lower street that ran along the western wall. The last gate was set above Robinson's Arch (13.5m broad) [fig. 36], which retained a staircase that led down to the street near the southwestern corner of the precinct. From there, according to Josephus, the road descended into the valley by a great number of steps. Sections of this street were uncovered, leading to the Siloam Pool, in the southern extremity of the city. Four shops were installed in the massive pilaster that supported Robinson's Arch.

On the south [fig. 26] there were two gates with broad staircases (still preserved) [fig. 37], in front: the Triple Gate served for entering,[101] while the Double Gate[102] was used

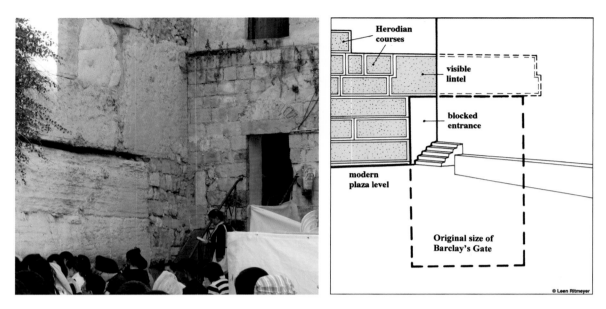

32   Left: The northern end of the lintel of Barclay's Gate as seen near the southeast corner of the Western Wall
33   Right: Barclay's Gate: reconstruction of original size (seen from the west)

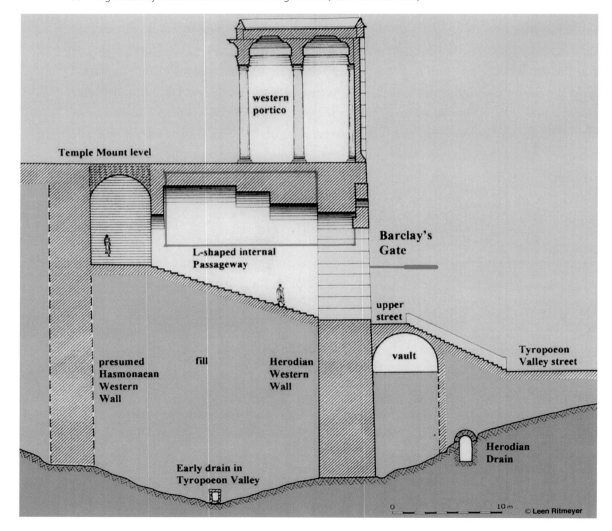

34   Barclay's Gate: The rear arch and blocked gate opening seen from within the Buraq Mosque, looking west
The mosque is located below the level of the Haram al-Sharif Esplanade. The staircase on the right possibly dates from the Mamluk period

35   Opposite: Reconstructed section drawing of Barclay's Gate and the Western Wall
The red lines indicate the location of the Buraq Mosque seen in fig. 34 and the level of the present-day prayer plaza in front of the Western Wall

by those going out. They are regularly identified as the Hulda Gates mentioned above, though this designation had referred to the Hasmonaean southern gates that preceded the Herodian ones. Behind these gates, long underground passages, shaped like graded tunnels, led forth into the precinct [fig. 38, 39]. A graded street on top of vaults ran along the western [fig. 40] and southern walls, with shops located in the vaults.

Inside, along the southern wall, stood the Royal Stoa, one stade long with four colonnades (the fourth being attached to the wall) and three walks, or aisles. The middle walk was twice as high and 1.5 times wider than the other two, that measured 50 ft. (ca. 16.5m) in height

36 Robinson's Arch

and 30 ft. (ca. 10m) in width. It was a magnificent two-storied basilica, rising to an enormous elevation relative to the area outside. The thickness of each pillar was such that three men extending their arms were required in order to circle it. Its height, including the base, was twenty-seven feet. Altogether there were 162 pillars, of the Corinthian order. The Royal Stoa served non-cultic commercial purposes, normal for any Roman civil basilica (oblong colonnaded hall): sale of sacrificial materials, money-changing by pilgrims from different parts of the world,[103] and in one end a court of law conducted trials.[104] A staircase resting on wide arches—one of them Robinson's Arch—led there from the junction of the streets underneath that ran along the western and southern walls of the precinct.

37   Remains of the broad staircase leading to the Double Gate

The entire Herodian compound comprised a central temple surrounded by porticos on three sides, and a broad basilica occupying the fourth. Such a compound resembles a caesareum—a definite religious complex of Roman architecture, said to be consecrated to the emperor cult, like those known in Cyrene, and elsewhere.[105]

It was customary for one of the priests to announce, by sounding the trumpet, the approach and end of the Sabbath from the roof of the priests' chambers.[106] A Hebrew inscription found in the debris on the Herodian street below the southwestern corner of the precinct suggests that the place of announcement was on top of a tower there, to the west of the basilica, overlooking large parts of the lower and upper city and the markets below.

38 A decorated dome of the Double Gate

L.RITMEYER

39 Reconstructed interior view of the underground passageway of the Double Gate

The Tower of Antonia, actually a fortress,[107] stood at the corner where the northern and western porticos of the precinct met. It was built by Herod between 37 and 31 BCE, on the site of the older castle (*baris*) erected by John Hyrcanus I (134–104 BCE), and serving as his residence before the Hasmonaean palace was built in the upper city.[108] Here the last Hasmonean, Mattathias Antigonus, found refuge from Herod and Sosius, the Roman governor of Syria.[109] It is the barracks of Acts 21.34, into which Paul was dispatched from

40   The Herodian street near the southwest corner of the Herodian precinct, below Robinson's Arch, looking north

the Temple precinct by the Roman guard. This citadel afforded a splendid view of the Temple precinct and the cult conducted therein. Situated on a lofty site, it was fortified by a number of towers built of sizeable stones right up to the top. Catapults and a variety of engines were positioned upon the towers, and a guard of 500 soldiers was stationed there. It served to guard the Temple and the area around it, and was also protected by a moat already before Pompey's siege against Aristobulus II in 63 BCE.[110]

Herod's Antonia was no mere reconstruction of the Hasmonaean *baris*, damaged in the war with Pompey and Sosius. He made the *baris* stronger than before, for the safety and protection of the Temple, and named it after Marc Antony, his Roman patron at that time. It also served as his residence in Jerusalem before his palace was constructed on the western hill. A secret subterranean passage led from the Antonia to the inner Temple.[111]

What can be still seen today of the Second Temple and of the Herodian building project? The Temple itself has disappeared, of course, but many of the water cisterns under the Haram al-Sharif date from that period. Of particular significance is Cistern Five, which determines the exact location of the altar, the Temple, and its courts. Since the beginning of archaeological research in this area, in the nineteenth century, it is well known that the outer walls of the Haram al-Sharif are founded on the walls of the Herodian precinct, except in the north, where it is delineated by the rock escarpment of the Antonia. The courses of the Herodian walls, founded on bedrock, are easily recognizable in the southeastern corner and on the south and west, being much larger than the overlying Muslim courses. The original western wall is preserved in the area of the Western (Wailing) Wall to a height of 14m above rock level. Farther north one can follow its entire course in an underground tunnel that was cut in recent years under the foundations of the mediaeval structures above, to serve tourists. In the southwestern corner the original walls rise to a height of 20m. In the southeastern corner, where the elevation of the bedrock was 20m below the Herodian street level, the preserved wall is almost twice as high. All entrances on the west and on the south are partially preserved. The passages leading in from Warren's Gate and Barclay's Gate were converted to water cisterns; of the other two western gates, marked by Robinson's Arch and Wilson's Arch, only arches are partially preserved, not the gates on top of them. The post-1967 excavations have dramatically enhanced our knowledge. Mazar's excavation and later ones on the west and south exposed the network of streets, sewage system, shops, ritual baths, and other installations that were built on the outside, below the precinct walls. Most impressive are the piazza-like staircases that extended in front of the two southern gates—the Double Gate and the Triple Gate. These are mute echoes of the multitudes of pilgrims who once ascended and descended. The gates themselves, Herodian in origin and leading into the outer court of the Temple through underground tunnels, are blocked at present.[112] On the east, near the corner, a spring course of another arch is recognizable. The Herodian extension on this side is marked by a seam; the wall seen extending farther north is pre-Herodian [figs. 21, 22].

41 Herodian decorated fragment, found ca. 1970 near the Temple Mount in the excavations of Benjamin Mazar and Meir Ben-Dov. Most probably originating from the Herodian Temple Mount. On permanent exhibition in the Hecht Museum, Haifa

Conclusion

The Temple was prominently located in the city, and in many respects—religious, political, judicial, social, cultural, and economic—it dominated and dictated the life of the city and of the entire nation. It was the only temple common to the entire nation. A tribute of half a sheqel was collected each year from every adult in the Land of Israel and abroad as tribute to the Temple. It was a meeting place for various sects and an objective of pilgrimage for Jews from Judaea, Galilee, and the Diaspora—especially since the time of Herod and later. Their number was especially numerous in the three annual pilgrimages of Passover, Sukkot (Tabernacles), and Shavu'ot (Pentecost).[113] This is well reflected in a passage of the philosopher Philo (ca. 20 BCE–45CE):

> Countless multitudes from countless cities come, some over land, others over sea, from east and west and north and south at every feast. They take the Temple for their port as a general haven and safe refuge from the bustle of the great turmoil of life, and there they seek to find calm weather [...]. In fact, practically in every city there are banking places for the holy money where people regularly come and give their offerings. And at stated times there are appointed to carry the sacred tribute envoys selected on their merits, from every city those of the highest repute, under whose conduct the hopes of each and all will travel safely.[114]

A lively description of a Pentecost pilgrimage to the Temple from towns and villages near and far, during the reign of King Agrippa I, is given in the Mishnah:

> Those [who come] from nearby bring figs and grapes, but those [who come] from afar bring dried figs and raisins. And an ox walks before them, its horns overlaid with gold, and a wreath of olive [leaves] on its head. A flutist plays before them until they arrive near Jerusalem. [Once] they arrived near Jerusalem, they sent [a messenger] ahead of them [to announce their arrival], and they decorated their firstfruits. The high officers, chiefs, and treasurer [of the Temple] come out to meet them. According to the rank of the entrants, they would [determine which of these officials would] go out. And all the craftsmen of Jerusalem stand before them and greet them, [saying], "Brothers, men of such and such a place, you have come in peace."
>
> A flutist plays before them, until they reach the Temple Mount. [Once] they reached the Temple Mount, even Agrippa the King puts the basket [of firstfruits] on his shoulder, and enters, [and goes forth] until he reaches the Temple court. [Once] he reached the Temple court, the Levites sang the song, "I will extol thee, O Lord, for thou hast drawn me up, and has not let my foes rejoice over me" (Ps. 30.1).[115]

The Mishnah also includes similar detailed descriptions of the ceremonies and the sacrifices pertaining to all other feasts related to the Temple rite. The broad, well-paved streets, wide staircases, and lofty gates allowed the pilgrims convenient access and easy circulation. The vast water cisterns on the Temple platform provided plenty of water for their needs, as well as for the rite. They could gather in the Royal Stoa and in the porticos before or after worship. There were people who ascended to hear the words of the Law. An academy (*beyt midrash*) was located on the Temple Mount, where the Sanhedrin used to convene on the Sabbath and holidays as an academic, rather than a judicial, body.[116]

Several episodes in the life of Jesus Christ took place in the Temple courts. As a firstborn male Jewish infant he was presented in the Temple, dedicated to the Lord by a sacrifice of two turtledoves, or two young pigeons, as prescribed in the Bible.[117] The Firstlings Gate, on the northern side of the Inner Court, was the site of registration associated with this sacrifice. The episode that follows—of Simeon, a just and devout man who foresaw the infant Jesus to be the Messiah—could have taken place nearby, outside this gate. Growing up, at the age of twelve, Jesus left his parents who were back home from a Passover pilgrimage to the Temple, impressing the Sages by his knowledge, listening to them and asking them questions.[118] This could have occurred near the stairs leading up from the south to the Triple Gate.[119] The eastern portico is Solomon's Porch; there, during the feast of Hanukkah, took place the encounter between Jesus and Jews wishing to know if he was indeed the Messiah.[120] The Beautiful Gate of Acts 3.2, where the apostle Peter, accompanied by John, cured a lame beggar, seems to be the adjacent gate, leading to the Women's Court from the east. The site of the temptation of Christ "on the pinnacle of the Temple,"[121] should apparently be located in the southeastern corner of the Temple Mount, or perhaps in that corner on the roof of the Royal Stoa. The location of the stalls of the money changers, and of the vendors of pigeons and other sacrificial animals reproached by Jesus before the feast of Passover, his last feast,[122] seems to have been in the Royal Stoa. The next day, returning to the Temple where he was teaching the people, he gave his prophecy about the destruction of the Temple, after contesting there with the Pharisees and the Sadducees.[123]

The Temple was destroyed some forty years later. On the 10th of Av (29 August) 70 CE the Herodian Temple was set afire by the troops of Titus.[124] Since then this event is commemorated by the Jewish People as a day of grief and fasting (set in later years on the 9th of Av—the date the First Temple was destroyed). This was the result of the Great Jewish Revolt against Rome that had erupted under the Roman emperor Nero, in 66 CE, when governor Florus stole seventeen talents from the Temple treasury and caused many other humiliations and much killing in Jerusalem.[125] As a result of all these, at the instigation of the son of the High Priest, it was decided to suspend the daily sacrifice for the emperor. This was a clear declaration of revolt against Rome, and all efforts of the peace party in the city to revoke this dangerous decision were fruitless. The people adhered to this decision.[126] Vespasian, sent by Nero to suppress the revolt, conquered Galilee, the Golan, and the whole of the northern parts of the province of Judaea. But suppression of the revolt was hindered as a result of struggles in Rome between four who claimed the throne after Nero committed suicide on 9 June 68. Meanwhile Jerusalem was struck by civil war. Many were killed in acts of terror as buildings were destroyed and stocks of food and other provisions were set on fire. When Vespasian ascended to the throne in 69 CE, the war was resumed. After the conquest of Judaea came the turn of Jerusalem. The city was surrounded by three massive walls that seemed impregnable. Inside, the Herodian Temple Mount, with its prominent walls, resembled a fortress. It was the stronghold of the zealots, headed by John of Gischala, who erected there four towers: on the northeast and southwest corners, on the west controlling the bridge, and the fourth above the roof of the Temple chambers, overlooking the Antonia. The chief Roman commander was Titus, Vespasian's elder son. The Jewish historian Josephus, who surrendered to the Romans in Galilee, was now in the service of Titus, trying in long and articulate discourses to persuade the Jews to surrender, this being the will of God. He was an eyewitness to the events. The attack came from the north. The Third Wall was the first to be stormed, in the month of Iyar (April/May). Nine days later fell the Second Wall. The Antonia fortress, located in the northwestern corner of the Temple Mount, against which four ramparts were laid, was finally conquered by night when its wall were secretly scaled. After its capture, the Antonia was razed to the ground.[127] The day it was demolished, 17 Tammuz (June/July), the daily sacrifices in the Temple ceased.[128] The way to the Temple was laid open. The gates of the outer court were set on fire on the 8th of Av. On the following day (9 Av) Titus held a war council, attended by all his officers, to decide about the fate of the Temple proper. This is Josephus' narrative:

> Titus brought forward for debate the subject of the temple. Some were of the opinion that the law of war should be enforced, since the Jews would never cease from rebellion while the temple remained as the focus for concourse from every quarter. Others advised that if the Jews abandoned it and placed no weapons whatever upon it, it should be saved, but that if they mounted it for purposes of warfare, it should be burnt; as it would then be no longer a temple, but a fortress, and thenceforward the impiety would be chargeable, not to the Romans but to those who forced them to take such measures. Titus, however, declared that, even were the Jews to mount it and fight therefrom, he would not wreak vengeance on inanimate objects instead of men, nor under any circumstances burn down so magnificent a work; for the loss would affect the Romans, inasmuch as it would be an ornament to the empire if it stood.[129]

Titus decided to spare the Temple. But on the next day (10 Av/29 August), while repelling a Jewish attack coming out of the inner court, one of the soldiers threw a firebrand into the chamber of the Temple proper, and it was set on fire.[130] Efforts to extinguish it by the orders of Titus were futile and the flames took an ever increasing hold as more and more firebrands were thrown in by the soldiers in the fury of battle. Titus managed to inspect the interior before it was entirely overwhelmed. Only the holy vessels were saved, to be demonstrated later to the Roman populace in the triumphal parade. These are depicted to the present on the Arch of Titus in Rome [fig. 42]. It took another month to conquer the upper city. Before leaving for Caesarea, Titus gave an order to raze the Temple to the ground.[131] The deliberate destruction of the western portico can still be seen near the southwestern corner—huge fallen stones lying over the paved street.[132]

The destruction of the Temple marked a new stage in the history of the Jewish people and in the fate of its sacred precinct. A new, rabbinic leadership took the lead from the previous priestly elite. The synagogue replaced the Temple as the central institution of the Jewish nation. The Temple was never rebuilt, but its past grandeur nourished for generations hopes and aspirations for redemption.

42 The menorah on the Arch of Titus, Rome

70-638: The Temple-less Mountain

Yoram Tsafrir

The Hebrew University of Jerusalem

The Destruction of the Temple Mount by the Romans (70 CE)

For several days and nights flames continued to consume the Jewish temple and the surrounding buildings on the Temple Mount.[1] Flavius Josephus described the fate of the Temple in the sixth book of his history of *The Jewish War* (6.272): "The roar of the flames streaming far and wide mingled with the groans of the falling victims; and, owing to the height of the hill and the mass of the burning pile, one would have thought that the whole city was ablaze."[2] He describes the great courage of the Roman soldiers who conquered the Temple Mount and the heroic struggle of the defenders, and mourns the loss of the sacred Temple. The complete destruction took place, after three days of bitter fighting, on the 10th day of the month of Av, on exactly the same day as the destruction of the First Temple.[3] However, Jewish national collective memory dates both destructions, as well as some other calamities, to the 9th of Av. Although the fall of Jerusalem took place about a month later (on the 8th of Elul), the day remembered by all as the date on which Jerusalem fell, accompanied by massacres and expulsions, is the day on which the Temple fell, the 9th of Av. It is commemorated by Jews to this very day with prayers and fasting.

Titus came to know the Jewish spirit. Even after the complete fall of the city and its burning to ashes, he continued with systematic destruction of the city wall and the city's buildings, except for the wall on the west and the adjacent monumental towers, which were preserved to be part of the Roman legionary camp. The remaining walls and porticoes atop the Herodian enclosure on the Temple Mount were almost completely dismantled. The Romans even captured the liturgical implements, vestments, and the entire treasury of the Temple. Josephus resumes the story of the fall of Jerusalem at the beginning of the seventh book of *The Jewish War* (7.1–3):

> [...] Caesar ordered the whole city and the temple to be razed to the ground [...] (except of the towers and the wall in the west, where the Roman garrison was

43   A Herodian street covered by collapse of stones from the Western Wall of the Temple Mount, looking south

placed) [...] All the rest of the wall encompassing the city was so completely leveled to the ground as to leave future visitors to the spot no ground for believing that it had ever been inhabited.

Archaeological proof that stones were rolled down the walls appeared in the excavations of the streets along the western and southern walls of the Temple Mount near its southwestern corner.[4] Huge blocks had fallen from the area of the upper porticoes to the streets, including an upper stone of a tower with an inscription, "To the place of trumpeting to declare(?)," perhaps referring to the tower from which the priests announced the beginning of the Sabbath. Since no ashes were found on the streets, we can associate the huge concentration of rubble with the deliberate project of dismantling the Temple and the buildings that surrounded it, including the basilica and the porticoes around the temenos. In most of its circumference, except on the north and northeast, the blocks of the original Herodian wall (or of the Hasmonaean wall on the east) have survived below the present ground level of the enclosure of the Temple Mount. However, some rather poor remains of the walls of the Temple itself and the buildings around it remained, which later attracted the interest of both Jews and Christians. These scanty remains most probably disappeared during the early Muslim building activity in the seventh century.

Titus' command to destroy Jerusalem and its walls, and in particular the Temple, resulted from his assumption that the Jews had not given up. In fact, the last battle of the war was the fall of Masada three (or four) years after the destruction of Jerusalem.

After the war the ruined city began gradually to be resettled, probably in the vicinity of the legionary camp on the west side of the city. The pattern of building civil quarters (*canabae*) near legionary camps is known also from other places. It is reasonable to assume that the ratio of Jews and Christians among the new settlers (some of them were, perhaps, veterans of the Roman army) was substantial. Still, the total number of inhabitants remained very small.

It is difficult to assess the enormous impact of the loss of the Temple on Jewish life and Jewish thinking. More than a religious and national center, the Temple was the focus of Jewish life in Judaea and the Diaspora. Its destruction was a severe blow for Jewish communities and individuals. A new reality would gradually be adopted, in which synagogues, prayers, and study replaced the rites, sacrifices, pilgrimage, and mandatory donations of money to the Temple by every Jew all over the world. The priests were replaced by rabbis.[5]

Pilgrimages to Jerusalem and the Temple Mount continued, although on a small scale.[6] One of these pilgrims was Rabbi Akiva, the great sage who declared his belief in the rebuilding of Jerusalem and the Temple. Indeed, R. Akiva represented the activist circles among the Jews, who decided to fight and rebuild Jerusalem and the Temple. This took place in 132 CE, with the uprising led by Bar Kokhba, some 62 years after the destruction of the Temple by Titus.

The Bar Kokhba Revolt (132–135 CE) and Its Aftermath: The Temple Mount during the Time of Aelia Capitolina and the Early Christian Period

The Bar Kokhba War

The war against the Romans began in 132 CE and lasted until 135 CE, during the reign of Emperor Hadrian. There is no comprehensive and systematic report about this war similar to Josephus' account of the First Jewish War. Scholars, therefore, must avail themselves of a variety of literary and archaeological sources that can be interpreted in more than one way. Most prominent among the surviving literary sources is Cassius Dio's *Roman History* written in the late second or early third century (Book 69.12), but even this report is no more than an epitome composed by the Byzantine monk Xiphilinus in the eleventh century. Although the text seems very trustworthy, it might well be that the epitomizer changed, or corrected, sections—or even single phrases—of Dio's report, which have become keystones in scholarly interpretation of the war.[7]

Further information is found in the writings of Christian authors. Among these, the most prominent are Eusebius of Caesarea, who wrote in the late third and early fourth centuries, and Jerome at the end of the fourth and the beginning of the fifth centuries. The Christians were mostly attracted by the realization of Jesus' prophecy that the Temple would be destroyed, but also by other biblical prophecies which the Evangelists repeated.

Jewish rabbinic literature supplies some information, usually in a legendary form, about the revolt and its leader, Simon Ben-Khosba, known as Bar Kokhba (=Son of the Star).[8] Of great importance are the archaeological finds, including letters and legal documents from Bar Kokhba's headquarters. Also important are the coins minted by the rebels' leadership bearing inscriptions such as "For the Freedom of Jerusalem" and "For the Redemption of Israel."

The main issue concerning the history of the Temple Mount is whether Bar Kokhba indeed conquered Jerusalem during the revolt. It should be borne in mind that there were already people living in the city, even if it lay mostly in ruins, and some of them may have been Jews and Christians. An additional question relates to whether at some point during the war Bar Kokhba took possession of the city. If so, did he then begin to build a new temple atop the ruins of the older one? Most scholars agree that because of the brutal warfare the answer to this question must be in the negative.[9]

Yet, there is no doubt that Jerusalem and the Temple provided the main impetus for the uprising. Emperor Hadrian's plan to rebuild Jerusalem from its ruins, perhaps following his voyage to the East around 130 CE, most probably acted as a catalyst on anti-Roman feelings among the Jews. Dio's text, in *Roman History* (69.12.1), is very explicit:

> At Jerusalem he [Hadrian] built a new city in place of the one which was razed to the ground, naming it Aelia Capitolina, and on the place of the temple of God he

raised a new temple to Zeus. This brought on a war of no slight importance nor of brief duration.[10]

Although the text as presented by Xiphilinus clearly indicates that the emperor's intention was to build a city to be named Aelia Capitolina, it is reasonable to consider an alternative possibility: that Hadrian had no intention of acting against the Jews when restoring the famous city from its ashes. As a neo-classicist builder, Hadrian may even have believed that this enterprise would appease the Jews and earn their praise. It is also difficult to believe that he intended to abandon the historic name Hierosolyma, or Jerusalem.[11]

The Jews, however, rejected Hadrian's program. They realized that restoration of Jerusalem as a new Hellenized-Roman polis would bring an end to their aspirations to rebuild Jerusalem as a Jewish capital with a new Temple as its crown. The coins minted during the war by the Jewish administration reflect the intention of Bar Kokhba and his people to encourage fighting for Jerusalem. The relatively large silver *tetradrachms*, or *sela'im*, minted during the revolt show (among other symbols) the façade of the Temple and the inscription "For the freedom of Jerusalem" while other coins display the trumpets used in the Temple service [figs. 44, 45]. Coins, a tool of propaganda in the Roman world, were employed by the rebels to represent their struggle as a battle for the liberation of Jerusalem and building of a new Temple.

The brutal war continued for three-and-a-half years. The Romans suffered heavy losses, while the number of dead among the Jews was enormous, and many thousands were enslaved and expelled from Judaea. Jewish settlements in the central Judaean Hills, mostly around Jerusalem, were destroyed, resulting in the transfer of the Jewish leadership from Judaea to the Galilee.

The emperor issued decrees against the practice of the Jewish religion accompanied by persecutions, but also sought additional acts of punishment that would suppress the Jewish nationalistic spirit. He changed the name of the province from Iudaea to Syria-Palaestina (usually abbreviated as Palaestina). He also changed the name of the city, now holding the high status of a Roman colony [fig. 46]. It was no longer called Jerusalem but Aelia Capitolina, commemorating his own name—Aelius Hadrianus—and the god Jupiter of the Capitoline temple in Rome. The third act was perhaps the most painful: the Jews were expelled from Jerusalem and the surrounding area, and were not permitted to re-settle, or even visit, the new city and its close vicinity. For most Jews the Temple and the Temple Mount became a memory, commemorated in Jewish literature, study, and prayers.[12] Descriptions of the Temple or parts of it appeared in synagogue mosaics in Palestine and elsewhere during the Roman, Byzantine, and Early Islamic periods.[13] The Temple's menorah became the most important Jewish symbol in Palestine and the Diaspora.

The Christian community which remained in Jerusalem until the Bar Kokhba Revolt

44   A large silver coin (Hebrew: *sela'*) with a schematic depiction of the Temple's façade and the legend Shim'on (=Bar Kokhba). On verso: "For the Freedom of Jerusalem"

45   A small silver coin of Bar Kokhba showing the trumpets of the Temple with an inscription: "Year Two for the Freedom of Israel"

46   Verso of a large bronze coin that shows Hadrian ploughing with an ox and a cow the *pomerium*, that is, the furrow symbolizing the boundaries of the newly founded Aelia Capitolina
The inscription reads: "The Colony of Aelia Capitolina founded." (The emperor's portrait appears on the front side)

was led by bishops who were "Hebrew by origin," i.e., were circumcised Judeo-Christians.[14] The fact that both Jews and Christians returned to the ruined city shortly after its destruction by Titus in 70 CE is of great significance. It explains the continuity in identification of sites and traditions from the Second Temple period into Roman and Byzantine times and even to our very days. Among those traditions are the location of the Tomb of Christ and sites on and around the Temple Mount. The expulsion of the Jews from Aelia Capitolina had great significance for Christians. Eusebius writes that from the time of Hadrian the bishops of the Christian congregation of Jerusalem were no longer of Jewish descent but Gentiles.

Since the Christians conceived of themselves as the "true Israel" (*verus Israel*), they took great interest in the Bible and Jewish history prior to Jesus, which was common to them and the Jews. The fate of the Temple Mount was particularly close to their hearts. On the one hand, it was revered as the place where David had built an altar and Solomon had erected the Temple, while on the other hand, its ruined condition proved Jesus' prophecy: "There will not be left here a stone upon a stone that will not be thrown down."[15] Daniel's prophecy about the "abomination of desolation,"[16] that originally referred to the sacrilege committed by Antiochus IV who sacrificed to the Olympian Zeus on the altar in 168 BCE,[17] enabled Jerome to make reference to the Roman sculptures which were installed on the site of the ruined Temple in his own time.

Pagan Buildings on the Temple Mount

The temenos of the Temple Mount, even if less important than other structures, remained the most prominent man-made topographical component in Jerusalem. The huge enclosure built by Herod to provide space for many thousands of pilgrims gathering around the Temple during the three annual festivals, now filled almost no function. The porticoes surrounding it, as well as its gates, had not been reconstructed. On the contrary, the site became a stone quarry. Because of their very large size, the stones were used in the construction of public buildings. At the end of the third century, in his *Demonstratio Evangelica* (Proof of the Gospel) Church Father and scholar Eusebius (ca. 260–340) interpreted Micah's prophecy about the destruction of Jerusalem: "Therefore shall Zion for your sake be plowed as a field, and Jerusalem shall become heaps and the Mountain of the House as a wooded height."[18] He described the desolate state of Roman Aelia, at least parts if it: "And it is possible to perceive with our own eyes the sad sight of the stones being taken from the Temple and the Holy of Holies of the past, to be carried to the temples of the idols and to the constructions for the public spectacle."[19]

The present state of preservation of the Herodian Temple Mount walls clearly illustrates this situation. The walls had severely collapsed or been dismantled. This condition can easily be observed on three sides: east, south, and west. A most accurate survey of the remains carried out by Charles Warren and his team around 1870 illustrates this phenomenon.[20] As a rule, the corners of the Esplanade have been preserved better than the walls between them (the difference may be more than 12m) and looked like towers. One of them, probably the southeastern "tower," was later identified by Christians as the Corner Tower (*pinna templi*), the place where St. James the Less suffered martyrdom [figs 47, 48]. The Herodian courses at that point were preserved to a height of some 42m above the rock level (out of which some 20m remain today—and in large part also in the past—below the surface). These ruined walls were restored using smaller blocks in later periods, beginning with the Muslim building activity in the late seventh and early eighth centuries. Several further restorations took place after being damaged by earthquakes and erosion in later periods. Such restoration has continued until the present.

It seems, therefore, that during the Late Roman and Byzantine period the enclosure had no clear boundaries. In parts it was surrounded by straight walls (that hardly reached the level of occupation on top of the Esplanade) but mostly by heaps of stones that created inclined, even steep, slopes.[21] It seems that most of the original gates in the circumference of the Esplanade were ruined or blocked by rubble. The discovery of flagstones of the Roman street going east–west (probably the so-called *decumanus*) along the line of today's Chain Street, near Wilson's Arch, points to the possibility that one of the few entrances to the Esplanade was located above the Arch or very near to it.[22]

As no archaeological excavations have been conducted atop the platform that could supply information about Roman building activity, we must depend mostly on the written sources while also taking into account some of the finds outside of the enclosure's walls.[23] In a certain sector of the Esplanade, probably near the site of the ruined Temple (in the close vicinity of the later Dome of the Rock),[24] a sacred site of a Roman cult was established embellished with monuments.

The architectural nature of this cultic enclosure is still under dispute. The main issue

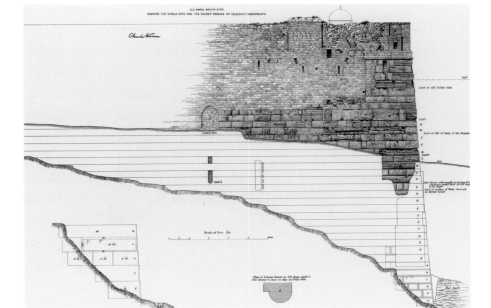

47 A drawing by Charles Warren of the southeastern corner of the Temple Mount, late nineteenth century

48 The southeastern corner of the Temple Mount, with the courses of large Herodian building stones creating the shape of a tower

is whether the colony's Capitolium, namely the temple of the Capitoline Triad (Jupiter, Juno, and Minerva), was located in the sacred area on the Temple Mount or somewhere else in the city, preferably near the later compound of the Holy Sepulchre. The Capitolium was the official and most important temple of a Roman colony, though not necessarily the largest and most decorated. Its location on the Temple Mount supports the hypothesis that this area continued to be the most important place within Aelia Capitolina, and vice versa.[25] Other scholars tend to locate the Capitoline temple in the city center, probably in or around the compound of the later Holy Sepulchre, not far from the city's forum.[26] According to this opinion, the cult place on the Temple Mount was an open sacred space, or at most included a minor built shrine.

Most important among the relevant texts is the paragraph of Cassius Dio (69.12.1) mentioned above. The epitome of Xiphilinus states that Hadrian built a city named Aelia Capitolina on top of the ruins of Jerusalem. He mentions that "on site (Greek: *topos*) of the Temple of the God he raised a new temple for Zeus."[27] It is very plausible that Xiphilinus was the one who emphasized that Hadrian's edifice was built atop the ruined Temple of God (a term which was probably strange to Dio himself) in order to point to the humiliation of the Jews.[28] Moreover, the term *topos* may point to the exact spot of the former Temple, but it may also be understood in a wider sense pointing to the City of the Temple in general. This second interpretation leaves room to locate the new temple of Jupiter in another place within the city.

Of great importance is the report, in Latin, of the anonymous Pilgrim of Burdigala (present-day Bordeaux) who made a pilgrimage to Jerusalem around the year 333 CE, when he thoroughly inspected the Temple Mount. He saw the fresh traces of the blood of Zacharias (the priest Zechariah) "in the marble in front of the altar."[29] This description echoes Matthew and Luke who locate the place of the martyrdom "between the shrine and the altar." The Bordeaux Pilgrim writes that an *aedes* (a Latin term for a built temple) stood on the site of the Temple of Solomon. One may take the description as the evidence of an eye-witness for the existence of an actual Roman temple, namely the Capitolium, on the site of the Temple of Solomon. It is possible, though less likely, that the pilgrim pointed to the Roman temple and altar of his time as a reference for the "altar and temple" of the ancient Jewish Temple mentioned in the Scriptures. Therefore, there is a strong possibility that the term *aedes* in his description refers to vestigial interior parts of the ruined Jewish Temple. Other important Roman monuments mentioned by the Bordeaux Pilgrim are two statues of Hadrian standing at the same site.[30]

While the Bordeaux Pilgrim presents the local popular traditions which were transmitted to him by his local guide, Jerome, the famous Christian author and theologian (who lived in Bethlehem from 384 until his death in 420) presents a scholarly as well as a theological (and anti-Jewish) approach. In his Commentary on Matthew 23.15, he

49 Part of a Latin inscription embedded upside down in the southern wall of the Temple Mount, near the Double Gate. It forms part of a monument honoring Emperor Antoninus Pius (138–61 CE). See also note 30

mentions an equestrian statue of Hadrian, placed on the site of the ancient Holy of Holies (with echoes of the prophecy of Daniel about the "abomination of desolation" approach noted above).[31] In his later Commentary on Isaiah 2.9 he goes even further and mentions a statue of Hadrian and another one of Jupiter installed on the site of the ruined Temple.

During Jerome's time there was no active temple on the Temple Mount. At that period Roman temples had already been abandoned or even lay in ruins (or at least did their inner shrines and the divine statue, as well as the altars in front of the temples). This was in accord with the edicts against the temples issued by Emperor Theodosius I since 391 CE. If there was a Roman temple on the Temple Mount it was already in ruins. Statues, on the other hand, were not removed from public and private places until the fifth or even sixth century, but they were usually defaced or even beheaded to mutilate their demonic powers as early as the late fourth and fifth centuries.[32]

No other text supplies even a hint that may prove the existence of a Capitoline temple on the Temple Mount. But the name Capitolium in connection with the Temple Mount appears again in two episodes from the second half of the seventh century, one preserved in Georgian and the other in Greek. The stories (both seem to come from the same milieu and perhaps are presented by the same author) are typical monk's tales rich in piety and miracles. One story mentions the building of the mosque (probably the first wooden mosque that preceded the Aqsa Mosque) in a place named the Capitol. The Greek text includes memories of a monk who had lived on the Mount of Olives thirty years before his report, when the Capitol was cleared (to enable building the mosque).[33] Bernard Flusin, who published the texts, and Cyril Mango, who discussed them, find here conclusive evidence that at one time the Capitoline temple of Roman Jerusalem had stood on the Temple Mount, and that the name survived in the memory of local residents throughout the Byzantine period. This opinion is favored by several other scholars and is strengthened by the fact that the name Capitolion is mentioned incidentally; the author simply tells a story and has no special interest in the name.

However, this conclusion, too, remains a hypothetical one. Although it is not impossible that the tradition about the Capitolium being on this site continued to exist more than three hundred years after the Christianization of the city, it is strange that it has not been mentioned in even one of the various descriptions of Jerusalem and the Temple Mount. One must, therefore, also consider other possibilities, such as the emergence of popular identification of the Temple Mount with a Roman Capitolium during the Byzantine or early Islamic period.[34] The existence of Latin inscriptions and Roman monuments on and around the Temple Mount might encourage the emergence of such a later local tradition.

Scholars who deny the existence of a Capitoline temple on the Temple mount tend to locate the Capitolium of Aelia in another part of the city. The most likely location for Jupiter's temple seems be a prominent high place adjacent to the city's central forum—where Capitoline temples were usually built in Roman colonies. It is reasonable to situate this forum to the south of the compound of the Church of the Holy Sepulchre. One can even identify the Capitolium with the Temple which was destroyed by Helena, mother of Constantine—the first Christian emperor—in 326 CE and called by Eusebius the Temple of Aphrodite, in order to discover the Tomb of Christ underneath it.[35] The latter suggestion is supported by the Church Father and scholar Jerome (letter 58.3) who knew that until the days of Emperor Constantine a statue of Jupiter had stood at the site of the Resurrection and that a statue of Venus (Aphrodite) had stood on the rock of the Cross. Both sites, which are close to one another, were later incorporated into the compound of Constantine's basilica of the Holy Sepulchre.

To sum up: The ruined enclosure of the Temple Mount attracted the Romans who installed there monumental sculptures of the emperors and other monuments. The area may have been used as an open cult place, perhaps connected with the Roman ruler-cult. It is possible that a built temple (*aedes*) was erected on the site, whether a small shrine or, less likely, the Capitoline temple (namely, the main temple of Aelia Capitolina). The exact location of this Roman cult center on the Temple Mount is unknown, but it was probably situated in the center of the Esplanade, near the site of the ruined Jewish Temple.

The Christians and the Temple Mount

Christians, still a minority, shared with the Jews many of the biblical traditions concerning the Temple Mount, but they also had their own traditions concerning the life and deeds of Jesus and the early Church Fathers.

On the one hand, they were pleased by the destruction of the Temple because it was confirmation of Jesus' prophecy that "There will not be left here a stone upon a stone that will not be thrown down." As indicated above, Christians also pointed out that the poor, profane, and defiled state of the site of the Temple fulfilled other biblical prophecies.

Eusebius and Jerome represent the milieu of the "purists"—educated theologians, but most people, both local residents and pilgrims, were looking for tangible sacred sites or relics that one could see, touch, and enter, in which they could hear voices or even taste and drink water from holy relics. The Temple Mount was one of these desired places.

It is possible that already before the Bar Kokhba revolt, and by no means later than the second century CE, Christians revered the place where St. James the Less, Jesus' brother and the first bishop of the Christian congregation of Jerusalem, had suffered martyrdom. According to the second-century description of Hegesippus[36] and of some apocryphal Christian texts, Jews had thrown James from a tower and then killed him. Perhaps he was even buried in the area of the Temple, although this could not have occurred in Jewish Jerusalem according to the Jewish laws of purity. The martyrdom allegedly took place at a site known as the Pinnacle, or the Corner Tower. This site is usually located in one of the southern corners of the Temple platform, preferably the southeastern one. According to one opinion, in the second and third centuries the site of the martyrdom was shown as being on the platform itself, since one of the surviving walls of the ruined Temple complex could be identified as the Pinnacle or Corner Tower.[37] According to this opinion, the Pinnacle was later transferred to the southeastern corner of the Esplanade during the Early Byzantine period.

The description of the Bordeaux Pilgrim is one of the best sources of information.[38] Although he, most likely, entered Jerusalem through the northern Porta Neapolitana (Neapolis [Nablus] Gate, today's Damascus Gate), he begins his description from the east. Near the Temple Mount, outside the city, he saw two big pools "built by Solomon," while inside it he saw the Bethesda (Probatica) pools where sick people were miraculously cured ever since the time of Jesus, as related in John 5.2. Solomon is the major hero of the scene. A cave was shown to the pilgrim where Solomon tortured the demons, though the exact site, whether inside or outside the precinct, is not clear. There were underground rooms in the place where Solomon's palace stood, in one of which he composed the Book of Wisdom (*Sapientia Solomonis*), one of the works included in Christian apocryphal literature. The ceiling was of one stone. At the Temple Mount there were, above all, the ruins of Solomon's Temple. Part of the Temple is identified as the *aedes*. In this place, as mentioned above, the blood of Zacharias was shown on the marble slabs.[39] One could also see around the marks "left by the sandals of the soldiers who killed him, incised in the pavement like in wax." Nearby were two statues of Hadrian. Of great interest for the Christian was the Tower (Pinnacle) of Temptation where Satan tempted Jesus,[40] and the "cornerstone," the one which "the builders rejected" and "has become the head of the corner."[41] Not far away was a "pierced stone" above which the Jews mourned. In close vicinity was the house of Hezekiah, king of Judaea. Further on, the pilgrim describes the elaborate ancient water system within the area of the Temple Mount and around it which was, most likely, in re-use, at least in part.[42]

Some of the sites were also mentioned by other, later, sources: Jerome, in addition to his references to the statues on the site of the Temple, mentions the traces of Zacharias' blood, while the place of the Temptation was noted by later pilgrims as well. However, it becomes clear that from the later part of the fourth century, Christian interest in the Temple Mount had significantly declined.

After leaving the Temple Mount, the Bordeaux Pilgrim went southwest to Mount Sion and then returned northward toward the Porta Neapolitana. On his way he passed through the Hill of Golgotha (Calvary), the place of the Crucifixion next to Christ's Tomb. There he saw the new Basilica of the Lord (*basilica id est Dominicum*), namely the new Church of the Holy Sepulchre which was under construction by order of Emperor Constantine. The building of the Basilica became the apex of a great development in Christian thought. In it the Temple was indeed rebuilt anew, though no longer on the Temple Mount but above the Tomb of Christ and the site of the Resurrection (*Anastasis*). This was the New Jerusalem.[43] As a consequence, the importance of the Temple Mount diminished. The Jerusalem liturgy was characterized by its "processional" character; priests and believers proceeded from one place to another.[44] They prayed appropriately, "according to the time and the place," as the pilgrim Egeria characterized it, not only in the complex of the Holy Sepulchre, the focus of the Jerusalem liturgy, but also in Zion, on the Mount of Olives, and even in Bethlehem, and they used to move from one place to another. The Temple Mount is not mentioned and seems to have played no role in the liturgy. It was mentioned only rarely in the writing of later pilgrims or Church Fathers. Clearly, the triumph of New Jerusalem and the New Temple at the site of the Resurrection over the historical Temple was total.

Even "tourist" interest in the Holy Places was confined to the margins of the Temple Mount, mainly to the Pinnacle at the corner of the Esplanade where St. James suffered martyrdom. Yet the transfer of the "Temple" from the Temple Mount to its new site at the complex of the Holy Sepulchre does not explain the neglect of the Temple Mount and its sites. The absence of such interest is particularly astonishing in an age in which the discovery of relics and new sites became popular.[45] It seems that this phenomenon was connected to a striking political event in the second half of the fourth century. This was the attempt by the Jews to build a new Temple on the Temple Mount during the reign of Emperor Julian (361–63).

The Jews and the Temple Mount

Since the suppression of the Bar Kokhba Revolt, the Jews had confined their interest, as described above, to the spiritual realm—studying and praying. They studied the tractates of the Mishnah which dealt with the physical Temple, the sacrifices, and rules of purification. Jerusalem and the Temple were mentioned in daily prayers and on holy days. From the sayings of R. Aha in the fourth century we learn that he believed that "The Divine Presence [*Shekhinah*] shall never move from the western wall of the Temple."[46] It should be emphasized that R. Aha referred to the remains of the supposed western wall of the ruined Temple, and not to the present Western Wall, which is the supporting wall of the precinct of the Temple Mount.

Settlement of Jews in Jerusalem continued to be prohibited, but it seems that a small Jewish congregation found its way into the city and lived there. This community is known in the Talmudic literature as the "Holy Congregation in Jerusalem."[47] The prohibition against settlement of Jews was reinstituted by Constantine, the first Christian emperor, in the early fourth century, perhaps under pressure from the Christian bishops.[48]

The itinerary of the Christian Bordeaux Pilgrim in Jerusalem and the Temple Mount refers to traditions that were shared by Jews and Christians and are reflected in rabbinic literature, either as learned discourses or as popular beliefs. It may well be that some of these common traditions, mostly concerning the monuments related to biblical heroes (such as Solomon), had a Jewish origin, even if they were sometimes derived from the Gospels, such as the tradition about Zechariah the priest, who was killed between the altar and the Temple. There were genuine Christian traditions which the Jews rejected, and undoubtedly there were specific Jewish traditions that the Christian pilgrim did not learn about, or if he was aware of them refrained from mentioning them.

The Bordeaux Pilgrim described a few monuments from the point of view of a "tourist guide" as features that had no Christian connotation but were still a matter of interest. These were the impressive pools and cisterns cut in the rock at the site, many of them, undoubtedly, still in use, and the "perforated (or pierced) stone" (Latin: *lapis pertusus*) located not far from Hadrian's statues. About this stone he says: "Jews come to anoint (it) every year. They mourn and rend their garments and then depart."[49] The day is probably the 9th of Av, or one of the three festivals—Passover, Pentecost, and Tabernacles—on which pilgrimage to the Temple took place in the past.[50]

Jewish pilgrimage to mourn at the ruins of the Temple is also attested in Jerome's exegesis on the Book of Zephaniah 1.15–16.[51] The prophet described the terrible fate of Jerusalem on the Day of Yahweh, which will be "A day of wrath that day, a day of distress and agony, a day of ruins and devastation, a day of darkness and gloom, a day of cloud and blackness, a day of trumpet blast and battle cry, against fortified town and high corner-tower." Although without any sympathy for the Jews, Jerome described the moving realization of this prophecy:

> But to this very day the faithless inhabitants, after they killed the servants of God, and finally his Son, are forbidden to enter Jerusalem, except for lamentation; and they acquire for a price the right of bewailing the ruin of their city, so that those who once bought the blood of Christ, now buy their own tears, and not even the weeping is free for them. On the day of the capture of Jerusalem you can see the people coming in mourning attire, decrepit women flocking together, and old men loaded with rags and years, showing the wrath of God. A crowd of miserable people gathers together, and as the place of the Lord's passion glitters and (the place of) Resurrection sparkles and on the Mount of Olives too the standard of the Cross flashes with light, the pitiable nation weeps over the ruin of its Temple […].

During the stormy reign of Emperor Julian ("the Apostate") between 361 and 363,[52] a last attempt was made in the Roman Empire to stop the process of Christianization and revive polytheism. Although Julian criticized Jewish monotheism, he accepted the Jewish God as one of the numerous God-messengers that fill the space between the one superior God, the creator of all, and human beings.[53] In such capacity he encouraged the Jews to rebuild their Temple in Jerusalem. In his letter to the "Community of the Jews," he wrote: "This you ought to do, in order that, when I have successfully concluded the war in Persia, I may rebuild by my own efforts the sacred city of Jerusalem, which for so many years you have longed to see inhabited, and may bring settlers there, and, together with you, may glorify the Most High God therein."[54] Other Christian writers confirm this event and inform us that the Jews reacted with great enthusiasm. It is surprising that the Jewish rabbinic sources do not mention this episode (at least not directly.)

Christians conceived of Julian's activity as intended to disprove the major demonstration of their belief: the prophecy of Jesus about the eternal destruction of the Jewish Temple. It is likely that both Julian and the Jews took this consideration into account, even if it was only a side effect of the new program. The building project began in the last year of Julian's rule and ceased with his death in battle at the Persian frontier (363 CE). According to Christian legends, it was brought to a halt—by supernatural powers—on the very night it had been begun. An earthquake was followed by mysterious eruptions of fire that caused many Jewish casualties as well as some Christian. Scholars have in vain attempted to provide a rational explanation of the miraculous eruption of fire. This earthquake may have been the major one that occurred in the same year and shook cities in many parts of the country—from Petra to the Galilee, including Jerusalem (18–19 May 363 CE). The most detailed description is found in a late manuscript containing an early fifth-century report in Syriac, falsely attributed to Cyril, the bishop of Jerusalem in the mid-fourth century. Other reports of this event are found in Histories of the Church written by Socrates, Sozomenus, and Theodoretus, and in other chronicles and literary compositions.[55] The Syriac text, although legendary and motivated by extreme anti-Jewish feelings, contains several details that prove the authenticity of its nucleus. The information, that the Jews dug out and removed the monumental statue of Herodes, which was later hurriedly restored by the citizens of Jerusalem, seems to be real. The statue was most probably the one of Hadrian which the author of the letter confused with Herod. This event indicates that the city was at that time still inhabited in part by polytheists. It also shows that the city's municipal authority maintained the Roman concepts of urbanism. This re-erection of the statue enabled Jerome, some 30–40 years after the event, to see it and report as an eye-witness that it was standing on the site of the former Temple.

This was the fate of the last Jewish attempt to build a new Temple on the Temple Mount. A Hebrew inscription was found incised on one of the blocks of the western wall of the Temple platform: "And when you see this your heart shall rejoice, and your bones [shall flourish] like an herb [...]" [fig. 50]. This is a part of a phrase from Isaiah 66.14, referring to the day of Resurrection at the End of Days. The excavator, as many other scholars, related this inscription to the rebuilding of the Temple in the days of Julian, since both the level of the excavation and the paleography of the inscription support this suggestion.[56] Yet such an interpretation remains, of course, hypothetical.

Christian sources report that the impact of the miraculous victory of Christianity over Judaism and polytheism was very persuasive and that many joined the Church. But it seems that Christian self-confidence was shaken as well. The fragility of the situation and the fear that the old Temple Mount would replace the New Temple, namely the Church of the Holy Sepulchre, called for a new policy. It seems that the Temple Mount was, henceforth, concealed and erased from the mind and memory of Christian believers. As we shall see below, the Christian monuments on the Esplanade were forgotten; the only one that continued to be venerated by Christians was the Tower of the Temptation, the Pinnacle or Corner Tower, which was easily visible from the outside. The triumph of Christianity was expressed in neglect of the Temple Mount, both in mind and in practice.

50   A stone in the Western Wall of the Temple Mount, with the Hebrew inscription "And when you see this your heart shall rejoice, and your bones [shall flourish] like an herb […]."
This is part of Isaiah 66, verse 14, referring to the day of Resurrection at the End of Days

The Temple Mount and the Urban Planning of Jerusalem from the Foundation of Aelia Capitolina to the End of the Fourth Century

No archaeological remains from the Roman period have been found atop the Temple Mount, and the possibility that some will be found in the future is very slight. Most of the pre-Islamic remains had, most probably, been removed already in ancient times. The Temple Mount platform has been surveyed, but no systematic excavations have taken place within the walls of the Muslim Haram al-Sharif. On the other hand, numerous archaeological finds outside the walls of the Temple Mount give us some information about the situation of the Temple Mount within the living city.

As described above, in 135 CE Hadrian inaugurated Aelia Capitolina. The new city, settled among others by veterans of the Tenth Legion, received the higher status of a Roman colony.[57] The headquarters of the Roman Tenth Legion, and probably some of

51 A World War I German aerial photo looking northwest. The central valley (Valley Street, Arabic: Tariq al-Wad) and the southwestern hill beyond it are visible to the west of (=above) the Temple Mount

its units, were encamped within it. There is no agreement among scholars about the city's plan, its expansion, the location of the legion's camp, and the importance and centrality of the Temple Mount within the new city.[58]

There is a consensus among scholars that the town plan of Aelia Capitolina can be detected in the layout of today's Old City of Jerusalem [fig. 51]. The city plan of Aelia is a compromise between the common Roman method of urban planning according to an orthogonal system, creating a grid of parallel and perpendicular streets, and the need to adjust to the topographical conditions and the rough terrain of the city. The latter forced the Roman engineers to create two main arteries, usually defined in our days as *cardines*, which became the main thoroughfares of the city.[59] These streets are not parallel to each

52   A segment of the Eastern Cardo, west of the Western Wall plaza, during excavations in 2008

53   The pavement of the Eastern Cardo south of the Dung Gate

54 Jerusalem on the Madaba Mosaic Map. The entrance to the Church of the Holy Sepulchre is situated in the center of the city, while the Temple Mount is not marked

other; both began their course, one toward the south and the other toward the southeast, from the square inside Porta Neapolitana (today's Damascus Gate; Arabic: Bab al-'Amud). In that period the gate was free standing; the city wall was added, probably, around the year 300 CE. The eastern *cardo* stretched along the central valley of Jerusalem (today's Valley Street, Arabic: Tariq al-Wad), and sloped down toward the Siloam Pool. This was the natural course, dictated by the city's topography, and also the course of Jerusalem's main thoroughfare in the Second Temple period. Segments of its pavement were discovered west and southwest of the western wall of the Temple Mount [figs. 52, 53].[60]

Because of the ruinous condition of the Temple Mount at the eastern edge of the new town, and the minor importance of the eastern part of the city, the eastern *cardo* lost some of its importance and another thoroughfare was built, which ran through the center of the city. This street became the main artery of Aelia. The modern street, which was built above it and is known in its northern part as Olive Press Street (Arabic: Tariq Khan al-Zeit), has remained the main street of the Old City today. The depiction of Jerusalem on the Madaba mosaic map, dating from the late sixth or very early seventh century, presents a clear graphic scheme of the main streets of Jerusalem [fig. 54].[61]

Perpendicular streets, known in the Roman engineering manuals as *decumani*, proceeded from the city gates in the east (today's St. Stephen Gate) and the west (today's

55 Lower part of an almost life-size marble statue of a Roman goddess found in excavations south of the Temple Mount, and dedicated by a lady named Valeria Aemiliana in fulfilment of a vow (now at the Israel Academy of Sciences and Humanities)

Jaffa Gate) and connected the main streets. The most important perpendicular street led from the western gate to the Temple Mount (along the course of today's David Street and Street of the Chain). Remains of this street came to light in excavations on the eastern end of the Street of the Chain near the present Chain Gate of the Temple Mount. At that place (or perhaps above the neighboring Wilson's Arch) may have stood the gate that Jerome mentions in his commentary on Matthew 23.35 when he writes about the blood

56 A rounded brick with the stamp of the workshop of the Roman Tenth Legion of the Straights (*Legio X Fretensis*)

of Zacharias being visible amongst the ruins of the Temple and the altar near the gates that go down to Siloam.[62]

The Temple Mount was situated at the southeastern corner of the new colony. Having lost its significance as a Jewish temple, the platform of the Temple Mount lost much of its importance, despite that there were statues of the emperors upon it and possibly a Roman cult place as well.

Aelia Capitolina developed gradually, and the most important monuments were positioned in its northern part, while in the area of today's Jewish Quarter only scattered remains of Late Roman buildings have been found. Thus it has been suggested that the Temple Mount remained actually outside of the inhabited city,[63] but this opinion seems less likely. The semi-deserted temenos of the Temple Mount remained an integral part of the city. Indeed, many architectural and other finds have appeared in every excavated area in close proximity to the western and southern walls of the enclosure [fig. 55].[64] Among the finds were numerous bricks and roof tiles with the stamps of the brick factory of the Tenth Legion located west of Jerusalem [fig. 56].[65] It has even been suggested that a unit of the Tenth Legion was encamped in the vicinity of the southwestern corner of the Temple Mount.[66] The suggestion that the precinct of the Temple Mount itself was used as the location of the Tenth Legion is highly unlikely.[67]

While discussing the place of the Temple Mount within the urban fabric of Aelia Capitolina, we must take into account that even if it lay half ruined and played a minor role in city life, it remained the largest single architectural unit and the major element in the urban topography of Jerusalem. No other Roman sources concerned with the Temple Mount are known in addition to those mentioned above. Yet it has been suggested that the huge precinct was an unknown monument called (in Greek) Kodra, which is most probably a Greek form of the Latin Quadra (square).[68] This name is found in a list of monuments of local character that was inserted into a world chronicle known as the *Chronicon Paschale*, composed in the early seventh century. While dealing with the outcome of the Bar Kokhba Revolt and the foundation of Aelia Capitolina, the *Chronicon* provides a list of monuments that Hadrian built in the town. There is no hint of a Christian hand in this paragraph, so the list predates the Christianization of the city. On the other hand, the source mentions a division of Aelia into quarters that was in effect "until our days." It is clear, therefore, that the paragraph does not belong to the time of Hadrian but is somewhat later, perhaps from the third century. It lists monuments with bizarre names which were known to local citizens of Aelia, but are unknown to us. The suggestion to identify the Kodra or Quadra with the enclosure of the Temple Mount is attractive, but remains hypothetical.

The Temple Mount in the Byzantine Period, from the Late Fourth Century to the Muslim Conquest (638 CE)

During the Byzantine period Jerusalem, now officially called Aelia and not Aelia Capitolina, expanded in area and population [fig. 57]. Numerous pilgrims filled the streets and churches of the Christian city, and many remained there, giving Jerusalem a cosmopolitan flavor.[69] Religious life, liturgy, and theological writing flourished.[70] But the condition of the Temple Mount continued to be poor. The area might even have been used, where possible, for agriculture, and the cisterns continued to collect water. According to later legends, it became a place for dumping refuse.[71] The Muslims, according to tradition, had to dig down in order to discover the Rock.[72] Though there were gates through which people could enter the precinct, in general it was deserted. The pilgrim Egeria, who recorded details of the liturgy of Jerusalem in the early 380s, did not mention even a single prayer or liturgical procession which passed through the Temple Mount, although there were frequent processions from the Mount of Olives through Gethsemane, on the opposite side of the valley, to the Holy Sepulchre. It is neither listed in the Armenian liturgical calendar of the fifth century, probably translated from the Greek, nor in the tenth-century Georgian calendar which in part reflects ancient traditions.

As noted above, the main reason for this neglect was the rivalry between the two Temples—the old, historical one which was still revered and longed for by the Jews, and the New Temple around Golgotha and the site of Christ's Tomb. However, when we check the lists of holy places within Jerusalem and its surroundings, we are astonished by the large number of cult places and invented relics. Almost none of those sites are found above the ruins of the Temple itself, the only venerated place being, as mentioned, the Pinnacle or Corner Tower at the southwest—or more likely the southeast—corner of the Esplanade. The change, therefore, should be sought in the political, or even psychological, sphere. The attempt by the Jews to build the Temple under the auspices and encouragement of Emperor Julian jeopardized the Christian triumph over Judaism. The historical perspective shows that Julian's attempt to revive polytheism was no more than a hopeless episode, but at the

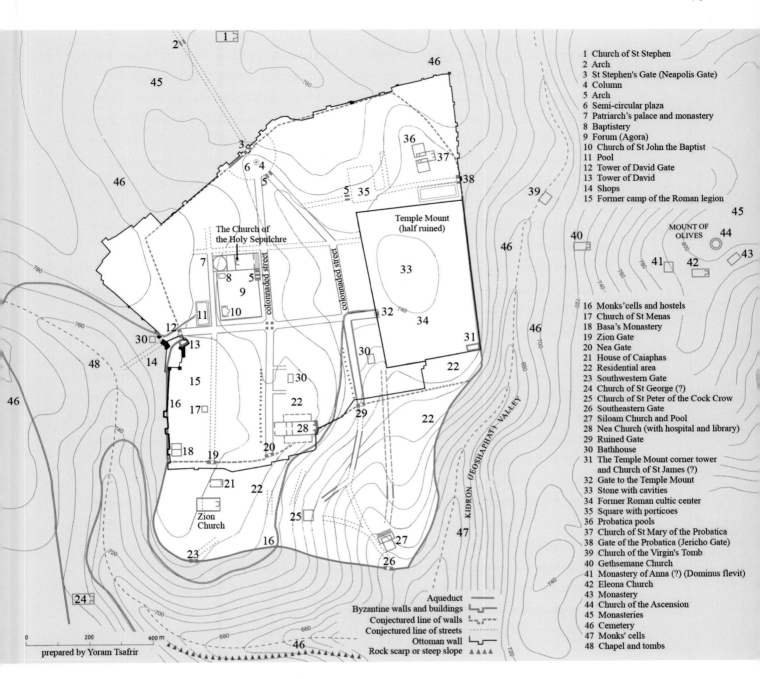

1 Church of St Stephen
2 Arch
3 St Stephen's Gate (Neapolis Gate)
4 Column
5 Arch
6 Semi-circular plaza
7 Patriarch's palace and monastery
8 Baptistery
9 Forum (Agora)
10 Church of St John the Baptist
11 Pool
12 Tower of David Gate
13 Tower of David
14 Shops
15 Former camp of the Roman legion
16 Monks' cells and hostels
17 Church of St Menas
18 Basa's Monastery
19 Zion Gate
20 Nea Gate
21 House of Caiaphas
22 Residential area
23 Southwestern Gate
24 Church of St George (?)
25 Church of St Peter of the Cock Crow
26 Southeastern Gate
27 Siloam Church and Pool
28 Nea Church (with hospital and library)
29 Ruined Gate
30 Bathhouse
31 The Temple Mount corner tower and Church of St James (?)
32 Gate to the Temple Mount
33 Stone with cavities
34 Former Roman cultic center
35 Square with porticoes
36 Probatica pools
37 Church of St Mary of the Probatica
38 Gate of the Probatica (Jericho Gate)
39 Church of the Virgin's Tomb
40 Gethsemane Church
41 Monastery of Anna (?) (Dominus flevit)
42 Eleona Church
43 Monastery
44 Church of the Ascension
45 Monasteries
46 Cemetery
47 Monks' cells
48 Chapel and tombs

Aqueduct
Byzantine walls and buildings
Conjectured line of walls
Conjectured line of streets
Ottoman wall
Rock scarp or steep slope

prepared by Yoram Tsafrir

57 Map of Jerusalem in the Byzantine period

time it occurred nobody was aware of that. The immediate Christian reaction was very effective: the Temple Mount was abandoned, not only mentally but physically as well.

A brief survey of the writings of Christian pilgrims whose descriptions of Jerusalem have survived will clarify the point.[73] They display an elaborate gallery of holy sites and relics in every part of the city, except for the Temple Mount. Jerome, who mentioned sites on the Esplanade in his commentaries on the Bible, does not mention this place in the description of the pious journey, in 386 CE, of the nun Paula, for whom he was most probably the guide. Eucherius, around 445 CE, compiled a short guidebook, based on earlier descriptions, without personal memories. He mentions that the site of the Temple is in ruins, and that one single tower (of the Temptation?) survived. He was also aware of a few cisterns on the site. Theodosius, between 518–530 CE, knows that St. James was thrown down from the Pinnacle of the Temple (the *pinna templi*) and then killed and buried on the Mount of Olives. The short pilgrim guidebook known as the *Breviarius* (early sixth century) includes Solomon's Temple among the sites to be visited on the way to the Pinnacle (Tower) of the Temptation. He makes it clear that nothing remained of the Temple except one cave.

Much more significant is the report that in front of Christ's Tomb was an altar in front of which Zachariah was murdered, and that the traces of his blood are shown to pilgrims. This tradition, too, had been transferred from the old ruined Temple to the new Christian one. The anonymous pilgrim from Placentia (Piacenza) in Italy (ca. 570) adds some more information. While entering into the city from the east he saw the "Beautiful Gate" (Acts 3.2), of which one could see the threshold and floor. These are, most probably, the remains of an old gate that could be seen near the Golden Gate, but on a lower level.[74] This pilgrim knows that the "corner stone which the builders rejected"[75] is in the Church of Zion. Thus this tradition had also been removed to this place from the Temple Mount. He attests that the altar of the sacrifice of Isaac, believed by the Jews to be on the Temple Mount, which is also Mount Moriah,[76] is to be found below the rock of Golgotha.[77]

The most explicit indication of the change in status of the Temple Mount is in the depiction of Jerusalem in the Madaba mosaic map [fig. 54]. This map is unique in that it tries to display real depictions of some cities in the Holy Land, most important among them Jerusalem.[78] In fact, however, since the artist had no room to show the entire city he chose the monuments of greatest importance, but its main colonnaded streets and most important churches are easily identified. Not only did artistic limitations shape the map, however, for ideology and theology also played an important role, more than the real topography. The entrance to the Church of the Holy Sepulchre, namely the new Temple, is located in the very center of the Holy City, which is also the center of the map of the Holy Land, a position undoubtedly intending to indicate that this was the navel of the world.[79] Thus, the church was shifted from its real location north of the center toward the south. The Temple Mount, on the other hand, the single architectural unit within the city, is not depicted at all. The artist or his patron deliberately ignored this area which they considered of no importance.

The Jews, for their part, did not forget the Temple Mount. Hopes were now diminished. They requested a regular permit to visit the Temple Mount on special occasions: the 9th of Av and the three pilgrimage festivals. In 438/9 CE Empress Eudocia,[80] who was on a pilgrimage to Jerusalem, granted such permission. The story is related in the biography of Barsauma, an ascetic and monk who, in the first half of the fifth century, acted with great zeal against Jews and Samaritans.[81] The story is legendary, full of miraculous events and exaggerations, but scholars agree that it contains a kernel of truth.[82] According to the biographer of Barsauma, the Jews requested the Empress' permission to pray at the ruins of Solomon's Temple. Her positive response, circulated by the "Priests and heads of the Galilee" to the "Great Jewish people," informed them:

> The time of our exile has passed; the day has come for the ingathering of our tribes, because the kings of the Romans have decided to give us back Jerusalem. Hasten and go up to Jerusalem for the feast of the Tabernacles, because our kingdom shall rise in Jerusalem again.[83]

The surviving text of the letter is undoubtedly full of exaggeration. Such an imperial promise to the Jews, to return Jerusalem to them, is beyond imagination. But the biographer of Barsauma relates this story in order to explain another incident connected with the holy man himself. Some twenty of his disciples, who visited the Corner Tower of the Temptation, confronted 103,000 (sic!) Jews making a pilgrimage to the Temple Mount. This happened during the Feast of Tabernacles. The monks were saved by a miracle but complained that the authorities, inspired by Eudocia herself, acted in favor of the Jews.

There is no trace of this event either in other Christian sources or in Jewish ones. It is clear, however, that Jewish efforts to visit the Temple Mount did not cease. During the sixth century anti-Jewish legislation continued and the pressure on Jews in Palestine and elsewhere increased (and even more so against Samaritans). The latter rose up against Byzantine rule and lost the battles at the end of the fifth and during the first half of the sixth centuries. No similar activity against Byzantine rule occurred among the Jews. Archaeological discoveries even show that synagogues continued to be built in the sixth century, mostly during its first half.

Several Hebrew inscriptions were incised by Jewish pilgrims around the walls of the Temple Mount, most of which can be dated to the medieval period. One of them contains a vocation to God for rebuilding the Temple and mentions both Jewish and Greek names. Both the paleographic consideration and the names led the scholar who published it, Leo A. Mayer, to date the inscription to the later part of the Byzantine period [fig. 58].[84]

But everything changed at the beginning of the seventh century, when the Sassanian Persians began their war against Byzantium, and during the early years of that century even seemed be winning the upper hand. The anti-Byzantine and anti-Christian reaction of the Jews, and the hope to free the Land of Israel from Christian rule, erupted with much anger and aggression. The Jews became allies of the Persians.

The Persian war against Byzantium reached its peak in 614 CE with the conquest

58   Jewish vocation for rebuilding the Temple, probably in the late Byzantine period.
"O God Sebaoth / build this House / in the lifetime of Jacob, the son / of Joseph and Theophylactos / and Sisinia and Anastasia / Amen and Amen / Selah"
The inscription was discovered in the late 1920s on a wall of the Is'irdiyya College in the northern part of the Haram

59   A lintel with a cross coated with plaster and a depiction of two seven-branched candelabra (*menorot*) from the time of the Persian conquest (after 614) or more probably from the Early Islamic period (after 638)

of Jerusalem and the capture of the True Cross from the Church of the Holy Sepulchre. The conquest was accompanied by the massacre of many thousands of Christians in Jerusalem.[85] According to the Christian sources the Jews collaborated with the Persians and took an active part in killing numerous Christians. These sources are biased and full of exaggerations, and it is almost impossible to discern when a report of historical facts changes into a legendary description.

The massacre of Christians in Jerusalem was very extensive; the number of people who were buried, probably in mass graves, was enormous. The manuscripts provide different statistics of the victims, but even the lowest reports (none of the manuscripts is complete) may add up to tens of thousands. Bodies were found all over the city, mostly in and around churches.[86] Many were exiled to Persia, 37,000 according to the reports, headed by the patriarch Zacharias together with the True Cross. The Temple Mount is not explicitly mentioned in any of the sources concerning the events in Jerusalem, not even in the list of places where bodies were found. There are only a few hints of a messianic nature in Jewish literature, expressing feelings and hopes to return to Jerusalem and the Temple Mount.[87] Jewish hopes to receive Jerusalem from the Persians and renew the Jewish rite on the Temple Mount ended in great frustration. The Persians, after realizing the real balance of political and demographic power, restored the rule of Jerusalem to Christian hands. Intensive rebuilding of the ruined churches began under the leadership of the monk Modestus, who acted as unofficial patriarch. Several years later, in 628 CE, the Persians were defeated and, probably in 630 CE, Emperor Heraclius brought the True Cross back to Jerusalem.

It seems likely that there was a period during which the Jews could freely go to the Temple Mount and pray there, but it was of very short duration.[88] A building was discovered near the southwest corner of the Temple Mount in which depictions of seven-branched candelabra (menorot) were found, painted on a cross which had been covered by plaster. Clearly, a Christian house had come into the possession of a Jewish owner [fig. 59].[89] However it is unclear whether the change of ownership took place during the Persian conquest or, more plausibly, in the Early Islamic period.[90]

It seems therefore that nothing changed on the Temple Mount. It remained abandoned under the Christians, except for the Corner Tower (pinna), probably at the southeast corner of the temple platform, which was revered as the Tower of the Temptation and as the place of the martyrdom of St. James.

It has been suggested that the revival of the Temple Mount, which reached its peak in the Early Muslim period, commenced already in the late Byzantine period. According to this thesis, the best expression of this revival was the building of the magnificent Golden Gate in the eastern wall of the Temple Mount.[91] Christian traditions maintain that Heraclius passed through this gate with a great procession while bringing back the True Cross from Persia to Jerusalem.[92]

It seems that there has been some confusion among scholars regarding the Golden Gate. Indeed there are remains of an ancient gate under the present Golden Gate, which seems to have belonged to the Second Temple period and could even have been the Beautiful Gate.[93] This is the ruined gate that was shown to the pilgrim of Placentia, as noted earlier. On top of this gate a new monumental one was built—the present Golden Gate. This new gate was constructed by the Muslims at the beginning of the seventh century, as part of their ambitious building program on the Temple Mount.[94]

A new climate emerged in which the faithful again held the holiness of the Temple Mount in high regard, but this was a sanctity that Jews and Christians could observe only from afar.

635/638–1099: The Mosque of Jerusalem (Masjid Bayt al-Maqdis)

Andreas Kaplony

University of Zurich

From the seventh to the eleventh centuries, the area of the Haram is mainly associated with the former Temple of Jerusalem.[1] This results in an impressive bulk of information from visitors coming from all over the Islamic and Christian worlds, mostly Muslims, but also Jews and Christians. The surviving descriptions are mostly in Arabic but also in Latin, Greek, Syriac, and Persian. Jerusalem is indeed better known than any other city of that time.

These visitors perceive the Haram mostly through three conceptions. For them this is the *Former and Future Temple*. This is also a Friday mosque, i.e., the one *Mosque of Jerusalem* where on Friday the Muslims gather for congregational prayer. And this is, thirdly, a *place of spiritual power*. These conceptions are realised in four ways, by *names and traditions* of salvation history, by *architecture and furniture*, by *ritual and custom*, and by *visions and dreams*.

Obviously each of these four realisations has its own rules. Architecture, for example, allows individuals to express their personal conceptions, but requires considerable funds for building and maintenance. Ritual and custom are much slower to change and much more difficult to hinder. Dreams and visions provide legitimacy where no other legitimacy can be found.

The three conceptions and the four realisations change with time. Our best strategy is to define four periods. *After their conquest of Jerusalem*, the Muslims, a religiously inspired loose confederation of Arab clans and tribes round the two cities of Mecca and Medina in Western Arabia, build a modest mosque amidst the ruins of the former Temple (635/638–85). In the *Umayyad period* (685–750) the caliphs 'Abd al-Malik and al-Walid start to build a real Muslim state with Syria-Palestine as its heart. As part of this, they construct the imperial architectural complex we still know today. Up to the civil war between the Abbasid caliphs al-Amin and al-Ma'mun (809–13) the area is considered to be both the Temple rebuilt and the Mosque of Jerusalem. For the *'Abbasids* (813–969) in

60 Carved wooden panel of the eighth century found originally on the ceiling of the Aqsa Mosque, now in the Rockefeller Museum, Jerusalem

Iraq, who have their power base in remote Central Asia, the conception of the Temple falls into oblivion and the Haram is reduced to what it officially still is today, i.e., the Mosque of Jerusalem. Things change with the *Fatimids* (969–1099), this North African-Egyptian dynasty with their undisputed control of the West African gold trade and very strong Shi'ite missionary concerns. Mainly after the earthquakes of the 1030s, they transform the Haram into a Fatimid imperial mosque. The period ends with the Crusader conquest of Jerusalem and the death and exodus of Muslims and Jews.

Each of these four periods has its own profile in the sources. For the Byzantine period, we mostly rely on the *reports of Christian pilgrims* from Western Europe.[2] Their authors lead the reader through a spiritual landscape full of allusions to the Bible and to Christian tradition. The physical experience of these places is meant to deepen their spiritual meaning; travelling is primarily a spiritual experience.

For the Umayyad period, the most important source are the *remains of buildings*, i.e., the general layout of the Haram, its wall, and the Dome of the Rock.[3] Their architectural language is still Late Antique, but the topics they deal with are already Islamic—they speak Late Antique, but think Islamic. *Inscriptions* provide a bridge from architecture to written sources,[4] especially the long inscription of 'Abd al-Malik inside the Dome of the Rock and the two inscriptions which used to be above two of its gates, but now are kept in the Islamic Museum. The vast literature related to *Muslim tradition* many times locates allusions to the Qur'an and Muslim tradition, explains peculiar features and customs, attributes them to the Islamic conquerors, etc.[5] Their brevity, however, pushes individual spirituality far into the background and stresses instead the aspects of teaching and explaining.

For the 'Abbasid period, our main sources are the *Muslim geographers* with their interest in physical shape and customs.[6] Both the geographers and the first *Jewish pilgrim guides* like to enumerate traditions in a tour-like order.[7]

For the Fatimid period, the Persian *travel report of Nasir-i Khusraw* is especially informative. A series of remarks in one of the collections of Muslim traditions has been found to be the *first Muslim pilgrim* guide to Jerusalem,[8] i.e., a survey of the places which really matter to a Muslim pilgrim, all the rituals performed at them, and the legitimizations given for these rituals. For this period the written sources are rich and quite reliable, but the *remains of the buildings* still have a significance similar to what they had for the Umayyad period: what have been preserved are mainly the layout and the decoration of the Aqsa Mosque and a number of gates in the Haram wall, even if the language and use of this architecture are still not fully understood. *Inscriptions*, primarily the monumental inscriptions inside the Dome of the Rock and the Aqsa Mosque, are at least as important as the Umayyad inscriptions. Finally, there are more than one hundred and twenty *Judeo-Arabic letters* with individual and collective prayers.[9]

Tracing the history of the Haram remains a didactic challenge. How is one to describe a complex change which, apart from the two great rebuildings mentioned, consists mostly of tiny shifts? Our survey starts with the Byzantine ruins and the first modest mosque. Then, we deal with the conception of the Temple through all three periods left, then turn back to discuss the conception of the imperial mosque, and finally review the conception of a powerful holy place. To avoid repetitions, details recurring in all periods will be presented at their first occurrence, and later just mentioned. Within each period most space will be devoted to Muslim conceptions, since the Christian and Jewish ones seem to be a kind of annex. This is due to the fact that Muslim sources are much more eloquent. Muslim, Jewish, and Christian perceptions of the Haram interact, adjust to each other, and move in separate directions to mark the difference.

The Background: The Ruins of the Temple

Prior to the great rebuilding at the end of the seventh century, the Haram is part of the scrub which typically surround the cities and villages of Palestine, a place where people dump things.[10] We should not misunderstand the character of the place. This is no garbage dump in the modern sense of the word. There are cisterns there, and people are certainly careful not to pollute them, even if later Jews and Muslims consider the place as ritually impure. To allow the Haram to crumble and be overgrown is a deliberate act of the *Christian* authorities to show that once it was important but now it is not any more, and therefore has been reclaimed by nature.

The massive enclosing wall seems to have been built for eternity. It is made of giant ashlars of stone joined with great precision, despite their dimensions. The upper ridge of the wall is uneven, most impressively at the southeast corner where the wall is quite high and the outside level quite low. The former gates must have been monumental, but now are in ruins: the east gate has just its threshold and jambs standing, while in the south an underground gate leads through a corridor inside the Haram. Inside the walls, there are some remains of walls standing with a few pieces of marble floor in between, mostly overgrown by thorns and bushes and interspersed with caves which are partially transformed into cisterns. In between the ruins of the south gate there is a kind of altar, as well as—somewhere on the Haram— two statues. The ruinous impression of the area is further stressed by its low elevation in between the glittering crosses and the main gates of two splendid churches above, i.e., the Church of the Holy Sepulchre on a terrace in the centre of the city and the Eleona Church (or the Church of the Ascension) on the Mount of Olives.

The Christians consider the Haram the place where the Temple had been and in short call it the Temple of Solomon. The ruins of the east gate are believed to be the gate through which Jesus entered the city on Palm Sunday and the Beautiful Gate where Peter healed the lame man. The southeast corner is supposed to be the Pinnacle of the Temple, a great stone there the Cornerstone, some rooms nearby the palace of Solomon. The ruins and rocks east of the south gate and the imprints on the floor all over the Haram are connected with the killing of Zechariah. The Rock, later so important, plays no role.

Architectural neglect, names and traditions, and the deliberate absence of ritual give the Haram its due part in Christian veneration, but simultaneously restrict its importance to the past—at an earlier stage of salvation history, in the Old Testament, this place had been important, but is no more. This enhances the importance of the Church of the Holy Sepulchre with the empty Tomb of Christ, representing the current stage of salvation history, the New Testament, to which traditions and rituals from the Old Testament are transferred. The End of Time and the promised return of Christ to judge the living and the dead are recalled and hoped for on the Mount of Olives. Thus the ruins of the former Temple are part of a whole ensemble whose importance lies in the fact that it represents the first of these three stages of salvation history. This is obviously part of how Christians deal with salvation history, and the ruins of the former Temple are aimed at a Christian public.

Yet there is another conception. The *Jews* are the one religious group stigmatized by its theological approach which is near to and yet insurmountably different from the Christian one. In the reign of the neo-pagan emperor Julian (361–63) and under Sasanian occupation (614–28), they try to rebuild the Temple, but this does not leave any traces.

For them, the Haram is not only the place of the Former Temple. Every year on the Ninth of Av men and women gather to mourn its destruction while rending their black garments, blowing trumpets, and anointing a certain pierced stone—thus reassuring themselves of its future rebuilding. Christian monks are especially hostile to the ritual and at a major gathering of this kind during the time of Empress Eudokia some Jews are even killed by stones thrown at them by the monks.[11] Due to the political weakness of the Jews, both the attempts to rebuild the Temple and this mourning ritual do not change the Haram, but in the diaspora they daily, on the Sabbath, and at the high feasts remember Jerusalem in their prayers, while in the synagogue the Torah niche marks the Jewish prayer direction towards Jerusalem.

When the *Muslims* conquer the city, they are, or very soon become, aware that the ruins east of the city are identified with the Former Temple. Sometime later they erect there a simple, but large, mosque and thus split the area into a Muslim southern section and a northern section, roughly around the rock peak, which is open to all. By conducting their Friday service, a ritual of both religious and political meaning, in between the ruins of the Temple they pay respect to it, even claim it as their own, but stress that its position is subordinate to the Ka'ba in Mecca. They thereby accept its former—but reject its current—importance, an ambiguous attitude quite similar to the Christian one.

This first mosque does not speak the architectural language of the monumental churches. It does not refer to the Church of the Holy Sepulchre west of it and the Eleona

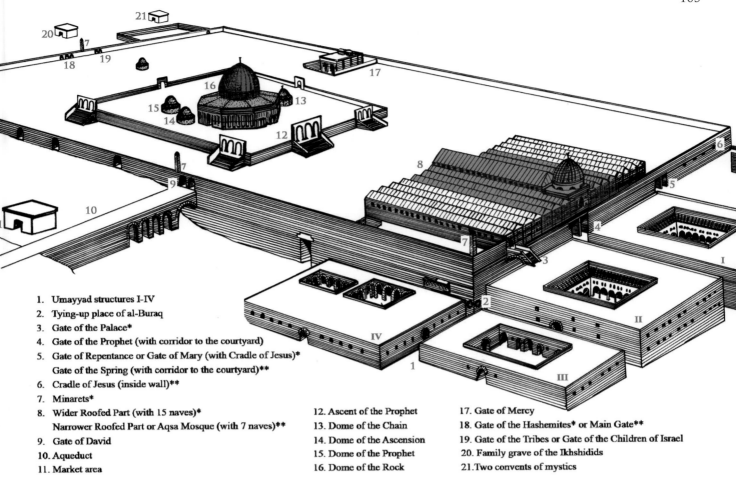

1. Umayyad structures I–IV
2. Tying-up place of al-Buraq
3. Gate of the Palace*
4. Gate of the Prophet (with corridor to the courtyard)
5. Gate of Repentance or Gate of Mary (with Cradle of Jesus)*
   Gate of the Spring (with corridor to the courtyard)**
6. Cradle of Jesus (inside wall)**
7. Minarets*
8. Wider Roofed Part (with 15 naves)*
   Narrower Roofed Part or Aqsa Mosque (with 7 naves)**
9. Gate of David
10. Aqueduct
11. Market area

12. Ascent of the Prophet
13. Dome of the Chain
14. Dome of the Ascension
15. Dome of the Prophet
16. Dome of the Rock

17. Gate of Mercy
18. Gate of the Hashemites* or Main Gate**
19. Gate of the Tribes or Gate of the Children of Israel
20. Family grave of the Ikhshidids
21. Two convents of mystics

61 The Mosque of Jerusalem, the so-called "Temple" (*Bayt al-Maqdis, al-Quds*) or "Furthest Mosque" (*al-Masjid al-Aqsa*), from the Umayyad rebuilding (685) to the Crusader conquest (1099), showing parts that existed only before (*) and after (**) the earthquakes of the 1030s

Church to the east, i.e., to the three stages of the Christian salvation history, but rather to the Ka'ba. It is intended for the Muslim public only and thereby indicates how the two societies—the indigenous Christian Palestinians and the Muslim conquerors—are living side by side, quite independently, with almost no interaction. But it also emphasises the Muslim claim of political leadership over all other communities having an interest in the site, i.e., the Christians and the Jews. The *Christians* react pragmatically to the building and simply call it the prayer-house or mosque of the Muslims at the place of the Former Temple.

The Temple Rebuilt

The Umayyad Period

At the end of the seventh century, the Muslim authorities rebuild the Temple, and therewith attempt what is definitely the most far-reaching reshaping since its destruction by the Romans.[12]

Their plan is to rebuild as a *Muslim* mosque the destroyed Temple (*Bayt al-Maqdis, al-Quds*), i.e., the Qur'anic Furthest Mosque (*al-Masjid al-Aqsa*) visited by Muhammad on his Night Journey.[13] Although the conceptions of the Temple and of the mosque have contradicting features, they are actually considered to be two sides of one and the same coin.

(Re)building the Temple, in *architectural terms*, means first of all drawing a system of concentric frames around the Rock [fig. 61]. A first set of circles consists of the enclosing wall around the whole Haram, the edge of the platform, and the outer wall of the Dome of the Rock. Each of these walls is pierced by gates. The enclosing wall has a monumental east gate on the ruins of the former east gate, two south gates, one of them leading through an underground corridor into the Haram, and between five and ten gates to the west and the north. The platform is reached by six staircases. Of these six, four are situated opposite the four gates of the Dome of the Rock. The Dome of the Rock has its outside walls richly decorated with white marble below and polychrome gold mosaic above (only in the sixteenth century is the mosaic replaced by blue tiles), its roof coated with gold, and carries an extraordinarily high gold dome, which both dominates the Haram and marks its spiritual centre, the Rock proper. This dome glitters in the sunshine and can be seen from far away; it is higher than the dome of the Church of the Holy Sepulchre and thus shows the superiority of Islam over Christianity. The building has no main axis, which is best shown by the fact that it has four gates of the same size, one in each direction, north, south, east, and west. Inside the Dome of the Rock a second set of circles surrounds the Rock: the exterior wall, the octagonal arcade, and the circular arcade with its curtains and the fence. The part inside the circular arcade is located under the high dome, which fills the space beneath with brilliant light. Inside the building all lower surfaces are covered with white marble, all upper ones with polychrome gold mosaic [fig. 62].[14]

Concentricity being in both Christian and Jewish tradition a formative element of both the Former and the eschatological Temple, these circles declare the Haram the Temple, and the Rock the navel of the earth. The mosaics inside and outside the Dome of the Rock make it a part of Heaven. The column of brilliant light hovering over the Rock possibly represents the column of fire leading the Israelites through the desert and fits in with the Muslim tradition according to which the Rock is the Nearest Throne of God, the place where God himself resides.

By integrating pieces of bedrock and ruins, architecture stresses that the Haram is the Former Temple rebuilt. The enclosing wall has a lower layer with large stones and an upper one with small stones, and at the southeast corner the upper layer even reaches the

62   The original cover of the Dome of the Rock: a riot of gilded copper, mosaic cubes, and white marble
H.R. Allen's model, prepared in 1986 for the Tower of David Museum, Jerusalem, attempts to recreate the edifice's appearance at its completion in 691. © Tower of David Museum of the History of Jerusalem / Photo: Rani Lurie

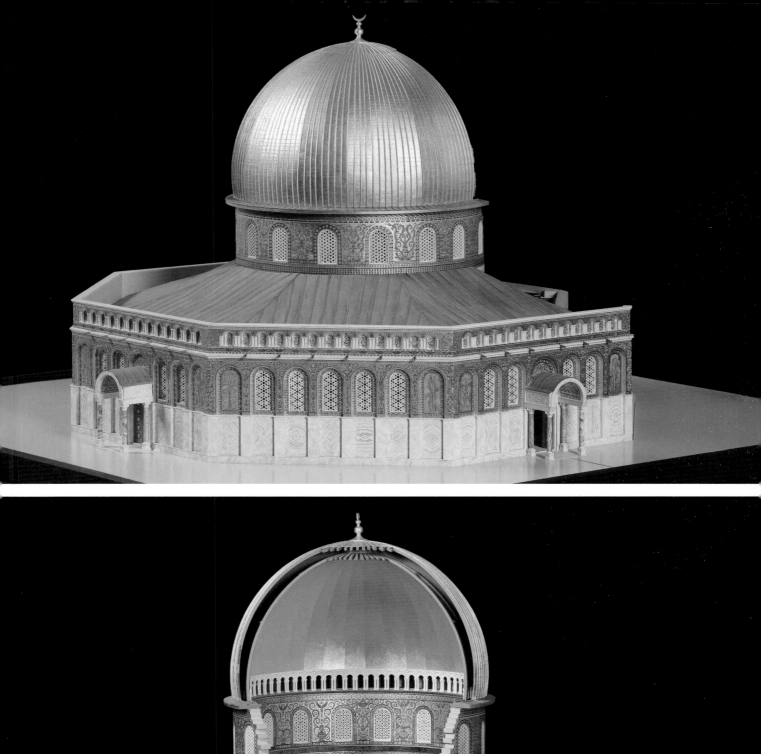

top of the wall. The monumental east gate, the two south gates, the southwest gate, and possibly even the two north gates, contain remains of earlier gates. The rather irregular position of some minor domes on the platform probably reflects the position of older structures beneath that are considered to be remains of the Temple.

Muslim *traditions* identify the Haram again and again with the Temple of David and Solomon, from where the Ark of the Covenant and God's Presence had been removed, where the Children of Israel killed John, the son of Zechariah (the biblical prophet Zechariah), and Nebuchadnezzar in revenge slaughtered them; with the sanctuary destroyed and transformed into the city's garbage dumps by Helena, mother of the first Christian emperor, Constantine, when she built the Church of the Holy Sepulchre, but recognised and cleaned by 'Umar; and with the Furthest Mosque[15] visited by Muhammad on his Night Journey.[16] To cut a long story short: this is the Former Temple rebuilt, the Qur'an is the true Torah, and the Muslims are the true People of Israel.

A great number of parts of the Haram are more explicitly connected to events which happened in the Temple; for our purpose, a few examples will suffice. At the Gate of Mercy to the east the Chain of Granting and Revelation had been suspended; there, God used to enter the Temple in the shape of a lion of fire. In the north part of the Haram lies the Qur'anic Chamber of David where two enemies came to have their cause judged. On the Throne of Solomon King Solomon prayed when he had finished building the Temple.[17] From the Gate of God's Presence the angels took the Ark of the Covenant away.[18] At the Chamber of Zechariah the latter stood in prayer when the birth of John was announced to him. At the Gate of Repentance Mary had been locked up by Zechariah, looked after by the angels, and it was there the birth of Jesus was announced to her. When Muhammad came here on his Night Journey he tied his fabulous riding animal al-Buraq to a stone ring in the wall; then, as the earlier prophets had done, he entered the Temple at the Gate of the Prophet (as, much later, did 'Umar and the *patrikios*/patriarch of Jerusalem), walked from the Aqsa Mosque to the Dome of the Rock, climbed the platform at the Ascent of the Prophet, saw the virgins of Paradise at the Dome of the Chain, led the ritual prayer of all prophets at the Dome of the Prophet while the archangel Gabriel took part in the prayer at the Standing-place of Gabriel. Muhammad mounted al-Buraq at the Dome of Gabriel, put his hand on the Rock, and ascended to heaven from the Dome of the Ascension, if not from the Rock.

A Muslim tradition on how the Muslims discovered the Haram after their conquest of Jerusalem:

When 'Umar ibn al-Khattab [the second caliph] had finished writing the document of truce with the people of Jerusalem (*Bayt al-Maqdis*), he said to the *patrikios* of the city: "Show me the Mosque of David." [...] The *patrikios* went to the Mosque of the Temple (*Bayt al-Maqdis*) and brought 'Umar to its gate which is [now] called the Gate of Muhammad. All the debris inside the mosque had fallen on the steps of the gate, even on the street in which the gate is, and it had become as much that it almost reached the ceiling of the gate. The *patrikios* said: "The only way to enter would be by crawling." And 'Umar said: "So, let us crawl!" And the *patrikios* crawled in front of 'Umar, 'Umar crawled after him, and we crawled after them, until, finally, we came out at the Rock of the Temple and were able to stand up. 'Umar looked, and considered things for a good while, then he said: "By the One in whose hand my soul is, this is what the Prophet has described to us [when he came back from his Night Journey]."[19]

The Rock inside the Dome of the Rock [fig. 63] is especially loaded with Temple traditions. This is one of the rocks of Paradise[20] and from beneath it originate the four rivers of Paradise and all the sweet water of the earth.[21] Before God began with Creation, he stood on it for forty years and from there he rose to heaven.[22] There Adam was created, and there he performed ritual prayer. This is the First Prayer-direction set up by Abraham,[23] Moses, and Solomon. This is the stone comprised of twelve stones which Jacob had under his head when he had his dream, the rock over which Isaac walked when he came here with Abraham for the sacrifice, and the place where David thanked God for ending the pestilence.

Muslim scholars vividly discuss the holiness of the Rock:
[...] Then said 'Ubayda ibn as-Samit: "No, by the One who, for forty years, used the Rock of the Temple [in Jerusalem] as a Standing-place (*maqam*), this is wrong and the scholars contemporary [with the Prophet] quote it [as follows] from previous revelations [the Torah?]—although I am not sure about that: 'God honoured and praised the Rock before He showed Himself to men and men then praised the Rock for forty years.'" This is made plausible by what al-Bukhari said, quoting the Prophet: "The Ka'ba was built forty years earlier than the Temple, and later, the Mosque of the Temple was built and men praised it. Before God showed Himself to men, he called the Rock holy, blessed it, honoured it and praised it for forty years."[24]

The authorities even installed a kind of Temple *ritual*. They employ Christian and Jewish mosque servants for general maintenance work, and forty acolytes who in shifts stay inside the Dome of the Rock and every Tuesday and Thursday conduct a service.[25] For this, they first eat, bathe, and don special clothes. They anoint the Rock, circumambulate it in a procession with their censers inside the closed curtains of the circular arcade until the dome is filled with incense, then open the curtains so that the incense spreads to the market in the city where at the same time a town-crier calls all to prayer. The service itself is remarkably simple and short, the faithful performing individually or together just two or four prostrations.

63 The interior of the
Dome of the Rock

How the servants prepare the Muslim Temple service in Umayyad times:
And on every Tuesday and Thursday, they order saffron to be pounded and milled
and they prepare it, for one night, with musk, ambergris, and sandal wood perfumed
rose water, and let it ferment this night. Then the servants are ordered to eat and
they enter the Bath of Sulaymān ibn ʿAbd al-Malik to wash and to purify themselves.
Then, they go to the wardrobe where the robes are, undress and come out with new,
red and blue clothes and a band [around their heads] and bring with them belts
with which they gird their waists. Then, they lift the lower parts of their robes and
go to the Stone, the Stone of the Dome of the Rock, and anoint what their hands
might reach until it is well anointed.[26]

The brevity and simplicity of the service, similar to the short and unstructured
congregational prayers Muslims hold on certain exceptional occasions, leaves no doubt
that this is a Muslim service, the Temple service as Muslims think it should be. Its existence
is surprising only at first glance. The history of Christian liturgy gives us at least two close
parallels: the liturgies in the fourth-century Church of the Holy Sepulchre and in the
Crusader Dome of the Rock both re-enact the Temple Service.

There are recommendations as to how individuals ought to pray on the Haram. One
says that within one mile of the city visitors should stop speaking about secular matters,
enter the mosque by the Gate of the Tribes, perform five ritual prayers, leave it, and return
to normal talk only when a mile distant. Another model suggests entering the Dome of
the Rock by the North Gate and praying inside at the black paving-stone. Both stress the
importance of places north of the Rock where Muslim ritual prayer is directed not only
towards the Kaʿba but also towards the Rock of Jerusalem, towards both the present and
the former prayer-direction.

Architecture,[27] traditions,[28] and ritual emphasize the Haram's authenticity. The
Umayyad caliphs responsible for the master-plan obviously consider possession of and
rebuilding in the authentic place of the Temple a very strong point in favour of their
political and religious claims to underline the authenticity of the Muslim faith and its
identity with the faith of David and Solomon.

This is also the central aim of the *inscription* of ʿAbd al-Malik (caliph 685–705) in the
Dome of the Rock, which stresses that God is one, that Muhammad is a prophet, and
Christ like him a prophet and a human being, not the son of God [fig. 64]. The inscription
declares that the Muslims are the legitimate heirs of the faithful of old and admonishes
the contemporary Christians to renounce their new and distorting characterisations of
Christ: Islam is the original undistorted faith, i.e., original undistorted Christianity, and
contemporary Christianity is only a travesty.

The assertion that the Haram is the rebuilt Temple continues the Byzantine idea that

64 Part of the inscription of 'Abd al-Malik inside the Dome of the Rock claiming that Jesus is God's messenger, not his incarnation *(Parts in round brackets are not shown in the photo, but are necessary for understanding)*:
The inscription reads: "(People of the Book, go not beyond the bounds in your religion, and say not as to God but the truth.) The Messiah, **Jesus, the son of Mary, is the Messenger of God, and His Word that He sen**(t to Mary, as a Spirit from Him. So believe in God and His Messengers, and say not, 'Three'. Refrain; better is it for you. God is only One God. Glory be to Him – He is far from having a son! To Him belongs all that is in the heavens and on earth; God suffices for a guardian.)" [Qur'an 4.171]

the emperor builds a New Temple and thereby declares himself the legitimate heir of King David, installed by God to rule over His People. Building the Church of the Holy Sepulchre in Jerusalem had thus legitimised the rule of Constantine (emperor 306–37) and building the Hagia Sophia in Constantinople the rule of Justinian (emperor 518–27); later, building the *Pfalzkapelle* at Aachen legitimises the rule of Charlemagne (Western emperor 800–14). The claim to be the legitimate heir of the Christian emperor leads to the caliphs' attempts to conquer Constantinople, the capital of what is left of the Byzantine Empire, an integral part of Muslim foreign policy until 'Umar ibn 'Abd al-'Aziz (caliph 717–20). The whole conception is obviously aimed at people living in Syria-Palestine and acquainted with Byzantine political categories—the Christian officials of the Muslim reign.

The rebuilding of the Temple alludes as well to the Jewish belief that the Temple will be rebuilt when the End of Days draws near. Rebuilding is thus also aimed at a Jewish public. What many prophets have been foretelling over the centuries is now happening—this is the eschatological Temple, this is the End of Days, and the caliph is the Messiah the Jews have been awaiting. This is the tone of the Jewish traditions praising 'Abd al-Malik for rebuilding the Temple and of the Muslim traditions referring to him as [the Second] David, King of Israel.

But the Muslim building with its impressive appearance of Byzantine monumental architecture has, first of all, a clear message to a Muslim public, i.e., the Muslims of Syria-Palestine. The caliph thus shows his will and power to use the enormous resources of Byzantine skill and experience to promote the Muslim cause. This gives him not only a powerful position vis-à-vis his rivals, but also considerably increases his authority: obviously, he is able to harness all this knowledge and make it productive on behalf of the Muslims. This is the Umayyad claim of building a Muslim Late Antique society, a society shaped and led by the Muslims, incorporating the heritage of its Christian subjects.

Christian sources rarely mention the Haram and point out any specific places in it. They continue calling it the Former Temple which the Jews wanted to rebuild, where they indeed built a synagogue, but from where they were soon after evicted by the Muslims. To consider the Muslim mosque a synagogue refers to the widespread Christian idea that the Muslims are basically nothing but Jews. Some interpret the Muslim building as the eschatological Temple—a short-sighted conception as this implies accepting the Muslim claims. Its opponents emphasise that the Muslim buildings are definitely not the Temple. The solution is to play down the topic, to deal with it as little as possible.

The 'Abbasid Period

In the 'Abbasid period we basically witness a shift in emphasis, as the Haram partially loses the charisma of being the Temple. The extent of this shift, however, depends on the manner of its realisation.

Muslim traditions which identify the Haram with the Temple, for instance, flourish more than ever. Many Umayyad traditions only now attain their full power. On the Haram itself, in *architecture*, concentricity and authenticity continue to be the two main features. Although no new buildings are added, Umayyad structures are well maintained, further enlarged, and embellished. These additions bear *inscriptions* mentioning who ordered them, but never refering to the Temple. The existing buildings obviously attract attention, but in architecture at least, the conception of the Haram as the Temple is no longer active and neither stimulates new investment nor prompts people to destroy anything.

The same holds true for *ritual*. The well-established system of servants and slaves in charge of the Haram works properly, but the Umayyad Temple service, clearly an expensive duty, has fallen into oblivion.

We thus find a gap between names and traditions firmly declaring the Haram the Temple, on the one hand, and ritual disappearing, on the other hand, with architecture maintained, but not extended, in between. The Muslim authorities care for the conception but do not invest in new buildings or in state-owned servants which would require continuous financial support. The conception of the Haram as the Temple joins the list of outdated conceptions carefully transmitted and still shaping the city's appearance, even after the historical circumstances which created them are long gone.

All this is indicative of Muslim emancipation from a Byzantine way of thinking. The claim of succeeding the Byzantine emperors loses importance with the end of the civil war between al-Amin and al-Ma'mun in 813, if not already with the 'Abbasid revolution in 750, and enters the stock of still valid but only secondary claims. But traditions develop their own dynamic and this probably makes the caliphs maintain the splendour of the place—not least to display their generosity to and responsibility for a place hallowed by traditions.

Christian traditions. The Muslims slowly forget what the New Temple was meant to signify and that particular conception loses its aggressiveness. This enables the Christian traditions to exchange the outdated conception of the Temple in ruins for the now harmless Muslim view that the Haram is the Temple of Solomon.[29] For Christians, the Rock becomes the place where Jacob in his dream heard God speaking, as well as the altar of the Former Temple. The Dome of the Rock is now the Holy of Holies. The eastern Gate of Mercy is the gate through which Jesus entered on Palm Sunday, the gate which first closed down when Heraclius wanted to enter with the relic of the True Cross, in imperial splendour. And the Aqsa Mosque is the Stoa of Solomon.

The monumental East Gate is used in a Christian sermon on pride and humbleness:

When the emperor descended from the Mount of Olives, by the very same gate by which the Lord had entered when He came to suffer, he also wished to enter, embellished with his royal diadem and his imperial ornaments and sitting [on his war charriot]. But suddenly the stones of the gate descended and closed in front of him and the wall became one piece. And when everybody was astonished and struck by great fear, they looked up and saw high up the sign of the Holy Cross, shining in the sky with a blazing sheen. And the angel of the Lord stood over the gate, looking at it [the Cross] in his hands, and said: "When the King of Heavens, the Lord of the whole World [Jesus] entered through this gate to complete the mysteries of suffering, he did not show up in purple nor embellished with a diadem, nor did he ask for a chariot with a mighty mare, but sat on the back of a humble ass and gave to his followers the example of humbleness." In that, the emperor rejoiced in the Lord having seen the angel, laid down the sign of reign [...] and the door granted him free access.[30]

After the existing buildings had been identified as the ruins of the Former Temple in the Byzantine period, and the topic of the Temple had been downplayed in the Umayyad period, the 'Abbasid period now proceeds to identify them with the Former Temple, despite their Muslim appearance and the many Muslim traditions connected with them. Their architectural unity and outstanding beauty may have furthered the identification, not to mention the obvious uselessness of the old conception which, confronted with these buildings, neither convinces nor helps to explain their existence. The political implications of a Muslim New Temple are now irrelevant for both Muslims and Christians.

Considering the Haram to be the Temple subsequently becomes one of the most successful conceptions of the city. Later, the Crusaders integrate the Haram into their Christian Jerusalem and consider the Dome of the Rock the Temple of the Lord [Jesus] (*Templum Domini*) and the Aqsa Mosque the Temple of Solomon (*Templum Solomonis*). And from Mamluk times till today the view of the Haram with the Dome of the Rock, both from the east—from the Mount of Olives—and from the west with the Western Wall, are the most popular Christian and Jewish representations of the Former Temple.

Jewish traditions. After having dealt with the Haram only summarily in the Umayyad period, Jewish traditions now begin once again to mention it at length. It is no longer only the place of the Former and Future Temple, but the existing buildings now are themselves considered to be the Temple as it had been. Some parts are considered as surviving from the Former Temple, but this does not imply that all the other buildings are new constructions—the Muslim buildings are not simply commented upon. The Rock becomes the Foundation Rock (*even shetiyyah*) from which the Ark of the Covenant had been taken away.[31] The Gate of Mercy is the Gate of Nikanor where the high priest purified men, women, and lepers and gave women suspected of adultery the water of curse, while the ruins beneath it are considered the East Gate rebuilt by Nehemiah where Ezekiel saw the glory of God entering the Temple.[32] The Gates of the Chamber of Mary are claimed to be the Water Gate—where Ezra re-installed the Feast of the Tabernacles, the Song Gate, and the Women's Gate. The Gate of the Prophet and its corridor is the

Gate of the prophetess Huldah and the *Mishneh*. And the Mount of Olives with the Chair of the Cantors, a piece of bedrock, now becomes the Place of the Ascent of God's Presence and God's Footstool where God's Glory was standing after the destruction of the Temple by the Babylonians and to which it will return.[33]

Ritual and custom emphasise the centrality of the Haram. Prayer is directed towards the Rock. On the Feast of the Tabernacles, the main feast of the year, a procession circumambulates the gates of the Haram from the southwestern Gate of Huldah to the eastern Gate of the Priest, and the latter is favoured for individual prayer.[34]

Jewish names and traditions, ritual, and custom declare that the Haram is the Temple. This may again be influenced, at least partly, by its outstanding beauty and architectural unity, as well as by the Muslim double conception of the Temple which is also a mosque. The Muslim conception has become harmless and does not imply recognition of Muslim rule as the eschatological fulfilment of Jewish hopes. Attention focuses on the wall, especially on the gates, and on the Mount of Olives, from where there is the best view of the Haram. Jews are not necessarily forbidden to enter the interior—Muslim devotion just occupies the centre, marginalises Jewish devotion, and relegates it to the borders.

The Fatimid Period

Muslim conceptions. In the Fatimid period the Muslim authorities continue using the conception of the Temple in the same ambiguous way. They neither change the concentric layout of the Haram, in architecture, nor the features which emphasised its authenticity. They maintain it and make repairs where necessary. When the heavy earthquakes of 1015 and 1033 damage Jerusalem and, inside the Haram, first and foremost the Aqsa Mosque and all of the south part which is supported by huge arches, the Fatimid al-Zahir (ruled 1021–36) rebuilds it.[35] On a monumental inscription inside the new Aqsa Mosque, he stresses his role as a patron and connects the building with Muhammad's Night Journey. The Fatimids maintain the Haram at great expense, most probably to sustain their political legitimacy. As will be shown later, they even transfer features from the Temple to the conception of an imperial mosque.

Names and traditions proclaim the Haram to be the Temple and the centre of the world; traditions flourish and now have a life of their own. What we thus have is the gap, described above, between names and traditions on the one hand and architecture on the other. Ritual plays no role.

This too changes with the earthquakes of 1015 and 1033 and the following rebuilding of the south of the Haram. The Gate of Mary, till now just a room in the south wall, is connected by an underground corridor to the courtyard and thus becomes a second entry from the south. The Prayer-niches of Zechariah and Mary, which had been in the same room, are moved to a new room in the southeast corner of the Haram, and are combined with the Cradle of Jesus, most probably to relieve the Church of the Nativity in Bethlehem of the burden of Muslim veneration.

Christian traditions continue to call the Haram the Temple and the Dome of the Rock the Holy of Holies. But they also continue to use the 'Abbasid conception, although only seldom, which shows that they are not particularly concerned with the Haram.

Jewish interest. This is in sharp contrast to a growing Jewish interest. The Jews sometimes distinguish between the destroyed Temple, to be rebuilt, and the present buildings, but mostly equate one with the other.

Names and traditions focus as before on the Rock, for them the Holy of Holies, and the Foundation Rock from which the Ark of the Covenant had been taken away, the gates, and the Mount of Olives.

Ritual and custom declare the Haram the centre of the world. The faithful individually visit the gates throughout the year. At the great feasts a procession goes praying and singing round the Haram from gate to gate and up to the Mount of Olives from where the Dome of the Rock—a place rarely, if ever, accessed by Jews—is best viewed. Although they obviously know that the Former Temple had been destroyed and, in the End of Days will have to be rebuilt, they nevertheless identify the existing Muslim buildings with the Temple.

In a letter, a Jewish leader mentions the prayer procession at the Feast of Tabernacles:
Our prayers are constant for you and the dear elders with you, on the Mount of Olives opposite the Temple of God [the Haram], i.e., at the Place of Our God's Footstool, and at the Gate of the Priest, and at the gates of the Temple of God [the Haram], in the community of all of Israel, at the feast, the feast of God, the Feast of Tabernacles.[36]

The Imperial Mosque of Jerusalem

The Umayyad Period
Muslim traditions. Let us now return to the Umayyad period and to the conception of the Muslim imperial mosque. An official inscription in the north wall which gives the dimensions of the Haram *calls* it a mosque (*masjid*). The sources describe the Haram's physical shape by relying on the technical terms used for great mosques. They speak of minarets, ablution places, a courtyard with cisterns, and a treasury, and call the Aqsa Mosque a roofed hall with a main gate, a gable roof, and a pulpit or standing-place (*maqam*).

An Iraqi geographer describes the layout of the Haram:

And in Jerusalem there is a mosque [the Haram]... This mosque has, in the southwest corner, a roofed building [the Aqsa Mosque]. This roofing covers about half of the width of the mosque and all other space of the mosque is empty, with no buildings, except the Place of the Rock [the Dome of the Rock].[37]

A Muslim tradition explains the position of the Aqsa Mosque exactly in front of the Dome of the Rock:

And 'Umar said to Ka'b [a Muslim convert of Jewish origin]: "Where would you put the mosque?" Ka'b said: "Put it behind the Rock [to its North] to combine the Prayer-direction of Moses and the Prayer-direction of Muhammad." But 'Umar said: "You have shown some Jewishness! By God, the best part of the mosque is the one in front of the Rock [to its south]." And he built it in the front part of the mosque.[38]

Architecture shows the same ambiguous picture. The buildings might easily be interpreted as a mosque. The Haram is oriented towards the south as are all mosques in Palestine. It has all the parts which are characteristic of contemporary imperial mosques like the Umayyad Mosque in Damascus and the Mosque of the Prophet in Medina: four minarets (three in the west wall, one of them in the southwest corner, and one in the north wall), ablution places near the gates, arcades (inside the west and north walls), a paved courtyard, a treasury, cisterns (fed by an aqueduct), a roofed hall (the Aqsa Mosque) with a main gate, (fifteen) naves and (eleven) vertical naves, a gable roof with a dome, and a pulpit.

Architecture emphasises the pre-eminence of the Aqsa Mosque, i.e., the place where the first simple mosque had been. It thus stresses the superiority of the Ka'ba in Mecca to the Rock in Jerusalem. The monumental north façade of the building (with its mosaic-covered gable wall, a main copper gate and additional seven large gates on each side, the central gate of each group of seven being also a copper gate), the wide central nave under the gable roof, and the main prayer-niche are all in line with the Rock and thus emphasise the position of the Aqsa Mosque in front of the Rock.

Rituals and customs bear the same dual message. Some rituals define the whole Haram a mosque: the prayer call comes from the minarets atop the west and north walls, ritual ablution is performed at ablution places just outside the gates, and individual ritual prayer may be performed all over the area. But the main ritual, which defines a mosque as such, i.e., congregational prayer, is performed in the Aqsa Mosque only, with the *imam* leading and preaching from the pulpit there. There is not a single reference to congregational prayer performed anywhere else on the Haram.

What does this mean? The Umayyads extend the mosque in the south of the Haram to the four corners of the Former Temple, to equate the mosque with the Temple. But the former conception continues to exist. This results in two contradicting positions: the new one of a greater mosque (the whole Haram) and the old one of a smaller mosque (the Aqsa Mosque)—a mosque with another mosque inside it. The authorities propagate the new conception through architecture, names, and ritual, but the old conception is surprisingly persistent and deeply rooted: the south building continues to be called a mosque, and traditions and rituals clearly maintain that this is the only place where congregational prayer may be performed.

Both conceptions, as well as the emphasis on the idea that the Ka'ba is superior to the Rock, are obviously part of a Muslim way of thinking and aimed at a Muslim public. The complex combination of two overlapping conceptions may even mirror a Muslim society only partly secluded from the indigenous Christian majority, certain groups being more, and others less, involved with Christians.

The 'Abbasid Period

In the 'Abbasid period the conception of the Haram as the Mosque of Jerusalem gains in importance, mainly due to the fact that the other conception, the Haram as Temple, slowly falls into oblivion. The definition of this imperial mosque remains as ambiguous as previously, with the Haram as a wider mosque and the Aqsa Mosque as a smaller mosque inside it.

The Fatimid Period

Muslim traditions. This conception develops, in the Fatimid period, into one of a mosque complex (the Haram) with minor mosques on all four sides, the Aqsa Mosque being one of those minor mosques. When the Fatimid authorities rebuild the Aqsa Mosque after the earthquakes of 1015 and 1033 they seize upon the opportunity to transfer a number of features from the conception of the Temple unto it.

Visitors describing the Haram use the same terms as they employ for imperial mosques. They see a Main Gate, ablution places, a courtyard, and pools and cisterns. There is a Roofed Hall (the Aqsa Mosque) with a main gate, a space with restricted access (*maqsura*) next to the prayer-niche and, till the rebuilding of the 1030s, a pulpit. In addition to the Aqsa Mosque, there are other places called mosques: a west gate and the monumental east gate, both locked, the Chamber of David in the north, and the Mosque of the Cradle of Jesus in the southeast corner. The two convents of mystics just outside the north wall have their own separate mosques.

Architecture clearly makes the Haram a Fatimid imperial mosque. Its (official) main gate is a monumental portal-minaret in the north wall in line with the monumental north staircase to the platform; there are no other minarets. A splendid double gate in the west wall embellishes the real main entrance from the market. There are ablution places and cisterns, in part supplied with water by the aqueduct. The courtyard has a stone floor and is surrounded by arcades, one in the southwest, one in the west, and three in the north.

After the earthquakes the new Aqsa Mosque is of the same length, but much less wide, and it has a north and an east façade (both with an arcade in front), together with an additional west arcade. There are five naves and eleven vertical naves, a main prayer-niche and further prayer-niches, but no pulpit. This is basically the building as it exists today.

This much smaller new Aqsa Mosque has its north arcade, the monumental main gate, the wider central nave, and the monumental arch with the inscription in front of the prayer-niche all exactly in front of the Rock, thus emphasising the precedence of the Ka'ba over the Rock. This axis even becomes the all-dominant axis of the Haram, from the monumental portal-minaret in the north over the monumental north staircase to the platform and the Dome of the Rock to the Aqsa Mosque. All other minor mosques are marked as such by prayer-niches: the west gate, the monumental east gate, the Mosque of the Cradle of Jesus, the mosques of the two convents of mystics, the Dome of the Chain, and the Dome of Gabriel.

The rebuilding not only transforms the Haram into a mosque complex, but also adds to the existing system of concentric zones around the Rock a second system around the main prayer-niche inside the Aqsa Mosque. These zones become more and more splendid the nearer they draw to the centre. They are separated by walls, each with many entries but one splendid mosaic-covered, inscription-bearing main gate: the monumental portal-minaret in the north wall of the Haram (or the Gate of David in the west wall), the main copper gate of the Aqsa Mosque, and the monumental arch in front of the prayer-niche. The main prayer-niche, with its marble decoration and two splendid red marble columns to the left and right, becomes its new centre.

The key to this layout can be found on the monumental arch where the Fatimid caliph al-Zahir mentions himself, his ancestors, and descendants, side by side with the Furthest Mosque [fig. 65]. This does not place the Night Journey inside this building—traditions place it all over the Haram, but never here—but rather declares its main prayer-niche the centre of the Haram. This obviously alludes to the older system of concentric circles around the Rock. The Fatimid rebuilding thus causes the Umayyad dual conception of the Temple around the Rock and the imperial mosque oriented towards the Ka'ba to merge, and further develops the Umayyad conception of the wider and the smaller mosque. If we consider the immense financial investment the rebuilding demanded, we cannot doubt that the Fatimid caliphs took it quite seriously.

Traditions and rituals do not keep pace with architecture, but just repeat the well known conception of a wider mosque with a smaller mosque inside it. Where the authorities build permanent facilities they consider the whole of the Haram a mosque:

65   The Aqsa Mosque: Triumphal Arch of the Fatimid caliph Abu al-Hasan 'Ali al-Zahir li-I'zaz Din Allah (1021-36)
The inscription reads *(Parts in round brackets are not shown in the photo, but are necessary for understanding)*:
"(In the name of God, the Merciful, the Compassionate.) Glory be to Him, who carried His servant by night from the Holy Mosque to the Furthest Mosque, the precincts of which We have blessed" [Qur'an 17.1]. [Has ordered] its construction our Lord 'Ali Abu al-Hasan the Imam, the Manifest to Strengthen the Religion of God, (Commander of the Faithful, son of the Ruling by the Command of God, Commander of the Faithdul --- blessings of God on him, on his pure fathers and on his most noble sons. ...)

the ablution places are now outside the wall (or under the Aqsa Mosque), and the prayer-call comes from the portal-minaret in the north wall. But congregational prayer, the main ritual defining a mosque, is performed only at the Aqsa Mosque. This is where the *imam*, standing near the main prayer-niche, directs the congregational prayer and where he preaches the Friday sermon.

We thus find the same discrepancy again. Architecture makes the Haram a mosque complex with minor mosques girding it from all four sides, and shifts the emphasis from the Rock inside the Dome of the Rock to the main prayer-niche inside the Aqsa Mosque, whereas traditions and ritual know only the old dual conception of a wider mosque with a smaller mosque inside.

The Haram as a Place of Spiritual Power

The Umayyad Period

The two conceptions mentioned so far are supported by the authorities and mainly expressed in architecture and traditions. But upon reading the sources, one has the strong impression that all this is somehow too sophisticated. On a deeper level the Haram is mostly perceived in accordance with a third, less explicit, conception which is obviously related to that of the Temple, but nevertheless, with time, becomes almost independent: this is a place of extraordinary spiritual power, of distinct holiness.

Muslim traditions charge the whole Haram with spiritual power and make the Dome of the Rock the most holy place on earth. This holiness gravitates around a number of topics.

First of all, the Haram has been *touched by God*. Before creating everything, God was standing on the Rock and from there rose to heaven. From here, the Ark of the Covenant and God's Presence (*al-Sakina*) were taken away. Because of this holiness, a good deed is more valuable and a bad one more wrongful if performed here than elsewhere.[39] In addition, this is one of the three great mosques every Muslim should visit, the other two being in Mecca and Medina.[40]

This is a *place of visions*. Here Jacob had his dream of angels and the Rock is the stone which he had under his head. At the Gate of Mercy God used to enter the Temple in the shape of a lion of fire. At the Chamber of Zechariah an angel announced the birth of John to Zechariah. At the Chamber of Mary the angels provided Mary with fruits and announced to her the birth of Jesus, who was born here, at the Birth-place of Jesus.

This is a *favourite place to ask God for healing, forgiving and answering prayers*. Dew falling here has the power to heal. Whosoever starts his pilgrimage to Mecca from here has all prior and future sins forgiven. Here God freed David and the Children of Israel from pestilence. At the Dome of the Chain David had a chain hanging down from heaven, which in a lawsuit only the innocent party could touch, but not the guilty. At the Throne of Solomon, Solomon prayed when he had finished building the Temple, and God granted him everything he asked for. People even know the places most effective for prayer: God is said to answer all prayer at the east wall with its Gate of Mercy, at the Gate of Repentance and the Hitta Gate, at the Dome of the Chain, the Dome of the Prophet, and the Dome of the Rock (especially west and east of the Rock and at the black paving-stone), etc.

The Haram is considered *near to Paradise*.[41] Dew falling here originates from Paradise. The Rock is a piece of Paradise and from beneath it flow the four rivers of Paradise. The ladder Jacob saw while dreaming at this spot reached up to a gate of heaven. Muhammad on his Night Journey to Paradise came to this Furthest Mosque, and his visit is recalled at a number of places. And Sharik an-Numayri, one of the heroes of Early Islam, entered Paradise from a pit here.

This is the scene of *eschatological events*.[42] At the End of Days the eschatological *Sufyani* will be killed at the Gate of Mercy. The *Mahdi*, the Messiah, will die after the Ark of the Covenant was put in front of him here, and most of the Jews will, when looking at the Ark, become Muslims. The Ka'ba with the Black Stone will be brought here, along with all people who ever made the pilgrimage to Mecca, as well as Hell and Paradise. And on the Day of Judgment the archangel Israfil will resurrect mankind by blowing his trumpet from the Rock.

Architecture accentuates the holiness of some places. Some domes are gilded: the Dome of the Rock, the Dome of the Chain, and at first two—later even six—minor domes, as well as the dome of the Aqsa Mosque and all of its roof. Of these, the Dome of the Rock is by far the most important one, which is shown by its sheer dimensions, the white marble covering of its lower part, the polychrome gold mosaic of its higher parts, and the massive gold covering of its dome and roofs. The Rock inside it gains additional holiness by the shaft of brilliant light hovering over it and by a chain suspended from above to which are attached the two Horns of the Ram of Abraham, a pearl called "the Unique" (*al-Yatima*), and the Crown of Khosroes.

Suspending lamps are another, non-permanent means to emphasise holiness. The Haram has 5,000 (later 1,500) lamps burning all day, with an additional 2,000 candles on Friday nights, the nights of the two high feasts, and the Nights of the Ascension, of the Creation, and of 'Ashura'. The Dome of the Rock, where incense is spread and about one fourth of all lamps burn all day, is definitely the centre of holiness.

Ritual. Today the monumental architecture of the Haram impresses us most. In those times, traditions were very powerful. Nevertheless, we should not forget that for most people ritual was and still is the *one* appropriate way to express veneration. Within a mile of the city one has to stop speaking of secular matters. Ritual prayer on the Haram is considered very effective and the Haram is a favourite place for those who want to spend the night in ritual prayer. Prayers are even more powerful if said at the places mentioned above. The Dome of the Rock is the site of the official service held twice a week, with the Rock anointed and circumambulated in a procession carrying censers. Only the Dome of the Rock has forty servants especially assigned and adherents staying there permanently.

Visions interpreted are a last, very powerful way to attribute a distinct holiness to certain places. In the Umayyad period, we know only of one vision, in which God appears in the shape of a lion of fire.

Traditions, architecture, and this vision make the Haram a place of extraordinary holiness, an area both promising and dangerous, with a number of especially holy places, the Dome of the Rock being the most sacred of them. Borders around the whole Haram and between the zones are precisely defined, to be crossed only at some few well-defined places. The faithful react to this holiness by performing ritual prayer, twice a week in a common ritual, or individually, and by having visions. This is obviously the well-known conception of a Haram, with well-defined borders, accessible only under certain conditions. All this is deeply imbued with local Palestinian custom and has the features characteristic of the Palestinian reverence for holy places. This is the conception local people have independently of their religious affiliation, the conception which they transmit to foreign visitors and which theologians here and abroad further explain and justify. The distinction between Muslims and non-Muslims, an important topic in the conception of the imperial mosque, plays no role at all.

The ʿAbbasid Period

In this period, in addition to *Muslim traditions* which do not change much, there are two new ways of realising conceptions.

Architecture. Burial allows people to participate in the holiness of the Haram: next to one of the north gates, there is the family grave of the Ikhshidids (935–61), a dynasty of Central Asian origin ruling Egypt.

Dreams and visions now become important. Dreams accompanied by interpretations create beautiful but enigmatic images of well-known traditions. Thus, the Gate of Mercy is, from inside the Haram, a gate made of light while from outside it is made of iron. An avenue as white as snow leading from the Aqsa Mosque to the Dome of the Rock is interpreted as the way followed by Muhammad on his Night Journey and the way the faithful go with God. The Dome of the Chain is said to be made of invisible light. The Dome of the Ascension shines green and red like a rainbow. The Dome of the Rock appears as a large and high dome of white light with a pearl on top, the Rock itself as a red ruby, and light coming from beneath it represents the four rivers of Paradise. Inside the Aqsa Mosque people swallowed up by the earth with only their heads sticking out are said to be those who hate the ancestors. Muhammad is seen as he leaves the Dome of the Rock with a group of companions to perform ritual prayer at the Ascent of the Prophet. Of three men standing between the South Ascent and the Dome of the Rock two are lifted up and disappear; this is explained as meaning that after reliability and the cutting of the ties of kinship [in favour of God's cause] have disappeared, ritual prayer must be carefully maintained.

> **From the dream of Abu Muhammad 'Abd Allah al-Hawli about the Haram, on the 'Ashura' Night A.H. 335/10–11 August 946:**
> Then, I left the dome [the Dome of the Rock] and there were trees of light reaching from the Gate of the Dome of the Rock to the Copper Gate [the Main Gate of the Aqsa Mosque] which is opposite the prayer-niche. And I said: "What are these trees?" And it was said to me: "This is the street of the believers in God." I said: "And what about those who oppose them?" He said: "Look, their way is blocked." Then, I asked about the Prophet, what kind of traces remained from his Night Journey. It was said to me: "Look at the earth!" And there was a light, white like snow, the traces of feet, which had become a street.[43]

Traditions, architecture, dreams, and visions definitely focus on the holiness of certain places standing out as more sacred than the already holy Haram. Dreams introduce a new dimension insofar as they furnish images of well-known traditions. Traditions dealing with Muhammad's Night Journey and Ascension are especially popular. The growing importance of minor places reduces the predominance of the Dome of the Rock. The 'Abbasid Dome of the Rock is still a very powerful place but begins being accompanied by a number of minor ones—whereas the Umayyad Dome of the Rock had been absolutely pre-eminent and unchallenged by any other place.

The Fatimid Period

The Fatimid Haram is the Temple focussed on the Rock and on the prayer-niche inside the Aqsa Mosque, and an imperial mosque complex with minor mosques inside it. But visitors are mainly concerned with the incredible power of the place, with its holiness.

Muslim architecture declares that this is a holy landscape containing a number of extremely holy places. Till the great rebuilding of the 1030s, this landscape culminates in one peak, i.e., the Rock inside the Dome of the Rock. After the great rebuilding there is a second peak, the main prayer-niche of the Aqsa Mosque. In addition to domes and lamps, precious carpets and prayer-niches also mark holiness. Carpets are found in the Dome of the Rock, the Aqsa Mosque—the space of restricted access (*maqsura*) next to the prayer-niche even being covered with extremely precious North African mats, and

66 The minor domes on the Esplanade: minor holy places in a wider holy area

the monumental east gate. Prayer-niches multiply inside the Aqsa Mosque, in the minor mosques in the west, north, east, and southeast, and are even found in two minor domes on the platform [fig. 66]. All holy places now have prayer-niches and sometimes domes, lamps, and carpets—a rather inconsistent picture. Only the peak(s) of holiness, at first only the Dome of the Rock but later also the space of restricted access (*maqsura*) inside the Aqsa Mosque, are marked by all four features: a prayer-niche, a dome, lamps, and carpets.

Ritual prayer is considered appropriate and most effective all over the Haram. It might be combined, in some places, with certain prayer formulas and gestures, making it even more effective. The first written Muslim pilgrim guide extant explains how to visit the holy places. Such guides may have already existed previously and might be reflected in the careful lists of holy places provided by the Muslim geographers.

A Muslim prayer recommended in the Dome of the Chain:

It is recommended to make ritual prayer in the Dome of the Chain and to stay at the gate of the Dome of the Rock, which is called the Gate of Israfil, and to pray there. This is the place where the Children of Israel used to go if they had committed a sin, and where they asked God to forgive them. And one of the prayers recommended for this place is what the shaykh Abu l-Hasan Ahmad ibn 'Abd Allah told me in Damascus ..., I heard 'Ali ibn al-Hasan saying: "Oh Khy's [one of the mysterious names of God, see Qur'an 19.1], oh Light of Light, oh Holy, oh God, oh Merciful." He repeated that three times, then he said: "Forgive me the sins which pierce certitude, forgive me the sins which make ordeal descend, forgive me the sins which hold oath back, forgive me the sins which make enemies increase, forgive me the sins which hold prayer back, forgive me the sins which accelerate passing away and forgive me the sins which withdraw the veil.[44]

The times in which only the Dome of the Rock had its own servants are gone. Servants and adherents stay both in the Aqsa Mosque and the monumental east gate. The mystics previously mentioned live and pray in the two convents in the north but on Fridays join the congregational prayer on the Haram. A recluse possibly lives at the west staircase to the platform.

Touching the holy places is openly declared important. The Rock inside the Dome of the Rock is touched and kissed, despite the marble fence round it. People are encouraged to pray on top of the Cradle of Jesus.

Traditions and architecture, ritual and custom present a rather inconsistent but lively picture. Against the background of a general holiness a growing number of places gain a special status. This uneven picture with many small, embellished places is quite different from that of the impressive building projects with their all-embracing master-plans. Building a small dome, or donating a precious carpet or a lamp with some oil is not beyond the financial means and influence of an individual, a family, or a group wishing to mark their presence. The existence of a Muslim pilgrim-guide, the use of lamps and carpets, and individuals spending time there might be explained by informal, personal involvement. The Haram now becomes a place in which not only the authorities and those close to them invest but where more and more people become personally involved.

67 A tombstone of the Fatimid period, excavated ca. 1970 near Robinson's Arch. The deceased, whose name was deliberately effaced, died in 1002

The same holds true for the *Jews*. There is no doubt that the identification of the Haram with the Temple already implies its holiness, but this becomes more and more prominent.

Traditions attribute an extreme holiness to the Foundation Rock (the Rock inside the Dome of the Rock) and the place of the Ascent of God's Presence, also called the Place of the Presence of God's Strength and God's Footstool (on the Mount of Olives).

Architecture lends reality to the traditions. Mosaic decoration and precious carpets, well known means of characterising Fatimid Muslim holy places, now also embellish the so-called Cave, a Jewish holy place deep inside the west Haram wall.[45] The Haram, ruled and shaped as it is by Muslim conceptions, thus includes a piece of Jewish architecture. Architecture declares the Jewish claims vis-à-vis a Jewish, not a Muslim, public and gives them a share in the Haram's holiness.

Rituals and customs declare the gates of the wall and the Mount of Olives to be holy places. People circumambulate the gates and ascend the Mount of Olives, singing and praying, individually throughout the year, and on the Feast of Tabernacles, Passover, and Pentecost in a procession. Prayers recited are considered as effective as if said after a congregational service. Favoured places to pray at are the Gate of Judah in the west, where people ask God to explain their dreams, and the Gate of Mercy in the east.

Ritual concerned with a number of holy places thereby comes to the foreground, and this resembles the growing importance of Muslim ritual at many places on the Haram. But there are two basic differences: Jewish ritual is one-dimensional, around the gates and up to the Mount of Olives, and people may choose certain places and leave other places out, while Muslim ritual is concerned with two dimensions—if not three—and people may combine the holy places in many different ways. Jewish ritual connected with holiness is performed both individually and collectively while Muslim ritual focused on holiness is, as far as we know, performed only individually.

Ritual defines the Cave as the centre of the Jewish community in the city. It is here that the Torah scrolls are taken out for the service and that, if necessary, excommunications are pronounced. This invites a comparison between the Jewish Cave and the Jewish Chair of the Cantors on the Mount of Olives. Both are strongly related to the Rock as they are directly west and east of it. The Cave has the obvious advantage of being much nearer to the Rock and of being accessible to a Jewish public only. The Chair of the Cantors had the advantage of overlooking the Former Temple, but the serious disadvantage of being farther away and exposed to Muslim harassment. The changeover from the Chair of the Cantors to the Cave probably indicates a Fatimid policy of giving the Jewish minority a place under Jewish control, unharassed by the Muslim public.

The Fatimid Cave is maintained by pious foundations from the diaspora, giving people abroad the opportunity to participate in the Haram's holiness,[46] a feature to be compared to the increasing number of minor places on the Haram sponsored by Muslims outside Palestine.

Rituals and customs, and in one instance even architecture, attribute a distinct power to the Haram, i.e., to its wall, the central Rock, and the Mount of Olives. Restriction to the gates and to the Mount of Olives does not imply that the other parts of the Haram are not holy, but rather once again reflects Muslim control of the Haram, which leaves to the Jews mainly the gates—and the so-called Cave—as points of direct contact, and the Mount of Olives as a point of visual contact.

Conclusions

Contemporary sources show a surprisingly clear picture of the Haram, a picture which, despite the diversity of sources, is almost perfectly coherent in itself. For our period, we know of about fifty individual places on the Haram, related Muslim, Christian, and Jewish names and traditions, contemporary events, rituals and customs, visions and dreams. All these closely interact. Many features have close parallels in contemporary Jerusalem and Palestine.

The people of the period under discussion have a number of conceptions of perceiving the Haram which cannot be reconciled with each other. However problematic contradictions of this kind seem to be for the modern researcher, a careful look at the sources shows that they pose no problem for the people of those times. To get an all-encompassing conception which explains everything is no issue. The discovery of the simultaneous use of disparate conceptions has been one of the most striking results of our research.[47]

Of the three conceptions mentioned, the first—the perception of the Haram as the Temple—suits most of the different political situations and religious traditions, and therefore appears in a number of variations. Compared to this, the second—that this is the one mosque of Jerusalem—is much more straightforward. Both are officially maintained, but the people visiting the Haram are mostly concerned with the third one—that this is an area of extraordinary spiritual power.

For the four-and-a-half centuries of the Early Muslim period, the Haram of Jerusalem was the effective focus not of one religion, but of Jews and Muslims—and to some extent also of Christians—alike, a place of mutual adaptation and distinction, i.e., a place of interaction, as shared holiness is characteristic of Jerusalem.

1099–1187: The Lord's Temple (*Templum Domini*) and Solomon's Palace (*Palatium Salomonis*)

Benjamin Z. Kedar
The Hebrew University of Jerusalem

Denys Pringle
Cardiff University

The Frankish or Crusader presence on the Esplanade began with a massacre. On the morning of 15 July 1099, the Crusaders of Godfrey of Bouillon forced their way across Jerusalem's northern wall and chased the Muslim defenders all the way to the Esplanade, where hard fighting took place for several hours. When Muslim resistance ceased, the Crusaders went on killing people, men and women, until "they were wading up to their ankles in blood." About 300 Muslims escaped to the roof of the Aqsa Mosque, and Tancred, the Norman Crusader from southern Italy who had just pillaged the Dome of the Rock, gave them a banner signifying his grant of protection. The next morning, the Crusaders cautiously ascended the roof, rushed upon the Muslims who were huddling there and beheaded them, men and women alike, by the sword—to Tancred's great chagrin.[1] Some of the Muslims chose to fling themselves headlong from the roof. Non-eyewitness Latin chroniclers, writing several years later, gave the number of Muslims killed in the mosque as 10,000, while much later Muslim chroniclers gave the figure as 70,000 or even 100,000. However, the well-informed Ibn al-'Arabi—a Muslim from

68a The Frankish false lantern on the top of the Dome of the Ascension (*Qubbat al-Mi'raj*), possibly the erstwhile baptistery of the Lord's Temple. For a view of the entire building see fig. 86

68b Squeeze of a fragment of a Latin inscription mentioning the MILITIA TE(M)PLI (the Order of the Knights Templar). The fragment was found in the Aqsa Mosque during the restoration works of Kamal al-Din Bey in the 1920s

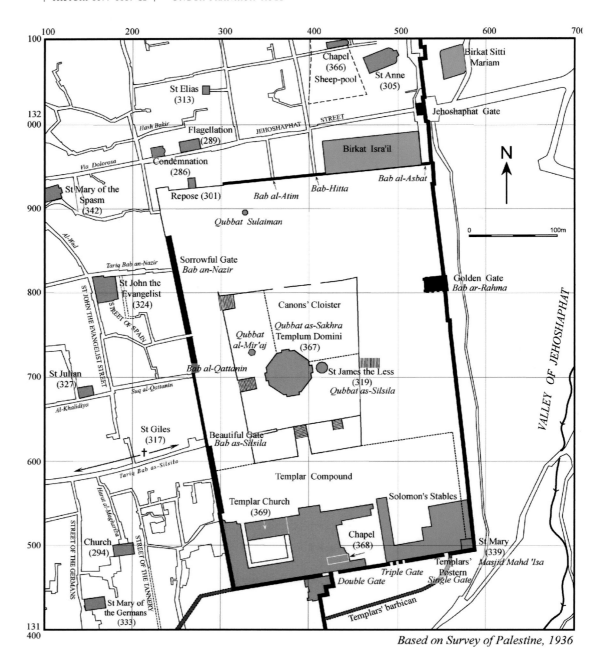

Based on Survey of Palestine, 1936

69 Plan of the Esplanade under Frankish rule

Seville who had studied in Jerusalem between 1092 and 1095, passed through Palestine again in December 1098, and was in Egypt in 1099—wrote that 3,000 people, "including God-fearing and learned worshippers," were killed in the Aqsa Mosque. "The learned woman from Shiraz [Persia]," he adds, "was killed in the Dome of the Chain along with other women."[2]

Henceforward, Jerusalem was under Frankish rule. Non-Christians—that is, Muslims and Jews—were not allowed to dwell in the city, although they were permitted to visit it.

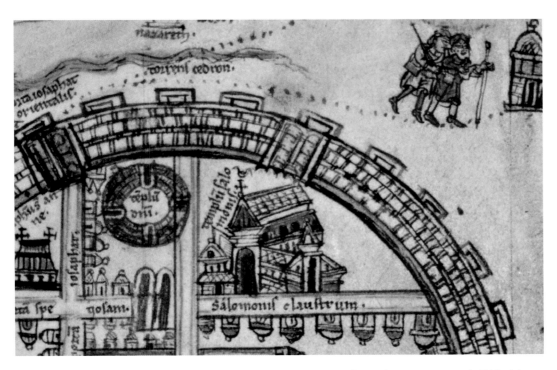

70 The Lord's Temple and Solomon's Palace on a twelfth-century map of Jerusalem, now in Brussels (Bibliothèque Royale de Belgique, MS No. 9823-4, fol. 157r)

This state of affairs continued until the Muslim reconquest of Jerusalem under Saladin on 2 October 1187.

Frankish rule over Jerusalem lasted just 88 years, during which, for the first time since the demise of the Second Jewish Commonwealth, Jerusalem was a capital city—the capital of the Latin Kingdom of Jerusalem, which extended, at the height of its expansion, from Beirut in the north to the head of the Gulf of Aqaba in the south.

These 88 years occupy a special place in the Esplanade's history, for it was only during this period that its Islamic shrines came under Christian control. Christian rule was symbolized by a huge golden cross set atop the Dome of the Rock. This caused grave offence to Muslims, some of whom offered the Franks much gold to secure its removal, but without success.[3] The Dome of the Rock became an abbey church, served by Augustinian canons and known as the Lord's Temple (*Templum Domini*). The Aqsa Mosque came to be known as the Temple or Palace of Solomon (*Templum/Palatium Salomonis*), serving first as the palace of the Frankish kings and later as the headquarters of the military order of the Knights Templar.

The pilgrim John of Würzburg, who visited Jerusalem in the early 1160s, reports that Muslim worshippers were allowed to pray on a spot just south of the Dome of the Rock, at a sundial which the Franks regarded as originally having been the altar at which the Old Testament priest Zechariah met his death.[4] At least one Jew managed to pray at the Esplanade or even within the Dome, for Maimonides writes: "I entered the Great and Holy House and I prayed in it on Thursday, the sixth day of Marheshvan [4926]," that is, 14 October 1165.[5] Some prominent Muslim visitors were allowed to enter the Dome and al-Aqsa. However, the two shrines, and the entire Esplanade, were thoroughly Christianized.

Under Frankish rule, uniquely, Christian Jerusalem possessed two sacred foci: the Church of the Holy Sepulchre and the Lord's Temple. Before 1099, the rivalry between the two was open, with the Islamic dome above the Rock erected expressly to outshine the Christian dome above the Sepulchre. After 1099, with both shrines in Christian hands, a more harmonious relationship evolved between them, although this did not prevent some rivalry between the clergy attached to them emerging from time to time.[6]

Of the two, the Holy Sepulchre had the full force of Christian tradition on its side, while the Lord's Temple had to be established from scratch as a Christian shrine. Achard of Arrouaise, the Temple's prior in the years 1112–36, left behind a long poem in which he attempted to do just that.[7] He surveys the site's history in considerable detail, from David and Solomon down to Vespasian and Titus. Then, without wasting a word on the period subsequent to the destruction of the Jewish Temple, he proceeds to present the shrine of his own days as the work of some Byzantine emperor—Justinian or Heraclius—or of Helena, the mother of Constantine;[8] its erection by Caliph 'Abd al-Malik is simply blotted out of existence. Achard does not tackle the question of why a Christian ruler should have rebuilt the Temple whose destruction Jesus had foretold. He goes on to thank God for having recently liberated "His Temple with the Sepulchre" from Turkish hands. The order in which he mentions the two shrines—for him, equally Christian—is hardly accidental: The Lord's Temple comes first, the Church of the Holy Sepulchre, second. Achard notes that the three historical dedications of the Temple—by King Solomon, by the Jews returning from Babylonian captivity, and by Judas Maccabeus—took place, respectively, in autumn, spring, and winter. A future, fourth dedication, he declares, will take place in the summer, completing the four seasons. The first to be undertaken not by Jews but by Christians, this dedication will also be the last, to be commemorated forever. Achard chooses to present the shrine under his custody as the fourth and final embodiment of the biblical Temple.

Thus, the Dome of the Rock gets a new Christian past and significance. Various events of sacred history are now said to have happened there. Saewulf, the Anglo-Saxon pilgrim who visited Jerusalem in 1102–1103, already asserts that it was in the Lord's Temple that Jacob saw the heavenly ladder, betraying the influence of an Islamic tradition, apparently transmitted to the Franks by some Oriental Christians. John of Würzburg was shown the imprint left by Jesus' foot in the rock when he was expelling the merchants from the Temple. This must have been a Christian appropriation of what Islamic tradition sees as the imprint of Muhammad's foot upon his ascension to heaven.[9]

The bulk of the shrine's new Christian content, however, derived directly from the Bible—from the identification of the rock in the shrine's centre with the Holy of Holies of the Solomonic Temple, to that of a nearby crypt as the location of Christ's encounter with the adulterous woman. Abraham's sacrifice of Isaac and the slaying of Zechariah, which originally had pertained to the Temple and were transferred in the Byzantine period to Calvary, now tended to move back to their original location.[10] Mosaic inscriptions in Latin added to the shrine's exterior mostly reproduced biblical passages exalting the Temple as the House of the Lord,[11] and aimed at imbuing the literate visitor with the certainty that he was indeed facing the rebuilt Temple. Achard's long poem and the mosaic inscriptions broadcast the same message.

If Achard believed that his poem would effectively obliterate the memory of the shrine's Islamic origin, he was to be proven wrong. Jerusalem's Oriental Christians must have known the true facts all along. The Russian pilgrim Daniel, who visited Jerusalem between 1106 and 1108, relates that the shrine was built "by a Saracen [Muslim] chieftain called Amor," evidently a distortion of 'Umar.[12] Some Latins, too, had an inkling or more of the truth. In 1137, Fretellus, a canon of the cathedral of Nazareth, wrote a description of the holy places in which he devoted much more attention to the Temple than to the Sepulchre. He must have shared the same source as Achard, for he, too, mentions that the shrine, which he explicitly presents as the Fourth Temple, was built either by Helena or by Heraclius or Justinian. He adds, however, that some believed the builder to have been an *Ammyrator* (emir) of Memphis in Egypt, who erected it "in honor of *Allachiber* [probably an attempt at transcribing the Arabic words *Allah kabir*], that is to say, God most high, and seeing that it is reverently adored, in His worship, by all tongues." Fretellus remarks that this last possibility was the more likely one, since an Arabic inscription supported it; a derivative, anonymous description adds that before the coming of the Franks there was nothing relating to the Law of Moses and nothing in Greek written on the building.[13] Yet Fretellus does not appear to have been certain on this point, or more likely found it troublesome. In a second redaction of his work, he no longer declared the greater likelihood of the last possibility and omitted the reference to the Arabic inscription.[14]

John of Würzburg copied Fretellus' second, diluted version almost verbatim, thus presenting the four candidates—three Christian, one Muslim—as equally likely.[15] The German pilgrim Theoderich, probably writing in 1172, is certain that it was Helena who erected the shrine.[16] Writing in the 1170s or the early 1180s, William of Tyre, the great historian of the Frankish Kingdom of Jerusalem, also has no doubts about the shrine's builder; for him, however, it is not Helena, but the caliph 'Umar. William claims to make this statement on the basis of Arabic mosaic inscriptions on the shrine's interior and exterior[17]—a statement that casts grave doubts on his knowledge of Arabic, since no such inscription existed.[18] William also knows of the shrine's continued importance for Muslims. He mentions that Turks of the tribe that had ruled Jerusalem before the Crusader conquest came from afar to the Mount of Olives in 1152, and observed from there "the Lord's Temple, which they hold in uppermost and exceptional respect."[19] Evidently, the attempts to obliterate the shrine's Muslim past were only partially successful.

Against this background, it is remarkable that the Damascene mystic, theologian, and poet 'Abd al-Ghani al-Nabulusi (1641–1731)—a descendant of the Banu Qudama who fled their homes in the Frankish-ruled area around Nablus and settled down in Muslim Damascus after 1156—assumed that the Dome of the Rock had been erected by the Franks. Al-Nabulusi, who visited Jerusalem in 1690, believed that the Rock was miraculously suspended between heaven and earth and that the Franks built the Dome in order to conceal

> this conspicuous wonder that testifies to the distinction of Islam and the dazzling power of God most high. Especially since what is widely known among people had reached [the Franks]—that when our Prophet Muhammad, may God's prayer and salutation be upon him, ascended to heaven from the Rock on the night of Ascension, the Rock ascended behind him, but was held back by the angels and so remained hanging between heaven and earth.

Al-Nabulusi explained that on Saladin's reconquest of Jerusalem the Muslims thought that the Frankish-built edifice had been there originally and therefore did not demolish it. And he concluded that in the final analysis it was God who made the Franks conceal the miracle of the Rock.[20] Thus, similarly to Fretellus and John of Würzburg half a millennium earlier, al-Nabulusi contemplated the possibility that Infidels erected a God-inspired building.

The process by which the Lord's Temple became a major shrine of Frankish Jerusalem started soon after the Crusader conquest. The earliest Latin accounts relate that when the fighting ended, the victorious conquerors came to pray in the Church of the Holy Sepulchre. Just a few years later, Fulcher of Chartres, a chronicler writing in Jerusalem, asserts that the conquerors went "to the Lord's Sepulchre and His glorious Temple"; and when the True Cross was found a few weeks later, the Franks went to the Sepulchre and thence to the Temple, singing psalms and thanking God.[21] The Temple was also the setting for prayers offered by Godfrey of Bouillon, his men, and the citizens of Jerusalem before the victory over the Muslims at Ascalon in August 1099. And at Easter in 1101, the Holy Fire appeared in the Sepulchre only after the king, patriarch, papal legate, clergy, and people had gone to the Temple as penitents early on Sunday morning.[22]

This bi-focality of Sepulchre and Temple was institutionalized in the liturgy evolved by the Frankish clergy. On Palm Sunday the procession coming from Bethany dispersed at the Temple, and on Holy Saturday the Miraculous Fire was carried to the Temple as soon

71 Royal lead seal of King Amaury of Jerusalem, 1163-74 [Unpublished]
The obverse shows the king seated on a throne, surrounded by a circular Latin inscription: AMALRI[CVS] DEI GR[ATIA] REX
IERUSALEM (=Amaury, by the grace of God, king of Jerusalem). On the reverse are depicted, from left to right, Jerusalem's
three principal monuments: the Holy Sepulchre, the Tower of David and the Lord's Temple. The legend reads: CIVITAS [REGIS]
REGVM OMNIVM (=City of the King of all Kings)

as it appeared in the Sepulchre. On 15 July, a procession made its way from the Sepulchre to the spot at which the Crusaders had stormed the city in 1099; after stopping at the Temple, it then dispersed back at the Sepulchre. Likewise, on the feast of the Purification of the Virgin the procession would start at the Sepulchre and proceed to the south door of the Temple.[23] The two shrines also played central roles in the coronation ceremonies of Jerusalem's Frankish rulers. The king was crowned in the Sepulchre and immediately thereafter offered his crown in the Temple, at the altar where Jesus had been presented to the Lord. He thereupon proceeded to the Temple of Solomon (the Aqsa Mosque) for the coronation banquet.[24] The seal of the kings of Jerusalem showed the Tower of David in the centre, flanked by the Sepulchre on the left and the Temple on the right [fig.71].[25] In his version of the call of Pope Urban II for the First Crusade, Jerusalem-born William of Tyre has the pope lament the desecration of the *two* shrines, symptomatically mentioning the Temple first and the Sepulchre only thereafter.[26]

The written sources contain many details about the appearance of the Lord's Temple under Frankish rule.[27] According to Fulcher of Chartres, for the first fifteen years after the conquest, the rock remained exposed; but because it disfigured the building, it was then covered over and paved in marble. By the time he wrote, in the 1120s, an altar had been placed over it and a choir fitted out for the canons. A Muslim chronicler, Ibn al-Athir, later reported that one of the Frankish kings had ordered the rock to be covered because the Frankish priests used to break off fragments of it to sell to pilgrims. It is possible that the wrought-iron grille with which the Franks enclosed the rock—first mentioned in an Icelandic account ca. 1150—served for its protection, besides acting as a chancel screen [fig. 72]. Images decorated the walls, and numerous Latin mosaic inscriptions covered the building's exterior and interior.

72   The Frankish grille around the Rock

John of Würzburg offers a detailed description of the building and the sites in and around it, quoting the inscriptions to be seen there. For example:

It is said that the Blessed Virgin Mary, when already three years old, was presented in the Temple of the Lord on 21 November, as these verses which are written there teach us:

Here the Virgin, accompanied by seven virgin girls,
was offered as a servant to God at the age of three.

There, indeed, she frequently received solace from the angels, whence the verse:

The Virgin is supported by attendant angels.

The Lord Jesus Christ cast out from the Temple the buyers and sellers, as a token of which on the right-hand [southwest] side of the Temple, there is displayed with a great veneration of lamps and ornamentation a stone, which was trodden on and marked, so to speak, by the Lord's foot, when He alone by divine virtue stood up to so many and threw them out. This stone is joined to another stone. Our Lord is represented as having been presented on this, as if on an altar, as is shown in a picture and by the words written above it, thus:

Here was presented the King of kings, born of the Virgin,
Wherefore this has rightfully been called a holy place,
Whence this place is adorned and by right is called holy.
Here Jacob saw the ladder and built an altar.
But although Jacob is depicted as having laid his head on that stone when he saw in his sleep the ladder stretching into heaven, by which angels ascended and descended, with all respect to the Temple, this is not true. And this verse is placed there:
This land shall be for you, Jacob, and your descendants.[28]

John's reason for doubt was that the Franks also associated the place where Jacob had his dream, Bethel, with the village of Baitin, near present-day al-Bira, 16 km north of Jerusalem. Describing the entrance to the Temple from the west, John mentions:
Inside the porch there is an image of Christ, around which is this epigram:
This my house shall be called a house of prayer.[29]

Inscriptions recorded around 1172 by another German pilgrim, Theoderich, suggest that the work of Christianizing and embellishing the Lord's Temple went on almost continuously throughout the twelfth century.[30] Yet the Franks left its original Qur'anic inscriptions untouched, even though the oldest of these rejected the Trinity and Jesus as the Son of God, and extolled Muhammad as God's Messenger and the Muslims' intercessor at the Last Judgment[31] [see fig. 64]. Probably the Franks were unaware of their content.

Today only a few features bear witness to the Frankish presence in the Dome of the Rock. Of the wrought-iron grille that ran between the columns and piers of the central circular arcade there remains *in situ* only one piece, reused in the aedicule enclosing the hairs from Muhammad's beard. While the building contains a number of pieces of Frankish architectural sculpture, none appears to be *in situ*, and it is uncertain which, if any, originally came from this building. They include the doorway to the cave, which consists of a moulded arch carried on Corinthianesque capitals with matching abaci and a lintel decorated with a wet acanthus rinceau. The *mihrab* is flanked by two Corinthianesque capitals with human heads, while the shrine to the left of the stair as one descends into the crypt has a trefoil arch with wet swirling acanthus rosettes in the spandrels, carried on double and triple intertwined colonnettes. Other pieces of Frankish sculpture reused in the building were more obviously brought from elsewhere at a later date. Numerous Frankish masonry marks have been recorded on masonry reused in and around the building.

Some 20 metres northwest of the Dome of the Rock stands the Dome of the Ascension of the Prophet Muhammad (*Qubbat al-Mi'raj*). Although composed almost entirely of Frankish dressed or sculpted stonework, including a large number of columns and capitals [fig. 73], there still remains some doubt as to whether this was an original Frankish building adapted by the Ayyubids or one built by them *de novo* from Frankish *spolia*. If the former, it might perhaps have served as the baptistery of the Lord's Temple or for some other public liturgical function, such as the blessing of the palms on Palm Sunday.

On the east side of the Dome of the Rock stands the Dome of the Chain (*Qubbat al-Silsila*), which the Franks turned into a dependent chapel of the Lord's Temple. It was dedicated to St James the Less, brother of Jesus and first bishop of Jerusalem, who in medieval times was believed to have been martyred by being thrown from the Temple's roof. John of Würzburg reproduces the verses applied to the chapel's wall:

> *James, son of Alphaeus, similar to the Lord in countenance,*
> *Died for Christ, cast from the nearby Temple:*
> *Thus James the Just publicly preaching Christ*
> *Was beaten by the evil crowd and felled by a fuller's club.*[32]

North of this dome was the cloister of the Augustinian canons who served the Lord's Temple.[33]

As for the other major Islamic shrine on the Esplanade, the Aqsa Mosque, its outward appearance under Frankish rule is far less documented in the written sources. Although called the "Temple or Palace of Solomon," it served not as a church but as a royal palace, and, from the 1120s onward as the headquarters of the Knights Templar. Consequently, it was less accessible to pilgrims and appears but sketchily in their accounts. Yet the edifice played a major role in the Frankish Kingdom, first as a royal residence and then as the centre of the Templar Order, which boldly merged a knight's way of life with that of a religious vocation and made a major contribution to the kingdom's military capacity.

Around 1170, Benjamin of Tudela, a Jewish traveller from Spain, wrote of "the Temple of Solomon" that it was:

> the palace built by Solomon, king of Israel. The knights are quartered there, and each day 300 of them ride out to war, besides those knights who come from the land of the Franks and the land of Edom [= Christendom], vowing to stay there for days or years until their vow's fullfilment.[34]

The Rule of the Templar Order prescribes in great detail the daily conduct of the knights, down to the injunction that they may not leave their dwellings to go into town without permission of the Master of the Order, unless they wish to go by night to the Church of the Holy Sepulchre and other places of prayer within the town's walls.[35]

The Aqsa Mosque that the crusaders found when they captured Jerusalem would have been larger than the present building. With a width of 15 aisles, it extended some 100 m (east to west) by 68 m (north to south). However, it is likely that the outer aisles

73   Frankish capitals of the Dome of the Ascension (*Qubbat al-Mi'raj*)

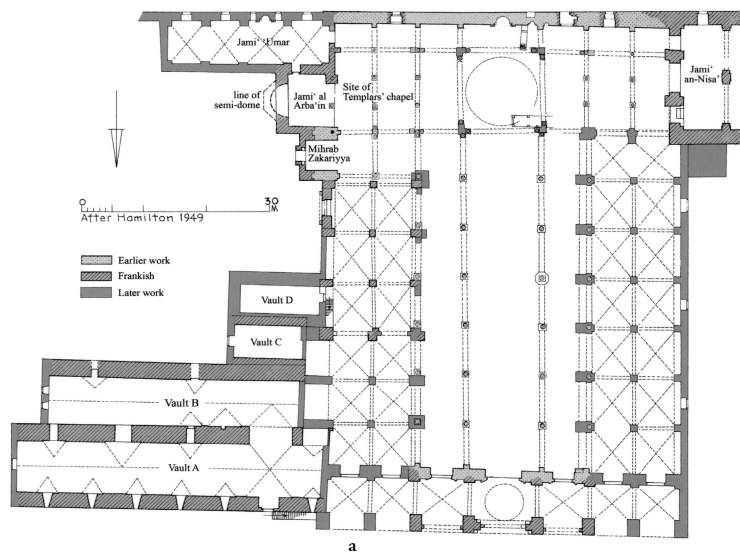

a

b

c

74 Solomon's Palace (the Christianized Aqsa Mosque)
a. Plan highlighting Frankish work
b. Frankish masons' marks on piers in the southern half of the Aqsa Mosque's east aisles
c. Frankish masons' marks on stones re-used in the northern bays of the Aqsa Mosque's east aisles

75 An aerial photograph from the 1930s showing the now non-existent Templar vaults that adjoined the Aqsa Mosque in the east

were already ruinous by the early twelfth century, for Fulcher of Chartres records King Baldwin I (1100–1118) demolishing those parts of the building that it was difficult to maintain. In the twelfth century the building had seven aisles, as it does today. The three central ones probably formed a large open-aisled hall, which was used for grand ceremonial occasions of state such as coronation feasts, when the the king reasserted his ownership of the palace in which the Templars technically were only tenants. The outer aisles and the domed "crossing" and "transept" parallel to the southern *qibla* wall were divided up by the Templars into a series of smaller rooms and chambers. These included a chapel with an apse whose outline still survives in the east wall of the Mosque of the Forty (*Jami' al-Arba'in*), and near it a refectory.

After the Muslim reconquest in 1187, 'Imad al-Din, Saladin's secretary, wrote that the Templars had built a wall before the *mihrab* of the Aqsa Mosque and turned it into a granary or even a latrine, and that they had built "a spacious house and a high church" west of the *qibla*.[36] The construction of this second church was already in progress in the 1160s and 1170s, as attested by John of Würzburg and Theoderich. It probably closed off the north side of the courtyard, nowadays enclosed on the south by the Women's Mosque (itself a Frankish structure) and on the west by the Islamic Museum. Other Frankish additions still evident in the present-day Aqsa Mosque include the three central bays of the porch (albeit modified by al-Mu'azzam 'Isa in 1217–18), six vaulted bays in the

76   Historians of the Crusades in the deserted Solomon's Stables, 1983. From left to right: Sylvia Schein, Hans Eberhard Mayer, a student, Joan and 'Otto' (R.C.) Smail, a student, David Jacoby

two eastern aisles, and a rose window in the east wall of the Mihrab Zakariya. Until the 1940s there also survived a series of three Frankish barrel-vaults on the eastern side of the mosque [see figs. 69, 75, 125].

The vaulted substructure under the southeastern part of the Esplanade was used by the Templars as an underground stable for their horses—known as Solomon's Stables [fig. 76], to which external access was provided by a new postern gate (the so-called "Single Gate") made in the south wall of the precinct. A larger gate was provided by walling up the eastern opening of the Herodian Double Gate below al-Aqsa and constructing a defensive gate-tower in front of the western one. Outside both gates was another defensive wall, forming a barbican. The Templars also had their own cemetery, which was probably located outside the Golden Gate, east of the Esplanade. In it were buried the two murderers of St. Thomas Becket, archbishop of Canterbury (d. 1170).

During repair works in the Aqsa Mosque in the 1920s, a small piece of parchment

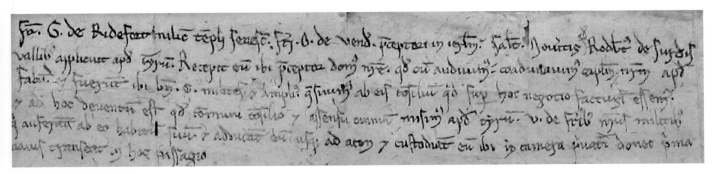

77 Gerard de Ridefort's letter, now in the Islamic Museum

came to light, containing a letter written in Latin by the seneschal of the Order of the Knights Templar, Gerard de Ridefort, to the commander of the Order in Jerusalem. Most probably dating from 1184, it deals with a knight by the name of Robert of Sourdeval who, upon landing in Tyre, was arrested, deprived of his habit, and sent under guard to Acre, where he was to await his despatch to the West. It is the only Latin document found to date in the entire Frankish Levant, which spread from Antioch in the north to the Gulf of Aqaba in the south—and it deals with an obscure disciplinary act. The letter is now on display in the Islamic Museum [fig. 77].[37]

The Golden Gate in the compound's eastern wall, which served as a mosque before the Crusader conquest, was opened under Frankish rule only twice a year: on Palm Sunday, in commemoration of Christ's triumphal entry into Jerusalem, and on the day of the Exaltation of the Cross (14 September), in commemoration of the recovery of the True Cross by the Byzantine emperor Heraclius in 629. The service book of the Church of the Holy Sepulchre describes in detail how the Palm Sunday procession, comprising the patriarch (carrying the relic of the Cross in his own hands), the priors of Mount Zion and of the Mount of Olives, and the abbot of St Mary in the Valley of Jehoshaphat, with their respective congregations, would approach the gate from the Mount of Olives. Those who had remained in Jerusalem, including the canons of the Holy Sepulchre and the convents of the Hospital of St John, St Mary Latin, and St Mary of Mount Zion, would congregate with the people at the Lord's Temple, where one of the bishops would bless the palm and olive branches before everyone proceeded into the valley of Jehoshaphat to meet the Cross. As the combined procession approached the Golden Gate, various festival antiphons were sung.

> And the cantor begins the festival antiphon *Before the day of Easter.* Then the subcantor and the master of the school, accompanied by the boys, go up on top of the gate through which the Lord Jesus entered when He came, and there they wait until the procession has assembled inside. When they have foregathered, the cantor alone begins this antiphon: *Glory, praise and honour.* And the chorus below responds: *Christ, O King.* And only the boys sing the verse [...] and the others.

When these are finished, the boys or the patriarch begin the response *When the Lord entered.* Thereupon, having formed a procession, they enter the court of the Lord's Temple, descend the steps towards the Temple of Solomon and ascend some other steps towards the Lord's Temple, on the south, where, arranged in procession, they make a station.[38]

John of Würzburg mentions the existence of a cemetery around the Golden Gate, where lay those who fell in the conquest of Jerusalem in 1099.[39] A large number of east–west oriented graves covered with stone slabs was found there in 1891, when accumulated earth was dug away from the walls of the gate inside the Esplanade, a few feet above the gate's floor level; these probably formed part of that cemetery. But any structural alterations that the Franks may have made to the gate are not obviously apparent in what survives of it today, except perhaps for the domes raised on drums and pendentives over the two eastern bays, which must have existed by the time when the Frankish Palm Sunday liturgy was formalized.

The underground Mosque of Jesus' Cradle (*Masjid Mahd 'Isa*), located in the southeastern corner of the compound, was adopted by the Franks as a Christian holy place, where Jesus' wooden cradle, his bath, and the Virgin's bed were shown. From the 1160s onward, pilgrims also began to identify the place as the dwelling of Saint Simeon, to which the Virgin brought the Child Jesus 40 days after his birth. The addition of the Simeon tradition to the site may have been accompanied by new building work: Whereas earlier accounts speak only of an underground chamber, John of Würzburg refers to a chapel described as Saint Simeon's dwelling standing above the city wall. It thus appears that a chapel, identified as the dwelling of Saint Simeon and containing his tomb, had been built over the underground chapel of Saint Mary, which thereafter served in effect as its crypt. In the extant building there is little that can be attributed to the Frankish period. Elsewhere on the Haram, however, there are many examples of Frankish architectural sculpture, re-used in various Islamic structures [see figs. 79, 84, 85, 88, 90, 117].

For Jews, the Lord's Temple was the site of the Temple, for whose rebuilding in the messianic age they continued to pray.[40] The longing to behold its ruins was given eloquent expression by the famed Hebrew poet Judah Halevi (ca.1075–1141), who in his latter years left his native Spain for Jerusalem and apparently died on the way. One of his best-known poems reads:

My heart is in the east, and I in the uttermost west—
How can I find savour in food? How shall it be sweet to me?
How shall I render my vows and my bonds, while yet
Zion lieth beneath the fetter of Edom, and I in Arab chains?
A light thing would it seem to me to leave all the good things of Spain—
Seeing how precious in mine eyes to behold the dust of the desolate sanctuary.[41]

In reply to "one who reproved him for his longing to go to the Land of Israel," he exclaims:

> Have we any heritage save the sanctuaries of God?—
> Then how should we forget His holy Mount?
> Have we either in the east or in the west
> A place of hope wherein we may trust,
> Except the land that is full of gates,
> Toward which the gates of Heaven are open?[42]

In Muslim eyes, the loss of Jerusalem to the Crusaders enhanced its position among the holy places of Islam. The Christianization of the Dome of the Rock and the Aqsa Mosque was increasingly perceived as a dishonour and act of defilement that must be brought to an end. The treatises on the Merits of Jerusalem (*Fada'il al-Quds*), which regained prominence from the 1160s onward, repeatedly dwelt on the importance of Jerusalem's two holy shrines, and the yearning for their liberation played a central role in the Jihad propaganda of the sultans Nur al-Din and Saladin. In 1168–69, Nur al-Din commissioned a wooden preacher's pulpit (*minbar*), earmarked for eventual installation in reconquered Jerusalem. In 1173 he wrote to the caliph of Baghdad that his principal aim was "to banish the worshippers of the Cross from the Aqsa Mosque [...] to conquer Jerusalem [...] to hold sway over the Syrian coast." Saladin's secretary 'Imad al-Din announced in 1186 that "the swords of Jihad stir gaily in their scabbards; Allah's cavalry is ready to charge. The Dome of the Rock rejoices at the good news that the Qur'an of which it was deprived is about to return."[43]

After Saladin's decisive victory at the Battle of Hattin on 3–4 July 1187 and his swift conquest of most of the Frankish Kingdom, the reconquest of Jerusalem was imminent. Patriarch Eraclius sent letters to Pope Urban III and other western leaders, desperately imploring them to send immediate help,[44] but when Saladin laid siege to Jerusalem on 20 September, the Franks could rely only on their own meagre remaining manpower. Eraclius and Balian of Ibelin resisted to the best of their ability; faced with Saladin's final assault, however, they decided to negotiate for a peaceful evacuation. Evidently wishing to revenge the Crusader massacre of July 1099, Saladin initially declined to accept a Frankish surrender, but when Balian threatened to pull down the Dome, tear up the Rock, and kill all Muslim prisoners, Saladin agreed to allow the Franks to leave Jerusalem, in return for a ransom.[45] On 2 October 1187 the victorious Muslims took possession of the city, and the Franks began to leave it soon thereafter. The large gilt cross on top of the dome of the Lord's Temple was brought down in triumph and dragged through the streets of Jerusalem as far as David's Gate, where it was smashed to pieces.

1187–1260: The Furthest Mosque (al-Masjid al-Aqsa) under Ayyubid rule

Michael Hamilton Burgoyne

Historic Scotland, Edinburgh

As Saladin prepared for the final assault on Jerusalem, the view from the Mount of Olives over the Dome of the Rock and the Aqsa Mosque, in the fabulous setting of the Noble Sanctuary (al-Haram al-Sharif), would surely have been as inspiring then as it is now.[1] Saladin's secretary, the historian 'Imad al-Din al-Isfahani, declared:

> How could God not assist in the conquest of the mighty Jerusalem and of the Aqsa Mosque, founded in piety, since she is the seat of the prophets, the home of the saints, the place where the pious adore their God, the place that the great saints of the earth and angels of heaven visit? … There is the Rock, whose eternal splendour has been preserved from any deterioration, from which the Way of the Ascension [of the Prophet] leaves the earth … and from there al-Buraq [Muhammad's mystical steed] departed on the night of the heavenly journey. … Among its gates is the Gate of Mercy; who enters by it gains the right to dwell forever in Paradise. Within it are the Throne of Solomon and the Oratory of David and the Fountain of Aloes, which represents … the heavenly River Kauthar. Jerusalem is the first *qibla* [direction of Muslim prayer], the second of two houses of God, and the third sacred sanctuary.

When the force of Saladin's attack became apparent to the Franks, they sent a deputation to ask for terms. Saladin refused their request: "We shall deal with you just as you dealt with the population of Jerusalem when you took it in 1099, with murder and enslavement and other savageries."

Then the Frankish leader, Balian of Ibelin, presented himself before Saladin and once again asked for a general amnesty in return for surrender. The sultan maintained his refusal. Finally, despairing of this approach, Balian said:

> Know, O Sultan, that there are very many of us in this city. … If we see that death is inevitable, then by God we shall kill our children and our wives, burn our

78 The Aqsa Mosque: The wooden pulpit (*minbar*) installed by Saladin in 1187 beside the prayer niche in the mosque's south wall. The pulpit was destroyed in the 1969 fire

possessions so as not to leave you a dinar or a drachma or a single man or woman to enslave. When this is done, we shall pull down the Sanctuary of the Rock and the Aqsa Mosque and the other sacred places.

Whether or not because of this threat to destroy the shrines of the Noble Sanctuary, Saladin relented and agreed to allow the population to leave the city, on payment of a tribute of ten dinars per man, five per woman, and one or possibly two per child. What the Franks could not take with them, they sold to merchants and non-Latin Christians, who had sought and received Saladin's permission to remain in their homes if they paid the tax on non-Muslims. What could not be sold was left behind, including superb columns and slabs of marble and mosaic in large quantities.

The city surrendered on 2 October 1187, the anniversary of Muhammad's Night Journey. Saladin was determined to cleanse the Noble Sanctuary of Christian "contamination" and restore it to its pre-Crusader Islamic glory, much vaunted in the *fada'il* literature of the period lauding the "Merits of Jerusalem." Various Crusader structures, such as the conventual buildings of the Augustinian canons north of the Dome of the Rock, were demolished, leaving no recognisable trace, above ground at least.[2]

The cross finial on the Dome of the Rock was speedily replaced by an Islamic crescent. Religious trappings inside were likewise removed, including marble lining the surface of the Rock itself, Latin inscriptions, and Christian images, though the beautiful wrought-iron grille was left in place. The Rock was washed with rosewater brought by camel train from Damascus; a tribune (*sudda*) assembled largely from Crusader sculpture was installed (to be removed in the twentieth century); the interior of the dome was re-gilded and the lead outer covering renewed.

A wall had been erected by the Crusaders in the Aqsa Mosque, redirecting the focus of worship from Mecca in the south to the east, by forming an apse in the east wall; it was removed, exposing the prayer niche (*mihrab*), which was restored and redecorated with glass mosaics. Some twenty years earlier, a pulpit (*minbar*) of exquisitely carved wood had been ordered expressly for Jerusalem by Nur al-Din from the Ibn Ma'ali family in Aleppo, which was also responsible for the wooden prayer niche (now lost) in the Mosque of Abraham in the citadel of Aleppo. It was now placed beside the prayer niche. A raised platform (*dikka*) built almost entirely of finest-quality reused Crusader marble sculpture was provided, where the movements of prayer could be repeated in time with the imam for the benefit of those who could not see him directly in a mosque as large as al-Aqsa [fig. 79]. The Muslim character of the Dome of the Chain was re-asserted by the introduction of a prayer niche (uncovered behind a later Mamluk prayer niche during restoration work in 1976). It incorporates fragments of Crusader capitals and other architectural spolia, indicating that it was built after Saladin's recovery of Jerusalem, possibly when the ceiling and pavement of the building were restored in 1200.

79 South wall of the Aqsa Mosque: prayer niche, pulpit (the recently installed replica) and *dikka*

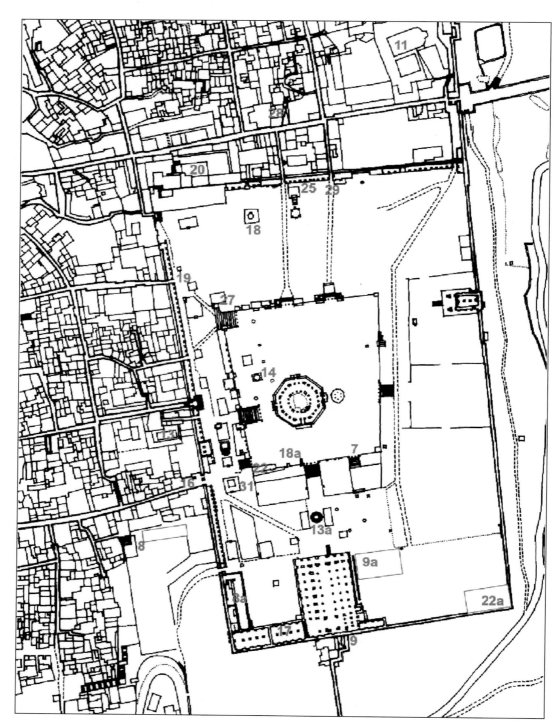

80 Plan showing locations of Ayyubid structures around the Noble Sanctuary[3]. **7**: Southwest Arcade (restored 1211–12) **8**: Approximate location of the former Afdaliyya Madrasa **8A**: North Africans' Mosque **9**: Khanthaniyya zawiya **9A**: Location of the former Eastern Annexes to the Aqsa Mosque **11**: Salahiyya College (1192) **13**: Ablution Place **13A**: The "Cup" **14**: Dome of the Ascension (1200–01) **16**: Chain Gate and Gate of the Divine Presence **17**: Former Women's Mosque **18**: Dome of Solomon **18A**: Dome of the Balance **19**: Superintendent's Gate **20**: Grave of Sheikh Darbas **22**: "Grammar School" (1207–08) **22A**: "Market of Knowledge" **25**: North Portico **27**: Sha'lan Fountain 1216–17) **28**: Mu'azzamiyya College (1217–18) **29**: Remission Gate **31**: Dome of Moses (1249)

81   Looking south towards the fountain known as "the Cup" and the façade of the Aqsa Mosque

Strategic considerations could not be ignored, however, with a Frankish counterattack always possible. Several Arabic inscriptions, none in its original location, attest to efforts by Saladin and his brother, his sons, and his amirs to strengthen the city's defences. Over a period of ten months in 1191 and 1192, sections of the city wall and its gates and towers were rebuilt—in places using stone quarried from a deep ditch cut into the bedrock, said to be so hard that it damaged the workers' tools. 'Imad al-Din reported that Frankish prisoners and local workers were involved in this major undertaking, together with a group of fifty stonecutters from Mosul as well as craftsmen from Egypt and Syria. The late-Mamluk chronicler of Jerusalem, Mujir al-Din, put the number of Frankish prisoners at 2,000. Rebuilding the city's wall would have been a popular move, helping to persuade new residents that their security was taken seriously, but the need for it diminished when Saladin concluded a truce with Richard the Lionheart in 1192.

The practical requirement in Islam for ritual ablution before prayer led Saladin's brother al-Malik al-'Adil to build a water basin [**13**] (and possibly latrines) in 1193, of which the entrance porch survives at the present ablution place west of the Noble Sanctuary. Al-'Adil also built a fountain for drinking and ablution, known as the Cup [**13a**; fig. 81], located between the Dome of the Rock and the Aqsa Mosque and still in use today, though much altered. Saladin fulfilled another practical function by establishing a hospital for people arriving to take up residence in the city, probably in the former nuns' abbey church of St Mary the Great, south of the Church of the Holy Sepulchre, in what is now the marketplace known as the Muristan.

Revitalization and repopulation meant the introduction of new pious institutions, or rather, their reintroduction, for several are known to have existed there before the Frankish conquest. In the tenth century, the famous geographer al-Muqaddasi, himself a native of Jerusalem, referred to convents (*khanqah*s) for members of the Karramiyya sect in the city; an Arabic inscription found at the present Remission Gate [**29**] commemorates the provision in 1053–54 of accommodation for visitors; and we know from Ibn al-'Arabi, who spent about three years in Jerusalem with his father from 1092 to 1095 on their way to Mecca, that there were two theological colleges (*madrasa*s) in the city on the eve of the First Crusade, one at the Gate of the Tribes and one opposite the Church of the Holy Sepulchre. Saladin's new religious foundations were in roughly the same places as these colleges: the Salahiyya College [**11**] was founded in 1192 in the former Church of St Anne; and a convent for Sufi mystics, the Salahiyya Khanqah (endowed in 1189, according to a deed preserved in the archives of the Ottoman Court in Jerusalem), was established in the former Latin patriarch's residence, immediately to the north of the Holy Sepulchre. Such reuse of abandoned buildings was typical of most Muslim foundations following the recapture. For example, a mosque, now known as the Mosque of 'Umar, was founded in 1193 by Saladin's eldest son, al-Malik al-Afdal, in the northwest corner of the former Hospitaller complex, south of the Holy Sepulchre. (Following the departure of the Latin clergy, the Sepulchre had been handed over to Eastern Christians, who resumed worship there and in several other churches in the city.)

In the northern part of the city, not far from the Salahiyya College, the Maymuniyya College was established by Saladin's treasurer in the Church of St Mary Magdalene and endowed in 1197. None of these conversions appears to have involved major structural interventions in the fabric of the buildings; little more was done than to add a prayer niche in the south wall or to place a foundation inscription over the entrance.

The same is true of various Crusader annexes to the Aqsa Mosque that survived the process of re-Islamization. Eastern annexes [**9a**] of a more or less utilitarian nature were retained, and though they were subsequently demolished during the 1938–42 restorations, we know them from the careful record made by R.W. Hamilton, and from old photographs [see figs. 75, 125]. A southern annex, built by the Crusaders over the southern salient in the city wall, was converted and endowed in 1189 as a *zawiya* (literally, a "corner," a residence for a Sufi *shaykh* and a meeting place for his followers), known as al-Khutniyya or al-Khatuniyya [**9**]. Only one of three original vaults over the main hall remains, but enough survives of the walls to indicate that few changes were involved in the conversion

82   The frontage of the Women's Mosque
to the west of the Aqsa Mosque

83   Entrance to the Afdaliyya Madrasa in a
pre-1967 photograph
IAA 27.478

process. Such triple-bayed assembly halls were to become a feature of all Sufi convents and
many colleges in Mamluk Jerusalem. A western annex, extending from the mosque to the
southwest corner of the enclosure, was converted to serve as the Women's Mosque [**17**;
fig. 82]. It survives today practically intact, now housing part of the Aqsa Mosque Library

and part of the Islamic Museum. The Crusader origin of this western annex is confirmed by the distinctive diagonal tooling of the stone surface and the presence of masons' marks, both reliable evidence of Crusader stonework when they are not mixed with other types of masonry but remain *in situ* and homogeneous, as here. In the absence of such dependable evidence, distinguishing between Crusader and Ayyubid construction is far from easy, because stones from demolished Crusader structures, including marble columns, bases and capitals, were collected for reuse in later constructions.

Around this time, al-Afdal endowed an area in the southern part of the city for the benefit of North African immigrants who were for the most part adherents of the Maliki school of religious law. He built a college there, named Afdaliyya [**8**; fig. 83] after him, which was demolished unrecorded in June 1967 and is now known only from old photographs and a short report in the archives of the British Mandate Department of Antiquities in the Palestine Archaeological (Rockefeller) Museum. That report describes the building as having a "medieval" doorway and a domed middle chamber flanked by two cross-vaulted chambers. The dome was carried on a drum with four windows, supported by a transition zone of four shallow arches in the cardinal axes and four deeper arches or squinches spanning the corners. In the central (domed) chamber was a prayer niche with a moulded arch. A wooden cenotaph in the west chamber was probably a later addition. This description suggests that, unusually, the building was a new Ayyubid construction rather than a converted Crusader one. The "medieval" doorway, to judge from the irregular way it and its mismatched hoodmould were fitted into the surrounding masonry (as shown in a photograph taken before its demolition), is a Crusader doorway salvaged and reused in an otherwise new construction.

The North Africans' Mosque [**8a**; fig. 84] at the south end of the west wall of the Noble Sanctuary, abutting the Crusader hall formerly housing the Women's Mosque along the south wall, was also built by al-Afdal. As al-ʿUmari observed around 1345, although both these mosques are popularly called *jami*ʿs (Friday mosques) they are in fact ordinary neighbourhood mosques (*masjid*s), in which an imam performs the five daily prayers. Jerusalem had only one Friday mosque in which the sermon was read: al-Aqsa.

Apart from this modest building programme in the first dozen or so years following the recapture, work in the Noble Sanctuary centred on the main monuments, with little in the way of new construction.

The struggle for power following Saladin's death in 1193 concentrated the attentions of the Ayyubid amirs on politics rather than architecture. Gradually, however, the situation stabilized. Al-ʿAdil gained control of Syria and successfully negotiated a series of truces with the Franks. As security was restored, new construction began. The main gateway leading from the markets of the town into the Noble Sanctuary, the double gate comprising the

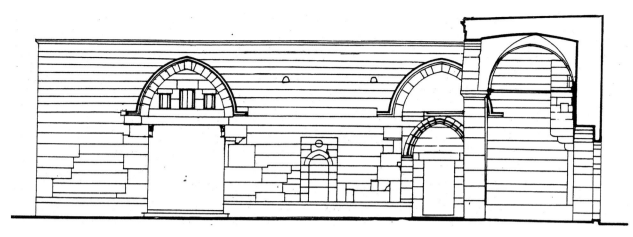

84   North Africans' Mosque

The North Africans' Mosque retains its decorated north front with two pointed-arched doorways placed more or less symmetrically on either side of the central axis, one for each of the halls. The doorways are built largely of re-used Crusader elements including hoodmoulds and, on the left-hand (eastern) doorway, elbow brackets supporting a lintel. Both doorways have undergone subsequent alteration. The tympanum of the left one is blocked save for three small windows; the tympanum of the right one remains open and, though the doorway is now partly blocked by a pointed arched recess (also composed of re-used Crusader elements) containing a smaller doorway, it is likely that both doorways were originally similar.

85 General view of the Gate of the Divine Presence and the Chain Gate from the west, showing the large amounts of re-used Frankish sculpture. The semicircular arch of the earlier Umayyad gate can be discerned above the "flat arch" of the Ayyubid gate.

Left: plan
Below: three details

Chain Gate and the Gate of the Divine Presence (*sakina*) [**16**; fig. 85], was provided with a twin-domed outer (western) porch, decorated with prodigious quantities of reused Crusader sculpture. Beside it, an inscription dated 1199 records the construction and endowment of a school where Muslim children would learn the Qur'an, their recitation doubtless appreciated by passers-by entering and leaving the Noble Sanctuary. In the Dome of the Rock, a beautiful *mashrabiyya*, a balustrade containing lattices of turned wooden spindles, was erected around the rock in about 1199. It bears the names not only of the carpenter who made it, Abu'l-Khayr ibn Abu'Ali b. Rahma, but also of two brothers, Abu Bakr and 'Uthman, who designed it, and of their patron, al-Malik al-'Aziz 'Uthman, another of Saladin's sons.

An intriguing structure, standing on the terrace just 20 m northwest of the Dome of the Rock, has a typically formulaic inscription over its entrance doorway:

> In the name of God, the Merciful, the Compassionate, may God bless and grant peace to Muhammad, His Prophet, and His family. Whatever good you do, God knows it (Qur'an, 2.196) … and who has done the smallest particle of good, [He] shall see it (Qur'an 99.8). This is the Dome of the Prophet—God bless Him and His family—which the historians mention in their books. Charged with its reinstatement after its loss and its construction after its destruction, on his own initiative and at his own expense, was the servant in need of the mercy of his Lord, the great amir, the great general, the unique, the glorious, the special, the confident, the hero of the holy war, the conqueror, the fighter at the frontiers, glory of the faith, beauty of Islam, happiest of the happy, sword of the prince of believers, Abu 'Umar 'Uthman b. 'Ali b. 'Abdallah al-Zanjili, governor of Jerusalem, in the months of the year 597 [1200–1201 CE].

This dome is now known as the Dome of the Ascension [of Muhammad] [**14**; fig. 86] and is considered by some to have been a Crusader baptistery, but it shows not much evidence of diagonal tooling or masons' marks, nor is it mentioned in any contemporary description. It seems more likely, therefore, that it is an original Ayyubid construction built in 1200–1201, making extensive use of a rich supply of Crusader sculpture, and so interpretable as part of the continuing process of restoring the Noble Sanctuary to its pre-Crusader form and sanctity. Early Islamic authors mention several commemorative structures dotted around the Noble Sanctuary, including a Dome of the Prophet; hence the reference to historical books in the inscription.

About 160 m to the north, a second, frustratingly anepigraphic structure, a free-standing octagonal domed edicule known as the Dome of Solomon [**18**; fig. 87], encloses a rock outcrop that may provide the reason for its particular location. In popular tradition, the outcrop is known as the Throne of Solomon, said to be the place where Solomon prayed when he had completed the construction of the Temple. It has also been called

86   The Dome of the Ascension (*Qubbat al-Mi'raj*)

Kursi 'Isa, the Throne of Jesus, which may refer not to Jesus Christ but to the Ayyubid, al-Malik al-Mu'azzam 'Isa (see below). Here, too, many Crusader columns are incorporated. Unmentioned in the Crusader historical sources, this building, too, is likely Ayyubid, reinstating some earlier shrine or commemorative structure that had disappeared by the time of Saladin's recapture of Jerusalem.

Another domed structure in the Noble Sanctuary stands to the west of the arcade at the top of the staircase leading south from the terrace down towards the Aqsa Mosque. Al-'Umari, who calls it the Dome of the Balance [**18a**; fig. 88], describes two marble cupolas, one above the other, each formed of a single piece, carried on twelve columns of speckled red and white marble and resting on "waxen" bases. The two-tiered dome fitting this description now has a staircase leading to the upper level, converting it into what is

87 The Dome of Solomon (*Qubbat Sulayman*)

called the Summer Pulpit or, alternatively, the pulpit of Burhan al-Din, the judge who restored it in the fourteenth century. Consisting of a square lower structure surmounted by a hexagonal upper one, it is composed almost entirely of reused Crusader sculpture [fig. 88]. Its original date of construction is not known, but, given the quantity of Crusader sculpture used, it appears likely that a pre-Crusader Dome of the Balance mentioned in historical sources was reinstated shortly after the recapture.

In 1198, al-'Adil had his second son, al-Malik al-Mu'azzam 'Isa, invested as ruler of Damascus, a position that included responsibility for Jerusalem. Under al-Mu'azzam's suzerainty, Jerusalem enjoyed a period of relative peace and prosperity. He took an especially close interest in completing the repair of the city wall and the refurbishment of the Noble Sanctuary, begun by his father and his uncle, Saladin. By 1204, he even chose the city as his main place of residence. An inscription in secondary use in the Citadel, and three others recovered in recent excavations along the southern and western lines of the city wall, commemorate the construction of towers and other repairs to the fortifications in the name of al-Mu'azzam, in 1202, 1203, 1212 and 1213–14. He is best remembered, however, for his significant contribution to the architectural embellishment of the Noble Sanctuary.

Al-Mu'azzam's most striking enterprise was perhaps his extension of the whole west side of the Dome of the Rock terrace a full 18 m to the west,[4] with the addition of some water tanks and, a little to the north of the terrace, a water fountain called Sabil Sha'lan [27]. It remains to be investigated why the Umayyad upper terrace, whose other boundaries appear to be the same as its present ones, was so much narrower on this west side, closest to the city.

By extending the upper terrace, al-Mu'azzam created a prestigious site for a new building known as the "Grammar School" (al-Madrasa al-Nahwiyya) [22; fig. 89], described in its foundation inscription as "this blessed dome and the construction which adjoins it," with the date of its foundation given as 1207–08. The building has been altered over the years. An idea of its original appearance may be gained from al-'Umari's description:

> Its external length is 36 dhira' [each of about 70 cm, and so about 25 m] and its width from south to north is 7 dhira'. It has two doors opening to the north. On both sides of them stand three marble columns, each column consisting of four individual parts, coiled like a serpent… Through the two aforementioned doors one enters a portico whose length is 18.5 dhira' and its width 6 dhira', and which has a gilded Syrian ceiling of 13 squares (murabba'). In its south front are three windows which look out on the Noble Sanctuary and the doors of the [Aqsa] Mosque. On its western side is a domed room on arches. The south, west and north sides each have three windows. In its [east] side is an entrance door from the aforementioned portico and a window into it. On the east side of the aforementioned portico there is a domed room smaller than the other. It serves as a residence for the imam… Al-Mu'azzam provided a single imam [for this school] to recite the five [daily] prayers. He also provided 25 men from among the students of grammar (nahw), and a shaykh, on condition that they be adherents of the Hanafi school of law and students of his theological college [al-Mu'azzamiyya] outside the Noble Sanctuary.

The present eastern domed chamber stands exactly in the position of the south-west corner of the Dome of the Rock terrace before it was extended by al-Mu'azzam. The low dome

88 The Dome of the Balance (*Qubbat al-Mizan*) incorporated into the Summer Pulpit in the Mamluk period and partly remodeled in the Ottoman period

89 The Grammar School (*al-Madrasa al-Nahwiyya*) built in 1207–08 by al-Mu'azzam 'Isa at the south end of his extension of the upper terrace

and the double window in its south wall plainly belong to alterations made some time in the Ottoman period, but it seems likely that an earlier structure had stood here, to which al-Mu'azzam added a portico and another dome. Early photographs show the exterior of the portico just as al-'Umari describes it: four arches (which had been blocked before the middle of the nineteenth century) resting on three twisted and intertwined reused Crusader columns. Two of these columns now flank an Ottoman doorway added in the late nineteenth century [fig. 90], and the third is in a collection of architectural sculpture outside the entrance to the former Women's Mosque. Of the gilded Syrian ceiling nothing else is known; the present ceiling is cross-vaulted in three bays.

Another structure consisting of two domes separated by a portico stood at the south-east corner of the Noble Sanctuary until the end of the nineteenth century, when it was

90　Frankish columns flanking an Ottoman doorway of the Grammar School

demolished. Known as the "Market of Knowledge" [**22a**], it is said to have been assigned by al-Mu'azzam to members of the Hanbali school of law as a place of prayer. The two domes, visible in early photographs and engravings, appear to be of similar construction: smooth ashlar masonry raised on moulded cornices resting on circular drums, like the west dome of the Nahwiyya. The eastern dome might, again, have belonged to an earlier structure, for there are reports of a chapel of St Simeon standing here in Crusader times, which might have survived Saladin's purge of the Noble Sanctuary.

A *zawiya* called al-Nasiriyya, on top of the Golden Gate in the east wall of the Noble Sanctuary, took its name from eleventh-century *shaykh* Nasir al-Muqaddasi, who for a long time gave lectures on the science of religion there, on the site where the famous Muslim philosopher and theologian al-Ghazali was to stay during his sojourn in Jerusalem

91   General view of the central part of the North Portico of the Noble Sanctuary. The building above the portico is
later, added in the Mamluk period

in around 1090. Rebuilt by al-Mu'azzam for those engaged in reading the Qur'an and
studying grammar (one of al-Mu'azzam's enthusiasms), it had fallen into disrepair by the
late fifteenth century, when it was mentioned by Mujir al-Din.

The central section of the North Portico [**25**; fig. 91] of the Noble Sanctuary, built by
al-Mu'azzam and bearing an inscription dated 1213–14, consists of ten cross-vaulted bays
on piers with sloping-topped buttresses extending westwards from the Umayyad double
gate once known as the Gate of the Tribes, whose eastern opening is Remission Gate [**29**]
(the other opening having been blocked by the construction of the Mamluk Awhadiyya
Mausoleum immediately outside the Noble Sanctuary; see the next chapter). This portico
follows a long tradition. The Herodian temple precinct was surrounded by porticoes, and
a regular series of sockets for beams belonging to the north one remains visible, cut in

92 The rock scarp at the west end of the north boundary of the Noble Sanctuary in which may be discerned empty grooves hewn into the rock face to take vaulting springers, evidently all that remains of porticoes along the north and west sides of the enclosure described in the tenth century by the writers Ibn al-Faqih and al-Muqaddasi

the rock scarp at the west end of the north boundary; below these may be seen a line of a dozen empty grooves fashioned to take the vaulting springers of an early Islamic portico [fig. 92; see also fig. 25]. Again, al-Muʻazzam would have had a personal interest in embellishing the northern part of the enclosure with a new portico, since the gate here led from the Noble Sanctuary to the site of a major new college, the Muʻazzamiyya [**28**], which he was building for students of his favoured Hanafi school of law; endowed in 1209, it was completed in 1217–18.

While the ten-bay section of the North Portico and the western extension of the upper terrace are both new Ayyubid constructions that used few salvaged Crusader materials, they are built very much in Crusader style, notably in their sloping-topped buttresses, this being the earliest known use of such features in Islamic architecture.

It seems hard to credit that the entrance porch of the Aqsa Mosque, added to the *Palatium Salomonis* by the Franks, lay partly in ruins until its restoration was begun by al-Mu'azzam. Making use of salvaged Crusader material, he repaired the central section, to which he added a pendentive dome over the main entrance [fig. 93] and a new façade on the central three bays, completed, according to inscriptions, in 1217–18. Remarkably, the voussoirs of the chevron arch in the central bay are carved in emulation of Crusader style on the backs of a group of Crusader and earlier architectural fragments. The restoration was not completed for another 130 years, when the east and west bays and the north end of the adjoining aisles of the mosque were added by the Mamluks.

Other aspects of the refurbishment of the Noble Sanctuary under al-Mu'azzam include the renovation in 1211–12 of the arcade [7] at the top of the eastern flight of steps on the south side of the Dome of the Rock terrace, originally built in 1020 or 1030 by Anushtiqin al-Dizbiri, governor of Damascus. Al-Mu'azzam also provided new door leaves for the Superintendent's Gate [19] in the west wall and for Remission Gate [29] in the north wall.

In Muslim (as in Jewish and Christian) eschatological tradition, Jerusalem was regarded as the future scene of the Last Judgment and Resurrection. Consequently, it became a popular place of burial, usually in one of the cemeteries outside the walls: Mamilla to the west, al-Sahira to the north, and at the Golden Gate immediately to the east of the Noble Sanctuary. Epitaphs of several amirs in Saladin's army have been recovered from these cemeteries, many of them Kurds like him, who had fallen in battle and been brought to Jerusalem for burial. Yet another Kurdish amir, Badr al-Din Muhammad al-Hakkari, one of al-Mu'azzam's closest advisers in Jerusalem, was buried in the Marzuban district in the city centre, not far from the main markets, in the courtyard of the Badriyya College founded by him in 1213–14 "for the followers of the Imam Shaf'i."

Earlier, in the mid-tenth century, the Ikhshidid rulers of Egypt built a family mausoleum for themselves, apparently within the city itself and close to the Noble Sanctuary, somewhere near the present Remission Gate. A small Seljuk cemetery dating from the late eleventh century, uncovered in 1969, lay outside the west wall of the Noble Sanctuary. In Ayyubid times we know of only two additional burials near the Noble Sanctuary. One is of another Kurd, described by Mujir al-Din as Sheikh Darbas al-Kurdi al-Hakkari, a virtuous and faithful man who died in 1217–18; his grave lies under a now ruinous ashlar dome on squinches [20] at the entrance to the Crusader Chapel of the Repose, at the site of the former Antonia tower in the northwest corner of the Noble Sanctuary. The second is of al-Malik al-Amjad Hasan, brother of al-Mu'azzam, who was buried in a college (which no longer survives) named after him, located beside one of the gates of the Noble Sanctuary. While burial within the Noble Sanctuary itself seems to have been forbidden, the popularity of burial near it was to grow in the Mamluk period.

93   Pendentive dome built in 1217–18 by Mu'azzam 'Isa at the entrance to the Aqsa Mosque

The apparent growing prosperity of Jerusalem under al-Mu'azzam's rule came to an abrupt halt with the Fifth Crusade and the siege and eventual Crusader occupation of Damietta in the Nile delta. There seemed to be a real possibility that Jerusalem would once more fall into Frankish hands. In these circumstances, to destroy its military strength, al-Mu'azzam ordered the dismantling of the walls in 1219. It is unlikely that the walls of the Noble Sanctuary were affected, but enough of the rest of Jerusalem's walls were destroyed to render the place effectively defenceless. The city was largely abandoned by its Muslim population, and for the following thirty years there seems to have been no attempt at new building in the Noble Sanctuary.

There is considerable evidence on Jewish life in Jerusalem in the Ayyubid period. With the Muslim recapture, Jews began to return, albeit in small numbers. In 1209–10, for example, 300 of them arrived from France and England. Before the Crusades, Jews had been in the habit of praying at the gates of the Noble Sanctuary, and this custom may have revived under the Ayyubids. The Noble Sanctuary remained in Muslim hands and in theory accessible to Christians and Jews if they asserted their faith to the Muslim guardians, but in effect it remained out of bounds. Judah Alharizi, the Jewish poet from Spain who made the pilgrimage to Jerusalem in 1217, lamented seeing—most probably from the Mount of Olives—the "place of the Temple and the inner court, from which our sins removed the candelabrum and lit an alien fire in its stead."[5]

The possibility of returning Jerusalem, but not the Noble Sanctuary or the Citadel, to Frankish control was first discussed in the negotiations of 1192, but it was never agreed. With the advent, amid incessant squabbling among the Ayyubids, of the Crusade of the Hohenstaufen Emperor Frederick II, the ruler of Egypt, al-Malik al-Kamil, decided to cede the defenceless city to Frederick for a period of ten years. The terms of the Treaty of Jaffa, signed in 1229, stated that the Noble Sanctuary was to remain under Muslim control, and the Muslim population had a right of free access for prayer.

Frederick, who had grown up in Sicily, which had a substantial Muslim population, was interested in Islamic culture. After the truce had been concluded, he asked to visit Jerusalem. Leave was granted to him, and the sultan commissioned the judge Shams al-Din, *qadi* of Nablus, to accompany the emperor during his visit. Shams al-Din gave the following account to the chronicler and diplomat Ibn Wasil (1208–98):

> When the emperor came to Jerusalem, I attended on him as al-Malik al-Kamil had commanded me, and I entered the Noble Sanctuary with him, and he saw the places of pilgrimage in it. Then I entered the Aqsa Mosque with him, and its construction and that of the Dome of the Rock delighted him. When he reached the prayer niche of the Aqsa, its beauty and the beauty of the pulpit enchanted him. He went up the stairs to the top [of the pulpit]. Then he came down and took my hand, and we came out of the Aqsa. There, he saw a priest with the gospels in his hand, who wanted to enter the Aqsa, so he shouted to him, "What's that you have brought here? By God, if one of you tries to get in here without my leave, I'll have his eyes out. We are the vassals and slaves of al-Malik al-Kamil. He has granted these churches to me and to you as an act of grace. Don't any of you step out of line!" The priest made off, shaking with fear.

The emperor then spent the night in a house prepared for him in Jerusalem. When Shams al-Din went to meet him the following morning, Frederick asked "O *qadi*, why did the muezzins not give the call to prayer last night in the usual way?" Shams al-Din replied, "This humble slave prevented them, out of regard and respect for Your Majesty." "You did wrong to do that," said Frederick, "for my chief aim in passing the night in Jerusalem was to hear the call to prayer given by the muezzins and their cries of praise to God during the night."

The truce was greeted with widespread hostility among the Muslim population, however. Reportedly, al-Kamil attempted to justify his action by saying: "We have conceded to them only ruined churches and monasteries. The Noble Sanctuary, the sacred Rock and all the other shrines there are in the hands of the Muslims as before."

This did not wash with al-Malik al-Nasir Dawud, who had succeeded al-Mu'azzam as ruler of Damascus. Appalled at his uncle al-Kamil's behaviour, he invited the renowned cleric Sibt b. al-Jawzi to preach in the Great Mosque of Damascus. Al-Jawzi, a famous author, had written: "When … news of the handover of Jerusalem arrived, all hell broke loose in the lands of Islam." Of his sermon, he reported:

> It was a memorable day, for not one of the people of Damascus remained outside. In the course of my oration, I said "The road to Jerusalem is closed to the company of pious visitors. O desolation for those pious men who live there; how many times have they prostrated themselves there in prayer, how many tears have they shed there? By God, if their eyes were living springs they could not pay their whole debt of grief; if their hearts burst with sorrow, they could not diminish their anguish. May God burnish the honour of the believers! O shame upon the Muslim rulers!"

On the expiry of the 1229 treaty in 1239, the city returned to Muslim control. But the intestine quarrels among the Ayyubid princes led to the Franks regaining the city in 1241. In 1243 they gained control of the Noble Sanctuary as well, in return for a promise to assist one Ayyubid faction against another.

This time, Frankish control did not last long. As the Mongol hordes under the leadership of Gengis Khan and his successors swept westward across Asia, threatened populations fled before them. One such group, the Khwarazmian Turks, had taken refuge in what is now Iraq after being dispossessed of their Central Asian homelands. The Ayyubid ruler of Egypt, al-Salih Ayyub, had designs on Syrian territory held by hostile Ayyubid kinsmen, and it was with his encouragement that the Khwarazmians, in 1244, fell on Jerusalem and sacked the city, apparently doing no damage to the shrines in the Noble Sanctuary. The Franks departed, never again to return.

In 1249, as some form of security was gradually being restored in Jerusalem (though the walls would not be rebuilt until the sixteenth century), the Ayyubid sultan al-Salih Ayyub erected a structure called the Dome of Moses [**31**; fig. 94] in the western part of the Noble Sanctuary, near the Chain Gate. It consists of a square base and an ashlar dome on corner squinches, all relatively plain, with a fine polychrome marble floor and a marble-lined prayer niche.

Conclusion

The Ayyubids regarded themselves as the new champions of orthodox Sunni Islam, and their consecration of the Noble Sanctuary parallels the Umayyad transformation of the site into a Muslim holy place. In "re-Islamizing" the Noble Sanctuary, the Ayyubids, like the Umayyads, made use of pre-existing Christian architecture.

The Ayyubid sway over Jerusalem may be divided roughly into four periods. In the first, the reign of Saladin, the major Ayyubid construction activities consisted in restoring the main shrines to Muslim worship and simple conversions of Christian property, with little alteration except for the introduction of prayer niches.

In the second period, the struggle for power following Saladin's death, Latin property continued to be converted to Muslim use. The few new structures that were built, such as the North Africans' Mosque and the Afdaliyya College, depended on the reuse of Crusader sculpture for architectural effect, or, in the case of the domed shrines in the Noble Sanctuary, the use of Crusader spolia in such quantities that consensus on their attribution to the Ayyubid period has not yet been reached. Indeed, such was the appreciation of Crusader sculpture that even figural representations that might have been expected to offend Muslim sensibilities were reused, sometimes after defacement, sometimes not.

The third period, the relatively calm and prosperous early rule of al-Mu'azzam 'Isa, was different. While use continued to be made of salvaged sculpture, it was in the context of new constructions of some architectural pretension, designed and built for Muslim patrons. None has survived wholly intact, but enough remains to allow us, with the aid of historical descriptions, to infer the involvement of skilled craftsmen trained in north Syria, like the carpenters responsible for the pulpit in the Aqsa Mosque. The domes, for example, are of smooth ashlar masonry, practically unknown in contemporary Muslim dome construction except in Aleppo. Frankish masons, too, were skilled in the construction of ashlar domes, but they used pendentives in zones of transition, rather than squinches. The Ayyubid ashlar dome on pendentives at the entrance porch to the Aqsa Mosque, and the new façade containing a Romanesque chevron arch, suggest that skilled construction techniques developed under Frankish rule remained in use in later periods, practised perhaps by some of the prisoners of war or their descendants who participated in Saladin's rebuilding of the walls.

Finally, the fourth period, from al-Mu'azzam's dismantling of the city walls to the establishment of Mamluk sovereignty in 1260, including a period of Frankish occupation, saw little in the way of architectural activity in the Noble Sanctuary, either constructive or destructive, except for the erection of the simple domed cube of the Dome of Moses.

94 The Dome of Moses (*Qubbat Musa*)

1260–1516: THE NOBLE SANCTUARY (AL-HARAM AL-SHARIF) UNDER MAMLUK RULE – HISTORY

DONALD P. LITTLE
MCGILL UNIVERSITY, MONTREAL

Inscriptions

Craning one's neck toward the interior of the dome of the Aqsa Mosque, eyes bedazzled by mosaics and gilded carvings, one can pick out a massive inscription which circles the upper dome in panels broken by roundels. With the help of experts in deciphering Arabic calligraphy, we know it reads:

> This blessed dome was renewed during the reign of Our Lord, the Sultan al-Malik al-Nasir, the Learned, the Just, the Warrior, Defender of the Frontiers, the Victorious Helper, Vanquisher of Dissidents and Rebels, Vindicator of Justice in the worlds, Sultan of Islam and the Muslims, Victor of this world and religion, Muhammad ibn al-Sultan the Martyr, al-Malik al-Mansur Qalawun al-Salihi, may God have mercy upon him, in the months of the year 728 [1328].[1]

From this inscription there is much to be inferred about the Haram under the Mamluk dynasty ruling Egypt and Greater Syria. First, the task of preserving this remote shrine was assumed centuries after its construction by a Muslim ruler in Egypt. Second, this ruler—sultan—was not a native of Jerusalem, or even Palestine, where the shrine was located, but a ruler, of slave-convert descent, resident in his capital in Cairo. Third, the honorific, but stereotypical, titles of the sultan inscribed in the dome, stress his role as militant defender of the faith, even though he was son of a Turkish slave convert to Islam and a Mongol mother.

The Mamluks' presence in the Haram, then, is conspicuous from this inscription and many others and proclaims their dedication in maintaining and restoring the splendor of al-Aqsa, still regarded, obviously, as one of the holiest shrines of Islam. But al-Malik al-Nasir's construction enterprises were not confined to the inscription in the dome of al-Aqsa. He also had the exterior replated with lead, and regilded the interior of the Dome of

95 Tankiziyya College (1328): glass mosaics in the semidome of the prayer niche in the south wall

the Rock, commemorating this with an even grander inscription crediting Saladin with an earlier regilding. He also erected new colonnades and arches on the Haram as well as other structures such as the minaret of Bab al-Silsila and the market and Gate of the Cotton Merchants (Suq al-Qattanin) [fig. 96].[2] It should also be noted that al-Nasir Muhammad was one of seven sultans known to have made a pilgrimage (*ziyara*) to Jerusalem. Nor was al-Nasir the only Mamluk ruler to sponsor and finance construction and embellishment on and around the Haram. Sixteen other sultans, whose reigns span practically the entire Mamluk period undertook either to build their own structures on the Haram, such as the college and fountain of Qa'itbay [fig. 95]—both still standing today—or to repair and maintain deteriorating structures and ornamental features of existing buildings.[3] Most if not all of these pious activities are commemorated in inscriptions.

Travellers' Reports

For the impressions the Haram made on its beholders during the Mamluk period and the significance it held for the devout, both Muslims and non-Muslims, we are indebted largely to visitors. Among the former was the most celebrated Muslim traveller of the Middle Ages, Ibn Battuta, who visited Jerusalem in A.H. 726 [1326] as part of his grand tour of the Muslim world. While he acknowledged the impressive size of the Haram area, which he claims constituted the largest mosque in the world, and admired the beauty of al-Aqsa, his fervent wonder was aroused by viewing the Dome of the Rock:

> This is one of the most marvellous of buildings, of the most perfect in architecture and strangest in shape; it has been endowed with a plentiful share of loveliness, and has received a choice portion of every rare beauty.... Both on its exterior and inside it is adorned with such a variety of decoration and such brilliance of execution to defy description. The greater part of this decoration is surfaced with gold, so that it glows like a mass of light and flashes with the gleam of lightning; the eyes of him who would gaze on its splendour are dazzled and the tongue of the beholder finds no words to represent them.[4]

Besides this over-all impression Ibn Battuta mentions other features of the layout and construction of the site, most notably the central place of "the blessed Rock of which mention is made in the Traditions, for the Prophet (God bless him and give him peace) ascended from it to heaven."[5]

While there is nothing strikingly original in this description, it is important nevertheless as an indication that the general effect of the Dome of the Rock on Muslim viewers during the Mamluk period must have been much as it is today, meaning that concerted efforts had been made to maintain its splendour and that its main religious significance, as the site of

96 Entrance to the Market of the Cotton Merchants (1336–37) from the Noble Sanctuary

Muhammad's ascent to heaven, had apparently not changed in the nearly six centuries that had passed since its construction.

Non-Muslims were routinely denied permission to enter the Haram, the whole area being considered a mosque forbidden—*haram*—to unbelievers. But this did not prevent them from viewing its wonders from outside the sanctuary from elevations such as Mount Zion and the Mount of Olives, or one or another of the gates opening on the interior of the Haram. In 1483 a German Dominican pilgrim, Friar Felix Fabri, and a group of fellow pilgrims succeeded in gaining access to al-Madrasa al-Ashrafiyya [fig. 97], then being decorated under the patronage of Sultan Qa'itbay. Besides admiring the marble panels and gilded ceiling of this, "one of the three jewels" of the Haram, these Christians were able to see through its windows the Temple (the Dome of the Rock) in close proximity: "a noble and exceedingly costly building, great and round … with mosaics where the field of the pictures gleams with gold."[6] Other Christians, such as the German knight Arnold von Harff, in 1496 bribed a Mamluk to smuggle him into the Haram in disguise, where he was able to explore the Temple of Solomon (Dome of the Rock) as it was known to Christian pilgrims of the Middle Ages, "with many lamps burning, at least five hundred, as I was in fact told and saw with my own eyes."[7] From the Dome von Harff proceeded with his Mamluk guide to the Porch of Solomon (al-Aqsa), "a mosque or church," where eight hundred lamps," he said "burn there daily."[8] "But no Christian or Jew is suffered to enter there [the Dome] or draw near, since they [Muslims] say and maintain that we are base dogs, and not worthy to go the holy places on pain of death."[9]

Jews, too, revered the Haram, as the site of Solomon's Temple. Quite apart from Muslims' interdictions regarding entrance to the Haram, Jews had taboos against treading the sacred ground. The Italian rabbi Obadiah da Bertinoro observes around 1487 that

> No Jew may enter the enclosure of the temple. Although sometimes the Arabs are anxious to admit carpenters and goldsmiths to perform work there, nobody will go in, for we have all been defiled (by touching the bodies of the dead), I do not know whether the Arabs enter the Holy of Holies or not.[10]

Jewish travellers showed awareness of a community of their brothers in Jerusalem, unlike the Christian pilgrims who rarely mentioned co-religionists residing in the city other than Franciscans in their monastery. The importance of Jewish scholars in the city is stressed by Elijah of Ferrara, who in 1434 lectured on Maimonides and other Jewish legists in a Jerusalem synagogue. Elijah also observed the abundance and affordability of provisions at this—post-plague—time.[11]

Muslim Commentaries

So far, visitors' impressions of the sanctity of the Haram have been stressed, whether they be Muslims, Christians, or Jews. But what about the views of Muslim natives of Jerusalem? For these, during the Mamluk period, we turn to the principal medieval Muslim historian, Mujir al-Din al-'Ulaymi al-Hanbali, a scholar and judge, who lived in Jerusalem during the reigns of the late Mamluk sultans—including one of the greatest, Qa'itbay (reigned A.H. 872–901 [1468–96]). As a long-time resident of the city, educated by some of its leading scholars and, during an extended period, chief Hanbali judge Mujir al-Din was certainly well acquainted with its religious and political affairs and conscious of its sacral significance. His book, *Precious Familiarity with the History of Jerusalem and Hebron*,[12] is the most comprehensive study of Jerusalem and its significance written during the Mamluk period.[13] In this respect it is important to note that the city did not exist in isolation but was paired with its Palestinian sister, Hebron, known to Muslims as al-Khalil (the Friend of God), the Arabic designation of the prophet Abraham, where his tomb, along with those of other patriarchs and their wives, was located. In accordance with Muslim veneration of the great forefathers of monotheism. their tombs in Hebron became the site of a mosque maintained by the Mamluks, under whose supervision it became known as one of the two noble *haram*s, the other being Jerusalem. It is no accident, of course, that the two sanctuaries par excellence were, and are, Mecca and Medina, and Mujir al-Din expatiates on the lofty status of Jerusalem as the counterpart of Mecca in Muslim tradition and belief. This view of Jerusalem is paramount for Mujir al-Din. The focus of his book is the centrality of the city, not only in the Muslim era with Muhammad's miraculous ascent to heaven and his reception there by the monotheistic prophets, but also in pre-Islamic times as the homeland of these precursors of the Islamic revelation, and in the future, too, as the site of Judgement Day. In order to develop these themes of the historical significance of Jerusalem in the past, the fifteenth-century present, and the future, Mujir al-Din divides his work into four parts. By far the longest section is the first: a history of Jerusalem (and the Holy Land) in general and the Haram in particular, beginning with the Creation and continuing through the Ayyubid period.[14] Here the emphasis is on the Jewish forerunners (and the Christian Messiah) of Muhammad, the last prophet, and the continuity of the monotheistic revelation from time immemorial through the Muslim conquest in A.H. 6 [638] and reconquest from the Franks by Saladin in A.H. 583 [1187]. Mixed with an account of political and military events is a spiritual history recounting the deeds of the prophets, climaxing in Muhammad's Night Journey from Mecca to Jerusalem. This link between the two *haram*s was prefigured by the equally aerial transport of Solomon from Bayt al-Maqdis, after he had completed its reconstruction, to Mecca, where he foretold the emergence of an Arabian prophet of monotheism. The link with Hebron is also maintained when the angel Gabriel is said to have conducted Muhammad not only to Jerusalem but also to the tomb of Abraham in Hebron and instructed him to pray there.

In the second section of *al-Uns*, Mujir al-Din switches from sacred to topographical history.[15] Here he describes the greater and lesser shrines of the Haram and its surroundings along with those of the Holy Land (*al-ard al-muqaddasa*) in general. In this section Mujir al-Din's methodology is based on personal observation, including the measurements he made, as he tries to record the physical dimensions of the Muslim shrines of the city. His survey of the shrines is systematic, beginning with the spiritual core in the Haram and proceeding to the religious colleges and retreats on the periphery of the sacred area and outside it, which were obviously meant to share in the sacrality of the two main shrines.

The third section of *al-Uns* consists of biographies of Jerusalem's Muslim notables, including rulers, judges, and scholars.[16] From the data in this section can be gleaned an idea of the political, judicial, and religious administration of the city under the Mamluks. Mujir al-Din begins with thumbnail sketches of all the Mamluk sultans, whether or not they were active in the city because, he says, "they had jurisdiction over Bayt al-Maqdis, and prayers were said for them on its pulpit."[17] Nevertheless, since many of them had only this peripheral connection with the city they receive only brief notice while those sultans who made positive contributions to the governance of the city and the Holy Land, either on the battlefield or in institutions located, for the most part, in the Haram area, are discussed more fully.

After the sketches of the sultans Mujir al-Din turns to Mamluk amirs and, in a few cases, judges who ruled as viceroys on behalf of the sultans in Cairo. In fact, Mujir al-Din devotes a separate part of Section III to these rulers, entitled "The Names of Those Who Assumed the Supervision and the Viceroyship in Jerusalem and Hebron."[18] By these terms the author refers to the dual titles of the rulers of Jerusalem: Superintendent of the Two Noble Sanctuaries (*Nazir al-Haramayn al-Sharifayn*) and Viceroy of Jerusalem the Noble (*Na'ib al-Saltana bil-Quds al-Sharif*). Sometimes these offices were held by two individuals, but for most of the Mamluk period one person held both jointly, subject to the power of appointment and dismissal of the Sultan in Cairo or as exercised by his subordinates in Syria. Mujir al-Din's biographies of these officers do not make clear the exact nature of their functions or who consistently appointed them, or to whose jurisdiction they were immediately subject. Mujir al-Din does state, however, that beginning in A.H. 800 [1397/98] Sultan Barquq began appointing these officials from Cairo, whereas previously the Viceroy of Damascus had done so.[19]

This date is contradicted by other historians but only by a decade more or less. For present purposes the specific date is not so important as the fact that around A.H. 800 the Sultan did decide to intervene more directly in the governance of Jerusalem at the expense of his viceroys in Damascus. The first Mamluk amir to whom Mujir al-Din refers as *Nazir al-Haramayn* is one Aydughdi; he ruled during the reign of Baybars until that of Qalawun. Praised by Mujir al-Din for his obedience and dignity, he was responsible for building and maintaining several structures in the two *harams*. The first governor to be referred to as holder of both the viceroyship and the supervision of Jerusalem was al-Amir Sanjar (d. A.H. 745 [1345])—an expert in Shafi'i law!—who was appointed to the offices during the reign of al-Nasir Muhammad. In this dual capacity he built a *madrasa* in the city which was to become a residence of the viceroys of Jerusalem during Mujir al-Din's lifetime. He is also credited with establishing many pious endowments (*awqaf*) in Jerusalem, Gaza, and Hebron, which was certainly a natural activity for the superintendent responsible for the endowments of two of these cities. Although many subsequent governors held both offices, some occupied only one. This is especially true during the reign of Sultan Faraj

(A.H. 801 [1399]; A.H. 808 [1405]), who decreed that the two offices should not be held by the same man, in an obvious attempt to circumvent the concentration of power—political, economic, and even religious—in one person.[20] Adding to the complexity is the fact that it was not always a Mamluk who held one or the other or both of these offices. Moreover, there was another official who was charged with administering endowments in Jerusalem. We know this most clearly from the career of a Shafi'i judge, al-Qadi Sharaf al-Din 'Isa b. Ghanim al-Khazraji al-Ansari (d. A.H. 797 [1395]). In addition to serving as chief Shafi'i judge of Jerusalem and *Shaykh* of the Sufi Khanqah al-Salahiyya, he is referred to in documents from the period as *Nazir al-Awqaf al-Mabrura bil-Quds al-Sharif* (Superintendent of the Blessed Pious Endowments in Jerusalem). This title may refer mainly to his supervision of the endowments for the hospital and Sufi monastery founded by Saladin, but the point is that administration of the waqfs of the city did not rest solely in the hands of one official in Mamluk governance.[21]

Nevertheless, Mujir al-Din's biographical notices of the viceroys/superintendents of the city and the Haram make it clear that many of these officials took an active interest in maintaining and enhancing shrines within the Haram.

The longest part of Section III of *al-Uns* is devoted to the religious dignitaries of the city—members of the legal profession mainly as judges, scholars, and teachers. Mujir al-Din sketches the careers of hundreds of such men, who flourished in the city from the late twelfth century until 1500, many of whom conducted their legal and scholarly activities in the mosques and colleges within the Haram and adjacent areas. Some of these persons came from foreign places—Iran, Anatolia, Syria, Egypt, Iraq, the Maghrib, etc.—and were clearly attracted to living and working in the city because of its sacred character. On the other hand, certain scholarly families were natives, long established in Jerusalem, and were assured of repeated appointments to some of its chief offices and institutions. The Ghanim family of the above-mentioned Qadi Sharaf al-Din al-Shafi'i, for example, had held the *shaykh*-dom of the Khanqah al-Salahiyya for over three hundred years at the time Mujir al-Din was writing.

Section IV of *al-Uns* is devoted to a history of the city during the reign of Mujir al-Din's contemporary, Sultan Qa'itbay, starting with the year of his enthronement and ending with A.H. 900 [1495].[22] This period is significant for the history of the city under the Mamluks not only because Mujir al-Din records it in so much detail but also because Qa'itbay adopted a policy of keeping the city, its governance, and its religious affairs under his thumb. Enduring evidence of this sultan's interest in the Haram can be found in two of its monuments: the Madrasa al-Ashrafiyya [fig. 97] on the western border of the Haram and the Sabil (Fountain) Qa'itbay [fig. 95], which stands near the former. The Sultan's visit to Jerusalem (and Hebron) in A.H. 880 [1475], accompanied by top Mamluk officers and eminent judges, reflects not only his concern for the holy places but also his determination to monitor and control its governance from the capital in Egypt. During this visit he sat in state at his *madrasa* as well as at Qubbat Musa, also in the precincts of the Haram, to hear complaints against the tyranny of his viceroy, al-Amir Jar Qutli. As a result of these complaints the Sultan forced the viceroy to pay reparations to those persons he had wronged and threatened him with death for any subsequent misconduct of his office. Similar attention was given to an alleged judicial miscreant, a judge, who was expelled from the city for his misdeeds. Qa'itbay also paid homage to the two main shrines of the Haram, both of which were ablaze with the lamps which so impressed all pilgrims. In al-Aqsa, surrounded by political and religious dignitaries, he heard Qur'an recitations performed by three professional reciters whom he had brought with him from Cairo. Finally the Sultan performed prayer in the mosque under the leadership of one of the dignitaries he had installed at the Haram.

Qa'itbay's presence was felt in the city even when he was not there because of his insistence on appointing, recalling, and dismissing its officials—political, judicial, and religious. Of these the most important, of course, were the viceroys/superintendents. For the first twenty-one years of his reign, Qa'itbay had kept the two offices separate, but in A.H. 893 [1488] he consolidated them in a single Mamluk amir, who henceforth combined political administration of the city as the Sultan's deputy with oversight of the pious endowments of the Haram. It is worth mentioning that this office must have been lucrative since one *na'ib/ nazir*, al-Amir Duqmaq, paid 10,000 dinars plus various gratuities to the treasury when he was appointed in A.H. 893 [1488]. It would seem, furthermore, that he managed to stay in office despite flagrant misdeeds—including failure to keep al-Aqsa in good repair—only by bribing officials in Cairo, until he was finally dismissed in A.H. 896 [1491]. Members of the judiciary, especially the four chief judges, were also appointed and dismissed by the sultanate in Cairo and were sometimes summoned there for interrogation.

Striking evidence of Qa'itbay's supervision of the judiciary is provided by two well-documented disputes between the Muslim religious establishment in Jerusalem and the subject communities, both Jewish and Christian.[23] The first case involved a synagogue and house in the Jewish Quarter which blocked access to an adjacent mosque. When the house, also belonging to Jews, collapsed under heavy rain Muslims expropriated the site to insure easy entry to the mosque and even claimed that the synagogue was of recent construction and should therefore be destroyed. Claims and counterclaims were made by the concerned parties to the Sultan in Cairo. To sort out the matter, in A.H. 879–80 [1474–76] no less than eight councils of political and judicial officials were convoked in either Jerusalem or Cairo. It is noteworthy that some of those held in Jerusalem met in Haram edifices—al-Aqsa, al-Madrasa al-Tankiziyya [fig. 95] (seat of the Superintendent

97 Entrance to the Ashrafiyya College (1482)
The striped stonework within the frame moulding of the portal has lead instead of mortar in the horizontal beds, apparently to give it a more defined and precise appearance

of Pious Endowments), and Qubbat Musa—demonstrating the use of the Haram for purposes other than visitation and prayer. All but one of the councils met at the initiative of the Sultan and were clearly part of his policy to impose his will on Jerusalem judicial officials from Cairo. In this he was successful, and the synagogue was restored to the Jews, not without resentment from the Muslims of Jerusalem. The second incident involved a contest over a shrine on Mount Zion—the Tomb of David—claimed as a holy place at this time by both Christians and Muslims. Again, in A.H. 894–96 [1489–91], councils were held in the Haram, this time at the Dar al-Niyaba (Viceregal Palace, located in the Madrasa al-Jawiliyya), as well as al-Madrasa al-Tankiziyya, and al-Aqsa. Again Sultan Qa'itbay intervened in the case, this time by sending decrees to Jerusalem expressing his wishes to the judiciary. Oddly enough the case also involved allegations against the na'ib/nazir Duqmaq, who as mentioned above was accused of neglecting his duty to maintain al-Aqsa in good repair. In the end matters were settled in conformity with the wishes of both the Sultan and the Muslim judiciary of Jerusalem, and the dome that had been constructed by Christians at the Tomb was demolished not once, but twice for good measure!

Although Mujir al-Din's *al-Uns* is the longest and fullest source for the history of the Haram and Jerusalem, it is by no means the only work of the Mamluk period celebrating the merits (*fada'il*) of the city; at least thirty such works are known to have been written between 1250–1517.[24]

Of special interest are the books on visitation or pilgrimage (*ziyara*). These, reminiscent of guides to Christian holy places in Palestine, provide a guide to the numerous minor shrines located in the Haram in addition to the two major ones, complete with the spiritual benefits to be gained from prayers properly performed at them. In view of the exaggerated significance assigned by these guides to performance of these rites by Muslim pilgrims, such as "the reward of 1000 martyrs for a single visit," and coupling *ziyara* with the *hajj* to Mecca, it is not surprising that a reaction should have occurred.[25] This came most forcefully and dramatically with the pamphlet written by the celebrated and controversial Hanbali Ibn Taymiyya (d. A.H. 728 [1328]) on the occasion of visitations made in A.H. 716 [1316] by the famous jurist Badr al-Din ibn Jama'a and the Mamluk governor of Damascus, al-Amir Tankiz, whose *madrasa* at the Haram bears his name. In *Jerusalem Visitation (Ziyarat Bayt al-Maqdis)*, Ibn Taymiyya accepted the authenticity of the Prophetic tradition recommending visits to Jerusalem, Mecca, and Medina, but he utterly rejected the superstitious sanctification of the Jerusalem shrines by scholars and populace alike.[26] Nevertheless, as was the case with many if not most of Ibn Taymiyya's pronouncements on religious matters, for which he was repeatedly imprisoned by the Mamluk regime, this one did not find widespread acceptance and probably did not stem the flow of Muslim pilgrims to the city. Pilgrimage, after all, whether Muslim, Christian, or Jewish, was one of the bases of the economy of Jerusalem under the Mamluks.

Documents

As indicated at the beginning of this article, monumental inscriptions for shrines within and without the Haram have long been conspicuous in Jerusalem. These have been recorded and analyzed by several scholars, most notably van Berchem, and testify to the interest of Mamluk sultans, lesser officials, and private persons in adorning the city, perpetuating their own names and spiritual welfare. More recently, other rich primary sources for Mamluk activities in the Haram have come to light which reinforce the evidence gained from literary sources and inscriptions. These are the Haram documents, consisting of almost 900 papers discovered during the 1970s in the Islamic Museum located in the southwestern corner of the Haram and consisting for the most part of remnants from the archives of the above mentioned, late fourteenth-century Shafiʿi judge, Sharaf al-Din ʿIsa plus other assorted pieces . Though only a few of the documents have so far been published, they have been catalogued for the most part[27] and even in this tentative state testify convincingly to Mamluk concern for the welfare of the Haram shrines. Most salient in this respect, certainly, are the royal—sultanic—decrees which refer to pious endowments in support of Haram edifices. There are seven of these, ranging from Baybars in A.H. 664 [1266] through Khushqadam (A.H. 886 [1481]). Six of these definitely refer to the *haram*s in Jerusalem and Hebron and possibly the seventh as well and instruct Mamluk officials in Greater Syria to insure that endowment income from properties there be spent for the benefit of al-Aqsa and the Dome of the Rock as specified in the deeds. In document #308, for example, dated 844/1441, Sultan Jaqmaq decrees that the waqf for al-Masjid al-Aqsa is to be maintained and appoints administrators to do so. In #1, dated A.H. 866 [1461], Sultan Khushqadam orders that the poll tax on non-Muslims resident in a village in the vicinity of Jerusalem be disbursed for the benefit of the Dome of the Rock. Document #6, dated A.H. 766 [1365], signed by Sultan Shaʿban, pertains to "the servants of al-Haram al-Sharif" in general. Other decrees originate with Mamluk amirs resident in Jerusalem who wished to appoint religious scholars to various pious duties, such as recitation of the Qurʾan and Prophetic tradition, in institutions in and around the Haram. In document #2, dated A.H. 788 [1386], for example, al-Amir Aqbugha Yanki appoints a local *shaykh* as reciter of the Qurʾan, exegesis, and tradition at the Dome of the Rock. In document #4, dated A.H. 781 [1379], al-Amir Shihab al-Din b. al-ʿAskari appoints the same *shaykh* as reciter in three Haram venues. While it is not clear whether these and other amirs were serving as officials in Jerusalem or, like many Mamluks, had retired or been exiled there, they obviously wanted to participate in maintaining and sharing the sacrality of the city. By so doing they actively maintained a Muslim tradition of long standing despite lapses during the Ayyubid period.

1260–1516: The Noble Sanctuary (al-Haram al-Sharif) under Mamluk Rule - Architecture

Michael Hamilton Burgoyne
Historic Scotland, Edinburgh

The flurry of building activity following Saladin's recovery of Jerusalem from the Franks and during the early part of al-Muʿazzam ʿIsa's rule came to a more or less abrupt halt. As we have seen in the previous chapter, the only Ayyubid structure of any significance erected after the advent of the Fifth Crusade in 1218 was the Dome of Moses, built in 1249. This apparent neglect did not change immediately under the Mamluk sultans who in 1260 assumed their Ayyubid predecessors' responsibilities for the embellishment and maintenance of the Noble Sanctuary and its two great monuments.[1]

Sultan Baybars, who had seen off the Mongols at the Battle of Goliath Spring in 1260 and did much to improve communications throughout the Mamluk territories, building bridges and caravanserais as well as developing an efficient postal system, also devoted attention to religious foundations. In his reign (1260–77) the upper terrace was re-paved and the mosaics on the Dome of the Rock repaired. The mosaics [fig. 100] in the Dome of the Chain were probably repaired at the same time when a polychrome marble lining was added to the prayer niche [fig. 101]. Kitbugha (1294–97) was to make further repairs to the mosaics of the Dome of the Rock a few decades later. While the relatively harsh winter weather must have made regular maintenance necessary, no further repairs appear to have been made before the Ottoman sultan Sulayman the Magnificent replaced the mosaics with glazed tiles in the sixteenth century. The dome was restored and regilded under al-Nasir Muhammad (three reigns: 1294–95, 1299–1309 and 1309–40) and roof repairs were made by Jaqmaq (1438–53) following a fire, presumably in the ambulatories since the structural timber ribs of the dome itself are inscribed with the date of their earlier restoration in 1022–23.

The Aqsa Mosque also underwent occasional maintenance and repair. Qalawun (1280–90) and later his son, al-Nasir Muhammad, repaired the roof, and al-Nasir Muhammad's viceroy, Tankiz, opened two new windows in the south wall in 1330–31.

98 Fountain of Qaʾitbay (ca. 1482) – The dome

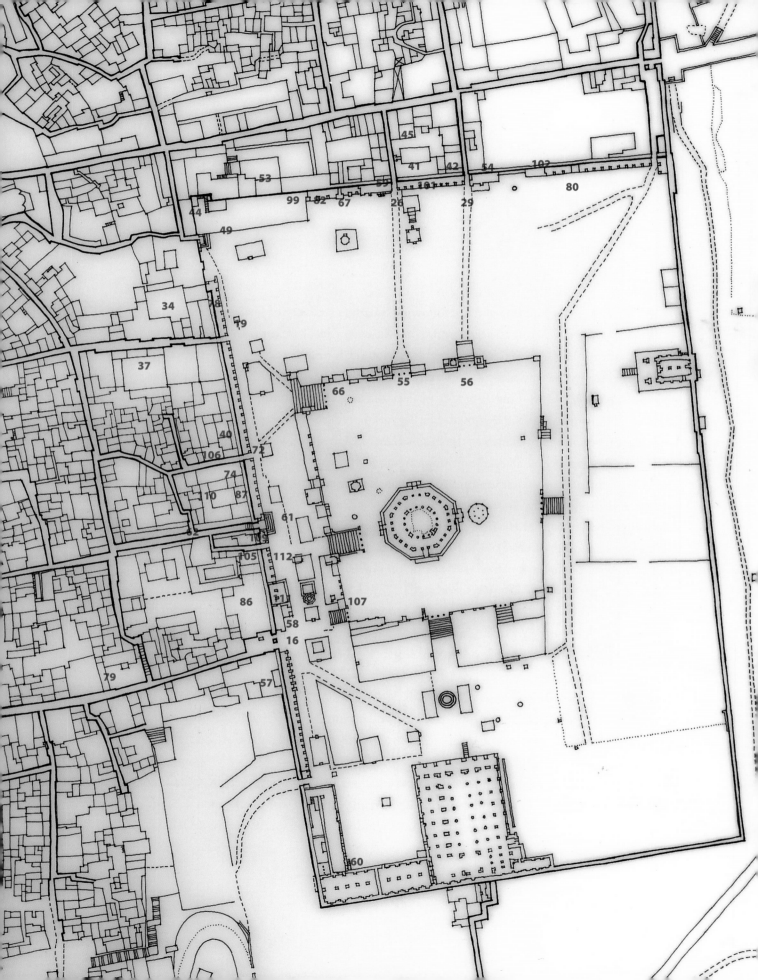

Sha'ban (1345–46) restored the doors. The porch begun by al-Mu'azzam 'Isa was finally completed by sultans Hasan (two reigns: 1347–51 and 1354–61) and Salih (1351–54). Further work is recorded during the reigns of Inal (1453–61), Qa'itbay (1468–96), and Qansuh al-Ghawri (1501–17).

In the reign of Lajin (1297–99) the Ghawanima minaret [44; fig. 102] was erected at the northwest corner of the Noble Sanctuary. A further three minarets were added, two at the west [58, 60] and one at the north border [80], at various times in the fourteenth century. Al-Nasir Muhammad built two new arcades [55, 56] at the north edge of the upper terrace, Sha'ban restored the north-west arcade [66], and Qa'itbay built the southwest one [107]. The south wall of the Noble Sanctuary also received attention during al-Nasir Muhammad's reign when, more significantly, the west portico was reinstated in three stages between 1307 and 1337, including a beautiful domed porch [fig. 103] at the Superintendent's Gate [19].

Commercial establishments were also set up to help finance the Noble Sanctuary, its staff and its monuments; these included caravanserais (*khans*), covered markets (*qaysariyyas*) and bathhouses (*hammams*).

Institutions Founded by Individuals

Although they embellished and maintained the main monuments, the Mamluk sultans had little interest in keeping the city walls in good repair or in adding major new buildings within the Noble Sanctuary. During two and a half centuries under their rule, however, there was a remarkable expansion in new building on a grand scale by a wide range of individual patrons, notably at the borders of the Noble Sanctuary, creating façades that are still a striking feature today.

99 Plan showing locations of Mamluk buildings mentioned in the text.[2] **16**: Chain Gate and Gate of the Divine Presence (pre-Mamluk origin) **19**: Superintendent's Gate (pre-Mamluk origin) **26**: Gate of Darkness (pre-Mamluk origin) **29**: Remission Gate (pre-Mamluk origin) **34**: Hospice of 'Ala al-Din (1267–68) **37**: Hospice of Sultan Qalawun (1282–83) **40**: Hospice of Kurt al-Mansuri (1293–94) **41**: Dawadariyya Convent (endowed 1295) **42**: Awhadiyya Mausoleum (endowed 1298) **44**: Ghawanima Minaret (ca. 1297–99) **45**: Sallamiyya College (ca. 1338) **49**: Ghawanima Gate (pre-Mamluk origin) **53**: Jawiliyya College (1315–20) **54**: Karimiyya College (endowed 1318) **55**: North Arcade (1321) **56**: Northeast Arcade (1326) **57**: Tankiziyya (1328–29) **58**: Chain Gate Minaret (1329–30) **59**: Aminiyya College (1329–30) **60**: Fakhriyya Minaret (ca. 1330) **61**: Cotton Merchants Gate 1335–36) **62**: Market of the Cotton Merchants (ca. 1336–37) **66**: Northwest Arcade (rebuilt 1376–77) **67**: Almalikiyya College (1340) **72**: Iron Gate (restored 1357) **74**: Arghuniyya College (1357) **78**: Manjakiyya (1361) **79**: Taziyya (1362) **80**: Gate of the Tribes Minaret (1367–68) **82**: Is'irdiyya College (before 1345) **86**: Baladiyya College (before 1380) **87**: Khatuniyya College (endowed 1354 and 1380) **99**: Subaybiyya College (before 1406) **101**: Basitiyya College (endowed 1431) **102**: Ghadiriyya College (1432) **105**: 'Uthmaniyya College (1437) **106**: Jawhariyya College (1440) **107**: Southwest Arcade (1472) **109**: Zamani Hospice (1476–77) **110**: Muzhiriyya College (1480–81) **111**: Ashrafiyya College (1482) **112**: Qa'itbay Fountain (ca. 1482).

100 Mosaics in windows of the drum of the Dome of the Chain
These windows were blocked when the glazed tiles were applied in the sixteenth century and revealed—and subsequently covered up again—during late twentieth-century repairs

101 Marble lining provided by Sultan Baybars (1260–77) on the prayer niche in the Dome of the Chain
Subsequently removed during late twentieth-century repairs

102 The Ghawanima minaret at the northwest corner of the Noble Sanctuary and, to the right of it, the striped *ablaq* façade of the Jawiliyya College

103 View looking up at the domed porch at Superintendent's Gate

Philanthropic institutions of all kinds were established: theological colleges (*madrasa*s), convents for Sufis (*khanqah*s), hospices for pilgrims (*ribat*s), a school of Prophetic tradition (*dar hadith*), a school for orphans (*maktab aytam*), *zawiya*s (literally "corners," meeting places for members of Sufi orders and often the residence of their local leader), drinking fountains (*sabil*s), and so on. Attached to many of these institutions was a mausoleum where the founder might be buried, and occasionally living accommodation for the founder. Each foundation was provided with an endowment in perpetuity (a *waqf*) usually of land or property from which revenues were reserved for the salaries of staff, for the sustenance of students, and for the upkeep of the buildings.

Such philanthropic institutions are typical for any large town of the period. What makes them exceptional in Jerusalem is their distinct relation to the Noble Sanctuary. In no other medieval Islamic town can one find such a conglomeration of religiously inspired buildings, often several storeys high, frequently incorporating earlier remains. Indeed, except for the Dome of the Rock and the Aqsa Mosque, the Noble Sanctuary is largely the product of Mamluk patrons and builders, whose legacy has survived remarkably intact.

Pilgrimage

With the Crusaders confined to the coast and soon to be expelled from the Holy Land, Jerusalem's political significance was negligible. Her religious importance, on the other hand, was inestimable. Pilgrims and religious scholars from all over the Muslim world arrived to worship and study there, particularly around the Noble Sanctuary.

The earliest Mamluk foundation near the border of the Noble Sanctuary is a pilgrim hospice [34] endowed in 1267–68 "in favour of the poor who come on pilgrimage to Jerusalem" by 'Ala al-Din Aydughdi who, though blind, served for many years as superintendent of the two sanctuaries of Jerusalem and Hebron.

Such was the need to provide accommodation for visitors that three of the next four buildings in chronological order are hospices and the fourth is a Sufi convent. The second hospice, the Mansuri Ribat [37; fig. 104], was founded by al-Malik al-Mansur Qalawun in 1282–83 according to an inscription above the entrance, for the benefit of "the poor and pilgrims to Jerusalem." The third hospice [40] was founded beside the Iron Gate in 1293–94 by one of Qalawun's amirs, Kurt al-Mansuri.

These three pilgrim hospices are close to the Noble Sanctuary, the object of the pilgrims' devotion. The first two, built when big sites were readily available, have courtyards that are exceptionally large by Jerusalem standards. They face one another across the Street of the Superintendent's Gate, an ancient street leading to this gate in the west wall of the Noble Sanctuary. North of the street the bedrock rises so that the northernmost gate in the west wall, the Ghawanima Gate, is reached by a passage cut in the rock. South of the street the

104 Street frontage of the Mansuri Hospice founded by Sultan Qalawun

ground falls away rapidly and the early gates into the Noble Sanctuary were either from low level with stairs rising to the Esplanade ("Warren's Gate" and "Barclay's Gate") or were reached by a street carried on a bridge as at the Chain Gate. The Iron Gate in the west wall is not an ancient gate, and it seems likely that it was opened to provide access to the narrow undeveloped site on which the hospice of Kurt was built at a level somewhat lower than that of the Noble Sanctuary, presumably on debris that had accumulated at the foot of the wall when Titus demolished the Temple enclosure in 70 CE. Additional hospices continued to be provided for pilgrims throughout the Mamluk period. The Haram documents include reference to no less than 17 hospices, although several are likely to be the same institutions but registered under slightly different names.

The North Border of the Noble Sanctuary

Three gates give access to the Noble Sanctuary from the north. Two of them were built in the Umayyad period and had multiple openings; the western gate had three and the middle gate two or three. Of the western one only the present Gate of Darkness (so called because the street leading to it is covered by a vault) [26] and of the middle one only the present Remission Gate [29] remain open. There was an area of ground outside these two gates at much the same level as the Esplanade of the Noble Sanctuary. It is likely that this site was occupied by earlier buildings such as the "places of prayer of the Sufis" mentioned by Nasir-i Khusraw, or the family mausoleum of the Ikhshidids, or two houses endowed in favour of pilgrims from Diyarbekir according to an inscription found at Remission Gate. The site is now occupied by two adjoining Mamluk buildings, the Dawadariyya (endowed in 1295) and the Awhadiyya (endowed in 1298).

The Dawadariyya Convent [41; fig. 105] was founded by the amir Sanjar al-Dawadari, who had been responsible in 1291 for organising the siege artillery and for dismantling the fortifications of Acre following the capture of the last Frankish stronghold in the Holy Land. According to a long and detailed foundation inscription below the magnificent stalactite vault of the entrance portal, the convent was endowed

> … in favour of 30 persons from the community of Sufis and novices, Arab and non-Arab, of whom 20 shall be unmarried and 10 married, to dwell there without leaving, not in summer, winter, spring, nor autumn, except on specific business; and to give hospitality to those Sufis and novices who visit [and who can stay] for [up to] 10 days.…

The inscription goes on to list the endowments made in favour of the foundation and

> … for a sheikh to give instruction in Prophetic tradition and a Koran teacher with whom the Koran will be studied, and for 10 persons to study the Traditions, and for 10 persons to recite the Book of God (i.e., the Koran) in full each day, and for a panegyrist to chant praises of the Prophet, all in the Aqsa Mosque.

The convent consists of residential cells around an open courtyard with a three-bay assembly hall in the south side; a north annex seems to belong to an earlier Frankish structure that was simply incorporated into the new foundation. The two eastern openings of the Umayyad triple gate were blocked by the construction of the convent leaving only a grilled window in each of the blocked openings.

The Awhadiyya Mausoleum [42] is the first of many Mamluk mausoleums at the border of the Noble Sanctuary. It stands immediately east of the Dawadariyya and was endowed by a Superintendent of the Two Sanctuaries of Jerusalem and Hebron, al-Malik

105 The entrance to the Dawadariyya (1295) built by the master builder 'Ali b. Salama

al-Awhad, grandson of the Ayyubid al-Mu'azzam 'Isa, in 1298. The tomb chamber, with a window opening on the street and another on the Noble Sanctuary, has a fine stone dome supported by pendentives of a particular Frankish type. Except for the dome at the Aqsa Mosque porch (see previous chapter), it is the only one of this type built after the period of Crusader rule in Jerusalem.

As in other towns, the founding of a funerary monument in the form of a tomb chamber along with a philanthropic institution, usually a college, became a regular occurrence in

Jerusalem. In the case of the Awhadiyya the tomb is combined with a small hospice, evidence of the continuing need to provide accommodation for pilgrims.

The first colleges in Jerusalem were founded before the Crusades. The first Mamluk one to be founded at the border of the Noble Sanctuary is the Karimiyya [54], endowed in 1318 by a high court official, Karim al-Din 'Abd al-Karim, a Copt who converted to Islam. It is perched opposite the Awhadiyya on the other side of the street. The propinquity of the street to the west and the Pool of the Children of Israel, a large open reservoir that was part of the city's elaborate water supply and storage system, to the east, has created an attenuated layout, and its selection implies that by this time more spacious sites had already been taken. In future more imaginative ways would be needed to build at the borders of the Noble Sanctuary.

One, used in the construction about this time of Sanjar al-Jawili's college [53], was to build it high on the rock scarp from where the Herodian tower Antonia had once dominated the Temple precinct. Sanjar was governor of the district of Gaza, which at that time included Jerusalem, as well as Superintendent of the Two Sanctuaries, and he would naturally have chosen a site in keeping with his status. Substantial remains of the solid south wall of Antonia blocked the view of the Noble Sanctuary, however, and the massive wall was cut away in places to allow new windows to be introduced. The ancient wall was also partly refaced with striped masonry (*ablaq*) to form a symmetrical façade [fig. 102].

The subsequent constructions at the north border included a college called the Aminiyya (1329–30) [59; fig. 106] where the exiguousness of the site, bounded by the eastern spur of the Antonia rock scarp to the west and the street to the east, forced the builders, following the precedent of the Tankiziyya at the west border (see below), to use the roof of the portico which allowed them to create a fine façade on the Noble Sanctuary. The absence of a decorated portal to mark the entrance from the street demonstrates the shift in emphasis from the street to the Noble Sanctuary frontage at this time.

The Sallamiyya College [45] was founded immediately to the north of the Dawadariyya around 1338 by al-Majd al-Sallami, probably having access to a team of royal builders (see below). He was the most important merchant of his day, who had acted as ambassador to the Mongol court and was instrumental in negotiating a peace treaty signed by the Mamluks and the Ilkhanids in 1323. Another merchant, from the town of Siirt in modern Turkey, built the Is'irdiyya College [82; fig. 107] at about the same time (before 1345) over an extension to the north portico he had built to support it, copying the solution first adopted at the neighbouring Almalikiyya College (1340) [67; fig. 107]. At this point in the north border there was once a *zawiya* called al-Lawi (of the Levite) and, perhaps by coincidence, some Hebrew inscriptions were found nearby. Building on the portico provided the opportunity to present a decorative façade on the Noble Sanctuary as had first been done at the Jawiliyya. The Almalikiyya College was followed at the north border by others, including the Subaybiyya (before 1406) [99], the Basitiyya (endowed in 1431) [101], and the Ghadiriyya (1432) [102; fig. 108]. A

106 Façade of the Aminiyya (1329–30) above the portico
The bay directly under the centre of the façade leads to the Gate of Darkness, also known as King Faysal Gate because it was
through this gate that King Faysal of Iraq entered the Noble Sanctuary during his visit in 1930

107 Façades of the Is'irdiyya College (before 1345) with the Almalikiyya (1340) on its right above the porticoes built specially to carry them

108 The Ghadiriyya College (1432) built into and over the north portico

further three colleges are known from historical sources to have stood on the north portico near the Pool of the Children of Israel, but they no longer survive: the Hasaniyya (ca. 1360), the Tuluniyya (before 1397), and the Fanariyya (before 1412).

The West Border of the Noble Sanctuary

If Sanjar al-Jawili demanded a prestigious location for his foundation, for Tankiz, viceroy of all Syria, only the best would do. Therefore, the foundation bearing his name, the Tankiziyya (1328–29) [**57**; fig. 95], had to be adjacent to the Noble Sanctuary, and preferably at a focal point of urban life. The site chosen, beside the principal and most-frequented gate, the Chain Gate, could hardly be better. Tankiz proposed a complex foundation, called simply "place" in its inscription, comprising a college and a Sufi convent, a school of Tradition, a school for orphans, residential accommodation including a small bathhouse presumably for the use of the residents, and shops beside the street to help pay for its upkeep, as well as a hospice for twelve pious and poor aged women on the opposite side of the street. The site was not large enough to accommodate all this on one level and so upper floors were added. The college, exquisitely decorated, occupies the ground floor and is the first in Jerusalem to adopt the four-*iwan* layout—four vaulted halls arranged in a cruciform pattern, each with one end opening on a central courtyard—then fashionable in Cairo. In the centre of its vaulted courtyard is a fountain supplied by the main aqueduct, restored by Tankiz in 1328. On the upper floors, a small mezzanine and a series of rooms including the bathhouse provided lodgings for the students of the college and the Sufis of the convent. For the convent itself Tankiz's architect had an inspiration that was to transform future development of the borders. He constructed the convent, including a three-bay assembly hall furnished with a decorative façade overlooking the Noble Sanctuary, on the roof of the west portico, which had been completed about 15 years earlier.

Tankiz, acting for Sultan al-Nasir Muhammad, was also instrumental in the construction in 1336–37 of a new commercial centre known as the Market of the Cotton Merchants [**62**]. Its revenues were to be divided partly for the upkeep of the Tankiziyya and partly for the maintenance of the Noble Sanctuary. It is an impressive complex including a covered market in the form of a street of shops, possibly incorporating an earlier shopping street, extending to the Noble Sanctuary where a magnificent new portal, the Cotton Merchants Gate [**61**; fig. 96], was erected, through which visitors are drawn down a flight of twenty steps into the complex. Besides the shopping street there were two bathhouses and a caravanserai and, at first-floor level above the shops, living quarters. The substantial difference in level (more than 4m) between the shopping street and the Noble Sanctuary and the posited presence of an earlier market street may explain why this part of the west border had not been developed earlier.

The only way to accommodate such variations in level without resorting to the expensive alternative of filling up the lower level to match the higher, was to build on both levels. This is what happened at the Khatuniyya College (endowed in 1354 and again in 1380) [87] immediately to the north of the Market of the Cotton Merchants, where the most important parts of the foundation—a tomb chamber, an assembly hall and two iwans—are at the higher level beside the Noble Sanctuary, while cells for habitation around the courtyard are at the lower level. In order to take advantage of the existing north wall of the Market of the Cotton Merchants, the college is set well back from the street leading to the Iron Gate, which gives access to it. Illuminated leaves of a beautiful Koran given in 1358 to the college by its founder, a lady from Baghdad called Ughul Khatun, are now in the collection of the Islamic Museum.

In the same year, 1358, the Arghuniyya College [74] was built on the site between the Khatuniyya and the street, comprising a tomb chamber—situated at the favoured location beside a Noble Sanctuary gate with a window opening on the street and one opening on the Noble Sanctuary—and a college on the ground floor and, on the upper floor, living quarters. Arghun was a former governor of Aleppo (where he built a well-known hospital) and of Damascus, who was put on the inactive list (battal) and retired to Jerusalem where he died in 1357 before his college was finished. The inscription over the entrance includes two cartouches containing the heraldic blazon of the Master of the Sultan's Robes, the office held by Arghun.

At this time, Jerusalem was becoming a favoured place of exile for high-ranking amirs who had fallen out of favour or had reached retirement on completion of service. One of them, the amir Taz al-Nasiri, chose to retire to Jerusalem, and an inscription refers to his mausoleum in what seems to have been his grand residence [79] in the Street of the Chain Gate, although most evidence points to his having been buried in Damascus where he died in 1362.

Another prominent amir, Manjak al-Yusufi, chose for his pious foundation [78; fig. 109] a site at the west border beside the Superintendent's Gate. Because at this time—around 1361—earlier buildings occupied the area next to the wall of the Noble Sanctuary, Manjak could not build at street level. Instead he erected his foundation partly on the roof of the portico, following the example of the Tankiziyya. To accommodate a college and living quarters required more than an unoccupied section of portico roof, however, and there was the consideration, too, of access to the roof. The building was therefore extended westwards into pre-Mamluk structures and upwards over earlier Mamluk structures, thus accommodating both stairs and an entrance portal. Included within the foundation is an elaborately decorated domed loggia designed to take advantage of the magnificent view of the Noble Sanctuary through a handsome double-arched window. It is likely that the rooms over the portico were intended as private living quarters for Manjak, who had

109 Façade of the Manjakiyya (ca. 1361) with the double window of its domed loggia
overlooking the Noble Sanctuary

chosen to spend his retirement in Jerusalem and, if so, he was the first to make use of the
area over the portico—with its fine outlook—for private, non-religious purposes.

The site of the Baladiyya College (before 1380) [**86**] next to the Chain Gate between
the bridge over Wilson's Arch to the south and the ablutions place to the north lies some
5m below the level of the Noble Sanctuary. A massive cruciform substructure was required

to support the four-*iwan* college at the level of the Noble Sanctuary, the high cost of which might explain why this site was not occupied sooner. The costs involved seem to have drained the resources of the founder, Manklibugha al-Ahmadi, governor of Aleppo, for it is the only major Mamluk institution at the border to have neither a monumental entrance portal nor an elaborate façade. The layout is conventional except for its central courtyard being open to the sky. This is the only example of a four-*iwan* college with an open courtyard in Jerusalem, since the cold and often rainy winter weather demands a roof. The absence of one may be explained by the size of the courtyard, approximately 13m square, which was too large to vault.

Following the intensive building activity that transformed the north and west borders of the Noble Sanctuary, there were few sites left for future development. Nevertheless, the sacred and historical importance of the place remained a powerful attraction, and sites at the borders continued to be sought.

Much of the roof of the west portico between the Tankiziyya to the south and the Manjakiyya to the north remained empty. The problem of building on this roof was, as it had been at the north border, one of access, for most of the land adjoining the Noble Sanctuary wall was already built up. A site immediately south of the Ablutions Gate was available, but it had two obvious disadvantages. First, it overlooked the public latrines to the west and second, it was more than 2m below the level of the Esplanade and so required a substantial substructure to raise the level. Notwithstanding these drawbacks, it was the best site still available, and on it the 'Uthmaniyya College [**105**; fig. 110] was erected in 1437 for a lady from Anatolia called Isfahan Shah al-'Uthmaniyya. Her college includes a tomb chamber where she lies buried next to the Noble Sanctuary beside the Ablutions Gate. Her foundation included a series of imposing rooms on the roof of the portico, including a loggia with a wonderful view of the Dome of the Rock.

The architect of the Jawhariyya College (1440) [**106**] found a novel solution to the problem of gaining access to the roof of the portico. On the north side of the Street of the Iron Gate, the college is on two floors separated from the Noble Sanctuary by the hospice of Kurt al-Mansuri. By extending the upper floor of the college over the roof of the single-storey hospice, it was possible to achieve contact with the Noble Sanctuary wall where an assembly hall and loggia were added on the portico roof, though they no longer survive.

The last three buildings at the west border, the Zamani Hospice (1476–77) [**109**], the Muzhiriyya College (1480–81) [**110**] and the Ashrafiyya College (1482) [**111**; fig. 97] are all built in a distinctive style developed in Cairo using angular cells in the stalactite corbelling (*muqarnas*) rather than the curvilinear types commonly used in Syria.

The Zamani Hospice occupies a tiny site immediately south of the Cotton Merchants Gate opposite the 'Uthmaniyya. The Muzhiriyya College on the Street of the Iron Gate is separated from the Noble Sanctuary by the intervening Arghuniyya College but,

110 Façade of the 'Uthmaniyya College (1437) with the double window of its domed loggia overlooking the Noble Sanctuary (dome removed in the late nineteenth century)

undeterred, the builders erected an assembly hall on the roof of the portico, which the students could reach simply by walking across the flat roof of the Arghuniyya.

Finally, the Ashrafiyya College was begun by Sultan al-Ashraf Khushqadam around 1465 but left unfinished when he died in 1467. The work was being overseen by the Superintendent of the Two Sanctuaries who, on the accession of al-Ashraf Qa'itbay, travelled to Cairo to persuade the Sultan to complete the construction. An inscription in the west portico records Qa'itbay's ordering the new building work in 1470. However, when in 1475, seventeen years into his long reign, the sultan visited Jerusalem and saw the college he had inherited and endowed, "he did not like it," according to Mujir al-Din who added that "it was built after the fashion of Jerusalem colleges, which are not up to much." Qa'itbay consequently determined to have it demolished and rebuilt on a grander scale. Years passed with nothing happening until Qa'itbay dispatched in 1479–80 an officer from his court to oversee the demolition and start the reconstruction. The digging of foundations began on 19 October 1480 and in the following year the sultan sent a team of builders, engineers, and stonemasons, led by a Coptic architect. The resulting building, completed in August 1482, the "third jewel" of the Noble Sanctuary according to Mujir al-Din, projects beyond the line of the portico into the enclosure: the only one to do so. The living accommodation for staff and students was at first-floor level above the Baladiyya College. The main feature was a central court with *iwans* opening on three sides, all covered by gilded ceilings and a lead-clad timber roof (the only timber roof outside the Dome of the Rock and the Aqsa Mosque at the time). On the fourth, east, side of the court was a three-bay loggia with windows of "Frankish glass" overlooking the Dome of the Rock. Mujir al-Din wrote a long description of the building, and its endowment deed has survived, which means that we know more about this college than any other in Jerusalem (and practically anywhere else, for that matter). Sadly, it was damaged by earthquake in the sixteenth century and, though it remained in use, its timber roof decayed and the upper floor fell into ruin. Little of the upper part of the façade survives, but enough is known to allow convincing reconstruction. During repairs made in the 1990s substantial sections were exposed of the beautiful pavement of inlaid marble and polished limestone described by eyewitnesses to the construction, Felix Faber and Mujir al-Din.

Christel Kessler has suggested that, having completed their work on the Ashrafiyya and leaving the marble workers to take over, the team of skilled builders led by the Coptic architect was to give a similar makeover to a small free-standing fountain built by Sultan Inal on the Esplanade near the Ashrafiyya, now known as Sabil Qa'itbay [**112**; fig. 98]. Despite some late-Ottoman remodelling, it retains its Egyptian sculptured stone dome, the only one outside Cairo and a fitting climax to two-and-a-half centuries of Mamluk construction activity in Jerusalem.

Conclusion

Pious institutions in the Mamluk period were founded by wealthy individuals who had the means to acquire sites close to the Noble Sanctuary: sultans, ladies of rank, provincial governors including several in voluntary or enforced retirement in Jerusalem, Superintendents of the Two Sanctuaries, merchants, religious scholars, and at least one eunuch.

The materials were by and large the same as in earlier periods: the excellent local cream-coloured limestone bound with lime mortar. Internal walls were usually plastered, sometimes with incised decoration in the plaster.

Crusader columns remained available for re-use: the Ghawanima minaret contains no fewer than 31, for example, and the Awhadiyya contains six. Such quantities were exceptional, however, and few other building have more than two or three, usually placed on either side of the prayer niche or to support the springing of an arch. The marble used in the most lavish foundations for wall panelling and pavements must also have been cut from salvaged Crusader material, for there are no marble quarries in Palestine and none seems to have been imported in the Ayyubid and Mamluk periods.

The early Mamluk buildings tend to be rather austere in the Crusader/Ayyubid tradition with little in the way of decoration apart from more or less imposing entrances and a number of foundation inscriptions. Later, buildings incorporated increasingly intricate decorative elements. Thus, while the royal hospice founded by Qalawun displays little of the grandeur of his huge funerary complex in Cairo, it is the first instance in Jerusalem of striped masonry (*ablaq*), courses of cream limestone alternating with stone of a different colour, commonly red but also yellow and black. The red "Palestinian marble" is still quarried near Bethlehem, and the yellow variety favoured towards the end of the fifteenth century was quarried at Dayr Yassin, 5km west of the city. The black stone that was used in small quantities is a bituminous limestone known as "Moses stone (*hajar Musa*)," which came from the Dead Sea region near the shrine of Moses about 30km east of Jerusalem. Stones of alternating colour (*ablaq*) were also used for decorative effect in the construction of arches and other features. Initially the arch stones or voussoirs were wedge-shaped in the usual fashion but increasingly the voussoirs of arches and string courses were interlocked in a fanciful system of indented or fretwork joggles to produce a counterchange effect and, at the entrance to the Dawadariyya, joggling in the soffit as well as the face which, with the contrasting *ablaq* stone colours heightens the dramatic effect. This is among the most elaborate stonework of any age [fig. 105].

Timber was in short supply and its use was usually restricted to doors and window shutters, though a cenotaph dated 1402 in the tomb chamber of the 'Uthmaniyya is made of beautifully inscribed and carved wood. Doors were often plated with sheets of iron held

111 Iron grille at the tomb chamber in the Is'irdiyya College (before 1345)

in place with large nails. Window openings at lower floor levels were protected by iron grilles and, in the altogether exceptional Ashrafiyya, fitted with glass.

The similar appearance of Qalawun's hospices in Jerusalem and in Hebron (the latter no longer extant but known from an inscription dated 1280 and from photographs) suggests that they were built by the same construction team and, to judge by corbel table cornices in Jerusalem and Hebron reminiscent of Frankish and Ayyubid details elsewhere in Jerusalem, this team was locally based. It is probable that local tradesmen were responsible for most of the plain arched monumental door recesses and for general construction work, but for particularly important buildings specialists were brought in, as we have seen at the Ashrafiyya.

Architects and craftsmen are not as a rule named in the historical literature. Occasionally, however, "signatures" are found of the craftsman or atelier responsible for the work. The foundation inscription of the Dawadariyya, for example, bears the inscribed signature of the master builder, 'Ali b. Salama, and names the clerk of the works, Sanjar al-Qaymari. The entrance portal, with its suspended impost seeming to defy structural logic, belongs to a sequence developed first in Damascus at the Nuriyya College (1172) followed by the 'Adiliyya College (1222–23) and the Qilijiyya College (1253–54), and also used at the Ayyubid palace of the 'Ajami family in Aleppo.

A very fine iron grille [fig. 111] in the tomb chamber in the Is'irdiyya is signed by the metalworker Muhammad b. al-Zayn 'Ali and must have been made in his workshop.

Travelling workshops certainly existed. The entrance portal of the Tankiziyya is very similar to those at Tankiz's mosque in Damascus, where he resided as viceroy, and it is probable that the builders responsible for it were sent from there to Jerusalem at Tankiz's request. We know also that the glass mosaic conch of the prayer niche in his Jerusalem foundation was done by specialists from Damascus, and the marble panelling in the same building is undoubtedly the work of specialists who made panelling for the Aqsa Mosque and the sanctuary in Hebron at much the same time.

Another signature, on a stalactite cupola in the Market of the Cotton Merchants, is of Muhammad b. Ghulaysh. The same signature, with the addition of "al-Shami" (signifying that he originally came from Syria), is inscribed in the grand entrance doorway of the Palace of Qawsun in Cairo, built around 1337. The doorway of this palace belongs to a group of four built in the fourth decade of the fourteenth century in Cairo, which bear a striking resemblance to each other. Of these, the Mosque of Bashtak (1336) in particular is similar in its vaulting to that of the entrance to the Sallamiyya in Jerusalem. All were built for prominent members of the Mamluk administration in the reign of al-Nasir Muhammad, who is known to have made contributions to the building activities of his senior amirs. These contributions ranged from supplying building materials to providing skilled workmen. As a mark of special favour the sultan might authorise master craftsmen attached to the court to work for his amirs. In the case of al-Majd al-Sallami, it seems likely that the sultan allowed Muhammad b. Ghulaysh al-Shami, who was working in Jerusalem on the Market of the Cotton Merchants at the time, to be deployed on his long-serving ambassador's new foundation.

1516–1917: *Haram-i-Şerif* – The Temple Mount under Ottoman Rule

Amnon Cohen
The Hebrew University of Jerusalem

The poor state of the dilapidated walls surrounding Jerusalem in the late Mamluk period indicates a low rate of importance in the order of priorities of that Muslim Sultanate. This was not just an outward appearance; rather it had a direct, accumulated effect on life in the town as a whole. Major market places (e.g., Khan al-Sultan, on the main street leading to Bab al-Silsila) looked like deserted sites and were hardly functioning, while the town's entire population reached the humble figure of 5000. The general situation in Palestine and in greater Syria was no better, making these provinces easy prey for the advancing Ottoman army. In this context Jerusalem had neither any meaningful economic appeal for the Ottomans, nor should its conquest be ascribed to particular religious zeal. It should rather be seen as part of an overall strategic scheme of uprooting the rival Sultanate of Cairo and replacing it by the new, emerging Muslim potentate—the Ottoman sultan. Palestine, situated on the Ottoman route of advance to Cairo, was a potential stumbling block, hence its inevitable, and almost uneventful, takeover in late 1516.[1]

Once they became masters of the Arabic-speaking provinces of the eastern Mediterranean, the Ottomans started transforming the entire scene. The first half of the sixteenth century witnessed major changes in Palestine, as it did in the neighboring regions, changes that were highlighted in Jerusalem. An a priori condition was the re-introduction of law and order into this town, administratively upgraded when it became the center of a newly created district (*sancak*) bearing its name. The seat of a *vali*, it could benefit from the permanent presence of a military garrison (Janissaries, cavalry, and artillery personnel) stationed in its citadel.[2] Cavalry officers, *sipahis*, who were supposed to reside in their respective rural leases within the *hinterland* of Jerusalem, preferred, from a relatively early stage, to live in town, thus increasing its military importance.

112 Gustav Bauernfeind, "At the Entrance to the Temple Mount," 1886
The Arabic inscription on the wooden gate at the left reads: "Enter it [=the Haram al-Sharif] in peace, with God's permission."

Reconstructing the Walls of Jerusalem and Other Projects

Of even greater military (and symbolic) significance was the decision taken in Istanbul to launch a major project there: the reconstruction of the walls of Jerusalem. Taking the existing fortifications as a basic architectural layout, specific arrangements were made to ensure effective implementation of the scheme. A high-ranking official (Muhammad Çelebi al-Naqqash) was sent in the late 1530s from Istanbul, expert builders were enlisted in other Syrian towns and dispatched to Jerusalem, and—most importantly—an adequate budget was allocated for the several years it would take for the completion of this project.

The importance of the official entrusted with this project may be gleaned from the honorific titles preceding his name in the Jerusalem court proceedings (*mawlana mafkhar al-akabir wa'l-amathil wa'l-amajid*—"our master the most glorious of the very great and the most eminent and the most illustrious"). His surname Naqqash, meaning in Ottoman times "an artist who embellishes surfaces" or "a wall-decorator,"[3] may be taken as an allusion to the nature of this major construction project, most probably indicating his family's involvement in building activities in earlier generations and other, different, places. His actual role, however, had hardly any artistic dimension, since his responsibility was first and foremost an administrative-fiscal one. His official title was "the superintendent for the collection of the taxes due to the sultan" (*al-amin ' ala' l-amwal al-sultaniyya*, also: *al-nazir*), and his name comes up in the Jerusalem court proceedings in several cases of tax collection, as of the middle of the 1530s.[4] Towards the end of 1536 his title changes abruptly, and he becomes "the superintendent of the wall" (*al-amin 'ala'l-sur*).[5] From then onwards, his name is followed by either of these two titles, or by both.[6] This combination seems quite natural, since the construction of the Jerusalem walls involved exorbitant expenses which could easily be funneled through this high-ranking tax collector.

Independently of this particular project, Muhammad Çelebi was also put in charge of the financial arrangements involving other schemes carried out in and around the town in the 1530s and 1540s: when the Franciscan monks of the Mount Zion monastery were apprehended by the local authorities in 1538, he was entrusted with the money seized from them; the following year he forwarded a substantial amount of money for the upkeep of the Janissary units stationed in the Citadel.[7] In 1540–41 he attended a public meeting on the Temple Mount, where he reported on another project he had just completed, that of supplying Jerusalem with fresh, running water through the repaired aqueduct running from Solomon's Pools, south of Bethlehem.[8] All of these indicate a high degree of public activities and, under different headings, they fall into the general pattern of providing Jerusalem and its inhabitants with better and safer standards of living. By the same token, only in a much more meaningful manner and on a much larger scale, al-Naqqash undertook his major assignment, that of building the walls of Jerusalem.

Scattered references in the court proceedings of Jerusalem, as well as one detailed document recorded therein, provide us with meaningful data concerning the budgeting of this project. In the course of the two years that preceded the actual building of the walls, between 1536 and 1538, large sums of money collected as regular taxes in various parts of Palestine and Syria were diverted to Jerusalem for this particular project. The total sum recorded for those two years that preceded actual construction was about 800,000 *para*, and it was made up of two major entries: 60 percent were sent from Damascus, the capital of the *eyalet*, and the other 40 percent came from the different *sancak*s of Palestine. Comparing the specific entries of taxes transferred from their regular goal to the budget of these fortifications one may largely conclude that a high percentage, perhaps most, of the fiscal income due from Palestine was earmarked, during the four to five years of construction, for the financing of this project. However, since much larger sums of money were needed for this ambitious plan, the provincial fiscus of Damascus was instructed by Istanbul to shoulder (with the active participation of the central authorities) the additional costs, hence it sent a military unit to escort the actual contribution, in gold coins, all the way to Jerusalem. In other words, the immediate neighboring districts, as well as the central and provincial administrations, became deeply involved in the fulfillment of this scheme.[9]

The actual building of the walls stretched over more than four consecutive years, 1538–1541, as one may easily ascertain from the inscriptions over the gates surrounding the town. These were summed up by Max Van Berchem, more than eighty years ago, as follows:

> In 944 the northern and northwestern walls, the most exposed ones, are built, since they are dominated by their immediate approaching grounds. The following year the eastern wall is erected, from the northeastern angle up to Saint-Stephen's Gate, maybe even beyond it, and parallel with this the western wall [is built] up to the Citadel. The following year, which is not indicated by any specific date, must have undoubtedly seen the completion of these two sides; finally, the year 947 is devoted to repairs of the southern wall.[10]

However, more recent findings indicate that architectural information may sometimes prove to be not as fully reliable as one might otherwise surmise. Reading through the proceedings of the Jerusalem court,[11] one comes across evidence to the effect that a fifth year should be added to the actual timetable of the building process of this project. At least as late as the end of Ramadan 948, i.e., January 1542, this project was referred to as barely finished. Complaints had allegedly been made by one of the expert builders employed on the project, *al-mu'allim* Darwish from Aleppo, to the chief financial authority in Damascus (*al-daftardar bi'l-mamalik al-sharifa al-islamiya*—"the Treasurer of the Sublime Islamic territories"), claiming negligence displayed by Muhammad al-Naqqash in the allegedly

113 Fountain of the Gate of the Chain (*Sabil Bab al-Silsila*)
Constructed by Sultan Sulayman I in 1537. The rosette in the tympanum and the spandrels are Frankish, in secondary use

sloppy and slow conduct of his work. This negligence, as alleged by the reports arriving from Damascus, was the direct responsibility of al-Naqqash, since he had at his disposal all the necessary elements for the proper fulfillment of his task, including a sufficient number of "expert builders, porters, and workers." In a public hearing convened at the Jerusalem court and attended by a large audience of religious dignitaries, the above-mentioned Darwish took a diametrically opposed position. According to his oral testimony delivered there, he denied having ever complained to Damascus and praised al-Naqqash for the efficient and highly professional manner in which he executed this project "day and night," up until its completion at the time of the court session. Which of the two versions was the correct one is beyond the scope of our present interest, but the entire episode confirms that actual construction extended over an additional year to the period suggested by Van Berchem, and that it involved experts from other major towns of Syria and Egypt—all of this under the direct responsibility (both professional and financial) of al-Naqqash. Final touches were added in the following years, for example in January 1557 when special orders, together with an appropriate budget, arrived from Istanbul for furthering the fortification of Jerusalem by digging a moat around certain parts of the walls as well as supplementing them by more fortifications on the neighboring Mount of Olives.[12]

As a result of all these activities, the local population could enjoy the security the walls provided from the early 1550s onwards. This was not just a passing mood: the Ottoman census system recorded a clear and steady trend of demographic growth during the following years,[13] which was undoubtedly an outcome of the sense of security inspired by this, as well as by related Ottoman policies. The steadily growing population of Jerusalem meant increasing recourse to the various services this town could offer its inhabitants: improved economic facilities such as marketplaces,[14] reduced taxation on imported goods thereto,[15] government support for the production of local commodities aimed at local consumption as well as export (e.g., olive oil and its derivatives, such as soap),[16] provision of free daily meals to the poor of Jerusalem by the newly endowed and constructed soup-kitchen of Khasseki Sultan,[17] and an increased water supply for regular usage, as well as for sanitary and ritual purposes.[18] The latter, i.e., water supply for ritual purposes, was predominantly related to the Temple Mount and the mandatory ablution prior to each of the five daily prayers. No wonder, therefore, that in order to provide the Believers with the appropriate means to perform this regular religious duty, an entire set of public water fountains (*sebil*) was constructed in and around the Temple Mount Esplanade in 1536–37.[19]

All these, and similar acts of the new Ottoman administration, were not local manifestations of steps taken in other parts of Palestine, but rather a particular policy applied in Jerusalem only. However, Jerusalem was neither regarded as capital of the country nor did it have any particular administrative role or status: it was the head-town, the district center, of a *sancak* bearing the same name, just like other central towns in

Palestine (Safed, Nablus, Gaza). The different projects carried out within its precinct stemmed from one major consideration: its historic religious importance. In early Islamic days it was the first direction of prayer prescribed by the Prophet, and the third holy place after Mecca and Medina (*ula'l-qiblatayn wa-thalith al-haramayn*). This change from "first" to "third" is indicative of a general trend undergone by the status of Jerusalem in the course of later years of Muslim rule: although no attempt was made to reduce its historical and religious importance, politically and otherwise it lost much of its former grandeur. Under the Mamluks, for example, the breakdown of Palestine into two administrative units —*niyaba*—highlighted Safed and Gaza, rather than Jerusalem. True, different Mamluk rulers, although residing in Cairo, chose to commemorate themselves by having impressive *madrasa*s bearing their respective names built in and around the Temple Mount. However, the general state of the town and its inhabitants appears to have been of little concern to them. The arrival of the Ottomans brought about, as we saw above, a variety of changes in the relative importance of this town. All of these were undertaken with one specific intention in mind: raising the relevance of Jerusalem in the eyes of the local population and augmenting its importance in Palestine as well as among the neigboring provinces. The Temple Mount was one of the major means towards achieving this goal: improving its physical condition would enhance the actual relevance of the town for its inhabitants, as well as for the increasing number of pilgrims who would come to pray there.

Improvements on the Temple Mount

Variegated projects were initiated by Istanbul for the Temple Mount. An annual donation (*surre*—"a purse, or bag of money") was regularly sent from Istanbul, to be distributed as salaries (*waza'if*) for the religious functionaries of the Haram and its shrines. Among the recipients of this annual charity were also people whose role was ritual rather than functional: *mujawirin* students of the Holy Law, public readers of sections of the Qur'an, and those who were supposed to recite prayers to the Almighty for the well-being and success of the Ottoman sultan and his dominions. Structural improvements were made in the walls and roofs of both al-Aqsa Mosque and the Dome of the Rock, which were renovated and restored by applying new faïence and lead tiles to their outer walls and roofs, respectively.[20]

Unfortunately, very little of this was recorded in the usually most informative and helpful proceedings of the Shar'i court, hence, when seeking evidence one should turn to other sources. It appears that the major project there was undertaken between 1545–52, when parts of the Dome of the Rock were restored, both on the interior and the exterior of the dome itself. Persian craftsmen, as one gathers from their signatures on the tiles, produced and installed them during these seven years.[21] Inscriptions found above

114 Fountain of the Gate of the Superintendent (*Sabil Bab al-Nazir*)
Constructed by Sultan Sulayman I in 1537. The arches as well as their sculpted elements are Frankish, in secondary use

the northern entrance of the Dome of the Rock (registering the renovation of the dome itself in 1552), as well as above its western entrance (referring to additional renovations carried out in 1565) provide more information. The overall impression one gathers is that building activities on the Temple Mount continued throughout the entire rule of Suleiman the Magnificent.[22] All of the above were positive steps taken to improve the physical conditions on the Temple Mount area. There were also certain negative steps initiated, targeting the Jewish (and most probably the Christian) population of Jerusalem. Special regulations were issued, proclaiming a general prohibition of entry of non-Muslims

115 The Dome and Prayer Niche of the Prophet (*Qubbat wa-mihrab al-Nabi*), with the Dome of the Rock in the background. The walled prayer niche dates from 1538–39; the dome was restored in 1620

116 The Dome of Joseph (*Qubbat Yusuf*)
The dome was built in 1681 by Yusuf Agha, possibly a governor of Jerusalem

into the Temple Mount area and threatening potential intruders with severe punishment. Although, generally speaking, the Jews of Jerusalem heeded this policy and limited their rituals to the external periphery of the compound, i.e., the Wailing [or: Western] Wall, several cases recorded by the Shar'i court indicate repeated attempts to circumvent it. In the early 1550s, for example, a substantial group (six Jewish men and six women) climbed in broad daylight onto the roof of the Ottoman college (*al-madrasa al-'uthmaniyya*) [see fig. 110], then on the colonnade bordering the western side of the Temple Mount (*riwaq al-masjid al-aqsa*). When brought before the *qadi* they claimed to have done so upon a permit granted by the Mufti of Jerusalem. The latter denied this allegation in court, whereupon each of the male transgressors was dealt an "exemplary punishment" (*ta'zir mithli*) of flagellation.[23]

All of these steps notwithstanding, they did not bring about the peaceful atmosphere and conditions sought. Around the middle of the sixteenth century a renewed look was taken by Istanbul at the way things were actually happening on the Temple Mount, and upon request, a detailed report was submitted by the commanding officer (*dizdar*) of the citadel of Jerusalem. It provided the following description:

On Fridays, as well as on Lord's days and other festive occasions, the Temple

117 Fountain (*Sabil*) of Mustafa Agha
Founded in 1740–41 by Mustafa Agha, governor of Jerusalem. The Arabic inscription announces that
the fountain's water "is similar to that of Paradise, it is sweet, it is a cure, it deserves to be drunk"[24]

Mount is visited by large crowds of Believers, men and women alike. The mingling together of both sexes creates a licentious atmosphere that generates "all kinds of reprehensible acts [*munkarat*]." Moreover, a variety of building materials, left over from the different repairs and renovation projects carried out there, add an element of filthiness and squalor to this place which should have been kept immaculately clean and tidy. It seems that neither the dispatch of repeated orders from Istanbul and Damascus, nor the insistence by the local authorities on the need to pay proper attention to, and preservation of, proper conditions among the Believers on this highly revered site would rectify this situation. In order to systematically bring an end to this shameful situation, permanent military presence should be introduced there. A well-trained and accomplished soldier, a member of the garrison stationed at the citadel of Jerusalem, whose name is provided, was therefore put in charge of imposing law and order on the Temple Mount. This would not be just an impromptu measure: a new institution was thus created—that of an official "guard" [*yasaqji*] to be permanently stationed on the Temple Mount. To assure its permanent nature, a special budget was allocated for this particular project. Although this soldier will no longer be subject to the duties of other Janissary members of his military unit, he will be entitled to the same daily salary he has been collecting so far. A special document of appointment [*berat*] to this effect was issued in Istanbul, and it was seconded by a financial note [*tezkere*] provided by the *defterdar* of Aleppo.[25]

The patterns laid during the first decades of Ottoman rule were followed in the course of the following 300 years. We shall examine these in three different contexts: personnel, *surre*, repairs and renovations.

Personnel

The rationale for maintaining an ongoing presence of security staff on the Temple Mount did not change with the passing of time. The diminishing standards of the Janissary soldiers of the Empire during the seventeenth and eighteenth centuries could not have skipped Jerusalem, and the growing involvement of members of the local garrison in regular economic activities and social links with the local population further reduced their motivation and ability to enforce law and order. The *yasaqji* stationed there (now apparently upgraded and referred to as an "officer"—*dabit*) may have continued to collect his salary as well as receive his instructions as before, but his presence there was hardly felt. Early in the nineteenth century, when the Governor of Damascus visited Jerusalem, he discovered great discrepancies between the regrettable daily reality and the praiseworthy norms introduced some two hundred years earlier. People were entering the compound while totally disregarding the prohibition of wearing their footwear (*ni'al, qibqab*) therein, and no one was posted at the gates to stop this reprehensible behavior. The Jibali[26] public sweepers (*kannasin*), on the other hand, were not implementing their daily, unremitting responsibility of keeping that entire compound area clean. Likewise, other members of the Temple Mount staff were systematically collecting their salaries while neglecting their duties: preachers (*khatib*), prayer leaders (*imam*), teachers (*mudarris*), attendants of lamps (*sha'al*), spreaders of carpets (*farrash*), gardeners, general attendants (*khadim*) of the Dome of the Rock and the Temple Mount, "and others." This culpable behavior should immediately be discontinued, wrote the *vali* to the local governor and the religious dignitaries in Jerusalem, and whoever fails in systematically fulfilling their duties should immediately be replaced. Special attention should be paid to the presence of women on the Temple Mount: it should be limited to hours of prayer, and for praying purposes only. Dogs should be totally barred from entering the entire complex. As for the entrances of al-Aqsa Mosque and the Dome of the Rock, ten special armed doorkeepers (*anfar bawwabin*) should be appointed thereto, with a monthly salary of 2.5 *ghirsh asadi* each, to be allocated from Damascus, as well as a daily bowl of soup (*çorba*) and 4 *'uqqa*s of bread that each of them will be served from the Khasseki Sultan soup-kitchen.[27]

These new appointments and renewed regulations were not an isolated event. In the following years (1813, 1816, 1820, and 1830) special orders of a similar nature, with a few modifications, were sent by the Governor of Damascus to Jerusalem (four doorkeepers—rather than the former ten—to the four "gates of the Haram"; two new sweepers who will collect their salaries, like the doorkeepers, from Damascus, hence they will be answerable to the provincial governor rather than the local authorities; mandatory introduction of long benches at the inner side of all the entrances to the Haram aimed, undoubtedly, at facilitating the act of mandatory removal of the shoes of the worshippers).[28] These repeated orders (to be applied invariably "to rich people as well as to [poor] students"), issued at such a steady pace during the early nineteenth century, indicate an increasing relevance of the Temple Mount, perhaps as a result of a growing awareness in Istanbul, but more likely because it was visited by an increasing number of worshippers due to the constant growth of the population of Jerusalem.[29]

At this point, reference to the dereliction of duties by the staff, just reported, is called for. This negligence may be related to the general decline of the Ottoman administration touched upon above. However, these functionaries were devout local people who should have shared both a conviction and an interest in properly preserving the serene, revered atmosphere of ongoing reciting of prayers and other rituals on the Temple Mount. Moreover, they were supposed to be remunerated for the fulfillment of their duties. This brings us back to the "purse" (*surre*) of money sent annually from Istanbul, as early as the sixteenth century.

Surre

Reading through the court proceedings of the following years, one finds out that these stipends were regularly distributed in Jerusalem up until the nineteenth century. Their value, quoted in gold coins, tended to be less affected by the constant devaluation of the Ottoman currency. There were, however, two major flaws in the intrinsic connection between duty and remuneration. First, scattered cases reported in the *sijill* show that this specific budget item was regarded by the local families as a "given" asset, as their own, to be inherited—like any other piece of property—by their descendants after their death, according to the prescriptions of the Shari'a. This means that second-generation members of the family kept receiving these regular payments although many of them—minors or women[30] in particular, but not exclusively—could not provide the service for which they were remunerated (e.g., reciting parts of the Qur'an in public). But even when entitled to collect these allocations for services actually rendered (e.g., a *khadim* attendant at al-Aqsa Mosque), there was no inevitable connection of cause and effect maintained. These stipends, once again, were regarded by the grantees as pieces of property, hence they could be sold—i.e., legally disposed of—to the highest bidder.[31]

A case in point is that of Suleiman b. Muhammad Qutayna, a member of a respectable family in Jerusalem in the late eighteenth and early nineteenth centuries. Suleiman was a respectable merchant, referred to as 'umdat al-sada wa'l-tujjar ("the support of the descendants of the Prophet and of the merchants"), also 'ayn al-tujjar ("the most eminent merchant"), and from an endowment he established in 1810 one may gather the extent of his properties: these included several buildings (or parts thereof) in various neighborhoods of Jerusalem, several vegetable gardens, an oil-press, an oven, and a weaving workshop. Half of the annual proceeds of this endowment he committed to the gardener of the Temple Mount grounds, the other half to people who would recite Qur'an verses at al-Aqsa Mosque every night.[32] This pious act is hardly surprising if we bear in mind that a large part of his belongings had been incrementally purchased by him from different religious functionaries of the Haram during his lifetime. The procedure he followed emerges clearly from the many cases recorded: he would pay the religious functionary, or his heirs, a lump-sum, usually amounting to about ten times their annual expected income from the surre, and in return the other party declared to the court the forfeiture of their right to that particular income. The qadi's approval would then pronounce the deal formally binding, just like any other real-estate transaction.[33]

In other words, this routine, while granting the buyer full ownership of that particular part of the "purse," severed the link between the religious service and the functionary who was supposed to conduct it. From the perspective that is the focus of our attention, that of the Temple Mount, there was no incentive left for the grantee to attend any more to that part of the religious service for which this annuity had originally been allocated. Little doubt, therefore, that the above "dereliction of duty" became a widespread phenomenon. One may add that in several cases where the economic status of these functionaries could be established, they were quite well-off people who owned a variety of real-estate properties in town, and the lack of these annuities did not seem to have had a meaningful effect, neither on their life nor on their social status.[34] The accumulated effect, however, of all of these transactions on conditions on the compound of the Temple Mount, was devastating.

Repairs and Renovations

Last but not least is the actual state of the buildings themselves. Once a full survey of the proceedings of the Jerusalem Shar'i court is undertaken, detailed information is bound to emerge. In the meantime, relying on St Laurent's summary of several available archival documents from Istanbul and Jerusalem we concur with her general conclusion: "Beginning in 1705, and continuing until 1780, there were at least four major restorations to the Dome of the Rock and al-Aqsa Mosque."[35] Very little is known about the seventeenth-

118 The Temple Mount / al-Haram al-Sharif, based on a plan drawn by Charles W. Wilson, 1864–65

119 A nineteenth-century "aerial view" of the Dome of the Rock and the Aqsa Mosque
Conrad Schick's model (scale 1:200) of the Haram al-Sharif, prepared for the Vienna World Fair of 1873;
now at St Chrischona near Basel

century restorations, and a few references are available with regard to the late-nineteenth century (mainly 1874–75) repairs. Aref al-Aref refers briefly to renovations conducted in the second half of the nineteenth century at al-Aqsa Mosque and the Dome of the Rock: important repairs done in 1853 by an Armenian architect sent from Istanbul together with his fellow Armenian expert builders who attended mainly to the dome itself, as well as to various inscriptions and decorations in both buildings. Aref also mentions later repairs done in the mid-1870s, and he briefly touches upon marble renovations in 1818.[36]

This last episode deserves greater attention, since this was actually part of the most significant repairs done on the Temple mount in the early nineteenth century. As a prelude to the actual buildings repairs, special attention was paid in Istanbul to the water supply system of the Temple Mount. After a certain period of preparatory research and investigations, we hear (31 March 1812) of a detailed plan of repairs to the aqueduct bringing water from Solomon's Pools to the Temple Mount. A special budget, says the document, has been allocated for this particular project from the endowment of the Dome of the Rock, out of which the assigned builders were promised 4 *asadi ghirsh* a day, so that they may start their work right away. Two months later (29 May 1812), a *firman* cites written reports, describing the poor state of al-Aqsa Mosque and the Dome ("about to disintegrate"—*mushrif-i harab olduğundan*), that had reached Istanbul from Jerusalem. These reports estimated the total budget needed for repairs at 200,000 *ghirsh*, and requested an immediate dispatch of about 10 percent of that sum. This overall estimate must have been prepared by way of complying with earlier instructions, sent in mid-December to the *vali* of Damascus, ordering him to attend to the needs of this particular site. We do not know whether this requested down-payment was fulfilled; the immediate reply by the Sultan was an order to prepare a precise description of all repairs needed and follow it up by dispatching a detailed budget needed for the entire project. Two-and-a-half months later (17 August 1812), most probably after having complied with these instructions, the *vali* of Damascus sent specific orders to the Jerusalem authorities to commence executing this project. In order to ensure proper standards of the survey, as well as the adequate execution of the plan, special builders were sent from Istanbul.[37]

It is not clear whether the actual work started immediately afterwards; it definitely was not completed, nor meaningfully progressed, during that particular year. A Jesuit manuscript[38] found in Beirut, undoubtedly based on official Ottoman documentation, describes a still unchanged picture of the Temple Mount some time afterwards. A certain Kusa Kiahya, a high-ranking official at the Sublime Porte, visited Jerusalem on his way back from the annual *hajj* pilgrimage in late 1816. He was appalled by the state of the Temple Mount, which seemed to have fallen into oblivion. When he asked for the reasons for that unfortunate state of affairs he was told that the regular income of the local *waqf* authorities was insufficient to properly maintain the place. Back in Istanbul, he kept his promise to the Jerusalemites, lobbied for the introduction of improvements on the Temple Mount, and apparently hit a positive chord. The Sultan agreed to focus on a major repair project there, and charged it to the account of Damascus. Since this province (Jerusalem included) was temporarily entrusted in 1817 to the *vali* of Sidon, Sulayman Pasha, he was charged with drawing up the immediate plans (and bearing the financial burden) of the Temple Mount repairs. Sulayman set out to work upon receipt of his master's *firman*: from his permanent residence in Acre he sent to Jerusalem the expert builders who had arrived by sea from Istanbul, along with auxiliary staff carrying his general instructions to conduct a detailed survey and to prepare a budget estimate and work plan for the entire project. He also instructed the Jerusalem religious and technical functionaries to extend any help necessary for this plan. The reports he got back from Jerusalem pointed at the main elements that had to be attended to: the lead tiles and the *kashani* faïences covering of the roofs, as well as the walls, of al-Aqsa Mosque and the Dome of the Rock. As for the *kashani* faïence tiles, it turned out that the most efficient way to proceed would be to have them produced in Jerusalem itself. Orders were sent from Acre to the Governor of Tripoli to dig out and send to Jerusalem a consignment of soil from a certain cave near Antakya, famous for its quality for the production of tiles, and a special enamel kiln was built in Jerusalem for that purpose. Amir Bashir Shihabi, the governor of Mount Lebanon (an underling of the Governor of Damascus), was put in charge of the supply of wooden panels, and especially the wooden cedar beams (from Mount Lebanon's famous cedar trees) needed to replace the old, decrepit ones upholding the ceilings and supporting the arches. He had them dispatched by sea from Beirut to Jaffa and Gaza, then transported by camel caravans uphill to Jerusalem. This seems to have been a fairly complicated assignment, which reportedly caused the death of many (more than 200) camels, along with quite a number of human casualties. Special paints, as well as gold leaves, were sent from Istanbul, and many other building materials (ropes, iron, lead, nails, etc.) were forwarded from Acre. When the magnitude of the project was reported to Istanbul, various construction experts were also sent to Jerusalem. The actual work went on for 21 months, in the years 1817–18.

September 1818 was a most bountiful month in terms of reports about the progress of this project. An order sent by the Governor of Damascus (Salih, not Sulayman any more) arrived in Jerusalem after less than a week and was registered at the court on the 5th of the month. It was addressed (in the following order) to: the religious authorities there (*qadi*, *mufti*, *qa'immaqam naqib al-ashraf*), the administrative and military officials (local governor —*mutasallim*, *mir-alay*, *yeniçeri bashi*), the supervisor of the Khasseki Sultan soup-kitchen (*wakil al-takkiyaa al-'amira*), the religious dignitaries (*ulema*, preachers—*khutaba*), and more generally to the dignitaries of the town—*wujuh al-balda*. The Governor notified all of them that he had been entrusted with the repairs and reconstruction of al-Aqsa Mosque and the Dome of the Rock. This was, no doubt, yet another copy of the older *firmans* sent to him beforehand, as one gathers from another *buyuruldu* order dated just a week later and registered in Jerusalem on 14 September.[39]

The latter speaks of a very similar order sent from Istanbul much earlier, followed up by instructions dispatched to Jerusalem, and then by a detailed progress report (*mahdar*) sent back from Jerusalem by all of the above. Moreover, the Governor mentioned his personal involvement for more than a year in the actual execution of the project, and his insistence on receiving a detailed report before its completion (*qabla khalas wurshat al-ta'mir*). No doubt, therefore, that we are dealing here with a major operation that goes back to 1817 or even 1816, related here in hindsight. When the above-mentioned *mahdar* arrived, pointing out that the work has just about been completed, repeated instructions were sent demanding that all the work accomplished should be double-checked and then a listing of all the unfinished parts be compiled and sent to the Governor. "All the repairs were meticulously done and very solidly completed" went their report.

120 The German Emperor Wilhelm II near the Dome of the Rock, 2 November 1898
The photo was taken by Empress Auguste Viktoria

121 Enver Pasha and Cemal (Jamal) Pasha, members of the triumvirate that ruled the Ottoman Empire during World War I, at the Dome of the Rock, March 1916

There were, however, several elements still missing. Part of the lead cylinders covering the roofs of both buildings had been replaced, but there was still a certain quantity that had to be added, particularly on the outside of al-Aqsa Mosque. The same applied to the porcelain faïences on the walls of both buildings, which still needed either replacement or repair. Additional repairs had to be performed in other locations on the Haram platform: the vaulted portico structures flanking it, where some of the overriding *madrasa*s had seriously deteriorated and needed urgent attention; the arch of Bab al-Silsila had to be reconstructed, as well as several other entrances and their doors; the public lavatories were in need of serious attention and repairs, as were several other smaller buildings close to the Dome of the Rock; the courtyard (*sahn*) surrounding the Dome had grown overwhelming weeds, hence it needed new pavement. The most urgent of all these addenda were the missing tiles and cylinders, hence specific instructions were issued to the effect of dispatching another 3500 *uqqa* of lead from Damascus for the production of the cylinders. No further reports were registered in the court proceedings indicating whether all the work had actually been completed, or, as one may surmise, some loose ends were left. The lengthy time-span of the actual execution and the very detailed reports of the missing links lead us to believe that major repairs had been performed, and in the eyes of the authorities the project had reached its prescribed end. A detailed list dated from the middle of 1819 records the leftover building materials on the Haram platform: these (wood, lead, marble, various paints) were to be stored and locked by the *qadi* of Jerusalem who would keep the relevant keys at his disposal. This entry in the court records, indicating that these may be used for future renovations and repairs, sends a very clear message: much has been achieved, but there will definitely be room for more repairs in years to come. As we know, later years in the nineteenthth century (e.g. 1874–75) witnessed additional repairs there, but never did they reach the volume of budget allocated and work performed as was the case during the second decade of that century, described above.[40]

The Political Context of the Renovations

One final question remains to be dealt with: why were the years 1817–18 chosen for this major project? Was it just because, as suggested in the manuscript cited above, a certain high-ranking official visited the place and reported to Istanbul? Was there any other trigger, perhaps a physical one, for the poor state of that site, or did it stem from an ideological consideration? We do not know of any major earthquake in Jerusalem around the turn of the century, hence the cracks, the missing tiles, and the dilapidated walls should be regarded as a result of a centuries-long process of gradual disintegration, due to natural causes, aggravated by many years of insufficient attention bordering on neglect by the local administration and diminishing available funds either at the level of the local endowment authorities or at that of the central government. As for ideology, we are not aware of any particular rise in the religious zeal of the Ottoman sultans during these specific years.

Perusal of the central policies of the state leads to the very opposite conclusions: ever since the accession of Selim III to power in 1789, special attention was paid at the highest echelon of the Empire to identify the reasons for Europe's ascendancy, and a series of reforms was gradually initiated in order to implement "a new order" (*nizam-i cedid*), heavily imbued with European influence. These policies were amplified by Mahmud II (1808–39), who agreed to stop his interminable wars with Russia, and as soon as he signed the treaty of Bucharest in May 1812, writes the Ottoman official historian Cevdet, the Sultan felt free to launch "internal reforms."[41] Palestine, just like Syria and Egypt, had long been neglected by the Sultans whose political attention was focussed on Europe. In the course of the seventeenth and eighteenth centuries, occasional attention was paid by the central administration of the Empire to the deterioration of the Temple Mount complex. These, however, seem to have been far from satisfactory. Renewed interest in that particular area of Arabic-speaking provinces emerged as a result of Napoleon's invasion, followed by Muhammad Ali's growing autonomy in Egypt and the Wahhabi religious threat gathering in Arabia. The *Tanzimat* reforms, aiming, inter alia, to quell autonomy of any kind in the Empire, meant also increased involvement in the internal affairs of these provinces, and the Temple Mount in Jerusalem seemed to be a case in point. A major renovation project was not only long overdue; it would indicate renewed interest, as well as a pious posture very becoming to the central government which wished to signal its intention to hold on to its power and rule for generations to come.

Ottoman policies thus came a full circle: the reconstruction activity on the Temple Mount in the nineteenth century, just like the erection of the walls of Jerusalem in the early sixteenth century and the repairs initiated immediately after their conquests, were intended to play up the religious importance of Jerusalem as a useful tool in the political game and reality. As such, it was reminiscent of tunes played and distinctly heard much later, in years to come.

Jerusalem was occupied by the British army on 9 December 1917, following a decision by the German-Ottoman command to evacuate it. Franz von Papen, who was a member of the German-Ottoman high command, claims in his memoirs that he argued for a voluntary evacuation so as to save the city from destruction, and that General Falkenhayn finally agreed. The British official history of World War I presents the evacuation as the result of military considerations and so does the official Turkish history.[42] Thus we come full circle again: precisely as had been the case in late 1516, when occupied by the Ottomans, Jerusalem was given up by them without any serious battle.

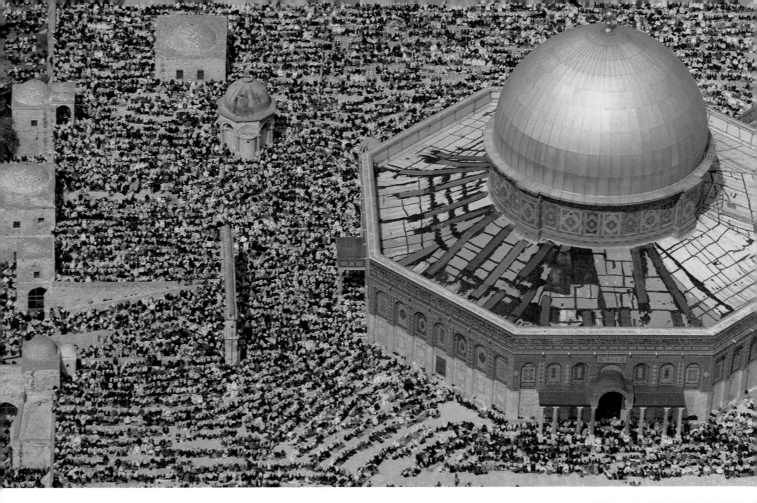

1917 to the Present:
Al-Haram al-Sharif / Temple Mount (Har ha-Bayit) and the Western Wall

Not used

Yitzhak Reiter
The Hebrew University of Jerusalem

Jon Seligman
Israel Antiquities Authority

Introduction

The demise of the Ottoman Empire, based as it was on lethargic inaction, and the arrival on the scene in Palestine of a dynamic western power in the form of the British Mandate, were to have major consequences upon the relationship between the new Christian authorities and the Muslim guardians of the Haram al-Sharif. Furthermore, the rise of Zionism and the consequential influx of an ideologically vibrant Jewish community, whose clear aim was the formation of a renewed Jewish homeland, was a source of conflict between this community and the indigenous Arab population not only concerning the future of the country as a whole, but also in relation to the status of the holy sites within that future. The short period of Jordanian rule (1948–67), and following that Israeli control from 1967 onward, have left the issues of rights, ownership, control, maintenance, conservation, inspection, and law open and subjects of vigorous debate, that due to diametrically opposed interests are not likely to be resolved in the near future.

This conflict between the Jewish Zionist entity (and since 1948—the State of Israel), on the one hand, and the Palestinian Muslims and the Muslim world at large, on the other, has focused inter alia on the Sacred Esplanade—called by Muslims the Haram al-Sharif and by Jews the Temple Mount (*Har ha-Bayit*). Increasing political importance boosted the Sacred Esplanade's significance both as a powerful religious and a national symbol for both parties to the conflict. The fact that the Esplanade is sacred to Jews and Muslims alike has been an ongoing source of tension, particularly since Israel assumed control of East Jerusalem in 1967. Archaeology, as a state tool, as a field of enquiry that challenges basic assumptions of faith, and as a professional discipline that makes demands of those maintaining the Esplanade, has always been part and parcel of that tension. As shall be seen, the perception of the Esplanade for both sides and the way in which that

122 Above: Muslims praying at the Haram al-Sharif
123 Below: Jews praying at the Western Wall
Priests with heads covered with prayer shawls are blessing the worshipers

perception is presented often uses, exploits, and misrepresents archaeological scholarship and method.

With the British conquest of southern Palestine in late 1917 and the disintegration of the Ottoman Empire, Palestine came under non-Muslim rule after some 1,300 years of Islamic rule interrupted only by the Crusader interlude of the twelfth century. The struggle of the Arabs of Palestine (later identified as Palestinians) against both Zionism and the British Mandate in Palestine and the later ongoing conflict between the Palestinians and Israel significantly affected both the ideology and the reality of the Sacred Esplanade of Jerusalem. Since the 1920s the Haram al-Sharif / Temple Mount and the Western Wall have become religio-nationalist symbols for both Jews and Palestinian Muslims. The 1948 and 1967 wars, as well as the first and the second Palestinian uprisings (*Intifadas*), are landmarks in the history of the Esplanade.

The Haram al-Sharif / Temple Mount, the Islamic Waqf, and Archaeological Research

Modern scholarly interest in the Haram al-Sharif / Temple Mount began in the nineteenth century as the result of a series of motives, not all of them scholarly. These included religious—especially Christian—belief, romantic adventurism, imperial intrigue of the major western powers, and often also genuine scientific enquiry. Still, the results of often illicit sorties into the precincts of the site, that was closed to non-Muslims till the end of the Crimean War, form the basis for modern understanding of the site. Foremost of these early visitors were Frederick Catherwood (who produced a cartographic impression of the Haram), Titus Tobler, Melchior de Vogüé, James Turner Barclay, and others. The most important survey of this period, and indeed one of the most significant conducted ever, was the well-known works of Charles Wilson (1865) and Charles Warren (1884).[1] The knowledge they accumulated, both of standing and subterranean structures, is still the basis for all modern research of the Haram al-Sharif.

During the British Mandate period, two comprehensive studies were carried out, focusing on the Dome of the Rock and the Aqsa Mosque. In 1924 Ernest T. Richmond published the results of an extensive survey of the Dome of the Rock, carried out in 1918,[2] and in 1938–42 Robert W. Hamilton, the British Mandate's Director of Antiquities, documented the Aqsa Mosque and conducted limited excavations in the building while wide-ranging repairs were underway.[3] This scholarship was augmented by the descriptions and study of textual material by the Dominican fathers Louis-Hugues Vincent and Félix-Marie Abel (1914–26) on Jerusalem and the Temple Mount.[4] In the 1920s an expert on Arabic inscriptions, Max van Berchem, documented and published dozens of ancient inscriptions discovered on the Temple Mount and in the surrounding buildings.[5]

Later Keppel A.C. Creswell compiled a detailed study of the structures of the Temple Mount, including many drawings and photographs, some of which were published in his monumental book.[6] In 1967 Kathleen Kenyon carried out a small excavation south of the Aqsa Mosque, uncovering a section of the building that would later be identified as one of the Umayyad palaces.[7] After the Six Day War, Israeli scholars made their contribution to the documentation of the buildings on the Temple Mount. Myriam Rosen-Ayalon published a comprehensive study of structures from the Early Muslim period[8] and other researchers dealt with the reconstruction of the form of the Temple Mount in the Second Temple period, based on the written sources and the physical remains collated by their predecessors.[9] Large scale excavations by Benjamin Mazar and Meir Ben-Dov in the area south of the Temple Mount exposed important remains of the Herodian structures around the Temple Mount and uncovered huge Umayyad buildings that transformed archaeological understanding of that period.[10] The study of the Umayyad rebuilding and construction of the Haram al-Sharif was intensively highlighted by Andreas Kaplony's monumental study of all known data for that period.[11]

During the past few decades extensive surveys of the Crusader, Mamluk, and Ottoman construction on the Temple Mount had been conducted as a joint effort of the British School of Archaeology in Jerusalem and the Archaeological Department of the Islamic Waqf.[12] The contribution of these studies to our knowledge of the Temple Mount, its structure, history, and development, has been considerable. Nevertheless, it must be emphasised that due to the religious importance and sensitivities of the site, no proper scientific archaeological excavation has ever been conducted, save for limited work during the Aqsa Mosque repairs in the Mandatory period.

The attitude of the Waqf authorities to archaeological research and archaeologists is demonstrated by both their formal and informal relations with government authorities and the official archaeological authorities, from the Mandatory period till the present.[13] In general, the Waqf exhibited a consistent reservation to archaeological research and architectural documentation by external organisations. This reservation escalated throughout the periods of the British Mandate, Jordanian rule, and into that of Israeli control. Parts of the Muslim establishment considered the study of the Temple Mount by western scholars not as academic inquiry into the historical development of the site and its archaeological remains, but rather as an attempt to undermine the central status of the Islamic monuments of the Haram al-Sharif / Temple Mount—the Dome of the Rock and the Aqsa Mosque. On the other hand, side by side with its suspicion of foreign scholars, the Waqf was always prepared to cooperate with professional archaeological and conservation organisations concerning themselves with the Islamic monuments of the site, an approach that changed with the involvement of the Israeli Islamic Movement in the development of the site from 1996.

The British Mandate Period

In the wake of World War I and the British conquest of Palestine, the new rulers left the Muslim administration of the Haram al-Sharif in place, regarding the site as possessing an informal immunity.[14] The Supreme Muslim Council (SMC), established with the blessing of the Mandatory government, enjoyed wide-ranging autonomy over all Muslim religious matters. It administered the Haram al-Sharif, and situated both the Shari'a (Muslim law) Court and its own offices on the site.[15] For the most part, the British police avoided entering the Temple Mount. The position of the SMC was further reaffirmed in July 1922 by articles 9 and 13 of the League of Nations' provision for a Mandate in Palestine:

> … nothing in this mandate shall be construed as conferring upon the Mandatory authority to interfere with the fabric or the management of purely Moslem sacred shrines, the immunities of which are guaranteed.

This immunity was later reinforced by the provisos of the Palestine (Holy Places) Order in Council 1924 which endorsed the Status Quo arrangement in the Holy Sites adopted by the Great Powers in the Treaty of Paris of 1856.[16]

Shortly after the British occupation of Jerusalem in December 1917 it became clear that the historic monuments on the Temple Mount were in a very poor state of preservation, owing to continual neglect during the last phase of Ottoman rule [fig. 124]. In a revealing letter dated 4 December 1918 the Grand Mufti, Muhammad Kamil al-Husayni, eloquently described the atrocious state of the monuments of the Haram al-Sharif in an appeal to fellow Muslims:

> …This sacred Mosque, to which Allah translated His Prophet one night from the Mosque in Mecca … is neglected and for several decades was overlooked, until decay has set in its frame, and its ornamentation has faded, and the whole edifice stands in peril of disruption, which may God avert. … Now, when the men of the Occupying Power, and in particular H.E. Colonel Storrs, Governor of the Holy City, saw the ruined state in which stood the Mosque … he expressed his deep regret … and applied for an able engineer of those who have specialized in the repairs of ancient places of worship. … His appeal met with prompt response, for very soon the British Government sent … the most celebrated engineer … Major Richmond. … Having examined everything bit by bit, … he drew up a report fully explaining what was required for the restoration and preservation of this noble edifice ….[17]

Ernest Tatham Richmond, who would later be appointed director of the Department of Antiquities, was an architect who had worked previously on the preservation of Islamic

124 A partial view of the Dome of the Rock, ca. 1921, showing the damage to its mosaics
This early color photograph is preserved in the collection of the École Biblique et Archéologique Française de Jérusalem

monuments in Cairo. Upon the invitation of Ronald Storrs he conducted a detailed architectural survey of the Dome of the Rock published in a magnificent volume that provided the first modern overview of the site, including analysis of previous attempts to maintain the building.[18] The attitude to preservation presented by Richmond was both modern and extremely professional, with clear understanding of the fact that an edifice like the Dome of the Rock is a living structure, changing with time in order to continue its existence, for, as he states: "Had there been no change the building would have disappeared."[19]

The Dome of the Rock, especially the tiles that covered the building, required immediate attention, but it wasn't till 1921 that the administrative structure of the SMC and the Waqf (the official administration of Islamic endowments, an Ottoman apparatus which has continued to operate ever since) adapted itself to provide the framework for the task. The restoration of the Dome of the Rock continued for much of the twentieth century but started with a small grant from the Pro-Jerusalem Society, an intercommunity society formed by the British Military authorities for the "preservation and advancement of the interests of Jerusalem." The grant provided for the initial preservation of tiles by the Armenian ceramicist David Ohanessian.[20]

In that same year the SMC established a Technical Department, under the Turkish architect Kamal al-Din Bey, with the aim of maintaining the monuments of the Temple Mount. One of the first actions undertaken by this department was the preparation of a plan to treat the ceramic tiles adorning the Dome of the Rock. In time, the Technical Department—which still exists—became an organ that documented and studied the monuments in the field of conservation, often in cooperation with recognised international institutions. Thus, between 1924–28 the Supreme Muslim Council (SMC), in cooperation with the British Mandatory government, undertook a project for the restoration of the Haram al-Sharif. Kamal al-Din planned the renovation and supervised its implementation. A committee of six experts, including two Egyptians and three British, approved the plan. The SMC dispatched six delegations to Muslim countries (Egypt, the Hijaz, Iraq, Kuwait, Bahrain, Iran, and India), two of them headed by the Grand Mufti, Hajj Amin al-Husayni, to raise the money needed for the restoration.[21] The delegations also sought to arouse awareness in the Muslim world to the struggle for Palestine as an Islamic territory, with the Haram at its center. When restoration began, Kamal al-Din engaged 104 foremen and 75 workers. Several crafts such as iron, wood, and wickerwork skills, were locally promoted, and mosaic tiles were obtained from Kütahya in Turkey.

The renovations included not only the two shrines but also al-Madrasa al-Manjakiyya, which housed the SMC and Waqf offices, al-Madrasa al-Tankiziyya, which housed the Shari'a Court (known as al-Mahkama—court building), and the complex of four *madrasas* on the western side, al-Jawliyya, al-Wajihiyya, al-Subaybiyya, and al-Muhaddathiyya. The last named, which had been used by the Ottomans as barracks, was renovated and placed at the disposal of the Rawdat al-Ma'arif College.[22] Two other buildings on the same side were renovated—al-Khanqah al-Dawadariyya and al-Madrasa al-Basitiyya—to serve the Islamic College. The Qubbah al-Nahwiyya (Dome of Grammar), a small building close to the Dome of the Rock, was restored and turned into an Islamic library (today serving as the Shari'a Court of Appeals). An Islamic Museum was established at the Maghribi Mosque on the southwest side of the Haram. Other small repairs were also undertaken to the gates, fountains, water reservoirs, and windows.[23] Already in 1925, a *Brief Guide to the Haram al-Sharif* was published in English by the SMC and reprinted several times. The SMC aimed to elevate the importance of the Haram al-Sharif, and of Jerusalem in general, in the minds of Muslims everywhere.

From the archival material of the Mandatory Department of Antiquities we learn of a wide range of professional contacts that developed between SMC officials and those of the Department.[24] Immediately after the British had set up their military government in Jerusalem, the first formal contacts were made between the authorities and the SMC. Inspectors working for the Department of Antiquities had free access to almost every place on the Haram / Temple Mount and were allowed to record, measure, and photograph its major monuments. Through the years of Mandatory rule, documentation and surveys continued on the Temple Mount for preservation purposes, including that of the Dome of the Rock and the Aqsa Mosque. These professional ties were maintained by the directors of the Department of Antiquities, who were personally active in the documentation work.[25]

However, this system of chiefly professional contacts was not backed up by any legal authority of the Mandatory Government of Palestine, for according to law the Temple Mount was a recognised Holy Place and therefore the jurisdiction of the civil authorities, including those of the Department of Antiquities, was subject to certain restrictions.[26] Despite this, throughout the years of British rule good professional relations were maintained between the authorities and the Muslim religious authority, and the Waqf was generally willing to cooperate in professional matters with the Department of Antiquities or with other government agencies, such as the Public Works Department, or with government officials, scholars, and the High Commissioner himself. Department of Antiquities inspectors routinely visited the Temple Mount together with SMC officials to comprehensively document both the monuments and everyday activities. The visiting inspectors were often accompanied by professional teams from the Department of Antiquities and from other government agencies.[27]

Good professional contacts between the Muslim religious establishment and the official archaeological and architectural organs of the Mandatory government continued till the end of British rule in Palestine. Surveys and documentation of the Temple Mount were conducted throughout the 1940s as a joint effort of the Department of Antiquities, the Public Works Department, and the SMC.

On 11 July 1927 an earthquake, whose epicenter was in the Jordan Valley, rocked Jerusalem. Within a year the SMC was ready to celebrate completion of the renovations in the Haram. The ceremony took place on 29 August 1928, to coincide with the birthday of the Prophet Muhammad (*al-mawlid al-nabawi*). This occurred one month before the Jewish Day of Atonement and inflamed the struggle over the rights at the adjacent Western Wall. Coinciding with the event the SMC decided to introduce, for the first time in the history of the Sacred Esplanade, entrance fees for non-Muslim visitors.

125 An aerial view of the Haram from the southeast, ca. 1930

In a narrow area, only 3.5 metres wide in the Magharibah (Hebrew: Mughrabim) Quarter of the Old City, a remaining section of the Herodian temenos wall of the Temple Mount was still visible. Jewish prayer had, since the sixteenth century, been concentrated in the small space in front of the Western Wall (also known as the Wall of Lamentations or Wailing Wall) in which a tense de facto status quo had developed allowing Jews limited access to the site for prayer—backed by payment to the authorities (mainly the administrator of the Abu Midyan Magharibah Waqf), while strictly restricting Jewish requests to renovate the site.[28] Since the increase of Jewish immigration to Palestine in the 1880s there was a gradual growth in the number of Jews who came to pray and visit at the Western Wall and hence it developed into a collective symbol of the Jewish community.

Sensing the importance of the site to the Jews, the Arab owners consistently rebuffed Jewish attempts to purchase the area for prayer, though in essence the practice had developed by the end of Ottoman rule of allowing unrestricted Jewish access to the holy site.

The Muslims considered the Western Wall as part of the retaining wall of the Haram al-Sharif, and as such an integral part of that monument. An old Muslim tradition tells of a place at "the entrance of al-Aqsa" where the prophet Muhammad tethered his wondrous beast of burden, al-Buraq, following the nocturnal flight (al-mi'raj) from Mecca.[29] During the 1920s Muslims pointed to the Western Wall as this particular place. Furthermore, the tiny plaza fronting the Western Wall constituted part of the Abu Midyan al-Ghawth Waqf, a charitable institution of a North African who endowed the land and houses in 1320 CE in favour of North African Muslim immigrants to Jerusalem, the endowments being documented fully in the Shari'a Court records.

Zionist efforts to acquire ownership of the Wall were renewed immediately after the British occupation of Palestine. Speaking to members of the Zionist Commission in March 1918 while underway to Palestine, Chaim Weizmann maintained that the Western Wall is one of the Jewish holy places "which we must have," adding that the Commission will attempt to immediately obtain permission from the British authorities in Palestine to clean up the place and deploy a Jewish guard there. On 1 May 1918 he sent a letter to William Ormsby-Gore—the liaison officer between the Commission and the British military administration in Palestine—in which he requested permission to explore the possibility of transferring the site to Jewish control. The British governor of Jerusalem, Ronald Storrs, attempted to help Weizmann, but this proved unsuccessful.[30] Following a protest by dignitaries of Jerusalem's Muslim community against any infringement of the pre-existing status quo, and due to the delicate intercommunal relations between Jews and Muslims in Palestine, the Zionist officials were requested by the new British administration to cease their efforts in this matter.[31] During this early period of the Mandate the condition of the Wall also became a subject for concern. In 1920 the SMC began repairs of the upper courses of the Western Wall, leading this time to protests by prominent Jews and a temporary suspension of the work. A decision was then taken to place the maintenance of the small upper stone courses under the authority of the SMC, while the lower Herodian and Umayyad masonry were to be preserved by the Department of Antiquities, a decision protested by the Mufti of Jerusalem. This pattern of division of responsibility would repeat itself in later years.

Considering the situation that had developed, Jerusalem District Commissioner Ronald Storrs stated in a memorandum of 1925 that:

> … though it is sometimes asserted by Moslems that they could legally erect a wall debarring public approach [to the Western Wall], no Mandatory Government could countenance so flagrant an infringement of the Status Quo. On the other

hand the Jewish right is no more than a right of way and of station, and involves no title, expressed or implied, of ownership, either of the surface of the Wall or of the pavement in front of it.[32]

In this atmosphere of jockeying for an advantageous position, with neither side being really prepared to accept the compromises presented by the new British arbitrators, it was only a question of time before the next conflict would arise. This emerged around the right to bring seating to the site for prayer and placing a cloth partition to separate the genders in accordance with Jewish religious practice. Following Muslim objections, the British adopted the previous ruling of the Ottoman Government preventing the placing of any installation, even temporary, on the pavement before the Wall to prevent any challenge to established rights, until agreement could be reached between the communities on the matter. With time Jewish challenges of this ruling, Muslim protest, and British enforcement became one of the pretexts for an attack by a Muslim crowd upon Jewish worshippers at the Wall in August 1929. The unrest that followed led to widespread rioting in Jerusalem, during which more than 130 Jews were massacred in Hebron, Safed, and elsewhere, centered round the claim that Jewish prayer at the Western Wall endangered the sanctity of the Haram al-Sharif.

A Commission of Inquiry was appointed by the British government in May 1930 to investigate what became known as "the Western Wall incidents" and the conflicting Jewish and Muslim claims regarding the Wall. This Commission submitted its report in December of the same year and its recommendations formed the basis for an ordinance adopted by the Mandatory government—The Palestine (Western or Wailing Wall) Order in Council, 1931. The commission concluded that:

…the established custom should be a proper basis for deciding the existing rights of the Jews at the Wall…

A. To the Moslems belong the sole ownership of, and the sole proprietary right to, the Western Wall, seeing that it forms an integral part of the Haram-esh-Sherif area, which is a Waqf property. To the Moslems there also belongs the ownership of the Pavement in front of the Wall and of the adjacent so-called Moghrabi (Moroccan) Quarter opposite the Wall, inasmuch as the last-mentioned property was made Waqf under Moslem Sharia Law, it being dedicated to charitable purposes.

Such appurtenances of worship and/or such other objects as the Jews may be entitled to place near the Wall either in conformity with the provisions of this present Verdict or by agreement come to between the Parties shall under no circumstances be considered as, or have the effect of, establishing for them any sort of proprietary right to the Wall or to the adjacent Pavement.

On the other hand the Moslems shall be under the obligation not to construct or

126 A British police post at the entrance to the Western Wall, 1933

127 A British checkpost in the Chain Gate Street of Jerusalem's Old City, 1938

build any edifice or to demolish or repair any building within the Waqf property (Haram area and Moghrabi Quarter) adjacent to the Wall, in such a manner that the said work would encroach on the Pavement or impair the access of the Jews to the Wall or involve any disturbance to, or interference with, the Jews during the times of their devotional visits to the Wall, if it can in any way be avoided. B. The Jews shall have free access to the Western Wall for the purpose of devotions at all times subject to the explicit stipulations...[33]

The stipulation stated that the Jews had a proprietary right to pray at the site according to arrangements dating from the Ottoman era,[34] but they were not permitted to bring chairs or benches, to build a partition between men and women, or to blow the *shofar*. Thus, the British ruled that the status quo should prevail. Responsibility for maintenance of the Wall was placed upon the British administration in consultation with the SMC and the Rabbinical Council. This ruling would be challenged by Jewish groups and continue to be a source of tension until the end of the British Mandate in Palestine in 1948.

A major Islamic event associated with the Haram during this period was the Islamic Congress, which convened in Jerusalem in 1931 on the initiative of Hajj Amin al-Husayni, the SMC's president. Some of its sessions were conducted at Rawdat al-Ma'arif, adjacent to the Haram. The Congress resolved to establish a university in Jerusalem to be named Al-Aqsa University, but the resolution was never implemented. In 1931 al-Husayni also opted to turn the western external portico of the Haram into a pantheon for important Muslim figures. Muhammad 'Ali, the leader of the Indian *Khilafat* (Caliphate) movement, and al-Husayn ibn 'Ali, the Hashemite leader of the 1916 Arab revolt, were both buried there in tomb chambers. In 1934, the president of the Arab Executive, Musa Kazim al-Husayni, was interred there, as was his son, 'Abd al-Qadir al-Husayni—a prominent Palestinian hero, commander of irregular forces fighting the Jews in Palestine in 1948. In 2001, 'Abd al-Qadir's son, Faysal al-Husayni—a Palestinian Authority cabinet member—was buried in the same site.

After the outbreak of the Arab Revolt in 1936, Hajj Amin al-Husayni was sought for his involvement in the riots. He took refuge in the Haram al-Sharif, which he knew the British officials would not dare to enter to arrest him, because of the recognized immunity of the site.[35] In October 1937, after Hajj Amin had escaped and fled the country, the Mandatory government appointed a three-man committee to oversee the SMC's activities. Finally, in 1938—before the end of the Arab Revolt in 1939—the government established a police post on the Sacred Esplanade (based on an Ottoman precedent) manned by Muslim officers.

On 12 October 1937 a further tremor was felt in the city. While the Dome of the Rock remained relatively unscathed, the Aqsa Mosque, built above ancient vaults on the Umayyad reconstruction of the Herodian extension of the Temple Mount, was severely damaged, including collapse of the roof together with many of the ancient timbers. In view of this the Waqf commissioned a report on the physical state of the monument from Mahmud Ahmad Pasha, Director of the Department for the Preservation of Arab Monuments of Egypt, which was presented in May 1938. Major repair works, involving the heavy dismantling and rebuilding of extensive sections of the Mosque [figs. 128–131], were conducted from 1938 to 1942 under Egyptian supervision and sponsorship.[36] In a break from earlier practice the repairs were professionally, if partially, documented by Robert W. Hamilton and included for the first time limited archaeological excavation within the Mosque and documentation of the large twelfth-century Frankish vaulted structures east of the building prior to their removal around 1940. Hamilton sums it up thus: "It [the documentation] … preserved some record, however imperfect, of an ancient building that has now suffered radical and irreversible transformation."[37]

In another ground-breaking effort the decorated timbers which had previously adorned the Aqsa Mosque were removed for preservation to the newly founded Palestine (Rockefeller) Museum and are today divided between that institution and the Islamic Museum.

During the 1930s work was conducted to restore the magnificent Umayyad mosaics and further treat the tiles, for which the SMC was encouraged by R.W. Hamilton, the director of the Antiquities Department, to engage a specialist to deal with the surveying and preservation of the tiles.[38] After eight years of indecision the SMC turned to Arthur Hubert Stanley Megaw, then director of the Cyprus Department of Antiquities.

128 A defaced carving used as a paving stone in the nave
IAA 26.263

129 Uncovering a column and a capital within a pier
IAA 20.445

130 Placing a new column
IAA 22.011

131 Two rows of new columns set up in the nave, near the temporarily freestanding inner northern façade.
The monolithic marble columns were imported from Italy. IAA 22.124

132 9 April 1948: 'Abd al-Qadir al-Husayni's funeral procession passing near the Dome of the Rock.
'Abd al-Qadir al-Husayni, commander of the Palestinian Arab forces in the Jerusalem area, fell in battle with the Haganah at
al-Qastal, a village overlooking the Tel Aviv-Jerusalem road

The detailed report Megaw presented in 1946, and submitted finally to the Jordanian
Department of Antiquities and the Waqf in 1952, showed that even though conservation
had been conducted throughout the Mandatory period, the building was still in a very
poor condition due to water leakage into the core of the walls. This report would form the
basis for the repairs conducted under Jordanian rule.[39]

Under Jordanian Rule—1948–67

In 1947 the political situation in Palestine deteriorated, leading to the departure of the
British Mandatory government and UN resolution 181 for partition of Palestine, including
provision for the internationalization of Jerusalem and its environs. The hostilities of
1948 left Jerusalem divided, with the Old City and East Jerusalem under Jordanian
control. The Jews, who had been evacuated from their quarter in the Old City, expected
that a special committee be formed, as guaranteed under article VIII of the Armistice
Agreement of 1949 between the newly established State of Israel and Jordan, allowing
access to Jewish holy sites—including the Western Wall—for devotional purposes, an
agreement never implemented.

The Hashemite regime's attitude to the Holy City was ambivalent during its period
of rule over the West Bank. On the one hand, Jerusalem, with the Haram al-Sharif at its
heart, was the political stronghold of the Hashemite dynasty's enemies—the Husaynis

133 20 July 1951: Jordanian officials in the Aqsa Mosque; in front of them, the body of Mustafa Shuqri Ashu, the Palestinian extremist who assassinated King Abdullah I of Jordan while he was attending Friday prayers on the Haram

and their allies. On the other hand, Jordan's association with the Holy City enhanced its status in the Muslim world and provided legitimacy for the Hashemites. As the instigators of the Arab revolt against Ottoman rule, the Hashemites saw themselves as the liberators of Jerusalem in 1948 and the legitimate custodians of Islam's holy sites.[40] Furthermore, the Jordanians realized that Jerusalem was of considerable tourist and economic value.

Thus, the Jordanians pursued a middle ground for their Jerusalem policy. They developed the city economically and provided political supporters (many of them of Hebronite descent and long-time supporters of King Abdullah I) with important posts in the municipality and in the Haram al-Sharif's Waqf. Simultaneously, the regime developed Amman into the monarchy's most significant political centre at the expense of Jerusalem.[41]

King Abdullah I often attended Friday prayers at the Aqsa Mosque and liked to have the Jordanian army's military band play when he entered the Haram al-Sharif.[42] This offended the sensibilities of the Palestinian religious leadership, who considered a British-style military band a violation of the site's sanctity. The annexation of the West Bank to Jordan in 1950 did not reduce tensions between the Palestinians and the Hashemite regime. King Abdullah was assassinated at the entrance of the Aqsa Mosque on 20 July 1951. According to one version, the assassin's trail led to Hajj Amin al-Husayni [fig. 133].[43] For several years after his coronation, the young King Hussein also attended public prayers at the Aqsa Mosque.

To a great extent, the Jordanians continued the Ottoman tradition of the site's

134 A part of the Frankish grille in the Islamic Museum

administration, which had been preserved by the British.[44] Some of the Muslim officials in Jerusalem who had been involved in the administration of the Haram al-Sharif during the Mandatory period continued in their posts after 1948. They became officials of the Waqf administration, subordinate at first to the prime minister's office and later to an independent ministry—the Religious Endowments (or Waqf) Ministry.

Seemingly, the good professional contacts between the Jordanian Department of Antiquities, under the leadership of Gerald Lankester Harding, and the professional functionaries of the Waqf were initially maintained, but soon a tendency developed pointing to a deterioration of that cooperation. This is indicated by a seemingly small incident in 1953, when documentation was required following the collapse of part of the mosaic covering the internal walls of the Dome of the Rock. In a letter sent by Lankester Harding to the renowned expert on Muslim architecture, K.A.C. Creswell, responding to his request to erect scaffolding so that the mosaics could be examined, Lankester Harding observed: "By the law I have no control over any religious buildings which are actually in use, but I might be able to pull a few strings."[45] In a curt reply the Waqf refused the request, explaining that it was unwilling for worshippers to be disturbed by photography.

In 1952 the Jordanians launched an appeal, based on Megaw's report, for the renewal of restoration of the Dome of the Rock, augmented in 1954 by the passing of a special law for this purpose by King Hussein.[46] Money donated by various Arab states led to the initiation of the work in 1956 by a Saudi contractor. Work proceeded slowly because of Jordan's lack of economic resources and the reservations of the Arab nations, whose

135 An aerial view of the Haram al-Sharif, the Western Wall and the destroyed Jewish Quarter to its west, under Jordanian rule

Lt.-Gen. Yitzhak Rabin donated in 1964 this photo, taken by the Israel Air Force, to Professor Joshua Prawer of the Hebrew University of Jerusalem. The red arrows point at the locations where the two main synagogues of Jerusalem's Old City had been standing until their destruction in 1948. The red arrows at fig. 51 point at the synagogues' domes while still intact. The domes are also visible on fig. 176

donations were small and slow in coming. During the works the foundations were reinforced, the mosaic ceiling decoration repaired, the twelfth-century Frankish grille around the *Sakhra* (the Dome's sacred Rock) dismantled and deposited partially in the Islamic Museum on the Haram [fig. 134], and the heavy lead dome—which had crushed its own supporting structure—was replaced by a gilded aluminium sheeting. Professional architectural and technical supervision was provided by the Egyptian government and the edifice was later carpeted by the Moroccan crown. The work was conducted without involvement or interference on the part of the Jordanian Department of Antiquities.

With the completion of the repairs on the Dome of the Rock in 1964,[47] Jordan celebrated the event with the attendance of heads of Arab and Muslim countries, and a special commemorative postage stamp was issued showing the Dome of the Rock and a portrait of King Hussein.[48] Subsequently, the Jordanians were able to attract many more Muslim pilgrims and tourists to the Haram al-Sharif and the Old City. They did not, however, enjoy the fruits of their labours for very long. In June 1967 the Six Day War broke out, and Israel took East Jerusalem.

Post-1967 Policy: Waqf Administration under Israeli Rule

Israel's conquest of East Jerusalem during the Six Day War, including the Old City, the Haram al-Sharif, and other Muslim holy sites, was a traumatic event for Muslims. Islam's third most important site had fallen to the Jews, who regarded the Haram al-Sharif as the site of their ancient Temples. Soon after the raising of the Israeli flag over the Dome of the Rock, Israel's Defense Minister Moshe Dayan, understanding the symbolic sensitivity of this action, ordered its removal.

Following Dayan's decision of 17 June 1967, the Waqf was granted full civil administrative authority and was returned to the area which had been taken by the Israel Defense Forces (IDF) only ten days earlier,[49] while responsibility for security affairs was invested with the Israel Police. With this single decision Dayan had created the basis for the status quo that has existed till the present day. In his description of the events of that day Uzi Narkiss, at the time the IDF Chief of the Central Command, succinctly describes this new state of affairs:

> The IDF will clear the Temple Mount platform and will redeploy outside it. The Israeli administration will be responsible for general security, but will not interfere with the internal guarding and the internal inspection of the running of the Mount.[50]

The decision to leave the administration of the Sacred Esplanade in the hands of the Muslim clergy momentarily calmed both the Palestinians and the Muslim world. The Israeli government's policy was backed by the Chief Rabbinical Council's decision according to which Jewish religious law forbids Jews to enter the Temple Mount.

136 7 June 1967: Israeli paratroopers advancing from the east to Lions' Gate (Saint Stephen's Gate; Bab Sitti Maryam), on their way to the Temple Mount

Although Israel ceded the day-to-day administration of the Sacred Esplanade, the government did not feel that it was bound by the status quo. In fact, the opposite was true: it sought to initiate changes that would reflect Jerusalem's new political reality. East Jerusalem was unilaterally annexed by Israel immediately after the war.[51] The state extended the jurisdiction of its laws and administration to East Jerusalem and thus the Temple Mount, obviously an active religious site, was from the 31 August 1967 also part of a registered antiquities site consisting of the Old City and its surroundings.[52] The interpretation of civil control soon became a point of contention within the Israeli public over the level of control that could be exercised by the Israeli government and administrative authorities.[53] The Waqf and the Palestinian public viewed the Israeli occupation as temporary, rejecting the

137 7 June 1967: Paratroopers gazing for the first time at the Western Wall
David Rubinger

138 7 June 1967: Paratroopers at the Dome of the Rock

139 A soldier about to smash the street sign "Tariq al-Buraq," the Arabic name of the lane in front of the Western Wall

140 7 June 1967: Maj.-Gen. Shlomo Goren, chief rabbi of the Israel Defense Forces, in the Dome of the Rock, holding a Torah scroll and a *shofar*

141 Bulldozing part of the Magharibah Quarter

imposition of Israeli civil rule while claiming that as occupied territory the Haram al-Sharif was to be dealt with within the context of international law which prohibited conquerors from changing the status quo. On the same grounds, they argued that Jordanian law, which had prevailed in the territories prior to their conquest, should continue to be in force.[54]

Jewish exultation—even messianic fervour—that followed the speedy victory in Jerusalem presented the new authorities with a dilemma concerning the fate of the Western Wall. Nineteen years of Jewish exclusion from their most holy site and what had been seen by many as the site of Jewish humiliation led to the quick decision to clear the space fronting the wall. Despite international condemnation and Arab consternation,[55] the Magharibah (Mughrabim) Quarter, including a number of Islamic monuments (such as the Afdaliyya Zawiya and the small al-Buraq Mosque), was bulldozed beginning on the evening of 8 June 1967, leaving a large esplanade in front of the Wall to which thousands of Israelis flocked [figs. 141–143]. The conclusions of the 1930 Shaw Commission and the consequent rulings of the Order in Council of 1931, which had so dismayed the Jewish community, could now freely be ignored and uninterrupted Jewish prayer could be conducted with all the previously prohibited accoutrements, a situation that for Israel was never to be reversed. Israel unilaterally expropriated as national Jewish sites the Western Wall plaza as well as two sites in the Jewish Quarter that also included religious buildings and assets belonging to the Waqf.

142–143 14 June 1967, *Shavu`ot* (Feast of Weeks):
West Jerusalemites streaming into the recently
conquered Old City and trudging through
the remains of the Magharibah Quarter to the
Western Wall

On 11 July Israel's Minister of Religious Affairs Zerach Wahrhaftig informed the leading Muslim clerics that Israeli laws governing the status of the Muslim community in the State of Israel would henceforth apply to East Jerusalem's Muslims as well. This would include the right to monitor the Friday sermons delivered at al-Aqsa and the other mosques and to appoint a government committee to supervise the Waqf's administration (including the Haram al-Sharif).[56] In reaction, a group of 22 Muslim dignitaries convened on 24 July 1967 and wrote a memorandum, addressed to the Israeli military governor of the West Bank, claiming that the annexation of East Jerusalem was illegal and that the city is an "inseparable part of the Kingdom of Jordan." They declared themselves the Supreme Muslim Authority (*al-hay'a al-islamiyya al-'ulya*). The memorandum, that was accorded the force and effect of a religious legal opinion (*fatwa*),[57] stated the following:

> Because Muslim religious law clearly stipulates that Muslims must take the initiative and run their religious affairs by themselves in the situations that exist today, and because Muslim religious law prohibits non-Muslims from running the religious affairs of Muslims … therefore the signatories have appointed themselves the "Supreme Muslim Authority Responsible for all Muslim Matters in the West Bank including Jerusalem," until the end of the occupation.

A significant portion of the Supreme Muslim Authority's protest activities focused on protecting the Haram al-Sharif's status and preventing Israel from reducing the autonomy of the Waqf administration that controlled the site. In 1984, Shaykh Sa'd al-Din al-'Alami, who headed the West Bank's Islamic establishment, published a book containing hundreds of documents concerning these activities.[58] Subsequently, a book written by 'Abd al-Salam al-'Abadi, the Jordanian Waqf minister, credits Jordan with assisting the Supreme Muslim Authority in its struggle against Israel's attempts to expand its authority and influence on the Sacred Esplanade.[59]

In fact, at the day-to-day level, the same Palestinian-Jordanian officials and clergymen who had administered the site before June 1967 continued to do so under Israeli rule by remote control from Amman, with Israel's tacit consent. They continued their administrative subordination to instructions from Jordan's Waqf Ministry and received their salaries as Jordanian government employees. Every local high-level bureaucrat had a corresponding official in the Jordanian Waqf Ministry in Amman to whom he was subordinate. Consequently the Haram al-Sharif's official administrator, Shaykh Muhammad Husayn, held the title "assistant director of the Haram al-Sharif" and was subordinate to the administrator in Amman.

Disturbances and Incidents, 1967–87

Throughout the twenty years from Israel's 1967 conquest to the outbreak of the first Intifada, there were ongoing tensions associated with the Haram al-Sharif. The first incident was the act of an Australian Christian fundamentalist, Michael Dennis Rohan, who saw the re-establishment of the Temple as a precursor for the return of the Messiah. On 21 August 1969 a fire he set caused heavy damage to the Aqsa Mosque [fig. 144], destroying the unique *minbar* created by Nur al-Din Zangi and donated to the mosque by Saladin. The extensive repairs following this event continued for the next two decades; the substitute *minbar* was installed in the mosque in February 2007. The arson attack was exploited by Arabs to mount a campaign to liberate Jerusalem from Israeli rule by employing the Aqsa Mosque as a religious symbol.[60] Two days after the fire the UN Security Council convened at the urging of Arab countries and adopted a resolution expressing deep concern over the desecration of the Haram al-Sharif.[61] The Muslim claim was that the fire was set deliberately and Israel was held responsible.[62] Egyptian President Gamal 'Abd al-Nasser called for a war of purification against Israel, while Saudi King Faisal and other Arab political leaders called upon all Muslims to mobilize for *jihad* to liberate Jerusalem.[63] The event also served as Saudi King Faisal's impetus for the founding of the Organisation of the Islamic Conference (*munazhzhamat al-mu'tamar al-islami*), an intergovernmental grouping of 57 Muslim states.[64] In the fire's wake, King Hussein appointed the Royal Jordanian Commission for Jerusalem Affairs, headed by his brother, Crown Prince Hassan.

Another significant incident was a shooting attack staged on the Temple Mount on 11 April 1982 by Allen Goodman, a recent American immigrant to Israel who had been conscripted into the IDF and used his weapon to shoot at Muslims.[65] This incident was followed by various other events that offended the Palestinian Muslims. Violent demonstrations were conducted after the Goodman attack, in which a Waqf guard was killed and others were injured.[66]

In 1984 an illegal Jewish underground cell of well-known activists of the settler movement Gush Emunim was uncovered whose plan had been the destruction of the Aqsa Mosque. Their arrest, jailing, and eventual pardoning did nothing to allay Muslim fears of actions by various Jewish groups and by the government, actions which they viewed as aiming "to de-Islamize and Judaize" the character of the sacred space and its surroundings.

A demonstrative visit to the Temple Mount by the Knesset Internal Affairs Committee in January 1986 also triggered Muslim demonstrations and violent encounters between Muslims and the security forces, resulting in harsh reactions from the Arab world.[67] During this period Rabbi Mordechai Eliyahu, Israel's Sephardic Chief Rabbi, issued a ruling in favour of building a synagogue on the Temple Mount. The Muslims viewed this with alarm as an official Israeli initiative, and their reactions intensified accordingly.[68]

144 21 August 1969: The fire at the Aqsa Mosque

New Modus Vivendi (Waqf–Israel)

Despite the official discourse of conflict, ongoing informal meetings have been held regularly since 1967 between the Waqf's leaders and representatives of the Israeli police, the Jerusalem municipality, and the Israel Antiquities Authority (previously known as the Israel Department of Antiquities and Museums). These gradually created a modus vivendi between the Israeli government and the Waqf officials, as well as the Jordanian government.[69] In practice, the Israeli government essentially abandoned the enforcement of its law wherever the Temple Mount / the Haram al-Sharif was concerned. The site's administrators were moderate Palestinian figures appointed by Jordan, and they generally adhered to all the tacit understandings that were reached with Israel's representatives.

The post-1967 modus vivendi was based on the following understandings: The Waqf administers the site, controls the gates, dictates the rules of behaviour, employs Muslim guards (today there are 210 guards, 70 in each of the three shifts), is responsible for the ongoing maintenance and physical upkeep, and collects entrance fees from non-Muslim visitors to the Dome of the Rock and the Aqsa Mosque. However, the Waqf is not allowed to raise flags within the Sacred Esplanade. Significant renovations and constructions were, until September 1996, unofficially coordinated with the Israeli Antiquities Authority. One of the physical changes conducted by the Waqf during this period and in accordance with these understandings was extensive planting of trees and landscaping to the northeast of the Dome of the Rock.

Israel, on the other hand controls the Mahkama building (al-Madrasa al-Tankiziyya), which houses a Border Police unit to overlook the Sacred Esplanade and the Western Wall plaza and to intervene in cases of violation of public order. It also demanded the keys to the Magharibah Gate, thus controling the entrance of non-Muslim visitors through it. Israeli police guard the site from the outer circle and entrances and from a police post on the fringe of the Dome of the Rock platform to maintain public order on the Sacred Esplanade. However, some of the authority Israel claims to hold according to its post-1967 law is limited by the fear of large-scale Muslim violence. The major outstanding issues are the entrance of Jews into the Esplanade for prayer and the gradually reduced effectiveness of consultation concerning digging and construction. Some matters are coordinated between Waqf and Israeli authorities, such as visiting hours and the visits by high-ranking foreign officials.

The modus vivendi based on the above regulations and understandings prevailed until September 1996, when Muslim riots erupted following Israel's action to open the northern exit of the Western Wall Tunnel.

The Tunnel, the Western Wall, and the Israeli-Jewish Challenge

Soon after the inauguration of the plaza in front of the Western Wall the Chief Rabbinate and the Israeli Ministry of Religious Affairs initiated a project to cut a 320-metre long tunnel along the outer side of the Western Wall of the Temple Mount, from the vaults under Wilson's Arch to the so-called Hasmonaean aqueduct which connected to the Struthion Pool at the northwest corner of the Mount. The work continued for over ten years without archaeological supervision—a source of tension between the religious authorities and the Israel Department of Antiquities—and without permission from the owners of the overlying structures, a further cause for Arab protest and international condemnation. Fear was expressed that the tunnelling would cause subsidence of the buildings above and that the tunnel would be used as a pretext to access the Temple Mount from below. Tension was increased by the discovery of cracks in the walls of al-Madrasa al-Jawhariyya, al-Madrasa al-Manjakiyya, and Ribat al-Kurd, buildings adjacent to the Wall and above the tunnel. These cracks were blamed on the tunnelling activities, and only consolidation of the buildings calmed the situation. The Muslims also viewed the tunnel endeavour as an effort to change the Islamic character of the area.

In 1981 another incident in the tunnel caused anxiety amongst Muslim officials. During excavation work near the Warren Gate, which was revealed in the process of excavating the site, the Rabbi of the Western Wall, Yehuda Getz, started to remove stones separating the tunnel from Bir Sabil al-Qa'itbay (Cistern 31), located within the Haram and only 80 metres from the Dome of the Rock. A short fist fight ensued between Waqf employees and workmen under Getz's supervision. After the police put and end to the fight, the Government, aware of the consequences of the incident, ordered the opening's immediate sealing.

The Waqf, Arab governments, and Islamic organisations expressed concern about the physical consequences of the archaeological excavations conducted to the south and west of the Temple Mount and the excavation of the tunnel along the Western Wall, claiming destabilization of the walls of the Haram al-Sharif and the undermining of the Aqsa Mosque and the Mamluk *madrasas* to the west of the Sacred Esplanade. Complaints lodged with UNESCO by Jordan and other Arab states regarding the state of the Old City in general and the Haram al-Sharif in particular resulted in a long series of visits by Professor Raymond Lemaire as the personal representative of the Directors-General of that body. The conclusions of his reports[70] and the superior numbers and political clout of the Arab states led to annual condemnations of Israeli practice relating to the Haram al-Sharif area, to refuting the legal validity of the Israeli excavations south of the Temple Mount, and to the registering of Jerusalem on the list of "World Heritage Sites in Danger" in 1982.

Operation of the tunnel as a major tourist attraction, allowing the visitor to view the whole length of the Western Wall, the corner of the Antonia Fortress, the karstic fissure used for the aqueduct and the Struthion Pool, was limited by the fact that the tunnel was accessed only from the south. The site could not be truly opened to the public without a northern exit, inside the Muslim Quarter. Attempts to purchase a suitable exit failed and it was eventually decided to quarry a tunnel from the pool to a point on the Via Dolorosa, opposite the First Station of the Cross. The Israeli government procrastinated about the appropriate time to open the exit till September 1996, when some officials mistakenly viewed the opening of the northern exit as part of a quid-pro-quo arrangement between the government and the Waqf to allow the opening of the Hasmonaean Tunnel in return for the government's acceptance of the opening of Solomon's Stables for Muslim prayer.[71] The results were catastrophic as the newly formed Palestinian Authority (PA) used the ill-timed Israeli decision as a catalyst for yet another round of violence, focusing on the conflict between the two peoples over the definition of rights in the Temple Mount area. In the clashes between protesters and the police three Muslims were killed and 31 people were injured, including 11 policemen.[72] The riots quickly spread to East Jerusalem and the territories of the West Bank and the Gaza Strip. The events took on the character of

145 September 1996: Palestinian youths throwing stones on the Haram in the wake of the opening of the Hasmonaean tunnel

a popular uprising, which was supported by members of the PA's police, who even opened fire on Israelis, with 57 Palestinians and 15 Israelis being killed in the riots. A consequence of this event as well as of similar ones has been Israel's intermittent restriction of access of Palestinian Muslims to the Haram according to criteria of age and residence.

Incidentally, radical Islamic factions called the Palestinian activities in reaction to the opening of the Western Wall Tunnel the "al-Aqsa Intifada"[73]—the name that four years later was to be given to the Second Intifada. At the time it was claimed that the Israeli excavations constituted a physical threat to the Aqsa Mosque.[74] In the wake of this incident, the Islamic Movement in Israel organized the first convention (*mihrajan*) under the banner "al-Aqsa is in danger." This slogan transmitted to the Muslim public the message that Israel is seeking, in a deliberate and systematic manner, to destroy the Aqsa Mosque in order to build the Third Temple in its place.

The developments on the Jewish side after 1967 challenged the Palestinian Muslims and added fuel to the conflict. Despite the Israeli government's secular nature, the post-1967 nationalist-messianic wave and the Jewish settler movement in the Palestinian territories were religiously-motivated phenomena that increasingly influenced Israeli mainstream positions. The Temple Mount, together with the Western Wall, gradually developed into a national symbol. IDF induction ceremonies take place at the Western Wall, as well as other memorials and commemorations with the participation of Israel's president.

146 Memorial Day Ceremony at the Western Wall, honoring the fallen in Israel's wars

A few radical Jewish movements which aim to revive Temple construction and worship have been formed since 1967 (some of them funded by evangelical Christian organisations) and although they are marginal and opposed to government policy, their activity has offended Muslims.[75] Since the Oslo process there has been a significant rise in Israeli-Jewish awareness (including Jews who are not religiously observant) of the Temple Mount as a symbol of national and cultural identity.

Arab fear for the security of the sacred Muslim sites was reinforced by a number of incidents that Palestinians considered a threat to the very existence of the Haram al-Sharif. The fact that these actions came from the fringes of Israeli society, or even beyond it, did not affect their exploitation by the ascendant fundamentalist Islamic movements within Palestinian society, often with complete disregard for actual events. Although the official policy of the Israeli government is to prevent a change of the status quo on the Sacred Esplanade, many Muslims fear that Israel seeks to demolish the mosques and establish the Third Temple in their place—or alternatively, to change the status quo and permit corresponding Jewish worship on the site. Indeed, even though Jewish prayer upon the Temple Mount had been strictly prohibited by successive Israeli governments[76] there have, for a number of years, been a series of proposals made by ultra-nationalist Israelis to utilise the vast space of Solomon's Stables for Jewish prayer. In this context it must be remembered that *halakhah* (Jewish religious law) forbids Jews from coming up to the Temple Mount due to the sanctity of the site. This ban was reinforced by the Chief Rabbinate following the Six Day War [fig. 147] and by other halakhic authorities on numerous occasions since then,[77] the ban receiving political clout through the decision to reassert the administrative control of the Waqf on the Temple Mount.[78] However a group of rabbis, led by Chief Rabbi Shlomo Goren, provided ritual backing for the visit of Jews to the site as long as they stayed outside the original 500 square cubit space occupied by Solomon's Temple,[79] including the Herodian expansion of the Temple platform of which Solomon's Stables was a part.[80] Pressure mounted to sanction Jewish prayer at the site;[81] suggestions were even made to construct a synagogue above Solomon's Stables[82] or to allow prayer within the confines of that structure.[83] These appeals did not pass unnoticed by Muslim ultra-nationalists and the decision by the Waqf and the Islamic movement to transform the site into a mosque was probably hastened to block any future possibility of the realisation of these proposals.

First Intifada and the Events of October 1990

The First Palestinian Uprising (Intifada) which erupted in December 1987 turned the Sacred Esplanade into a central locus of the national conflict. The Palestinian Muslims used the relative immunity of the site—where large crowds gathered after the Friday service and its large open space which Israeli forces usually do not enter—as a venue of political demonstrations and unrest. The deputy of the Mufti of Jerusalem, Shaykh Muhammad-Sa'id al-Jamal, stated that the Haram al-Sharif is an inseparable part of the land of Palestine and that it therefore was only natural that the Intifada should be conducted in the mosques as well.[84]

The stormiest event in the history of Palestinian–Israeli violence at the Esplanade took place in October 1990, which the Muslims refer to as the "al-Aqsa Massacre." This occurred when the radical Jewish Faithful of the Temple Mount Movement publicised provocative plans, including a cornerstone-laying ceremony for the Third Temple near the Dung Gate and the erection of a *sukkah* (a booth commemorating the Jews' wanderings in the desert after the Exodus from Egypt) next to the Magharibah Gate. In the Muslim version of the events, the Faithful of the Temple Mount Movement's cornerstone-laying ceremony was taken seriously by many Muslims, who organised for pre-emptive action. A month prior to this incident, al-Aqsa preacher Shaykh Fathallah Silwadi called upon Muslims to come and defend the Aqsa Mosque with their own bodies.[85] The police prohibited the planned ceremony from taking place near the Sacred Esplanade but permitted it to be conducted in the nearby Silwan area. In reaction, Muslims showered rocks from the Haram al-Sharif Esplanade onto Jewish worshippers praying below at the adjacent Western Wall. The police, summoned to the Temple Mount in order to disperse the demonstrators and stop the rock-throwing, opened fire killing 17 Muslims. Another 53 Muslims and 30 Jews (police and

147 The Chief Rabbinate's announcement prominently displayed at the entrance of the bridge leading to Bab al-Magharibah, the only of the Haram's gates open to Jewish visitors
The photo was taken in December 2008

worshippers) were injured.[86] In the aftermath two books entitled *The Aqsa Massacre* were published in Arabic.[87] The Waqf also mounted an exhibition of photos and other artefacts of the incident at the Islamic Museum next to the Aqsa Mosque. Furthermore, the UN Security Council unanimously passed a resolution condemning the acts of violence committed by the Israeli security forces resulting in loss of human life and injury to many Muslims on the Haram al-Sharif, and decided to have the Secretary-General send a mission to the region to investigate the incident. The US also supported this decision,[88] but Israel did not consent to receive the delegation. One of the outcomes of the October 1990 events was the beginning of a campaign launched by Shaykh Ra'id Salah, the leader of the Northern Branch of the Islamic Movement in Israel, claiming that Israel intended to bring about the destruction of the Aqsa Mosque (see below).

Arab-Muslim Competition for Involvement and Control of the Sacred Esplanade

The centrality of the Haram al-Sharif as a religious and political symbol resulted in competition between Arab and Muslim states and organisations as to who would control, or at least have a symbolic affiliation to, the Sacred Esplanade. Three Arab states actively seek to gain control or at least increase their standing in the Haram al-Sharif: Jordan, Saudi Arabia, and Morocco. Other Arab leaders, however, see Islam's holy sites in Jerusalem as belonging to the entire Muslim nation—that is, they too wish to play a role, if only a symbolic one.

As noted, Jordan has played a central role in the administration of the Haram al-Sharif since 1948. Indeed, King Hussein regarded this responsibility an essential tool for strengthening the Hashemite regime's legitimacy. Since the 1970s, the Saudis have provided financial support for radical bodies in Jerusalem. In the 1980s, a chapter of the General Islamic Congress headquartered in Saudi Arabia was active in the Haram al-Sharif. This fund financed renovations of the Aqsa Mosque and other Waqf assets. It also supplemented the salaries of the Waqf's employees (seventy five dinars each) and assisted various welfare and educational institutions in East Jerusalem, the West Bank, and Israel.[89] Moroccan involvement with the Sacred Esplanade included a personal contribution by King Hassan II, who donated

148 Israeli policemen at a deserted Western Wall, fleeing rocks which Palestinians are throwing from the Haram in the wake of the Hebron massacre of 25 February 1994

149 A Palestinian wounded near the Aqsa Mosque during a clash with Israeli police, 25 February 1994

carpets to the Aqsa Mosque in the 1980s, as well as by his chairing the "Al-Quds [Jerusalem] Committee of the Organisation of the Islamic Conference." As for Egyptian involvement, one can point to President Muhammad Anwar al-Sadat who, during his visit to Jerusalem, insisted on praying at al-Aqsa Mosque. He then declared: "No Arab nation will agree to relinquish the Aqsa Mosque or the Dome of the Rock."[90] After the visit, his deputy, Hassan Tohami, informed Jerusalem's mayor Teddy Kollek that the Egyptian government had decided to send engineers to help renovate the Aqsa Mosque.[91]

An incident reflecting inter-Arab competition over involvement with the Esplanade took place in 1992 when money was needed to conduct urgent renovations of the Dome of the Rock and the Aqsa Mosque. Both King Hussein of Jordan and King Fahd of Saudi Arabia competed over who would donate the required funding. Finally King Hussein decided to contribute 8,249,000 dollars of his private and family fortune to the Haram al-Sharif's renovation. The request of King Fahd of Saudi Arabia to contribute to the renovations through UNESCO (so as to circumvent the need for Jordanian approval) was rejected by King Hussein.

In the Oslo Accords signed between Israel and the Palestine Liberation Organisation (PLO) in September 1993, it was agreed that the issue of Jerusalem would be deferred to the negotiations over the permanent status agreements. Jerusalem was not among the jurisdictions granted to the Palestinian Authority that was established in the territories of the Gaza Strip and the West Bank as part of the Oslo Accords. However, on 11 October

1993 Israel's Minister of Foreign Affairs, Shimon Peres, sent a letter to Norwegian Foreign Minister Johan Jorgen Holst assuring him of the following:

> I wish to confirm that the Palestinian institutions of East Jerusalem and the interest and well-being of the Palestinians of East Jerusalem are of great importance and will be preserved. Therefore, all the Palestinian institutions of East Jerusalem, including the economic, social, educational and cultural, and the holy Christian and Moslem places, are performing an essential task for the Palestinian population. Needless to say, we will not hamper their activity; on the contrary, the fulfilment of this important mission is to be encouraged.[92]

This letter was used as a trade-off in the negotiations for the agreement of the PLO chairman to establish the PA's centre outside Jerusalem, namely in Ramallah.[93] The formation of the PA in 1994 immediately created tensions between the Palestinians and Jordan, and between the two of them and Israel.

While negotiations between Jordan and Israel were being conducted, King Hussein insisted that the peace treaty between the two countries include a clause—which later became Article 9(2) of the agreement—stipulating that when Israel negotiates a permanent agreement with the Palestinians, it will give precedence to the Hashemite monarchy's historic and current role in Islam's holy sites in Jerusalem.[94] Shortly after, the Palestinians pressured Jordan into reaching an agreement with the PA whereby it stated that it is holding the Haram al-Sharif and the other holy places on a temporary basis only, until the PA is able to take full control following agreement with Israel.[95]

On the ground, Jerusalem's Muslim establishment underwent a major transformation with the establishment of the PA in 1994. The PA immediately began intervening in the affairs of the Haram al-Sharif. For example, in July 1994, when Jerusalem's mayor Teddy Kollek invited King Hussein to pray at the Aqsa Mosque,[96] PA Chairman Yasser Arafat reacted by declaring that "Arab Jerusalem is under Palestinian jurisdiction," and thus Israel has no authority to proffer such an invitation. Only he could invite the king to come and pray with him.[97] These threats resulted in the cancellation of the visit.

The PA was also successful, in October 1994, in imposing its own candidate—Shaykh Ikrima Sabri—as Mufti of Jerusalem and the Palestinian areas, instead of the Jordanian nominee. At the beginning of 1999, Sabri moved his offices from a building that was adjacent to the outer section of the Sacred Esplanade, near the Gate of the Chain, to a building adjacent to its inner section. This manoeuvre established the seat of the Mufti of the PA within the Haram al-Sharif, as was the situation during the British Mandate period.[98]

The post-Oslo peace process situation produced a new modus vivendi between the Palestinian Authority and Jordan. Most of the administrative policies regarding the Sacred Esplanade were coordinated by the Waqf administrators with both Jordan and the PA. In 2006, Jordan still financed most of the Jerusalem Waqf's payroll, and the PA supplemented it. Thus, despite the efforts of the other players, Jordan has remained the major Arab country associated with the Haram al-Sharif.

The Muslim Campaign for al-Aqsa and the Rise of the Islamic Movement among Israeli Arabs

The political struggle over Jerusalem and its holy sites since June 1967 has enhanced the status of the Temple Mount / the Haram al-Sharif in the minds of Jews and Muslims alike. The Muslim side, which is the weaker side in the conflict, developed a new ethos of Jerusalem and its Sacred Esplanade. It is based on renewing, emphasising, and marketing to the masses early Muslim traditions (taken from the medieval literature in praise of al-Quds—the *Fada'il*) and introducing them into the forefront of public discourse.[99] Thus, al-Aqsa is often mentioned today in the context of its connection to the Sacred Mosque in Mecca through frequent emphasis on, and reference to, the Qur'anic verse (1.17) which tells of the Prophet Muhammad's night journey "from the Sacred Sanctuary to the Furthest Sanctuary"—in Arabic, al-Aqsa. It also revives the traditions according to which al-Aqsa was built by Adam 40 years after the Ka'ba of Mecca. According to this narrative, the Aqsa Mosque has been in existence since the dawn of mankind. This effort also employs eschatological and apocalyptic traditions which relate that on the Day of Judgement the Ka'ba will be transported to Jerusalem as a bride, along with all of the pilgrims who have visited it. The entire human race will then rise up on the Mount of Olives and from there a bridge will extend to the Rock—the place of judgement.[100]

The Prophet's night journey (*isra'*) and the tradition concerning his ascension to heaven (*mi'raj*) have been elevated to a special celebration in the last two generations. In 1953 the Jordanians introduced *al-isra' wal-mi'raj* day, which traditionally takes place on the 27th of the Islamic month Rajab, as a formal holy day, with special prayers and official ceremonies and speeches.[101]

Early Muslim writers acknowledge that the Haram al-Sharif is the site of the Jewish Temple. Thus, *A Brief Guide to the Haram al-Sharif*, published in 1929 by the Supreme Muslim Council, maintains the following referring to the Haram:

> Its identity with the site of Solomon's Temple is beyond dispute. This, too, is the spot, according to the universal belief, on which David built there an altar unto the Lord, and offered burnt offerings and peace offerings (2 Samuel XXIV, 25).[102]

However, since 1967 there is a growing tendency among Muslim writers in general and among Palestinian authors and politicians in particular to deny the Jewish attachment to the Sacred Esplanade. Firstly, they refer to the Jewish Temple (*haykal*) by adding the term *al-maz'um*, whose literal meaning is "alleged." Moreover, PA Chairman Yasser Arafat used to claim that the Jewish Temple had been in Yemen, not in Jerusalem.[103] His cabinet member Saeb Arikat was quoted by then Israeli Minister of Foreign Affairs Shlomo Ben-Ami as having said, during the July 2000 Camp David II negotiations: "This whole issue of the Temple … is a Jewish invention lacking any basis."[104] Sometimes such a denial is grounded in archaeology, although no excavations could ever be conducted under the Dome of the Rock. As an example, Palestinian-Jordanian historian Kamil al-'Asali maintained that "modern archaeology has not succeeded in proving that the site on which the Temple stood is located in this place, since no remnants of the Temple have survived."[105]

Secondly, current Islamic writing also tends to deny an authentic Jewish connection to the Western Wall. For example, the Mufti of the Palestinian Authority, Shaykh Ikrima Sabri, stated in an interview broadcast by the al-Jazeera television channel that the Western Wall was never, even for a single second, a Jewish structure and that the Jews have no connection to it. "Who decided that the Western Wall is a remnant of the Temple?" asked Sabri, answering with the rhetorical question: "Is it scientifically or archaeologically conceivable that Herod, who built the temple to Augustus in Caesarea, also built a temple for the Jews?"[106] According to Sabri, the Jews only began to pray at the Western Wall during the nineteenth century, when they began to develop nationalist aspirations. Shortly afterwards, in April 2001, Egyptian Waqf Minister Mahmoud Hamdi Zaqzuq stated that the Jews have no connection to the Western Wall which, according to him, "was never a holy site for them." Zaqzuq added that no historical evidence exists to support Jewish claims regarding the existence of Solomon's "alleged" Temple anywhere in the city.[107]

Another interesting phenomenon related to the growing importance of the Sacred Esplanade in the national conflict over Palestine is the usage to designate the entire Esplanade as "al-Aqsa" rather than "al-Haram al-Sharif." Since the post-Crusader era, Jerusalem's Sacred Esplanade was upgraded to a *haram* by naming it "al-Haram al-Sharif." However since the 1980s Palestinians gradually abandoned that designation, given in honor of Jerusalem's status, in favour of its more traditional name: "al-Aqsa." Evidently, since "al-Aqsa" appears in the Qur'an, all Muslims around the world should be familiar with it.

Increased use of the name "al-Aqsa" is particularly striking against the background of what is written on the website of the Jerusalem Waqf, headed by PA's Mufti Shaykh Ikrima Sabri. There, it is asserted that "al Masjid al-Aqsa was erroneously called by the name the Haram al-Qudsi al-Sharif," and that the site's correct name is al-Aqsa.[108] In proof of this, Sabri quotes Ibn Taymiyya (1263–1328), a precursor of modern Islamic fundamentalism, who denied the existence of a *haram* in Jerusalem. Sabri also states that Arab historians such as Mujir al-Din al-Hanbali, author of the famed fifteenth-century work on Jerusalem, did not make use of the term *haram* in connection with the Aqsa site.[109] Since Hanbali sources are being cited by Sabri, one should ask whether this is indicative of Saudi Arabian influence or pressure. The "al-Aqsa" designation has thus become popular and prevalent. The previous term is still used by official bodies (the Organisation of the Islamic Conference, the Arab League) and by ordinary people, in contrast to religious entities.

The growing political importance of the site for Muslims and the religious traditions associated with it entailed, since the late 1980s, a significant increase in the number of Muslim worshippers who arrive for Friday prayers on the site, especially during the holy month of Ramadan. This can be as many as 400,000 people on the last Friday of Ramadan, according to police counts.

The Arab Muslim citizens of Israel (about 350,000 in 1967 and 800,000 in 2007, not including Muslim residents in East Jerusalem and the Druze in the Golan Heights) have a vested interest in both a permanent solution to the Palestinian–Israeli conflict and in Palestinian Muslim sovereignty over the Haram al-Sharif. In June 1967 Israel's Muslim citizens were able to access the Haram al-Sharif after a nineteen-year period of exclusion during Jordanian rule over East Jerusalem. Shortly after taking over East Jerusalem on 7 June, the Israeli government had an interest to show that Muslim worship in the Aqsa Mosque would be unhindered. The first prayer conducted there was broadcast in Arabic over the Israeli government radio station by religious programming editor Nur al-Din Darini (Abu Jarir), a Muslim citizen of Israel. The authorities also provided transportation for Israeli Muslims to attend the first Friday prayers after the war.

There are two interesting examples for the identification of Israeli Arabs with the Palestinian side regarding the battle over the Sacred Esplanade. After a demonstrative tour of the Temple Mount by members of the Knesset's Internal Affairs Committee in 1986 and the publication of rabbinic decisions permitting Jews to enter the site, Ibrahim Nimr Husayn, chairman of the National Committee of Arab Mayors, issued the following declaration: "We shall not rest nor shall we remain silent until the status quo is preserved in the place we hold dear."[110] Another example is the declaration issued by *qadi*s and employees of Israel's Shari'a courts (Muslim religious courts) in February 1986 which stated that any attempt to violate the accepted agreements on the Temple Mount is liable to end in a clash between religions.

The Islamic Movement of Israel's Arab citizens played a special role in the enhancement of the Haram al-Sharif's political and religious status. Its Northern Branch coined the slogan "Al-Aqsa is in danger" and ingrained this in the consciousness of Muslims in Israel, the Palestinian territories, and throughout the Muslim world. This led to the movement taking an active leadership role in developments inside the Haram, especially in Solomon's Stables and beneath the Aqsa Mosque. This issue will be dealt with in detail below.

On 10 October 1996 the Islamic Movement held a mass assembly under the slogan "Al-Aqsa is in danger" in Umm al-Fahm's sports stadium, where a painted model of the

150 Shaykh Ra'id Salah, leader of the Islamic Movement (Northern Branch), at the annnual mass rally in Umm al-Fahm, 16 September 2005

Dome of the Rock was erected. This assembly has become an annual event, attended by some 100,000 Israeli Muslims [fig. 150].

Encouraged by its success at Solomon's Stables, the Islamic Movement continued to raise funds among its local supporters and from the Persian Gulf. Its leaders visited these countries, dwelling on the danger of a Jewish takeover of Islamic holy sites in Jerusalem. The funds were used to prepare additional prayer halls on the Haram al-Sharif's lower level, namely preparing the passage below the Aqsa Mosque, called al-Aqsa al-Qadima, as an additional roofed prayer hall. These comprehensive development projects had two objectives. One was to take over the lower level and thus prevent the Jews from finding a place for worship on the Temple Mount and from digging a tunnel underneath the site. A second objective was to develop as many prayer sites as possible, both covered and open, in order to transform the Haram al-Sharif into a Muslim focal point whose status would be equivalent to that of Mecca and which would attract Muslims from throughout the world.

Inspection of Antiquities and Relations with the Israeli Department of Antiquities and the Israel Antiquities Authority, 1967–96

During the first twenty years of Israeli rule in East Jerusalem, the Department of Antiquities and Museums of the Ministry of Education and Culture maintained regular contacts with the Waqf in all matters concerning the Temple Mount. From time to time departmental inspectors would visit the mount, sometimes accompanied by police officers or government representatives. On occasion, mainly when the Waqf was engaged in construction or earth-moving operations on the Mount, questions arose concerning archaeological supervision and prevention of damage to antiquities. Such questions frequently had to be settled at the political level.[111]

During this period of time, in particular from the mid-1980s onward, informal relations were established between representatives of the Israeli Department of Antiquities and the professional staff of the Waqf, mainly the engineers and architects responsible on behalf of the Waqf for development and maintenance work on the Mount. These relationships amounted primarily to occasional personal meetings in which views and positions were presented in various areas relating to activity in and around the Temple Mount. At the same time, the Waqf consistently declined to inform Israeli authorities, in an official capacity, of their plans for construction and development on the Temple Mount.

From 1988 the legal situation on the Mount changed following an appeal brought before the Israel Supreme Court by the Faithful of the Temple Mount Movement and in light of the directives issued by the Government Attorney General that reviewed the authority and the modus operandi of government agencies in relation to works on the Mount.[112] In accordance with these directives the Israel Department of Antiquities and Museums, and later the Israel Antiquities Authority (IAA), conducted regular tours of inspection on the Temple Mount, monitoring work of various types (construction, development, and conservation) and submitted regular reports of this inspection to the Attorney General.[113] During the years 1990–96 good informal relations were maintained between the IAA staff and the professional personnel active on the Mount. These relations included regular meetings, during which information was received and updated and opinions exchanged as to activities on the Mount. In the course of these conversations, the Waqf staff gave the IAA representatives advance notice of planned activities, such as extensive repairs to the Dome of the Rock and preparation of the underground vaults in Solomon's Stables for visitors and worshippers. The IAA representatives, for their part, showed the Waqf staff their plans for excavation south of the Temple Mount and for developing the area for tourism.

It should be noted that work conducted at this time on the Mount, under the direction of the professional departments of the Waqf, generally adhered to universally accepted principles and rules for the treatment of historical monuments, with the cooperation and supervision of international professional agencies. Thus differences of opinion between the IAA staff and the Waqf on professional matters were almost non-existent.

Notable in this context is the extensive renovation, by an Irish contractor, of the Dome of the Rock in 1992–94, during which large portions of the dome were replaced. The work, including an extensive conservational survey of the existing dome, was commissioned by the Waqf and involved many foreign experts who conducted their work over many months inside the Temple Mount. During the work, access to the site by Israeli professionals was possible and they were able to communicate their advice.

The situation changed drastically in autumn 1996, with the active entry of the Islamic

Movement of Israel's Arab citizens into development projects and into the management of the Temple Mount. The work to prepare Solomon's Stables for worship was conducted for the first time with the participation of the Islamic Movement under the stewardship of Shaykh Ra'id Salah, mayor of Umm al-Fahm (and leader of the movement's radical Northern Branch). Utilising funds collected from supporters in Israel, the movement invested about $500,000 in construction materials and converted Solomon's Stables into a huge prayer hall renamed the Marwani Hall or Mosque. This construction involved hundreds of volunteers, who carried out the project.[114] The process involved operations in violation of conservation principles for the treatment of historical monuments; in some places antiquities were actually damaged (e.g., by drilling holes into ancient walls).

It came to the IAA's knowledge that some of the work had even been done without the consent of the professional staff of the Waqf, who had been barred at some points from entering the site of operations. During these years the IAA's ability to inspect the site and to conduct informal discussion with the Waqf was severely curtailed.

In 1998–2000 further work was carried out in the ancient underground passages and vaults beneath the southern part of the Temple Mount, encompassing, in addition to the work in Solomon's Stables, the renovation and utilisation of the derelict passage below the Aqsa Mosque, known as al-Aqsa al-Qadima. The works reached a zenith toward the end of 1999, when a monumental staircase and entrance were cut down into Solomon's Stables.[115] In the process a tremendous pit was dug with heavy mechanical machinery without any archaeological supervision, causing major irrevocable changes to the site, in complete contravention of internationally recognised standards of management of sites of universal cultural value and sparking worldwide controversy over the management of the archaeological patrimony of the Temple Mount.[116] The Director of the IAA, Amir Drori, described the event as an "archaeological crime." However the Waqf could not bring into the Haram heavy machinery without consent of the Israeli police and perhaps other high political authorities. The resulting political uproar in the Israeli body-politic has not subsided, with the ostensibly a-political Committee for the Prevention of Destruction to Antiquities on the Temple Mount placing an intense scrutiny upon the actions of the Waqf, Israel Police, IAA, and the Government within the site. Periodic petitions to the Supreme Court have been made challenging the decisions of the official bodies noted, these motions usually rejected as being beyond the jurisdiction of the court due to the highly sensitive nature of the site.[117]

One of the rare cases in which Israel implemented its control over construction works on the site took place in August 1999. The Waqf carved out a window in the southern wall of al-Zawiyya al-Khanthaniyya in order to provide light and air to the underground prayer hall. Israeli authorities viewed this action as endangering the site's character, fearing that the Waqf will turn this window into a Muslim-controlled exit leading to the Israeli exclusively controlled excavation area south of the Esplanade. The closing of the window could be carried out since the work could be done from outside the Esplanade. In contrast to this case, when the Waqf opened a large exit to the Marwani Mosque and caused damage to antiquities, Israel's Attorney General Elyakim Rubinstein recommended not implementing Israeli law because "Restoring the pre-existing situation might bring to bloodshed and to a situation that might inflame Judea, Samaria and the entire territory of Israel." His position was backed by a ruling of Israel's Supreme Court.[118]

Two bulges, one each on the southern and eastern walls, were noted in 2000. While the structural causes of these bulges was a matter for some debate, with the usual mutual recriminations, the inherent danger of collapse, on the one hand, and the clear understanding that such a collapse would drag unwanted responses from extremists of both sides, on the other, created an urgent necessity to treat the problem. A debate ensued concerning the thorny subject who had the competence to repair the wall and especially who had the right. With the decline of the influence of the Palestinian Authority on the Temple Mount it was decided at prime ministerial level that the repair would be used as a pretext to enhance the influence of the Jordanians over the site. A specialist team from the Hashemite Kingdom was invited to investigate the structural needs and entrusted with the supervision of the works which were completed in 2006.

Camp David II Summit, Sharon's Visit, and the Outbreak of the Aqsa Intifada

The Sacred Esplanade issue was the bone of contention at the Camp David peace talks of July 2000 between Israel and the Palestinian Authority with US President Bill Clinton's mediation. The final compromise proposal suggested by Clinton was a vertical division of sovereignty, according to which the Palestinians would have supreme sovereignty over the surface levels and the buildings of the Haram, while Israel would have sovereignty beneath the surface at the level of the Western Wall and its plaza. The proposal was rejected by the Palestinians.[119] Israelis were offended by Yasser Arafat's denial of the existence of the Jewish Temple. Israelis and Palestinians continued to discuss the issue of sovereignty over the Temple Mount at Taba. However, with the release to the media of information about Palestinian denials of a Jewish Temple, combined with information about the additional works that the Waqf was carrying out on the Temple Mount, the Israeli opposition exerted pressure on the government and on the Chief Rabbinical Council to change its traditional opposition to Jewish entry onto the Haram al-Sharif.

Finally, the demonstrative visit of Ariel Sharon (who was then leader of the opposition), six other Knesset members from his Likud party, and a large police escort on 28 September 2000 culminated in a violent clash. During the visit and the subsequent days of violence, three Palestinians were killed and many more were injured. The incident was the cause

151 1999: Large-scale mechanical earth-removal north of Solomon's Stables, in preparation of a new staircase and entrance

152 2008: The new staircase leading down to the Stables, now known as al-Musalla al-Marwani

for the outbreak of turbulent riots in Israel, the West Bank, and the Gaza Strip, which the Arabs named the "Aqsa Intifada." Three weeks after the intifada's eruption an Arab summit was convened in Cairo (21 October 2000)—a summit which received the title of the "Aqsa Summit."

One of the outcomes of Sharon's visit was the prohibition of all non-Muslim visitors from entering the Sacred Esplanade for about three years and a parallel intensification of Israeli access restrictions for Palestinians to the site. Israel restored the visits with the tacit consent of the Waqf (in cooperation with Jordan, when Yasser Arafat was isolated in Ramallah) in August 2003. However, the repercussions of Sharon's visit were much more wide-ranging for the Israeli–Palestinian struggle.

In 2004 part of the ramp leading up to the Magharibah Gate collapsed, requiring the construction of a temporary wooden bridge. Israel decided unilaterally to remodel the ascent by excavation, partial demolition, and the future construction of a permanent bridge to the Magharibah entrance. The works regenerated Muslim condemnation and protest resulting in the dispatch of a UNESCO technical mission to investigate the issue which recommended the immediate cessation of the work. Excavation continued for some time and more modest proposals were submitted to the planning commissions for a simple bridge set upon the remains of the ascent. At the time of writing, the matter has yet to be resolved.

Conclusion

Since the 1920s the Sacred Esplanade of Jerusalem came to symbolise the bone of contention in the conflict over Palestine. The Haram renovations, side by side with the struggle over the rights to the Western Wall, have proven a strong tool in pulling together Palestinian Muslims and the Muslim world ever since the British Mandate period.

The maintenance and even definition of the lines of division between the communities was a clear aim of the British authorities, a situation which left neither side fully content and resulted in a series of incidents which the Mandatory government never succeeded in controlling on the political level. At the same time, the British authorities succeeded in introducing modern conservation methods for maintenance of the monuments on the site, though scholars were never able to carry out archaeological excavations or to properly document the subterranean spaces, due to a basic reticence of the Muslim guardians to activities which might, in their view, weaken the hold of Islam on the Mount by the exposure of early "non-Muslim" remains.

The period of exclusive Muslim control under Jordanian rule was characterised by two incidents displaying the continuation of the same inbuilt tension. The assassination of King Abdullah showed that the attraction of the site for extremists was not dimmed by Islam's full control of the Haram, while the important restoration of the Dome of the Rock demonstrated that the necessity for modern management, underscored by the British, was well understood by the site's new rulers. During the nineteen years of Jordanian rule, the Hashemites capitalised on their control of the Haram, using its renovation to enhance their legitimacy in the Arab and Muslim arena, and they have retained an element of control since then.

This conflict intensified after 1967 with the Israeli capture of East Jerusalem and other Arab-populated territory. From this time on Israeli Jews were also able to develop areas near the Esplanade, including the Western Wall, as a national symbol founded on their claim for

153 Ariel Sharon's visit, 28 September 2000

historical rights. Israel expected the Arab party to the conflict to recognise at least the Jews' historical connection to the Temple Mount. Tension was manifested in repeated attempts by nationalist religious Jewish groups of exremists to actively express their aspiration to renew Jewish rule over the Mount and even bring it about by force. These attempts have heightened the fears of the Muslim religious establishment of any challenge that might undermine the historical connection of Islam to the site. Accordingly, archaeological research by Israeli scholars close to the Temple Mount, and especially the excavations conducted south of the Mount between 1968 and 1982, are presented as a tool in the political and national conflict and as an Israeli attempt to test the Muslim control of the site.

For Jews and Muslims, Israelis and Palestinians, the Temple Mount and the Haram al-Sharif respectively are the physical embodiment of their religious and national aspirations. Both groups have at times tested the fragile lines of—often informal—understandings that provided periods of artificial tranquillity. Challenges to that delicate status quo were always a reason for discord. According to a poll conducted in February 2005, only 9 percent of the Jewish public is willing for sovereignty over the Temple Mount to pass entirely into Palestinian hands, while 51 percent insist on exclusive Israeli control of the site and 36 percent are prepared for joint Palestinian-Israeli control.[120]

Without doubt, the Sacred Esplanade has been and will continue to remain a contentious issue between Israel and the Palestinians and is a major stumbling block to peace.

1917 to the Present:

Basic Changes, but Not Dramatic: *Al-Haram al-Sharif* in the Aftermath of 1967

Nazmi Al-Jubeh

Riwaq, Centre for Architectural Conservation, Ramallah

In the year 2000, the Palestinian and Israeli negotiators at Camp David and Taba failed to reach a comprehensive and final solution of the long-lasting conflict. There were several reasons for this state of affairs, the exploration of which is beyond the scope of this paper, but one of the most complex reasons was *sovereignty* over the Haram al-Sharif and finding solutions for Jewish attachment to the site, as requested by the Israeli negotiators. This was the first time that Israel formally sought recognition of Jewish attachment as well as, to a certain extent, a share in sovereignty over the site. Despite the new agenda on the negotiation table, Israel had worked to reach this status by creating a long list of facts on the ground since 7 June 1967.[1]

Immediately after the Israeli occupation of East Jerusalem the Israeli flag was raised by Israeli soldiers atop the Dome of the Rock, declaring the Israeli occupation of "all of Jerusalem" and sending clear messages to the Palestinian population and much beyond it. The struggle over the meaning of that event is not yet finished, so the history of the Haram al-Sharif since June 1967 until the present is the history of a conflict over the means of control of the site in particular and of the adjacent areas in general. True, Israeli Minister of Defense Moshe Dayan ordered that the flag be taken down after Shaykh 'Abdulhamid al-Sa'ih, the Grand Imam of the Aqsa Mosque, refused to call for prayer and to "act normally" unless this be done.[2] Israeli policy towards the site was not well defined from the beginning and actually went into several stages, some planned while others were only a reaction to certain developments.

The object of this paper is to trace the various administrative as well as physical changes that took place in the Haram al-Sharif and the adjacent area from June 1967 until the present. One of the major problems of this review of developments on the site is not only the sensitivity of the subject, a crucial and emotionally loaded aspect, but also the

154 6 May 1995: An aerial view showing the Dome of the Rock at bottom and the prayer plaza in front of the Western Wall close to the upper right corner, where a ceremony is taking place
Photo: Moshe Milner

lack of references; therefore I will depend to a great deal on my private observation as well on statements issued by various parties to the conflict.

Changing the Status Quo

"Status quo" is a term which is widely used in Jerusalem with different meanings. Its original interpretation was an agreement concluded by various Christian communities in Jerusalem to regulate the rights and uses of Christian Holy Places in both Jerusalem and Bethlehem under the Ottoman Empire since 1852.[3] Regardless of this formal agreement, which was respected by and expanded during the British Mandate over Palestine and fully respected by Jordan, it took the form of a social compact among the citizens of Jerusalem, interpreted as respecting the de facto situation or modus vivendi in the city's holy places sacred to all three religions. Thus, whenever a conflict arises over any holy place, the reaction is the automatic use of the term "status quo."

Since Israel considered its occupation of East Jerusalem as "liberation and an opportunity to correct an historical injustice," most Israeli actions in Jerusalem are to be understood in this framework, which can be summarized by the long-declared slogan, that "the United Jerusalem is the Eternal Capital of Israel." This led to dramatic changes in the status quo of the Holy Places in general, and of the Haram al-Sharif in particular.

For Jerusalem's Palestinian Muslims the Israeli actions, which will be detailed below, were a challenge to their very existence in the city in particular and in Palestine in general; they therefore converted the Haram al-Sharif into a symbol of this conflict. The sensitivity of the site, with all its surrounding areas (along the western and southern walls of the Haram), was so clear during the past four decades and a reason for several bloody conflicts between both sides. Issues such as attacks against the Haram, archaeological excavations around and beneath it, Jewish settlement activities adjacent to the Haram, projects to reconstruct the Third Temple, exercising freedom of access to the Haram, the presence of Israeli police, the Western Wall tunnel, the Magharibah Gate of the Haram al-Sharif, and so forth, are all of great importance for tracing the development of the site since 1967 and also for an understanding of the Palestinian reaction to them.[4]

Since it was convenient for both Israelis and Palestinians to maintain Jordanian control over the site, dramatic changes in the aftermath of 1967 were not welcomed, for they could lead to a dramatization of the conflict. The replacement of the Jordanian administration—which had begun in the early 1950s—could be seen as a total change of the political game. For Israel, it was easier to deal with a modest Jordanian presence (through arrangements or a gentlemen's agreement) than with complicated and vague Palestinian structures.[5] Till now, in spite of the establishment of the Palestinian Authority in 1995, Jordanian rule has proven to be the fallback position for both Israelis and Palestinians. The recent events related to the restoration of the southeastern corner of the city and the Haram[6] (Solomon's Stables / al-Musalla al-Marwani) were clear evidence that Jordan can play a vital role in stabilizing the sensitive situation on the site.[7] This is also a proof that any changing of the "status quo" can be dangerous to all parties concerned and, above all, to the site itself, taking into consideration the different interpretations of the meaning of that term.

After the removal of the Israeli flag from atop the Dome of the Rock, the muezzin called for prayer in the Haram al-Sharif, a sign of "normality." Is "normality" a proper terminology to be used to describe the post-1967 realities in and around the Haram al-Sharif?

Immediate Developments and the Creation of "New Realities"

Three major changes took place directly after the Israeli occupation of the Old City in June 1967, arousing suspicion within the Muslim community in Jerusalem, in particular, and among Palestinians and the Muslim world, in general. These were the destruction of the Magharibah Quarter, confiscation of the key to the Magharibah Gate (a Haram Gate on the western wall that leads from the Haram to the Wailing Wall plaza), and the confiscation of the Madrasa Tankiziyya.

The first change led to the destruction of an entire community that had existed in Jerusalem since the thirteenth century, as well as the destruction of several holy places, changing the status quo (at least that which had been in effect since 1929) by creating a huge plaza in front of the Wailing Wall.[8] The second change challenged total Muslim control over the Haram al-Sharif, securing access to its plaza without the permission of the Muslim Waqf, a development that was strengthened through later actions. Confiscation of the Madrasa Tankiziyya (adjacent to the Chain Gate, a major gate of the Haram al-Sharif in the western wall), which is a huge building overlooking both the plazas of the Haram al-Sharif and the newly created plaza of the Wailing Wall,[9] also led to actual control by Israel (through different organizations and agencies) of a large section of the western wall of the Haram al-Sharif.

These developments were crowned by declaring the plazas of the Haram al-Sharif as "public open spaces," a de facto appropriation of the Muslim Waqf's authority over them. This declaration of intent dictates the current relationship between the Muslim Waqf Administration in Jerusalem and the Israeli authorities. For example, as a result of Ariel Sharon's "visit" to the Haram in 2000 and the events which came in its wake (Palestinian demonstrators throwing stones onto the plaza of the Wailing Wall, the killing of thirteen Palestinians in the plazas of the Haram al-Sharif, and the outbreak of the Aqsa Intifada), the Waqf Administration froze visits by non-Muslims to the Haram al-Sharif. This stance was unacceptable to the Israeli authorities who insisted, despite the Waqf's objection, that the plazas are public spaces, finally using control of the key to the Magharibah Gate to

155 The pre-1967 Magharibah Quarter

156 The post-1967 Western Wall prayer plaza

organize visits of Israelis and non-Israelis alike to the plazas of the Haram, escorted by Israeli police. These visits are taking place today on a large scale, but the Waqf authorities are still in control of the covered buildings—the Aqsa Mosque, the Dome of the Rock, and the tens of buildings inside the Haram al-Sharif complex—to which visitors are not allowed without special permission of the Waqf Administration.

Bab al-Magharibah First—A Case of Challenge

In August 1967, shortly after Israel had occupied Arab Jerusalem and before the Magharibah Quarter had been completely demolished and leveled, Israeli Minister of Defense Moshe Dayan ordered the director of the Jerusalem Awqaf (pl. of *waqf*) Hassan Tahbub, to hand over to Israeli forces the keys to Bab al-Magharibah (the gate to the Haram al-Sharif). Upon consultation with members of the newly formed Islamic Council, Hassan Tahbub rejected the demand on the grounds that the gates to the Haram al-Sharif are an inseparable component of the compound. He argued that the Haram al-Sharif is solely and irrefutably Islamic property—guaranteed and supported as such by international law and the site's long Islamic history.

On 31 August Israeli troops were then sent to the Islamic Awqaf headquarters at the al-Manjakiyya School near Bab al-Majlis to seize the keys to the gate under threat of force. The gate's keys, and hence the gate itself, thereby came under control of the Israeli forces which stationed Israeli military police at the site. Some Israelis believed that Israeli military control of Bab al-Magharibah dashed extremist Jews' dreams of controlling the entire Aqsa Mosque compound.[10] The Islamic Awqaf, however, viewed the takeover as a break in complete Islamic control of the site and the beginning of increasing Israeli interference in the compound's administration, freedom of worship, and Muslim access to their holy sites. The tug of war between the Islamic Awqaf and the Israeli government over Bab al-Magharibah began to manifest itself through a variety of incidents, reaching its peak with the setting on fire of the Aqsa Mosque on 21 August 1969 by an Australian. Immediately afterwards, Israel closed the gate for fear that Jews would rush the compound upon seeing smoke rise from the mosque structure. Likewise, the Awqaf closed all of the compound's gates to non-Muslim visitors, and demanded that Bab al-Magharibah be returned to Islamic control before the compound was reopened to non-Muslim guests.

The Islamic Awqaf linked the fire to Israeli control of Bab al-Magharibah, on the grounds that the arsonist had smuggled in the materials used to set alight the mosque's wooden ceiling and dome via that particular gate, within eyesight and earshot of the Israeli forces. On that basis, the Islamic Awqaf insisted that control of the gate be returned to its offices. Israel, on the other hand, had its own fears that the Islamic Awqaf had solidified control over the entire Aqsa Mosque compound by charging that the burning of the mosque had inflamed the emotions of Muslims around the world.[11] The incident gained such importance that the Israeli government held a cabinet meeting on 19 October 1969 to discuss the issue at length. The cabinet decided to re-open the compound to visitors in order to "return normalcy to the area." Indeed, the following day, Israeli forces opened Bab al-Magharibah to non-Muslim visitors in a direct challenge to the Islamic Awqaf. Doing so underscored that control over the Haram al-Sharif was not entirely Muslim, or at least not recognized by Israel as being completely under Awqaf control.

One month later, the Awqaf attempted to reassert authority by opening the remaining compound gates. At the same time, it kept the mosques themselves closed to visitors, allowing them to enter only the compound's courtyards. This lasted until 24 October 1972, when the Awqaf decided to reopen both of the mosques (the Dome of the Rock and the Aqsa Mosque) to non-Muslim guests. The Islamic Awqaf did not however cease its loud declarations, made both domestically and internationally, that it feared and rejected out of hand any Israeli control over Bab al-Magharibah. To give one example of these protestations, on 18 February 1976 the Islamic Council issued a statement addressing the gate's condition: "... it suffices to say that the Islamic Awqaf, which is entrusted with protecting the Aqsa Mosque, does not possess effective supervision over its entrances and gates, for the [Israeli] authorities continue to this day to hold the keys to one of the main gates, Bab al-Magharibah."[12]

Nor did the Islamic Awqaf hesitate to follow up. On 9 August 1977 it sent a letter to the United States secretary of state protesting the confiscation of Bab al-Magharibah's keys and other Israeli measures.[13] The Islamic Awqaf viewed even the smallest attempt to alter circumstances to be a serious transgression of its control over the compound. It issued a statement on 29 December 1978 protesting the fact that Israel had painted and renovated the wooden door to Bab al-Magharibah, despite that the door remained the property of the Islamic Awqaf.[14] This incident was considered a further Israeli attempt to weaken the Islamic Awqaf's control over the Haram al-Sharif.

On 11 April 1982 an Israeli soldier attacked the Dome of the Rock, firing his automatic weapon both inside the mosque and around it. The Islamic Awqaf subsequently closed the compound once again to non-Muslim visitors, maintaining that the soldier had entered the compound with his weapons via Bab al-Magharibah. The Awqaf issued a statement that read: "The practice of opening and closing the gates of the Haram al- Sharif is solely the right of Muslims."[15] Israel subsequently used that same incident to secure Israeli control over the remaining gates by positioning Israeli border police (under supervision of the Israeli police) at all of the compound's entrances. Those guards controlled movement to and from the Haram al-Sharif. The Israeli police also controlled which of the compound's gates were open or shut, under the pretext of making security arrangements to protect the compound from extremist Jews.

This situation had serious ramifications for Muslim freedom of access to holy sites. Muslims waited in long lines before the compound's gates at prayer times, particularly on Fridays, in order to be searched by the Israeli police. The concept of protecting the compound's gates was gradually widened to allow Israeli border police and regular police into the compound's courtyards, where they conducted armed patrols.

Dramatic Transformations

Following the Palestinian–Israeli Oslo Accords of 1993, Israeli attempts to consolidate its control over Jerusalem only increased. During this period, Israel attempted to create facts on the ground and pre-empt the outcome of planned final negotiations (including negotiations over the city's future) by reinforcing its control over land and by superimposing symbols of Israeli sovereignty on the holy city.[16]

Despite top-level Israeli and American representation at negotiations at both Camp David II and Sharm al-Sheikh (2000),[17] it has been argued that truly serious negotiations over Jerusalem's future were never conducted. At those negotiations it was proposed that the city be divided into two areas of sovereignty, one Israeli and the other Palestinian, using as a guideline the Israeli and Palestinian presence in the city at the time of the talks. The reality was, however, that Israel's perpetual expansion and rather public policy of Judaization has turned Jerusalem into a city difficult to divide.[18]

Just before those talks commenced, in 1997, the Islamic Awqaf began the rather daring process of renovating "Solomon's Stables"[19] (now known as the Marwani Mosque) in the southeastern corner of the Haram al-Sharif. This was accomplished by excavating the ground in that section of the compound's courtyard, an area of 4,500 square meters below the level of the Aqsa Mosque. Doing so created a third mosque with an area larger than that of al-Aqsa and the Dome of the Rock combined, thereby providing a vast new space for additional worshippers. The project also stymied plans promoted by some Israelis to turn part of the Haram, that under renovation, into a Jewish temple. Moreover, the mosque connects directly to the outside of Jerusalem's Old City via several sealed gates that are easy to open and link to the Wailing Wall through the archaeological park. This endeavor intensified the struggle for sovereignty over the Haram al-Sharif. Since work began, the Islamic Awqaf has consistently refused to allow any interference from the Israeli Antiquities Authority in the renovation or the opening of the gates to Solomon's Stables. The Awqaf has held firmly to its position that it retains the sole right to undertake renovation and maintenance of the Haram al-Sharif, on the grounds that it enjoys total sovereignty over the compound and on the basis of the operative British Mandate and Jordanian antiquities laws.[20] These laws do not allow the Jordanian Antiquities Department to interfere with the affairs of holy sites. The relevant religious authorities, in this case the Islamic Awqaf, retain sole rights.

As a result, Israel kicked up quite a fuss. The government has enlisted Knesset members, "antiquities experts," and clerics to support its opposition to the Awqaf project.[21] Some of these parties went so far as to claim that the Islamic Awqaf was destroying the remains of the Second Temple when in September 1999 it opened two gates leading from the compound's plazas into the Marwani Mosque. The charges were made when construction crews disposed materials that had filled the stable area over decades, but Awqaf officials insist that the earth removed was merely dirt and rubble with little archaeological significance.

Enter Ariel Sharon. On 28 September 2000, the then opposition Likud Party leader (later Israeli prime minister) used Bab al-Magharibah as his entry point to "visit" the Haram al-Sharif [see fig. 153], igniting a firestorm of protest. One day later, several worshippers were killed in the compound's courtyard when clashes broke out and Israeli troops fired live ammunition after Friday prayers. In retaliation, the Awqaf closed the Haram al-Sharif to non-Muslim visitors, making the point that it alone retained control over the site. Israel responded by tightening its soldiers' control over the compound's gates, intensifying the search of worshippers, and preventing worshippers under the age of 45 from entering the Haram, particularly on Fridays [fig. 157]. The most serious of Israel's decisions, however—and one that remains in effect at the time of writing—is Israel's prohibition on renovation materials entering the holy site. While both sides acknowledge that renovations are necessary on the southern wall of the Aqsa Mosque compound, which is also the southern wall of Jerusalem's Old City,[22] those repairs have been impeded by Israeli attempts to establish a precedent. When the Awqaf attempted to renovate the wall, Israeli authorities rejected the effort and subsequently tried to make the repairs themselves on the grounds that the wall posed a threat to public safety and the preservation of antiquities. The Islamic Awqaf, for its part, charged Israel with exaggerating reports on the site's hazards—reports maintaining that the wall was near collapse. In the end, the two sides "agreed" after multilateral intervention, including the USA, UNESCO, and Egypt, that the Jordanian government would either renovate the walls or directly supervise their renovation.[23]

The keys to Bab al-Magharibah have become "Joha's nail"[24] in all dimensions. With these keys, Israel has imposed a "partnership" on the Haram al-Sharif, later using that partnership at the Camp David negotiations to demand joint sovereignty over the mosque area, as well as Palestinian recognition of world Jewry's religious and historical ties to the site.

The 1969 Fire, a Non-Stop Flame

On 21 August 1969, Michael Dennis Rohan set fires in different locations within the Aqsa Mosque [fig. 144]. Rohan was an Australian Protestant follower of an evangelical sect known as the Church of God. By his own admission, Rohan hoped to hasten the coming of the Messiah by burning down the Aqsa Mosque. He told the court that he acted

157 Israeli border policemen limiting worshipers' access to the Haram al-Sharif

as "the Lord's emissary" on Divine instructions, in accordance with the Book of Zechariah, and that he had tried to destroy the Aqsa Mosque in order to rebuild the Jewish Temple on the Temple Mount. The flames were very difficult to control due to the lack of fire extinguishing systems, the absence of proper water pumps in the plazas of the Haram, the late arrival of the fire fighting teams, and—above all—the wooden structures of the Aqsa Mosque. The result was a large-scale catastrophe to the mosque itself, to the cultural heritage, for the history of Islamic Art, to the Muslim community in Palestine and all over the world, and surely for Palestinian–Israeli relations, and is still tangible. The restoration works began immediately and are still going on.

The fire, which led to continuous demonstrations in Palestine and throughout the Muslim world, caused great damage to the mosque. The wooden ceiling of the southeastern part of the mosque was totally burned, and all the wooden beams which supported that section had to be replaced. The stones of the southern arch, opposite the *mihrab* (prayer niche) were damaged and had to be replaced, for they support the dome of the mosque.

158 A remnant of the destroyed *minbar*

Some of the columns and their capitals have been also damaged. In general the entire southern façade with all its components: *minbar* (pulpit), *mihrab*, and the decorations (wooden windows, stucco, stone, mosaics, and inscriptions) were partially or totally damaged. The lower interior wooden structure of the dome of the Aqsa mosque was also totally damaged as well as the dome's stone rotunda. The ceiling above the *mihrab* was also no less influenced by the fire wreaking through the whole structure. Some of the damage was reparable; other parts were a total loss. The *minbar*, which is of great artistic value in addition to its symbolic value, was lost for ever; just very small parts of it have survived the fire (now on exhibit in the Aqsa Mosque Museum [fig. 158]).[25]

As a result of this fire, the Haram al-Sharif was slowly converted into a construction site, money was collected from the local communities and the Arab and Muslim world, but Jordan—through its local Awqaf Administration as well as by establishing "The Committee for the Restoration of the Aqsa Mosque" under the leadership of the Grand Muslim Qadi (*Qadi al-Qudat*)—took the lead. The expertise of local craftsmen was not sufficient to undertake such a very challenging renovation undertaking, which includes different aspects of restoration: structure, stone, glass mosaics, stucco, wood, iron, glass, plaster, marble, and so forth.[26] It was very quickly realized that the needs exceeded the local capabilities.

With the help of Jordan, Egypt, Turkey, Italy, and UNESCO, damage assessment was made, followed by training and enhancement of building skills. As a result of a lengthy process, a capable local team was created. The local on-site workshops of marble, glass mosaic, stone carving, stucco windows, and more have managed to undertake most of the needed restorations. One thing the technicians were unable to repair was the mistrust and fear that such a nightmare might be repeated. These efforts attracted the attention of the Agha Khan, resulting in the Agha Khan Award for Architecture (The Third Award Cycle 1984–86)[27] being given to the committee of restoration.

Series of Attacks: "Security" is the Key

In this part of the paper, world "security" is the most important prism through which developments could be viewed. Of course, most of the time security had been used as a façade for further control of the site by the Israeli authorities. In addition to major attacks against the Haram al-Sharif, every month, or even week, incidents took place which caused severe problems and made the situation on the site impossible. For instance, on 14 August 1970 Gershon Salomon's group, the Faithful of the Temple Mount (Hebrew: *Ne-emney Har ha-Bayit*), which is an ultra-fanatic group dedicated to the rebuilding of the Temple of Solomon on the site of the Haram al-Sharif, forcibly entered the premises of the Haram, leading to confrontation between the Muslims, on one side, and the group together with Israeli police, on the other. This event is repeated every year in various forms; the Gershon Salomon group is holding an Israeli Supreme Court decision allowing them to conduct prayer at the site as a "Jewish right," but the court left actual implementation to the police dependent upon security considerations. Such permission was issued again. On 25 July 1995 the Israeli High Court of Justice issued a ruling allowing Jews to pray on the "Temple Mount." The decision sparked widespread protests among Muslims. The protests were not enough to prevent this, so on 21 August 1995 the Israeli police permitted Jewish extremists to hold prayers within the confines of the Haram premises. Of course another wave of protests soon followed.

On 19 April 1980 a group of rabbis and Jewish activists held a semi-secret conference devoted to exploring ways and means to liberate the Temple Mount from Muslim hands. And on 4 August 1986 another group of rabbis issued a final ruling allowing Jews to pray at the Haram al-Sharif and demanded the establishment of a synagogue in the area.

The attacks continued despite the security arrangements and heavy presence of the Israeli police. On 11 April 1982, an Israeli soldier named Allen Goodman stormed the interior of the Dome of the Rock, spraying worshippers with bullets from his M-16 assault rifle, killing and wounding over 60 Palestinians. On 12 May 1988 Israeli soldiers opened fire on a Muslim procession at the Haram, killing and wounding about a hundred Palestinians. And on 8 October 1990 the Israeli authorities committed a grisly massacre at the Haram, killing 22 worshipers and injuring over 200. These events, including those of 2000, were proof for the Palestinians that the objective of the Israeli police and border police presence at the Haram al-Sharif is to control the Palestinians and protect Israeli interests in the site—and not to protect the site from Israeli extremists, as is officially declared.

159 Restoration of the Dome of the Rock

Early in the 1980s Israel, through various agencies, began to dig the tunnel along the western wall of the Haram which came to be known by Israelis as the "Hasmonaean Tunnel." The Muslim Waqf saw this as another step towards changing the status quo, endangering the various Islamic buildings above it, and most important—a form of conquest of the underground of the Haram al-Sharif, which meant another form of control. For Israel this activity was a way of exploring the history of underground Jerusalem, including searching for remains of the Second Temple, expanding the Wailing Wall, and of course coming closer to the Temple Mount. The sensitivity of this tunnel was expressed in several UNESCO reports, but its effect was also clear on the ground. On 26 March 1983 the main entrance and staircase to the Jerusalem Waqf Department, al-Madrasa al-Manjakiyya (a Mamluk building located above the tunnel), collapsed as a result of the tunneling activities, and cracks were discovered in several other buildings along the western wall of the Haram, including the Ribat al-Kurd and al-Madrasa al-Jawhariyya (both are Mamluk buildings).

Three examples of restoration on the Haram al-Sharif: **160** Above: The frontage of the Women's Mosque to the west of the Aqsa Mosque **161** Center: The Ghadiriyya College **162** Below: Façade of the Aminiyya College

Solomon's Stables / al-Musalla al-Marwani

The inauguration of the staircase in the archaeological garden to the south of the Aqsa Mosque by the Israeli prime minister increased the sensitivity of the Islamic Waqf and the citizens of East Jerusalem, for it leads directly to the Triple Gate, which in turn leads to Solomon's Stables. The Israeli "archaeological" activities outside Solomon's Stables led the Waqf Administration to rediscover the site and to take action that could prevent Israeli expansion in the direction of the Haram. The stables (ca. 4000 sq. m) were never used since the Crusader period; in fact, the name "Solomon's Stables" was also given to this elevated structure by the Crusaders. They date most probably from the Umayyad period, but Roman ashlars were re-used in constructing the building to create a large elevated space upon which the large Aqsa Mosque could be constructed. Various Israeli and Jewish attempts to control any place related or close to the Haram are mostly the background for interventions at the site.

The Islamic Waqf considers itself a sovereign entity inside the Haram, due to the status quo as well as practice during the British Mandate and the period of Jordanian rule. Permission for activity of any kind, such as restoration, rehabilitation, or construction inside the Haram, was not needed except from the Waqf Department.

Various Israeli actions around the Haram al-Sharif included reconstruction of the stairs leading from the archaeological sector to the south of the Aqsa Mosque directly to Solomon's Stables. Much fear has been engendered by the various activities in the underground tunnels, both to the south and the east of the Haram complex. Some of these tunnels lead to the Haram complex, including also direct access to Solomon's Stables. To this is added the Israeli (mostly unofficial) continuous demand to establish a synagogue on/in the complex. The complex situation is made more difficult due to the fact that the Israeli authorities do not share information with Palestinian concerned parties, in spite of the fact that all of the above mentioned activities are directly affecting the complex.

The underground structure that received the name "Solomon's Stables" from the Crusaders who used it as a stable for their horses, was later abandoned and parts of it were used as storage space for different materials. Pre-Crusader use is uncertain, but there is a tradition of mentioning it as a theological school (*madrasa*). The physical condition was generally good, except in the southeastern corner, which is part of the city wall. The building consists of sixteen aisles divided by elegant pillars constructed of well-dressed stone, some of which are of Herodian style or imitations of it. Historically, the only opening, which connected the stables with the Haram complex was a small and narrow staircase (less than one meter in width) on the eastern wall, very close to the southeastern corner of the Haram complex, leading to a wider staircase through a small hall containing a small memorial wooden dome of the Cradle of Jesus (*mahd 'Isa*), from where the staircase leads

163 Muslims at prayer in the Musalla al-Marwani/ Solomon's Stables

to the huge halls of the structure. Ventilation was very limited and insufficient, mainly through very small windows in the southeastern city wall.

All these elements led local Muslims to focus their attention on the site and also attracted the attention of the Islamic Movement in Israel (Aqsa Association for Rehabilitation of the Islamic Holy Sites). Under the supervision of the Aqsa Mosque Rehabilitation Committee and the Awqaf Administration, this body began a full rehabilitation program of Solomon's Stables. The first phase, begun in July 1996, continued until November 1996. It included the full cleaning of the interior walls, removing the thin stratum of rubbish, consolidating some of the interior walls, as well as paving the floors with marble and adding electrical wiring for lighting the whole area. These activities converted the halls into a prayer site, after adding a wooden prayer niche (*mihrab*). Later, one of the archways was opened in the roof of the structure (northeast of the Aqsa Mosque) to lead to the complex, so that access to it became possible. In this process its name was also changed, becoming "al-Musalla al-Marwani," after the Marwanids ('Abd al-Malik b. Marwan and his son al-Walid bin 'Abd al-Malik) who were the major builders of the Haram al-Sharif complex during the Umayyad period.

Immediately after conclusion of the rehabilitation works, prayer began at the site. The newly opened halls soon became very attractive for visitors, both Muslims and non-Muslims, and thousands pray there every day, especially during the winter season, and on Fridays.

A PHOTOGRAPHIC DOSSIER

Saïd Nuseibeh
Damascus, Amman, San Francisco

167 Qubbat al-Sakhra and the Old City from the top of Bab-al-'Amud (Damascus Gate), at sunset

Previouse pages:
164 Qubbat al-Sakhra and the Golden Gate (Bab al-Dhahabi) from the Mount of Olives, at dawn

Opposite page:
165 Above: The southern wall of Masjid al-Aqsa, seen from the foundations of the Umayyad structures
166 Below: Masjid al-Aqsa from the southeast, with some Byzantine and Umayyad remains in the foreground

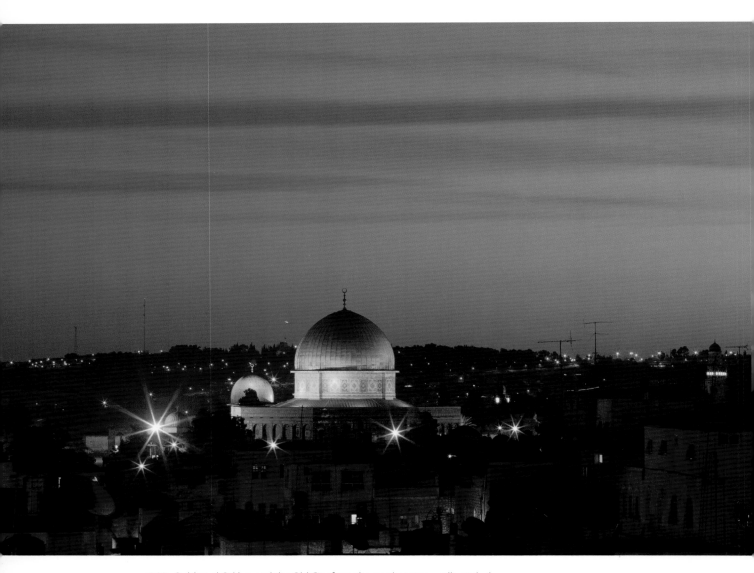

168 Qubbat al-Sakhra and the Old City from the northeastern walls, at dusk

Opposite page:
169 Qubbat al-Sakhra and Sabil Qa'itbay through the arched portal of the western *riwaq*

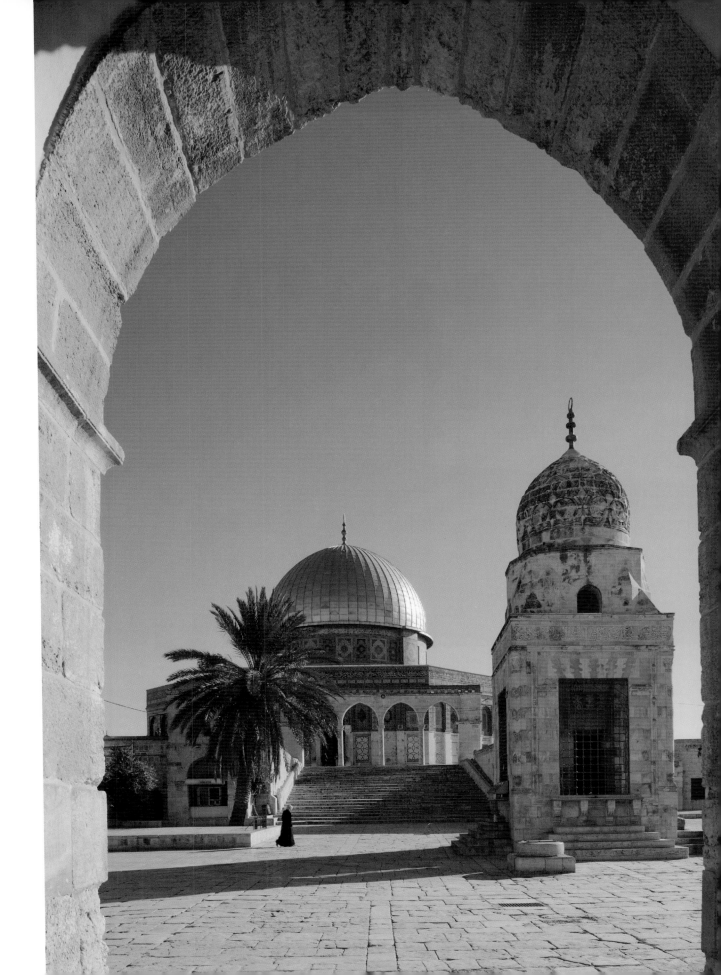

170 View from the Ashrafiyya Madrasa toward the southwestern corner of the Upper Esplanade

Opposite page:
171 Above: View from Bab al-Nizar toward Qubbat al-Sakhra and the Upper Esplanade
172 Below: Qubbat al-Sakhra from the southwest, seen through capitals and trees

175 Afternoon view from the southeastern corner of the Lower Esplanade

Opposite Page:
173 Above: View southwest from the roof of the Golden Gate (Bab al-Dhahabi)
174 Below: Qubbat al-Sakhra and Qubbat al-Silsila seen through the olive orchard to the east of the Upper Esplanade

THE *HARAM AL-SHARIF* AS A WORK OF ART

OLEG GRABAR

INSTITUTE FOR ADVANCED STUDY, PRINCETON

My remarks are an attempt to depart from the traditional ways of looking at Jerusalem in general and the Haram in particular. This preliminary attempt needs discussion and refinement, on two levels. One level is that of the city of Jerusalem, with the aim of verifying the accuracy and appropriateness of the approach. The other is the comparative level, as the point of my argument will be that the existence of a space like the Haram within an urban setting transforms that setting in ways that belong to a rare but important set of cities, perhaps exclusively cities with a sacred program.

Why propose a new or different approach to Jerusalem? Let us consider the current scholarly practice, and to some degree the cultural practice as well. Like the city of Jerusalem itself (by which I mean the walled Old City and its immediate surroundings), the Haram al-Sharif has mostly been considered from two points of view. One approach, which dominates the contributions to this volume, is historical. Its objective is to unravel the chronological sequence of constructions, functions or associations that define and then modify a space. History always deals with concrete moments of time (the degree of concreteness depending on the precision of the available information), but it also needs to concern itself with what preceded the moment, and it usually cannot help mentioning what will follow. As everyone knows, history is synchronic and diachronic. However accomplished it is in the case of any one specific place, history provides us with descriptive chronicles of events or activities and with suggested explanations of what is to be found there now, or what was there earlier, or what might have been there. It does not judge or evaluate its reconstruction, at least not in theory.

The second prevalent point of view or approach regarding the Haram al-Sharif is that of religion. It focuses on the relationship between the space and systems of belief, pious behavior, and memories; that is, on the key components of religion—belief, behavior, commemoration—at least insofar as they affect space. A religious approach can focus on a single religious system or on broad religious practices shared by several systems of

176 The Haram al-Sharif from the Mount of Olives, ca. 1917

faith, but it is always defined by something that happened or is happening outside of the physical environment.

I would like to argue that there is at least one additional dimension to the understanding of the Haram, and perhaps of the Old City of Jerusalem itself: the understanding of the place as a work of art. The Haram is an artificial, man-made construction, composed in order to be seen and not only to be used, and its presence affected the growth and development of the city without necessarily taking into consideration specific ideological or religious objectives. It is possible to define that artistic dimension in esthetic terms—that is, in terms of beauty, of a reaction of pleasure affecting the senses; in terms of other, more complicated ways in which we are affected by what we see; or in terms of constituent forms, regardless of what they meant. These very general concepts can be broken down into smaller categories; for instance, what I will call vectorial or directional terms: issues like visual access or domination by height, which affect and control what we see, and so on. For the purposes of our discussion, I associate with esthetic terms the notion of space creation, which, as proposed in a recent book by David Summers is the very essence of art.[1] In fact, it is interesting that the author, a specialist in the Italian renaissance, uses the case of Jerusalem for his discussion of urban space.

Let me elaborate a bit on these definitions by way of one remark, and a reflection upon its implications. Since Breydenbach in the fifteenth century, nearly all the drawings made of Jerusalem, as well as the vast majority of the photographs taken of the city or of the Haram—and even the movie *A Fallen Angel* by Uri Aloni, describing his attempt to understand his relationship to the city and to the Jewish past—look first from the east, from the Mount of Olives. These images can be primitively schematic, as in a popular old postcard from Aleppo, or dramatically romantic, as with the sunset picture in so many travel books, but as a group they imply a consistent point of view in the perception of the city, one that is not connected with any route of access to the city or to the Haram. In fact, it always shows the one gate, the Golden Gate, that has been closed for most of the city's history. Nor does this point of view suggest a particular meaning, religious or ideological, to anything. It is a physical reaction to the way in which natural space has been harnessed by man's transformations and by the quality given to these transformations.

Looking at the Haram from the east, we may also note the almost total absence of symbols identifiable as such, whether one knows their actual meanings or not. This can be explained by the fact that those who know will always recognize their own in whatever one sees from the east, and others do not need to know. Matters are slightly different inside the city. There are two Mamluk minarets attached to small mosques, framing the Holy Sepulchre. Much taller late-nineteenth century Catholic and Lutheran towers then frame the Mamluk ones. But these towers do not matter much, it seems, to most viewers today, and I have always been struck that the intentional dominance of these minarets' visual position is rarely mentioned in travel guides. The main reason for the relative absence of symbols is that there is a sensory self-sufficiency in what one sees from the east. One can almost say that the less you know about the Haram, the more likely it is that you can deal with it visually only from the east. That, in part, is what the western traveler Arculfus did in the later seventh century. His actual understanding of what he saw was minimal, but he became aware of a Mount of Olives-to-Haram axis in the city.

On the other hand, this was not the point of view taken by Nasir-i-Khusraw, a pious and learned agent of the Fatimids who visited Jerusalem in the middle of the eleventh century. The Fatimids had just erected a fancy, mosaic decorated gateway on the west side of the Haram and thereby compelled a western point of view, which Nasir transformed into an anthropologist's walk through the site, with a notebook filled with measurements and details and no overall appreciation of the whole space. In fact, we can probably argue that while a vision of the Haram from the east predominated after the thirteenth century, it did not do so earlier. There would have been an evolution in the visual perception of the Haram, or else there were several perceptions, each one identified with a different social or religious group, or, as we shall see, with a different time.

My main point, however, is that the impact of the Haram was and still is largely a visual one, and therefore that the historical and religious and probably also the ideological explanations and descriptions so often provided for it represent only parts of the information provided by that space. I should add that this esthetic, visual definition of the Haram is not necessarily the only additional one. A recent article by Erwin Reidinger is an interesting example of the use of metrological principles to imagine and reconstruct space,[2] and I can imagine several further studies seeing the Haram and its monuments by way of mathematical and engineering principles, not religious or esthetic ones. This is all the more possible since descriptions of the Haram often provide numerical values to the space; moreover, these values were recorded in inscriptions and thus became part of the fabric of the space.

How, then, can one deal with the visually perceived space of the Haram? I would like, very preliminarily, to propose three moments in the creation of the space of the Haram, each of which contributed a specific feature of that space as it exists now. These moments are defined by periods of time, but, on the level of the visual and esthetic understanding that I am trying to develop, they constitute the creation of a space and then two transformations of that space.

Creation of a Space

The space of the Haram as we know it was created under and by order of Herod the Great for the third (or second) Jewish Temple. There is a huge literature on this Temple, and I would like only to argue the following about it.

First, its dimensions were approximately those of the present Haram. Some have argued otherwise, especially about its northern end, where the archaeological evidence may not be as clear as one would like; but, in my judgment, the arguments for making Herod's Esplanade shorter are neither necessary nor useful. In any event, this does not significantly affect my second proposition, which is that, whatever other routes of entry existed for it, Herod's enclosure was primarily meant to be *seen* from the south, and that includes the southwestern area, whose steps and bridges, illustrated by Robinson's Arch, are visible in all the reconstructions. The great colonnade was on that side, as was at least one of the more dramatic entrances to the Temple area, the Double Gate. The reason why the point of view of the Temple enclosure was toward the south and the southwest is that much of the city was there, and the Temple, with its complement of dynastic, military, and private establishments to the north, served as a backdrop to the city and dominated it [fig. 177].

The destruction of the Temple brought a loss of direction; there was no focus any more, not only spiritual (which was maintained only in part, on a folk level), but especially visual or vectorial. Should we assume the maintenance of a south-to-north or down-to-up direction, simply because of an infrastructure that was probably still there? The east-to-west direction was primarily religious and would have been destroyed and became invisible. However, the size, coherence, and quality of Herod's creation could not be destroyed, and the space he created remained an unavoidable part of the city. A new Roman-type military city apparently incorporated that space for its official monuments and developed to the west of it. The standard explanation is that the ruined Temple area became a Roman visual focus, probably to be seen or visited from the south or the west.

Then, after Constantine and Helena, the area became simply an empty space of ruins—what later Arabic sources dealing with other urban centers call a *khirab*, a ruin, apparently a characteristic feature of most medieval cities. With the creation of Christian Jerusalem, all foci switched to the western part of the city. The Holy Sepulchre, the Nea of Justinian (now totally ruined), and whatever was built on Mount Zion dominated a city whose southeastern section may have had symbolic and commemorative meanings, but these were no longer bolstered by visual or spatial force or value in defining the city. From an urban point of view, the city was "handicapped," with a significant section of it present but withered and senseless.[3]

First Islamic Transformation

The first rehabilitation of the Haram began with the Umayyads and, for visual purposes, with the building of the Dome of the Rock in 691. Over several decades, the Herodian space was refurbished and again became the city's major visual magnet. Accessible primarily from the south, its visual axis consisted of a south-to-north sequence of new

177 Looking at a model of the Herodian Temple from the southwest
The temple forms part of Michael Avi-Yonah's model of Jerusalem at the time of the Second Temple (scale 1:50), now in the grounds of the Israel Museum, Jerusalem[4]

buildings (Aqsa, the Dome of the Rock, and the Dome of the Chain), and the southern and probably the southwestern entrances were restored [fig. 61]. The visual impact of these changes was twofold:

A. The eastern hill was formally set as an answer to the western one; Jerusalem became a city with two monumental foci, only one of which, the eastern one, was meant to be seen from both outside and inside the city. This rejuvenated focus proclaims the Rock, the highest point of the space, which now acquires a holiness missing for centuries, and it also reflects the political power of the Muslim caliphate.

B. The second change is more curious: The planning of the surface of the Herodian space seems, at least in large part, haphazard. It is true that the Aqsa Mosque is on the axis of the Dome of the Rock, but it is not in line with the borders of the space itself. The platform of the Dome of the Rock is not in the center of anything, and the Dome of the Rock is not in the center of the platform. Except for one of the southern ones, none of the *maqams*, the sets of steps leading up or down from the platform, is on any understandable geometrical axis. Only the Dome of the Chain is in the geometrical center of the whole space, but it is the one building whose function and purpose have not been well recorded, and which we therefore cannot explain. There were probably perfectly valid and reasonable ideological, religious, and perhaps simply practical reasons, still undiscovered, for these peculiarities, but none of the axes was meant to be seen; they were only to be felt. The result is a fascinating paradox: The highly geometrical Dome of the Rock and the even more peculiarly geometrical Dome of the Chain dominate an area that conforms to other rules of organization than those of geometrical planning.

This arrangement was subject to one major change early in the eleventh century, when the southern entrances were either closed or downgraded and a fancy new western gate was erected, more or less in the place of the present Bab al-Silsila.

Second Islamic Transformation

The second transformation took place under the Mamluks. The Haram is now entered from the north and west, but it is only seen from the east [see for example fig. 176]. The important point is the creation of a backdrop of buildings of the highest architectural quality to the west and north of the main sanctuaries. Until trees were planted on the Haram, these buildings, which also line up with the streets leading to the Haram, transformed it into a kind of stage. It is possible to interpret quite a few events recorded for the seventeenth century, or today, as staged performances in a sort of theatrical setting. In fact, a local dignitary of the time, Abu al-Fath al-Dajani, complained that the Haram had become a public space, with women showing off fancy perfumes and young men misbehaving after a sermon delivered from the roof of the Dome of the Rock. The Haram became an open space, without clear foci and axes, but with opportunities for a wide range of activities. It was no longer a unified work of art, but it could contain remarkable works of art like the fountain of Qa'itbay [fig. 98] or the entrance to the Suq al-Qattanin (the Market of the Cotton Merchants, [fig. 96]), which are architecturally significant but play no role in the structure of the Haram as a whole. This second transformation is still the one that dominates our perception of the Haram, although I suspect that major changes in the surrounding area, especially to the west and the southwest, and a new political and ideological atmosphere are modifying the ways in which the Haram is perceived.

To sum up, the development of the visual or esthetic components of the Haram consists in the following:

a. Height, whose importance is strengthened by the absence of surrounding structures; this development is now final, in the sense that nothing taller than the Dome of the Rock is likely to be built.

b. Axes of access, each of which provides a different set of visual values (note the failure of the eastern access—the Golden Gate, the Bab al-Rahma, and Bab al-Tawba of the Muslim tradition—to affect the space of the Haram).

c. A vast stage, with few constraints and considerable freedom for adaptation to new needs.

Each of these features has a history and a spiritual or pious explanation, but they are also formal aspects of a space that, for 2000 years or more, has defined the city of Jerusalem. And here we have yet another topic for further investigation: how the existence of the Haram affected and perhaps even directed the settlement of various human groups within the city.

178 The Dome of the Rock from the Phasael Tower Observatory in Jerusalem's Citadel

The text of the first six lines reads: I remember thee for blessing, O Zion; with all my might have I loved thee. May thy memory be blessed for ever! Great is thy hope, O Zion: that peace and thy longed-for salvation will come. Generation after generation will dwell in thee and generations of saints will be thy splendor: Those who yearn for the day of thy salvation that they may rejoice in the greatness of thy glory. On [the] abundance of thy glory they are nourished; and in thy splendid squares will they toddle. The merits of thy prophets wilt thou remember, and in the deeds of thy pious ones wilt thou glory.

From Priestly (and Early Christian) Mount Zion to Rabbinic Temple Mount

Rachel Elior
The Hebrew University of Jerusalem

For almost a thousand years there was a Temple in Jerusalem that was meant to reflect a complex cosmic order representing the duration of time, the continuity of cycles of life, and the perpetual Divine Presence in creation. The Temple was conceived as the conjunction between heaven and earth and between the macro-cosmic order reflected in the daily cycles of nature and the micro-cosmic worship reflected in the repetitive cycles of sacrificial rites and liturgy.

This focus on eternal cycles and an everlasting divine order was consolidated around a divine solar calendar of fifty-two Sabbaths or fifty-two weeks, forming a year of 364 days which was also divided into four seasons, each consisting of 91 days or 13 weeks. The year, that was carefully observed and monitored in the Temple, was divided into two divisions of time: visible and audible divisions that were combined and synchronized. The order of the perceivable natural *visible* divisions of time related to the movements of the sun and of the *fourfold divisions* of the year (the natural cycles of days and nights, the four seasons, further divided by vernal and autumnal equinox and summer and winter solstice). The heavenly *audible* and ritual divisions of the year related to the numerical, consecutive pre-calculated *sevenfold cycles* (Sabbaths, seven "appointed times of the Lord" in the first seven months of the year, Sabbaths of each seventh fallow year, and Jubilees). Together they constituted the essence of the eternal priestly solar calendar preserved and implemented in the Temple which formed the foundation for the ritual order and sacrificial cycle.

The eternal sequences of time and its predestined, calculated cosmic changes, as represented in the permanent astronomical courses and constant cycles of creation, were noted and preserved by the Levitical priests who were invested with the office of "sentinels of the holy course of time." According to the biblical tradition, the Temple was built in the days of David and Solomon, in the tenth century BCE, in a sacred place designated by divine revelation. The twenty-four priestly watches responsible for Temple worship were mainly intended to preserve the audible and visible divine cycles of time through the cycles of sacrifices and sacred liturgy and were inaugurated by King David and by the High Priest Zadok (1 Chron. 24:3–19) during the same period.

The Jerusalem Temple was destroyed in 586 BCE by Nebuchadnezzar of Babylon and rebuilt seventy years later in 516 BCE following the Persian conquest of the Babylonian empire. The Second Temple period began with four centuries (516 BCE–175 BCE) in which the priestly hegemony of the biblical House of Zadok continued to prevail. The following three centuries of turmoil and dispute (175 BCE–70 CE) brought the end of the Zadokite priestly leadership and the sacred solar calendar. First, an illegitimate Hellenized priesthood emerged (175 BCE–159 BCE); then high priesthood and kingship were usurped by the Hasmonaeans, who ruled Judaea and officiated in the Temple contrary to the biblical order (152 BCE–37 BCE). The usurpation entailed a bitter dispute between the Hasmonaean regime and the former Temple leadership of the priests of the House of Zadok, later known as Zedokim or Sadducees, followers of the written foundations of divine worship and its ritual implementation. The last hundred years of the Jerusalem Temple (37 BCE–70 CE), marked by Roman rule and the emergence of the Herodian dynasty, generated profound disputes between various religious and political parties. The stormy period that commenced in 175 BCE produced a great body of literature concerning the Temple, the priesthood, and the divine worship.

The Temple, while still standing, was the symbol of the archetypal divine order of an ideal mythical past when Divine Presence and human experience were united. After its destruction it was perceived as the symbol of yearned-for redemption and reinstitution of divine order, since from its inception it constituted both the earthly dwelling of the infinite Divine Presence, source of life, and cycles of time, and the representation of the ideal eternal cosmic order within temporal confinements. In the Temple sacred ritual was performed in order to unite the hidden God with an eternal earthly representation in sacred time and sacred place. The Temple was associated with "sacred geography," standing within transcendental mythical space as well as on actual terra firma, invested with ancient memories and sacred history.

Sacred Geography and Changing Names

"Sacred geography" has been a characteristic of religious creativity in diverse cultures from antiquity to the present. The term refers to the singling out of a place in mythological, cultic, or literary contexts linked to divine revelation or angelic appearance, celestial election, unique sanctity, and an etiological story whose sacred importance transcends the boundaries of time and space.[1] It bases the uniqueness of the sacred terrestrial place in its connection to its cosmic, mythic, or celestial counterpart, situated beyond time and space. And it grounds its premises in sacred writings derived from a heavenly source.[2]

Because of the importance and centrality of sacred sites at which heaven and earth touch and the divine appears on earth, their locations and names are not always the subject

לבית התקיעה להכריז

180 Right: The Hebrew inscription reads: "Of the house of blowing, [to announce]"
The inscription is engraved on a stone that fell to the street level below the corner of the southwest tower of the Herodian precinct and was discovered during the post-1967 excavations. The stone most probably marks the place where trumpet-blowing priests used to announce the Sabbath
181 Left: A priest blowing a trumpet announcing the Sabbath, standing on the southwest corner of the southwest tower of the Herodian precinct. A reconstruction

of universal agreement within their traditions. The changes repeatedly reflect various stages of tension, disagreement, and dispute over the traditions and their terrestrial representations in shifting historical circumstances.

In Jewish Antiquity, the sacred place, that is, the place associated with God's dwelling, divine or angelic revelation, covenant and Temple, altar of cultic sacrifice, and the Binding of Isaac (*ʿaqedah*), was identified with two mountains: Mount Moriah and Mount Zion. The relationship between the two is far from clear. Today there is no mountain bearing the name "Mount Moriah"; Judaism's sacred mountain is nowadays referred to as the "Temple Mount (*Har ha-Bayit*; literally, the mountain of the house [of the Lord])." The only circles in which the Temple Mount is today referred to as Mount Moriah are associated with groups that want to return to the mountain and build the Third Temple. The biblical-period sources that speak of Mount Zion throughout the first millennium BCE do not refer to the Mount Zion known to us today as the site of David's Tomb[3] and the Dormition Abbey. They refer, rather, to the mountain that is today called *Har ha-Bayit* or the Temple Mount. In the pages that follow, which pertain only to Antiquity, I attempt to show that the changes in the name of the sacred place and in the memories associated with it are connected to a dispute among various groups over the nature of the sacred place, sacred time, and sacred memory.[4]

The Second Book of Chronicles, written in the fourth century BCE toward the end of the period of return from the Babylonian Exile, tells that King Solomon built his Temple on Mount Moriah.[5] Why did the Chronicler locate the Temple on Mount Moriah? The book of Genesis mentions "the Land of Moriah" in connection with the offering known in Jewish tradition as the Binding of Isaac: "And He said: 'Take your son, your favored one, Isaac, whom you love, and go to the land of Moriah, and offer him there as a burnt offering on one of the mountains that I will point out to you."[6] Noticeably, the Septuagint here omits any reference to the Land of Moriah. It says: "and go into the high land, and offer him there for a whole burnt offering." The omission is prominent as well in the parallel account in Jubilees 18.2 which mentions "the high land" and knows nothing of Mount Moriah.

In calling the site of the altar in early monarchic times—associated with the appearance to David of an angel of God[7]—by the name of the site of the offering and an angel's appearance in patriarchal times, the Chronicler may have meant to invest Solomon's Temple on Mount Moriah with the memory of the site of the Binding of Isaac in the Land of Moriah. He may have intended likewise to associate the site with a founding moment in the life of the nation and the eternal covenant between God and His people.

The alternative biblical tradition that identifies Mount Zion as the holy mountain and dwelling place of God is much more widely attested, frequently appearing in traditions that predate the composition of Chronicles by hundreds of years.[8] Still, some second-century-BCE traditions explicitly identify Mount Zion as the site of the Binding of Isaac. These traditions also see Mount Zion as "the navel of the earth" and the sacred dwelling-place of the deity;[9] the place where God was revealed to Abraham;[10] and as the place where the angel of the presence appeared at the time of the Binding of Isaac and rescued him from sacrifice.[11]

In the early prophetic books and in Psalms, Mount Zion is referred to dozens of times as the holy mountain in Jerusalem or as the place selected by God to be sanctified as His dwelling. It is explicitly referred to as the place of eternal blessing and as the site of divine revelation. Zion became also a synonym for the City of David and a cognomen of Jerusalem. Yet, for the most part "Mount Zion" is a synonym for the holy mountain, the place where the divine and the terrestrial touch.[12]

In about 700 BCE, Isaiah's prophecies of destruction portray Mount Zion as a place fraught with meaning,[13] and the site is similarly treated in the prophecies of consolation associated with the return to Zion.[14] It is mentioned as the site of God's sovereignty in prophecies that stress the identity between the holy mountain and Mount Zion: "And you shall know that I the Lord your God dwell in Zion, my holy mount"[15]; "Blow a horn in Zion, sound an alarm on my holy mount."[16] Interestingly, not one of the pre-exilic references to Mount Zion limits God's place to a particular edifice. Instead, they all relate God's dwelling place to the entire mountain, and make no mention of the Temple.

Texts composed after the destruction of Solomon's Temple in 586 BCE refer to the dirge imagery of Lamentations, used repeatedly in rabbinic literature and *midrash* to convey the intensity of the disaster: "Because of Mount Zion, which lies desolate, jackals prowl over it."[17] The image is connected to Third Isaiah's description of the contrast between the

182 A stone weight incised with the word *qorban* ("offering") and a drawing of a dove, discovered during the post-1967 excavations

183 Part of a sarcophagus lid with the inscription "Son of the high priest"
The lid, probably dating from the last decades of the Second Temple, was found in 2008 in excavations northwest of Jerusalem

source of life and the wasteland: "Your holy cities have become a desert: Zion has become a desert, Jerusalem a desolation. Our holy Temple, our pride, where our fathers praised You, has been consumed by fire; and all that was dear to us is ruined."[18] Desolation and consolation in regard to the Temple on Mount Zion is further attested at the end of the second and during the first century BCE in the books of Maccabees, where the Second Temple on Mount Zion figures as the focus of the Maccabaean revolt: "'Behold, our enemies are crushed; let us go up to cleanse the sanctuary and dedicate it.' So all the army assembled and they went up to Mount Zion. And they saw the sanctuary desolate, the altar profaned, and the gates burned."[19] And the post-Second-Temple liturgical tradition dwelled time and again on Zion as God's sacred dwelling place.[20]

Much earlier traditions, composed while the Second Temple still existed, contain associations between Mount Zion and the sacred site that expand the biblical tradition, suggest an alternative recollection to that known from rabbinic traditions, and clarify the nature of the sanctity associated with it. These appear in the multifaceted priestly literature found in the Qumran scrolls—written and preserved in Hebrew and Aramaic during the final centuries BCE by the "the priests of the House of Zadok and the keepers of their covenant"[21]—and in the books of Enoch, Jubilees, and the Testament of the Twelve Patriarchs, which had been known in the pseudepigraphic literature before their Hebrew and Aramaic originals were discovered at Qumran.

In these texts, God's dwelling place, suspended above Mount Zion, is described as a heavenly garden, an expansive source of life encompassing mountains, trees of life, running water, fragrant trees, and holy angels. It is described also as a magnificent house, a heavenly sanctuary, whose expanse extends beyond the boundaries of time and space and encompasses the chariot and cherubim. The garden is linked to the place from which life flows and to the source of eternal blessing, a place subject to no earthly temporal flaws and in which the holy angels serve. The house (Temple) is connected to a sacred and pure place, situated beyond the bounds of time and space. The Divine is present there and death has no dominion over either the garden or the house. In both, the Divine Presence is connected to various traditions surrounding the chariot of the cherubim, whose first representation in a cultic context is as "two cherubim of gold" with outstretched wings, mounted on the cover of the Ark of the Covenant in the desert sanctuary, and as standing in the Holy of Holies of Solomon's Temple.[22]

The terrestrial Temple is the focal point for maintaining the sacred cycle of life and for preserving eternal, cyclical time, connected to the weekly and quarterly cultic cycles maintained by the assigned groups of priests who bring the fixed sacrifices and burn incense on a fixed cycle corresponding to the cycles of song described in the Psalms Scroll found among the Dead Sea Scrolls.[23] God's celestial sanctuary is the Garden of Eden, while the Temple is the terrestrial one, the sacred mountain chosen by God for His dwelling place within His Land; the two sanctuaries are linked by cosmographic, mythic, mystic, and liturgical traditions.[24]

The terrestrial sanctuary is described at the beginning of the Book of Jubilees, where it is explicitly linked to Mount Zion. After the giving of the Torah, as Moses stands on Mount Sinai, God's mountain, God depicts for him the future in which the Temple will be created on Mount Zion, whose sanctity is given threefold mention:

> And I shall build my *sanctuary* (*miqdash*) in their midst, and I shall dwell with them. And I shall be their God and they will be My people truly and rightly ... until My *sanctuary* is built in their midst forever and ever. And the Lord will appear in the sight of all. And everyone will know that I am the God of Israel and the father of all the children of Jacob and king upon **Mount Zion** forever and ever. And Zion and Jerusalem will be holy ... until the *sanctuary of the Lord* is created in Jerusalem upon **Mount Zion**.[25]

The Book of Jubilees also asserts that Mount Zion, along with the Garden of Eden and Mount Sinai, is one of the three or four places in which God dwells.[26] The author states explicitly, describing Noah's knowledge about the portion of Shem: "And he knew that the Garden of Eden was the Holy of Holies and the dwelling of the Lord. And Mount Sinai (was) in the midst of the desert and Mount Zion (was) in the midst of the navel of the earth. The three of these were created as holy places, one facing the other" (Jub. 8.19–20).

The Garden of Eden, Mount Sinai, and Mount Zion correspond to the foci of priestly myth and its seven protagonists who transcend the boundaries of heaven and earth: Enoch and Melchizedek (Garden of Eden); Moses and Aaron (Mount Sinai); and Abraham, Isaac, and David (Mount Zion). The Garden of Eden is the heavenly "Holy of Holies," the place of the cherubim and angels and the abode of the man who attained immortality, known as Enoch son of Jared, the founder of priesthood, who was assumed into heaven in the 1/1 month, (the first of the first month, Alef Nisan [Exod. 12.2]) on the day that the calendar commenced.[27] He was the first to burn incense in the heavenly Temple and the first to master reading, writing, and counting. It was he who brought the calendar of Sabbaths and seasons from heaven to earth.[28] A further individual of crucial importance in priestly myth resided in the Garden of Eden: Melchizedek the King of Shalem, the son of Enoch's great-grandson, on whom it was said in the Melchizedek Scroll in Qumran[29] that he will be a high priest on Mount Zion. According to the tradition recorded in the concluding chapters of 2 Enoch, Melchizedek, priest of God Most High, was taken to the Garden of Eden and "kept there" so as to transmit to Abraham and his descendants the ancient priestly tradition going back to Enoch.[30]

Mount Zion is associated with "the place of Araunah," the site from which Enoch was transported heavenward in order to learn and bequeath the tradition of the solar calendar (2 Enoch, chapters 16–23), as well as the site on which his son, Methuselah, was consecrated as a priest and offered sacrifices on the altar upon the return of his father from heaven. The place of Araunah is the site of the angelic revelation to David, where it was disclosed that the Temple will be built on Mount Zion.[31]

Transformation and Appropriation of Holy Place and Holy Time in Early Christianity

The Book of Jubilees explicitly associates Mount Zion with the Binding of Isaac, which it places in the middle of the first month—that is, the time of the future Passover holiday.[32] Likewise it associates a sacred time called "the feast of the Lord" with the time of the Passover holiday and the lamb offered in sacrifice. It thereby calls to mind a religious tradition, later than that of Jubilees by more than two centuries, that uses that place, that time, and the story of a human sacrificial offering as the background for a founding story of sacred time, sacred place, and sacred memory. I refer, of course, to the Crucifixion of Jesus, "the lamb of God," at the paschal festival, in the midst of the first month, connected to Mount Zion.

Within Christian tradition, there is a significant departure from, as well as an intertwining of, several traditions regarding the burnt offering, the lamb, the Binding of Isaac, Passover, and Mount Zion. Using a typological mode of interpretation that regards past events as a mirror reflecting the future, the Christians identified Jesus as "the bound lamb" on Mount Zion and as the paschal sacrifice—that is, they identified the crucified one as the lamb given as a burnt offering instead of Isaac, and they set the fifteenth of Nisan as the time of the crucifixion.[33] While the biblical Passover, at the midpoint of the first month, is regarded in Jubilees as the time of Isaac's Binding, in Christian tradition it prefigures the Crucifixion at Passover, and Jesus corresponds allegorically to both Isaac and to the bound lamb, *agnus dei*, the lamb of God. According to legends about Isaac's Binding, Isaac was sacrificed, died, taken up to the Garden of Eden, and returned from there when he was healed.[34] Similarly, Jesus, once crucified, entered the celestial Temple or the Garden of Eden, and his terrestrial symbol, the lamb, stood opposite the Garden of Eden on Mount Zion: "Then I looked, and there was the Lamb, standing on Mount Zion!"[35]

In some verses of the Epistle to the Hebrews, Mount Zion is removed from terrestrial geography and transformed into part of the sacred tapestry of Christian tradition: "But you have come to Mount Zion and to the city of the living God, the heavenly Jerusalem …"[36] In Christian tradition, Mount Zion, the sacred place, becomes the site where the Holy Spirit descended on the apostles on Pentecost, as described in Acts 2.1–4.

The relationship between the Jewish and Christian traditions during the first centuries of the Common Era has been described as one of mutual rejection and mutual acceptance.[37] An example of this process is provided by the transformations in the tradition concerning Mount Zion. At the present, Jews identify Mount Zion with Old Jerusalem's upper city; but this notion is Christian, reflecting the wish to annul the Temple Mount's sanctity and to transfer it to the mountain on which the tomb of King David, the prototype of Jesus, is traditionally located.[38] Jews who regard Jerusalem's upper city as Mount Zion are oblivious of the fact that originally Mount Zion was the name of the Temple Mount itself.

The Dispute over Holy Time and Holy Place

The rabbinic tradition, consolidated in the centuries that followed the destruction of the Second Temple and the Bar Kokhba Rebellion (132–35 CE), stands in contrast to the priestly tradition that united holy time and holy place, or the solar priestly calendar and the tradition of the chariot of the cherubim on Mount Zion. Rabbinic tradition suppressed Mount Zion's name, declined to maintain the many biblical-priestly foundational traditions which located central events on it, and discarded the tradition regarding Enoch and Melchizedek and their relations to the solar calendar and Mount Zion.

The rabbinic tradition likewise obliterated the idea that Mount Zion was the sacred site of Isaac's Binding and adopted the biblical Land of Moriah as an alternative site lacking prominent priestly associations. It even adopted a new calendar, replacing the biblical-priestly calendar, said to have been brought down from the heavens by Enoch. In this ancient priestly calendar the year began on the first day of the first month, the month of Aviv (or Nisan). That was the day on which Enoch was taken to Paradise to study the calendar.[39] The first month was associated with Passover, the festival of redemption and the time of Isaac's Binding. The rabbis' new lunar calendar, on the other hand, began the year on the first day of the seventh month, the month of Tishri—the day, according to rabbinic tradition, on which Enoch was killed by God.[40] Rabbinic tradition also moved the time of Isaac's Binding to the month of Tishri—the month associated with the New Year festival (*Rosh ha-Shanah*), a holiday not mentioned as such in the Torah or the Scrolls.[41]

What accounts for these far-reaching changes in sacred time, sacred place, and sacred memory? Were they made by the rabbis only vis-à-vis Christianity, which transferred Mount Zion to a new place (today's Mount Zion) and connected it to the "Lamb of God" and to the ancient time of Isaac's Binding at Passover? Or were they made also vis-à-vis the ancient priestly tradition, which had maintained its hegemony through the First-Temple Zadokite priestly dynasty down to the Hasmonean period?

The struggle by the Zadokite priestly tradition to retain its standing during the Hasmonaean and early rabbinic periods is the struggle otherwise known as that between Sadducees and Pharisees—a conflict not always fully understood. The Sadducees are "the Zadokite priests and their allies," whose writings appear in the Dead Sea Scrolls. As the source of their authority, they look to the biblical tradition assigning the high priesthood to Aaron's descendants in a direct line to the end of the biblical canon,[42] and to traditions related to angels, the world of the celestial chariot and a calendar based on a fixed solar year. The Pharisees, who interpreted the Torah through the use of sovereign human power and ancestral tradition, are those who shaped a social order distinct from the priestly way of life and pre-calculated calendar. They and the rabbis reckoned time according to a new lunar calendar that does not fix in advance the number of days in a year or any particular month. As noted, the priestly calendar maintained by the Zadokites was connected to Enoch son of Jared, who had been taken up to heaven from the Place of Araunah, on Mount Zion, on the first of the month of Nisan; the Pharisee calendar, which began on the first of the month of Tishri, was not linked to a particular place or person and lacked all support in biblical tradition, which consistently counts Nisan as the first month.[43]

Christians associated some of the priestly tradition's heroes—the immortal Enoch and Melchizedek, who breached the boundaries of time and space and dwelled in the holy of holies, the Garden of Eden—with Jesus, who came to be regarded as immortal. This too may have led to the rabbinical rejection of the priestly tradition involving the heavenly sanctuary and the chariot, and the Garden of Eden "facing" Mount Zion. One may assume that the dispute between Sadducees and Pharisees over the time of the Festival of Shavu'ot—the central festival in the priestly covenant tradition as reflected in Jubilees and in the Rule of the Community—led to the sages' rejection of association of Shavu'ot with the tradition of the chariot and with the renewal of the covenant. And it may be inferred as well that the new role assumed by Shavu'ot in the Christian tradition as Pentecost—the time when the Holy Spirit descended on the Apostles—and as the renewal of the covenant that took place on Mount Zion according to later tradition, is what brought about its displacement from the rabbinic tradition.

It is almost certain that the disagreement over the holy place and holy time predates the rise of Christianity. From the time the Second Temple was destroyed and the terrestrial center ceased to be a meaningful sacred site, various dislocations took place in the Jewish world and outside it. During the first centuries CE, priestly groups called Descenders to the Chariot produced the *Heykhalot* literature focused on the seven eternal, heavenly sanctuaries that preserve the glory of the destroyed terrestrial Temple. The celestial protagonist of this literature is Enoch son of Jared, the hero of the priestly tradition, who resides in the Garden of Eden or Garden of Truth, "facing Mount Zion." The literature carries on the tradition of the chariot and the cherubim situated in the seven heavenly sanctuaries, a tradition that began with texts written after the destruction of the First Temple and continued in the literature of the Dead Sea Scrolls, which connected the tradition of the chariot to the Festival of Shavu'ot and to Ezekiel's vision of the chariot.

The rabbis, for their part, forbade study of the account of the chariot[44] and disallowed use of Ezekiel's vision of the chariot as the prophetic reading for Shavu'ot.[45] They thereby declined to direct attention to the world of the sacred, a heavenly expanse whose earthly embodiment is called Zion. In contrast to the priests and prophets who excelled in their praise for Mount Zion and the mythic and mystical dimensions associated with it, the sages neutralized the priestly-mystical "chariot of the cherubim" dwelling place tradition and denigrated its hero. In their version of events, Enoch son of Jared—Metatron, the celestial High Priest,[46] the hero of the priestly solar calendar—was displaced from his celestial dwelling in the Garden of Truth facing Mount Zion and struck with sixty pulses of fire;[47] Enoch is also spoken of disparagingly in *Targum Onqelos* on Gen. 5.24 and in *Genesis Rabba* sec. 25. In these rabbinical texts his eternal righteous life in Paradise attested widely in the priestly tradition, was exchanged with punishment, humiliation, and death in the rabbinic tradition.

Moreover, the sages transformed the desolate Mount Zion, on which the Temple no longer stood, into "the mountain of the house" (*Har ha-Bayit*) on which no house any longer stood, thus accentuating the empty void. Having eliminated the word "sanctuary" or "temple" from the site's name, they prohibited public discussion of the chariot of the cherubim that had stood in it.[48] Though listing the cultic recollections associated with the lost Temple, they did so using the past tense. Yet, they forbade directing attention to the heavenly counterpart of the Temple situated in the Garden of Eden. Even though the celestial temple continued to operate in the realm of the chariot and of the angels and to figure in the ramified Enoch literature and in the poetic world of the *Heykhalot* and *Merkavah* literature that developed in parallel to the Mishnah and the Talmud,[49] the sages shied away from involvement with it.

Their opposition was certainly nourished to a substantial degree by the fact that in the early centuries CE, the Christians transformed Mount Zion into an aspect of their myth, connected to the Lamb of God, the Binding, and the Crucifixion.[50] The Christians likewise depicted Jesus as a high priest[51] and as a priest to the Most High God on the pattern of Melchizedek,[52] situated in the celestial temple.[53] Jesus is also associated with Enoch son of Jared, the founder of the priesthood who serves as heavenly high priest offering incense in the Temple in the Garden of Eden, and with his great-grandson Melchizedek, described as a priest dwelling forever in the Garden of Eden.[54]

The priestly traditions reviewed above that connected holy place (Mount Zion as the place of the altar of the Binding and the place of the chariot in the Temple Mount), with holy time (the 364-day calendar kept in the Temple by the priestly watch) and with holy memory of a priestly dynasty starting with Enoch who brought the solar calendar from heaven and continued with Melkizedek who officiated as high priest on Mount Zion, reflect a set of alternative memories to those that coalesced in rabbinic thought. The latter, which gained hegemony within the Jewish world following the destruction of the Temple, blurred the biblical vision of the sacred Mount Zion and the associated mystical-priestly memory related to the chariot, the Garden of Eden, the navel of the earth, the Binding, Enoch, Melchizedek, and the 364-day solar calendar. The rabbinical circles preferred Mount Moriah, lunar calendar, and the seventh month to Mount Zion, solar calendar, and the first month. Alternative memories of the priestly mystical tradition from before the Common Era linked these motifs with the mystical *Heykhalot* literature that was written after the destruction of the Temple. This literature included Enoch-Metatron, seven heavenly sanctuaries, chariot tradition, solar calendar, and angelic liturgy that were supressed by the rival rabbinic tradition. Some parts of the chariot tradition associated with Mount Zion, the Binding in the middle of the first month, and Melkizedek as eternal priest were continued within Christian tradition.

Christian Memories and Visions of Jerusalem in Jewish and Islamic Context

Guy G. Stroumsa

Oxford University

A Sacred Place and Its Religious Overdetermination

From the perspective of the comparative historian of religion, the real peculiarity of the Temple Mount lies in its resilience and versatility. In striking contrast to the Delphic *omphalos*—the navel of the earth—this *axis mundi* has, throughout history, symbolized more a border between clashing civilizations than the epicenter of a culture. There are other places that are sacred to more than one religious tradition.[1] But no other place on earth, to my knowledge, has retained to such a degree, over centuries, its deeply attractive power as the venue for a series of cultures transforming themselves and replacing one another.[2]

If religious history, to a great extent, is the history of the devaluations and revalorizations of various manifestations of the sacred, then the Temple Mount can be said to model a significant portion of it. Over the last two thousand years, at least, the Temple Mount has constituted a unique pole of attraction for competing myths and rituals, both successive and juxtaposed. Moreover, the transmission of sacral power from one tradition to another has always been compounded by the interaction between those traditions and the dialectics of their own transformation.

As far as we know, the Temple Mount first owed its sacredness to Solomon's construction of his Temple there. In other words, its holiness was acquired rather than native. What is perhaps most striking is the retention of its sacred character for the Jews even after repeated destructions. Rather than losing its sacred character, it seems to have become, more than ever before, the locus of God's dwelling, His *Shekhinah*—a concept that developed only in rabbinic literature, after Titus' destruction of the Temple. As long as the Temple stood, there was no need to emphasize that it was the dwelling place of the divinity. In a sense, the emptiness of the Temple Mount during the Byzantine period reflected the aniconic nature

184 A partial view of the Dome of the Chain (*Qubbat al-Silsila*), ca. 1921
This early color photograph is preserved in the collection of the École Biblique et Archéologique Française de Jérusalem

of God in the former Temple. Indeed, to the puzzlement of pagans, the Temple of the Jews contained no statue of their God, not even in the Holy of Holies. Pagans could thus easily consider the Temple to be empty. Incidentally, the Temple's emptiness is reflected, as it were, in the Cenotaph of the Anastasis and in the empty space of a mosque, in particular that of the *mihrab*, the niche indicating the *qibla*, Mecca's direction.

As from the destruction of the Second Temple, however, the Jews were no longer the only community concerned with the Temple Mount. Between the fourth and the seventh centuries, Christian leaders sought to erase the memory of the Temple (in contradistinction to the splendor of the Basilica of the Anastasis)—to accomplish, in a sense, what the Romans called the damnation of memory (*damnatio memoriae*) of the barren Mount. But for the Jews, despite its barrenness, the Mount became the place that most powerfully recorded the glory that was once Jerusalem.[3] It became what French historians call a "place of memory" (*lieu de mémoire*), or rather: a memory of the place (*mémoire du lieu*). Notwithstanding the report of Dio Cassius (69.12), the Hadrianic Capitolium or temple of Zeus, which stood until the fourth century, was not built on the Temple Mount. Though there may have been some imperial statues, the holy place, in the main, stood desolate and empty, pointing—for the Jews—to a future rebuilding. In the Christian mind, too, the Temple would play a part in the future, but only in the eschatological future, when the Antichrist would establish his throne there.[4] The eschatological dimension of Christian thought, however, paled with time, particularly after Constantine—or so it seemed. For the Jews, on the other hand, the reconstruction of the Temple not only was conceivable in theory—and of course prayed for three times daily—but was also considered achievable in practice, as showed by the events surrounding the Emperor Julian's authorization of its reconstruction in 361.

As highlighted by both Christian and Jewish attitudes to the future of the Temple Mount, there can be no sacred place without a sacred time. While the Temple was standing, sacred times were those of sacrifices, of holy days. After its destruction, the sacred time, the temporal axis around which history was developing, became the eschatological time of its reconstruction. The barren Temple Mount, then, points to a time as well as to the building that once stood there. Or, rather, it points to two opposite moments in time, past and future—when the Temple stood, and when it will stand again—and to Israel and humankind at the beginning and end of history, the *Urzeit* and the *Endzeit*. In a sense, one can say that the sacredness of time is a projection of the sacredness of space. Between Christians and Jews, then, the Temple Mount stood at the core of a dialectic: the one's loss was the other's gain. For the Jews, the reconstruction of the Temple would herald the advent of the Messiah, while for the Christians it would announce that of the Antichrist.[5] Hence, the Temple Mount played (and plays) a role in clashing visions of the end, at the core of the competition between the two clashing religions.

Various clashes between civilizations, focusing on the Jerusalem Temple, had occurred in the past: the Babylonians, from the East, and the Romans, from the West, had each in turn destroyed it for its reflection of a vanquished people's identity. Later, the invaders of the seventh century CE, for a brief but violent time the Persians, and then the Arabs, would bring back, with a vengeance, the eschatological expectations of earlier times, which the Christians had thought banished to the back of their consciousness.

Two highly different vignettes, both from Christian sources, symbolize the Christian reaction to the victorious entry of Caliph 'Umar into Jerusalem. The first portrays him, still dusty from the way, dismounting his horse to be invited by Patriarch Sophronius to pray in the Anastasis (today's Holy Sepulchre). 'Umar allegedly replied politely but firmly in the negative. Had he accepted, he added, Muslims would have transformed the church into a mosque. In the second vignette, Sophronius laments seeing 'Umar on the Temple Mount; for him, indeed, it is nothing less than the repudiation of the desolation announced by Christ.

By transforming the Dome of the Rock into a church, baptized the Templum Domini, the Crusaders, at least for a while, changed the parameters of the opposition between the Mount and the Anastasis. In 1099 they could exclaim: "Ad Dominicum sepulcrum, dehinc etiam ad Templum!" ("Up to the tomb of the Lord, hence, up to the Temple!"). The Crusaders, indeed, are a reminder of the Christians' ultimate inability to settle for a spiritual Temple or forget the old one of stone.[6] But this inability could only be due to the dominating presence of the Qubbat al-Sakhra—the Dome of the Rock.

Eschatological Beliefs

Moving between the *even shetiyyah*, the Holy of Holies, the Temple, Jerusalem, and the Holy Land, we have before us, as it were, a series of Russian dolls. All seem alike; all reflect the same sacred character. In order to understand more precisely the religious dimensions of the Temple Mount, we must also reflect upon the power encapsulated in the name of Jerusalem in religious and cultural history and memory. Originally, to be sure, it is from the Temple that Jerusalem received its sacred character. Later, however, the Holy City became emblematic of the sacred locus where the Temple had once stood, and where it would eventually be rebuilt. It would be a mistake, therefore, to limit our inquiry to the Temple Mount itself, without calling attention to Jerusalem's metaphorical dimension in cultural memory.

The concept of cultural memory (*kulturelles Gedächtnis*) was developed, in particular, by art historian Aby Warburg between the two world wars. In order to be really useful, this concept should be connected to that of collective memory (*mémoire collective*), a term invented in the 1930s by French sociologist Maurice Halbwachs. Any cultural memory, indeed, belongs ipso facto to collective memory.[7] The early Christian thinkers whom we call the Church Fathers launched the process through which the name of Jerusalem was transformed into a major icon of Western cultural memory. This process was directly related to what Christoph Markschies has recently called its *devaluation* in early Christianity.[8] Cultural memory does not necessarily stand in contradistinction to religious memory, but rather to the radical intensification of religious feelings involved in eschatology.

The earliest Christian attitudes toward Jerusalem seem to have been related directly to the millenarian or chiliastic view founded upon the announcement of Jesus' reign of a millennium (*chilia etè*) in Jerusalem. Although this view was not the only one available (the African bishop Cyprian never mentions Jerusalem), it seems to have been dominant.[9] As Ernst Käsemann put it, "Apocalyptics is the mother of Christian theology."[10] In the second century, Papias and Justin Martyr espoused millenarian views of this kind. Enthusiastic expectations of a return of Christ in glory (*parousia*) and a restitution of things past (*apokatastasis*) seem to have been inseparably bound up with the Christian faith down to the middle of the second century. This tendency was broken only by Marcion; and Marcion's opponents, such as Irenaeus, returned even afterwards to broaching the End of Time.

Can we detect the mechanism by which such eschatological views were contested, and so ceased to prevail in the mainstream tradition? Marcion, a contemporary of Justin in the mid-second century, rejected the Old Testament (as well as major parts of the New Testament), arguing that Christianity was a religion of a new kind and possessed no Jewish roots. He seems to have been the first opponent of chiliastic ideas in early Christianity. As Stefan Heid has shown, the argument around millenarianism in the second century was directly related to the controversy between Jews and Christians.[11] The Jewish wars, especially the revolt launched by Bar Kokhba in 132–35 CE, form the background to this controversy and to the debate over millenarianism and the role of Jerusalem. For most Church Fathers, the Holy Land remained the land of the Jews, and a reconstruction of the Temple meant a Jewish victory, at least from a spiritual perspective. Indeed, expectations of this kind were to be found among the various Jewish-Christian groups, such as the Ebionites, for whom the rebuilding (*restitutio, apokatastasis*) of the Temple was a central eschatological belief.

Marcion rejected all that, including beliefs in the *eschaton* and about the role of Jerusalem at the End of Time. For him, such beliefs were simply irrelevant to the Christian faith. No wonder Irenaeus—for whom Marcion, along with various dualist and Gnostic thinkers, was the arch-enemy—insists precisely on eschatology. Deservedly called "the theologian of chiliasm," Irenaeus is the greatest writer on eschatological Jerusalem. The last chapters of his magnum opus, *Against the Heresies*, are devoted to the battle between Christ and Antichrist that was to precede the reign of Christ in Jerusalem, waged up to the ruins of the Temple. Eschatology is the principal insurance against the metaphorization of Christian beliefs; it possesses an irrevocably concrete element.

It is no accident that Tertullian, the late-second and early-third-century North African Church Father, who first established the antinomy of "Athens versus Jerusalem," eventually joined the ecstatic and prophetic Montanist movement. For the followers of Montanus, in the second half of the second century, a new prophecy, delivered to women, announced the imminent descent to earth of the Heavenly Jerusalem.[12] Montanism, then, exhibits with particular clarity the direct connection between the role played by (heavenly or earthly) Jerusalem at the End of Time and the intensity of eschatological expectations.[13]

The Christian idea of *translatio Hierosolymae*, the holy city's travel in space, seems first to appear with Montanus, who, according to Eusebius, "gave the name of Jerusalem to Pepuza and Tymion, which are little towns in Phrygia."[14] As confirmed by Tertullian, who had inside knowledge of Montanist beliefs, this probably meant that the heavenly Jerusalem was seen as having descended upon Pepuza and Tymion. The heretical status of the Montanists in the third century, and the Christian invention of the Holy Land in the fourth century, probably forestalled the implantation of *translatio Hierosolymae* in Patristic literature. Nevertheless, this concept never quite disappeared. Throughout Christian history, it emerged as an expression of sectarian eschatology in such phenomena as the Hussite reconstitution of the Holy Land in fifteenth-century Bohemia, the Taborites' Tabor, and the expectations of the New Zion sectarians in nineteenth-century Russia for the descent of the Heavenly Jerusalem.[15]

If the new Jerusalem can descend from heaven onto Pepuza, a small town in Asia Minor, who needs the city of David anymore?[16] Indeed, new Zions exist in various cultural surroundings. A famous case is that of the churches carved in the rock in Lâlibalâ, in Ethiopia. This new Jerusalem became a major pilgrimage destination in periods when Axum was inaccessible.[17] Today we think mainly of Baptist churches in the southern United States or in black Africa, or of the Swedenborgian churches of "the New Jerusalem."[18]

The failure of early Christian apocalyptical movements, illustrated by the perception of the Montanists as heretics and the postponement to the End of Days of Christ's Second Coming, his *parousia*, had direct implications for the representations of Jerusalem. Rather than earthly alternative locations, or the idea of an eschatological *renovatio*, it is the metaphor of a *spiritual* Jerusalem that was to become prevalent in the early Christian mind. This Jerusalem was the Christian's true fatherland, and it was in heaven—from which, according to Rev. 21.2, the New Jerusalem was to descend. In this regard, the early Christian writers were following in the footsteps of Jewish apocalypticism. In IV Esdras, a Jewish text redacted at the end of the first century CE, the eschatological element is still prominent: Jerusalem would be established by God in the messianic era. The Syriac Apocalypse of Baruch weakens this element by describing the Heavenly Jerusalem as having been prepared by God at the origin of the world, thus pointing to the direct relationship between the origins of the world and the End of Time.

The transformation of the ideal city is completed in the late second century with Clement of Alexandria, who recalls that the Stoics referred to the heavens as the true city.[19] For him, as a Christian, the obvious parallel to the heavenly city of the Stoics was the Heavenly Jerusalem, which he calls "my Jerusalem."[20] We touch here on the roots of Jerusalem's mystical meaning. Origen takes up and develops Clement's views on the holy city (*polis*): Jerusalem, whose Hebrew name (*Yerushalayim*) is interpreted as meaning "vision of peace" (*yir'eh shalom*), can mean the Church, but also, in the tropological sense, the soul.[21] A similar allegorical interpretation appears in the writings of the fourth-century Origenist Didymus the Blind. For him, too, the significance of Jerusalem is threefold: It is at once the virtuous soul, the Church, and the heavenly city of the living God. We shall return to the "vision of peace" (*visio pacis*) metaphor of Jerusalem, which runs as a thread through the centuries.[22] One further formative metaphor stems directly from Paul: The supernal Jerusalem, mother of the Christians, is also called *eleuthera*—free (Gal. 4.26).[23]

For Marcion and the Gnostics, the whole Jewish heritage was a stumbling block on the way to a fully emancipated Christianity. The Gnostics did not need Judaism's traditional eschatological expectations, since they claimed to live in the redeemed time of "realized eschatology." In their struggle against such objectors, Church Fathers such as Irenaeus were led to insist, precisely, upon the hopes of Christ's *parousia* and the last, decisive battle between the forces of good and evil. But such hopes were also those of the Jews and of the Jewish-Christians, with whom the same Church Fathers were also engaged in intensive competition about the proper understanding of the Scriptures.

Thus, concerning Jerusalem, two distinct phenomena can be observed in early Christianity. The first is the distinction, made more and more clearly with time, between the Earthly and the Heavenly Jerusalem. This distinction, which, again, is of Jewish origin, received a new impulse in early Christian writings, already with Paul. The two Jerusalems became completely disconnected, as they never had been in Jewish writings. The Earthly Jerusalem remained identified, essentially, as the city of the Jews, who had killed Christ and whose Temple had been destroyed in divine punishment. This Temple would not be rebuilt. "And I saw no Temple in it"—that is, in the New Jerusalem to come down from heaven—says the visionary in the Apocalypse of John, the most topical of all early Christian eschatological texts (Rev. 21.22). The Heavenly Jerusalem soon became a metaphor for the community of the saints, or the "city of God," in Augustine's parlance. It was invested with all the dreams and qualities attributed to Jerusalem in eschatological thought, but very little remained here of the original meaning of the name.

The Augustinian typology of the two cities has its roots in Tyconius, whose *Commentary on the Apocalypse* referred to two cities, Babylon and Jerusalem.[24] For Augustine, Babylon represents power and politics, while the Heavenly Jerusalem—of which he sings, "Quando de illa loquor, finire nolo"[25]—represents the Church, wife of Christ. Babylon refers to life in the present, in this world, Jerusalem to the future life, in which the boundaries of time will be overcome and God will be praised forever, *in saecula saeculorum*. The major formative influence of this typology on medieval perceptions needs no further stressing.[26]

The second phenomenon is the weakening of eschatological beliefs, expressed in the progressive erosion, from the second to the fourth century, of the expectation of Christ's second coming. As it became more and more difficult to maintain intensive hope of an imminent advent, the acme of the Christian message became clearly entrenched in the past. With the fading of its future, Jerusalem itself, a small, marginal city in the Empire with the forever destroyed Temple and Golgotha at its heart, was bound to lose almost all significance. Paradoxically, the less important the city of Jerusalem became, the more the name "Jerusalem" seemed to gain in evocative power. Late antique Christianity, indeed, bequeathed the overwhelming resonance of Jerusalem to European culture, eastern and western. Jerusalem was now Rome: In the words of Jerome, "Romam factam Hierosolymam." It was also Byzantium; Constantinople is often called "the second Jerusalem," while Moscow, later, would become "the third Jerusalem." The whole world would eventually become Jerusalem. This is literally true in the *Commentary on the Apocalypse* written in the fourth century by Victorinus of Poetovio (Ptuj in present-day Slovenia): At the End of Time, Jerusalem will expand and cover the face of the earth.[27] Similar conceptions appear in rabbinic literature as well.

In both the fourth and the sixth centuries, major architectural achievements sought to offer new, Christianized versions of the old Jewish Temple. Eusebius, the bishop of Caesarea Maritima, who was Constantine's spiritual herald, described the Basilica of the Anastasis as "the new Temple," while Justinian, upon entering the newly built Hagia Sophia in Constantinople, allegedly declared: "I have outdone you, O Solomon!"[28]

It is traditionally assumed that by the fourth century, the chiliastic trends so prominent in the early stages of Christianity had more or less burnt themselves out; yet they seem to reappear with renewed strength in the seventh century, with the same old scenario being played out in Jerusalem, in particular around the Temple Mount. Indeed, the seventh century, a period of dramatic religious and political transformations in the Near East, has long been recognized as a time when eschatological beliefs were particularly activated in the Byzantine Empire.

The Temple Mount Islamicized

In ancient Israel, as we learn from Max Weber, a major tension revolved around the Temple and its service. The prophets' charisma versus the priests' routine: two radically different kinds of religious action confronted one another, one pushing for change, the other for stability. In the seventh century CE, centuries after the destruction of the Temple, the very place where it had been built, its locus, seems to have been once more at the epicenter of a prophetic movement.

At least as from the conquest of Jerusalem by the Sasanians in 614 and the capture of the Holy Cross, the Christian world was rife with expectations of the *Endzeit*, with its traditional imagery of cosmic war between the forces of light and darkness. The Byzantines were slow in understanding the true faith of the new conquerors. For too long, they perceived the Arabs as barbarians from the desert and Muhammad as a false prophet, whose faith could be understood only in the categories of Christian theology—namely, as a heresy.[29] What would eventually settle into a centuries-long, deep-seated political and religious conflict, sometimes more overt and sometimes relatively dormant, started as a "big bang," epitomized more than anything else by the conquest of Jerusalem by the Arabs in 638 and the ensuing dramatic changes in the city's religious topography.

In a series of important publications, distinguished Byzantinists such as Gilbert Dagron, Averil Cameron, Cyril Mango, and Vincent Deroche have done much to provide us with a clearer understanding of the complex interface between Jews and Christians in seventh-century Byzantium, in particular from the perspective of the Greek texts.[30] These and other scholars have underlined the renewed importance of polemics between Jews and Christians in the Eastern Roman Empire. In particular, they have highlighted the centrality in these polemics of the Holy Land, the Holy City, and its core, the Temple Mount, as well as their direct impact on the earliest Islamic program in Jerusalem.[31]

The spiritual demotion of the old Israel by *Verus Israel* was spatially represented by the relocation of the sanctified locus from the Temple Mount, whose emptiness should have remained striking, visible to all, to the new Basilica of the Anastasis. Oleg Grabar has called this process of relocation an *eislithosis*,[32] while Annabel Wharton refers to the "erasure" of the Jewish dimension of Jerusalem.[33] The city's Islamic conquerors, seeking to accomplish what we could call, in the Hegelian sense, an *Aufhebung* of both Judaism and Christianity, moved its sacred core back to the Temple Mount. For the Byzantine historiographer Theophanes, it was 'Umar's devilish pretension that made him seek to emulate Solomon.[34] As Andreas Kaplony argues convincingly in this volume, there is reason to believe that the early Muslim rulers intended to rebuild the Temple and even to install a kind of Temple ritual. This perception of things was also aimed at convincing the Jews that the End of Time was drawing near, and that the Caliph was the expected Messiah. In the Umayyad period, at least, the Temple Mount, not yet called the Haram al-Sharif, was viewed both as the Temple rebuilt and as the Mosque of Jerusalem. If some of the Jews, however, might have been tempted to place the dramatic events in an eschatological perspective, they soon were disappointed. For them, the construction of a new kind of Temple in place of the old was perceived as no less an erasure of the Jewish dimension than the Christian dislocation of the sacred. Moreover, since the Anastasis remained standing, it would retain its sacredness (albeit lessened) under the Islamic regime.

The new clash of civilizations between the Christian and the Islamic imperial states was nurtured in the cocoon of the Jewish–Christian clash of interpretations, which only superficially appeared essentially to reiterate, again and again, old arguments over a long-decided issue. The argumentation of these polemics, which centered upon the interpretation of biblical prophecies, revolved mainly around the image of Christ as the Messiah announced by the prophets of Israel. For the Jews, the Messiah was yet to come; for the Christians, he was to return in full glory and establish his kingdom, at long last, over all the earth. For the Chiliasts of the first centuries—most clearly exemplified, perhaps, by Irenaeus—Jerusalem, and in particular the Temple Mount, was to be the epicenter of the cosmic events that would occur at the End of Time.[35] The debate focused on the inheritance of the Holy Land and the restoration to it of the Jews. Early Christian Chiliastic expectations had very strong Jewish roots. In particular, the Antichrist is strikingly similar to the figure of the false prophet in the pre-Christian Jewish sources and was probably constructed from the latter.[36]

For the Christians, the Messiah expected by the Jews would be the last impostor, the Antichrist. The Jews, on the other hand, believed that they were being ruled by believers in a false Messiah. Victory for one side would mean defeat for the other: in modern strategic terminology, this was a zero-sum game. The clearest expression of a Jewish vindication would be the re-establishment of the Temple. For the Christians, this was tantamount to the coming of the Antichrist, who had been envisioned, in Irenaeus' classical version of the myth as well as in the slightly later version of Hippolytus, as establishing his throne for three and a half years in the Temple itself, until his finally defeat by Jesus Christ. In the Christian psyche, this threat did not quite belong to the ancient past. The memories of the great anxiety generated by Julian's authorization of the Temple's reconstruction—and by the actual start of the work, before a providential earthquake brought these efforts to naught—seem to have been a long time in dissipating.[37] And now, with the violent conquest by the Persians and its deeply humiliating result, the exile of the Holy Cross, and then the new wave of successful invasion by the barbarian Arabs, the old questions were raised again, with a new urgency. These Arabs, streaming from their southern desert and claiming to follow the lead of their prophet—who could they really be, if not the powerful arm of the Jews, sent to reclaim their pretended possessions in the Holy Land and the Holy City? Paradoxically, the great fear of the Christians had more to do with the shadow of the Jews than with the Arab invaders.

'Umar's conquest of Jerusalem in 638 was bound to rekindle both the fears of the Christians and the hopes of the Jews and bring them to new levels of intensity. The Armenian historian Sebeos, bishop of Bagratunik in the seventh century and one of our best sources, seems to indicate quite clearly that the Jews began building a structure on the Temple Mount in the first years after the conquest:

... the plot of the Jewish rebels, who, finding support from the Hagarenes for a short time, planned to [re]build the Temple of Solomon. Locating the place called Holy of Holies, they constructed [the Temple] without a pedestal, to serve as their place of prayer. But the Ishmaelites envied [the Jews], expelled them from the place, and named the same building their own place of prayer. [The Jews] built a temple for their worship elsewhere.[38]

Apparently, the first Aqsa Mosque was built only later.

For the Christians, Muhammad, who thought of himself as both prophet and apostle, was simply an impostor, a false prophet. For the Jews, the matter seems to have been more complex. In their perception, Muhammad could have been either a prophet or a Messiah. Both these titles, indeed, had been attached to non-Israelite figures, such as Balaam, who was a prophet, and Cyrus the Great, who was called "God's Messiah." The Jewish sources from Arabia are scarce and difficult to interpret, but it seems that some Jews, at least, did at first see in Muhammad a messianic (or pre-messianic) figure. For the Christians, on the other hand, the concept of "Messiah" was bound to remain quite puzzling, since *Christos* (a literal translation into Greek of Hebrew *mashiah*, "anointed") was, for them, the name of the Savior.

According to the *Doctrina Jacobi*, a crucial Greek document dating from the very beginning of the Islamic conquests, the Jews considered Muhammad a false prophet (*pseudo-prophètès*). This would seem rather surprising, since the Jews viewed the "gates of prophecy" as having been closed long before that date. It may well be that the Jews were speaking of a false Messiah rather than a false prophet, and the Christians, who could not possibly have understood what such a term meant, decided that it was identical to the much more comprehensible "false prophet."

In this context, it is interesting to note that the concept of a false Messiah (*mashiah sheqer*) is extremely rare in rabbinic literature, occurring, as far as I know, only in the late seventh-century *Apocalypse of Zerubbabel*. The Syriac *Apocalypse of Pseudo-Methodius*, a fundamental witness to the eschatological perception of the Islamic conquest and a text that would become, in Latin translation, a major source of medieval eschatology, also mentions a false Messiah, *mashiha degala*.[39] This *Degala* seems to be the source of the *Dajjal*, the figure paralleling the Antichrist in Islamic eschatological texts.

For just one religious group, Jesus was at once Messiah and prophet: the Jewish-Christians, and particularly the Ebionites and the various groups that succeeded them. Notwithstanding the lack of scholarly consensus on this issue, I am convinced that the sources formally indicate that such groups were still in existence, at least in Palestine, in the seventh century (and beyond). In this respect, the "Jewish-Christian" formulations and Docetic conceptions in the Qur'an, according to which Jesus was not really crucified and only appeared (Greek *dokein*) to suffer, deserve fresh consideration.

Almost thirty years ago, Michael Cook and Patricia Crone, in their thought-provoking and very influential *Hagarism*, showed the extent to which earliest Islam must be understood as a product of Jewish messianic preaching in a gentile environment.[40] In recent years, the important epigraphic studies of Christian Robin have transformed our perception of the Jewish element in the background to Muhammad's preaching. Although Robin suggests that his findings weaken the need for appeal to Jewish ideas imported from Palestine, as proposed by Cook and Crone,[41] it seems that the cross-fertilization of Jewish and Christian beliefs, the centrality of the Holy Land and in particular of the Temple Mount, and the eschatological expectations of both Jews and Christians should be perceived as the true prelude to Islam.

Mystical Jerusalems

The Christian transformation of Jerusalem and of the Temple Mount, however, is not bound to happen only at the End of Time. The ubiquity of Jerusalem is also manifested in the representations of the Basilica of the Anastasis built in various European cities in the Latin Middle Ages. In certain cases, in particular in Bologna, it is the whole earthly city of Jerusalem that is reconstituted, a theme park of sorts, complete with Golgotha, the Mount of Olives, Kidron, and Gethsemane. One did not have to go on a crusade in order to reach Jerusalem; it could be reproduced anywhere, in any city or in any cloister.

The other regnant Christian transformation of Jerusalem is to be found in the mystical envisioning of the Heavenly Jerusalem, to which the religious virtuoso is called to ascend in heart and mind. Mysticism, with its insistence on immediacy and interiority, would seem to be the antipode of eschatology. But here, too, one should note that various mystical meanings of Jerusalem took on an eschatological dimension in Christian history.

An apocalyptic Christian spirituality was to survive through the centuries, permitting the actualization and vivification of perceptions often muted or neutralized in mainstream tradition. The great twelfth-century Calabrian visionary Joachim da Fiore is said to have experienced a conversion to the inner life during his pilgrimage to the Holy Land as a young man. He later made extensive use of the name of Jerusalem in his *Book of Figures*. The most puzzling antithesis in this book is perhaps that of Jerusalem/Ecclesia and Babylon/Rome. But for Joachim, the Roman Church is always Jerusalem, never Rome. If Babylon is the realm of the devil, the heavenly kingdom of God is symbolized by Jerusalem, whose sons "are pilgrims sojourning in the midst of Babylon."[42] At the end of history there will be a third apotheosis of Jerusalem, after the reign of David in the Earthly Jerusalem and the papacy of Sylvester in Rome. In a detailed description of the Heavenly Jerusalem in his *Eternal Gospel*, Joachim points to the precise symbolism of its various components, named in Rev. 21, such as the different precious stones of which it is built. He insists that in the

Heavenly Jerusalem there is no Temple built by men, since the Father and the Son are themselves the only Temple of the Spirit.

Via the intermediacy of Augustine and Isidore of Seville (ca. 560–636), the traditional etymology of Jerusalem as referring to a vision of peace became prominent in medieval texts.[43] The last avatar of the perception of the earthly Jerusalem, in the later Middle Ages and the Renaissance, reflects a new dimension to this mystical visio pacis. From a purely spiritual vision, it also becomes the best metaphor for an eschatological dream of peace on earth between religions and civilizations.

In his *Peace of the Faith*, Nicolas Cusanus (1401–64) dreams of a religious concordat agreed in heaven, the only rational region, by wise Christians, Jews, and Muslims. Given full powers, they then meet in Jerusalem, their common religious center, to receive in the name of all the single faith, and they establish perpetual peace within the city, "in order that in this peace, the Creator of all things be glorified in all *saecula*. Amen."[44]

The development of ethnological curiosity, also towards "Turks" (Muslims) and Jews, together with the sorrows generated by religious strife throughout Europe, encouraged a renewal of utopian thought, and in this context Jerusalem provided a ready-made symbol, understood by all. Tommaso Campanella, another visionary (this time a Dominican) from Calabria, dreamed at the beginning of the seventeenth century of a regaining of the Holy Land (*recuperatio Terrae Sanctae*) that would be the utmost expression of a historical restoration, a *renovatio saeculi*: "The Church was born in Jerusalem, and it is to Jerusalem that it will return, after having conquered the whole world." He perceived the erstwhile presence of the Crusaders in Jerusalem as a step toward the instauration in that city of the messianic kingdom: Jerusalem, indeed, is the Holy City, where Jews, Christians, and Muslims can become united in communion.[45]

In the religious history of Jerusalem and of its representations, each new historical stage has perforce reflected all the previous layers. The earliest Christian attitudes toward Jerusalem reflect contemporaneous Jewish apocalypticism, while early Islamic perceptions of Jerusalem are deeply indebted to both Jewish and Christian approaches. The various religions have not only succeeded one another in presiding over the political destinies of the city. They have also developed dialectical relationships between them. Today, as Israelis and Palestinians search (or should search) for a modus vivendi in the city, with the various Churches anxious and active in the background, the idea of the three monotheistic faiths having equal shares in the spiritual identity of the city might offer a reference point.

At the very core of this city and of Jewish and Christian eschatology stands the Temple Mount, the Haram al-Sharif. The main intention of the preceding pages has been to reflect upon the complexity of its character, and to show how this small locus has also, throughout its history, been at the core of the interaction between three religious traditions. Their constant transformations of both themselves and each another have been played out, at some crucial turns in their history, through their competing visions of this same locus.

The Temple Mount is indeed a pivotal point, at the intersection of cultures and religions. It may also appear, alas, as a tectonic fault line in history. It sometimes seems that evil may sprout not from the North, as Jeremiah has it, but from this place at the center. The Temple Mount appears to be a Rashomon of sorts: each side and its story. I have seen the photo-montages in which a reproduction of the Temple replaces the mosques on the Mount. And I have read about a Palestinian claim (supported by "the research of Israeli archaeologists") according to which the Jewish Temple was actually built elsewhere, not on the Haram al-Sharif.

The Mount is not only too small to allow for physical partition; one cannot even partition this small piece of holy land diachronically, allotting its past to the Jews, its future to the Christians, and its present to the Muslims: all three want to possess it throughout time. Let us only hope, then, that we are not living, as did Jews, Christians, and the first Muslims, at the End of Time. Regarding the Temple Mount, like so much else, the complexity of cultural memory offers safer horizons than the simplicity of eschatological beliefs.

185 Muslim women harvesting olives on the Haram al-Sharif

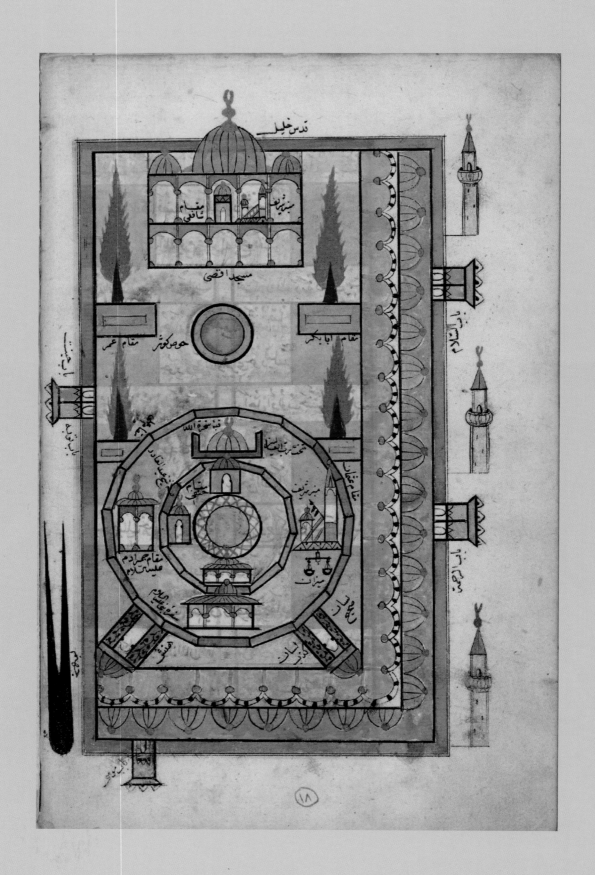

The Holy Land, Jerusalem, and the Aqsa Mosque in the Islamic Sources

Mustafa Abu Sway

Al-Quds University

Coming from the same divine source as previous revelations, Islam embodies many things that are common to them, such as the special status that the Holy Land and Jerusalem enjoy.[1] Islam recognizes the fact that the Holy Land is sacred to the People of the Book. When Muslims say that the Holy Land is the "Land of the Prophets," certainly the prophets of the Children of Israel are included and constitute a continuum in the line of prophecy, which culminated with Prophet Muhammad (Peace be upon them all). Almost every prophet lived in the Holy Land, or had a special relationship with it, including those who were born elsewhere. An example of the latter is Prophet Abraham, the prototype iconoclast. After he destroyed and mocked the idols of his people, they planned violence against him, but he was destined to go to the Holy Land. The following verse uses inclusive language to reflect the nature of Abraham's new home: "But We delivered him and [his nephew] Lot [and directed them] to the land which We have blessed *for the nations*" (Qur'an, 21.71) [emphasis mine].

An example of a prophet who had a special relationship with the Holy Land and Jerusalem in particular is that of Prophet Muhammad. The Qur'an stated in the chapter of the "Children of Israel" (*Banu Isra'il*), or the "Journey at Night" (*al-Isra'*), that he was taken in a night journey miraculously from the Sacred Mosque to the Farthest Mosque (*al-Masjid al-Aqsa*):

> Glory be to (Allah) Who did take His Servant for a journey by night from the Sacred Mosque [*al-Masjid al-Haram*] to the Farthest Mosque [*al-Masjid al-Aqsa*] whose precincts We did bless, in order that We might show him some of Our Signs: for He is the One who hears and sees [all things] (Qur'an, 17.1).

186 The Haram al-Sharif on an illustration in a mid-eighteenth century manuscript, National Library of Israel, Yah. Ms. Ar. 1117. The four minarets appear in their actual locations, but only the arcades on the northern and western sides of the Haram are depicted

The *hadith* scholars, Qur'an commentators, and all of Islamic tradition take this particular verse seriously and consider the Sacred Mosque to be in Mecca and the Farthest Mosque to be in Jerusalem. No Muslim scholar challenged this position throughout Islamic intellectual history which extends for more than fourteen centuries. The parameters of this blessed land go beyond what is between the Jordan River and the Mediterranean. Ibn Kathir (d. 774 AH/1373 CE), a medieval Muslim scholar, reported the commentary of several early Muslim scholars on verse 21.71.

According to the famous Ubayy Ibn Ka'b, the blessed land is *al-Sham* [i.e., Greater Syria, which includes Jerusalem]. The great early commentator, Qatadah, adopted the same position.[2] A more detailed account of the Night Journey and the Ascension [*al-Isra'* and *al-Mi'raj*] and their relation to Jerusalem will follow.

In addition, there is another verse in the Qur'an with reference to this line of blessing:

> Between them and the cities on which We had poured Our blessings, We had placed cities in prominent positions, and between them We had appointed stages of journey in due proportion: "Travel therein secure, by night and by day" (Qur'an, 34.18).

According to Mujahid, al-Hassan, Sa'id Ibn Jubayr, Malik, Qatadah, al-Dahhak, al-Sadiyy, Ibn Zayd, and many other respected early Muslim scholars, the blessed cities are those of al-Sham. Ibn 'Abbas (d. 68 AH/687 CE), the prominent early scholar of the Qur'an who was also a cousin and companion of the Prophet, maintained that the "blessed cities" is a reference to Bayt al-Maqdis [i.e. Jerusalem].[3]

Though there are several references to *the* land, the term "Holy Land" [*al-Ard al-Muqaddasa*] is mentioned only once in the Qur'an:

> Remember Moses said to his people: "O my People! Call in remembrance the favor of God unto you, when He produced prophets among you, made you kings, and gave you what He had not given to any other among the peoples. O my People! Enter the Holy Land which God has assigned unto you, and turn not back ignominiously, for then will you be overthrown, to your own ruin" (Qur'an, 5.20–21).

The context is that of Moses (peace be upon him) inviting the Children of Israel to enter the Holy Land after he delivered them miraculously from Egypt across the sea. The Children of Israel refused to enter the Holy Land, because it meant that they had to fight its people, who were known for their exceeding strength. This rejection earned them Divine punishment: God said: "Therefore will the land be out of their reach for forty years: in distraction will they wander through the land: but sorrow you not over these rebellious people" (Qur'an, 5.26).

This verse is read in two very different manners, each one arriving at a very different meaning. The first way, as shown above, divides the verse into two parts, the first of which ends after "years." This way of dividing the verse indicates that the Children of Israel were forbidden to enter the Land temporarily because of their disobedience. The second reading also divides the verse into two parts, the first of which ends after "reach." Some scholars interpreted this way of dividing the verse to mean that the Children of Israel were forbidden to enter the Land in an absolute sense, again as a result of their disobedience. I am personally inclined toward the first reading, which considers the prohibition temporarily, and the entry into the Holy Land as conditional.

Sayyid Qutb stated in his *In the Shade of the Qur'an*, a contemporary exegesis of the Qur'an, that the reason for this prohibition is to allow room for a new generation of Israelites to be brought up.[4] I would add that the new generation was ready to submit to the will of God, and therefore qualified for entry into the Holy Land as "Submitters," those who submit their personal will entirely to the will of God. The meaning of "Muslims" is also submitters. The Qur'an states in clear terms that righteousness is a prerequisite for inheriting lands: "Before this We wrote in the Zabur ("Psalms"!),[5] after the Message [given to Moses]: 'My servants, the righteous, shall inherit the earth'" (Qur'an, 21.105).

Other verses in the Qur'an directly associate the religious state of the Children of Israel to the inheritance of the land:

> And We made a people, considered weak [in Egypt], inheritors of the East and West of the land [i.e., all of it], whereon We sent down Our blessings. The fair promise of your Lord was fulfilled for the Children of Israel, because they had patience and constancy, and We leveled to the ground the great works and fine buildings which Pharaoh and his people erected (Qur'an, 7.137).

According to these verses, the proper relationship with God, which means submission to and peaceful alignment with His will, is the absolute criterion for inheritance of the Land. Of critical importance to the Qur'an is the fact that genetic or biological descent is never sufficient in itself to merit such inheritance. It is a non-factor in this respect.

Jerusalem or *Bayt al-Maqdis* (House of the Holy) is, by definition, a holy place. It is included in verse 17.1, either by referring to the Aqsa Mosque or to its precincts about which God said: "We did bless." The great fourteenth-century Muslim scholar Ibn Kathir said that the Aqsa Mosque is Bayt al-Maqdis.[6] Indeed, "the Aqsa Mosque" and "Bayt al-Maqdis" are used interchangeably whereby one of them is used as a metaphor of the other, as in the following hadith:

> Maimuna said: "O Messenger of Allah! Inform us about Bayt al-Maqdis!" He said: "It is the land where people will be gathered and resurrected [on the Day of Judgment]. Go [grammatically imperative!] and pray in it, for a prayer in it is the equivalent of a thousand prayers in other [mosques]." I said: "What if I couldn't

reach it?" He said: "Then you send a gift of oil to it in order to be lit in its lanterns, for the one who does so is the same like the one who has been there."[7]

The *hadith* shows that it is the religious duty of Muslims all over the world to maintain the Aqsa Mosque both physically and spiritually. The relationship with the Aqsa Mosque is primarily fulfilled through acts of worship, but the physical maintenance of the Mosque is also part of the responsibility of all Muslims. The fulfillment of both duties will be impaired as long as the Aqsa Mosque remains under occupation! The truth of the matter is that under Israeli occupation, Muslims do not have free access to the Mosque. Those who are prevented from having freedom of worship at the Aqsa Mosque include, but not restricted to, all Palestinians from the Gaza Strip, the West Bank, and occasional restrictions for Jerusalemite men younger than 45 years of age.

Since the miraculous Night Journey of Prophet Muhammad (Peace be upon him), *al-Isra' wa al-Mi'raj*, took place more than fourteen centuries ago, Muslims have established a sublime and perpetual relationship with the Aqsa Mosque. The Prophet was taken from al-Masjid al-Haram in Mecca to al-Masjid al-Aqsa in Jerusalem. This event marked a twinning relation between the two mosques. The beginning of Sura *al-Isra'* (17.1) reminds Muslims and non-Muslims of this important event.

When the Prophet (Peace be upon him) reported the event to the people of Mecca, they challenged him to prove it by describing Jerusalem to them, because they were familiar with it through their caravan trading. They used this story to undermine his credibility as a prophet; they knew that the journey from Mecca to Jerusalem would take several weeks during that time in each direction. They were considering Prophet Muhammad's abilities, not that of the Omnipotent God!

The greatest *hadith* scholars, al-Bukhari and Muslim, narrated that the Prophet (Peace be upon him) said: "When [the Meccan tribe of] Quraish did not believe me [about the Night Journey], I stood in the Hijr[8] and God revealed to me Bayt al-Maqdis [i.e., Jerusalem] and I began describing its signs to them while I was looking at it." This *hadith* provides the setting for interpreting verse 17.1, and explains why Muslims believe that the "Furthest Mosque" is in Jerusalem.

The twinning relationship manifests itself in the fact that another term, "the Sanctuary" or the Haram, also refers to the Aqsa Mosque, deriving from the name "the Noble Sanctuary" or al-Masjid al-Haram in Mecca. The reference to the Aqsa Mosque as "Haram" is a cultural development that reflects the very close relationship between the two mosques in Islamic consciousness. In other words, strictly speaking from a *fiqh* (Islamic jurisprudence) point of view, the laws that apply to the Haram in Mecca, such as the prohibition of hunting during the time of Hajj, do not apply to the Aqsa Mosque.

Mujir al-Din al-Hanbali (d. 1522) used "Al-Masjid al-Sharif al-Aqsa" in the first page of his introduction to *Al-Uns al-Jalil fi Tarikh al-Quds wal-Khalil*. But the order of the words differed in the chapter on the description of the Aqsa Mosque; he used "Al-Masjid al-Aqsa al-Sharif."⁹ Muslim scholars understood that the name "Al-Masjid al-Aqsa" predates the structures, and that no one building could be called as such. It is anachronistic to call the southernmost building the Aqsa Mosque; al-Hanbali called it "al-Jami' al-Kabir al-Qibliyy" (The Grand Southern Friday-Mosque).¹⁰ It is quite remarkable that al-Hanbali, who wrote *Al-Uns al-Jalil fi Tarikh al-Quds wal-Khalil* in the year AH 900 (1495), when there were no political disputes regarding the Aqsa Mosque, offered the following definition:

> Verily, "Al-Aqsa" is a name for the whole mosque which is surrounded by the wall, the length and width of which are mentioned here, for the building that exists in the southern part of the Mosque, and the other ones such as the Dome of the Rock and the corridors and other [buildings] are novel (*muhdatha*).¹¹

The paragraph that preceded the definition of the Aqsa Mosque was dedicated to its measurement. Twice, the measurements of the Mosque were taken under the supervision of al-Hanbali to ensure that they were accurate. He mentioned that the length of the Mosque was measured from the southern wall to the northern corridor near Bab al-Asbat (i.e., Lions' Gate; St. Stephen's Gate), and the width was measured from the wall overlooking the cemetery of Bab al-Rahma (i.e., Golden Gate) to the western corridor, beneath the Tankiziyya School. In both cases, the width of the walls themselves was excluded.

It should be noted that the Qur'anic reference to the Aqsa Mosque, as a mosque, took place years before the actual arrival of Muslims to Jerusalem. It means that part of what the Muslim believes is that the Aqsa Mosque was designated as a mosque by God. Other than the three Mosques of Mecca, Medina, and Jerusalem, Muslims are free to choose the site for a new mosque, but once it is established, it remains a mosque forever.

The journey by night had Jerusalem as a transit station or as a gate to the heavens. God could have taken His Prophet (Peace be upon him) directly from Mecca to heaven, but He didn't. The Aqsa Mosque has a very prominent place in the whole event. It was the place where the Prophet (Peace be upon him) led the other prophets and messengers in prayer. This act is interpreted, among other things, as inheriting the responsibility for and becoming custodians of the mosque.

Bayt al-Maqdis became the first *qibla*, or direction of prayer. Al-Bara' said: "We have prayed with the Messenger of Allah (Peace be upon him) in the direction of Bayt al-Maqdis for sixteen or seventeen months. Then we were directed to the Ka'ba [in Mecca]" (narrated by al-Bukhari and Muslim).

Despite the change of the *qibla*, the mere fact that Muslims prayed in the direction of Jerusalem is an indication of its prominence. According to the Qur'an, however, the mosque in Mecca was the first ever established by God for humanity, so it should not be surprising that the *qibla* was shifted back to it: "The first House [of worship] appointed for men, was that at Bakka [i.e., Mecca]: full of blessing and of guidance for all the worlds" (Qur'an, 3.96).

The same position is confirmed in a *hadith* narrated by al-Bukhari and Muslim:

Abu Dhar al-Ghafari—May God be pleased with him—said: "I said: O Messenger of Allah: Which mosque was established first on earth?
He said: al-Masjid al-Haram [in Mecca].
I said: Then which one?
He said: al-Masjid al-Aqsa [in Jerusalem].
I said: How much time was between them?
He said: Forty years, and when it is time for prayer, wherever you are, pray, for that where the merit is.

The Qur'an teaches that, while a single system of ethics and belief should be common to the revelations and Scriptures of all peoples, the specific laws of ritual and behavior [i.e., *Shari'a*] may vary among peoples and religions:

…To each among you have We prescribed a Law and an Open Way.
If Allah had so willed, He would have made you a single People, but
[His plan is] to test you in what He has given you: so strive as in a race
in all virtues (Qur'an, 5.48).

It should not be surprising, therefore, that Jews pray toward Jerusalem while Muslims pray toward Mecca. This fact does not reduce the sanctity of Jerusalem for Muslims. The second chapter of the Qur'an (verses 142–50) addresses the change of the *qibla* in detail. The basic message is that both directions of prayer are from God and that: "…the People of the Book know that that is Truth from their Lord."

In the sphere of *fiqh*, it is prohibited to relieve oneself (e.g., urinate) in the open space in the direction of both, al-Masjid al-Haram in Mecca and the Aqsa Mosque in Jerusalem. The *hadith* that declares such prohibition refers to these two mosques as the "two *qiblas*."[12]

Moreover, the importance of the Aqsa Mosque in the life of Muslims is reflected in the many other traditions of the Prophet. One of these traditions—narrated by al-Bukhari (# 1115) and Muslim (# 2475)—makes it clear that traveling in order to visit mosques for religious purposes is permitted to three mosques only: al-Masjid al-Haram (in Mecca), al-Masjid al-Nabawi (in Medina), and al-Masjid al-Aqsa (in Jerusalem).

The language of the abovementioned *hadith* in Arabic gives the impression that it is prohibited to travel to mosques other than these three. This led the prominent Shafi'i scholar Imam al-Juwayni (d.1085) to issue a religious ruling that it is prohibited to do so. Imam al-Nawawi (d.1277), who belonged to the same school of *fiqh*, rendered the position of al-Juwayni erroneous, and that the majority of scholars (*jumhur al-'Ulama'*) understand the hadith as saying that "there is no [extra] merit in traveling to other mosques."[13]

The Aqsa Mosque was developed and the buildings expanded on a large scale during the reign of the two Umayyad Caliphs, 'Abd al-Malik ibn Marwan (685–705) and his son al-Walid (705–15), to the extent that it surpassed the architectural grandeur of all mosques. The magnificence of the architecture of the Dome of the Rock and the southernmost building within the parameters of the Aqsa Mosque is witness to the importance of these holy sites in Islam.

Calligraphy is used at the Aqsa Mosque to reflect its status in the Islamic worldview, and to stress God's oneness and uniqueness (i.e., *tawhid*). Several chapters of the Qur'an and various other verses can be found inscribed inside and outside the buildings. One of these inscriptions, chapter 17 (i.e., *al-Isra'*), asserts the status of the Aqsa Mosque in the Islamic worldview. Like a necklace, it is inscribed on the neck of the Dome of the Rock, on the outside. The first verse of this chapter has a direct reference to the Aqsa Mosque in the context of the "Night Journey." The rest of this chapter, another 110 verses, is about the story of the "*Children of Israel*," which is the second name of this chapter. The narrative shifts from talking about Prophet Muhammad and his journey to the Aqsa Mosque, to Prophet Moses: "We gave unto Moses the Scripture, and We appointed it a guidance for the children of Israel, saying: Choose no guardian beside Me" (Qur'an, 17.2).

It should be noted that the same chapter is also inscribed over the niche in the southernmost building. The inscription, black on golden background mosaic with multi-colored leaves, begins immediately to the right side of the niche, facing south, and continues anti-clockwise in the direction of the east and then continues north and stops before the beginning of the two eastern "halls," the most northern of which has the rose window. The southern one has a hand-carved wood of a small part of chapter 17. It seems that most of this apparently old work of art was lost in the arson of 21 August 1969 which devastated that southeastern corner of the building. Some of the next verses could be considered either as a report on historical events that have taken place already, or as a prophecy that will unfold in the future, with the Children of Israel and the Aqsa Mosque being at the center of these events (Qur'an, 17.7).

Another chapter of the Qur'an is written on the outside of the Dome of the Rock. Like a crown, chapter 36 (i.e., *YaSeen*) covers the uppermost part of the octagonal walls. There are several prophetic traditions of various strengths about the virtues of this chapter of the Qur'an. One of them, categorized as having a "weak" chain of narrators, considers it the "heart of the Qur'an."[14] *YaSeen* does begin with confirming the messengership of Prophet Muhammad, but then it moves to other topics including life, death, and resurrection.

The inner side of the octagonal walls is adorned with short chapters and parts of longer ones, in addition to other non-Qur'anic inscriptions. It should be noted that the beginning and end of the following inscriptions don't always coincide with the beginning and end of the mentioned walls. Anti-clockwise, the southeastern, eastern, northeastern, and northern walls have the following anti-Trinitarian message:

> O People of the Book! Do not exaggerate in your religion nor utter aught concerning Allah save the truth. The Messiah, Jesus son of Mary, was only a messenger of Allah, and His word which He conveyed unto Mary, and a spirit from Him. So believe in Allah and His messengers, and say not "Three" – Cease! (it is) better for you! – Allah is only One Allah. Far is it removed from His Transcendent Majesty that He should have a son. His is all that is in the heavens and all that is in the earth. And Allah is sufficient as Defender. The Messiah does by no means disdain that he should be a servant of Allah, nor do the angels who are near to Him, and whoever disdains His service and is proud, He will gather them all together to Himself (Qur'an, 4.171).

Beginning with the northwestern wall, we find the following verses from chapter 19 which is named after Maryam (i.e., Mary, mother of Jesus Christ), the only woman in the Qur'an to be mentioned by name:

> And peace on me on the day I was born, and on the day I die, and on the day I am raised to life. Such is 'Isa, son of Maryam; [this is] the saying of truth about which they dispute. It befits not [the Majesty of] Allah that He should take to Himself a son. Glory to be Him. When He has decreed a matter He only says to it "Be," and it is. And surely Allah is my Lord and your Lord, therefore serve Him; this is the right path (Qur'an, 19.33–36).

The western and southwestern walls have the following verses from chapter of the "*Family of 'Imran*":

> Allah bears witness that there is no god but He, and (so do) the angels and those possessed of knowledge, maintaining His creation with justice; there is no god but He, the Mighty, the Wise. Surely the [true] religion with Allah is Islam, and those to whom the Book had been given did not show opposition but after knowledge had come to them, out of envy among themselves; and whoever disbelieves in the revelations of Allah then surely Allah is quick in reckoning (Qur'an, 3.18–19).

Chapter 20 (i.e., *Ta-Ha*) is written on the neck of the Dome of the Rock on the inside. It reflects certain similarities with chapter 17 which is written on the outside; both chapters "begin" with Prophet Muhammad and move to Prophet Moses. The Qur'an narrates, in the case of the latter, some essential stories about him including receiving revelation, his struggle against the Pharaoh, liberating the Children of Israel from servitude, the story of the golden calf, splitting the sea, and more.

Some critics of Islam have claimed that because Jerusalem was never a political center of the Islamic world, it could not have been held in high esteem by Islam. This is a false argument, for even Mecca, the most sacred religious site of the Islamic world, was never the capital of any Islamic state. This certainly does not negate the importance of sacred religious sites. One should remember that the Umayyads developed the site of the Aqsa Mosque before the end of the first century AH. They moved their capital from Medina to Damascus. Thereafter, no Muslim ruler took any of the three sacred cities, Mecca, Medina, or Jerusalem, as a capital. It is rather the religious importance of these cities that led them to their decisions, not the opposite.

There are many other traditions extolling the special merits of Jerusalem, including the view that praying at the Aqsa Mosque is far more efficacious than prayers in other locations (with the exception of the two mosques of Mecca and Medina). In addition, Um Salamah, wife of the Prophet said: "I have heard the Messenger of God (Peace be upon him) saying: 'He who initiates the minor Hajj [the 'Umrah] or Hajj at the Aqsa Mosque, God will forgive his prior sins.'"[15]

There is an addendum to the previous hadith stating that Um Hakim, daughter of Umayyah Ibn al-Akhnas, who reported the hadith of Um Salamah, traveled from Medina all the way to the Aqsa Mosque and initiated the minor Hajj from there.

There are many other traditions that reflect the importance of Jerusalem and the Aqsa Mosque in Islam that for brevity I did not include in this article. Yet, to conclude, I would like once again to refer to 'Umar ibn al-Khattab. After entering the city, the bishop of Jerusalem invited him to pray inside the Church of the Holy Sepulchre. 'Umar declined politely and stepped outside the church to pray. This act, I believe, established a practical module for interfaith relationship, especially in relation to the religious space of the other.

The sacredness of the Holy Land does not mean that spirituality could only be achieved in such places. In a tradition narrated in Imam Malik's greatly respected hadith collection known as Al-Muwatta', two prominent companions of the prophet had the following exchange of letters regarding Jerusalem: Abu Darda' invited Salman al-Farisi to come to Bayt al-Maqdis (literally, the House of the Sanctified). Salman replied by saying that the land cannot sanctify anyone. Only one's good deeds may bring one true sanctity.

THE DIVINE PRESENCE NEVER MOVES FROM THE WESTERN WALL

Jewish tradition teaches that the Temple
Mount is the focal point of Creation.
In the center of the mountain lies the
"Foundation Stone" of the world.
Here Adam came into being.
Here Abraham, Isaac and Jacob served God.
The First and Second Temples were built
upon this mountain.
The Ark of the Covenant was set upon the
Foundation Stone itself.
Jerusalem was chosen by God as the dwelling
place of the Shechinah.
David longed to build the Temple, and
Solomon his son built the First Temple here
about 3000 years ago.
It was destroyed by Nevuchadnezzar
of Babylon.
The Second Temple was rebuilt on its ruins
seventy years later.
It was razed by the Roman legions over
1900 years ago.
The present Western Wall before you is a
remnant of the western Temple Mount
retaining walls.
Jews have prayed in its shadow for
hundreds of years, an expression of their
faith in the rebuilding of the Temple.
The Sages said about it: "The Divine Presence
never moves from the Western Wall."
The Temple Mount continues to be the focus
of prayer for Jews from all over the world.

"My House Is A House Of Prayer...
For All Peoples"

Isaiah 56:7

Bs"d
Dear Visitors.
You are approaching the holy site of the
Western Wall where the Divine Presence
always rests. Please make sure you are
appropriately and modestly dressed so as
not to cause harm to this holy place or to
the feelings of the worshippers.
Sincerely,
Rabbi of the Western Wall and Holy Sites.

187 Announcements at the entrance to the
Western Wall prayer plaza

THE TEMPLE MOUNT IN JEWISH THOUGHT (70 CE TO THE PRESENT)

MIRIAM FRENKEL

THE HEBREW UNIVERSITY OF JERUSALEM

After the Destruction of the Temple

The destruction of the Second Temple in 70 CE was a traumatic event for the Jews. It shattered basic assumptions as to the destiny of the nation in the world and God's eternal covenant with it. The assumptions rested on the words of the Prophets, who maintained that the covenant between the People of Israel and the Lord was an eternal one. But now the Temple had been destroyed and, together with it, the ability had been lost to atone for the nation's sins through offering sacrifices. Seemingly, this event could only be explained as abandonment of the covenant by the wrathful, silent God who had been exiled from His abode. The rabbinical Sages took upon themselves the complex, delicate task of moderating the terminal meaning of the Temple's destruction.[1] This they accomplished in various manners.

A. The first was through a new interpretation of the biblical text by means of homiletic elaboration on the Bible (*midrash*). It created an order of priorities which gave precedence to the nation, while the Temple was assigned secondary priority and described merely as a structure, "trees and rocks." Instead of bemoaning its ruin, the Sages called for giving thanks that the nation had been saved. By means of the *midrash*, the Sages now directed the people towards study of the Torah: synagogues and study houses in which the Torah was studied were identified as places from which the Jews would draw their confidence in the continued existence of the covenant and would also serve as a temporary substitute for the Temple. Though they did not all in all deny the importance of the Temple, they postponed its rebuilding—which would signify the renewal of the covenant—till an unknown end time.

B. The second was by means of Jewish religious law (*halakhah*). After the destruction of the Temple, the Sages composed and collected many parts of the *halakhah* relating to details of the Temple ritual into two central bodies of religious law: the Mishnah and the Talmud. The laws governing sacrifices, the various utensils of the Temple, its measurements and its sanctity, all these greatly occupied the early Sages, and many tractates of the

Mishnah and the Talmud are devoted to these subjects. Some of these texts are written in the past tense, as if relating a story of what was and is no longer, and diffuse a sense of nostalgia for the glorious worship of God that had been practiced in the Temple, along with a desire to preserve its memory to the minutest detail. Other texts are phrased in the present tense. They comprise clear, detailed instructions and teach the laws of sacrifices and the worship of God as if the Temple was still standing and functioning, while totally overlooking the reality of the Destruction. By adopting this approach, the Sages applied a tendency, also found in the *midrash*, to divert the center of gravity from the actual Temple ritual to reading and studying about that ritual as a substitute for it. In their own words: "Whoever occupies himself with the laws of sin offering is as if he had sacrificed a sin offering. And all who occupy themselves with the law of guilt offering it is as if they had made a guilt offering."[2]

Outside the circles of the Sages, additional approaches developed to contend with the sense of loss that the Destruction had created:

C. After the Destruction, apocalyptic literature—a rich mystical literature that preserved the transcendental significance and numinous nature of the Temple—gained momentum.[3]

D. In the field of liturgy, a unique kind of liturgical poem (*piyyut*) emerged, known as an *'avodah*, whose purpose was to describe the high priest's ritual acts in the Temple in the minutest detail and with great accuracy. Alongside the *'avodah* poems, there also developed liturgical poems about the several watches into which the priests were divided when the Temple existed.

E. Post-Destruction ritual worship underwent changes and took on new meanings and content. Daily prayer commemorated the sacrifices and liturgy of the Temple, and time and again called for its rebuilding. Jews began making pilgrimage to Jerusalem to visit the destroyed Temple very soon after the Destruction. After the suppression of the Bar Kokhba Revolt in 135 CE, the Romans prohibited the entry of Jews into Jerusalem. However, this edict was apparently not very strictly applied; Jews continued to reach Jerusalem and once a year, on the Ninth of Av—the anniversary of the Destruction—and were even permitted to visit the site of the ruined Temple.[4] A ritual of mourning developed on the Mount around a perforated rock which was identified as the Foundation Rock (*even shetiyyah*). Indeed, in the generations after the Bar Kokhba Revolt a tradition developed according to which the Foundation Rock was the navel of the world from which Creation had begun. According to tradition, at this spot, which contains the essence of holiness, the Ark of the Covenant had also stood, as well as the Holy of Holies, the place where incense had burned in the Temple.[5] The ceremony around the Foundation Rock was the highlight of the pilgrimage route that included arrival at Jerusalem, ascent of the Temple Mount, and walking around on it until one reached the site of the Holy of Holies where a ceremony was held at the foot of the Rock comprising lamentations, tearing one's garments, and anointing the Rock with oil. Each stage was accompanied by structured, fixed readings of biblical verses.

Under Muslim Rule

The Muslim conquest of Jerusalem in 638 aroused apocalyptic expectations among Jews. Liberation from the Byzantine yoke and 'Abd al-Malik's building of the Dome of the Rock on the site identified as the Temple's Holy of Holies infused the Jews with faith that redemption was near, to be accompanied by the restoration of the Temple. The "Little Horn," the last among the Beast's horns symbolizing the several empires in Daniel's vision (Dan. 7.8), was interpreted to refer to the Islamic empire, after which Redemption was expected to come. This, apparently, was why Jews participated alongside Muslims in cleansing the Temple Mount, with the intention of uncovering the site of the Foundation Rock. The event is mentioned in several Jewish, Muslim, and Christian traditions. Perhaps this was also what lay behind the tradition according to which Jews regularly participated in cleansing the Aqsa Mosque, down to the times of the Caliph 'Umar b. 'Abd al-'Aziz (717–20).[6] The identification of the Muslim structures on the Temple Mount with the Temple ended at the beginning of the eighth century after the Jews had been explicitly forbidden to pray on the Temple Mount by a decree of 'Umar b. 'Abd al-'Aziz. Indeed, when the Dome of the Rock was damaged in 1015 by an earthquake, Solomon ben Judah, the Head of the Jerusalem Academy, reporting on the event in a letter, expressed an explicit hope: "The splendid place built upon it fell ... May it be [His] will that a lasting structure be built." "The splendid place" is the magnificent structure that the Muslims built "upon it," the site of the Temple. This event was enough to infuse Solomon ben Judah with the hope that in its stead the Temple itself will be built that will stand for ever and ever.[7]

'Umar b. 'Abd al-'Aziz's edict prohibiting Jewish prayer on the Temple Mount entailed significant changes in the ritual. The prayers and mourning ceremonies on the Mount itself were replaced by a "circuit of the gates" and by ascending the Mount of Olives. A book found in the Cairo Geniza spelled out the order of prayer for the Temple gates. The pilgrim customarily circumambulated the Temple Mount, pausing at each of the ten gates in order to say set prayers. The circuit was made by solitary pilgrims or small groups. This was in contrast to the public ceremony of blessing the communities and of proclaiming the festivals of the Jewish calendar, performed annually on the Mount of Olives in the presence of the Head of the Academy. The ceremony on the Mount of Olives, which faces the site of the Temple from the east (see fig. 176), served as a substitute for the Temple Mount.

The prohibition against Jews praying on the Temple Mount was not meticulously observed. It is related of Shmuel ben Paltiel, a ninth-century pilgrim from southern Italy, that he donated "...for the oil of the sanctuary at the western wall of the inner altar....". From this we may conclude that Jewish worship was conducted around the remnants of the Temple's outer walls.[8] Apparently, it was also permitted to enter and visit the Temple complex itself, for an eleventh-century guide for Jewish pilgrims notes sites found on the Mount, such as the gigantic column that was located "in the middle of the domes that rise up in the middle of the mosque where the Ishmaelites pray."[9]

An important role in developing the special attitude towards the Temple Mount was played by the "Mourners of Zion." This was an ascetic sect that developed within the Karaite movement which placed dwelling in Jerusalem, self-mortification, and mourning ceremonies on the Mount of Olives—i.e., opposite the gates to the Temple—at the center of its religious activity. As early as the tenth century, the Mourners of Zion had a fixed cycle of lamentations, recited while making a circuit around the Temple Mount and standing before its gates and also on the summit of the Mount of Olives.[10]

Mourning the destruction of the Temple was also a major theme in poems of lamentation composed during the Middle Ages. An example is the famous wine poem of Dunash Ben Labrat (Fez, 10th century) in which he rejected an invitation to a banquet, since "the Temple is in ruins and foxes run about in Zion."[11] Rabbi Sa'adyah Gaon (882–942) too, in a prayer of entreaty that he composed and included in his prayer book, implored God to show kindness towards His people in view of the destruction of the Temple and the abandonment of Jerusalem.[12]

In the Period of the Crusades

Even before the Crusader conquest in 1099, the Jerusalem Academy was on the decline, and with it the ceremonies on the Mount of Olives. The Crusader regime and the prohibition it imposed forbidding Jews to live in the city put a total stop to these traditions. Despite the prohibition, Jewish pilgrimage ceremonies continued; however, their character was drastically transformed. The holy places connected with the Temple Mount that had served as locations of Jewish worship up to the Crusader conquest, such as the Temple Mount gates and the Mount of Olives, became Christian holy places to which Jewish access was denied. The absence of a regular Jewish community in the city transformed pilgrimage into an individual endeavor very limited in time, as was Maimonides' visit to the city in 1165.[13] The Spanish-Jewish traveler Benjamin of Tudela, a contemporary of Maimonides, provided details, explaining that the usual place of prayer at that time was "facing the 'azarah" (the main forecourt of the Temple), that is, near the gate west of the Dome of the Rock.

After Saladin's conquest of Jerusalem in 1187 its Jewish community was established anew and Jewish pilgrims from Christian Europe and Muslim countries arrived. Shmuel bar Shimshon described the journey of a group of Provençal pilgrims ca. 1210. He told of Jewish public ceremonies which had been resumed on the Mount of Olives and about a ceremony of entry into Jerusalem which began at the western gate of the city and ended at the Temple Mount's Gate of the Chain. Similarly, Spanish-Jewish poet Judah Alharizi, who came to Jerusalem in 1216/17, recounted the holding of a ritual, apparently of private character, on the Mount of Olives.[14]

Anticipation of the Temple's restoration played a significant role in the thoughts and feelings of medieval Jews. They expressed these sentiments in the oral language of everyday speech and in the written language of correspondence. Merchants' letters and missives of friendship found in the Cairo Geniza abound in expressions such as: "May God grant me the privilege to meet you in the courtyards of the Temple in Jerusalem"; "May God grant you many years of happiness and joy, and may He grant you to behold the beauty of the Lord and to visit His Temple"; "And may He bring us and all Israel together to His sanctuary, when His congregation will be assembled and His Temple renovated."[15]

Medieval Jewish philosophers, too, attributed major significance to the Temple Mount's holiness. Judah Halevi (ca.1075–1141) elaborated the theory which maintained that men's character and manner of behavior were conditioned by their climatic environment. He regarded the Land of Israel as the ideal climatic region that was also the source from which stemmed the uniqueness of the Jewish nation. Within the Land, the predominance of Jerusalem stood out and all the more so that of the Temple, where men could be nearest to Divine Providence, the *Shekhinah*. Manifestation of the *Shekhinah* in Jerusalem was conditional upon establishing a reciprocal relationship between the people and the place. Only if the people lived a full collective life in that place would it be transformed into the Gate of Heaven, renewal of the Temple ritual be possible, and prophecy be restored. His conception was reflected in his philosophical treatise *Kuzari*, in his poems of longing for Zion, and in his journey to the Land of Israel towards the end of his life.

Maimonides (1135–1204) continued to a great extent the intentions of the Sages in that he dedicated sizable sections of his teachings on religious law to detailed discussions relating to the rules governing the worship of God in the Temple. In fact, he is considered to this day to be the chief authority on Temple matters. He saw the importance of the Temple in the ingathering of the entire nation on regular festivals to worship God by offering sacrifices. Rebuilding the Temple, he believed, was an element of messianic times, and one of the clear signs of a true Messiah would be if he succeeded in rebuilding the Temple on its site and gathering the dispersed of Israel.[16] Nevertheless, Maimonides believed that prior to the building of the Temple, he and the nation would have to "arise and restore the kingdom of David"[17] and only then could they approach rebuilding the Temple. Since the Temple's holiness was "due to the *Shekhinah*," it was in effect even at the time of its destruction. For that reason, he argued that the Jews must be imbued with "awe of the Temple" and that one may approach it only in a state of holiness. As all Jews are considered impure since the Destruction, he ruled that one must not go up onto the Temple Mount at all.

In contrast to Maimonides, who thought that the Temple would be rebuilt by the King-Messiah, Rashi (Rabbi Shlomo ben Yitzhak, the eleventh-century leading commentator on the Bible and the Talmud) and most of the Sages of Ashkenaz (northwestern medieval Europe) viewed Redemption in apocalyptic terms and believed that the Temple would descend from heaven in complete and perfect form. One of the outstanding Sages who disagreed with Maimonides was Rabbi Abraham ben Daud (Rabad), who wrote: "This is his own opinion and I don't know whence it came to him." Rabad permitted going up to the entire area of the Temple Mount since he saw the holiness of the Temple as "holiness in the future," not a present sanctity.

Maimonides' sweeping prohibition against Jews going up onto the Temple Mount attests to the immense physical transformation which that compound had undergone by his time. During the first centuries following the Destruction, in traditions handed down from generation to generation Jews preserved knowledge of the bounds of the holy places on the Temple Mount: the courtyards, the altar, the Sanctuary, the Holy of Holies, and the Foundation Rock. Intensive construction carried out on the Mount since the Muslim conquest had changed its topography to such an extent that it was no longer possible to retrace its ancient bounds. That is what brought Maimonides to sweepingly forbid any entry onto the Mount.

This situation is reflected in the words of Nahmanides, Rabbi Moshe ben Nahman, the most outstanding Jewish scholar of Spain in the thirteenth century. For him, Jewish settlement in the Land of Israel was one of the 613 biblical commandments. He himself came to the Land of Israel in his old age in 1267. In a letter from Jerusalem, he wrote: "One destroys and tears up the boundaries, the other erects and sets up idols."[18] Nahmanides' pupil, who accompanied him to Jerusalem, also wrote in the same spirit:

> When the Muslims set out to build their buildings on the Temple Mount, they destroyed and razed the holy places to the foundations and ruined and destroyed the surface of the ground of the Temple, leveling the ground until the confines and boundaries of the holy ritual baths were no longer known. Because it is known that the Temple was not on a plateau, but that people went up to it …. And now all of it is level ground and its location is lower than the city.[19]

When in 1229 Jerusalem was restored to Crusader rule for a period of fifteen years, the Jews were once again expelled and until 1236 were not allowed to enter the city, not even as pilgrims. When Nahmanides arrived at the beginning of Mamluk rule in Jerusalem, only a handful of Jews were living there, but he documented the beginnings of a revival of

Jewish life in the city as well as of Jewish pilgrimage. He himself did not go up onto the Temple Mount but instead ascended the Mount of Olives.

The Mamluk and Ottoman Periods

During the period of Mamluk rule Jews kept a greater distance from the Haram al-Sharif. The Jewish traveler Rabbi Eshtori ha-Parhi wrote in his travel itinerary between 1316 and 1322 that the Jews customarily prayed only at the gates.[20] Expanding upon the discussion of the boundaries of the Temple Mount, he provided a description of his own which reflects the fact that he did not visit the Mount due to his principled position that entering it was absolutely forbidden. When the Jewish traveler from Italy, Meshullam of Volterra, visited Jerusalem in 1481, he provided a very detailed description of the Temple Mount enclosure, but from the viewpoint of an observer on the summit of the Mount of Olives. It is quite obvious from his account that Jews identified the Dome of the Rock with certainty as the location of the Holy of Holies and the Aqsa Mosque as the structure containing the walls of the Temple.[21]

After the Ottoman conquest and with the arrival of Jewish exiles from Spain, a change took place in the ritual conducted at the Temple Mount. The Western Wall of the Temple Mount precinct, whose remnants had been mentioned and described by travelers and visitors in earlier centuries as well, began to serve as a place of gathering and prayer for Jews and to play an important role in Jewish consciousness. This process, already begun in the late Mamluk period after the Jewish Quarter was relocated,[22] was accelerated, probably as a consequence of the explicit decree forbidding Jews to enter the confines of the Mount under threat of punishment.[23] Rabbi Ovadiah of Bertinoro, who visited Jerusalem in 1488 and described the Western Wall, did not yet indicate any worship being performed there, whereas Rabbi Yisrael Ashkenazi, who served as a judge in a religious court in Jerusalem, wrote in 1520 in a letter to Rabbi Abraham Perugia, that he is "raising his hands [in blessing]" and praying for him and the members of his family while standing before the Western Wall. Ashkenazi also added an explanation why prayer was conducted specifically at this site: no Jew entered the Temple Mount itself "because of the prohibition," the halakhic prohibition deriving from the holiness of the place, as well as because "in any case, the Ishmaelites do not allow [Jews] to approach."[24] In 1572, when Rabbi Isaac Luria (a leading sixteenth-century kabbalist) visited the Western Wall, it is related that he "laid his hand" on it. We may assume that by doing so he confirmed identification of the site with the Western Wall and approved the ritual performed there.

In the sixteenth century, a circle of pietists and kabbalists was active in Jerusalem, headed by the leader of the Jewish community, Rabbi Isaac Solal, and the kabbalist Rabbi Abraham bar Eliezer ha-Levi. Its members calculated the End of Days and the time of Redemption, which they believed to be drawing near. Renewal of the Temple was a focal point of their apocalyptic visions. For that reason, they interpreted the destruction of Muslim structures on the Temple Mount in the earthquake of 1546 as a sign of the beginning of Redemption and described the destruction dramatically in their letters. The hope for redemption and longings for the Temple were also expressed in many liturgical poems composed in this period. The most famous is *Lekhah Dodi* (Come, My Beloved) by Shlomo Alkabez (Safed, 1505–84) which became an inseparable part of the Friday evening synagogue service everywhere:

> O Temple of the King, O royal city,
>
> Arise, go forth from your downtrodden state,
>
> You have too long dwelt in the Vale of Weeping,
>
> And He will truly show you compassion.

Despite the prohibition, we still hear in the sixteenth century of Jews who entered the Temple Mount precinct. A lively dispute continued in this period over the boundaries of the Mount and the holy place and about the halakhic prohibition against entry onto the Mount. These matters were reflected by Rabbi David ben Zimra (Radbaz, 1480–1574) in a responsum to a query directed to him about Jewish entry onto the steps built around the Mount. Radbaz, who had moved to Jerusalem in 1553, attested that he himself had not entered the Temple Mount and knew the precinct only from the descriptions of others who had visited it. Thus, he recommended that his questioner, too, avoid entering the Mount out of caution, lest he come too close to the Foundation Rock, which he identified with certainty as that beneath the Dome of the Rock. Nevertheless, he admitted "that in the main this law is a matter of controversy." This query and responsum indicate that not a few Jews were accustomed to going up into the Temple Mount enclosure, whether onto the steps surrounding it or "into the underground cavern whose opening is in the west and which stretches to a place underneath the Dome," but the rabbi goes on to say that this is forbidden.[25] Such action constantly decreased and by the seventeenth century nearly all Jewish worship was concentrated around the Western Wall. An anonymous Italian traveler who visited Jerusalem in 1626 wrote: "I kissed it and prostrated myself at its feet and there I said regular prayers."[26] Similar testimonies are found in Karaite writings from this period.

How did Jews explain the new place of worship at the Western Wall, on the fringes of the Temple Mount—in fact outside it? The clearest tendency was to attribute the distancing from the Temple Mount to halakhic reasons deriving from the holiness of the place. The more worship at the Wall became established, the greater the belief as to the holiness of the Mount, which now took on mystical dimensions entailing a real danger to life. For example, the story spread about a group of Jews that had arrived with the army of Ottoman sultan Selim II immediately after the conquest of Jerusalem in 1516, and came to the Temple Mount with him: "... and they entered into it and they all died."[27] At the same time, worship at the Western Wall was becoming established practice. According to a belief that was gaining strength, the Western Wall was an authentic remnant from the time of King Solomon, and its stones had been hewn and laid in place by a Divine miracle rather than by human hands. This was one reason for its holiness; the other reason was that the *Shekhinah* had never abandoned the Wall and would never abandon it. The biblical prooftext for this belief was generally the verse from Song of Songs 2.9: "Behold, there He stands behind our wall." This was interpreted as referring to the *Shekhinah* that was always present behind the Western Wall.

Consequently, Jews tried to purchase homes or to dwell in places overlooking the Wall, and a special prayer was even set to be recited on Sabbaths and holidays when gazing at the Wall. Many Jews made the effort to come to the Wall in person, particularly on Sabbaths and holidays after the synagogue service. A special prayer service at the Wall was taking shape. Rabbi Gedaliah of Siemiatycze, Poland, who arrived in Jerusalem in 1700, reported that Jews used to pray at the Western Wall on various days of fasting. Rabbi Yehudah Poliastro, who visited the city in 1743, presented a depiction of the Wall in his book *Memory of Jerusalem (Zikhron Yerushalayim)*. His book also included the prayer services at the Wall for the Sabbath, for the beginning of a new month, for Rosh ha-Shanah, and for the festivals. The Wall became a place where Jews uttered prayers for the whole Jewish nation in Exile together with private prayers for one's immediate family and relatives. The presence of women was especially prominent at the site, praying, lamenting, and weeping in loud voices. Prayer at the Wall, particularly at night, became a way of expressing piety and awe of Heaven. Rabbi Shalom Shar'abi (Yemen, 1720–Jerusalem, 1777) used to come alone every night to the Wall and say the midnight prayer in memory of the Destruction of the Temple and for the Land of Israel's restoration.

Belief in the holiness of the Western Wall took on popular expressions, such as stories about Jews who had been attacked on the way to it and had been miraculously saved. A typical story was that about Rabbi Shalom Shar'abi himself whom a group of Muslims had tried to attack as he made his way to the Wall, but found themselves riveted to the ground without the capacity to move until he finished his prayer and left. In general, Jews could pray at the Wall without being molested, but there are also reports about repeated attacks. Rabbi Moshe Hagiz (1672–1750) wrote in his book that in such instances the city authorities generally defended the Jews praying at the Wall. His remarks implied that the Jews themselves sought to play down the significance of these events, even disregarding them.

The visits to the Wall, which became increasingly frequent, did not occur without criticism from Jews themselves. A hint of this is found in the book *Ruins of Jerusalem (Horvot Yerushalayim*, 1627) from whose introduction it emerges that there were Jews who called for avoiding trips to Jerusalem which involved a heavy financial burden. The writer reprimanded those who expressed such opinions, arguing that financial distress need not stand in the way of the desire to shelter in the shadow of the *Shekhinah*.

The late nineteenth century was a time of Jewish national awakening. The central stream in the Zionist movement concentrated on establishing a national home for the Jews, while not attaching great importance to the Temple Mount. The thought of rebuilding the Temple was far from and alien to the Zionist way of thinking. When Theodor Herzl, the founder of modern Zionism, visited Jerusalem, he indeed very much enjoyed "a view of the Temple area, the Mount of Olives and the whole storied landscape in the morning sunshine," but he described the Western Wall realistically without a bit of emotion: "We have been to the Wailing Wall. A deeper emotion refuses to come, because that place is pervaded by hideous, wretched, speculative beggary ... I am firmly convinced that a magnificent New Jerusalem could be built outside the old city's walls ... A very pretty, elegant town would be quite possible beside it."[28]

However, there were also Zionist circles that wished to bind the call to rebuild the national home with one to rebuild the Temple and renew the sacrifices therein. One of the powerful voices calling for renewal of the Temple was Rabbi Zevi Hirsch Kalischer (1795–1874), a founder of religious Zionism and one of the first Lovers of Zion (Hovevei Zion) who deliberated at length about the renewal of sacrifices in modern times.[29] Yet Kalischer's position aroused bitter opposition among members of his own circle. His mentor, Rabbi Akiva Eiger, sent him several letters in which he expressed opposition to conducting sacrifices in modern times. He based his opinion, among other things, on that of Maimonides as well as on the statements of Rabbi Elijah of Vilna (1720–97), one of the greatest spiritual leaders of Jewry in his days, and especially on his interpretation of the verse from Song of Songs 2.7: "I adjure you, O maidens of Jerusalem ... Do not wake or rouse love until it pleases!" According to Rabbi Elijah, the oath refers to an initiative to rebuild the Temple without explicit Divine command.[30]

While this controversy was going on, several attempts were also made to purchase land near the Western the Wall. In 1850, Hakham [= rabbi] 'Abdallah of Bombay unsuccessfully tried to purchase the Wall. Further, the attempts of Moses Montefiore to ease praying at the Wall by setting up chairs and awnings did not bear fruit. In 1887 Baron Edmond de Rothschild proposed a plan to purchase the area of the Magharibah neighborhood, facing the Wall, and turn it into a Jewish pious endowment. For various reasons his plan came to naught, among them the opposition of Jerusalem's rabbis.

With the increase in the Jewish population of Jerusalem and the growing numbers of visitors to the Wall, the emotional relationship to the remnant of the Temple gained strength. Further, the image of the Wall began to appear on religious artifacts as well as in artistic depictions. This was especially true of Boris Schatz and his students at the Bezalel School of Art, founded in Jerusalem in 1906.

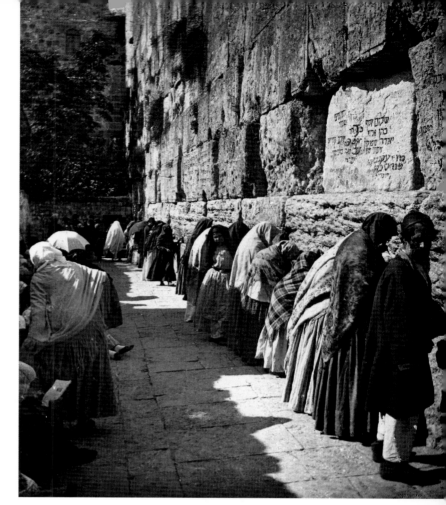

188 Jewish men and women praying together in the lane in front of the Western Wall, 1910

189 Soldiers of a Jewish battalion serving under the British flag, and local Jews, at the Western Wall, 1918

לשנה טובה
תכתבו

קבוצת חיילים עברים
אצל כותל המערבי

Under the British Mandate and Jordanian rule

Mainstream Zionism generally persisted in its indifference to the Temple Mount, continuing in its efforts to create modern, secular substitutes for the Temple. Religious Zionists, too, did not demand control of the Temple Mount. Their foremost leader, Rabbi Abraham Isaac Ha-Cohen Kook, distinguished between matters of Redemption which are in the power of Heaven and over which men have no control—including faith in the coming of the Messiah and in the restoration of the Temple—and, on the other hand, the nation's duty to settle in the Land of Israel and build it until the coming of the Messiah. He stressed that the Torah's commandments strictly prohibited Jews from even entering the site of the Temple. Nevertheless, as two opposed national movements developed in the country—Zionism and the Palestinian national movement—religious tension increased over the Western Wall. Violent disorders erupted there in 1929.[31]

Fierce clashes between Arabs and Jews took place in late 1947 after the UN resolution on Palestine. As a consequence, Jews were totally prevented from having access to the Wall. In May 1948 the Jewish Quarter in the Old City fell to Transjordan's Arab Legion and its synagogues were destroyed.

Under Jordanian rule (1948–67), Israeli Jews were barred from visiting the Western Wall and other Jewish holy places in Jordan's West Bank. Neither were Jews from other

190 Commemorating the millions of Jews murdered in Nazi-occupied Europe during a public prayer at the Western Wall, 1944

191 Tourists and a Jordanian soldier at the Western Wall, 1961
Published by permission, *Historic Views of the Holy Land: The 1960s: Photographs of Charles Lee Feinberg,* HYPERLINK "http://www.bibleplaces.com" www.bibleplaces.com, 2004

countries permitted to do so. While the Kingdom of Jordan vigorously promoted Muslim and Christian pilgrimage and tourism to Jerusalem's Muslim and Christian holy places, it categorically denied entry to Jews. The *Guide officiel* published by Jordan's Tourist Department in 1956 put it bluntly: "Les personnes professant la religion juive ne sont pas admises en Jordanie."[32] The English version of the *Guide* saw fit to strike a somewhat apologetic note: "Persons professing the Jewish faith are not admitted into Jordan. This prohibition is motivated purely by security reasons, as Jordan is still at war with the Jewish State Israel."[33]

The Jordanian *Guides* did not mention the Western, or Wailing, Wall among Jerusalem's places of interest. Still, some non-Jewish tourists did visit it [fig. 191].

Under Israeli Sovereignty[34]

In June 1967 the Israeli army conquered the Temple Mount. The liberation of the Temple Mount and the Western Wall evoked highly emotional feelings among the Jewish public. The most famous expression of the public mood in those days was Naomi Shemer's song, "Jerusalem of Gold." It had been composed a few weeks prior to the outbreak of hostilities and soon became the melody that accompanied those euphoric times. Her song expressed longing and yearning for the reunified city and the Temple Mount. However, despite its unprecedented popularity it did not arouse the public at large to demand a change in the status of the Temple Mount. The secular public took into account the danger of confrontation with the Muslim world and the damage to Israel's international status that might result, while both Religious Zionist and *Haredi* (Ultra-Orthodox) Jewry were explicitly and unambiguously reserved, each group for its own reasons, towards any action on the Temple Mount. Anti-Zionist *Haredi* Jewry, especially the *Neturei Karta*, believe that the State of Israel is of itself an obstacle to Redemption and the establishment of the Third Temple. Religious Zionism, including the Merkaz ha-Rav Yeshivah and Gush Emunim which hold militant nationalist viewpoints and see the State of Israel as a necessary stage on the path to full Redemption, conditioned any Jewish action on the spiritual preparedness and readiness of the whole Jewish people for such acts, while rejecting any practical initiative on the Temple Mount. The official position of the Chief Rabbinate was declared in an "Announcement and Warning" issued a few months after the Six Day War against entry into any area of the Temple Mount out of fear of "prejudicing the purity of the holy place" [see fig. 147].

Opposing them, as early as the first year after the Six Day War, were groups that challenged the new arrangements on the Temple Mount. The outstanding figure among them was the chief rabbi of the Israeli army, Shlomo Goren. On the Ninth of Av he went up to the Temple Mount with a large group of pupils and there conducted a mass prayer service. Other groups, the most noteworthy among them being "The Faithful of the Temple Mount," followed in Rabbi Goren's footsteps, persistently trying to pray on the Temple Mount and calling for application of Israeli-Jewish sovereignty over the Temple Mount so as to begin building the Third Temple. This group was comprised of people from the national-religious community and of veterans of the central faction of the radical LEHI (Fighters for the Freedom of Israel) underground movement which during the last stage of the Mandate Period strove to drive the British out of Palestine. The ideologue and intellectual leader of the movement was the poet Uri Tsvi Greenberg. The vision of the Third Temple was a central theme in his poetry and one around which his life revolved.

Several decades later the Habad Hasidim led by Menachem Mendel Schneerson, the Brooklyn-based Rabbi of Lubavitch, joined in calling to rebuild the Temple on the Temple Mount. In 1991, the rabbi instructed his followers to hold the joyous Sukkot water-drawing ceremony that used to be conducted in the Temple's courts, on "the Temple Mount itself … and thus to enter the site of the Temple in the areas permitted [by *halakhah*]." The initiative did not come to fruition, but the rabbi never retracted this decision by the time of his death in 1994, although neither did he try again to implement it. The main importance of the event was the precedent-setting rabbinical ruling which obviously contradicted the warning of the Chief Rabbinate Council.

Militant groups that called for applying Jewish sovereignty to the Temple Mount, such as *El Har HaShem* (To God's Mountain), did not find acceptance among national-religious circles. One political group that did agree with them was the Kakh movement, founded by Rabbi Meir Kahane, which focused ideologically on the commandment to build the Temple and called for "purifying the Mount of its abominations." The point of departure for the Kakh people was more national than religious. Restoration of the Temple was important in their view, but they were primarily disturbed by the Muslim presence on the Temple Mount, which they considered a national disgrace.

In the 1980s a new clandestine group came into being, later known as the "Jewish Underground." It too aspired to "cleanse" the Temple Mount. Prominent among its members was a branch which based its views on the Kabbalah of Rabbi Isaac Luria, elaborating upon and updating it. According to their belief, as long as the Jewish nation is, at least in part, under the control of the Gentile nations of the world, the Gentile nations are capable of existence only by absorbing vestiges of the holiness of the Jewish people. The Dome of the Rock, implanted atop of the Holy of Holies, is a source of spiritual inspiration for the Arabs which enables them to exist. Hence, Muslim rule over the Temple Mount is at the roots of the sorry state of the Jewish nation. Therefore, liberating the Temple Mount from Islam's grip is conceived as a necessary step on the way to Redemption. It should be noted that the Jewish Underground was unsuccessful in obtaining the blessing of any rabbinical spiritual authority, and in the final tally its members acted without it. The Underground was uncovered in 1984 and its members arrested and sentenced. The national-religious community publicly rejected the Underground's members who were termed "false messiahs." Secular leaders of the right-wing "Whole Land of Israel Movement" also expressed their opposition to the Underground and were horrified by its deeds.

A public dispute developed in Israel in the late 1970s as to the issue of sovereignty over the Temple Mount. Journalist Shmuel Schnitzer protested, in a series of articles, against what he considered the lax application by the Israeli authorities of Israeli-Jewish sovereignty over the Temple Mount. Professor Nathan Rotenstreich was a leading protagonist of the contrary approach. He distinguished between "ownership" and "sovereignty": while ownership means control over a property, sovereignty implies authority to impose domination and has no relationship whatsoever to property. Consequently, Rotenstreich asserted that the State of Israel was sovereign over the Mount, but it did not hold ownership of the mosques located there. He also warned that the eagerness to emphasize and enforce Israeli sovereignty over the Mount might blur the distinction between sovereignty and ownership, and indeed weaken Israeli sovereignty there.

In 1983 the Temple Institute, propagating the view that Jews are obligated to study and

192 At the edge of the Western Wall prayer plaza, "The Women of the Wall" are huddling together to prevent disruption of their service; an Ultra-Orthodox man (left) vehemently expressing his disapproval of the group; the Rabbi of the Wall and the Holy Places, Shmuel Rabinovitch, observes its doings[37]
Three frames from Yael Katzir's documentary, *Praying in Her Own Voice: The Struggle of the Women of the Wall for Freedom of Worship in Israel* (2007)

research halakhic issues linked to the Temple's re-building, was established in Jerusalem. As the Institute aims inter alia at identifying the exact location upon which the Temple had stood, it has been able to provide a common ground for rabbis from the religious establishment who forbid entry to the Temple Mount as well as for religious personalities who allow it. The Institute is carrying out much educational and public relations activity. Its "House of the Hebrew Craftsman" has conducted practical workshops where craftsmen recreate the Temple instruments and vessels. The Institute also strives to renew ceremonies such as the medieval circuiting of the gates of Jerusalem.[35]

The most prominent voice to come out against this trend was that of Professor Yeshayahu Leibowitz (1903–94), an Orthodox Jew well known for his consistent call for separation of religion and state. He regarded the possibility that the State of Israel, a fundamentally secular entity, would engage in rebuilding the Temple as absolutely groundless. Leibowitz did not view the Temple as an essential or central issue in Judaism, nor did he perceive a true link between it and religious life in Israel. Among Israel's secular Jews, author S. Yizhar argued that the trend to renew the Temple was essentially non-Zionist in nature.

Concomitantly with the vociferous dispute over the Temple Mount, the Western Wall increasingly became the central site of worship of the Jewish People. The plaza in front of the Wall became also a tourist attraction, a popular place for personal and family ceremonies, and a public space where national, state, and military ceremonies are conducted. The Western Wall as a Jewish holy place continued to draw much controversial fire. One of the outstanding disagreements revolved around "The Women of the Wall," a body comprising women of all Jewish religious denominations who, from 1988 onward, have sought to conduct services at the Wall as a female prayer group. They demand the right to pray out loud, wear ritual prayer shawls, and read from the Torah scroll. Their

193 3 July 2008: Against the background of the Dome of the Rock, Rabbi Tendler observes an imaginary rendition of the pilgrimage to the Temple

attempt aroused sharp, even violent, opposition, both from Ultra-Orthodox Jews—both men and women—and from the rabbinical establishment in charge of the Wall [fig. 192].[36] Parallel to the struggle of this group, the Wall served as an arena for the campaign by the Jewish Conservative and Reform religious movements for egalitarian prayer, that is, women and men in mixed prayer groups in the rear area of the Western Wall plaza, on the holiday of Shavu'ot and on the Ninth of Av. These efforts, too, led to violent reactions, verbal and physical, on the part of Ultra-Orthodox Jews. These struggles attest that the site of the Western Wall has been transformed into an arena for expressing the dominant ethos in Judaism, both inside and outside of Israel. At the same time, opinions have also been voiced expressing reservation with regard to the centrality the Wall has acquired over the years at the expense of the Temple Mount itself.

At the time of writing, the Temple Mount is still at the very heart of a bitter dispute among the Jewish Israeli public. Into this dispute have been drawn religious and secular Jews, intellectuals and politicians. In May 2005, some Religious-Zionist rabbis published a new halakhic ruling permitting the entry of Jews onto the Temple Mount "in a state of purity." This ruling elicited a sharp controversy within Religious Zionism itself, calling forth antagonists who saw it as a violation of holiness and stressed the spiritual power deriving precisely from keeping at a distance from the Temple Mount. The tendency to go up to the Temple Mount has also spread into Ashkenazi ultra-Orthodox circles. The ascent of the Mount, on 3 July 2008, by Rabbi Moshe Tendler [fig. 193], who is associated with these circles, ties in with the actions of the ultra-Orthodox "Faithful of the Temple Mount" who continue to visit the Mount despite the warnings and rigorous objections of leading ultra-Orthodox rabbis. In any event, until the present this halakhic ruling has not brought about a mass ascent of religious Jews to the Temple Mount. We are still in the eye of the storm.

ובקומה · צנים לכפר · שאן בת השובבה

צ יהגב החלשים · טרה והעלה מקלפי · צנה והגריל
לשם גבהה ולציון · ינשק כקולדים · רגש חטאת
צותתיו עצו לדי · ויקרבו את השם

צ בע זהרית · קשר בראש משתלח · יצאתו אימן
נגד בית שילוח · שלחהו בא · אנלפדי שינת
צהן מטהד · פב: יצור התעורה

וכר חיה אומ · אנא השם חטאתי עויתי פשעתי לפניך
אני וביתי ובני אהרן עם קדושיך " אנא בשם
כפר נא לחטאים ולעונות ולפשעים שחטאתי ושעויתי ושפשע
ושפשעדי לפניך אני וביתי ובני אהרן עם קדושיך '
מכה בתורת משה עבדך מפי כבודך ' כי ביום הזה יכפר

עליכם לטהר אתכם מכל חטאותיכם לפני י"

והכהנים והעם

העומדים בעזרה כשהיו שומעין את השם הנכבד והנורא מפרש
יוצא מפי כהן גדול בקדושה ובטהרה היו כורעים ומשתחוים
ונופלים על פניהם ואומרים ברוך שם כבוד מלכותו לע'

לעולם ועד "

ואת חרא יהב מתפניו לגמור את השם כנגד המברכים ואומ

תטהרו " ואתה בטובך מעורר רחמיך וס'

ומלה לשבט משרתיך '

קח מאכלת חדה ושחטו בסדר · וקיבלדם במזרק

ינתנו למעמרס · קדישתו ימס · עד עת הדריה
הפאו ' פן יהי · ותושעיר סליחה "

THE TEMPLE MOUNT—A PERSONAL ACCOUNT

MENACHEM MAGIDOR

PRESIDENT, THE HEBREW UNIVERSITY OF JERUSALEM

It took me a long time to write this very personal account of what the Temple Mount means to me. Partially this was because other matters cluttered my schedule, but there were deeper reasons. I literally agonized over the memories, dreams, and fantasies associated with this site that constantly fired my imagination even before it became accessible to Israelis of my generation in 1967. But this is exactly why I agonized: I could not quite fathom the flare of passion and excitement that mention of the Temple Mount was arousing in me. I was confronted with a very basic dilemma of my identity. You see, I consider myself to be a complete agnostic. But at the same time I am very Jewish. Jewish literary heritage, history—even Jewish religious rites, most of which I do not practice—are an important part of my life, but have nothing to do with religion. I do not believe that declaring my belonging to a particular historical and cultural chain requires any commitment to a particular belief in a transcendental being. So why does a space which is dedicated to man's access to God arouse in me, and in many of my secular friends, such deep emotions?

Even from a purely monotheistic perspective the notion of "God's place" is problematic. The very fact that one of God's names in the Jewish tradition is *ha-maqom*, that is, "the Place," indicates that the notion of a particular geographic location as "God's place" is fraught with tension and contradictions. It is said in *Bereshit Rabbah*, a Jewish commentary

194 The Day of Atonement in the Second Temple. A passage from the Yom Kippur service in the Worms Mahzor (thirteenth century), National Library of Israel, MS Heb. 4°781/1, fol. 134v. The text reads:

And thus did he [i.e., the high priest] use to say: "O Lord, I have sinned, committed iniquity, and transgressed before You, I and my household and the children of Aaron [the priests], Your holy people. O Lord, I beseech Thee, forgive the sins, iniquities, and transgressions which I have sinned, committed, and transgressed before You, I and my household and the children of Aaron, Your holy people. As it is written in the Torah of Moses, Your servant, out of the mouth of Your glory: 'For on this day He will grant atonement to you, to cleanse you from all your sins before the Lord.'" And when

THE PRIESTS AND THE PEOPLE

who stood in the forecourt heard the venerable and awesome Name [of God] issuing forth explicitly from the mouth of the high priest in holiness and purity, they would kneel, prostrate themselves, fall on their faces, and say: "Blessed be the name of the glory of His kingdom for ever and ever." And he strove to end the Name's utterance when they concluded their words of blessing, and said unto them: "You shall be clean."

on Genesis dating from ca. 400 CE: "Why is the Holy One, Blessed-Be-He, called 'the Place'? Because He is the place of the world." God is omnipresent; therefore the idea of "The House of the Lord" is antithetical to the universalist conception of God, one of monotheism's great contributions.

Therefore, how could a secular Jew like myself, or for that matter a committed monotheist, be so moved by a space whose significance stems from an attempt to find a physical location for the Holy of Holies? This is even more puzzling when I recall some of my first exposures to the idea of the Temple as the House of the Lord. From a very young age I was fascinated by the descriptions of the services in the Temple, the culmination of which was the entrance of the high priest into the Holy of Holies on the holiest day of the Jewish year, Yom Kippur—the Day of Atonement. I still shudder when I remember the excitement as the *seder ha-'avodah* (literally, "the order of the rite") was being read during the Yom Kippur service:

> And when the priests and the people who stood in the forecourt heard the venerable and awesome Name [of God] issuing forth explicitly from the mouth of the high priest in holiness and purity, they would kneel, prostrate themselves, and fall on their faces [see fig. 194].

In spite of my atheistic attitude I could not resist sharing the ecstasy and reverence felt by the multitude gathered in the Temple about two millennia ago. Even at a young age I was well aware that there were many aspects of the service that I would have found repulsive, like the sacrifice of animals, but the strong feeling that I share a very deep experience of a community with whom I have a very powerful bonding, in spite of the long time span separating us, is a fundamental part of my identity. This feeling was inseparable from the physical space which was the setting for that ancient solemn gathering. That is the reason why, even when the possibility of actually accessing that space seemed like a political never-never land, I was excited by the detailed study of the physical Temple. Comparing the descriptions in Tractate *Middot* of the Mishnah with the descriptions of the Temple in Josephus' *Antiquities* and *Jewish War* had been a favorite pastime of my youth. The fact that the Temple Mount was on the one hand a physical space but on the other hand an inaccessible object of the imagination, lent it a special charm.

This charm was not lost when in 1967 I was able to visit it for the first time. I was immediately struck by the sheer beauty of the place. The spectacular setting and the wonderful Muslim shrines were breathtaking, but the strongest feeling was that of continuity, of walking on the platform laid by Herod at the heyday of the Jewish Temple; the thought of directly connecting to the dreams and aspirations of my own roots was overwhelming. I was acutely aware that there are very few places that are so central to the joint narrative of my people. Let me make it very clear: I did not feel bothered at all by the fact that another religion was dominating the site. In some strange way the fact that over the physical and imagined layers that related directly to my heritage and culture, History superimposed the dreams and imaginations of other cultures added depth and meaning to my collective memory.

Then the skeptic in me raises his head again. Why do I need the physical presence to connect to the dreams and imaginations of previous generations? Does a modern secular Israeli like me need pilgrimage? A more serious reflection forces me to admit that we do have our sacred spaces and we do make our pilgrimages to our "holy places." Just think of the visits to the houses of people we admire. Many times we encounter very little physical reality directly linked to the person to whom we are trying to connect. Typically, there is even less connection between the physical space that many years ago contained the bodily existence of that person and his or her creations. Still, we feel that we need this physical presence to connect to a world of ideas. There is something about the way in which our mental processes are structured that causes us to need this direct connection to the physical space which is associated with the people, ideas, and the creations of the imagination that are to play a central role in our psyche. It is easier to imagine a past scene or event when you rationally know (or trick yourself into believing) that you are at the physical space in which the original scene or event took place. So when I am present on the Temple Mount I am transformed in time. In some strange way I connect to the ecstasy felt by my forefathers at the same space. Thus, the non-religious, atheistic, very modern rationalist is suddenly becoming a part of the attempt of a community of two thousand years ago to connect to a transcendental, sublime presence. The feeling of continuity, of being part of a long chain, is overwhelming.

Of course, I am well aware that the narrative to which I connect myself is not the site's exclusive narrative, but without underestimating the explosive potential of the conflicting narratives, somehow I believe that at the bottom of all of them there is a common endeavor to find a place which by the memories and mental images it generates, by its sheer sublime beauty, will facilitate men's attempt to transcend the depressingly limited physical existence of this world. I can only pray that this deep layer, shared by all the conflicting narratives woven into this most wonderful site, will be used to defuse what can potentially be the source of a great calamity. May the spirit of Isaiah 56.7 prevail: "Then I will bring them to My holy mountain and make them joyful in My house of prayer ... for My house will be called a house of prayer for all peoples."

Mount Scopus, Jerusalem, April 26, 2009

حوت که در یای کنش راندید | کرد سبک پای زر کو بلند | بر سر عرش آمد و کر سی کنند

تشنه زنه بحر بسوش دید | کرد زپا زحمت نعلین دور | کشت خرامان به بالا طم

زا طبع جبخ از فانشکم نقل | جون قدری برترازان زدم

بس که در و رفت ازاین راز | دو رشد ازخوش براه راز

شد بمکانی که مکانی ندا | وز خودی خویش نشانی بدا

کم شد ازا رحبسان که زمین بود | کم شدنش یافتن خویش بود | باک شدش خانه رصد کری | تن شدش از بستی صورتی سری

از همه سو عاست جهت خاسه | بلکه یکی کشت جنبش و نور | کشته خیال دویی از جسم

دست بدر یوز متصود | آنکه نگنجد بجهت روبرد | سیع جهت جون زمین سو سو د

هر جهتی کرد بسوی کریند | روی بطاعنکه معبود ا

ناظر دیدارلسبند کشت | وزپی دیدن ممتن دیده | وزپی دیدن ممتن دیده

THE HARAM AL-SHARIF

SARI NUSSEIBEH

PRESIDENT, AL-QUDS UNIVERSITY

Imagining the universe is an impossible task, for it stretches, and continues to stretch, to infinity. And though it may initially seem like less of a demanding task just imagining what it would be like to try to imagine the infinite rather than actually imagining it, even this concept of a second-order attempt seems obtuse, since for it to make sense would require us to be able to imagine what it might mean to imagine the infinite in the first place! Now let us see how we can understand this—a supposedly common-place concept: to imagine, of all the infinitely imaginable spots in the universe, one which is "the holiest" or "second holiest" site. What does that—could that—mean?

Consider the following verse from the Qur'an, where, after sixteen months of the practice of turning to Jerusalem in prayers, Muhammad is finally instructed to break from this Jewish tradition (apparently so he could draw the line between those among the peoples of the Book who have truly come to believe in him, and those who were simply "posing" or pretending to believe he was the genuine and ultimate messenger of God in the Abrahamic tradition), and is addressed thus by God:

> We may see your face turning about in the heavens in search of a praying focal point (*qibla*): and we shall provide you with one that you may like: turn your face to the Sacred Mosque; and from wherever you may be, turn your face henceforth towards it [...] (2.144).

Two verses earlier (2.142), in anticipation of those who will deride the prophet for changing the *qibla* from Jerusalem, God addresses his messenger thus: "The fools will deride you saying: what made them change their *qibla*? Say: the east and west belong to Allah [...]."

On a first reading, one doesn't get the impression that God Himself feels strongly about a particular spot, including the Ka'ba (the Sacred Mosque): notice that His assignment of it is textually predicated on Muhammad's preferences, and not on some mysteriously divine

195 Muhammad's Ascension from Jerusalem's Rock to Heaven
Khusraw Dilhawi, *Khamseh*, Topkapi Museum, Hazine 798, fol. 4v

quality inhering in the spot itself. Likewise, in providing a "defense" for the changeover of the *qibla* from Jerusalem, God reminds Muhammad of His infinite dominion: Jerusalem is important to God, but it is just one spot among many, stretching east and west.

God, then, in what seems to be a perfectly logical attitude, does not feign to "unveil" or "reveal" a divine quality inhering in some physical spot, one for which Man is called upon to turn in prayer: quite the opposite, God reminds Man of the objectively neutral status of any physical spot, assuring him that God's dominion is immanent, and unbound by physical dimension.

Nonetheless, physical spots, like the Rock and its environs in Jerusalem, or like the Ka'ba in Mecca, clearly do acquire "sacredness." Where, we may ask, does this sacredness come from?

One ready—and logical—answer is Man: if a physical spot is not inherently divine, then surely what is regarded as its divine status must be conferred upon it by Man. The spot's sacredness in this manner would be subjective rather than objective. Furthermore, being subjective, one could perhaps better understand such sacredness being a matter of degree—being "more" or "less" sacred—meaning, in this respect, being regarded as such by human beings, rather than meaning the presence of different material shades or hues of holiness in the object itself.

But another answer, more common in the case of idolatrous religions, may actually bring "God" Himself into the picture, for example by claiming that "God" dwells in such and such a spot, thus making the spot divine by virtue of God's own sacredness. The phrase "a/the House of God" is not uncommon, and may be a leftover from such primitive periods. Jerusalem's legendary Temple, for example, may have been such a House (where the *Shekhinah* dwelled, attended to and served by high priests).[1] Certainly, Mount Olympus where Zeus and the other, lesser gods dwelled was such a spot. The Ka'ba itself, we know, harbored fake "gods" right up to Muhammad's re-entry into Mecca.

Or, the spot may acquire sacredness for its being a "transitory meeting point" between the two worlds, the earthly and the divine. Thus, again, God's intervention at Abraham's sacrifice, or His intervention in Mount Sinai; thus, also, Muhammad's ascension from Jerusalem's Rock to Heaven, or Adam's descent from Heaven—according to an Islamic tradition—unto that same Rock on Earth.

Of course, to understand sacredness in this "homo-centered" manner is not in any way to diminish from the holiness of a holy place. To claim that Man confers holiness or sacredness to a place—or that its holiness appertained to it as a result of having been a spatially-accidental crossing-point between the earthly and the divine—does not make it less sacred, or less inspiring of awe or commanding of respect. If one can stand in awe before monuments that are totally secular, without a hint of a divinity about them, then how much more awe and respect must there be in those ethereal locations where, as legend would have it, God (or one of His angels) actually revealed Himself in one manner or another to Man!

It is not being argued here that God never actually *confers* sacredness to the mundane: Canaan's holiness is certainly conferred upon it by God, as when (e.g., 5.21) He addresses the children of Israel thus: "Enter Ye the Holy[2] Land which God has assigned for you [...]." Indeed, we are not told why God has blessed this land. But bless it He did. God also confers a certain distinction to Man himself. "Verily We have blessed the Son of Adam."[3]

But whether a spot is initially and inherently sacred, or becomes so through practice, or even following upon the occurrence of some miraculous experience, it is still hard to see how God can "be made to feel better" by men fighting over that spot, killing and getting killed over it, dismantling or demolishing it, or whatever. The only "party" or "parties" that can hope to "feel better" by such gruesome contestations must surely be men themselves. In the final analysis, spilling (human) blood over the Rock can only be a secular practice, not a divine wish or command!

Muslims of course continue to perform the rites of *animal* sacrifice. They do not await the Second Coming or the rebuilding of the Temple to do this. These rites are performed annually (typically, at the end of the pilgrimage to Mecca) to mark God's last-minute intervention as Abraham was about to offer his own son in sacrifice. Indeed, non-Muslims may pause at this fact: that Islam's major day of celebration is the Festival of the Sacrifice (*al-Adha*).[4] On the other hand, Muslims are on the whole not aware of, and should perhaps give pause to, this corollary fact: that Jews (and Christians) take Jerusalem's Rock to have been the location where Abraham was about to make this sacrifice (Muslims assume the location was Mecca).[5]

196 Abraham about to sacrifice his son Isaac. Mosaic of the sixth-century synagogue of Beth Alpha

Now imagine this: just as the son of Adam (viz., Abraham) was about to slaughter his own son in proof of his unflinching loyalty to God Almighty, God Himself intervenes and provides the son of Adam with an alternative: a lamb! Jerusalem's Rock being proposed as the location of that miracle, what better or clearer divine message can there be to the sons of Adam in this day and age, but that killing each other or themselves over the Rock in an attempt to prove their loyalty or faith to Him is not at all what He wishes us to do!

Indeed, given the earlier remarks concerning the sources and meaning of sanctity, it is often hard for us to own up to the fact that our zealotry is driven by our own "baser" instincts (such as our egos) than by some divine wish or calling. Our egos (our sense of our own importance) can often blind us (i.e., make us totally disrespectful of and oblivious to) "the other": consider, for example, the mutual (and justified) accusations between Jews and Arabs concerning the desecration, between '48 and '67, of their respective graveyards in Jerusalem (East and West). Closer to our time, consider the digs now underway in Bab al-Magharibah, where a one-dimensional pursuit of historical relics disrespectfully threatens to scatter the historical relics of another dimension. Surely, such practices, done in the name of God, totally flout what is divine!

The said digs (in Bab al-Magharibah) seem to be aimed at unveiling a (now-subterranean) doorway along the western wall, which, some say, can also open up to a staircase leading to a small mosque on the other side (i.e., within the Haram precinct) which Muslims call "the Buraq Mosque," after the prophet's winged horse (?). You could (in theory, but the window is closed) look out from this small mosque onto the Wailing Wall plaza, where the Jews congregate to perform their prayers.

Now consider how these digs, in that small area, happen to encapsulate the entire ethos of mutual denial between the followers of the two religions: the small mosque, we recall, is called "al-Buraq" (you could "smell" the etymological connection with the Arabic and Hebrew words for "lightning"): al-Buraq is the legendary animal which brought the prophet Muhammad to Jerusalem across the desert, where he ascended from the Rock to the Divine Presence, then returned him to Mecca, all within the lightning space of one night! (Conspicuously, by the way, this is the only miracle, besides the revelation itself, associated with Muhammad!) Because the legendary animal was tied to "that wall," Muslims have taken to calling the Wailing Wall "the Buraq Wall"—hence the name "the Buraq Mosque," adjoining the Wall from its eastern side!

Here, then, we have almost a physical point of contact between the two traditions, one on each side of the same wall, a point threatening like a powder-keg to explode if the Israeli Government decides unilaterally to pursue those digs. But there is more: it is not just a one-sided affair where a Jewish government department seems by its action to disrespect or disregard (or deny, at some deep psychological level) Muslim tradition. Likewise, Muslims seem similarly disposed to a state of denial, for if asked, "Was there a

197 The ramp leading to Bab al-Magharibah, with the temporary wooden bridge and the Western Wall prayer plaza to its north, and the Dome of the Rock and the Aqsa Mosque above them

reason or a significance for the prophet's legendary animal to be tied specifically to that wall (and hence for calling that wall 'the Buraq Wall')?" one would only manage on the whole and in all likelihood to elicit a blank stare in response.

So why was al-Buraq tied to that wall? Indeed, why was the Prophet flown to Jerusalem in the first place? Why didn't God simply import (fly over) the prophet directly from Mecca? After all, the prophet's angelic companion, Gabriel, did not seem to have any problems about descending directly from the heavenly spheres unto the mountains of Mecca, to reveal the Holy Qur'an to the Prophet. One imagines that a direct "return flight" was also possible. The Jerusalem detour, so to speak, must therefore have had an explanation.

We must, at this point, return to the Qur'an, and to an oft-cited verse: "Glory unto Him Who transported His minion from the sacred Mosque to the Farthest Mosque whose environs We have blessed [...]" (17.1). And now our question, beyond merely being one concerning the winged animal and the Wall, comes to be about this Furthest Mosque—al-Aqsa: if asked, "What Mosque?" many Muslims may again respond with a blank stare. Surely, this Mosque, some of them might say, pointing to one or both of the mosques now occupying the Noble Sanctuary (al-Haram al-Sharif). But, according to the tradition, neither mosque was there when Muhammad made his night-journey. So, which or what Mosque (*masjid*)[6] is being referred to in the Qur'an?

Of course, many "wise" interpretations may be forthcoming. But it is beyond doubt that the actual physical spot in question couldn't have first acquired its holiness or sanctity from Muhammad's visit: rather, Muhammad's visit must have been made because of the spot's already-existing sanctity ("[...] whose environs We have blessed"). And the episode unquestionably added—in the Islamic context—to that sanctity.

Muslim tradition also has it that Muhammad led all the other prophets in prayer in that spot, as if to confirm the sanctified continuity between the earlier prophets, and the last. The Haram precinct (the Noble Sanctuary) thus marks not only the point of contact between the earthly and the divine, but also that between the three Semitic religions.

In explaining how Buddhism easily fitted Shintoism in Japan one is sometimes told the reason is the distinct domains of the two religions: they deal with respectively different requirements of the earthly and the hereafter. Religions typically "conflict" with one another, on the other hand, when they address the same domain, but produce different stories. One example is that of the location of Abraham's attempted act of sacrifice of his son. The attempted sacrifice by Abraham of his son embodies what Islam is all about. The act explains the etymological origin of the name, to "surrender" one's will to that of God. And yet one wonders whether it is conceivable, in some imaginary world, or in this, for Muslims ever to identify that act which embodies what their faith is all about *with* that physical location, consistently with the Jewish belief? Could Muslims ever see Abraham leaning over *that* Rock, about to sacrifice Isaac? Or would there be an inherent contradiction in such a postulate, making its realization even logically impossible?[7]

And if it's impossible for the different religious narratives to somehow melt into one another; and if, furthermore, the various episodes associated with that holy precinct seem only to prod and push towards confrontation, hatred, disrespect, and even bloodshed, wouldn't all of that simply deflate from the divine status of the narratives themselves?

Sometimes, confronted with those questions, the beautiful serenity of the place threatens to be metamorphosed in my mind into an apocalyptic trap, where death in its ugliest forms voraciously stretches out its long fingers in sadistic hunger to throttle the multitudes of innocent human lambs scattered in its vicinity. I shudder to think about the excesses that can be practiced in the name of religions—at the human blood that has been, and can still be spilt. I ponder with disbelief how Man could believe in the ephemeral—conferring upon it a value that is worthier than that which He confers upon Himself, a status for which he is prepared to kill and be killed. But then, as I gaze onto the precinct's splendid serenity, at the trees interspersed with the smaller and larger domes, another thought presents itself to my mind: this is the thought that, in the noble human effort at "feeling out" the "farthest" horizons of the universe, to understand the spiritual core from which an entire existence proceeds forth, a place on earth may be marked. Before being marked, this spot may be just like any other; but by becoming marked, this spot comes to be conferred upon with a holy reverence that accumulates and grows by generation after generation of like-minded believers and worshippers, often becoming imbued as the generations pass with aspects of the divine that did not even cross the minds of the previous generation, so that in the end, though in one respect remaining the same spot of earth it began as, in another respect it becomes infused with a holiness that commands respect and imposes awe. So even if such a spot is not, as the religious narrative may tell us, made of wondrous stone transported from the heavens, it can still celebrate that which is noblest in Man: the yearning to discover, to fly out in one's imagination to the farthest corners of the universe, to try to probe into the core of existence, to defy the four-dimensional structure of time-space, to bring oneself into the presence of the mysterious origins of all things – in short, it can still celebrate limitation's expression of the limitless.

"Could Muslims ever see Abraham leaning over that Rock [...]?" There is an implicit corollary to that question: Could Jews (and Christians) ever see Muhammad descending by Heavenly fiat into that precinct, and then being lifted up from that Rock unto the Divine presence? Could Jews in particular, who it would seem at first accepted Muhammad as their expected messenger, as Abraham's spiritual inheritor, and fell into performing their prayers after him towards Jerusalem, ever accept to see themselves still praying after him, as they perform their rites facing their Holy of Holies? Or is he (generically) condemned to having to separate between "his followers" and those of the earlier prophets? I look upon Muhammad's night-journey to the Haram as a first attempt to bring people (Abraham's spiritual inheritors) together. If the circumstances were not ripe, whether then or now, for the true believers in the one God to become united in their endeavors, can we still not entertain the hope that the holy precinct—what it is and what it symbolizes—will nonetheless one day succeed to inspire people who believe in the one God themselves to become united in their faith? That then would indeed be a reason for which any physical spot in this universe would be well-worth being considered sacred. Lifting the veils of prejudice and ignorance-through-denial concerning what this precinct is all about may well be a step in this direction. Perhaps scholarly works such as those contained in this volume may help bring that moment of revelation sooner.

East Jerusalem, Palestine, April 10, 2007

What Do I Think about When I Imagine Myself Walking on the Temple Esplanade—al-Haram al-Sharif?

Carlo Maria Cardinal Martini, S.I.
Former Archibishop of Milan

For various reasons, I have few opportunities nowadays to visit the extraordinary place, so rich in history, faith, and art, that has become known as the Temple Esplanade—the Haram al-Sharif. I visited it several times in the past, however, on which occasions I paid much attention to its grandiose sacred edifices. Allowing memory and fantasy to flow freely, I can easily imagine myself there.

As I am well aware, so many memories are linked to this place, and so many momentous events in the history of diverse religious traditions are remembered there, that it naturally gives rise to many different recollections. For my religious tradition, too, the events are so multiple and varied that I'm spoilt for choice, and so I shall dwell on only a few of the many memories that re-emerge in me while thinking about this remarkable place.

I think first of Abraham and the sacrifice of his only child, a story that has played a prominent role in my spiritual progress and prayers, and then of David and his joy at bringing the Ark of the Covenant to the Mount. Having solemnly consecrated about 200 sacred Christian buildings in my term as archbishop of Milan, I think of the exquisite prayer uttered by King Solomon at the consecration of the Temple, which appears in the Book of Kings and in Chronicles. How often have I meditated and commented on this text, the most ancient known consecration prayer of a sacred edifice.

Fantasy and memory then transport me to the time of the Prophets, in particular Isaiah and above all Jeremiah. It seems I can hear again his invective at the Temple's gate, shouted at those about to enter: "Hear the word of the Lord, all ye of Judah, who enter these gates to prostrate yourselves before Him. Thus says the Lord of Hosts, the God of Israel: Amend your ways and your doings, and I will cause you to dwell in this place. Trust ye not in lying words, saying, The Temple of the Lord, the Temple of the Lord, the Temple of the Lord, are these!" (Jer. 7.3–4).

198 Giotto: *The Presentation in the Temple* (ca. 1305)
Scrovegni Chapel, Padua © Photo Scala, Florence

Then I think of Ezekiel's description of God's glory leaving the Temple, and of his vision of the return of that glory to the renewed Temple. I'm particularly fascinated by his description of the prodigious stream of water issuing from the Temple's eastern side, becoming a torrent that descends into the Arabah and finally enters the Dead Sea, whose waters it heals (cf. Ezek. 47.1–12). This scene appears to prefigure the power of the water that flows with the blood from the pierced side of Christ on the Cross and heals the world (cf. John 19.33–37).

Many other chapters in the prophetic books crowd my thoughts, but the one that leads to what is dearest to my heart is the prophecy of Malachi about the things to come: "Behold, I will send my messenger to prepare the way before me; and the Lord whom you seek will suddenly come to His Temple; and the angel of the Covenant whom you desire, behold, he is coming, says the Lord of Hosts" (Mal. 3.1). As a Christian, I understand these words to refer to Jesus of Nazareth and his entries into the Temple, recounted above all by John the Evangelist.

But even before speaking of those, I cannot avoid recalling two episodes told in the second chapter of Luke about the parents of Jesus, who come to the Temple after his birth to offer him to the Lord and return there when he is twelve years old, first to lose and then to find him. I am particularly struck by the first of these episodes, in which I imagine them anonymously and silently lining up with all other parents, with no privileges and nothing to portend the meaning of the great mystery they carry in their arms.

Of the comings of the adult Jesus, I remember above all that in which he hurls himself at the animal dealers and moneychangers, shouting the words of Isaiah and Jeremiah: "My house shall be a house of prayer, but you have made it a den of thieves!" (Luke 19.45). And again: "Make not the house of my Father a house of traffic" (John 2.16). John the Evangelist tells of several of Jesus' visits to the Temple and of the lengthy discussions in its courtyards, particularly under Solomon's arcade (cf. John 10.23). But, over and above these episodes, I am struck by the prophetic words pronounced by Jesus near Jacob's Well in Samaria. To the woman who asks him whether one should adore the Lord in Jerusalem or on Mount Gerizim, he answers: "Woman, believe me, the hour cometh, when ye shall neither in this mountain, nor yet at Jerusalem, worship the Father. Ye worship ye know not what: we know what we worship: for salvation is of the Jews. But the hour cometh, and now is, when the true worshippers shall worship the Father in spirit and in truth" (John 4.21–22).

Nevertheless, the Acts of the Apostles show us that the first disciples still called at the Temple. Attempting today to locate the Beautiful Gate, I recall the miracle accomplished there by Peter in curing a crippled beggar. I think also of Paul, who, having come to the Temple to fulfil a vow, is captured by a furious crowd that drags him out of the Temple and attempts to kill him, stopping only when a Roman cohort arrives and arrests him. It is the start of a long imprisonment that will ultimately lead him to Rome, giving him the opportunity to bear witness to his faith before several tribunals.

The following decades and centuries were strewn with the great tragedies and destructions that render this place one of the most coveted and ravaged spots on earth. I am thinking of the Romans, then the Persians, then the Arabs—who erected the splendid edifices still in use—then the Crusaders, and finally the Mamluks and Ottoman Turks. Not a few of the conquerors marked their presence with works of art visible to this day. It is these that make the Haram al-Sharif so rich in memories for so many people and for diverse religions, each drawn to some of the monuments and memories rather than others.

It is vital to maintain mutual respect among the diverse religious traditions, as exemplified, for instance, by a statement inscribed in a mosaic on the internal facade of the octagonal colonnade of the Dome of Rock, formulated by its Muslim builders in the seventh century. It reads: "And say not as to God but the truth: The Messiah, Jesus, the son of Mary, is the Messenger of God [...]" [see fig. 64]. This statement may not say everything about Jesus, but it attests to a respectful deference towards him. Thus we are all invited today to seek peace and harmony, above all with respect to the religious traditions and symbols that followed one another over the centuries. May this mutual respect, alongside an open heart, help us to seek the truth that will conclusively manifest itself at the end of time.

I would like to end these brief remarks by drawing attention to a text that comes to my mind whenever I think of the ancient Temple of Jerusalem. The Apocalypse of John announces that in the ultimate Jerusalem there will be no temple, "for the Lord God Almighty, and the Lamb, are His temple" (Rev. 21.22). Thus, all things human are destined to disappear, leaving room only for the shining light of the glory of God and for a world in which "death shall be no more, nor mourning, nor crying, nor sorrow shall be any more, for the former things are passed away" (Rev. 21.4).

Jerusalem/Gallarate, Italy, 20 December 2006

Epilogue

Benjamin Z. Kedar

The Hebrew University of Jerusalem

Oleg Grabar

Institute for Advanced Study, Princeton

The Esplanade is not just a breathtaking historic monument. It is also a living space that has repeatedly undergone transformations, some of them brutal. Let us recapitulate just those that have occurred during our lifetime.

In the years 1938–42, in the wake of a minor earth tremor, the Aqsa Mosque underwent comprehensive rebuilding during which much of the edifice was demolished to the foundations. The nave and eastern aisles were reconstructed on arches resting on marble columns imported from Italy. The roof's decorated timbers were taken down for preservation in the Rockefeller Museum. The outer construction—high at the center and sloping northward and southward—that had abutted the gabled roof on the eastern side, was totally dismantled. The buildings east of the mosque, erected by the Knights Templar in the twelfth century, were pulled down. Indeed, Robert W. Hamilton, director of the Department of Antiquities in British Palestine, went so far as to claim that, as a result of the 1938–42 works, "a great part of the old Aqsa was […] replaced by a new building."[1] A comparison of photos taken in 1917 and in 1997 from the Mount of Olives [figs. 199, 200] demonstrates how the removal of the Templar buildings, and of other irregular accretions east of the mosque, dramatically changed its appearance; one sees now an almost straight eastern wall with five equal-size blind arches, each framing two small windows. The vanished Templar buildings are still visible on aerial photographs from the 1930s [figs. 75, 125].

The Dome of the Rock was massively renovated, under Jordanian rule, in the years 1956–64. The iron grille the Franks had installed around the Rock in the twelfth century was removed. The many hanging lamps around the building were replaced by interior lighting that accentuates the central drum and the dome. Some 45,000 ceramic tiles, installed on much of the building's exterior in the days of Suleyman the Magnificent, were replaced by new ones endeavoring to reproduce the original designs, and the 52 windows

199–200 The Aqsa Mosque from the Mount of Olives, 1917 and 1997
Photo 200 by Moshe Milner

in the octagon and the drum, also dating from the sixteenth century, were substituted by modern copies. Most conspicuously, the dull gray dome was replaced by a gold-colored aluminum sheeting. It soon became Jerusalem's best-known icon.[2]

The advent of Israeli rule during the Six Day War of 1967 led to a radical transformation of the area south and west of the Esplanade. A few hours after that war's end, most of the inhabitants of the Magharibah (or Mughrabi) Quarter were summarily evicted and their houses hastily bulldozed. The Israeli authorities, keen on creating a *fait accompli* that would provide mass access to the Western (or Wailing) Wall—whose five lowest stone courses form part of the western supporting wall of Herod's Temple Mount—made no effort to identify or preserve the quarter's historic buildings, the oldest of which was the Afdaliyya Madrasa, established by Saladin's son al-Afdal a few years after the Muslim reconquest of Jerusalem in 1187. After the leveling of much of the Magharibah Quarter, a narrow, 28-meters-long lane adjacent to the Wall [fig. 188] gave way to a vast plaza fronting a stretch of the Wall twice as long. In 1968 the plaza was lowered by about 2 meters, revealing two more Herodian courses at the foot of the Wall; 12 additional ones remain buried underground. The new plaza facing the Wall quickly became a major focus of post-1967 Israeli religiosity and nationalism.

In the years 1968–78, Hebrew University archaeologists excavated a vast area south and southwest of the Esplanade, principally aiming at fully exposing the southern supporting wall of Herod's Temple Mount and the southern, 80-meter-long part of the western one. South of the Esplanade they laid bare a monumental stairway as well as underground corridors and conduits that had led northward to Herod's Temple. At the foot of the southern and western supporting walls, 9 meters below the surface, they unearthed paved Herodian streets, partially crushed by squared blocks probably toppled during the Roman destruction of the Temple and the precinct's enclosing walls in the year 70 AD. In the southwest they found four structures erected by Umayyad caliphs in the seventh-eighth centuries, whose exact purpose has not yet been elucidated.[3]

In 1968, concomitantly with the Hebrew University archaeological expedition, Israel's Ministry of Religious Affairs began to construct an underground passage along the remaining 320 meters of the Western Wall that are situated north of the new plaza. Primarily with the aim of exposing three to five Herodian stone courses all the way to the Wall's northern limit, the workers also cleared several halls and passageways dating from the Hasmonaean, Herodian, Early Muslim, Crusader, and Mamluk periods. The Western Wall Tunnel was completed in 1985.[4]

As a result of these and other activities in the vicinity of the Esplanade, the amount of observable Herodian remains has increased dramatically. A plan was also put forward to augment it in a still more spectacular manner. Moshe Safdie of *Habitat* fame prepared— for the Municipality of Jerusalem, the Jerusalem Foundation, and the Company for the

Reconstruction and Development of the Jewish Quarter—designs that called for the exposure of the 12 Herodian stone courses of the Western Wall now buried underground, and for unearthing the Herodian street along the entire length of the Wall, from the new, post-1967 plaza to the Wall's southern limit excavated by the Hebrew University expedition. The plan, which entailed also demolition of the makeshift walkway that leads to the Haram's Magharibah Gate atop some ruins of the Magharibah Quarter, would have doubled the Wall's height and allowed Jews to pray actually standing on a street paved at the time of the Second Temple. A series of terraced piazzas, integrating finds from later periods, were to gradually ascend from the Herodian street at the foot of the Wall to the rebuilt Jewish Quarter to its west. This ambitious plan was shelved in the 1980s but some of its elements have recently come again under discussion.[5]

Parallel to this radical transformation of the area south and west of the Esplanade, the Haram al-Sharif itself underwent still another major renovation. On 21 August 1969 a Protestant fundamentalist set fire to the Aqsa Mosque, causing heavy damage, especially to its woodwork, and almost totally destroying the elaborate *minbar*, or preacher's pulpit, installed by Saladin after his conquest of Jerusalem in 1187. In the wake of this disaster, comprehensive restoration work was begun at the Aqsa Mosque and gradually expanded to all buildings on the Haram. At the Dome of the Rock, the aluminum sheeting of the dome installed in the 1960s was replaced with gilded copper plates donated by King Hussein of Jordan. Trees were planted in various parts of the Esplanade. This vast renovation has continued down to the present: early in 2007 a substitute *minbar* was placed in the Aqsa Mosque.

In 1996 work started to turn the subterranean "Stables of Solomon" into a vast mosque that came to be known as the *Musalla al-Marwani* (the Prayer Grounds of Marwan, one of the Umayyad caliphs). From March 1998 to July 1999, digging, construction, and repairs took place in the elongated underground area beneath the Aqsa Mosque that is known as *al-Aqsa al-Qadima* (the Ancient Aqsa). This had been one of the underground tunnels that accessed the Second Temple. And during a weekend in late November 1999 heavy mechanical equipment was hastily employed to prepare a monumental northern entrance leading from the Esplanade down to the Musalla al-Marwani. Lorries transported vast quantities of rubble to dumps outside the Old City. This major dig, the first undertaken on the Esplanade in modern times and carried out without archaeological supervision, triggered an outcry by Israeli archaeologists and the Israeli public, and was halted by the Israeli government. Later examination of the rubble revealed finds mainly from Byzantine times onward. Consequently the Esplanade now contains four prayer areas—The Dome of the Rock, the Aqsa Mosque, al-Aqsa al-Qadima, and the Musalla al-Marwani—with the area of the latter surpassing that of the original two.

A wide staircase descends from the Esplanade to two gates of the "Stables of Solomon"

201 The prayer place (*mastaba*) southeast of the Dome of the Rock commemorating the Palestinians massacred in September 1982 in the Beirut refugee camps of Sabra and Shatila. The inscription reads:
In the name of God, the Merciful, the Compassionate. "Whosoever is slain unjustly, We have appointed to his next-of-kin authority [to enforce justice]. But let him not exceed in slaying; he shall be helped [by God Himself]." (Qur'an 17.33). Verily, God has spoken the Truth.

reopened during the November 1999 digging operation. A plan is also afoot to erect a fifth minaret on the Esplanade. And while the Wall has become a focus of Israeli nationalism, the Esplanade is a major symbol of Palestinian nationalism. It is also a nascent Palestinian pantheon, with three leaders—Musa Qazim al-Husayni, his son 'Abd al-Qadir and his grandson Faysal—buried on the Esplanade, and with plans to re-inter Yasser Arafat there one day. Their burial reflects the age-old perception of the area as the site of eventual resurrection, with the location of the graves in structures at the Haram's very edge manifesting the Muslim opposition to burial within a mosque proper.

Present-day visitors to the area are confronted with the outcome of these manifold transformations. Southwest of the Esplanade they encounter the Davidson Center, a partly transparent steel-and-glass building embedded within the basements of one of the Umayyad structures; a periscope-like oculus rising from the entrance level offers a view of the Aqsa Mosque. Opened to the public in 2001, the Center contains an exhibition of artifacts found at the site. Films are projected outlining the history of archaeological research in the area and presenting an imaginary pilgrimage to the Second Temple. Yet the Center's focal points are technological simulations of the Second Temple and of the Umayyad structures. The two displays, which employ state-of-the-art digital technology, aim at enabling visitors to undertake a virtual tour of these largely vanished monuments.[6]

The exit from the Davidson Center leads into the Archaeological Park, where visitors can observe the impressive results of the 1968–77 excavations south and southwest of the Esplanade. Near its southwestern corner they may occasionally watch a group of Jewish women who pray standing on the Herodian street at the foot of the Second Temple's western supporting wall. These "Women of the Wall," who insist on performing rites that Orthodox Judaism reserves for men, were banished from the vast praying plaza in front of the Western Wall and relegated, by Israel's Supreme Court, to this out-of-the-way location. Other non-Orthodox Jews also have chosen to pray there.

The Archaeological Park is separated from the post-1967 plaza that faces the Western Wall by an earthen ramp that leads up, over the remains of the demolished Magharibah Quarter, to the Magharibah Gate of the Haram. In February 2004 the ramp partially collapsed, and Israelis and tourists ascending to the Haram now use a makeshift wooden bridge just to its north. In February 2007 the Israel Antiquities Authority started to excavate parts of the ramp in order to document and save antiquities prior to the construction of a planned permanent bridge. These excavations have triggered demonstrations by Muslims, who fear that the work may endanger the stability of the Haram's walls and totally destroy the remains of the Magharibah Quarter, or even that the true aim is to open the blocked Barclay's Gate of the Herodian Temple. The demonstrations, which had repercussions throughout the Muslim world, were organized by the militant Northern Branch of Israel's Islamic Movement that yearns to turn Jerusalem into the capital of a re-established Caliphate, calls for the rescue of the Aqsa Mosque allegedly endangered by Israeli plots, and claims the Western Wall as an inseparable part of the Aqsa compound.[7] These demonstrations provide the most recent testimony to the exceptional sensitivity of the Esplanade and its surroundings, and to the uncanny ease by which doings on or near it are prone to stir up emotions and trigger collisions. Only when the Jerusalem Municipality announced that further deliberations about the planned permanent bridge will take place and the Israel Antiquities Authority subsequently limited its work to the ramp's consolidation, did tensions appreciably abate, at least for the time being.

The lower (eastern) section of the plaza in front of the Western Wall has served since 1967 as a huge open-air place for Jewish prayer, and gradually assumed the appearance of an Orthodox synagogue with a cast-iron partition dividing male from female worshippers. This section offers a variety of sights: men and women ecstatically touching the Wall's stones, clinging to them in private prayer, or discreetly inserting supplicatory notes between them; at some distance from the Wall, groups praying, each according to its particular rites; still farther from the Wall, worshippers and tourists intermingle. An array of new rites has emerged, from celebrating a *bar mitzvah* or a *brit milah* (circumcision) at the Wall, to visiting

202–205 Praying and placing supplicatory notes
at the Wall:
Above left: Israel's Prime Minister Menachem
Begin, 1981;
Above right: Pope John Paul II, 2000;
Below left: Israel's President Shimon Peres, 2007;
Below right: Senator Barack Obama, 2008

206 The Temple Institute's menorah

the Wall upon one's appointment to high office; a recent such visit was that by Shimon Peres after his election as President of Israel in June 2007. The plaza's upper (western) section has become the site for national ceremonies, such as the inauguration of Remembrance Day for Israel's fallen and the swearing in of new recruits of various military units.

At present visitors can observe, at the western extremity of the prayer plaza, a major new excavation that has already revealed vestiges of buildings of the Early Muslim and Mamluk periods and, underneath them, an 11-meter-wide street of Aelia Capitolina, the Roman city erected after the destruction of Jewish Jerusalem. Still farther to the west, one can visit the Temple Institute, intent on bringing about the building of the Third Temple in our time—a mirror image of sorts of Israel's Northern Islamic Movement. At the Institute, visitors are shown vessels including the incense altar and the table of the showbread, as well as a display of priestly vestments, all "fit and ready for use in the service of the Beit HaMikdash" (that is, the Third Temple), as a flyer distributed at the entrance frankly states.[8] The Institute's seven-branched *menorah* (or candelabrum), weighing more than 500 kilograms of which 43 are of gold, is on display near the eastern extremity of the Jewish Quarter, deliberately facing the Aqsa Mosque [fig. 206].

Just north of the prayer plaza, visitors are encouraged to "take a walk along the Jewish chain of generations."[9] Proceeding via a maze of dramatically illuminated chambers and passageways cleared after 1967, they encounter non-figurative sculptures of green glass, carved with Hebrew letters, that purport to tell the story of the Jewish people from the age of the Patriarchs down to the present: a 9-meter high column consisting of 2,000 glass layers symbolizes the yearning for the return to Zion during 2,000 years of exile, a glass block shattered into six pieces meant to evoke the Holocaust. Finally, visitors gather in a small auditorium to hear a bearded man whose image is projected as a hologram relate the story of a pious Jew who yearns for Jerusalem even in a Nazi concentration camp, and of his paratrooper son who participates in the liberation of the Western Wall.

An entrance to the west of the Generations Center leads to a tunnel that exposes the underground continuation of the Western Wall extending to the north of the prayer plaza. Visitors are led through halls and passages dating from various periods, some from the days of the Second Temple, others from Early Muslim, Ayyubid, and Mamluk times. The major highlights are the spot in the tunnel considered to be the closest to the Holy of Holies of the Second Temple, and the huge stone of the Wall's master course, which is 13.6 m long and 3.5 m high, and weighs approximately 570 metric tons. The demand for guided tours of the tunnel is soaring—in 2006, visitors numbered about half a million—and new customs are taking root, such as wedding couples coming to that point purportedly closest to the Holy of Holies.[10]

On the Haram, the subterranean Musalla al-Marwani is a counterpart of sorts to the Western Wall tunnel. In this vast mosque, too, new customs have sprung up, with old men or groups of youngsters, even entire families, praying and studying at various hours of the day. In a broader sense, the physical as well as social components of the Haram have changed a great deal over the past half century. The major monuments, gray and decrepit in the fifties, have been repaired and restored, so that they can once again shine over the city and its surroundings [figs. 207–208; see also figs. 160–162]. A new museum has been built to exhibit the architectural remains from various sites, including the Aqsa Mosque and the Dome of the Rock. An impressive library with state-of-the-art equipment has been set up for the preservation of rare manuscripts. The interiors of buildings, especially of the Dome of the Rock, have been cleaned up, and new lights and sophisticated acoustic systems installed. The whole Esplanade has become a major social space to which, especially on Fridays and holidays, men, women, and children come to be among their own, to pray, socialize, exchange information, acquire knowledge, play soccer, and picnic. It is, once again, the private, restricted, space for the Muslim population of Israel and Palestine. In a fascinating development, deeply reflective of our times, one monument, the Dome of the Rock, is becoming primarily associated with the piety of women, more so than the Aqsa Mosque. This development illustrates the deeply Muslim phenomenon of spaces adapting to needs rather than reflecting and imposing static liturgies. And, just as is happening with the Jewish uses of the sacred spaces of Jerusalem, some of the areas

207, 208 The Dome of the Ascension (*Qubbat al-Mi'raj*) before and after restoration

west of the Haram have been rejuvenated, if not always revitalized, by the national and social significance of the Haram. The spectacular fourteenth-century Bab al-Qattanin, Gate of the Cotton-Merchants, serves as a passageway from the Haram to the city and to a new Centre for Jerusalem Studies created by al-Quds University. The attendant shops are not particularly successful so far, but there have been attempts to restore some of the mostly Mamluk buildings which line the streets leading to the Haram. They have all been recorded and published and some, like the Khalidi Library, are once again potential centers for learning and knowledge. Altogether, they demonstrate how Jerusalem, because of the Haram and its surroundings, is still, after Cairo, the most striking museum of late medieval Islamic architecture. The main problem is that the northwestern and northern areas adjoining the Haram are also residential, rather than ceremonial, areas, therefore subject to constant demographic as well as social pressures. Renovations, some of which were honored with an award from the Aga Khan Foundation, have barely begun to make a dent in a very difficult problem of urban growth.

We conclude with two personal statements.

Oleg Grabar:

My own relationship to the Haram and to Jerusalem began when I arrived in the Fall of 1953 as a graduate student in the history of art and archaeology concentrating on early Islamic monuments. Romantically orientalist at that time, I could not but be impressed by the extraordinary size of the Haram and by the unique treasury of monuments found there, even if they were not in the best of physical shape, especially when compared to the pitiful and depressing complex of the Holy Sepulchre or to the for the most part recently built or rebuilt sanctuaries scattered all over the area of Jerusalem and reflecting dozens of very different Christian communities and attitudes toward their faith. Neither uniqueness nor size had, in my mind then, a religious or pious content. On the contrary, there were few Muslim visitors to the Haram and, anyway, expressions of belief struck me then as modes of behavior profoundly antithetic to the universal secular humanism I professed. I had not come to Jerusalem because of religious or ethnic associations, but as a professional historian of visual forms. Belief and ideologies often create monuments, but they rarely preserve them well. As I began to study the Haram and its context, I began to realize that there was a truly unique phenomenon: a space created for a purpose that was no longer active transformed into something else by fourteen centuries of a new culture and of a new faith. Only Rome and Istanbul preserve comparable instances of cultural transformations, and the Haram to me became a demonstration of how physical and esthetic quality can overcome cultural antagonisms.

In 1953 or 1954, the then Jordanian Inspector of Antiquities in Jerusalem, the late Dr. (he may not have completed his doctorate at that time) Awni Dajani and I descended into the cellars and basements of many of the houses which lined the western edge of the Haram and discovered the streets, walls, and other remains which have become part and parcel of what is known now as the Western Wall Tunnel. It was an exhilarating, even if messy, experience which is still with me fifty-five years later. When we emerged from one of these cellars, Awni, who was only a few years older than me, turned to me and asked rhetorically: "What should we do with these places?" And he answered: "We must develop discotheques there." These were the new fashion in major cities and I fully concurred.[11] At that time, neither religion nor politics seemed to be likely patrons for the future to be dominated by universal tourism. And I recall how in 1960 or 1961, the Egyptian engineers in charge of restoring the Dome of the Rock had made a tentative plan of transforming the "Stables of Solomon," now the Musalla al-Marwani or Marwani Mosque, into a parking lot for cars and buses, with a café and restrooms for weary visitors. I do not quite understand how highly educated young men of the time were not aware of the religious and political revolutions about to come, but I cannot but regret that these particular forms of our dreams were never realized and were replaced by often cruel and always ignorant antagonisms.

There are legal and technical mechanisms for the preservation of what is deemed beautiful and historically significant, but the implementation of these mechanisms requires decisions about governance and responsibility which cannot be exclusively in the hands of political and religious authorities. Alternate possibilities, through UNESCO for instance, have failed so far. But, if one meditates on the eschatological component of the Haram as the space where Good will be made to prevail and man will be judged, one can perhaps imagine that a space shaped by the Antique world long gone and constantly enhanced by the living culture of Islam could become a place for reconciliation and mutual understanding rather than of strife and contest. Hope springs eternal.

209 Dome of the Rock graffiti on house walls of the Muslim Quarter of Jerusalem's Old City; the Western Wall on popular Jewish New Year cards

Benjamin Kedar:

My earliest memory relating to the Esplanade is a mistaken notion. As a child in postwar Nitra, Czechoslovakia, I was convinced that the imposing domed building on the cover of a Passover haggadah we had at home was none other than the Temple of Jerusalem, for whose speedy rebuilding we implored God in a concluding hymn of the Passover rite as well as in sundry other prayers. Somewhat later, already in Kfar Netter, Israel, I realized that the domed building was the Hurva, the main synagogue in the Jewish Quarter of the Old City of Jerusalem, destroyed in 1948 by a victorious Arab Legion along with some 30 other synagogues. In 1956 I was surprised to learn, from a Hebrew volume on Jerusalem's early history, that a part of the southern supporting wall of Herod's Temple Mount—and not only the famous Western Wall—was still standing. As a student at the Hebrew University of Jerusalem around 1960, I often brought my guests to the observation post at Abu Tor, close to the Israel–Jordan armistice line, from which one could see the Aqsa Mosque and the Dome of the Rock, whose dull gray dome was at the time being replaced by a golden one. There was great curiosity; but I do not recollect a desire to visit those shrines, to say nothing of incorporating them into Israel. Later, as a graduate student in New Haven I was repeatedly asked how I could accept the fact that the Old City and the Temple Mount were part of the Kingdom of Jordan, and I remember how shocked my interlocutors were to hear that, in my opinion, the Almighty did a great favor to Israel by keeping those places outside its borders, for I could well imagine the frenzy their possession by Israel would have generated. Moreover, in those years I had already begun to explore the hypothesis that the destruction of the Second Temple was a windfall for the Jewish scholarly elite of that time and to some extent a blessing in disguise for Judaism in general.[12] And yet I was soon to learn that my stance was much more complex. Upon the outbreak of the Six Day War I hastily left New Haven, rushing to take part in what then appeared to be a perilous, desperate fight for Israel's survival. And when a few days later I joined the jubilant, several-miles-long procession of West Jerusalemites who streamed for the first time into the recently conquered Old City and trudged through the pulverized remains of the Magharibah Quarter down to the Western Wall, I found myself touching one of its stones while silently reciting the words of Judah Halevi, the twelfth-century Jewish poet from Spain:

Surely shall I take pity on your stones and kiss them

And the taste of your clods will please me more than honey.

Somewhat later I stood, alone, before the remains of the still deserted Southern Wall.

When, forty years afterwards, I think of Jerusalem's sacred Esplanade, what scenes come to my mind? Abraham making ready to sacrifice his second son, Isaac? King David conveying the Ark of the Covenant? King Solomon praying at the consecration of the First Temple or Judas Maccabaeus reconsecrating the Second? King Herod inspecting the progress of his grandiose building scheme? Mary and Joseph coming to the Temple to offer their infant son to the Lord? Muhammad descending onto the Rock amidst the Temple's ruins and ascending thence to the heavens? Archbishop Peter of Lyon consecrating the Dome of the Rock as "the Temple of the Lord" in 1141 or Saladin reconsecrating it as a Muslim shrine 46 years later? Yes, I am aware of these scenes, some historical, some mythical. But pomp and ritual, let alone the sacrificial slaughter of animals, leave me cold; to the extent that I'm capable of being attuned to religion, I may be tempted by the "still small voice" of 1 Kings 19.12. The scenes that come to mind most readily are the recurring doublets of victory and defeat, from 586 BC and 70 AD down to 1099, 1187, and 1967. Of these events I've studied in detail the Crusader massacre of about 3,000 Muslim men and women at the Aqsa Mosque upon the conquest of Jerusalem on 15 July 1099, and its variegated, sometimes blatantly biased, reconstructions by Western writers from the twelfth century to the present.[13] In short, for me the Esplanade connotes, first and foremost, the extremes of humankind's frenzy at a spot where the sacred and the cruel have mingled all too often.

So much for past scenes. The present one is dominated by the regained grandeur of the Herodian walls and streets and by the renovated splendor of the Dome of the Rock. Must grandeur and splendor be tarnished by further confrontations and explosions of violence? I hope not. For it has become obvious that a durable solution of the Arab-Israeli conflict, apparently drawing closer despite many a setback, must address the opposing claims to the area discussed in this book and set up mechanisms to allay Jewish fears lest Muslim activities on the Esplanade damage remains of the Second Temple buried underneath (or embedded in) the Haram, and Muslim fears lest Jewish activities in the Western Wall area endanger the Haram or its foundations.

In the wake of such a settlement, the place where heaven and earth are said to meet will hardly become an antechamber to Paradise, so powerfully evoked by the interior mosaics of the Dome of the Rock. But neither will it trigger bloodshed and destruction, the likes of which the Western Wall had witnessed two millennia ago.

Notes

Victor A. Hurowitz, House of the Lord (*Beyt YHWH*)

1   This article uses the transliteration YHWH for the Tetragrammaton, or four-letter ineffable name of the God of Israel, usually translated as Lord and pronounced by some Jehovah or Yahweh.

2   Several items to have appeared in recent years including an inscribed ivory pomegranate, an inscription purportedly of King Jehoash, and an ostracon mentioning a payment to the "House of the Lord," are considered by most scholars modern forgeries. Archaeological sifting supervised by Dr. Gabriel Barkay of rubble removed from the Temple Mount in the course of recent construction work has yielded some fragmentary items from the First Temple period but nothing that can be characterized as belonging to the Temple proper [see fig.1].

3   For this controversy, see the articles collected in Lowell K. Handy, *The Age of Solomon: Scholarship at the Turn of the Millennium*, Studies in the History and Culture of the Ancient Near East 11 (Leiden, 1997). For defenses of the historical existence of the First Temple in some form or other (not necessarily as described in 1 Kings), see David Ussishkin, "Solomon's Jerusalem: The Text and the Facts on the Ground," in *Jerusalem in the Bible and Archaeology: The First Temple Period*, eds. Andrew G. Vaughn and Ann E. Killebrew, SBL Symposium Series 18 (Atlanta, 2003), pp. 103–15; William G. Dever, "Were There Temples in Ancient Israel? The Archaeological Evidence," in *Text, Artifact and Image: Revealing Ancient Israelite Religion*, eds. Gary M. Beckman and Theodore J. Lewis, Brown Judaic Studies 346 (Providence, RI, 2006), pp. 300–16, esp. 303–10.

4   The basic structure of the Temple, namely a building with three spaces (forecourt, anteroom, inner chamber) arranged on the vertical axis is known already from the second millennium, and specific parallels have been found at Tell Ta'yinat and 'Ayn Dara in Syria. For numerous specific similarities between the Temple of Solomon and the 'Ayn Dara temple, see now John Monson, "The 'Ain Dara Temple and the Jerusalem Temple," in *Text, Artifact and Image*, pp. 273–99.

5   Isa. 2.1–4; Mic. 4.1–5; Ezek. 40.2; Zech. 14.10.

6   See Victor A. Hurowitz, "Babylon in Bethel: New Light on Jacob's Dream," in *Orientalism, Assyriology, and the Bible*, ed. Steven W. Holloway (Sheffield, 2006), pp. 434–46.

7   Many scholars attribute Zechariah 9–12 to a prophet other than Zechariah son of Berekhiah son of Iddo, after whom the book is named and whose prophecies make up the bulk of the book.

8   The *ulam* is considered by many a room, assumedly with walls and a roof. However, according to 1 Kings 7.12 describing the courtyard walls, this structure is included as a courtyard; see Carol L. Meyers, "Jachin and Boaz in Religious and Political Perspective," *Catholic Biblical Quarterly* 45 (1983), 167–78.

9   *yakhin YHWH kisse David umamlakhto 'al zar'o 'ad 'olam.*

10 *be'oz YHWH yismah melekh*

11 *Enlil Mukin palêja*

12 This term is often erroneously translated "snuffers" or "shears." For the understanding offered here, see Victor A. Hurowitz, "Solomon's Golden Vessels (1 Kings 7:48–50) and the Cult of the First Temple," in *Pomegranates and Golden Bells: Studies in Biblical, Jewish, and Near Eastern Ritual, Law, and Literature in Honor of Jacob Milgrom*, eds. David P. Wright, David N. Freedman, and Avi Hurvitz (Winona Lake, 1995), pp. 151–64.

13 For further, more detailed discussions of Solomon's Temple see Wolfgang Zwickel, *Der Salomonische Tempel*, Kulturgeschichte der antiken Welt 83 (Mainz am Rhein, 1999), with extensive bibliography; Victor A. Hurowitz, "YHWH's Exalted House – Aspects of Design and Symbolism of Solomon's Temple," in *Temple and Worship in Biblical Israel*, ed. John Day (London and New York, 2005), pp. 63–110, and note the other essays in that volume.

Joseph Patrich, The Temple (*Beyt Ha-Miqdash*) and Its Mount

1   *Natural History* 5.70 (Pliny, *Natural History*; English translation by Harris Rackham, Loeb Classical Library, 10 vols. [London and Cambridge, MA, 1938–63]); Menahem Stern, *Greek and Latin Authors on Jews and Judaism*, 3 vols. (Jerusalem 1974–84), no. 204, 1:471, 1:477–78.

2   Quoted by Josephus, *Antiquities* 12.136 (Josephus, *Jewish Antiquities, Books XII–XIV*, trans. Ralph Marcus, Loeb Classical Library [London and Cambridge, MA, 1943], pp. 68–69).

3   *The Histories* 5.8.1 (Tacitus, *The Histories*, with an English translation by Clifford H. Moore, Loeb Classical Library, 4 vols. [London and New York, 1925–37]); Stern, *Greek and Latin Authors*, no. 281, 2:28, 2:46–47.

4   See particularly Charles W. Wilson, *Ordnance Survey of Jerusalem in the Years 1864 to 1865*, rev. ed. (Southampton, 1876) and Sheet 1: "Haram Grounds & c"; Charles Warren, *Plans, Elevations, Sections, etc., Shewing the Results of the Excavations at Jerusalem, 1867–70* (London, 1884); Konrad Schick, *Die Stiftshütte, der Tempel in Jerusalem und der Tempelplatz der Jetztzeit* (Berlin, 1896). Among the numerous later studies of the Temple and its precinct, of particular importance are the following: Louis-Hugues Vincent and A.-M Stève, *Jérusalem de l'ancien testament*, 2ᵉᵐᵉ partie (Paris, 1956), pp. 373–610; Michael Avi Yonah, "The Second Temple," in *Sefer Yerushalayim* (The Book of Jerusalem) (Jerusalem, 1956), pp. 392–418 (Hebrew); Bellarmino Bagatti, "La posizione del tempio erodiano di Gerusalemme," *Biblica* 46 [1965], 428–44; Th. A. Busink, *Der Tempel von Jerusalem von Salomon bis Herodes: eine archäologisch-historische Studie unter Berücksichtigung des westsemitischen Tempelbaus*, vol. 2: *Von Ezekiel bis Middot* (Leiden, 1980); Dan Bahat, "The Herodian Temple," in *The Cambridge History of Judaism*, vol. III: *The Early Roman Period*, ed. William Horbury, W.D. Davies, and John Sturdy (Cambridge, 1999), pp. 38–58; Leen Ritmeyer, "Locating the Original Temple Mount," *Biblical Archaeology Review* 18, 2 (1992), 24–45, 64–65; idem, *The Quest: Revealing the Temple Mount in Jerusalem* (Jerusalem, 2006). As for the historical studies, one should consult Lee I. Levine, *Jerusalem: Portrait of the City in the Second Temple Period* (Philadelphia, 2002).

5   Benjamin Mazar, *The Mountain of the Lord* (New York, 1975); Meir Ben-Dov, *In the Shadow of the Temple: The Discovery of Ancient Jerusalem* (Jerusalem, 1985). See also Kathleen and Leen Ritmeyer, "Reconstructing Herod's Temple Mount in Jerusalem," *Biblical Archaeology Review* 15 (1989), 23–42.

6   Mishnah Eruvin, 10.14 (for the Mishnah in English see Jacob Neusner, *The Mishnah: A New Translation* (New Haven and London, 1988). (Further references to Mishnah tractates will be marked M.) On the water cisterns under the Haram al-Sharif see Shimon Gibson and David M. Jacobson, *Below the Temple Mount* (Oxford, 1996).

7   While the altitude of the lower platform of the Haram al-Sharif adjacent to the upper platform (738m above sea level) is in accord with the level of the base of the Herodian pilaster as preserved on the outside near the northern end of the western wall, the top altitude of the Rock is 743.7m, namely 1.3–1.5m below the level of the upper court of the Herodian Temple (depending on the length of the cubit in use), according to the relative levels given by Flavius Josephus and in the Mishnah. These differences were already noted since the mid-nineteenth century by many scholars, such as James T. Barclay, Th. A. Busink, Bellarmino Bagatti, David Jacobson, and Meir Ben-Dov; for references see Joseph Patrich, "The Second Temple and Its Courts: A New Proposal for Locating Them on the Temple Mount", *Eretz Israel* 28 (2007) (Teddy Kollek Volume), 173–83 (Hebrew); idem, "The Location of the Second Temple and the Layout of Its Court's Gates and Chambers: A New Proposal," in *The Jerusalem Perspective: 150 Years of Archaeological Research*, ed. Katharina Galor and Gideon Avni (forthcoming), n. 13. Yet there are scholars who maintain that the rock was a part of the altar, or the "Foundation Rock" in the Holy of Holies. For a variety of opinions, see Ritmeyer, "Locating"; idem, *The Quest*. See also, more recently, Ehud Netzer, "The Form and Function of the Courts and Gates that Surrounded the Second Temple," *Qadmoniot* 38, no. 130 (2005), 97–107 (Hebrew), who locates the Muslim stone at the Holy of Holies; David Jacobson, "The Jerusalem Temple of Herod the Great," in *The World of the Herods: Volume 1 of the International Conference The World of the Herods and the Nabataeans Held at the British Museum, 17–19 April 2001*, ed. Nikos Kokkinos, Oriens et Occidens 14 (Stuttgart, 2007), pp. 145–76, who locates it at the center of the sanctuary. Asher S. Kaufman, *The Temple Mount: Where is the Holy of Holies?* (Jerusalem, 2004) suggested that the Temple and its inner courts were located to the north of the Dome of the Rock, the Dome of the Spirits marking the place of the Holy of Holies. There is no real basis for this theory.

8   Jer. 29.10 and 37.8–10.

9   Ezra 1.2–4. All quotations from the Old Testament are based upon the translation of the Jewish Publication Society.

10 Ezra 6.2–5.

11 Ezra 1.8–10, 5.13–16; in Ezra 3.1–8 this is attributed to Zerubbabel and Jeshua, under Darius, ca. 20 years later. See also Zech. 4.9; Josephus, *Antiquities* 11.11–13. Diana V. Edelman, *The Origins of the 'Second' Temple: Persian Imperial Policy and the Rebuilding of Jerusalem* (London, 2005), questions the historicity of Ezra 1–6, Haggai, and Zechariah as sources for the "origins" of the Second Temple. She maintains that both the rebuilding of the Temple and Jerusalem's refortification took place at the time of Nehemiah, and that the return from exile under Zerubbabel and Jeshua should be dated around 465 BCE. Peter R. Bedford, *Temple Restoration in Early Achaemenid Judah* (Leiden, 2001), attributes the beginning of works of restoration to Zerubbabel and Jeshua, under Darius I.

12 Ezra 6.8–10.

13 Josephus, *Antiquities* 11.99.

14 Ezra 3.12–13.

15 M Sheqalim 6.1–2; M Yoma 5.2; Babylonian Talmud, Yoma 21b. (For an English translation for all references to the Babylonian Talmud, see *The Babylonian Talmud*, translated into English with notes, glossary and indices under the editorship of Isidore Epstein [London, 1935–48]. Further

references to the Babylonian Talmud will be marked TB.)

16　In later years it was raised to half a sheqel (equivalent to two Roman dinars) for every adult male; women were not obligated to contribute.

17　Josephus, *Antiquities* 11.297–301.

18　The entire story of the Bible translation is given in the *Letter of Aristeas*. For an English translation see Moses Hadas, *Aristeas to Philocrates: Letter of Aristeas* (New York, 1951); R.J.H. Shutt, "Letter of Aristeas," in *The Old Testament Pseudepigrapha*, ed. James H. Charlesworth, 2 vols. (Garden City, NY, 1983–85), 2:7–34.

19　Ptolemy IV Philopator's failed attempt to enter the Holy of Holies is documented in the apocryphal book 3 Maccabees (1.8–2.24). For discussion see Hugh Anderson, "3 Maccabees: A New Translation and Introduction," in *The Old Testament Pseudepigrapha*, ed. Charlesworth, 2:510–12.

20　Josephus, *Antiquities* 12.138–46. The custom of providing allocations for the Temple service is first attested under Cyrus and Darius and seems to have been maintained by the Ptolemies, as well as by the later Seleucids (2 Macc. 3.3—pertaining to Seleucus IV; see also 2 Macc. 9.16; 1 Macc. 10.39–44; Josephus, *Antiquities* 13.55, all relating to Demetrius I, 152 BCE).

21　Josephus, *Antiquities* 12.141.

22　Ibid., 12.129–44.

23　Ben Sira 50.1–12. English translation of the Hebrew text in *The Jewish Temple: a Non-biblical Sourcebook*, ed. Charles T.R. Hayward (London, 1996), pp. 41–43.

24　Ibid., 50.1–3. For an English translation of the Greek version see *The Jewish Temple*, ed. Hayward, pp. 73–75.

25　M Middot 2.1. These dimensions are in accordance with the LXX to Ezek. 42.15–20; 45.2.

26　*Letter of Aristeas*, paragraphs 84–91. Hadas, *Aristeas to Philocrates*, pp. 14–15, has suggested that the curtain may have been the one looted by Antiochus IV and donated by him to the temple of Zeus at Olympia.

27　See 2 Macc. 3.10–11. Some donations were placed in the open, to be seen and admired (Josephus, *War* 2.413; ibid., *Antiquities* 12.249–50). An English translation of all the writings of Josephus is in the Loeb Classical Library series. The English translation of *Jewish Antiquities*, Books 12–13 was done by Ralph Marcus; that of Books 14–17 by Marcus and Allen Wickgren; and that of Books 18–20, by Louis H. Feldman; the English translation of *The Jewish War, The Life*, and *Against Apion* was done by Henry St. J. Thackeray.

28　2 Macc. 3.7–30. On the historicity of this event relating to Heliodorus and his role in the Seleucid administration, see now Hannah M. Cotton and Michael Wörrle, "Seleukos IV to Heliodoros: A New Dossier of Royal Correspondence from Israel," *Zeitschrift für Papyrologie und Epigraphik* 159 (2007), 191–205.

29　2 Macc. 4.

30　1 Macc. 1.20–24; *The First Book of Maccabees*: Introduction, Hebrew translation, and commentary by Uriel Rappaport (Jerusalem, 2004), pp. 102–7 (Hebrew). (For English translations of 1 and 2 Maccabees, by Jonathan A. Goldstein, see *The Anchor Bible* [New York, 1976 and 1983 respectively]); Josephus, *Against Apion* 2.83–84.

31　2 Macc. 5.11–16, 21; Josephus, *Antiquities* 12.249.

32　1 Macc. 1.31–33.

33　1 Macc. 4.36–61; M Middot 2.3.

34　1 Macc. 4.60.

35　The inner court had another wall, which Alcimus tried to tear to the ground in May 159, but his plan failed (1 Macc. 9.54–57).

36　M Middot 1.6.

37　1 Macc. 4.52.

38　2 Macc. 11.25. See also 1 Macc. 10.18–20, 25–45, 11.27, 11.37, and 11.57; Josephus, *Antiquities* 13.45–46.

39　1 Macc. 14.35, 41.

40　1 Macc. 15.7.

41　The spiritual-religious leadership of the nation during the Second Temple period.

42　TB Kiddushin 66a.

43　Josephus, *Antiquities* 13.372–73. See also TB Sukkah 48b.

44　2 Macc. 3.4 ("*prostates*"); Acts 4.1, 5.24–26; Josephus, *Antiquities* 20.131; Josephus, *War* 2.409, 6.294 ("*strategos*").

45　M Sheqalim 5.1; M Yoma 3.11; Tosefta, Sheqalim 2.14; Jerusalem Talmud, Sheqalim V, 49a. (Further references to the Jerusalem Talmud will be marked Y.) See also M Tamid 7.3; M Sheqalim 5.2; Y Sheqalim V, 19a.

46　On the Temple officials, see Abraham Büchler, *Die Priester und der Cultus im letzten Jahrzent der jerusalemischen Tempels* (Vienna, 1895), pp. 90–118; Shmuel Safrai, "The Temple," in Shmuel Safrai and Menahem Stern, *The Jewish People in the First Century* (Amsterdam, 1976), pp. 865–907; Emil Schürer, *The History of the Jewish People in the Age of Jesus Christ (175 B.C.–A.D. 135)*, ed. Géza Vermes, Fergus Millar, and Martin Goodman, vol. 2 (Edinburgh, 1979), pp. 275–91;

47　If named after Coponius, the Roman prefect of 6–9 CE, this will set our text in post-Hasmonaean context, unless it was an anachronistic name. The Herodian precinct had four gates on this side. For more about the Hasmonaean temple, see Joseph Patrich, "Differences between Herod's Temple and that of the Hasmonaeans: Reflections on the 'House of the Utensils' and the 'House of the Laver' of the Temple Scroll," in *New Studies in the Archaeology of Jerusalem and its Region: Collected Papers*, vol. 1, ed. Joseph Patrich and David Amit (Jerusalem, 2007), pp. 41–53 (Hebrew).

Jostein Ådna, *Jerusalemer Tempel und Tempelmarkt im 1. Jahrhundert n. Chr.* (Wiesbaden, 1999), pp. 91–95.

48　M Middot 1.3.

49　Josephus, *Antiquities* 14.56–76; Tacitus, *Histories* 5.81.

50　Josephus, *Antiquities* 14.72-73; idem, *War* 1.152–54. But according to Dio Cassius, 27.16.4, all the vessels were plundered. See Marcus' comment ad. loc.

51　Josephus, *Antiquities* 14.190–200.

52　Josephus, *War* 1.343–75; idem, *Antiquities* 14.465–88.

53　Josephus, *Antiquities* 14.58; idem, *War* 1.143.

54　Josephus, *War* 2.184–203; idem, *Antiquities* 18.261–309; Philo, *The Embassy to Gaius* 181–261. For an English translation by Francis H. Colson, see *Philo*, vol. 10: *The Embassy to Gaius*, Loeb Classical Library (Cambridge, MA and London, 1962), pp. 92–135.

55　Josephus, *Antiquities* 19.278–91.

56　Philo, *The Embassy to Gaius* 157, 317–19 (English translation, pp. 80–81, 158–59).

57　Josephus, *Antiquities* 14.216; 16.162 ff.; Philo, *The Embassy to Gaius* 156, 311–16 (English translation, pp. 78–79; 156–59).

58　Schürer, *History*, vol. 2,1, pp. 116–23; Edith Mary Smallwood, *The Jews under Roman Rule: From Pompey to Diocletian* (Leiden, 1976), pp. 124–28.

59　TB Baba Bathra 4a; Philo, *On the Special Laws* 1.73. (For an English translation by Francis H. Colson, see *Philo*, vol. 7, Loeb Classical Library (London and Cambridge, MA, 1937), pp. 142–43.)

60　Josephus, *Antiquities* 15.380–90.

61　Philo, *The Embassy to Gaius* 157, 319 (English translation, pp. 80–81, 158–61). This custom of contributions for the Temple was followed by other Romans, the donations of whom could be seen and admired by all (Josephus, *War* 2.412–13, 4.181). During the final Roman siege of the city in the Great Revolt, John of Gischala melted down sacred vessels, among them costly gifts presented by Augustus and his wife Julia and other Roman emperors (ibid. 5.562–63).

62　Josephus, *Antiquities* 15.425.

63　Ibid., 15.421–23.

64　Ibid., 20.219. According to John 2.20, construction work went on for 46 years.

65　Josephus, *War* 5.36.

66　The major sections are in *War* 5.184–247 and *Antiquities* 15.391–425.

67　Lee I. Levine, "Josephus' Description of the Jerusalem Temple: 'War', 'Antiquities', and Other Sources," in *Josephus and the History of the Greco-Roman Period: Essays in Memory of Morton Smith*, ed. Fausto Parente and Joseph Sievers (Leiden, 1994), pp. 233–46.

68　M Middot 1, 2, and 5 seem to refer to the Hasmonaean period.

69　Josephus, *Antiquities* 15.391–92. For the archaeological remains, see Mazar, *The Mountain of the Lord*.

70　Ibid., 20.220–21.

71　Ibid., 15.402.

72　Ibid., 15.400; according to M Middot it was a square of 500x500 cubits.

73　Joseuphus, *War* 5.193-94; idem, *Antiquities* 15.417. See also Virgil R.L. Fry, "The Warning Inscriptions from the Herodian Temple," Ph.D diss., Southern Baptist Theological Seminary, 1974.

74　Schürer, *History*, vol. 1, p. 222, n. 85. The laws of purity also prohibited access of particular persons. Those ill with gonorrhea and leprosy were excluded from the city entirely; women during their period of menstruation were not allowed into the Temple, and when they were free from that impurity could not enter beyond the limit of the Women's Court (see below). Men too, if not absolutely pure, were prohibited from coming into the inner court of the Temple. And even the priests, if impure, were prohibited from entering it (Josephus, *War* 5.227). Agrippa I, a descendant of converts, was criticized by one Simeon for entering the Temple precinct (Josephus, *Antiquities* 19.332–34). Paul, himself a Jew of Tarsus, aroused the people's anger, who suspected that he let Gentiles into the holy precinct (Acts 21.27–36).

75　M Middot 1.4.

76　Josephus, *War* 5.199–200.

77　M Middot 2.5; M Kelim 1.8.

78　Josephus, *War* 5.193–99.

79　Ibid., 5.201–6; Josephus, *Antiquities* 18.259.

80　M Middot 2.3; M Yoma 3.10. For parallels from the Tosefta and the Talmudim, as well as the question of the origin of Nicanor, see Joshua Schwartz, "Once More on the Nicanor Gate," *Hebrew Union College Annual* 62 (1991), 245–83.

81　Josephus, *Antiquities* 15.424. Apparently this was the "Beautiful Gate" of Acts 3.2 and 3.10.

82 TB Sukkah 4.1; M Middot 2.5.

83 M Sukkah 5.5; Y Yoma 37b.

84 M Middot 3.3; M Tamid 1.4; M Yoma 2.1–6; 2 Chron. 4.1.

85 Josephus, *War* 5.225–26; idem, *Antiquities* 15.419; M Middot 3.4.

86 M Tamid 1.4.

87 Patrich, "Second Temple and Its Courts"; idem, "Location of the Second Temple."

88 There is a huge amount of literature about the shape of the Temple. For a detailed reconstruction presented in the illustrations for the present chapter, see Joseph Patrich, "The Structure of the Second Temple—A New Reconstruction," in *Ancient Jerusalem Revealed*, ed. Hillel Geva (Jerusalem, 1994), pp. 260–71.

89 Josephus, *War* 5.208, 6.264.

90 Ibid., 5.222–24.

91 M Middot 3.7; Josephus, *Antiquities* 17.151, 155. Some scholars have suggested that this was the great gate over which Herod hung a golden eagle, but this interpretation seems to be mistaken. It was rather set over the gate named after Marcus Vipsenius Agrippa (Josephus, *War* 1.416), the gifted aide and son-in-law of Emperor Augustus who visited the Temple in 15 BCE, making votive donations and offerings to the Temple (Philo, *The Embassy to Gaius* 295–97; English translation, pp. 148–49). This gate should apparently be identified with the one that stood above Robinson's Arch.

92 Josephus, *War* 5.208.

93 Joseph Patrich, "The Golden Vine, the Sanctuary Portal and its Depiction on the Bar-Kokhba Coins," *Jewish Art* 19/20 (1994), 56–61.

94 M Yoma 3.10.

95 Josephus, *War* 5.217. It was suggested that the lamp's stand as depicted on the Arch of Titus was not a part of the original lamp; see Rachel Hachlili, *The Menorah, the Ancient Seven-armed Candelabrum: Origin, Form and Significance* (Leiden, 2001), pp. 46–50.

96 M Yoma 5.2; TB Yoma 21b; Tacitus, *Histories* 5.8.1.

97 *War* 5.215–19 and 237; M Kelim 1.9; Philo, *On the Special Laws* 1.72 (English translation, pp. 140–41).

98 Joseph Patrich, "The *Mesibbah* of the Second Temple in Jerusalem according to the Tractate Middot," *Israel Exploration Journal* 36 (1986), 215–33.

99 Josephus, *War* 5.220–21; idem, *Antiquities* 15.391.

100 Josephus, *Antiquities* 15.410.

101 Ritmeyer, "Reconstructing," 49–53; Gibson and Jacobson, *Below the Temple Mount*, pp. 259–68.

102 Gibson and Jacobson, *Below the Temple Mount*, pp. 235–59; Eilat Mazar, *The Complete Guide to the Mount Temple Excavations* (Jerusalem, 2002), pp. 50–57.

103 Matt. 21.12–13; Mark 11.15–19; Luke 19.45–46; John 2.13–22.

104 Ådna, *Jerusalemer Tempel*, pp. 72–150.

105 Erik Sjöqvist, "Kaisareion," *Opuscula Romana* 1 (1954), 86–108; John Bryan Ward-Perkins and Michael H. Ballance, "The Caesareum at Cyrene and the Basilica at Cremna," *Papers of the British School at Rome* 26 (1958), 137–94; Benjamin Mazar, "The Royal Stoa in the Southern Part of the Temple Mount," *Proceedings of the American Academy for Jewish Research* 46–47 (1978–79), 381–87; Ådna, *Jerusalemer Tempel*, pp. 32–71. The Alexandria Caesareum, known as Sebasteum, is described by Philo, *The Embassy to Gaius* 151 (English translation, pp. 76–77).

106 Josephus, *War* 4.582.

107 Josephus, *War* 5.238–46; idem, *Antiquities* 15.403, 409.

108 Josephus, *Antiquities* 15.403, 18.91; idem, *War* 1.75.

109 Josephus, *Antiquities* 14.481; idem, *War* 1.353.

110 Josephus, *Antiquities* 14.61. On the Hellenistic citadel, see also *Letter of Aristeas* 100–4, where it is referred to as *Akra*.

111 Josephus, *Antiquities* 15.424. For the archaeological remains attributed to the Antonia, see Pierre Benoit, "L'Antonie d'Hérode le Grand et le forum oriental d'Aelia Capitolina," *Harvard Theological Review* 64 (1971), 135–67; idem, "De la forteresse Antonia: la reconstitution archéologique," *Australian Journal of Biblical Archaeology* 6 (1973), 16–23.

112 For a different opinion, see Ra'ya Shani and Doron Chen, "On the Umayyad Dating of the Double Gate in Jerusalem," *Muqarnas* 18 (2001), 1–40. This was refuted by Orit Peleg, "Was the Double Gate Built by King Herod or by the Caliph 'Abd al-Malik?" *New Studies on Jerusalem* 10 (2004), 81–88 (Hebrew).

113 Safrai, "The Temple," pp. 898–904.

114 Philo, *On the Special Laws* 1.69 and 78 (English translation, pp. 138–39, 144–45).

115 M Bikkurim 3.3–4 (English translation, pp. 172–73).

116 Safrai, "The Temple," pp. 865–66.

117 Luke 2.21–24.

118 Luke 2.41–50.

119 Dan Bahat, "Jesus and the Herodian Temple Mount," in *Jesus and Archaeology*, ed. James H. Charlesworth (Grand Rapids, MI and Cambridge, 2006), pp. 300–8.

120 John 10.22–24.

121 Matt. 4.5–7; Luke 4.9–12.

122 Matt. 21.12–14; Mark 11.15–17; Luke 19.45; John 2.15–18.

123 Matt. 21.18–24.2; Mark 11.27–13.2; Luke 20.1–21.38. Another account of teaching in the Temple, during the Feast of Tabernacles, is given in John 7.14–53.

124 Josephus, *War* 6.252–66.

125 Ibid., 2.293–308.

126 Ibid., 2.408–21; Schürer, *History*, vol. 1, p. 486.

127 Josephus, *War* 6.68–93.

128 Ibid., 6.93–95; M Ta'anit 4.6.

129 Josephus, *War* 6.237–43. This account of Josephus, drawing a sympathetic portrait of Titus, his patron, is at divergence with other sources narrating the destruction of the Temple. Thus Sulpicius Severus, a fourth-century Christian historian who derived his narrative from Tacitus, and Orosius, another Christian author and a contemporary of Sulpicius Severus, report that in the war council it was Titus who decided to destroy the Temple; see Schürer, *History*, vol. 1, pp. 506–7; Stern, Greek and Latin Authors, no. 282, 2:64–67.

130 Josephus, *War* 6.244–53.

131 Ibid., 7.1.

132 Ronny Reich and Yaacov Billig, "Excavations near the Temple Mount and Robinson's Arch, 1994–1996," in *Ancient Jerusalem Revealed*, expanded edition., ed. Hillel Geva (Jerusalem, 2000), pp. 340–50.

Yoram Tsafrir, The Temple-less Mountain

1 In writing this chapter the author depended to a large extent on the collection of articles by various authors in *The History of Jerusalem: The Roman and Byzantine Periods (70–638 CE)*, ed. Yoram Tsafrir and Shmuel Safrai (Jerusalem, 1999) (Hebrew), (henceforth: *Jerusalem*, ed. Tsafrir and Safrai) and Yaron Zvi Eliav, *God's Mountain: The Temple Mount in Time, Place, and Memory* (Baltimore, 2005) (henceforth: Eliav, *God's Mountain*). My debt to the authors is greater than is indicated by the footnote.

2 Flavius Josephus, *Josephus: The Jewish War*, tr. Henry St. J. Thackeray, Loeb Classical Library (Cambridge, MA, 1927).

3 Jer. 52.12.

4 Benjamin Mazar, *The Excavations in the Old City of Jerusalem near the Temple Mount: Preliminary Report of the Second and Third Seasons* (Jerusalem, 1971), pp. 2–4 and figs. 5, 10 (henceforth: B. Mazar, *Excavations*); idem, "The Archaeological Excavations near the Temple Mount," in *Jerusalem Revealed: Archaeology in the Holy City 1968–1974*, ed. Yigael Yadin (Jerusalem, 1975), pp. 32–35; Ronny Reich and Yaacov Bilig, "Excavations near the Temple Mount and Robinson's Arch, 1994–1996," in *Ancient Jerusalem Revealed*, expanded edition, ed. Hillel Geva (Jerusalem, 2000), pp. 340–50.

5 Gedaliah Alon, *The Jews in Their Land in the Talmudic Age*, vol. 1 (Jerusalem, 1980), pp. 41–55; Lee I. Levine, *The Synagogue* (New Haven and London, 2000), pp. 160–93.

6 Shmuel Safrai, "The Jews of Jerusalem during the Roman Period," in *Jerusalem*, ed. Tsafrir and Safrai, esp. pp. 15–24.

7 Yaron Zvi Eliav, "Hadrian's Actions in the Jerusalem Temple Mount according to Cassius Dio and Xiphilini Manus," *Jewish Studies Quarterly* 4 (1997), 125–44; see also recently, Eliav, *God's Mountain*, esp. pp. 85–87.

8 Among numerous publications, see, for example, the concise discussion in Emil Schürer, *The History of the Jewish People in the Age of Jesus Christ (175 B.C.–135 A.D.)*, vol. 1, rev. by Géza Vermes and Fergus Millar (Edinburgh, 1973), pp. 534–57; also recently the various discussions in *The Bar Kokhba War Reconsidered – New Perspectives on the Second Jewish Revolt against Rome*, ed. Peter Schäfer, Texts and Studies in Ancient Judaism 100 (Tübingen, 2003).

9 See discussion by Safrai, "Jews of Jerusalem," pp. 24–26.

10 Cassius Dio, *Roman History*, vol. 8, ed. Earnest Cary, Loeb Classical Library (London and Cambridge, MA, 1925), p. 447.

11 Yoram Tsafrir, "Numismatics and the Foundation of Aelia Capitolina: A Critical Review," in *The Bar Kokhba War Reconsidered*, ed. Schäfer, pp. 31–36.

12 Isaiah Gafni, "Jerusalem in Rabbinic Literature," in *Jerusalem*, ed. Tsafrir and Safrai, pp. 35–59; Eliav, *God's Mountain*, esp. pp. 189–236.

13 See recently, Z. Weiss, *The Sepphoris Synagogue: Deciphering an Ancient Message through Its Archaeological and Socio-historical Context* (Jerusalem, 2005), and the literature cited there.

14 Eusebius, *History of the Church*, 6.5.

15 Mark 13.2, and parallels in Matt. 24.2 and Luke 21.6.

16 Dan. 9.27, 11.31, 12.11.

17 1 Macc. 1.62

18 Mic. 3.12

19 Eusebius, *Demonstratio Evangelica* 8.3.12.

20 Charles Warren, *Plans, Elevations, Sections, Shewing the Results of the Excavations at Jerusalem 1867–70 for the Committee of the Palestine Exploration Fund* (London, 1884). The Temple Mount is designated on his map by three names: Haram Ash Sherif, Masjed al Aksa, and Moriah.

21 This situation makes the unconvincing suggestion to locate the Roman legionary camp on the Temple Mount even less attractive. For such an identification, see Eilat Mazar, "Hadrian's Legion Encamped on the Temple Mount," *Biblical Archaeology Review* 32, 6 (2006), 53–58, 82–83; see also n. 43 below.

22 Amos Kloner, "The Dating of the Southern Decumanus of Aelia Capitolina and Wilson's Arch," *New Studies on Jerusalem* 11 (2006), 239–48 (Hebrew). Recent excavations, directed by Alexander Onn (not yet published), strongly support the conclusion that a street leading to the Temple Mount was in use on the arches of "Wilson's Arch" during the Roman period. Among other discoveries from the Roman period near this entrance to the Temple Mount was a public latrine; see Alexander Onn and Avi Solomon, "A Window to Aelia Capitolina in the Wailing Wall Tunnels Excavations," in *New Studies in the Archaeology of Jerusalem and Its Region*, ed. Joseph Patrich and David Amit (Jerusalem, 2007), pp. 85–93 (Hebrew).

23 An exception is a fragment of a monumental Latin inscription, found accidentally in front of the Aqsa Mosque around 1996, which was a part of a monumental arch. It is reasonable to assume that it belonged to a monument that stood atop the Temple Mount or in its close vicinity. The inscription was dated by Grüll to Flavius Silva, the legate of the Tenth Legion, several years after the destruction of Jerusalem by Titus: Tibor Grüll, "A Fragment of a Monumental Roman Inscription at the Islamic Museum of the Haram ash-Sharif, Jerusalem," *Israel Exploration Journal* 56 (2006), 183–200. Cotton and Eck reject Grüll's reading and interpretation. They conclude that the arch was erected either on the Temple Mount or in its close vicinity during the third century CE: Hannah M. Cotton and Werner Eck, "An Imperial Arch in the Colonia Aelia Capitolina: A Fragment of a Latin Inscription in the Islamic Museum of the Haram ash Sharif" (forthcoming).

24 For the exact location see discussion by Joseph Patrich in this volume, pp. 55–58.

25 For the location of the Capitoline temple on the Temple Mount, see, for example, Joseph Germer-Durand, "Aelia Capitolina," *Revue Biblique* 1 (1892), 369–87 (esp. 371–81); Dan Bahat, *The Illustrated Atlas of Jerusalem* (Jerusalem, 1990), p. 65 and map on p. 59; Hillel Geva, "Jerusalem," *The New Encyclopedia of Archaeological Excavations in the Holy Land*, vol. 2 (Jerusalem, 1993), map on p. 758.

26 See above p. 82, and below, p. 35.

27 Another opinion maintains that the text should be interpreted as "instead of," namely that a Temple of Jupiter replaced the Jewish Temple, but not necessarily on the Temple Mount; see Glen W. Bowersock, "A Roman Perspective on the Bar-Kochba War," in *Approaches to Ancient Judaism*, II, ed. William S. Green (Missoula, 1980, pp. 131–41; Benjamin Isaac, *The Limits of the Empire: The Roman Army in the East*, rev. ed. (Oxford, 1992), p. 353; idem, "Jerusalem from the Great Revolt to the Reign of Constantine 70–312 CE," in *Jerusalem*, ed. Tsafrir and Safrai, pp. 1–13, esp. p. 6 (Hebrew).

28 See the two items by Eliav (n. 7 above). See also Jerome Murphy-O'Connor, "The Location of the Capitol in Aelia Capitolina," *Revue Biblique* 101 (1994), 407–15.

29 For the death of the priest Zechariah son of Jehoyadah, see 2 Chron. 24.21–22. This Zechariah was conflated in Christian tradition with the prophet Zechariah son of Berechiah (Zech. 1.1) and also with Zechariah the priest, the father of John the Baptist (Luke 1.5). The Christian tradition (Matt. 23.35; Luke 11.51) relates that Zechariah son of Berechiah was killed "between the altar and the Temple" (i.e., in front of the Temple).

30 Scholars have suggested that one of the two statues depicted the emperor Antoninus Pius, Hadrian's successor (138–61 CE). A stone, which may have been a pedestal of his statue, carrying his full name: Titus Aelius Hadrianus Antoninus Pius, is embedded in the southern wall of the Temple Mount. See, among others, Murphy-O'Connor, "Location of the Capitol," 410–11.

31 See above, n. 16.

32 See discussion in Yoram Tsafrir, "The Fate of Free Standing Sculptures in Palestine with an Emphasis on the Finds from Bet Shean," in *The Sculptural Environment of the Roman Near East: Reflection on Culture, Ideology, and Power*, ed. Yaron Z. Eliav, Elise A. Friedland, and Sharon Herbert (Leuven and Dudley, MA, 2008), pp. 117–42.

33 Bernard Flusin, "L'Esplanade du Temple a l'arrivée des Arabes d'après deux récits byzantins," in *Bayt al-Maqdis: Abd al-Malik's Jerusalem*, ed. Julian Raby and Jeremy Johns (Oxford, 1992), pp. 17–31; Cyril Mango, "The Temple Mount, AD 614-638," in ibid., pp. 1–16.

34 Murphy-O'Connor, "Location of the Capitol"; Eliav, *God's Mountain*, pp. 91–92.

35 See, for example in Louis-Hugues Vincent and Félix-Marie Abel, *Jérusalem – Recherches de topographie, d'archéologie et d'histoire*, II : *Jérusalem nouvelle* (Paris, 1914), pp. 7–10, 32–33, and map in Pl. 1; see also a suggestion of a reconstruction in Virgilio Corbo, *Il Santo Sepolcro de Gerusalemme: Aspetti archeologici dalle origini al periodo crociato*, I–II (Jerusalem, 1981–82), Pl. 68. See also Kenneth G. Holum, "Hadrian and St. Helena: Imperial Travel and the Origins of Christian Holy

36 In Eusebius, *History of the Church* 2.23–24, tr. Kirsopp Lake, Loeb Classical Library (London, 1926), p. 175.

37 For this suggestion and an extensive discussion of the traditions concerning St. James, see Eliav, *God's Mountain*, pp. 60–79.

38 *Itinerarium Burdigalense* 589–96, ed. Paul Geyer and Otto Cuntz, in *Itineraria et alia geographica*, CCSL 175 (Turnhout, 1965), pp. 14–18. Among the numerous publications about this source, see Robert W. Hamilton, "Jerusalem in the Fourth Century," *Palestine Exploration Quarterly* (1952), 83–90; John Wilkinson, *Egeria's Travels*, 3rd ed. (Warminster, 1999), pp. 22–34; Ora Limor, *Holy Land Travels: Christian Pilgrims in Late Antiquity* (Jerusalem, 1998), pp. 19–38 (Hebrew).

39 What the pilgrim called marble was probably the crystallized local *meleke* limestone. The "blood" was probably red veins of oxidized iron in the rock, which is also typical of Jerusalem. For Zacharias (=Zechariah), see n. 29 above.

40 Matt. 4.5–10; Luke 4.9–12

41 Ps. 118.22; Matt. 21.42

42 For a survey of the water system and reservoirs, see Shimon Gibson and David M. Jacobson, *Below the Temple Mount in Jerusalem*, BAR International Series 637 (Oxford, 1996).

43 Eusebius, *Vita Constantini* 33.1–2; see also Robert Wilken, *The Land Called Holy: Palestine in Christian History and Thought* (New Haven, 1992), esp. pp. 93–97; Joshua Prawer, "Jerusalem in the Christian and Jewish Perspectives of the Early Middle Ages," in *Settimane di Studio del Centro italiano di Studi sull'Alto Medioevo* 26, 2 (Spoleto, 1980), pp. 739–812; idem, "Christian Attitudes towards Jerusalem in the Early Middle Ages," in *The History of Jerusalem in the Early Muslim Period, 638–1099*, ed. Joshua Prawer and Haggai Ben-Shammai (Jerusalem and New York, 1996), pp. 311–47.

44 John F. Baldovin, *The Urban Character of Christian Worship: the Origins, Development and Meaning of Stational Liturgy*, Orientalia Analecta Christiana 228 (Rome, 1987).

45 Pierre Maraval, *Lieux saints et pèlerinages d'Orient: histoire et géographie des origines a la conquête arabe* (Paris, 1985). For Jerusalem and its close vicinity, see pp. 251–74; Jozef T. Milik, "Notes d'épigraphie et de topographie palestiniennes, IX: Sanctuaires chrétiens de Jérusalem a l'époque arabe (VIIe–Xe s.)," *Revue Biblique* 67 (1960), 354–67, 550–86.

46 See, for example, Exodus Rabba 2.2. See bibliography in Shmuel Safrai, "Jerusalem and the Jews from Constantine to the Muslim Conquest," in *Jerusalem*, ed. Tsafrir and Safrai, pp. 240–41 (Hebrew); Eliav, *God's Mountain*, pp. 221–24 and bibliography there.

47 Shmuel Safrai, "The Holy Congregation in Jerusalem," *Scripta Hierosolymitana* 23 (1972), 62–78.

48 Oded Irshai, "Constantine and the Jews: The Prohibition against Entering Jerusalem – History and Historiography," *Zion* 60 (1995), 129–78 (Hebrew).

49 Wilkinson, *Egeria's Travels* (n. 38 above).

50 Exod. 23.17; Deut. 16.6.

51 Hieronymus, *In Sophoniam*, in *Commentarii in prophetas minores*, ed. Marcus Adriaen, CCSL 76 (Turnhout, 1969), pp. 672–74.

52 On Julian see, among others, Robert Browning, *The Emperor Julian* (London, 1975); Glen W. Bowersock, *Julian the Apostate* (London, 1978).

53 Menahem Stern, *Greek and Latin Authors on Jews and Judaism*, II (Jerusalem, 1980), pp. 502–74; Joseph Geiger, "The Revolt against Gallus and the Building of the Temple under Julian," in *From the Destruction of the Second Temple to the Muslim Conquest*, ed. Zvi Baras et al. (Jerusalem, 1982), pp. 208–17 (Hebrew); Shmuel Safrai, "Jerusalem and the Jews," in *Jerusalem*, ed. Tsafrir and Safrai, pp. 241–49 (Hebrew); Zeev Rubin, "Jerusalem in the Byzantine Period – An Historical Survey," in ibid., pp. 209–14 (Hebrew).

54 See *The Works of the Emperor Julian*, vol. 3, tr. William C. Wright, Loeb Classical Library (London and New York, 1923), pp. 177–81.

55 Sebastian P. Brock, "A Letter Attributed to Cyril of Jerusalem on the Rebuilding of the Temple," *Bulletin of the School of Oriental and African Studies* 40 (1977), 267–86; Emanuela Guidoboni, *Catalogue of Ancient Earthquakes in the Mediterranean Area up to the 10th Century* (Rome, 1994), pp. 264–67; and bibliographies in both works.

56 B. Mazar, *Excavations*, p. 23; Meir Ben-Dov, *In the Shadow of the Temple – The Discovery of Ancient Jerusalem* (New York and Toronto, 1985), pp. 219–23 (henceforth: Ben-Dov, *Discovery*).

57 Benjamin Isaac, "Roman Colonies in Judaea: The Foundation of Aelia Capitolina," in *The Near East under Roman Rule: Selected Papers* (Leiden, New York, and Köln, 1998), pp. 87–111; idem, *Limits of the Empire*, pp. 323–25. See also his "Jerusalem from the Great Revolt to the Reign of Constantine, 70–312 CE," in *Jerusalem*, ed. Tsafrir and Safrai, pp. 1–13 (Hebrew).

58 Vincent–Abel, *Jérusalem*; Tsafrir, "Topography and Archaeology"; Geva, "Jerusalem," pp. 758–

67. See also a minimalist view in Eliav, *God's Mountain*, esp. pp. 83–124.

59 William L. MacDonald, *The Architecture of the Roman Empire*, II: *An Urban Appraisal* (New Haven and London, 1986), pp. 5–62.

60 Amos Kloner and Rachel Bar-Nathan, "The Eastern Cardo," *Eretz Israel* 28 (2007; Teddy Kollek memorial volume), 195–207 (Hebrew,). More remains of the pavement of this Roman street have recently been discovered opposite the Western Wall. See Shlomit Wexler-Bdolah, Alexander Onn, Brigitte Onona, and Miriam Avissar, "The Eastern Cardo of Roman Jerusalem and Its Later Phases in the Light of the Excavations in the Western Wall Plaza," in *New Studies in the Archaeology of Jerusalem and Its Region*, ed. Joseph Patrich and David Amit (Jerusalem 2007), pp. 75–93 (Hebrew).

61 Michael Avi-Yonah, *The Madaba Mosaic Map* (Jerusalem, 1954), pp. 50–60; Yoram Tsafrir, "The Holy City of Jerusalem in the Madaba Map," in *The Madaba Map Centenary, 1897–1997*, ed. Michele Piccirillo and Eugenio Alliata (Jerusalem, 1999), pp. 155–63.

62 This location, near the supposed site of the Temple, is much more reasonable than Mango's suggestion (the southern "Double Gate"), see Mango, "Temple Mount," p. 3.

63 Eliav, *God's Mountain*, pp. 83–124.

64 See, for example, B. Mazar, *Excavations*, pp. 4–12; Ben-Dov, *Discovery*, pp. 185–205; E. Mazar, "Hadrian's Legion"; idem, "The Camp of the Tenth Roman Legion at the Foot of the South-West Corner of the Temple Mount Enclosure Wall in Jerusalem," *New Studies on Jerusalem* 5 (1999), 52–67 (Hebrew); Guy D. Stiebel, "The Whereabouts of the Xth Legion and the Boundaries of Aelia Capitolina," ibid., 68–103 (Hebrew).

65 Benny Arubas and Haim Goldfus, "The Kilnworks of the Tenth Legion Fretensis," in *The Roman and Byzantine Near East: Some Recent Archaeological Research*, ed. John H. Humphrey, Journal of Roman Archaeology, Supp. 14 (Portsmouth, RI, 1999), pp. 95–107

66 See n. 64 above; see also Orit Peleg, "Roman Marble Sculpture from the Temple Mount Excavations," *New Studies on Jerusalem* 7 (2001), 129–49 (Hebrew).

67 See the two articles by E. Mazar (above n. 64).

68 Germer-Durand, "Aelia Capitolina," 373–74.

69 Yoram Tsafrir and Leah Di Segni, "Ethnic Composition of the Population of Jerusalem in the Byzantine Period," in *Jerusalem*, ed. Tsafrir and Safrai, pp. 261–80 (Hebrew).

70 Guy Stroumsa, "From Cyril to Sophronius: The Christian Literature of Byzantine Jerusalem," in *Jerusalem*, ed. Tsafrir and Safrai, pp. 417–40.

71 Moshe Gil, *A History of Palestine 634–1099* (Cambridge and New York, 1992), pp. 65–69.

72 Ibid., pp. 65–67.

73 Among numerous annotated translations from Latin see, for example, John Wilkinson, *Egeria's Travels* (London, 1971); idem, *Jerusalem Pilgrims before the Crusades* (Warminster, 1977); Herbert Donner, *Pilgerfahrt ins Heilige Land: Die ältesten Berichte christlicher Palästinapilger (4.-7. Jahrhundert)* (Stuttgart, 1979); Limor, *Holy Land Travels*.

74 George Giacumacis, "The Gate below the Golden Gate," *The Bulletin Series of the Near East Archaeology Society* 4 (1974), 23–26; James Fleming, "The Undiscovered Gate beneath Jerusalem's Golden Gate," *Biblical Archaeology Review* 9, 1 (1983), 24–37; the author's suggestion, that the remains belong to the complex of Solomon's Temple, seems to be too far going.

75 Ps. 118.22; Matt. 21.42.

76 2 Chron. 3.1.

77 See discussion in Eliav, *God's Mountain*, p. 184.

78 Avi-Yonah, *Madaba Mosaic Map*.

79 Tsafrir, "Holy City of Jerusalem"; more on artistic representations of Jerusalem and their symbolic significance, see in Bianca Kühnel, *From the Earthly to Heavenly Jerusalem: Representation of the Holy City in Christian Art of the First Millennium* (Freiburg, 1987).

80 For Eudocia, see Kenneth G. Holum, *Theodosian Empresses: Women and Imperial Dominion in Late Antiquity* (Berkeley, 1982), pp. 112–46.

81 The Syriac text was published in part and discussed by François Nau, "Résumé de monographies syriaques (Barsauma)," *Revue de l'Orient Chrétien* 19 (1914), esp. 118–24; idem, "Deux épisodes de l'histoire juive sous Théodose II (423 et 438)," *Revue des Études Juives* 83 (1927), 184–202.

82 Rubin, "Jerusalem in the Byzantine Period," pp. 227–28; Safrai, "Jerusalem and the Jews," pp. 249–51.

83 English translation after Michael Avi-Yonah, *The Jews of Palestine – A Political History from the Bar Kokhba War to the Arab Conquest* (Oxford, 1976), p. 224.

84 Leo A. Mayer, "Hebräische Inschriften im Haram zu Jerusalem," *Zeitschrift des Deutschen Palästina-Vereins* 53 (1930), 222–29. About the dating, see also Eliezer L. Sukenik, "The Jewish Inscriptions in the Temple Mount," *Zion* O.S. 4 (1934), 136–41 (Hebrew).

85 The main source for the events in Jerusalem and its surroundings is the composition by Antiochus Strategius, a monk of the monastery of Mar Saba in the Judean Desert. The original Greek text was lost and has survived in Arabic and Georgian translations. This source is full of anti-Jewish expressions, and the later Christian sources contain even more extreme accusations.

References for the various sources and description of the event are found, among others in Avi-Yonah, *The Jews of Palestine*, pp. 257–78, Zvi Baras, "The Persian Conquest and the Later Days of the Byzantine Regime," in *From the Destruction of the Second Temple to the Muslim Conquest*, ed. Zvi Baras et al. (Jerusalem, 1982), pp. 300–49 (Hebrew). For a general background and discussion of the Byzantine state at the time of war, see Walter E. Kaegi, *Heraclius, Emperor of Byzantium* (Cambridge, 2003).

86 See particularly Jozef T. Milik, "La topographie de Jérusalem vers la fin de l'époque byzantine," *Mélanges de L'Université Saint Joseph* 37 (1960–61), 127–89.

87 Safrai, "Jerusalem and the Jews," esp. pp. 251–59; Avi-Yonah, *The Jews of Palestine*, 266, emphasizes Jewish activities and their rule in Jerusalem: "Apparently Temple services were resumed for the third time (since the destruction by Titus)." Avi-Yonah bases his conclusion on the rather enigmatic and messianic Book of Zerubbabel, an eschatological composition which speaks of one Nehemiah, son of Hushiel, a messiah from the House of Joseph, who ruled Jerusalem and "made sacrifices." See Martha Himmelfarb, "Sefer Zerubbabel," in *Rabbinic Fantasies: Imaginative Narratives from Classical Hebrew Literature*, ed. David Stern and Mark. J. Mirsky (Philadelphia and New York, 1990), pp. 67–90. Most scholars believe this information should be read with much caution. See also an analysis of the events in Jerusalem and the relating sources in Mango, "The Temple Mount," pp. 3–7.

88 Avi-Yonah, *The Jews of Palestine*, p. 266.

89 Eilat Mazar and Orit Peleg suggested that this building was a synagogue of the early Islamic period; however, by its plan and masonry, it seems to have been no more than a regular dwelling house; see Eilat Mazar and Orit Peleg, "The 'House of the Menorot' in the Temple Mount Excavations: the Earliest Synagogue Discovered in Jerusalem," *Cathedra* 94 (1999), 55–74 (Hebrew); Eilat Mazar, *The Temple Mount Excavations in Jerusalem 1968–1978 Directed by Benjamin Mazar, Final Report* II: *The Byzantine and Early Islamic Period*, Qedem 43 (Jerusalem, 2003), pp. 163–86.

90 Ben-Dov, *In the Shadow of the Temple*, pp. 260–65.

91 Among the scholars who date the Golden Gate to the Byzantine period see, for example, Keppel A.S. Creswell, *Early Muslim Architecture*, new ed., vol. 1 (Oxford, 1969), pp. 463–65; see also the discussion by Mango, "The Temple Mount," pp. 6–16.

92 John Wilkinson, *Jerusalem Pilgrims before the Crusades*, new ed. (Warminster, 2002), p. 315.

93 See the literature cited in n. 74 above.

94 Among the numerous publications in favor of dating the Golden Gate to the Muslim period see, for example, Myriam Rosen-Ayalon, *The Early Islamic Monuments of al-Haram al-Sharif – An Iconographic Study*, Qedem 28 (Jerusalem, 1989), pp. 33–45. For the approach ramp from the Jericho road to this gate see Yoram Tsafrir, "The Massive Wall East of the Golden Gate, Jerusalem," *Israel Exploration Journal* 40 (1990), 280–86 and the literature cited there.

Andreas Kaplony, The Mosque of Jerusalem (*Masjid Bayt al-Maqdis*)

1 The following is an abridged and updated version of Andreas Kaplony, *The Haram of Jerusalem (324–1099)*, Freiburger Islamstudien 22 (Stuttgart, 2002), where almost all source texts and the full range of references are given. Within the framework of this paper, references are restricted to some few and, where possible, recent publications. For the general history of Jerusalem in this period, see Moshe Gil, *A History of Palestine, 634–1099*, trans. Ethel Broido (Cambridge, 1992; repr. 1997); *Bayt al-Maqdis*, ed. Julian Raby and Jeremy Johns, Oxford Studies in Islamic Art 9, 2 vols. (Oxford, 1992–99); *The History of Jerusalem: The Early Muslim Period 638–1099*, ed. Joshua Prawer and Haggai Ben-Shammai (Jerusalem, 1996); *Jerusalem: Its Sanctity and Centrality to Judaism, Christianity, and Islam*, ed. Lee I. Levine (New York, 1999). For a special issue, see Shimon Gat, "The Seljuks in Jerusalem," in *Towns and Material Culture in the Medieval Middle East*, ed. Yaacov Lev, The Medieval Mediterranean 39 (Leiden, 2002), pp. 1–39. For dating the Muslim conquest of Jerusalem to 635, see Heribert Busse, " 'Omar b. al-Hattab in Jerusalem," *Jerusalem Studies in Arabic and Islam* 5 (1984), 149–51; idem, " 'Omar's Image as the Conqueror of Jerusalem," ibid. 8 (1986), 149–68.

2 The Christian pilgrim guides have been collected in John Wilkinson, *Jerusalem Pilgrims before the Crusades* (Warminster, 1977); Herbert Donner, *Pilgerfahrt ins Heilige Land: die ältesten Berichte christlicher Palästinapilger (4.-7. Jahrhundert)* (Stuttgart, 1979).

3 The physical Haram has been described by Max van Berchem, *Matériaux pour un Corpus Inscriptionum Arabicarum*, vol. 2. b.3: *Jérusalem*, vol. 2–3, Mémoires publiés par les membres de l'Institut français d'archéologique orientale du Caire 44–45 (Cairo 1925–49); Keppel A.C. Creswell, *Early Muslim Architecture*, 2 vols. (Oxford, 1969; repr. New York, 1979); Th. A. Busink, *Der Tempel von Jerusalem von Salomo bis Herodes*, 2 vols. (Leiden, 1970–80); Michael H. Burgoyne, *Mamluk Jerusalem* (Jerusalem, 1987); Myriam Rosen-Ayalon, *The Early Islamic Monuments of al-Haram al-Sharif*, Qedem 28 (Jerusalem, 1989); Klaus Bieberstein and Hanswulf Bloedhorn, *Jerusalem: Grundzüge der Baugeschichte*, 3 vols., Beihefte zum Tübinger

Atlas des Vorderen Orients, Reihe B 100 (Wiesbaden, 1994) and the related maps of Klaus Bieberstein and Michael H. Burgoyne, *Jerusalem: Architectural Development*, Beihefte zum Tübinger Atlas des Vorderen Orients, Reihe B. IV.7 (Wiesbaden, 1992); Oleg Grabar, *The Shape of the Holy: Early Islamic Jerusalem*, (Princeton, 1996); *Ottoman Jerusalem*, ed. Sylvia Auld and Robert Hillenbrand, 2 vols. (London, 2000); Kaplony; *Haram*; Mahmoud Hawari, *Ayyubid Jerusalem (1187–1250)*, BAR International Series 1628 (London, 2007); Denys Pringle, *The Churches of the Crusader Kingdom of Jerusalem*, vol. 3: *The City of Jerusalem* (Cambridge, 2007).

4   Most inscriptions on the Haram are found in van Berchem, *Matériaux: Jérusalem* 2; Moshe Sharon, *Corpus Inscriptionum Arabicarum Palaestinae* (CIAP), vol. 5, Handbook of Oriental Studies: The Near and Middle East 30,5 (Leiden, etc., forthcoming).

5   For Muslim traditions on Jerusalem, see Ernst A. Gruber, *Verdienst und Rang: die Fada'il als literarisches und gesellschaftliches Problem im Islam*, Islamkundliche Untersuchungen 35 (Freiburg i. Br., 1975), pp. 49–82; Izhak Hasson, "The Muslim View of Jerusalem: the Qur'an and Hadith," in *History of Jerusalem*, ed. Prawer and Ben-Shammai, pp. 349–85; Haj-Yehia Kussai, *Die Heiligkeit Jerusalems im Spiegel der arabischen Überlieferung und Geschichtsschreibung*, (Göttingen, 1990); Amikam Elad, *Medieval Jerusalem and Islamic Worship*, Islamic History and Civilization: Studies and Texts 8 (Leiden, 1994); Ofer Livne-Kafri, "The Muslim Traditions in Praise of Jerusalem (Fada'il al-Quds)," *Annali dell'Istituto Orientale di Napoli* 58 (1998), 165–92 and the many articles of Heribert Busse mentioned below.

6   For Jerusalem in Arabic-Islamic geography, see Guy Le Strange, *Palestine under the Moslems* (Boston and New York 1890; repr. Beirut, 1965).

7   For the first Jewish guides to Jerusalem, see Joseph Braslavi et al., "Der älteste jüdische Jerusalem-Führer," in *Jerusalem: Texte—Bilder—Steine ... zum 100. Geburtstag von Hildi + Othmar Keel-Leu*, ed. Max Küchler and Christoph Uehlinger, Novum Testamentum et Orbis Antiquus 6 (Göttingen, 1987), pp. 37–81; Gil, *History of Palestine*, pp. 621–31.

8   For the first Muslim pilgrim guide to Jerusalem, see Elad, *Medieval Jerusalem*, pp. 68–77.

9   For Jerusalem in the Geniza documents, see Gil, *History of Palestine*; Gat, "Seljuks."

10   For the Haram prior to the Umayyad rebuilding, see Creswell, *Early Muslim Architecture* 1:29–35; Busink, *Tempel*, pp. 3–5, 907–14, 1525–28; Bellarmino Bagatti, *Recherches sur le site du Temple de Jérusalem (Ier–VIIe siècle)*, Publications du Studium Biblicum Franciscanum. Collectio minor 22 (Jerusalem, 1979); Heribert Busse, "The Church of the Holy Sepulchre, the Church of the Agony, and the Temple: The Reflection of a Christian Belief in Islamic Tradition," *Jerusalem Studies in Arabic and Islam* 9 (1987), 279–89; idem, "Tempel, Grabeskirche und Haram ash-sharif: Drei Heiligtümer und ihre gegenseitigen Beziehungen in Legende und Wirklichkeit," in *Jerusalemer Heiligtumstraditionen in altkirchlicher und frühislamischer Zeit*, ed. Heribert Busse and Georg Kretschmar, Abhandlungen des Deutschen Palästina-Vereins 8 (Wiesbaden, 1987), pp. 9–15; Gil, *History of Palestine*, pp. 65–74; Cyril Mango, "The Temple Mount AD 614–638," in *Bayt al-Maqdis*, ed. Raby and Johns, 1:1–16; Bernard Flusin, "L'esplanade du Temple à l'arrivée des Arabes, d'après deux récits byzantins," in ibid., 1:17–31; Heribert Busse, "The Destruction of the Temple and its Reconstruction in the Light of Muslim Exegesis of Sura 17:2–8," *Jerusalem Studies in Arabic and Islam* 20 (1996), 1–17, 293.

11   François Nau, "Deux épisodes de l'histoire juive sous Théodose II (423 et 438) d'après la Vie de Barsauma le Syrien," *Revue des Études Juives* 83 (1927), 184–206, esp. 194–200.

12   For the Umayyad rebuilding, see van Berchem, *Matériaux: Jérusalem* 2:232–35; Busse, "Tempel, Grabeskirche"; Rosen-Ayalon, *Early Islamic Monuments*; Heribert Busse, "Zur Geschichte und Deutung der frühislamischen Harambauten in Jerusalem," *Zeitschrift des Deutschen Palästina-Vereins* 107 (1991), 144–54; Gil, *History of Palestine*, pp. 92–104; Flusin, "L'esplanade"; Elad, *Medieval Jerusalem*; Heribert Busse, "The Temple of Jerusalem and Its Restitution by 'Abd al-Malik b. Marwan," *Jewish Art* 23–24 (1997–98), 23–33.

13   For the Muslim rebuilding of the Temple, see Nasser O. Rabbat, "The Meaning of the Umayyad Dome of the Rock," *Muqarnas* 6 (1989), 12–21; Gustav Kühnel, "Aachen, Byzanz und die frühislamische Architektur im Heiligen Land," in *Studien zur byzantinischen Kunstgeschichte: Festschrift für Horst Hallensleben*, ed. Birgitt Borkopp (Amsterdam, 1995), pp. 39–57 and pl. 1–24; Busse, "Destruction of the Temple"; idem, "Temple of Jerusalem."

14   See H.R. Allen, "Observations on the Original Appearance of the Dome of the Rock," in *Bayt al-Maqdis: Jerusalem and Early Islam*, ed. Jeremy Johns, Oxford Studies in Islamic Art 9.2 (London, 1999), pp. 197-213.

15   For the equation of the Furthest Mosque (al-Masjid al-Aqsa), the goal of Muhammad's Night Journey, with the Temple and the Haram, etc., see Kussai, *Heiligkeit Jerusalems*, pp. 57–84; Heribert Busse, "Jerusalem in the Story of Muhammad's Night Journey and Ascension," *Jerusalem Studies in Arabic and Islam* 14 (1991), 1–40; Angelika Neuwirth, "The Spiritual Meaning of Jerusalem in Islam," in *City of the Great King*, ed. Nitza Rosovsky (Cambridge, MA and London, 1996), pp. 93–116; 483–95; Josef van Ess, *Theologie und Gesellschaft im 2. und 3. Jahrhundert Hidschra*, vol. 4 (Berlin and New York 1997), pp. 387–91; Claude Gilliot, "Coran 17, Isra' dans la recherche occidentale," in *Le voyage initiatique en terre d'Islam*, ed. Mohammad 'Ali Amir-Moezzi, Bibliothèque de l'Ecole pratique des hautes

études, Sciences Religieuses 103 (Leuwen and Paris, 1996), pp. 1–26.

16   For 'Umar in Jerusalem, see Busse, " 'Omar b. al-Hattab in Jerusalem"; idem, "Church of the Holy Sepulchre"; idem, " 'Omar's Image"; Albrecht Noth, "Abgrenzungsprobleme zwischen Muslimen und Nicht-Muslimen," *Jerusalem Studies in Arabic and Islam* 9 (1987), 290–315; Gil, *History of Palestine*, pp. 52–56; 65–74; Heribert Busse, "Die 'Umar-Moschee im östlichen Atrium der Grabeskirche," *Zeitschrift des Deutschen Palästina-Vereins* 109 (1993), 73–82; Robert Schick, *The Christian Communities of Palestine from Byzantine to Islamic Rule*, Studies in Late Antiquity and Early Islam 2 (Princeton, 1995), pp. 159–70.

17   For Solomon in Islam, see Priscilla P. Soucek, "The Temple of Solomon in Islamic Legend and Art," in *The Temple of Solomon*, ed. Joseph Gutmann, Religion and the Arts 3 (Missoula, MO, 1973), pp. 73–123 and pl. 25–33; idem, "Solomon's Throne/Solomon's Bath: Model or Metaphor?" *Ars Orientalis* 23 (1993), 109–34; Heribert Busse, "Persepolis als Thron Gamsids oder Moschee Salomos," in *Sokhanvarih: 55 Papers in Memory of Parviz Natil Khanlari*, ed. Hans Robert Roemer and Iraj Afshar, Tus Publications 436 (Teheran, 1997), pp. 13– 16; J. Walker and Paul Fenton, "Sulayman b. Dawud," *Encyclopaedia of Islam*, 2nd ed., 9 (1997), cols. 822b–24a; Livne-Kafri, "Muslim Traditions": 173–76..

18   For God's Presence (al-Sakina) in Islam, see Ignaz Goldziher, "Über den Ausdruck 'Sakina'," in idem, *Abhandlungen zur arabischen Philologie* 1 (Leiden, 1896), pp. 177–212; 217; Toufiq Fahd, "Sakina," *Encyclopaedia of Islam*, 2nd ed., 8 (1995), cols. 888b–89b.

19   Ibn al-Murajja, *Fada'il Bayt al-Maqdis*, ed. Ofer Livne-Kafri [Shfar'am, 1995], p. 51, no. 37.

20   For God's Throne in Islam, see Clément Huart and Joseph Sadan, "Kursi," *Encyclopaedia of Islam*, 2nd ed., 5 (1986), cols. 509a–b; Gösta Vitestam, "'Arsh and Kursi: An Essay on the Throne Traditions in Islam," in *Living Waters: Scandinavian Orientalistic Studies Presented to Professor Dr. Frede Løkkegard ...*, ed. Egon Keck et al. (Copenhagen, 1990), pp. 369–78; Josef van Ess, "Abd al-Malik and the Dome of the Rock," in *Bayt al-Maqdis*, ed. Raby and Johns, 1:89–103.

21   For the rivers of Paradise originating beneath the Rock, in Islam, see Rosen-Ayalon, *Early Islamic Monuments*, pp. 53–62.

22   For God rising from the Rock to heaven, see van Berchem, *Matériaux: Jérusalem* 2:49–53; van Ess, "'Abd al-Malik."

23   For Abraham in Jerusalem, in Islam, see Suliman Bashear, "Abraham's Sacrifice of His Son and Related Issues," *Islam* 67 (1990), 265–67; Reuven Firestone, *Journeys in Holy Lands: The Evolution of Abraham-Ishmael Legends in Islamic Exegesis* (Albany, 1990), pp. 105–59.

24   Ibn al- Murajja, *Fada'il Bayt al-Maqdis*, p. 114, no. 132.

25   For the Haram servants and the Umayyad Temple service, see Elad, *Medieval Jerusalem*, pp. 51–61; Busse, "Temple of Jerusalem"; Julian Raby, "In Vitro Veritas: Glass Pilgrim Vessels from 7th-Century Jerusalem," in *Bayt al-Maqdis*, ed. Raby and Johns, 2:167–79.

26   al-Wasiti, *Fada'il Bayt al-Muqaddas*, ed. Izhak Hasson [Jerusalem, 1979], pp. 82–83, no. 136.

27   For the Church of the Holy Sepulchre serving as a model for the Umayyad Haram, see Creswell, *Early Muslim Architecture*, 1:101–09; Busse, "Tempel, Grabeskirche," pp. 2–6, 14–24; idem, "Temple of Jerusalem."

28   For the transfer of Temple-related traditions from the Church of the Holy Sepulchre to the Haram, see Heribert Busse, "Jerusalem and Mecca, the Temple and the Kaaba," in *The Holy Land in History and Thought*, ed. Moshe Sharon, Publications of the Eric Samson Chair in Jewish Civilization 1 (Leiden, 1988), pp. 236–46; idem, "Geschichte und Bedeutung der Kaaba im Licht der Bibel," in *Zion Ort der Begegnung: Festschrift für Laurentius Klein*, ed. Ferdinand Hahn et al., Bonner Biblische Beiträge 90 (Bodenheim, 1993), pp. 169–85; idem, "Temple of Jerusalem." For the transfer of such traditions further to the Ka'ba, see Busse, "Jerusalem in the Story"; idem, "Jerusalem and Mecca."

29   For the Muslim Haram identified by Christians as the Temple of Solomon, see van Berchem, *Matériaux: Jérusalem*, 2:373–76; Heribert Busse, "Vom Felsendom zum Templum Domini," in *Das Heilige Land im Mittelalter*, ed. Wolfdietrich Fischer and Jürgen Schneider, Schriften des Zentralinstituts... 22 (Neustadt a. d. Aisch, 1982), pp. 19–32; Sylvia Schein, "Between Mount Moriah and the Holy Sepulchre: The Changing Traditions of the Temple Mount in the Central Middle Ages," *Traditio* 40 (1984), 175–95; Kühnel, "Aachen, Byzanz," pp. 51–57; Daniel H. Weiss, "Hec Est Domus Domini Firmiter Edificata: The Image of the Temple in Crusader Art," *Jewish Art* 23–24 (1997–98), 210–17.

30   Hrabanus Maurus, *Homilia* 1.70, ed. Jacobus Pamelius and Georgius Colvenerius, *Patrologia Latina* 110 (Paris, 1864), cols. 131–34.

31   For the Foundation Rock, see Wilhelm H. Roscher, *Neue Omphalosstudien*, Abhandlungen der Philologisch-historischen Klasse der Königl. Sächsischen Gesellschaft der Wissenschaften 31,1 (Leipzig, 1915), pp. 15–18, 73–75; idem, *Der Omphalosgedanke bei verschiedenen Völkern, besonders den semitischen*, Berichte über die Verhandlungen der Sächsischen Gesellschaft der Wissenschaften zu Leipzig. Philologisch-historische Klasse 70,2 (Leipzig, 1918), pp. 14–17; Joachim Jeremias, *Golgotha*, Angelos Beihefte 1 (Leipzig, 1926); Busink, *Tempel*, pp. 1174–78; Kretschmar, "Festkalender und Memorialstätten," part 2, in *Jerusalemer Heiligtumstraditionen*, ed. Busse and Kretschmar, pp. 29–115, esp. 81–111.

32 For the East Gate in Judaism, see Gil, *History of Palestine*, pp. 645–47.

33 For God's Presence on the Mount of Olives, see Moshe Gil, "Aliya and Pilgrimage in the Early Arab Period (634-1099)," *The Jerusalem Cathedra* 3 (1983), 163–73; idem, *History of Palestine*, pp. 626–31; Ora Limor, "The Place of the End of Days: Eschatological Geography in Jerusalem," *Jewish Art* 23–24 (1997–98), 16–19.

34 For Jewish prayer in Jerusalem, see Gil, *History of Palestine*, pp. 148–49, 608, 621–31, 700–1; David Golinkin, "Jerusalem in Jewish Law and Custom," in *Jerusalem*, ed. Levine, pp. 408–23.

35 For the rebuilding of Jerusalem after the earthquakes of 1015 and 1030, see van Berchem, *Matériaux: Jérusalem*, 2:15–18, 261–88, 381–92; Creswell, *Early Muslim Architecture* 194–96, 375–77; Gil, *History of Palestine*, pp. 397–400, 477–80; G.J. Wightman, *The Walls of Jerusalem from the Canaanites to the Mamluks*, Mediterranean Archaeology Supplement 4 (Sydney, 1993), pp. 237–45.

36 "Letter of ha-gaʾon Ben Meʾir," in *Sefer ha-yishuv*, vol. 2, ed. Simha Assaf and Leo A. Mayer (Jerusalem, 1944), p. 21, no. 24 (Hebrew).

37 Ibn Hawqal, *Liber Imaginis Terrae*, ed. Johannes H. Kramers, Bibliotheca Geographorum Arabicorum 2, 2nd ed. (Leiden, 1938–39), p. 171.

38 Ibn al-Murajja, *Fadaʾil Bayt al-Maqdis*, p. 53, no. 39.

39 For the importance of prayer said in Jerusalem in Islam, see Gruber, *Verdienst und Rang*, pp. 66–70; Meir J. Kister, "'You Shall Only Set Out for Three Mosques': A Study of an Early Tradition," in idem, *Studies in Jahiliyya and Early Islam*, Collected Studies 28 (London, 1988), paper 13, pp. 184–90; Niels Henrik Olesen, *Culte des saints et pèlerinages chez Ibn Taymiyya* (661/1263–728/1328), Bibliothèque d'Etudes Islamiques 16 (Paris, 1991), pp. 72–79.

40 For the tradition of the three mosques to visit, see Kister, "You Shall Only Set Out"; Olesen, *Culte des saints*, pp. 72–79; Ofer Livne-Kafri, "The Early Shiʿa and Jerusalem," *Arabica* 48 (2001), 112–20.

41 For the proximity of the Haram to Paradise, see Rosen-Ayalon, *Early Islamic Monuments*, pp. 46–69.

42 For eschatological traditions on Jerusalem in Islam, see Khalil ʿAthamina, "Jerusalem in Eschatological Literature: the Case of Islamic Hadith," *Annali dell'Istituto Orientale di Napoli* 60–61 (2002), 115–26.

43 Ibn al-Murajja, *Fadaʾil Bayt al-Maqdis*, p. 53, no. 39.

44 Ibn al-Murajja, *Fadaʾil Bayt al-Maqdis*, p. 73, no. 62.

45 For the much discussed so-called Cave inside the West Wall, see Gil, *History of Palestine*, pp. 607–9, 648–50.

46 For Jewish pious foundations for the benefit of the Cave, see Gil, *History of Palestine*, pp. 601–9; Moshe Gil, "Dhimmi Donations and Foundations for Jerusalem (638-1099)," *Journal of the Economic and Social History of the Orient* 27 (1984), 156–74; Avraham Grossman, "The Yeshiva of Eretz Israel, Its Literary Output and Relationship with the Diaspora," in *History of Jerusalem*, ed. Prawer and Ben-Shammai, pp. 225–69.

47 Similarly, on the coexistence of incongruent conceptions in Hellenistic-Roman Jerusalem, see Lee I. Levine, "Second Temple Jerusalem: A Jewish City in the Greco-Roman Orbit," in *Jerusalem*, ed. Levine, pp. 65–66; Albert I. Baumgarten, "The Role of Jerusalem and the Temple in 'End of Days' Speculation in the Second Temple Period," in ibid., pp. 79, 86 n. 8.

Benjamin Z. Kedar and Denys Pringle, The Lord's Temple

1 This account is based on the chronicle of an anonymous Crusader, an eye-witness of the events. See *Gesta Francorum et Aliorum Hierosolimitanorum*, ed. and trans. Rosalind Hill (Oxford, 1962), pp. 90–92.

2 For a translation of Ibn al-ʿArabi's testimony see Joseph Drory, "Some Observations During a Visit to Palestine by Ibn al-ʿArabi of Seville in 1092–1095," *Crusades* 3 (2004), 120. For a detailed discussion see Benjamin Z. Kedar, "The Jerusalem Massacre of July 1099 in the Western Historiography of the Crusades," *Crusades* 3 (2004), 15–75.

3 John of Würzburg, in *Peregrinationes tres: Saewulf, Iohannes Wirziburgensis, Theodericus*, ed. R.B.C. Huygens, Corpus Christianorum: Continuatio Mediaeualis 139 (Turnhout, 1994), p. 94.

4 Ibid., p. 92. John follows Matt. 24.35 in confusing the priest Zechariah of 2 Chron. 24.20–21 with the prophet of the same name.

5 *Letters and Essays of Moses Maimonides*, ed. Isaac Shailat, 2 vols. (Maʿaleh Adumim, 1987–88), 1:225; for an English translation and discussion see Joshua Prawer, *The History of the Jews in the Latin Kingdom of Jerusalem* (Oxford, 1988), p. 142 (but the date is 14 October, not 16).

6 On the relationship between the domes see Al-Muqaddasi, *Ahsan al-Taqāsīm fī Maʿrifat al-Aqālīm* [The best divisions for knowledge of the regions], trans. B. Collins (Reading, 2001), p. 146; for the Frankish period see Nurith Kenaan-Kedar, "Symbolic Meaning in Crusader Architecture: The Twelfth-Century Dome of the Holy Sepulcher Church in Jerusalem," *Cahiers archéologiques* 34 (186), 109–17.

7 Achard's poem has been edited by Paul Lehmann, "Die mittellateinischen Dichtungen der Priorn des Tempels von Jerusalem Acardus und Gaufridus," in *Corona Quernea: Festgabe Karl Strecker*, MGH Schriften 6 (Leipzig, 1941), pp. 307–30.

8 Ibid., pp. 308, 329–30. Albert of Aachen likewise writes that the Temple was rebuilt by Christians: Albert of Aachen, *Historia Ierosolimitana* 6.24, ed. Susan B. Edginton (Oxford, 2007), pp. 432–34.

9 Saewulf in *Peregrinationes tres* (above, n. 3), p. 67; John of Würzburg, ibid., p. 90; see Heribert Busse, "Vom Felsendom zum Templum Domini," in *Das Heilige Land im Mittelalter: Begegnungsraum zwischen Orient und Okzident*, ed. Wolfdietrich Fischer and Jürgen Schneider (Neustadt a.d. Aisch, 1982), pp. 27–28, 30.

10 See Sylvia Schein, "Between Mount Moriah and the Holy Sepulchre: The Changing Traditions of the Temple Mount in the Central Middle Ages," *Traditio* 40 (1984), 188.

11 The inscriptions are quoted, with some variations, in the itineraries of John of Würzburg and Theoderich, in *Peregrinationes tres* (above, n. 3), pp. 94–95, 160–61; for a discussion of their exact locations see Jaroslav Folda, *The Art of the Crusaders in the Holy Land, 1098–1187* (Cambridge, 1995), p. 252.

12 Daniel the Abbot, in *Jerusalem Pilgrimage, 1095–1197*, trans. John Wilkinson et al. (London, 1988), p. 132.

13 Petrus C. Boeren, *Rorgo Fretellus de Nazareth et sa description de la Terre Sainte: Histoire et édition du texte* (Amsterdam, 1980), p. 32; *Descriptio locorum*, in Sabino de Sandoli, *Itinera hierosolymitana crucesignatorum*, 2 (Jerusalem, 1980), pp. 100–102.

14 Boeren, *Rorgo Fretellus*, p. 58.

15 John of Würzburg, in *Peregrinationes tres* (above, n. 3), p. 88.

16 Theoderich, ibid., p. 163.

17 William of Tyre, *Chronicon*, 1.2, 8.3, ed. R.B.C. Huygens, Corpus Christianorum, Continuation Mediaeualis 63 (Turnhout, 1986), pp. 106–7, 386. Benjamin of Tudela, the Spanish Jew who visited Jerusalem about the same time, wrote likewise that it was ʿUmar b. Khattab who built there "a large and very beautiful dome," *The Itinerary of Benjamin of Tudela*, ed. and trans. Marcus N. Adler (London, 1907), p 24 (text), p. 22 (translation).

18 See the convincing argumentation of Hannes Möhring, "Zu der Geschichte der orientalischen Herrscher des Wilhelm von Tyrus: Die Frage der Quellenabhängigkeiten," *Mittellateinisches Jahrbuch* 19 (1984), 173–75.

19 William of Tyre, *Chronicon*, 17.20, pp. 787–88.

20 See Samer Akkach, "The Poetics of Concealment: al-Nabulusi's Encounter with the Dome of the Rock," *Muqarnas: An Annual on the Visual Culture of the Islamic World* 22 (2005), 110–27, with the quotation appearing on p. 114; also, Oleg Grabar, *The Dome of the Rock* (Cambridge, MA, 2006), p. 201.

21 Fulcher of Chartres, *Historia Hierosolimitana (1095–1127)*, 1.29–30, ed. Heinrich Hagenmeyer (Heidelberg, 1913), pp. 305, 310.

22 Fulcher of Chartres, 2.8, pp. 395–96; see also pp. 831–37.

23 Charles Kohler, "Un rituel et un bréviaire du Saint-Sépulcre de Jérusalem (XIIe–XIIIe siècle)," *Revue de l'Orient latin* 8 (1900–01), 409–10, 425.

24 *Chronique d'Ernoul et de Bernard le Trésorier*, ed. Louis de Mas Latrie (Paris, 1871), p. 118; *L'Estoire de Eracles Empereur*, 23.5 in *Recueil des Historiens des Croisades: Historiens Occidentaux*, 2:8; *La Continuation de Guillaume de Tyr (1184–1197)*, 5, ed. M. Ruth Morgan (Paris, 1982), p. 21; John of Ibelin, *Le Livre des Assises*, 220, ed. Peter W. Edbury (Leiden, 2003), pp. 575–76. For a full description of the ceremony see Prawer, *Latin Kingdom* (above, n. 5), pp. 97–101; Schein, "Between Mount Moriah" (above, n. 10), pp. 184–86.

25 See Gustave Schlumberger, Ferdinand Chalandon, and Adrien Blanchet, *Sigillographie de l'Orient latin* (Paris, 1943), pp. 2, 4, 7, 9, 10, 14, Plates 1.1–3, 16.1–5, 7.

26 William of Tyre, *Chronicon* (above, n. 17), 1.15, p. 132. On the role of the Lord's Temple in Frankish Jerusalem see Benjamin Z. Kedar, "Intellectual Activities in a Holy City: Jerusalem in the Twelfth Century," in *Sacred Space: Shrine, City, Land: Proceedings of the International Conference in Memory of Joshua Prawer*, ed. B.Z. Kedar and R.J. Zwi Werblowsky (London and Jerusalem, 1988), pp. 128-29, repr. in idem, *Franks, Muslims and Oriental Christians in the Latin Levant: Studies in Frontier Acculturation* (Aldershot, 2006), Study IX; and more recently Sylvia Schein, *Gateway to the Heavenly City: Crusader Jerusalem and the Catholic West (1099-1187)* (Aldershot, 2005), pp. 98–107.

27 For a detailed discussion of the various buildings under Frankish rule see Denys Pringle, *The Churches of the Crusader Kingdom of Jerusalem: A Corpus*, 3: *The City of Jerusalem* (Cambridge, 2007), pp. 103–9 (no. 293), 182–85 (no. 319), 310–14 (no. 339), 397–434 (nos. 357–59).

28 John of Würzburg, in *Peregrinationes tres* (above, n. 3), pp. 90–91.

29 Ibid., pp. 90–91, 93.

30 Theodericus, ibid., p. 161.

31 See Hannes Möhring, "Die Kreuzfahrer, ihre muslimischen Untertanen und die Heiligen Stätten des Islam," in *Toleranz im Mittelalter*, ed. Alexander Patschovsky and H. Zimmermann (Sigmaringen, 1998), pp. 131–33.

32 John of Würzburg in *Peregrinationes tres*, p. 92.

33 'Ali al-Harawi, *Guide des lieux de pèlerinage*, trans. Janine Sourdel-Thomine (Damascus, 1957), pp. 64–66.

34 *The Itinerary of Benjamin of Tudela* (above, n. 17), pp. 23–24 (text), p. 22 (a less literal English translation).

35 Henri de Curzon, *La Règle du Temple* (Paris, 1886), pp. 45–46.

36 'Imad al-Din in *Storici arabi delle crociate*, ed. and trans. Francesco Gabrieli (Turin, 1987), p. 161.

37 Félix-Marie Abel, "Lettre d'un templier trouvée récemment à Jérusalem," *Revue biblique* 35 (1926), 288–95.

38 Kohler, "Un rituel," 413.

39 John of Würzburg in *Peregrinationes tres* (above, n. 3), pp. 96, 124.

40 *The Itinerary of Benjamin of Tudela* (above, n. 17), p. 24.

41 *Selected Poems of Judah Halevi*, ed. Heinrich Brody, trans. Nina Salaman (Philadelphia, 1924), p. 2.

42 Ibid., p. 15.

43 See Emmanuel Sivan, "Le caractère sacré de Jérusalem dans l'Islam aux XIIe–XIIIe siècles," *Studia Islamica* 27 (1967), 149–82; Carole Hillenbrand, *The Crusades: Islamic Perspectives* (Edinburgh, 1999), pp. 150–65.

44 Benjamin Z. Kedar, "Ein Hilferuf aus Jerusalem vom September 1187," *Deutsches Archiv* 38 (1982), 112–22; Nikolas Jaspert, "Zwei unbekannte Hilfsersuchen des Patriarchen Eraclius vor dem Fall Jerusalems (1187)," *Deutsches Archiv* 60 (2004), 483–516.

45 'Imad al-Din in *Storici arabi delle crociate* (above, n. 36), pp. 154–55.

Michael H. Burgoyne, The Furthest Mosque (*al-Masjid al-Aqsa*) under Ayyubid Rule

1 For detailed discussion of Jerusalem in the Ayyubid period, see *Ayyubid Jerusalem*, ed. Robert Hillenbrand and Sylvia Auld (London, 2009).

2 Except for limited trial excavations made by the British archaeologist Robert W. Hamilton, Director of Antiquities in Palestine, during repairs to the Aqsa Mosque between 1938 and 1942, there have been no scientific excavations within the precincts of the Noble Sanctuary.

3 Numbers based on those in Michael H. Burgoyne, *A Chronological Index to the Muslim Monuments of Jerusalem* (Jerusalem: The British School of Archaeology, 1976).

4 I should like to express my gratitude to Isam Awwad, formerly Chief Architect of the Aqsa Mosque and Dome of the Rock Restoration Committee, and Dr Yusuf Natsheh, Director of the Department of Islamic Archaeology, for access to structures under the upper terrace.

5 I am indebted to B. Z. Kedar for this translation of Alharizi's Hebrew text.

Donald P. Little, The Noble Sanctuary under Mamluk Rule–History

1 Max Van Berchem, *Matériaux pour un Corpus Inscriptionum Arabicarum, deuxième partie: Syrie du sud*, II: *Jérusalem "Haram"* (Cairo, 1925–27), p. 421.

2 Michael Hamilton Burgoyne with Donald S. Richards, *Mamluk Jerusalem: An Architectural Study* ([London], 1987), p. 77.

3 Ibid., pp. 77–78.

4 *The Travels of Ibn Battūta*, transl. Hamilton A. R. Gibb, vol. 1 (Cambridge, 1958), pp. 78–79.

5 Ibid., p. 79.

6 Quoted by Hilda F. M. Prescott, *Jerusalem Journey: Pilgrimage to the Holy Land in the Fifteenth Century* (London, 1954), p. 177.

7 *The Pilgrimage of Arnold von Harff: Knight*, transl. Malcolm Letts (London, 1946), pp. 209–10.

8 Ibid., p. 210.

9 Ibid., p. 208.

10 Quoted in *Jewish Travellers: A Treasury of Travelogues from 9 Centuries*, ed. Elkan N. Adler, 2nd ed. (New York, 1966), p. 239.

11 Ibid., p. 152.

12 *Al-Uns al-Jalil bi-Ta'rikh al-Quds wal-Khalil*, 2 vols. (Amman, 1973).

13 See Donald P. Little, "Mujīr al-Dīn al-'Ulaymī's Vision of Jerusalem in the Ninth/Fifteenth Century," *Journal of the American Oriental Society*, 115, 2 (1995), 23–47.

14 Mujir al-Din, *Al-Uns*, I, pp. 1–408; II, pp. 1–10.

15 Ibid., II, pp. 11–84.

16 Ibid., II, pp. 85–281.

17 Ibid., II, p. 85.

18 Ibid., II, pp. 269–82.

19 Ibid., II, p. 283. See Donald P. Little, "Relations between Jerusalem and Egypt during the Mamluk Period according to Literary and Documentary Sources," in *Egypt and Palestine: A*

Millennium of Association (868-1948), ed. Amnon Cohen and Gabriel Baer (New York and Jerusalem, 1984), p. 75

20 See Donald Richards, in Burgoyne, *Mamluk Jerusalem*, p. 60.

21 See Donald P. Little, *A Catalogue of the Islamic Documents from al-Haram ash-Sharif in Jerusalem* (Wiesbaden, 1984), p. 10.

22 Mujir al-Din, *Al-Uns*, II, pp. 282–383. See Donald P. Little, "The Governance of Jerusalem under Qāytbāy," in *The Mamluks in Egyptian and Syrian Politics and Society*, ed. Amalia Levanoni and Michael Winter (Leiden, 2004), pp. 143–61.

23 See Donald P. Little, "Communal Strife in Late Mamlūk Jerusalem," *Islamic Law and Society*, 6, 1 (1999), 69–96.

24 See Emmanuel Sivan, "Le caractère sacré de Jérusalem dans l'Islam aux XII–XIII siècles," *Studia Islamica*, 27 (1967), 181.

25 Muhammad Umar Memon, *Ibn Taymīya's Struggle against Popular Religion* (The Hague, 1976), vol. 1, pp. 74–75.

26 See Charles D. Matthews, "A Muslim Iconoclast (Ibn Taymiyyeh) on the 'Merits' of Jerusalem and Palestine," *Journal of the American Oriental Society*, 56 (1936), 1–21.

27 See Little, *Catalogue*.

Michael Hamilton Burgoyne, The Noble Sanctuary under Mamluk Rule–Architecture

1 For a detailed discussion, see Michael Burgoyne, *Mamluk Jerusalem* (Buckhurst Hill, 1987).

2 Numbers based on those in Michael H. Burgoyne, *A Chronological Index to the Muslim Monuments of Jerusalem* (Jerusalem: The British School of Archaeology, 1976).

Amnon Cohen, *Haram-i Şerif* under Ottoman Rule

1 Amnon Cohen and Bernard Lewis, *Population and Revenue in the Towns of Palestine in the Sixteenth Century* (Princeton, 1978), pp. 19–28, 92–94.

2 Uriel Heyd, *Ottoman Documents on Palestine, 1552–1615* (Oxford, 1960), pp.191–92; Amnon Cohen, "L'oeuvre de Soliman le Magnifique à Jérusalem: les murailles, la citadelle et leurs moyens de défense," in *Soliman le Magnifique et son temps*, ed. Gilles Veinstein (Paris, 1992), pp. 354–55.

3 James W. Redhouse, *A Turkish and English Lexicon* (Constantinople, 1921; new impression), p. 2096; Adrien C. Barbier de Meynard, *Dictionnaire Turc-Français*, 2 vols. (Paris, 1881–86; repr. Amsterdam, 1971), 2:826–87.

4 *Sijill* of Jerusalem, vol. 5, p. 386; vol. 6, p. 68.

5 *Sijill* of Jerusalem, vol. 6, p. 713.

6 *Sijill* of Jerusalem, vol. 10, p. 16. A shorter version (*al-nazir 'ala al-amwal al-sultaniyya wa-ghayriha*) appears in vol. 7, p. 260.

7 *Sijill* of Jerusalem, vol. 7, pp. 259, 260, 279; vol. 10, p. 546. See also Amnon Cohen, "The Expulsion of the Franciscans from Mount Zion: Old Documents and New Interpretation," *Turcica*, 18 (1986), 147–57.

8 The term "Solomon's Pools" predated the arrival of the Ottomans in Palestine, and was always related to the biblical King Solomon (Arabic: Sulayman). It should not be confounded with Sulayman the Magnificent, the Ottoman sultan, in whose name a *waqfiya* was endowed in 1542 for the maintenance of this aqueduct; see Muhammad As'ad al-Imam al-Husayni, *The Pure Spring in [Matters of] Waqf Endowment and Its Administration* (Jerusalem, 1982), pp. 109-16 (Arabic).

9 For a more detailed breakdown of the figures of this scheme, as well as discussion of other aspects related to it, see my "The Walls of Jerusalem," in *The Islamic World, from Classical to Modern Times: Essays in Honor of Bernard Lewis*, ed. Clifford E. Bosworth et al. (Princeton, NJ, 1989), pp. 467–77.

10 Max Van Berchem, *Matériaux pour un Corpus Inscriptionum Arabicarum*, part 2, vol. 1 (Le Caire, 1922), pp. 443–44.

11 *Sijill* of Jerusalem, vol. 14, p. 144.

12 *Sijill* of Jerusalem, vol. 33, p. 182; vol. 17, p. 584.

13 For statistical details, see Cohen and Lewis, *Population and Revenue*, pp. 92–94.

14 Amnon Cohen, "Local Trade, International Trade and Government Involvement in Jerusalem during the Early Ottoman Period," *Asian and African Studies* 12, 1 (March 1978), 6–12.

15 Robert Mantran and Jean Sauvaget, *Règlements fiscaux ottomans, les provinces Syriennes* (Beyrouth, 1951), p. 38.

16 Amnon Cohen, *Economic Life in Ottoman Jerusalem* (Cambridge, 1989), pp. 61–97.

17 Amy Singer, *Constructing Ottoman Beneficence: An Imperial Soup Kitchen in Jerusalem* (Albany, 2002); Heyd, *Ottoman Documents*, pp. 139, 143, 144, 147; Stephan H. Stephan, "An

Endowment Deed of Khasseki Sultan, Dated the 24th May 1552," *Quarterly of the Department of Antiquities in Palestine*, 10 (1944), 170–94.

18 Amnon Cohen, *The Guilds of Ottoman Jerusalem* (Leiden, 2001), pp. 63–64. See also idem, "Local Trade," p. 6 and n. 4.

19 For an architectural survey of all of these, as well as a map showing their location around the Temple Mount, see Myriam Rosen-Ayalon, "On Suleiman's Sabils in Jerusalem," in *The Islamic World*, ed. Bosworth et al., pp. 589–607.

20 Aptullah Kuran, "Suleyman the Magnificent's Architectural Patronage," in *Soliman le Magnifique*, ed. Veinstein, pp. 218–19.

21 Beatrice St Laurent, "The Dome of the Rock: Restorations and Significance, 1540–1918," in *Ottoman Jerusalem: the Living City 1517–1917*, ed. Sylvia Auld and Robert Hillenbrand (London, 2000), Part One, pp. 417–19.

22 Aref el-Aref, *A History of the Dome of the Rock and al-Aqsa Mosque* (Jerusalem, 1958), pp. 90–91, 168 (Arabic); *Sijill* of Jerusalem, vol. 44, p. 577, reporting the arrival in Jerusalem of a large consignment of copperplates and tiles sent in 1565 from Istanbul for the doors of the Dome of the Rock.

23 Amnon Cohen, *Jewish Life under Islam* (Cambridge, MA, 1984), pp. 73, 128. The nineteenth century witnessed a gradual relaxation of the prohibition of entry by non-Muslims, and many references by European travellers indicate that it was almost systematically disregarded by the local authorities during the second half of that century. For many details see Yehoshua Ben-Arieh, *Jerusalem in the Nineteenth Century: The Old City* (Jerusalem and New York, 1984), pp. 141–49. A document dating from the early eighteenth century relates the difficulties the Jewish community was facing even in its attempts to pray at the Wailing Wall (*sijill* of Jerusalem, vol. 222, p. 87). No wonder, therefore, that in the 1880s the Jewish community was looking for ways to purchase the entire area of the Wall and its surroundings with the financial help of the Rothschilds. On the eve of the First World War, a letter was sent by David Yellin to Henry Morgenthau, the U. S. ambassador in Istanbul, asking him to try receive an Ottoman order to that effect (copy in the Central Archives for the History of the Jewish People, Givat Ram campus of the Hebrew University of Jerusalem, file P 3 1063).

24 See Sylvia Auld and Robert Hillenbrand, *Ottoman Jerusalem: The Living City, 1517–1917* (London, 2000), vol. 2: Architectural survey by Yusuf Natsheh, p. 974.

25 *Sijill* of Jerusalem, vol. 32, pp. 171–72.

26 For the origin of this term, as well as the guild of scavengers in charge of collecting refuse in Jerusalem in earlier years, see my *Guilds of Ottoman Jerusalem*, pp. 72–74.

27 *Sijill* of Jerusalem, vol. 291, pp. 36–38, dated October 28/29, 1807. For Khasseki Sultan see Singer, *Constructing Ottoman Beneficence*, pp. 54–65. For references of Arab contemporary travellers to the gates of the Haram, see Abdul-Karim Rafeq, "Ottoman Jerusalem in the Writings of Arab Travellers" in *Ottoman Jerusalem*, ed. Auld and Hillebrand, Part One, pp. 66, 70–71.

28 *Sijill* of Jerusalem, vol. 296, p. 35; vol. 299, p. 115; vol. 303, p. 145; vol. 314, p. 73.

29 Interestingly, the pages preceding these new instructions for the Temple Mount include several orders by the same *vali* to the effect that the Christian and Jewish inhabitants of Jerusalem must be given just and equal treatment (*Sijill* of Jerusalem, vol. 291, pp. 35–36).

30 See, for example, *sijill* of Jerusalem, vol. 291, pp. 127–28; vol. 297, p. 21.

31 See, for example, *sijill* of Jerusalem, vol. 312, p. 97; vol. 319, p. 112.

32 *Sijill* of Jerusalem, vol. 294, pp. 62–65.

33 *Sijill* of Jerusalem, vol. 280, p. 38; vol. 292, pp. 2, 67, 82–83; vol. 294, pp. 22, 52, 70,145; vol. 295, pp. 2, 105, 108; vol. 298, pp. 122, 131, 138; vol. 299, p. 73.

34 The legacy of a certain attendant of the Dome of the Rock included, among other things, two expensive rifles, a watch, a variety of household effects, and many debts of other Jerusalemites (*Sijill* of Jerusalem, vol. 286, pp. 103–4); another attendant of the Dome of the Rock some thirty years later, in 1829, bought expensive buildings (vol. 312, p. 95).

35 St Laurent, "The Dome," pp. 419–24.

36 Aref, *Ta'rikh*, pp. 93–95, 168.

37 *Sijill* of Jerusalem, vol. 295, pp. 103, 166, 170.

38 Ibrahim al-'Aura, *A History of the Rule of Sulayman Pasha the Righteous* (Sidon, 1936), pp. 267–70, 289, 292–97 (Arabic).

39 *Sijill* of Jerusalem, vol. 302, pp. 12, 14–15.

40 Two lengthy documents, describing in great detail the expenses incurred during this major restoration project, have been found in the Islamic Museum, located on the Temple Mount. These set early August 1819 as the date of the actual completion of this project, indicating that some of these left-over building materials were actually used after the middle of 1819, as suggested above. See Khadr Salameh, "Aspects of the *Sijills* of the Shari'a Court in Jerusalem," in *Ottoman Jerusalem*, ed. Auld and Hillenbrand, Part One, pp. 104–5, 141–43. For several restoration campaigns in the eighteenth and nineteenth centuries, recorded inside the Dome of the Rock, see Oleg Grabar, *The Dome of the Rock* (Cambridge, MA, 2006), pp. 198–200.

41 Ahmet Cevdet, *A History* (Istanbul, 1309 [1891/92]), vol. 10, p. 87 (Turkish).

42 See Hans W. Neulen, *Feldgrau in Jerusalem: Das Levantekorps des kaiserlichen Deutschland* (München, 1991), pp. 244–45; Cyril Falls and Archibald F. Becke, *Military Operations, Egypt and Palestine, 2: From June 1917 to the End of the War*, Part 1 (London, 1930), p. 252; Yigal Sheffy, "Jerusalem in World War I – the Military Dimension" (Hebrew, forthcoming). I thank B. Z. Kedar and Y. Sheffy for drawing my attention to these sources.

Yitzhak Reiter and Jon Seligman, 1917 to the Present

1 Charles Wilson, *Ordnance Survey of Jerusalem* (London, 1865); Charles Warren, *Plans, Elevations, Sections Shewing the Results of Excavations at Jerusalem 1867–1870* (London, 1884).

2 Ernest T. Richmond, *The Dome of the Rock in Jerusalem—A Description of its Structure and Decoration* (Oxford, 1924).

3 **Robert W. Hamilton**, *The Structural History of the Aqsa Mosque—A Record of Archaeological Gleanings from the Repairs of 1938–1942* (London, 1949).

4 Louis-Hugues Vincent and Félix-Marie Abel, *Jérusalem—Récherches de toporahie, d'archéologie et d'histoire: Jérusalem nouvelle*, 4 vols. (Paris, 1914–26).

5 Max von Berchem, *Matériaux pour un Corpus Inscriptionum Arabicarum II, 1: Syrie du Sud - Jérusalem, Haram* (Cairo, 1925).

6 Keppel A. C. Creswell, *Early Muslim Architecture* (Oxford, 1969).

7 Kathleen M. Kenyon, *Digging Up Jerusalem* (London, 1974).

8 Myriam Rosen-Ayalon, *The Early Islamic Monuments of the Haram al-Sharif—An Iconographic Study*, Qedem 28 (Jerusalem, 1989).

9 For that collation, see *The Book of Jerusalem: Jerusalem—Its Natural Conditions, History and Development from the Origins to the Present Day*, ed. Michael Avi-Yonah (Jerusalem and Tel Aviv, 1956) (Hebrew).

10 Benjamin Mazar, *The Mountain of the Lord* (New York, 1975); Meir Ben-Dov, *In the Shadow of the Temple: The Discovery of Ancient Jerusalem* (New York, 1982).

11 Andreas Kaplony, *The Haram of Jerusalem 324–1099: Temple, Friday Mosque, Area of Spiritual Power*, Freiburger Islamstudien 22 (Stuttgart, 2002).

12 Michael H. Burgoyne, *Mamluk Jerusalem: An Architectural Study* (Buckhurst Hill, 1987); Yusuf Natsheh, *Architectural Survey, Part Two of Ottoman Jerusalem: The Living City 1517–1917*, ed. Sylvia Auld and Robert Hillenbrand (London, 2000); Denys Pringle, *The Churches of the Crusader Kingdom of Jerusalem—A Corpus*, Volume 3: *The City of Jerusalem* (Cambridge, 2007).

13 See Gideon Avni and Jon Seligman, *The Temple Mount 1917–2001: Building and Development, Documentation, Research and Inspection of Antiquities* (Jerusalem, 2001).

14 Yitzhak Reiter, *Islamic Institutions in Jerusalem: Palestinian Muslim Organisation under Jordanian and Israeli Rule* (The Hague, London, and Boston, 1997), p. 89.

15 See Uri M. Kupferschmidt, *The Supreme Muslim Council: Islam under British Mandate for Palestine* (Leiden, 1987).

16 Lionel G.A. Cust, *The Status Quo in the Holy Places* (London, 1929).

17 *Jerusalem 1918–1920—Being the Records of the Pro-Jerusalem Council during the Period of the British Military Administration*, ed. Charles R. Ashbee (London, 1921).

18 Richmond, *Dome of the Rock*.

19 Ibid., p. 4.

20 *Jerusalem 1918–1920*, p. 8.

21 Kupferschmidt, *Supreme Muslim Council*, p. 88.

22 Ibid., p. 132.

23 Ibid., loc. cit.

24 Avni and Seligman, *Temple Mount 1917–2001*, pp. 11–22.

25 Hamilton, *Structural History*; Avni and Seligman, *Temple Mount 1917–2001*, pp. 14–20.

26 Palestine (Holy Places) Order in Council 1924; Shmuel Berkovitz, *The Battle for the Holy Places: The Struggle for Jerusalem and the Holy Places in Israel, Judea, Samaria and the Gaza Strip* (Jerusalem, 2000), p. 26 (Hebrew).

27 Avni and Seligman, *Temple Mount 1917–2001*, pp. 14–20.

28 Yehoshua Ben-Arieh, *Jerusalem in the 19th Century: The Old City* (Jerusalem, 1984), pp. 308–14.

29 Sahih Muslim, *Kitab al-Iman* (The Book of Faith), ch. 75 (Arabic).

30 Benjamin Z. Kedar, "Laying the Foundation Stones of the Hebrew University of Jerusalem: July 24, 1918," in *The History of the Hebrew University: Origins and Beginnings*, ed. Shaul Katz and Michael Heyd (Jerusalem, 1997), pp. 92–93 (Hebrew). *The Letters and Papers of Chaim Weizmann*, vol. 8: *November 1917–October 1918*, ed. Dvorah Barzilay and Barnett Litvinoff (New Brunswick, NJ and Jerusalem, 1977), Letter 185, pp. 176–77; see also Letter 208, pp. 203–4.

31 Letters in Archives of Mandatory Department of Antiquities, File ATQ/939. The files are deposited in the archives of the Israel Antiquities Authority, Rockefeller Museum, Jerusalem.

32 Ronald Storrs, "Memorandum on the Wailing Wall," November 1925, Archives of Mandatory

Department of Antiquities, File ATQ/939.

33 *Report of the Commission Appointed by H. M. Government... to Determine the Rights and Claims of Moslems and Jews in Connection with the Western or Wailing Wall at Jerusalem, December 1930* (London, 1931), p. 57.

34 Ibid.

35 Kupferschmidt, *Supreme Muslim Council*, p. 55.

36 **Hamilton**, *Structural History*, p. iii; Avni and Seligman, *Temple Mount 1917–2001*, p. 17.

37 **Hamilton**, *Structural History*, p. iv.

38 Avni and Seligman, *Temple Mount 1917–2001*, p. 16.

39 Ibid., p. 20.

40 Eliezer Be'eri, *The Palestinians under Jordan Rule* (Jerusalem, 1978), p. 54 (Hebrew).

41 Ibid., p. 55.

42 See the photo in *Majalat al-Akhbar al-Islamiyya*, 13, 1–2 (Dec. 1971), p. 41, published by Israel's Ministry of Religion, Muslim Department.

43 Nachman Tal, *The Struggle at Home: Egypt and Jordan's Contention with Radical Islam* (Tel Aviv, 1999), p. 195 (Hebrew). Jerusalem's senior conspirator was Dr. Musa 'Abdallah al-Husayni. There are, however, other opinions regarding the plotters' identities. See, for example, Nasser al-Din al-Nashashibi, *Who Killed King Abdallah?* (Dar al-'Uruba, n. d.) (Arabic).

44 Section 13 of the Writ of Mandate required them to provide free access to and freedom of worship at the holy sites.

45 Avni and Seligman, *Temple Mount 1917–2001*, p. 22.

46 Law No. 33; see Abd al-Salam al-'Abadi, *The Jordanian Hashemite Care for Jerusalem and the Islamic Holy Places in Noble al-Quds* (Amman, 1995), p. 30 (Arabic).

47 *Majalat al-Akhbar al-Islamiyya*, 13, 1–2 (December 1971), p. 43.

48 Kimberly Katz, *Jordanian Jerusalem: Holy Places and National Spaces* (Gainesville, 2005), pp. 107–10.

49 Amnon Ramon, "Beyond the Western Wall: The Relation of the State of Israel and the Jewish Public to the Temple Mount (1967–1999)," in *Sovereignty of God and Man: Sanctity and Political Centrality on the Temple Mount*, ed. Yitzhak Reiter (Jerusalem, 2001), pp. 113–42 (Hebrew).

50 Uzi Narkiss, *Soldier of Jerusalem* (Tel Aviv, 1991), 341 (Hebrew).

51 Berkovitz, *The Battle for the Holy Places*, 15–17.

52 The scheduling of the Temple Mount as a declared antiquities site according to Israeli law appears in the Official Gazeteer No. 1390 published on 31 August 1967.

53 Nadav Shragai, *The Temple Mount Conflict: Jews and Muslims, Religion and Politics since 1967* (Jerusalem, 1995) (Hebrew); Berkovitz, *The Battle for the Holy Places*; idem, *The Temple Mount and the Western Wall in Israeli Law*, JIIS Study Series 90 (Jerusalem, 2001); Yitzhak Reiter, "The Third Most Holy, The First in Politics: The Haram al-Sharif in the Eyes of the Muslims," in *Sovereignty of God and Man: Sanctity and Political Centrality on the Temple Mount*, ed. Yitzhak Reiter (Jerusalem, 2001), pp. 155–79 (Hebrew); idem, "Status-Quo on the Temple Mount / the Haram al-Sharif under Israeli Rule (1967-2000)," in ibid., pp. 297–336 (Hebrew); Ramon, "Beyond the Western Wall"; Gershon Gorenberg, *The End of Days: Fundamentalism and the Struggle for the Temple Mount* (New York, 2000).

54 Sa'd al-Din al-'Alami, *The Supreme Muslim Authority's Documents, 1967–1984* (Jerusalem, 1984), p. 12 (Arabic); David Farhi, "The Muslim Authority in East Jerusalem and in Judea and Samaria since the Six Day War," *HaMizrah HeHadash* 28, 1–2 (1979), p. 6 (Hebrew).

55 Michael C. Hudson, "The Transformation of Jerusalem—1948–1987 AD," in *Jerusalem in History*, ed. Kamil J. Asali (Buckhurst Hill, 1989), pp. 249–78.

56 Reiter, *Islamic Institutions*, p. 7.

57 Sa'd al-Din al-'Alami, *Wath'iaq*, pp. 7–8; 12 (Arabic).

58 See n. 55 above.

59 Al-'Abadi, *The Jordanian Hashemite Care for Jerusalem*.

60 The East Jerusalem (Palestinian-operated) fire station's commander and staff were the first to reach the site and, upon discovering the extent of the blaze, called the main fire station in West Jerusalem; within a short time 16 fire trucks arrived at the site. The Muslims who gathered there accused the Israeli fire-fighters of bringing gasoline instead of water to fuel the fire; see Uzi Benziman, *Jerusalem, An Unwalled City* (Tel Aviv, 1973) p. 141 (Hebrew). See also Meron Benvenisti, *Jerusalem, the Torn City* (Jerusalem, 1976), p. 300; Shragai, *The Temple Mount Conflict*, p. 40.

61 Berkovitz, *The Battle for the Holy Places*, p. 88.

62 Ahmad Mahmud Muhammad al-Qasim, *The Encyclopedia of Jerusalem: 1000 Questions and Answers on Jerusalem* (Ramallah, 2002) p. 229 (Arabic).

63 *Ha'aretz*, 24 August 1969 (Hebrew); Shragai, *The Temple Mount Conflict*, p. 42.

64 Television interview with Shaykh Yusuf al-Qaradawi, 24 January 2001.

65 On this incident, see Shragai, *The Temple Mount Conflict*, pp. 161–69.

66 Al-'Alami, *The Supreme Muslim Authority's Documents*, pp. 376–87.

67 *Ha'aretz*, 10 January 1986.

68 Justice Ezra Kama, "Investigation of the the Causes of Death of Those Killed during the Events on the Temple Mount on 8 October 1990," Jerusalem Magistrate's Court, file HSM 37/90, 18 July 1991, pp. 29, 339 (Hebrew).

69 Yitzhak Reiter, "Jewish–Muslim Modus Vivendi at the Temple Mount/the Haram al-Sharif since 1967," in *Jerusalem: Essays towards Peacemaking*, ed. M.J. Breger and Ora Ahimeir (Syracuse, NY, 2002), pp. 269–95.

70 UNESCO resolution 24 C/15, 15 October 1987, and others.

71 Yitzhak Reiter, "Status-Quo on the Temple Mount / the Haram al-Sharif under Israeli Rule (1967–2000)," in *Sovereignty of God and Man: Sanctity and Political Centrality on the Temple Mount*, ed. Yitzhak Reiter (Jerusalem, 2001), pp. 315–36 (Hebrew).

72 *Ma'ariv*, 29 September 1996, quoted in Berkovitz, *The Battle for the Holy Places*, p. 116.

73 *Filastin al-Muslima*, November 1996, cover and p. 4.

74 See also the claim made by Palestinian Mufti Shaykh Ikrima Sabri in al-Sharq al-Awsat, 30 August 2002.

75 On changes in the positions adopted by Jewish religious individuals and bodies, see Ramon, "Beyond the Western Wall"; see also Moti Inbari, "The Oslo Accords and the Temple Mount, a Case Study: The Movement for the Establishment of the Temple," *Hebrew Union College Annual* 74 (2003), 1–45.

76 Berkovitz, *The Battle for the Holy Places*, p. 13.

77 Shragai, *The Temple Mount Conflict*, pp. 28, 61; Yoel Cohen, "The Political Role of the Israeli Chief Rabbinate in the Temple Mount Question," *Jewish Political Studies Review* 11, 1–2 (1999), 101–26; Ramon, "Beyond the Western Wall," pp. 119–21.

78 Benvenisti, *Jerusalem, the Torn City*, p. 101; Ramon, "Beyond the Western Wall," pp. 114–17.

79 Shragai, *The Temple Mount Conflict*, p. 62.

80 Yisrael Medad, *Jerusalem's Temple Mount: A Jewish-Muslim Flashpoint*, ACPR Policy Paper 111 (Shaarei Tikva, 2000).

81 Ramon, "Beyond the Western Wall," pp. 121–35.

82 Shragai, *The Temple Mount Conflict*, p. 65; Ramon, "Beyond the Western Wall," p. 122.

83 Reiter, "The Third Most Holy," p. 168; Reiter, "Status-Quo on the Temple Mount," p. 309.

84 From the end of the First Intifada until the opening of the Hasmonaean tunnel's exit in September 1996, there were no unusual disturbances at the Temple Mount except for the Hamas Movement's non-violent parade on 12 June 1996 in which demonstrators set fire to Israeli flags. For a survey of these events see Berkovitz, *The Battle for the Holy Places*, pp. 115–16.

85 Kama, "Investigation of the the Causes of Death," p. 15. Another book, written in the spirit of the Northern Branch of the Islamic Movement in Israel, describes the danger posed to al-Aqsa. See Yusuf Kamil Hasuna al-Husayni, *Palestine and Israeli Violations of the Islamic Holy Places* ([Hebron], 2000), p. 9 (Arabic).

86 Shragai, *The Temple Mount Conflict*, pp. 340–63.

87 Sa'id 'Iyad, *The al-Aqsa Massacre ... and the Extreme Provocation* (Acre, [n.d.]) (Arabic); Dawlat Filastin, *The al-Aqsa Massacre: Testimonies and Documents* ([n.p.], 1992) (Arabic).

88 Shragai, *The Temple Mount Conflict*, p. 357.

89 Reiter, "The Third Most Holy," p. 172.

90 Berkovitz, *The Battle for the Holy Places*, p. 58.

91 Reiter, "The Third Most Holy," p. 172.

92 Israel's Foreign Ministry Website: www.mfo.gov.il.

93 Menachem Klein, *Jerusalem the Contested City* (London, 2001), p. 149.

94 Reiter, *Islamic Institutions*, p. 18.

95 Menachem Klein, *The Jerusalem Question in the Arab–Israeli Peace Negotiations: Arab Stands* (Jerusalem, 1995), pp. 43–56 (Hebrew).

96 Foreign Minister Peres in an interview with *Yediot Aharonot*, 17 July 1994 (Hebrew). Quoted in Berkovitz, *The Battle for the Holy Places*, p. 203.

97 Ibid.

98 Reiter, "Status-Quo on the Temple Mount."

99 Yitzhak Reiter, *From Jerusalem to Mecca and Back: The Islamic Consolidation of Jerusalem* (Jerusalem, 2005), chap. 2 (Hebrew).

100 Emmanuel Sivan, *Mythes politiques arabes*, trans. Nicolas Weill (Paris, 1995 [1988]), p. 77.

101 Katz, *Jordanian Jerusalem*, pp. 111–17; al-Akhbar al-Islamiyya, 13, 1–2 (December 1971); 13 / 3–4 (1972), 4.

102 *A Brief Guide to the Haram al-Sharif Jerusalem* (Jerusalem, 1929), p. 4. [See also Sari Nusseibeh, *Once upon a Country: A Palestinian Life* (New York, 2007), p. 532: "Travel books printed in Syria a hundred years ago had no problem calling the Noble Sanctuary the Jewish Temple Mount." [The official guide published by the Jordan Tourist Department in 1956 states that the Temple was built on Mount Moriah by Solomon, restored by Herod and burnt down in 70 A.D. by Titus; "the Rock on the summit of Moriah is sacred to the Moslems." Jordan, *The Holy Land: Official Guide* (Amman, 1956), pp. 16, 20. Ed.].

103 Reiter, *From Jerusalem to Mecca and Back*, p. 31. [Cf. **Nusseibeh**, *Once upon a Country*, p. 426. Ed.]

104 Shlomo Ben-Ami, *Front without a Rearguard* (Tel Aviv, 2004), p. 219 (Hebrew).

105 Kamil Jamil al-'Asali, *Jerusalem in Arab and Muslim Travel Narratives* (Amman, 1992), pp. 39–40 (Arabic).

106 Sabri in an interview with *al-Jazeera*, 17 December 2000. See also *al-Ayam*, 22 November 1997.

107 Egypt, State Information Service, 28 April 2001.

108 Similar *fatwas* can also be found on leading Islamic websites delivering legal opinions. See, for example, two *fatwas* of 17 June and 21 December 2003 at www.alaqsa-online.net .

109 Fatwa of 21 Dec. 2002 on www.alaqsa-online.net .

110 *Davar*, 3 February 1986 (Hebrew).

111 Avni and Seligman, *Temple Mount 1917–2001*, pp. 25–26.

112 Ibid., pp. 27–29; Shragai, *The Temple Mount Conflict*, pp. 299–306; Berkovitz, *The Battle for the Holy Places*, pp. 94–95.

113 Avni and Seligman, *Temple Mount 1917–2001*, pp. 27–40.

114 *Ha'aretz*, 11 October 1996 (Hebrew).

115 Avni and Seligman, *Temple Mount 1917–2001*, pp. 34–37; Reiter, "Status-Quo on the Temple Mount," pp. 308–16; Berkovitz, *The Battle for the Holy Places*, p. 62; Jon Seligman, "Solomon's Stables, The Temple Mount, Jerusalem: The Events Concerning the Destruction of Antiquities 1999–2001," *'Atiqot* 56 (2007), 33*–54*.

116 Seligman, "Solomon's Stables." In the rubble from the pit, which the Waqf loaded on trucks and dumped outside the Temple Mount, Israeli archaeologists subsequently found sherds from the Iron Age down to the Ottoman period, as well as glass fragments, glazed tiles, stone vessels, metal objects, beads, and coins from various periods. See Yuval Baruch, "The Archaeological Finds in the Soil Debris Removed from the Temple Mount, Jerusalem, 1999–2000," *'Atiqot* 56 (2007), 55*–64*; see also Gabriel Barkay and Yitzhak Zweig, "New Objects Found While Sifting the Rubble from the Temple Mount," *Ariel* 175 (October 2006), 6–46 (Hebrew).

117 Inbari, "Oslo Accords."

118 Berkovitz, *The Temple Mount and the Western Wall*, p. 63.

119 Menachem Klein, *The Jerusalem Problem: The Struggle for Permanent Status* (Gainesville, FL, 2003), p. 74.

120 Nadav Shragai, "Opinion Poll: 91 Percent of Jews Unwilling to Relinquish the Western Wall for Peace," *Ha'aretz*, 10 March 2005 (Hebrew).

Nazmi Al-Jubeh, Basic Changes, but Not Dramatic: Al-Haram al-Sharif in the Aftermath of 1967

1 For more details on these negotiations, see Menachem Klein, *Shattering a Taboo: The Contacts toward a Permanent Status Agreement in Jerusalem 1994–2001* (Jerusalem, 2001), esp. chap. 3 (Hebrew). In these negotiations, Israel insisted on giving sovereignty over the site to any third party, but not to Palestine.

2 See Michael Dumper, *The Politics of Jerusalem since 1967* (New York, 1997), pp. 199–202.

3 For the legal discussion, including the status quo, see Shmuel Berkovitz, *The Battle for the Holy Places* (Jerusalem, 2000), p. 246 (Hebrew).

4 Details of the Muslim Waqf's position can be traced through Sa'd al-Din al-'Alami, *Documents of the Islamic Council* (Jerusalem, n.d.) (Arabic).

5 Dumper, *Politics of Jerusalem*, pp. 214–17.

6 The Haram al-Sharif, which is located in the southeastern corner of Jerusalem's Old City, shares here its walls with those of the city.

7 Article IX of the Peace Treaty between Israel and Jordan, signed on 25 October 1994, under the title "Places of Historical and Religious Significance and Interfaith Relations," includes the following paragraphs: "1. Each Party will provide freedom of access to places of religious and historical significance; 2. In this regard, in accordance with the Washington Declaration, Israel respects the present special role of the Hashemite Kingdom of Jordan in Muslim holy shrines in Jerusalem. When negotiations on the permanent status will take place, Israel will give high priority to the Jordanian historic role in these shrines; 3. Parties will act together to promote interfaith relations among the three monotheistic religions, with the aim of working towards religious understanding, moral commitments, freedom of religious worship and tolerance and peace."

8 The difference in the meaning of the differently used terminology became clear at Camp David 2000. President Clinton referred to the "Western Wall," a term also used by the Israelis, while the Palestinians spoke of the "Wailing Wall" or "Buraq Wall." The Western Wall could be the entire western wall of the Haram (ca. 470m long). The Buraq/Wailing Wall is just 28m long and 4–5m wide. After 1967 Israel enlarged the length of the wall from 28m to 60m by exposing it. Israel then formally registered a section of the "Western Wall" 155m long and 1.5m

wide as Israeli state property.

9 Abdul Latif Tibawi, *The Islamic Pious Foundations in Jerusalem: Origins, History, and Usurpation by Israel* (London, 1978). About the Tankiziyya, see Michael H. Burgoyne, *Mamluk Jerusalem: An Architectural Study* (London, 1987), pp. 223–40. Little historical evidence of Jewish sanctification of the Haram al-Sharif's western wall has been found prior to the sixteenth century. Earlier accounts tell of Jews performing religious rituals on the Mount of Olives, facing Jerusalem. It appears that Jewish leaders began to take interest in worshipping at the Western Wall during the Ottoman period (sixteenth century). Jews were permitted to perform their religious rituals in a small courtyard, no more than 5m wide and 28m long. This section of the wall was referred to by its Arabic name, al-Buraq Wall; Muslims believe that the Prophet Muhammad tied al-Buraq, the legendary flying horse, to this wall before entering the sanctuary of the Aqsa Mosque to pray together with the prophets the night of his ascension to heaven. Jews continued to use this section of the wall, without ownership or the possibility of placing fixed property, until 1925. Ownership remained in Muslim hands without debate. In September 1925 Jewish worshippers brought tables, chairs, and books to the site on the grounds that the wall was part of the remains of the Second Temple, which was destroyed by the Roman Titus in 70 AD. The British Mandate authorities intervened to end the conflict, upholding laws of "status quo." Three years later, in 1928, the dispute was revived when Jewish groups requested abrogation of the British ruling for the status quo. This request was advanced when Jewish worshippers brought a partition screen to the site on the Ninth of Av (9 August 1928), the anniversary of the Second Temple's destruction. The site's British guard once again removed the screen on the grounds that it challenged the British decision and could dangerously tip the balance of the status quo. That November, the first Islamic Conference was convened in Jerusalem. In addition to other issues on its agenda, representatives from all corners of the Islamic world reiterated Muslim opposition to any changes at the Buraq Wall. Notwithstanding, several minor incidents followed that brought the issue of the wall to the forefront, while equally expressing resistance to Zionism, Jewish immigration, and British policy of transferring Palestinian property to Jews. In August 1929 these events culminated in the uprising known in Palestinian political lore as the "Buraq Uprising," which left some 250 Arab and Jewish dead. The Sir Walter Shaw Commission was subsequently formed to investigate the factors leading to the uprising. British Mandate officials affirmed repeatedly that all components of the Haram al-Sharif's western wall remained solely Islamic property due to its sanctity to Muslims. The British Mandate administration also affirmed that Jews had the right to hold religious rituals at the site as prescribed by custom. The problem was eventually buried by the events of the 1948 War, despite its mention in Israeli–Jordanian truce talks and Jordan's subsequent decision to grant Jews right of access to the Wailing Wall. Jordan never implemented its decision, because of the ongoing state of war between it and the new Jewish state and on the basis of the claim that Israel prevented the return of the Palestinian refugees; in addition, Jordan could not assure the security of worshippers coming from Israel to pray at the Wailing Wall.

10 See Uzi Benziman, *Jerusalem: A City without Walls* (Jerusalem, 1976), p. 24 (Arabic). Originally published in Hebrew (Tel Aviv, 1973), I am using Muhammad Madi's translation into Arabic: *Al Quds: Madinah bila Aswar.*.

11 See the statement issued by the Muslim Waqf Council, in al-'Alami, *Documents of the Supreme Islamic Council*, p. 280.

12 Ibid., p. 268.

13 Ibid., p. 268. The letter was signed by Shaykh Hilmi al-Muhtasib, president of the Supreme Islamic Council at that time, and outlines the circumstances surrounding the Haram al-Sharif, as well as the Haram al-Ibrahimi in Hebron (the Tombs of the Patriarchs), while also addressing other political issues.

14 See the statement in al-'Alami, *Documents of the Supreme Islamic Council*, p. 280.

15 See the statement issued by the Islamic Council on that date, Islamic Council Archives, Jerusalem, and the *al-Quds* newspaper issued that day.

16 The growth of Israeli settlement activity in Jerusalem and its surroundings since Oslo can be taken as an example of such pre-emptive activities. See the report on settlement in Jerusalem prepared by the Negotiation Technical Unit in the Palestinian negotiations department, published in the newspaper *al-Quds*, 19 November 2002.

17 For more details on Jerusalem in the negotiations, see the comprehensive and illuminating book, Klein, *Shattering a Taboo*, esp. chap. 3. It is worth noting that Israel did not attempt to demand sovereignty or even divide sovereignty of the Haram al-Sharif prior to the Camp David II negotiations. During the negotiations, Israel exerted serious efforts to prevent control being granted to the Palestinian side, even if Israel lost sovereignty as a result. Israel suggested sovereignty above the ground and below the ground, or granting sovereignty to a third party— forms of sovereignty previously unheard of.

18 For more information on Israel's lack of seriousness in these negotiations and the measures taken to impose facts on the ground, see Nazmi Al-Ju'beh, "The Ghettoization of Arab

Jerusalem," *Jerusalem Quarterly File* 16 (November 2002), 5–11.

19   It is most likely that this name came into use during the period of Crusader control of Jerusalem (1099–1187). The name continued to be used in subsequent periods, only to be transformed during the initiative of the mid-nineties to name the area the Marwani Mosque.

20   The Islamic Awqaf in Jerusalem does not recognize Israeli law, which was unilaterally imposed on Jerusalem. To this day, it only honors Jordanian law and therefore does not deal with Israeli rulings, and if forced to, does so only indirectly.

21   On the Israeli response see, Nadav Shragai, "Rubinstein: The Opening on the Temple Mount is a Kick at Jewish History," *Ha'aretz,* 2 December 1999 (Hebrew).

22   See n. 6 above.

23   A similar idea was proposed by Ehud Barak (then Israeli Prime Minister, who led negotiations at Camp David and Taba in 2000) and other segments of the Labor Party, when it was proposed that a third party, neither Israeli nor Palestinian, hold sovereignty over the Haram al-Sharif. Jordan was discussed in this regard, and it is noteworthy that Jordan's interests in the Haram al-Sharif were respected in the Israeli–Jordanian peace accords (see n. 6 above). Moreover, Jordan did not entirely let go of the Haram al-Sharif when it severed its formal ties to the West Bank. It preserved its relationship to the Islamic Awqaf responsible for the compound.

24   Joha is a well-known character in popular Arabic lore. In the story of Joha's nail, he asks permission to hammer a nail into the wall of a house that he sold to somebody, and then insists upon entering the house every day to visit his sole possession in it: the nail.

25   Unpublished technical assessment report on the destruction of the Aqsa Mosque, prepared by the Aqsa Mosque Restoration Committee, Jerusalem, 1970. See also L. Lazzarini and P. M. Schwarzbaum, "The Technical Examination and Restoration of the Paintings of the Dome of the Al Aqsa Mosque, Jerusalem," *Studies in Conservation*, 30, 3 (August 1985), 129–35

26   Ibid.

27   See http://www.akdn.org/agency/akaa/thirdcycle/jerusalem.html

Oleg Grabar, *The Haram al-Sharif* as a Work of Art

1   David Summers, *Real Spaces* (New York, 2003), pp. 140–52.

2   Erwin Reidinger, "The Temple Mount Platform in Jerusalem from Solomon to Herod: an Archaeological Re-examination," *Assaph* 9 (2004), 1–64.

3   This conclusion is drawn from written sources of a later time, which I and most other scholars have accepted at face value, because their evidence was convenient for other theories about the architectural history of Jerusalem. Since trying to reconstruct a visual history of a space, I have begun to feel some doubts about the supposed desolation of the Herodian space in Christian times. It does not make sense from the point of view of urban space at a time of relative institutional and population growth, and I wonder whether we have not taken too literally the assertions made by early Islamic sources and by a Christian ideology, both of which demanded that the space be barren, each for reasons of its own.

4   This reconstruction differs from the one proposed by Prof. Patrich (see figs. 28–29). [Ed.]

Rachel Elior, From Priestly (and Early Christian) Mount Zion to Rabbinic Temple Mount

*   This article is an abbreviated version of a longer monograph that has been published in Hebrew in *Eretz Israel* 28: *The Memorial Volume for Teddy Kollek* (2008), pp. 1–13. A full version was also published in English in *Israel's God and Rebecca's Children: Christology and Community in Early Judaism and Christianity*, ed. David Capes, April DeConik, Helen Bond, and Troy Miller (Waco, TX, 2007), pp. 277–302, 439–49.

1   Jonathan Z. Smith, *Map is not Territory: Studies in the History of Religions* (Leiden, 1978); idem, *Imagining Religion: From Babylon to Jonestown* (Chicago, 1982); *Sacred Places and Profane Spaces: Essays in the Geographics of Judaism, Christianity and Islam*, ed. Jamie Scott and Paul Simpson-Housely (New York, 1991).

2   On cosmography in religious thought, see Mircea Eliade, *The Myth of the Eternal Return*, trans. Willard R. Trask (New York, 1954), esp. pp. 6–17. On the relationship between mountains and cosmic mountains on which heaven and earth commingle and on which the deity makes a terrestrial appearance, see Ronald E. Clements, *God and Temple* (Philadelphia, 1965); Richard J. Clifford, *The Cosmic Mountain in Canaan and the Old Testament* (Cambridge, 1972).

3   On David's tomb, whose identity as such developed first in the Christian tradition and was later adopted by the Jewish one, see Israel J. Yuval, *Two Nations in Your Womb: Perceptions of Jews and Christians in Late Antiquity and the Middle Ages*, trans. Barbara Harshav and Jonathan Chipman (Berkeley, 2006), pp. 23–24; Ora Limor, "The Origins of a Tradition: King David's

Tomb on Mount Zion," *Traditio* 44 (1988), 453–62.

4   For background on the nature of the controversy over sacred time and sacred space within the Jewish world of the second century BCE, see Rachel Elior, *The Three Temples: On the Emergence of Jewish Mysticism*, trans. David Louvish (Oxford, 2004).

5   2 Chron. 3.1.

6   Gen. 22.2.

7   2 Sam. 24.16–18, 25.

8   Mount Zion is mentioned hundreds of times in the Hebrew Bible, especially in the books of Isaiah, Jeremiah, Micah, Zechariah, Psalms, and Lamentations.

9   Jub. 8.19.

10   Jub. 18.14–16.

11   Jub. 18.13.

12   2 Sam. 5.7; 1 Kings 8.1; 1 Chron. 11.5; 2 Chron. 5.2 ; Isa. 8.:18.

13   2 Kings 19.31 and parallel in Isa. 37.32. Cf. Jon D. Levenson, "The Jerusalem Temple in Devotional and Visionary Experience," in *Jewish Spirituality from the Bible through the Middle Ages*, ed. Arthur Green (New York, 1986), pp. 32–61, quote on p. 47.

14   Isa. 35.10; cf. 51.11 and see also 52.1, 7; 4.3–5.

15   Joel 4.17; cf. 4.21—"And the Lord shall dwell in Zion"; 3.5—"for there shall be a remnant on Mount Zion and in Jerusalem, as the Lord promised."

16   Joel 2.1; cf. 3.5 and 4.16.

17   Lam. 5.18; cf. Jer. 26.18; *Lam. Rab.* 5.18 (Buber 80a); *Sifrei Devarim* 43 (Finkelstein, p. 95); b. Mak. 24b.

18   Isa. 64.9–10.

19   *1 Macc.* 4.26-40, especially vss. 36, 37, 38; cf. 5.54; 7.33.

20   See, e.g., "Have mercy, our God, on us and on Israel Your people; on Jerusalem Your city; on Zion, dwelling place of Your glory; on Your sanctuary and Your habitation." (From the blessing *Nahem*, added to the standard prayers on the Ninth of Av, the day commemorating the destruction of the First and Second Temples).

21   On the meaning of this term, see Community Rule 1.19–21; 2.2–4; 5.1–3, 5, 8; Damascus Document 3.1, 4–21; 3.4; 5.5. Except otherwise noted, quotations from the Dead Sea Scrolls are taken from Géza Vermes, *The Complete Dead Sea Scrolls in English* (New York, 1997). On the significance of the tie between the Zadokite priests and the Sadducees, see Yaacov Sussman, "The History of *Halakhah* and the Dead Sea Scrolls: Preliminary Talmudic Observations on MMT," in *Discoveries in the Judaean Desert (DJD)X, Qumran Cave 4. V*, ed. Elisha Qimron and John Strugnell (Oxford, 1994), pp. 179–200. On the significance of this priestly context in the literary history of Jewish mysticism, see Elior, *The Three Temples* (above, n. 4), pp. 24–28.

22   1 Kings 6.23–35; 8.6–7.

23   On the Psalms Scroll from Qumran and the cycle of songs associated with the cycle of sacrifices, see James A. Sanders, "The Psalms Scroll of Qumran Cave 11(11QPs) col. xxvii:2–11," in *DJD IV* (Oxford, 1965), pp. 48, 91–93. Cf. Elior, *The Three Temples*, pp. 50–55.

24   See Carol A. Newsom, *Songs of the Sabbath Sacrifice: a Critical Edition* (Atlanta, 1985), Introduction; cf. Martha Himmelfarb, "The Temple and the Garden of Eden in Ezekiel, The Book of Watchers and the Wisdom of Ben Sira," in *Sacred Places* (above, n. 4), pp. 63–78. See also Lea Mazor, "The Two-direction Connection between Garden of Eden and the Sanctuary," *Shenaton le-heqer ha-mizrah ha-qadum* 13 (2002), 5–42 (Hebrew); Jacques T. van Ruiten, "Eden and the Temple: The Rewriting of Genesis 2:4–3:24 in the Book of Jubilees," in *Paradise Interpreted: Representations of Biblical Paradise in Judaism and Christianity*, ed. Gerard P. Luttikhuizen (Leiden, 1999), pp. 63–94.

25   Jub. 1.17, 28–29 (emphasis supplied).

26   Jub. 4.26.

27   Gen. 5.21–24; Jub. 4.23. 2 Enoch 19.2 (Hebrew version); *The Old Testament Pseudepigrapha*, ed. James H. Charlesworth, 2 vols. (Garden City, NY, 1983–85, vol. 1, chap. 68; henceforth: Charlesworth).

28   See 1 Enoch chapters 1–36; Jub. 4.17–20. See James Vanderkam, *Enoch—A Man for Generations* (Columbia, SC, 1995) and cf. Rachel Elior, "You Have Chosen Enoch From among Men," in *On Creation and Re-creation in Jewish Thought: Festschrift for Joseph Dan*, ed. Rachel Elior and Peter Schäfer (Tübingen, 2005), pp. 15–64 (Hebrew).

29   11Q13. *DJD XXIII* (Oxford, 1998), pp. 221–42.

30   2 Enoch 23, 25–45, 52–63 in *The Apocrypha*, ed. Avraham Kahana, 2 vols. (Tel Aviv 1937) (Hebrew; henceforth: Kahana); 71 J:17–23, 28–37; 72A+J:1–6 in Charlesworth, vol. 1.

31   2 Sam. 24.16–25; 1 Chron. 21.15, 18–30.

32   Jub. 18.13.

33   On the fourteenth of Nisan as the time of the Crucifixion, see John 19:31, stating that it took place on Friday, the fourteenth of Nisan, and the eve of Passover, when the paschal sacrifice was offered. On that time in the early eastern Christian tradition and on the time of the Crucifixion on a Friday that fell on the fifteenth of Nisan in the three synoptic gospels, see Yuval, *Two Nations* (above, n.

3), pp. 60–61, 210, 229. On identification of the paschal sacrifice with Jesus, the lamb of God, see ibid., p. 73. During the fourth and fifth centuries, the descent of the Holy Spirit on Jesus' apostles on Pentecost (Acts 2,1–4) was associated with Mount Zion, as implied by Christian pilgrims in late antiquity; see John Wilkinson, *Egeria's Travels* (London, 1971), p.191.

34 See Shalom Spiegel, "From the Legends about Isaac's Binding: a *piyyut* by R. Ephraim of Bonn on the Slaughter and Resurrection of Isaac," in *Alexander Marx Jubilee Volume* (New York, 1950), pp. 471–547 (Hebrew); idem, *The Last Trial: On the Legends and Lore of the Command to Abraham to Offer Isaac as a Sacrifice*, translated with an introduction by Judah Goldin; new preface by Judah Goldin (Woodstock, VT, 1993). Spiegel cites legends telling of Abraham actually killing Isaac; and while those legends, derived from tannaitic *midrash*, postdate the New Testament, it is possible that they preserve earlier traditions. Yuval takes a an opposing view, maintaining that these legends represent a Jewish effort to present Isaac as a substitute for Jesus as one who is killed and resurrected; Yuval, *Two Nations*, p. 57, n. 62.

35 Rev. 14.1. Quotations from the New Testament are from the *New Revised Standard Version Bible*, 1989.

36 Heb. 12.22–24.

37 Yuval, *Two Nations*, p. 23.

38 Ibid., p. 38; Ora Limor, "Christian Sacred Space and the Jew," in *From Witness to Witchcraft: Jews and Judaism in Medieval Christian Thought*, ed. Jeremy Cohen (Wiesbaden, 1996), pp. 55–77; Yaron Z. Eliav, *God's Mountain: The Temple Mount in Time, Place and Memory* (Baltimore, 2005).

39 2 Enoch 19.2 in Kahana; 68,1 in Charlesworth, vol. 1.

40 *Tg. Onq.* on Gen 5.24; Gen. Rab. 25.

41 Views are divided on the transfer of Isaac's Binding from Nisan to Tishri. See Philip R. Davies, "Passover and the Dating of the Aqedah," *Journal of Jewish Studies* 30, 1 (1979), 59–67.

42 See 1 Chron. 5.27–41; 6.35–38; Ezra 7.1–5; cf. Deborah W. Rooke, *Zadok's Heirs: The Role and Development of the High Priesthood* (Oxford and New York, 2000).

43 cf. Exod. 12.2.

44 T. Hag. 2.1.

45 M. Meg. 4.8.

46 Num. Rab. sec. 12.

47 Hag. 15b

48 M. Hag. 2.1.

49 On the *Heykhalot* literature, including 3 Enoch, see Gershom Scholem, *Major Trends in Jewish Mysticism* (New York, 1954), pp. 68ff; idem, *Jewish Gnosticism, Merkabah Mysticism and Talmudic Tradition* (New York, 1960), pp. 41–42; 3 (Hebrew) Enoch, translated by Philip Alexander, in Charlesworth, vol. 1, pp. 223–316; David J. Halperin, *The Faces of the Chariot: Early Jewish Responses to Ezekiel's Vision*, (Tübingen, 1988). Cf. Rachel Elior, *Heykhlalot Literature and Merkavah Tradition: Ancient Jewish Mysticism and Its Sources* (Tel Aviv, 2004) (Hebrew).

50 Rev. 14.

51 Heb 3.1; 4.14; 10.21.

52 Heb. 5.5–6; 6.20; 7.1.

53 Heb. 7–8.

54 2 Enoch 23.24–26 in Kahana; cf. chapters 68–72 in Charlesworth, vol. 1.

Guy G. Stroumsa, Christian Memories and Visions of Jerusalem in Jewish and Islamic Context

1 One of the most obvious instances of a place sacred to more than one religious tradition is that of the Babri Mosque, built at the birthplace of the god Rama in Ayodhya, in the Indian state of Uttar Pradesh, and destroyed in 1992 during an eruption of violence launched by Hindu fundamentalists. For another instance of a disputed place, see Robert J. Franklin and Pamela A. Bunte, "When Sacred Land Is Sacred to Three Tribes: San Juan Paiute Sacred Sites and the Hopi-Navajo-Paiute Suit to Partition the Arizona Navajo Reservation," in *Sacred Sites, Sacred Places*, ed. David L. Carmichael et al. (London and New York, 1994), pp. 244–58.

2 There is remarkably little literature on the history of the Temple Mount from a comparative religious perspective. For an introductory study, see Rivka Gonen, *Contested Holiness: Jewish, Muslim and Christian Perspectives on the Temple Mount in Jerusalem* (Jerusalem, 2003). For contemporary perspectives, see Roger Friedland and Richard D. Hecht, "The Politics of Sacred Place: Jerusalem's Temple Mount/Al-Haram al-Sharif," in *Sacred Places and Profane Places: Essays in the Geographics of Judaism, Christianity, and Islam*, ed. Jamie Scott and Paul Simpson-Howley (New York, Westport, CT, and London, 1991), pp. 21–61. See further J. P. Burgess, "The Sacred Site in Civil Space: Meaning and Status of the Temple Mount/Haram al-Sharif," *Social Identities* 10 (2004), 311–23, and Gershom Gorenberg, *The End of Days: Fundamentalism and the Struggle for the Temple Mount* (Oxford, 2001). See also Simon Goldhill, *The Temple of*

Jerusalem (London, 2004), p. 16: "The history of the Temple is a history of clashing cultures."

3 On the formation of the early Christian *imaginaire* of the Temple Mount, see Yaron Z. Eliav, *God's Mountain: The Temple Mount in Time, Place and Memory* (Baltimore, 2005). On the Christian translation of sacred space in Jerusalem, see Jonathan Z. Smith, *To Take Place: Toward Theory in Ritual* (Chicago, 1987), chapter 4: "To Replace", pp. 74–95 and notes, pp. 154–70. On the creation of Christian holy space, see Robert A. Markus, "How on Earth Would Places Become Holy? Origins of the Christian Idea of Holy Space," *Journal of Early Christian Studies* 2 (1994), 257–71. See further Jules Lebreton, "Sacred Space," in *Encyclopedia of Religion*, 12:526–35.

4 See in particular Stefan Heid, *Chiliasmus und Antichrist-Mythos: Eine frühchristliche Kontroverse um das heilige Land*, Hereditas 6 (Bonn, 1993). For an excellent collection of texts, see *L'Anticristo, I: Il nemico dei tempi finali*, ed. Gian L. Potesta and E. Marco Rizzi (Milan, 2005).

5 See William Horbury, "Antichrist among Jews and Christians," in *Jews in a Graeco-Roman World*, ed. Martin Goodman (Oxford, 1998), pp. 113–33, and Oded Irshai, "Dating the Eschaton: Jewish and Christian Apocalyptic Calculations in Late Antiquity," in *Apocalyptic Time*, ed. Albert I. Baumgarten (Leiden, Boston, and Köln, 2000), pp. 113–53.

6 See Hugh Nibley, "Christian Envy of the Temple," *Jewish Quarterly Review* 50 (1959–1960), 97–123, 229–240.

7 On these concepts, see in particular Jan Assmann, *Das kulturelle Gedächtnis: Schrift, Erinnerung und politische Identität in frühen Hochkulturen* (Munich, 1992).

8 Christoph Markschies, "Die Bedeutung Jerusalems für die Christen," (unpublished; I thank Prof. Markschies for making this rich text available to me).

9 See for instance Manlio Simonetti, "Il millenarismo cristiano da 1 al 5 secolo," *Annali di Storia dell' Esegesi* 15 (1998), 7–20. See also Charles E. Hill, *Regnum Caelorum: Patterns of Future Hope in Early Christianity* (Oxford, 1992).

10 See Christopher Rowland, *The Open Heaven: A Study of Apocalyptic in Judaism and Early Christianity* (Oxford, 1982).

11 Heid, *Chiliasmus* (above, n. 4).

12 On the representations of heavenly Jerusalem throughout Christian literature, see E. Lamirande, "Jérusalem céleste," in *Dictionnaire de Spiritualité* 7 (1972), 944–58.

13 See A. M. Berruto, "Millenarismo e montanismo," *Annali di Storia dell' Esegesi* 15 (1998), 85–100.

14 Eusebius, *Historia Ecclesiastica* 5.18.2; Loeb Classical Library (Cambridge, 1926–32) II, pp. 486–87.

15 See Pierre Kovalesky, "Messianisme et millénarisme russes?" *Archives de sociologie des religions* 5 (1958), 47–70.

16 On Montanist conceptions of the heavenly Jerusalem, see Pierre de Labriolle, *La crise montaniste* (Paris, 1913), pp. 86–95, 330–32. See further Christine Trevett, *Montanism: Gender, Authority and the New Prophecy* (Cambridge, 1996), pp. 15–26.

17 See for instance Marilyn Heldman, "Legends of Lâlibalâ: the Development of an Ethiopian Pilgrimage Site," *Res* 27 (1995) 25–38.

18 For the meaning of "the Heavenly Jerusalem" in the thought of Emmanuel Swedenborg, see, for example, his *The True Christian Religion*, §782. The *Book of Mormon* offers another self-understanding of a modern religious movement issuing out of Protestant Christianity as "the New Jerusalem."

19 *Strom* 172.2ff. This text is quoted by Karl L. Schmidt, "Jerusalem as Urbild und Abbild," *Eranos Jahrbuch* 18 (1950), 239.

20 For a discussion of Clement's attitude, see Klaus Thraede, "Jerusalem II (Sinnbild)," *Reallexikon für Antike und Christentum*, vol. 17 (Stuttgart, 1995), pp. 718–64, esp. 729–31.

21 *Hom in Ier* 9, on Jer 11.2; Com. in Ioh 10.18: "It is Jesus, God's logos, which enters into the soul, called Jerusalem." See also the triple allegorical interpretation of Jerusalem by the fourth-century Origenist Didymos the Blind, in his *Commentary on Zacharias*, quoted by Henri de Lubac, *Exégèse médiévale: Les quatre sens de l'Ecriture*, I.2 (Paris, 1959), p. 645. See also Dom O. Rousseau, "Quelques textes patristiques sur la Jérusalem céleste," *La vie spirituelle* 85 (1952), 378–88.

22 Medieval references in De Lubac, *Exégèse médiévale*, p. 646.

23 "Caelestis Hierusalem, quae est mater libertatis, chorus libertatis": this is a leitmotif of mediaeval Latin Christian literature. See for instance Godefroy of Saint Victor, Glossa in Ex., 20.2, quoted by De Lubac, *Exégèse médiévale*, p. 646.

24 See Thraede, "Jerusalem, II (Sinnbild)," 752–54.

25 "When I start speaking of her, I can't stop." Augustine, *Enarrationes in Psalmos*, 93.24.

26 See Johannes van Oort, *Jerusalem and Babylon: A Study of Augustine's City of God and the Sources of His Doctrine of the Two Cities* (Leiden, 1988). For the *Fortleben* of the idea, see Etienne Gilson, *Métamorphoses de la Cité de Dieu* (Louvain, 1952). Perhaps the most interesting of Augustine's elaborations on Jerusalem occur in his *Commentaries on Psalms*. Commenting on Ps. 64.2, for example, Augustine refers to the respective etymologies of Babylon and Jerusalem—the one meaning confusion (Heb. *bilbul*); the other, vision of peace. Although these two opposing entities are inextricably mixed throughout history, Jerusalem eternally represents the love of

God, while Babylon signifies the love of the world. (cf. Eusebius, *Demonstratio Evangelica* IV, *in fine*). Hence, the criterion for recognizing one's own identity: Ask yourself what you love, and you'll know where you belong. Such an understanding of Jerusalem rules out localization: Jerusalem is everywhere, or more precisely, in the hearts of those who love God.

27 See Martine Dulaey, *Victorin de Poetovio, premier exégète latin* (Paris, 1993), 2 vols., esp. vol. 1, pp. 208–19 and 255–70.

28 Similarly, the *Disputatio Gregentii*, a text from the mid-seventh century, states that the church of the Anastasis is the new Temple, while the Temple Mount itself remains razed. This seems to reflect the renewed fear of the Christians that the Jews may rebuild their Temple, perhaps through the medium of the Saracens.

29 See for instance John of Damascus, *De Haeresibus*, 101. See further Robert G. Hoyland, *Seeing Islam as Others Saw It: A Survey and Evaluation of Christian, Jewish and Zoroastrian Writings on Early Islam* (Princeton, 1997).

30 See, for instance, Gilbert Dagron and Vincent Deroche, "Juifs et Chrétiens dans l'Orient du VIIe siècle," *Travaux et Mémoires* 11 (Paris, 1991), 17–274; Cyril Mango, "The Temple Mount, AD 614–638," in *Bayt al-Maqdis: 'Abd al-Malik's Jerusalem*, ed. Julian Raby and Jeremy Johns (Oxford, 1992), 1–16; Vincent Deroche, "Polémique anti-judaïque et émergence de l'Islam (7e–8e s.)," *Revue des Etudes Byzantines* 57 (1999), 141–61; Averil Cameron, "The Trophies of Damascus: the Church, the Temple and Sacred Space," in *Le Temple, Lieu de conflit, Cahiers du Centre d'Etude du Proche-Orient Ancien*, 7 (Leuven, 1998), 203–12.

31 See for instance Günter Stemberger, "Jerusalem in the Early Seventh Century: Hopes and Aspirations of Christians and Jews," in *Jerusalem: Its Sanctity and Centrality to Judaism, Christianity and Islam*, ed. Lee I. Levine (New York, 1999), pp. 260–70. See further Guy G. Stroumsa, "False Prophet, False Messiah and the Religious Scene in Seventh-Century Jerusalem," in *Redemption and Resistance in the Messianic Hopes of Jews and Christians in Antiquity: Essays in Honor of William Horbury*, ed. Markus Bockmuehl and James Carlton-Paget (London and New York, 2007), 278–89.

32 Oleg Grabar, "Space and Holiness in Medieval Jerusalem," in *Jerusalem*, ed. Levine, pp. 275–86 (=*Islamic Studies* 40 [2001], 681–92).

33 Annabel Wharton, "Erasure: Eliminating the Space of Late Ancient Judaism," in *From Dura to Sepphoris: Studies in Jewish Art and Society in Late Antiquity*, ed. Lee I. Levine and Zeev Weiss (Portsmouth, RI, 2000), pp. 195–213.

34 See Carl De Boor, *Theophanis Chronographia* (Leipzig, 1883), and *The Chronicle of Theophanes Confessor: Byzantine and Near Eastern History, AD 284–813*, translated with introduction and commentary by Cyril Mango and Roger Scott (Oxford, 1997).

35 See *Adv. Haer.* 5.25–30.

36 See Horbury, "Antichrist" (above, n. 5).

37 See Robert L. Wilken, *The Land Called Holy: Palestine in Christian History and Thought* (New Haven, 1992).

38 *Sebeos' History*, trans. Robert Bedrosian (New York, 1985), ch. 31.

39 On the wide circulation of the *Apocalypse of Pseudo-Methodius* in the Western Middle Ages, see Hannes Möhring, *Der Weltkaiser der Endzeit: Entstehung, Wandel und Wirkung einer tausendjährigen Weissagung* (Stuttgart, 2000), esp. pp. 54–104.

40 Patricia Crone and Michael Cook, *Hagarism: the Making of the Islamic World* (Cambridge, 1977).

41 See, for instance, Christian Robin, "Le judaïsme de Himyar," *Arabia* 1 (2003), 97–172.

42 As pointed out by Marjorie Reeves and Beatrice Hirsch-Reich in their magisterial study, *The Figurae of Joachim of Fiore* (Oxford, 1972), pp. 184–91.

43 See for instance Haymon of Auxerre: "Jerusalem quae interpretatur visio pacis, significat sanctam Ecclesiam Deum mente videntem ..."

44 Nicolas Cusanus, *De pace fidei*, XIX. With the dawn of modern times, such "interfaith dialogues," or rather "polylogues," have become more common. The most famous example of the genre, perhaps, is Jean Bodin's *Heptaplomeres*.

45 Alphonse Dupront, *Du sacré* (Paris, 1987), 301–303. Benjamin Z. Kedar reminds me that the idea appears already in Guibert of Nogent's version of Urban II's Clermont Address.

Mustafa Abu Sway, The Holy Land, Jerusalem, and al-Aqsa Mosque in the Islamic Sources

1 This paper is a modified version of a previous one, "The Holy Land, Jerusalem and Al-Aqsa Mosque in the Islamic Sources," *Journal of the Central Conference of American Rabbis (CCAR)* (Fall 2000), 60–68.

2 Ibn Kathir, *Tafsir* (Beirut, 1988), vol. 3, p. 180.

3 Ibid., vol. 3, p. 512.

4 Sayyid Qutb, *Fi Zilaal al-Qur'an*, 12th ed. (Beirut, 1986), vol. 2, p. 871. [For an English translation,

see Sayyid Qutb, *In the Shade of the Qur'an*, vol. 4, trans. Adil Salihi and Ashur Shamis (Markfield, Leicestershire, 2001), p. 76. Sayyid Qutb (1906–66) was a prominent Egyptian intellectual. A leading member of the Muslim Brethren movement, he was involved in propagating their Islamic ideology. After the botched attempt on Nasser's life in 1954 he was arrested for ten years. Sentenced to death in 1965 for an alleged plot against the regime, he was executed along with other activists. His most important books were *Ma'alim fi'l Tariq* ("Milestones") and a commentary on the Qur'an. He advocated the replacement of Western ideas and institutions in the Muslim world by an Islamic government based on the Shari'a. Ed.]

5 The Qur'an uses "Torah," "Psalms," and "Gospel" (Arabic: *Tawrah*, *Zabur*, and *Injil*) in reference to the original revealed books. The Qur'an considers these previous revealed books to be different from those that exist today, because they suffered from human edition.

6 Ibn Kathir, *Tafsir*, vol. 3, p. 3.

7 Abu Dawud, *Sunan* # 457; Ibn Majah, *Sunan* # 147; Ahmad Ibn Hanbal, *Musnad* # 6/463; al-Bayhaqi, *Sunan* # 2/441.

8 *Hijr Isma'il*, an area considered to be part of the Ka'bah but ended up outside it when it was rebuilt before Muhammad (Peace be upon him) became a prophet.

9 Mujir al-Din al-Hanbali, *Al-Uns al-Jalil fi Tarikh al-Quds wal-Khalil* (Beirut, 1973) vol. 2, p.11.

10 Ibid., vol. 2, p. 32.

11 Ibid., vol. 2, p. 24.

12 Abu Dawud, *Sunan* # 10; Ibn Majah, *Sunan* # 319; Ahmad Ibn Hanbal, *Musnad* # 4/210.

13 Al-Nawawi, *Sahih Muslim bi-Sharh al-Nawawi*, Commentary on Hadith # 2475.

14 Al-Tirmidhi, *Sunan* # 2812.

15 Ahmad Ibn Hanbal, *Musnad* # 25347.

Miriam Frenkel, The Temple Mount in Jewish Thought

1 Alan Mintz, *Hurban: Responses to Catastrophe in Hebrew Literature* (New York, 1984), chap. 2.

2 *The Babylonian Talmud*, trans. I. Epstein (London, 1948), Section V, vol. 2, Seder Kodashim, Menahot, 11b.

3 See the article by Rachel Elior in this volume.

4 Oded Irshai, "Constantine and the Jews: The Prohibition against Entering Jerusalem – History and Hagiography," *Zion* 60 (1995), 133–35 (Hebrew).

5 See the article by Andreas Kaplony in this volume.

6 Moshe Gil, *A History of Palestine, 614–1099* (Cambridge, 1992; repr. 1997), pp 72–74.

7 Moshe Gil, "The Jewish Community," in *The History of Jerusalem: The Early Muslim Period, 638–1099*, ed. Joshua Prawer and Haggai Ben-Shammai (Jerusalem, 1996), p. 198.

8 *The Chronicle of Ahimaaz*, translated with an introduction and notes by Marcus Salzman (New York, 1924), p. 97. It is unclear from this passage whether the author is referring to the Western Wall of the Temple Mount.

9 Moshe Gil, *Palestine during the First Muslim Period 634–1099): Part II: Cairo Geniza Documents* (Tel Aviv, 1983), doc. 2, ll. 3–5 (Hebrew).

10 Haggai Ben-Shammai, "Poetic Works and Lamentations of Karaite 'Mourners of Zion': Structure and Contents," in *Knesset Ezra: Literature and Life in the Synagogue – Studies Presented to Ezra Fleischer*, ed. Shulamit Elizur, Moshe D. Herr, Gershon Shaked, and Avigdor Shinan (Jerusalem, 1994), pp. 191–234 (Hebrew).

11 Hayyim Schirmann, *Hebrew Poetry in Spain and Provence*, vol. 1 (Jerusalem and Tel Aviv, 1956), p. 34 (Hebrew).

12 *The Prayer Book of Rabbi Sa'adyah Gaon*, ed. Israel Davidson, Simha Assaf, and Issachar Joel (Jerusalem, 1979), pp. 62–63 (Hebrew).

13 See p. 135 in this volume.

14 *The Wanderings of Judah Alharizi: Five Accounts of His Travels*, edited according to Hebrew manuscripts by Joseph Yahalom and according to Judeo-Arabic manuscripts by Joshua Blau (Jerusalem, 2002), p. 82 (Hebrew).

15 Shlomo D. Goitein, *A Mediterranean Society*, vol. 5 (Berkeley, 1988), pp. 393–94.

16 Maimonides, *Code*, Book 14: *The Book of Judges*, vol. 3, translated from the Hebrew by Abraham M. Hershman (New Haven, 1949), p. 240.

17 Ibid., p. 238.

18 The letter is printed at the end of his commentary on the Torah. See Ramban (Nahmanides), *Commentary on the Torah*, edited and annotated … by Charles B. Chavel, 2 vols. (Jerusalem, 1963) (Hebrew).

19 Ibid.

20 Eshtori ha-Parhi, *Kaftor va-Ferah* (Bud and Flower), ed. Abraham Moshe Luncz (Jerusalem, 1897), vol. 1, p. 94 (Hebrew).

21 "Rabbi Meshulam of Volterra (1481)," in Elkan Nathan (ed.), *Jewish Travellers* (London, 1930), pp. 189–92.

22 Elchanan Reiner, "'Since Jerusalem and Zion Stand Separately': The Jewish Quarter of Jerusalem in the Post-Crusade Period (13th–15th Centuries)," in *Studies in Geography and History in Honour of Yehoshua Ben-Arieh*, ed. Yossi Ben-Artzi, Israel Bartal, and Elchanan Reiner (Jerusalem, 1999), pp. 277–321 (Hebrew).

23 See the article by Amnon Cohen in this volume.

24 "Letters of Travelers, Inscriptions on Graves … concerning the Middle Ages," *Hame'amer* 3 (1919), 185 (Hebrew).

25 *Responsa of Rabbi David ben Zimra*, vol. 2 (Venice, 1749), §691 (Hebrew). See also the testimonies in this regard from the Shari'a court in Amnon Cohen's article in this volume.

26 *Kobez al Jad*, IV (Berlin, 1888), p. 25.

27 Cf. the letter of Rabbi Yisrael Ashkenazi (n. 24 above).

28 *The Complete Diaries of Theodor Herzl*, edited by Raphael Patai, translated by Harry Zohn, 5 vols. (New York and London, 1960), 2:746–47.

29 Zevi Hirsch Kalischer, *Derishat Ziyyon* (Jerusalem, 1919), section "Article on Holy Things" (Hebrew).

30 Elijah of Vilna, "Commentary on the Song of Songs," *The Prayerbook of the Gaon, Rabbi Elijah* (Jerusalem, 1918) (Hebrew).

31 For details, see the article by Yitzhak Reiter and Jon Seligman in this volume.

32 Jordanian, *La Terra Sainte – Guide officiel* (Amman, 1956), p. 51. The sentence is highlighted by italics.

33 Jordan, *The Holy Land – Official Guide* (Amman, 1956), p. 52. In *A Guide to Jordan, the Holy Land*, published by the Jordan Tourism Authority in 1962, the words after "security reasons" are omitted; elsewhere in the booklet the State of Israel is referred to as "Israel." A travel guide to Jordan published in about 1965 informs prospective tourists: "If you plan to obtain a visa at the Jordanian frontier, you should have a certificate of religious affiliation with you. Acceptable documents are: a letter of membership from your church; your baptismal certificate; or a notarized statement of your religious affiliation." Kay Showker, *Travel Jordan: A Modern Guide to the Holy Land* (Beirut, n.d.), p. 19.

34 This section is based on Nadav Shragai, *The Mount of Contention: The Struggle for the Temple Mount* (Jerusalem, 1995) (Hebrew).

35 Recently, Israel's Ministry of Education awarded Rabbi Israel Ariel, the Temple Institute's director, its annual prize for Jewish culture, on the grounds that "the Temple stands at the center of Jewish existence in the Bible, the [teachings of the] Sages, and the [religious] Commandments, and constitutes a central axis of Jewish history and the Israeli life experience. Rabbi Ariel took upon himself to render this idea perceptible to the general public and founded the Temple Institute for this purpose." *Ha'aretz*, 26 Oct. 2008 [Ed.].

36 See *Women of the Wall: Claiming Sacred Ground at Judaism's Holy Site*, ed. Phyllis Chesler and Rivka Haut (Woodstock, VT., 2003) [Ed.].

37 In a recent halakhic book, Rabbi Rabinovitch and Rabbi Yisrael Yosef Bronstein lay down that "those [Jews] who engage in tourism should not encourage members of the religion of Islam to come as tourists to the Land of Israel, because their main wish will most certainly be to ascend to the Temple Mount." *The Western Wall: Halakhot and Customs* (Jerusalem, 2009), pp. 298–99 (Hebrew).[Ed.].

Benjamin Z. Kedar and Oleg Grabar, Epilogue

1 Robert W. Hamilton, *The Structural History of the Aqsa Mosque: A Record of Archaeological Gleanings from the Repairs of 1938–1942* (London, 1949), p. iii.

2 See most recently Oleg Grabar, *The Dome of the Rock* (Cambridge, MA, 2006), pp. 192–93, 203–5.

3 For detailed descriptions of the finds see Benjamin Mazar, *The Temple of the Lord* (New York, 1975); Eilat Mazar, *The Complete Guide to the Temple Mount Excavations* (Jerusalem, 2002).

4 See the account by the archaeologist Dan Bahat, published by the Western Wall Heritage Foundation under the telling title *The Western Wall Tunnels: Touching the Stones of Our Heritage* (Jerusalem, 2002).

5 Moshe Safdie, *Plan for the Western Wall Precinct: Preliminary Submission* (Jerusalem, 1974); idem, *Jerusalem: The Future of the Past* (Montreal and Toronto, 1989), pp. 121–30, 215–22. For another plan for the full exposure of the Herodian Western Wall, from the praying area to its southern end, see Anshel Pfeffer, "His Is the Temple Mount," *Ha'aretz Weekly Supplement*, 23 February 2007, pp. 36–40 (Hebrew).

6 Originally, only the Second Temple model was on display. For a presentation of the architectural and museological concepts see Kimmel Eshkolot Architects, *Davidson Center Jerusalem* (Tel Aviv, 2005). The website www.archpark.org.il allows for a partial exploration of the Second Temple model. For a negative appraisal see Yousef Said al-Natsheh, "The Digital Temple Mount," *Jerusalem Quarterly File* 19 (2003), 53–58; www.jerusalemquarterly.org/details.php?cat=5&id=189. Al-Natsheh rejects the term "Second Temple Period" and goes so far as to place the Second Temple in "Roman Jerusalem" and even to speak of "the alleged Second Temple" and its "alleged reality."

7 For some of the views of Ra'id Salah, the leader of the Northern Islamic Movement, see "The Islamic Movement inside Israel: An Interview with Shaykh Ra'id Salah," *Journal of Palestine Studies* 36, no. 2 (Winter 2007), 66–76.

8 For further information about the Institute and its aims see www.templeinstitute.org.

9 See the flyer of the Generations Center at the Western Wall Plaza.

10 Both the Generations Center and the Western Wall Tunnels are administered by the Western Wall Heritage Foundation , the website of which is www.thekotel.org. Thanks are due to Mr. Aryeh Banner for his guidance through the tunnels and for information readily proffered.

11 It is not devoid of irony that Yeshayahu Leibowitz, the maverick Israeli thinker who vociferously criticized the national-religious cult of the Western Wall, proposed a short time after the Six Day War to turn the prayer plaza in front of the Wall (or Kotel) into Israel's largest discotheque, to be named "The Divine Presence Discotheque"—a fitting symbol of the State of Israel which he decried as an atheistic-clerical entity. Yeshayahu Leibowitz, "Diskotel (a letter to the editor)," *Ha'aretz*, 21 July 1967, p. 2. [BZ Kedar's note].

12 See my "Cultural Persistence despite Total Political Collapse," to appear shortly in a volume in memory of Aron Gurevich.

13 See my "The Jerusalem Massacre of July 1099 in the Western Historiography of the Crusades," *Crusades* 3 (2004), 15–75.

Sari Nusseibeh, The Haram al-Sharif

1 Note the semantically-related Arabic root *s-k-n*, from which the meaning for "to dwell" is derived, (*shakhan/mishkan*, etc. in Hebrew have related meanings), as well as the etymologically-related term "*maskoon*," i.e., haunted, meaning "lived in by some spirit," as well as "*sakinah*," or spiritual tranquility, said (in Islamic scriptures) to "descend" on one who reads the Qur'an.

2 "*Al-muqaddasah*," thus, at the heart of this land, "*al-Quds*" (Jerusalem). In other places (e.g., 34.18, or 21.81) the word "*barakna*" is used. In the next quoted aya the word "*akramna*" (for the conferring of blessings) is used.

3 17.70.

4 The other festival (called "the Small") marks the end of fasting.

5 Another "incongruity" of beliefs concerns the identity of the son Abraham was about to sacrifice.

6 Notice which House of God the term (*masjid*) refers to later on in the same *sura*.

7 Note that the disagreement over which son, Ishmael or Isaac, was targeted does not, by itself, constitute a disagreement over fundamentals. Sayyid Qutb, for example, in his exegesis, does not discount the son being Isaac. But taken in the present political context, the symbolic combination of Isaac with the Holy Rock can constitute a conceptual powder-keg.

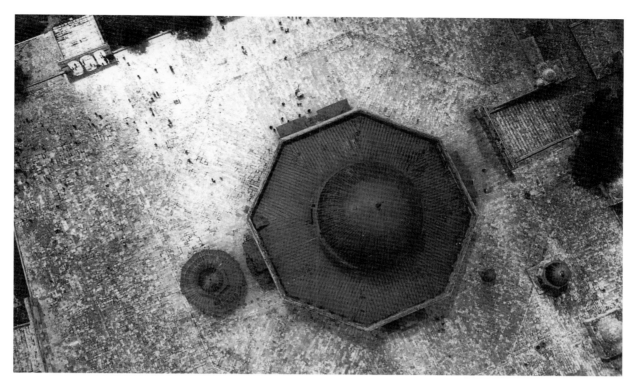

210 The Dome of the Rock, photographed from a Zeppelin airship, 1929/1933
Archiv der Luftschiffbau Zeppelin GmbH, Friedrichshafen, 193/138

211 The Aqsa Mosque, the Western Wall and the Magharibah Quarter, photographed from a Zeppelin airship, 1931
Archiv der Luftschiffbau Zeppelin GmbH, Friedrichshafen, 193/008

Glossary

'Abbasids—Muslim dynasty of caliphs 750–1258, based in Iraq, claiming the supreme leadership of the Islamic World

Aelia—official name of Jerusalem during the Byzantine period

Aelia Capitolina—name given Jerusalem by the Roman Emperor Hadrian (117–138)

amir (Arabic)—a Muslim commander, governor, prince

al-Aqsa Mosque (Jami' al-Aqsa)—see al-Masjid al-Aqsa

Ark of the Covenant—the ark in which the tablets of the Covenant were kept in the Holy of Holies

awqaf (Arabic; sing., **waqf**)—Muslim pious endowments

Ayyubids—Muslim dynasty that ruled Syria and Egypt in the 12th–13th centuries

Beyt ha-Miqdash (Hebrew)—The Sacred House; the Temple

cardo (Latin)—in Roman city planning, the main north–south street of a city

Church of the Holy Sepulchre—Jerusalem's main church, originally dedicated in ca. 335. According to Christian tradition, it contains the tomb in which Jesus was buried and from which he rose from the dead

decumanus (Latin)—in Roman city planning, the main east–west street of a city

devir (Hebrew)—inner sanctum of the Temple, the "Holy of Holies"

Dome of the Rock (Arabic: **Qubbat al-Sakhra**)—the Muslim shrine on the Esplanade, built over its rock peak, a sacred rock from which, in Muslim tradition, the Prophet Muhammad ascended to heaven

even shetiyyah (Hebrew)—"Foundation Rock"; in Jewish tradition, the rock from which the world was created, located in the Holy of Holies of the Temple, believed by Jews who wrote the Dead Sea Scrolls to be associated with the Rock of Zion

Fatimids—Shi'ite dynasty based in Egypt claiming the supreme leadership of the Islamic World from 909/969 to 1171

Franks—Christians from Western Europe and their descendants who lived in the Latin Kingdom of Jerusalem, established in the wake of the 1099 conquest by the First Crusade

Furthest Mosque (Arabic: **al-Masjid al-Aqsa**)—see al-Masjid al-Aqsa

hadith (Arabic)—a narration attributed to the Prophet Muhammad and his Companions; became a source of Islamic law

hajj (Arabic)—annual pilgrimage conducted by Muslim pilgrims to the Ka'ba in Mecca

halakhah (Hebrew)—Jewish religious law

Har ha-Bayit—"The Temple Mount"; Hebrew term denoting the Esplanade

haram (Arabic)—any sacred place with well-defined borders and accessible only under certain conditions

al-Haram al-Sharif—"The Noble Sanctuary"; Arabic term denoting the Esplanade that includes the Aqsa Mosque, the Dome of the Rock, and other sites

Hasmonaean Tunnel—the northern section of the Western Wall Tunnel

heykhal (Hebrew)—the outer sanctum of the Temple, where the main daily ritual was performed, located to the east of the devir

imam (Arabic)—any leader of Muslim ritual prayer; the leader of the community of all Muslims, the umma

Ka'ba— the building incorporating the Black Stone, the center of the Haram of Mecca, the most sacred site in Islam

khanqah (Arabic)—Muslim conventual building housing Sufi mystics

in situ (Latin)—archaeological term indicating that an object is "in its original place"

kavod (Hebrew)—term denoting Divine Glory

madrasa (Arabic)—Muslim theological college

Mamluks—imported slaves, mostly of Turkish or Caucasian stock, primarily destined for military service. They overthrew the Ayyubid dynasty to rule Egypt and Syria from the mid-thirteenth century to 1516

al-Masjid al-Aqsa—"The Furthest Mosque"; Arabic term denoting, in the Middle Ages, all of the Haram and later mainly the building in its southern part, the Aqsa Mosque

menorah (Hebrew)—seven-branched lampstand, one of the Temple implements

mihrab (Arabic)—prayer niche in a mosque

minbar (Arabic)—preacher's pulpit in a mosque

Mount of Olives—mountain east of the Esplanade and overviewing it

al-Musalla al-Marwani (Arabic)—recent name of Solomon's Stables

Night Journey (Arabic: **al-Isra'**)—in Muslim tradition, the journey of the Prophet Muhammad from Mecca to Jerusalem and his ascension (mi'raj) to the heavens in one night astride al-Buraq, the winged steed

Ottomans—people and empire that take their name from Osman I (14th century). The Ottomans ruled Jerusalem from 1516 to 1917

Palatium Salomonis (The Palace of Solomon)—one of the Frankish names for the Aqsa Mosque

portal-minaret—Fatimid imperial mosques had no minarets, but a magnificent main entry from where the prayer-call was issued

portico—a structure consisting of a roof supported by columns or piers

qadi (Arabic)—cadi; judge who rules according to Islamic religious law

qibla (Arabic)—the direction of prayer, towards Mecca, that Muslims face during daily prayers

Qubbat al-Sakhra (Arabic)—see Dome of the Rock

sancak (Turkish)—a district within an Ottoman province (vilayet)

shari'a (Arabic)—the way of life of a Muslim as explained in Islamic religious law

Shekhinah (Hebrew)—Divine Presence

Solomon's Stables (in Arabic recently called **al-Musalla al-Marwani**)—area under the southeastern corner of the Esplanade used by the Knights Templar as stables in the 12th century; converted into a mosque during the last decade of the 20th century

soreg (Hebrew)—a low partition delineating the sacred area of the outer court, beyond which access for gentiles was prohibited

stoa (Greek)—usually a detached portico that is used as a promenade or meeting place

Templum Domini (The Temple of the Lord)—Frankish name for the Dome of the Rock

Templum Salomonis (The Temple of Solomon)—Frankish name for the Aqsa Mosque

Umayyads—Sunnite Muslim dynasty based in Syria-Palestine, 661–750, claiming the supreme leadership of the Islamic World as caliphs

ulam (Hebrew)—a small forecourt, or porch, in front of the Temple, extending the width of the building

vali/wali (Turkish/Arabic)—governor of a province

vilayet (Turkish)—a province, and administrative unit of the Ottoman Empire; also eyelet

Wailing Wall—see Western Wall

waqf—see awqaf

Western Wall (**ha-Kotel ha-Ma'aravi**)—the major remnant of the walls surrounding the Herodian Temple

Western Wall Tunnel—320-meter-long tunnel created by Israel's Ministry of Religious Affairs along the outer side of the Western Wall

Yakhin and Boaz—two freestanding pillars in the forecourt of the Temple, flanking the entryway

YHWH—(Hebrew) transliteration of the Tetragrammaton, the ineffable four-letter name of God

Zadokites (**Sadducees**)—a priestly dynasty during the Second Temple period

zawiya (Arabic)—the residence of a Sufi shaykh and meeting place for his followers

ziyara (Arabic)—pilgrimage to holy places

Sources of illustrations

Albatross, Tel Aviv – **1**
Nazmi Al-Jubeh – **77, 134, 158, 197**
Pnina Arad – **9, 61**
Archiv der Luftschiffbau Zeppelin GmbH, Friedrichshafen – **210, 211**
Associated Press – **133, 144**
Dan Bahat – **151**
Yuval Baruch, IAA – **2**
Bayerisches Hauptstaatsarchiv, Abt. IV: Kriegsarchiv. Palästina-Bilder, No. 790 – **51**
Meir Ben-Dov – **56, 67**
Meir Ben-Dov, "Building Techniques in The Umayyad Palace near the Temple Mount," Eretz-Israel 11 (1973), 77 – **59**
Bibliothèque royale de Belgique – **70**
British Museum – **6, 11**
Michael H. Burgoyne – **34, 80** (map), **81, 82, 84, 85** (plan), **91, 95, 99** (map), **100–102, 106–111, 160a, 161a, 162a**
Alex Carmel and Hugo Schmid, *The Life and Work of Gustav Bauernfeind, Orientalist Painter, 1848-1904* (Stuttgart: Dr. Ernst Hauswedell & Co., 1990), pl. 170 – **112**
Central Zionist Archives, Jerusalem – **190**
Herman Chananya, GPO – **202**
Deutsches Archäologisches Institut, Berlin: Theodor Wiegand Collection, Aerial photo No. 308 – **199**
École Biblique et Archéologique Française de Jérusalem – **72, 124, 184**
Ejal Jakob Eisler – **120**
Baruch Gian – **85** (photo), **86, 87, 96, 207**
Government Press Office (GPO), Jerusalem – **132**
Oleg Grabar – **78**
R.C. Haines, Excavations in the Plain of Antioch, II, *Oriental Institute Publications* 125 (Chicago: University of Chicago Press, 1971), pl. 81A, pl. 103 – **8**
Robert W. Hamilton, *The Structural History of the Aqsa Mosque: A Record of Archaeological Gleanings of 1938-1942* (London: Oxford University Press, 1949), pp. 27, 28, 52 – **74**
Historic Views of the Holy Land: The 1960s: Photographs of Charles Lee Feinberg – **191**
Avi Hayun, GPO – **205**
Israel Antiquities Authority (IAA) – **12, 13, 68b, 83, 128-31, 155, 179, 183**
Israel Defence Forces, Film Archives – **140**
Israel Museum, Jerusalem – **5, 14, 18, 19, 44–46, 71**
Istanbul Archaeological Museums – **16**
Yael Katzir – **192**
Benjamin Z. Kedar – **20, 22–24, 32, 36, 37, 40, 49, 52, 55, 68a, 73, 76, 85** (3 details), **90, 92, 98, 105, 117, 147, 152, 177, 178, 187, 201, 206, 209a**
Benjamin Z. and Nurith Kedar Collection – **75, 119, 125, 176**

Gabi Laron, IAA – **48, 53**
Yoram Lehman – **43**
Nadav Mann/Bitmuna – **121**
Eric Matson, GPO – **127, 188**
L.A. Mayer, "Hebräische Inschriften im Haram zu Jerusalem," Zeitschrift des Deutschen Palästina-Vereins 53 (1930), Tafel 12A – **58**
Eilat Mazar – **182**
Moshe Milner, GPO – **122, 154, 156, 204**
Moshe Milner – **200**
Laura Minervini – **42**
Municipal Archives, Jerusalem (MAJ) – **142**
National Library of Israel – **186, 194**
Mark Neyman, GPO – **146**
Saïd Nuseibeh – **2–3, 63–65, 164–175**
Avner Offer – **136, 138**
Avi Ohayon, GPO – **148, 203**
Photo Scala, Florence – **198**
Hans Haim Pinn, MAJ – **139, 143**
Varda Polak Sahm – **159, 185**
Ehud Prawer – **135**
Denys Pringle – **69**
Zev Radovan/Bible Land Pictures – **4, 31, 41, 50, 60, 123, 180**
Leen Ritmeyer – **3, 17, 21, 26, 27, 28, 29, 30, 33, 35** (red lines added by Michael Burgoyne), **39, 181**
RMN - © Les frères Chuzeville – **10**
David Rubinger, GPO – **137**
Ely Shiller – **126, 141**
Hayim Shtayer – **209b**
The Temple Institute, Jerusalem – **193**
Olaf M. Teßmer, Vorderasiatisches Museum, Staatliche Museen zu Berlin – **7**
Topkapı Palace Museum, Istanbul – **195**
Tower of David Museum of the History of Jerusalem – **62**
Yoram Tsafrir – **54, 57, 118**
Sarit Uziely – **15**
Melchior de Vogüé, *Le Temple de Jérusalem, Monographie du Haram-ech-chérif* (Paris: Noblet et Baudrie, 1864), pl. VI – **38**
Charles Warren, *Plans, Elevations, Sections, &c., Shewing the Results of the Excavations at Jerusalem, 1867-70* (London: Palestine Exploration Fund, 1884), pl. 20 – **47**
Yad Izhak Ben-Zvi Photo Archives – **196**
Yad Izhak Ben-Zvi Photo Archives, Dov and Ruth Kantorowitz Collection – **189**
Khaled Zighari – **25, 66, 79, 88, 89, 93, 94, 97, 103, 104, 113–116, 145, 149, 150, 153, 157, 160b, 161b, 162b, 163, 208**

MAIN DATES

10th century BCE First Temple built by Solomon, King of Israel

586 BCE Destruction of the First Temple by the Babylonians

536–515 BCE Construction of the Second Temple by Judean returnees from Exile

168–169 BCE Antiochus IV Epiphanes confiscates the treasures of the Temple, now consecrated as a temple of Zeus Olympus; the Hasmonaean revolt begins

166–162 BCE The Temple is purified and restored by Judas Maccabaeus

19 BCE King Herod begins rebuilding and expansion of the Temple and its precinct

70 CE Destruction of the Second Temple by the Romans

135 Jerusalem declared Roman colony and renamed Aelia Capitolina by Roman Emperor Hadrian

363 Emperor Julian encourages the Jews to rebuild the Temple but his death in battle thwarts the attempt

614 Conquest of Jerusalem by the Sasanian Persians; Jewish plans to rebuild the Temple

629 Reconquest of Jerusalem by Byzantine Emperor Heraclius

635/638 Conquest of Jerusalem by the Muslims under Caliph 'Umar; up to the 680s, they build a modest mosque amidst the ruins of the former Temple

685–715 Rebuilding all of the Esplanade by the Umayyad Caliphs 'Abd al-Malik and al-Walid, including building the Dome of the Rock and the Aqsa Mosque, the latter twice as wide as at present

1015 and 1033 Heavy earthquakes damage the Aqsa Mosque

1034–36 Rebuilding and renovation of a much narrower Aqsa Mosque by the Fatimid Imam 'Ali al-Zahir (ruled 1021–36)

1073 Seljuk Turks wrest Jerusalem from the Fatimids

1098 Reconquest of Jerusalem by the Fatimids

1099 Conquest of Jerusalem and massacre of Muslims and Jews by the Crusaders

1099–1187 Frankish rule over Jerusalem

1120 The Aqsa Mosque becomes the headquarters of the Templar Order

1141 Dome of the Rock consecrated as the Church of the Lord's Temple

1187 Saladin conquers Jerusalem and reconsecrates the Dome of the Rock and the Aqsa Mosque

1229–1239, 1241–43 Frankish/Ayyubid condominium over Jerusalem, with the Esplanade under Muslim control

1244 Conquest of Jerusalem by Kwarazmian Turks; definite departure of the Franks

1260 Conquest of Jerusalem by the Mongols

1260–1516 Jerusalem ruled by the Mamluks

1516 Conquest of Jerusalem by the Ottoman Turks

1538–41 Walls of Jerusalem rebuilt by order of Sultan Sulayman the Magnificent; exterior of the Dome of the Rock covered with ceramic tiles

1817–18 Extensive renovation works on the Haram al-Sharif

1917 Conquest of Jerusalem by the British

1921 Establishment of the Supreme Muslim Council in Palestine; the offices of its president are located on the Haram al-Sharif

1924 Beginning of a program of restoration work on the Haram al-Sharif by the Supreme Muslim Council